Understanding Financial Management

To my wife, Linda, who as my mainstay patiently endured the long and arduous process that resulted in this book; and to my mother, who has provided a lifetime of support and encouragement.

H. Kent Baker

To my wife, Gloria, who patiently supported my work; to my mother, and in memory of my father.

Gary E. Powell

Understanding Financial Management

A Practical Guide

H. KENT BAKER AND GARY E. POWELL

Blackwell
Publishing

BLACKWELL PUBLISHING
350 Main Street, Malden, MA 02148-5020, USA
9600 Garsington Road, Oxford OX4 2DQ, UK
550 Swanston Street, Carlton, Victoria 3053, Australia

First published 2005 by Blackwell Publishing Ltd

4   2008

Library of Congress Cataloging-in-Publication Data

Baker, H. Kent (Harold Kent), 1944–
   Understanding financial management : a practical guide / H. Kent Baker and Gary E. Powell.— 1st ed.
      p. cm.
   Includes bibliographical references and index.
   ISBN 978-0-631-23100-4 (pbk : alk. paper)
   1. Business enterprises—Finance—Handbooks, manuals, etc.   I. Powell, Gary E.   II. Title.

   HG4027.3.B35 2005
   658.15—dc22

                                                        2004023529

A catalogue record for this title is available from the British Library.

Set in 10/12.5pt Dante
by Graphicraft Limited, Hong Kong
Printed and bound in Singapore
by Utopia Press Pte Ltd

The publisher's policy is to use permanent paper from mills that operate a sustainable forestry policy, and which has been manufactured from pulp processed using acid-free and elementary chlorine-free practices. Furthermore, the publisher ensures that the text paper and cover board used have met acceptable environmental accreditation standards.

For further information on
Blackwell Publishing, visit our website:
www.blackwellpublishing.com

Contents

Figures

Tables

About the Authors

H. Kent Baker is University Professor of Finance at the Kogod School of Business at American University in Washington, DC. He has more than 30 years of teaching experience in finance at the undergraduate and graduate levels as well as extensive administrative experience. He has received numerous teaching and research awards including the University Scholar/Teacher of the Year and the University Award for Outstanding Research Scholarship and Other Contributions, both from American University. Professor Baker has consulting and training experience with more than 100 organizations and has presented more than 650 executive development, management training, and CFA® prep programs.

Professor Baker has written or edited several books including *Financial Management* and *Financial Markets: Instruments and Concepts*. He has published more than 150 articles in accounting, finance, education, and management and 350 book reviews and article abstracts. His work has appeared in numerous academic and practitioner journals including *The Journal of Finance, Journal of Financial and Quantitative Analysis, Financial Management, The Journal of Financial Research, The Financial Review, Financial Analysts Journal, Journal of Portfolio Management,* and *Harvard Business Review.*

Professor Baker received a BSBA in management from Georgetown University; an MBA in finance, an MEd in educational administration, and a DBA in finance from the University of Maryland; an MS in quantitative methods, an MA in training and career development, a PhD in educational administration and organization development, and a PhD in counseling and student development from American University. He also holds CFA® and CMA® designations.

Gary E. Powell is Professor of Finance at Towson University in Towson, MD. He has more than 20 years of experience in the corporate world and academia. Professor Powell has trained more than 5,000 government officials, financial analysts, accountants, and engineers from more than 60 developing countries both in the US and abroad in areas related to project finance, financial analysis of infrastructure investments in electricity, telecom, and water, regulatory economics, privatization, pension fund reform, and utility restructuring. Professor Powell has served as an international consultant for various reform projects including national social security reform in Egypt, regulatory reform for the energy sector in

Zambia, and privatization and financial management of infrastructure services in Albania, Indonesia, Nigeria, and South Africa.

Professor Powell has published 20 research articles in areas related to dividend policy, share repurchases, corporate listing on organized stock exchanges, stock market anomalies, and corporate social responsibility. His articles have appeared in numerous academic and practitioner journals including *Financial Management, The Financial Review, Journal of Economics and Finance, Review of Financial Economics, Quarterly Review of Economics and Finance*, and *Quarterly Journal of Business and Economics*.

Professor Powell received his DBA in finance and MA in economics from Kent State University, and a BS in Chemical Engineering from the University of Akron. He is a Level III candidate for the CFA® designation.

Preface

Financial management plays a critical role in every business enterprise. Without money and its successful management, a firm would not survive much less grow and prosper. In today's rapidly changing business environment, financial management is more complex than in any time in history. This makes understanding corporate finance not only important and exciting but also challenging and sometimes bewildering. Similar to other business disciplines, financial management has its own terminology, conflicting theories, and varying practices.

Both the theory and practice of financial management continue to advance at an uncommonly rapid pace in response to shifts in economic conditions. Those involved with financial management in business organizations must run just to keep in place. Yet, the core principles underlying financial management have changed relatively little over time. Financial theory has added to the store of knowledge and provided needed structure, but these advances have generally been in the details. Often considerable time is required before meaningful financial developments or innovations become embedded in the fabric of finance.

The Need for the Book

Before undertaking this project, we asked ourselves "Does the market really need another book on financial management?" The answer, of course, depends on the type of book. Because many well-written financial management textbooks already exist, we reasoned that producing another lengthy book would have little marginal value. From experience we knew that few of these texts can be adequately covered in a single course because of their extensive breadth. Therefore, we decided to take a less well-traveled path and write a streamlined book dealing with a limited number of core topics in financial management. By targeting a somewhat different market than the standard textbook, we thought that we could add value. Although the market will be the ultimate judge on whether our decision was a correct one, we gained an immense amount of satisfaction by trying.

Our Goals in Writing the Book

In writing *Understanding Financial Management: A Practical Guide*, we have three major goals.

- Our first goal is to create a practical and understandable book that emphasizes the fundamentals needed to make better financial management decisions within business organizations. On the surface, financial management appears to be a collection of unrelated topics and decisions. This superficial view rapidly disappears after taking a closer look at the subject. At its core, financial management deals with decisions involving raising and allocating funds in order to create value. Throughout the book we try to illustrate how this is done by introducing the concepts, tools, and applications of finance. The book's perspective combines both the descriptive and prescriptive.
- Our next goal is to present financial management as an integrated business function, not as a stand-alone activity. Because financial decisions are interconnected, they must be incorporated into a firm's overall business strategy. In addition, we stress that interactions exist among investment, financing, and dividend policy decisions.
- Our final goal is to keep the book reasonably self-contained so that someone with only a modest background in accounting, economics, and statistics can understand its contents. Previous knowledge of these areas is useful but not essential to reading this book. The first five chapters provide sufficient background to understand the major types of financial decisions discussed in later chapters.

Intended Audience and Use

Understanding Financial Management can be used for several audiences. In a broad sense, the book is appropriate for anyone wanting to practice financial management or to improve their understanding about financial decision making in profit-oriented businesses. The book is ideally suited for participants in management and executive development programs, including Executive MBA programs. General managers, practicing finance professionals, and candidates preparing for various professional examinations such as Level I of the CFA® program will find the book helpful. Finally, the book may also serve as a refresher or reference for those who have previously taken coursework in financial management.

Organization of the Book

Understanding Financial Management follows a logical progression from developing basic principles and tools to applying them to specific situations, beginning with working capital decisions followed by long-term investment and financing decisions. The book consists of 12 chapters divided into four parts. Let's briefly look at each part.

I. The Foundation

These five chapters provide an overview of financial management and introduce tools of financial analysis and valuation needed for making sound financial decisions that create value. In Chapter 1, we present an introduction to financial management. We discuss the role of the financial manager and propose maximizing shareholder wealth as the major goal of the firm. In Chapters 2 and 3, we discuss the key financial statements and how to interpret them using ratio analysis. In Chapter 4, we explore one of the most important concepts in finance – the time value of money – and illustrate how to apply various formulas. Finally, in Chapter 5, we explore the topic of valuation. We explain various characteristics and features of securities and discuss how to value bonds, preferred stock, and common stock.

II. Working Capital Management Decisions

Chapter 6 focuses on working capital management decisions, which are made to support day-to-day operations of the firm. We examine various approaches to managing working capital and also discuss short-term financing.

III. Long-term Investment Decisions

The next three chapters examine long-term investment decisions. Chapter 7 provides an overview of capital investment decisions and focuses on estimating project cash flows. In Chapter 8, we consider capital budgeting. In Chapter 9, we examine common ways to describe, assess, and adjust for risk associated with capital investments.

IV. Long-term Financing Decisions

The final three chapters deal with long-term financing decisions. In Chapter 10, we discuss how business firms raise external capital and how investors trade securities. We also examine how firms estimate their cost of capital and determine an optimal capital budget. Chapter 11 investigates the financing mix for a firm and Chapter 12 focuses on dividends and share repurchases.

Features of the Book

The following are some key features.

- **Chapter overviews.** Each chapter contains a brief overview providing the key topics to be covered.
- **Learning objectives.** Every chapter begins with a set of learning objectives specifying what the reader should be able to do after completing the chapter. Thus, we clearly establish expectations for learning up front.
- **Readability.** To enhance readability, we use a direct writing style and strive to explain complex concepts in simplified terms. We relegate ancillary comments and references to footnotes so readers can continue with the main line of thought.
- **Concept checks.** At the end of each section within a chapter, we include a set of review questions designed to reinforce understanding and serve as a tool of active learning.
- **Focus on practice.** We use text boxes to provide examples of actual business applications to illustrate underlying concepts. In addition, we present the results of surveys to highlight the views of financial managers on different topic areas such as capital budgeting techniques and dividend policy.
- **Practical financial tips.** We use text boxes to provide numerous practical suggestions about key concepts. The intent of this feature is to capture the reader's interest and enhance the learning experience.

- **Key terms.** We place important terms in bold letters the first time they appear.
- **Numbered equations.** We highlight and number each equation.
- **Examples and illustrations.** We demonstrate the concepts using many examples and use a step-by-step approach to applying various mathematical concepts. We also develop numerous graphs and illustrations to clarify and visually reinforce key concepts.
- **Calculator and Excel spreadsheet examples.** We illustrate various techniques, especially those involving time value of money applications, using a financial calculator. Some examples include suggestions involving the use of Excel to solve the problem.
- **Chapter summaries.** Every chapter ends with a summary of the key points to reinforce learning.
- **References and Web sources.** Every chapter contains a list of references in addition to those specified in the footnotes. In several chapters we provide useful Web sources.
- **Web-based problems.** To provide flexibility, we include end-of-chapter problems and solutions on the following website: www.blackwellpublishing.com/baker. Using available technology enables us to periodically update and expand end-of-chapter problem sets.

Acknowledgments

This book reflects the efforts of many people both directly and indirectly. Although we cannot individually thank all of those who have provided help and encouragement such as our students, friends, colleagues, and former mentors, we would like to single out some individuals for special recognition. We thank Raluca Bancescu, David Fisher, Brian Fitzgerald, Robert Jaspersen, Kapres Meadows and Jurgen Niehaus, all former MBA students from the Kogod School of Business at American University, who painstakingly reviewed the chapters and provided useful inputs. Robert Jaspersen, Karla Kucerkova, Spencer Young, and Sabrina Vasconcelos also contributed to the problem sets. David Jones gave constructive feedback on chapters involving financial statements. In addition, we are grateful to the following reviewers – John Earl, University of Richmond, Ken Milani, University of Notre Dame, and Jay Prag, Claremont Graduate University – for comments and suggestions that helped to shape and improve the manuscript.

Finally, we wish to thank all the people associated with Blackwell Publishing who helped with this project, especially Seth Ditchik (Acquisitions Editor Economics and Finance), Linda Auld (Project Manager), Elizabeth Wald (Assistant Editor), and Laura Sterns (Assistant Editor), who ably guided the project to production. In-house production personnel include Joanna Pyke (Editorial Controller), Rhonda Pearce (Production Editor), Eloise Keating (Senior Marketing Controller, UK), and Desirée Zicko (Product Manager, US).

Although these individuals contributed to this book, we are ultimately responsible for any remaining errors. As Edward J. Phelps once stated "The man who makes no mistakes does not usually make anything." We hope that we created a useful book but perfection is beyond our grasp. Although we believe the book is relatively error free, some mistakes may have slipped by. If they have, we want to correct and post them on our Web address: www.blackwellpublishing.com/baker. Please report any errors to either author at the e-mail addresses shown below. We hope that *Understanding Financial Management* contributes to your understanding of the exciting world of finance.

H. Kent Baker   Gary E. Powell
American University   Towson University
kbaker@american.edu   gpowell@towson.edu

PART I

The Foundation

Chapter 1

Introduction to Financial Management

How do we want the firms in our economy to measure their own performance? How do we want them to determine what is better versus worse? Most economists would answer simply that managers have a criterion for evaluating performance and deciding between alternative courses of action, and that the criterion should be maximization of the long-term market value of the firm . . . This Value Maximization proposition has its roots in 200 years of research in economics and finance. (Michael C. Jensen, "Value Maximization, Stakeholder Theory, and the Corporate Objective Function," *Journal of Applied Corporate Finance* 14, Fall 2001, p. 8.)

Overview

Business firms make decisions everyday. Virtually all business decisions have financial implications. Consequently, finance matters to everybody. We start our study of financial management by discussing the meaning of financial management and the role of the financial manager. We then turn to the corporate form of business organization and its advantages and disadvantages compared with other forms of business organization. To make effective business decisions, the financial manager should have a single-valued objective function. Thus, we advocate the maximization of shareholder wealth as the goal of financial management. Achieving this goal requires that the financial manager focus on economic profit, rather than accounting profit. Finally, we discuss potential agency problems involving the separation of ownership and management and mechanisms for aligning the interests of owners and managers.

Learning Objectives

After completing this chapter, you should be able to:

- understand the nature of financial management;
- describe the three major functions of the financial manager;
- discuss the advantages and disadvantages of corporations;
- identify the goal of financial management;
- differentiate between accounting profit and economic profit;
- explain the agency relationship and mechanisms for aligning the interests of owners and managers.

1.1 Financial Management and the Financial Manager

Financial management is an integrated decision-making process concerned with acquiring, financing, and managing assets to accomplish some overall goal within a business entity. Other names for financial management include managerial finance, corporate finance, and business finance. Making financial decisions is an integral part of all forms and sizes of business organizations from small privately held firms to large publicly traded corporations. Virtually every decision that a business makes has financial implications. Thus, financial decisions are not limited to the chief executive officer (CEO) and a handful of finance specialists. Managers involved in many areas within an organization such as production, marketing, engineering, and human resources among others make or participate in financial decisions at least occasionally.

The person associated with the financial management function is usually a top officer of the firm such as a vice president of finance or chief financial officer (CFO). This individual typically reports directly to the president or the CEO. In today's rapidly changing environment, the financial manager must have the flexibility to adapt to external factors such as economic uncertainty, global competition, technological change, volatility of interest and exchange rates, changes in laws and regulations, and ethical concerns. As the head of one of the major functional areas of the firm, the financial manager plays a pivotal leadership role in a company's overall efforts to achieve its goals.

The duties and responsibilities of the financial manager are far reaching. In broad terms, the two main functions of the financial manager concern acquiring and allocating funds among a firm's activities. This individual has policy-making duties regarding these functions. The financial manager also acts as a liaison between others in the finance department and management personnel from other departments.

In large firms, the financial manager often coordinates the activities of the treasurer and the controller. The treasurer is responsible for handling external financial matters, such as managing cash and credit, capital budgeting, raising funds, and financial analysis and planning. The controller's responsibilities mainly deal with internal matters which are accounting in nature. These activities involve cost accounting, taxes, payroll, and management information systems as well as preparing financial statements, budgets, and forecasts.

Practical Financial Tip 1.1

Understanding financial management is a key ingredient in the success of any business organization. Financial management focuses on business decisions that add value to the firm.

The objective of this book is to provide an introduction to the principles and techniques needed to make financial decisions that create value within profit-oriented business organizations, specifically corporations. Unlike a privately held corporation, a **publicly held corporation** is a corporation that sells shares outside of a closed group of investors. Many of the principles and techniques that govern corporate finance also apply to nonprofit organizations. While the techniques of financial management change over time, the fundamentals remain remarkably constant.

Financial Management Decisions

Financial management involves three major types of decisions: (1) long-term investment decisions, (2) long-term financing decisions, and (3) working capital management decisions. These decisions concern the acquisition and allocation of resources among the firm's various activities. The first two decisions are long term in nature and the third is short term. Managers should not consider these decisions on a piecemeal basis but as an integrated whole because they are seldom independent of one another. Investment decisions typically affect financing decisions and vice versa. For example, a decision to build a new plant or to buy new equipment requires other decisions on how to obtain the funds needed to finance the project and to manage the asset once acquired.

The following analogy illustrates the relationship among these decisions. Figure 1.1 shows a three-legged stool with each leg representing one of the firm's three major types of decision activities in financial management. Long-term investment decisions represent the most important leg on the stool because a firm's growth and profitability come largely from making appropriate investment decisions. The long-term financing and working capital management legs of the stool are also important because without them the stool (or the firm) will not function properly. Let's take a closer look at the three major types of financial management decisions.

Investment decisions
Long-term investment decisions involve determining the type and amount of assets that the firm wants to hold. That is, investing concerns allocating or using funds. The financial manager makes investment decisions about all types of assets – items on the left-hand side of the balance sheet. These decisions often involve buying, holding, reducing, replacing, selling,

Figure 1.1 The three-legged stool analogy: Broad classification of decision activities in financial management

and managing assets. The process of planning and managing a firm's long-term investments is called **capital budgeting**. Common questions involving long-term investments include:

- In what lines of business should the firm engage?
- Should the firm acquire other companies?
- What sorts of property, plant, and equipment should the firm hold?
- Should the firm modernize or sell an old production facility?
- Should the firm introduce a more efficient distribution system than the current one?

As these examples show, investment decisions involve not only those that create revenues and profits, but also those that save money. The answers to these questions flow from the firm's long-term investment strategy.

Making investment decisions requires applying a key principle of financial management. The **investment principle** states that the firm should invest in assets and projects yielding a return greater than the minimum acceptable hurdle rate. A **hurdle rate** is the minimum acceptable rate of return for investing resources in a project. The financial manager should set the hurdle rate to reflect the riskiness of the project with higher hurdle rates for riskier projects.

Financing decisions

Long-term financing decisions involve the acquisition of funds needed to support long-term investments. Such decisions concern the firm's **capital structure**, which is the mix of long-term debt and equity the firm uses to finance its operations. These sources of financing are shown on the right-hand side of the balance sheet. Firms have much flexibility in choosing a capital structure.

Typical financing questions facing the financial manager include:

- Does the type of financing used make a difference?
- Is the existing capital structure the right one?
- How and where should the firm raise money?
- Should the firm use funds raised through its revenues?
- Should the firm raise money from outside the business?
- If the firm seeks external financing, should it bring in other owners or borrow the money?

The financial manager can obtain the needed funds for its investments and operations either internally or externally. Internally generated funds represent the amount of earnings that the firm decides to retain after paying a cash dividend, if any, to its stockholders. Dividend policy is intimately connected to a firm's investment and financing decisions because the dividend–payout ratio determines the amount of earnings that a firm can retain. According to the **dividend principle**, a firm should return cash to the owners if there are not enough investments that earn the hurdle rate. For publicly traded firms, a firm has the option of returning cash to owners either through dividends or stock repurchases. The form of return depends largely on the characteristics of the firm's stockholders.

If the firm decides to raise funds externally, the financial manager can do so by incurring debts, such as through bank loans or the sale of bonds, or by selling ownership interests through a stock offering. The choice of financing method involves various tradeoffs. For example, a firm must repay debt with interest over a specific period without typically sharing control with the lender. By issuing common stock, the firm dilutes the control of current owners but does not have to repay the funds obtained from the stock sale.

When making financing decisions, managers should keep the financing principle in mind. The **financing principle** states that the financial manager should choose a financing mix that maximizes the value of the investments made and matches the financing to the assets being financed. Matching the cash inflows from the assets being financed with the cash outflows used to finance these assets reduces the potential risk.

Working capital management decisions
So far we have focused on long-term investment and financing decisions. Now we turn to the day-to-day investment and financing decisions of a firm. Decisions involving a firm's short-term assets and liabilities refer to **working capital management**. **Net working capital** is defined as current assets minus current liabilities. The financial manager has varying degrees of operating responsibility over current assets and liabilities. Some key questions that the financial manager faces involving working capital management include:

- How much of a firm's total assets should the firm hold in each type of current asset such as cash, marketable securities, and inventory?
- How much credit should the firm grant to customers?
- How should the firm obtain needed short-term financing?

In summary, some of the more important concerns of financial management can be distilled into three questions:

1 What long-term investments should the firm undertake? (Investment decisions)
2 How should the firm raise money to fund these investments? (Financing decisions)
3 How should the firm manage its short-term assets and liabilities? (Working capital management decisions)

These decisions affect a firm's success and ultimately the overall economy. For example, misallocation of resources can affect a company's prospects of survival and growth and can be detrimental to the economy as a whole. Accordingly, we will examine each of these decision areas in the chapters ahead.

The financial manager's role is to help answer these and other important questions facing the firm. The balance-sheet model shown in Figure 1.2 is one way to graphically portray the three major types of decisions facing the financial manager and their effects on the firm.

As Figure 1.2 shows, the firm's long-term investment decisions concern the left-hand side of the balance sheet and result in fixed assets. Fixed assets last for a long time and can result in tangible fixed assets, such as buildings, machinery, and equipment, and intangible fixed assets, such as patents and trademarks. The firm's long-term financing decisions concern the right-hand side of the balance sheet. That is, the financial manager can obtain funds to pay for investments from creditors (long-term liabilities) or owners (stockholders' equity). Decisions involving short-lived assets and liabilities are working capital management decisions.

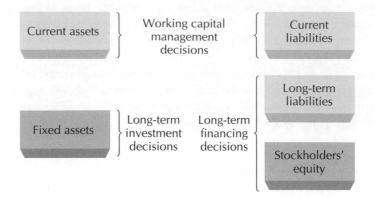

Figure 1.2 The balance-sheet model: Assets = Liabilities + Stockholders' Equity

Risk–Return Tradeoff

At the heart of most financial decisions is the concern about two specific factors: risk and return. An underlying assumption of finance is that investors should demand compensation for bearing risk. According to the concept of **risk aversion**, investors should expect a higher return for taking on higher levels of risk. Although considerable debate exists over the precise model for estimating risk and return, few contest the notion of a risk–return tradeoff. When making financial decisions, managers should assess the potential risk and rewards associated with these decisions. In fact, the foundation for maximizing shareholder wealth lies in understanding tradeoffs between risk and return.

Concept Check 1.1

1   What is financial management?
2   How do the roles of the firm's treasurer and controller differ?
3   What are three broad classifications of decisions within financial management? How are they related?
4   How does the notion of a risk–return tradeoff affect the behavior of financial managers?

1.2 Corporate Form of Business Organization

Although we focus on corporations in the chapters ahead, most principles and concepts underlying financial management apply across the three major forms of business organization.

- **Sole proprietorship**: a business owned and controlled by a single person.
- **Partnership**: a business owned by two or more individuals.
- **Corporation**: a legal entity separate and distinct from its owners.

Each of these legal forms of organizing firms has distinct advantages and disadvantages. As a firm grows in size, the advantages of the corporate form generally outweigh its disadvantages. In particular, the corporate form of business solves the problems associated with raising large amounts of cash. Not surprisingly, the corporation has emerged as the dominant force in today's global economy.

A sole proprietorship is the simplest, cheapest business to form, least regulated, and most common form of business organization. Despite these facts, corporations and their many variations around the world are the most important in terms of size and amount of business income generated. As a legal "person," a corporation has many of the rights, duties, and privileges of an actual person. For example, a corporation can enter into contractual agreements, own property, borrow money, sue others and be sued. Let's examine the major advantages and disadvantages of a corporation.

Advantages of Corporations

The corporate form offers several distinct advantages over other forms of business.

- *Unlimited life.* As a distinct legal entity, the corporation has a perpetual life. That is, the corporation can continue to operate after the original owners have withdrawn.
- *Limited liability.* Because the owners, who are the stockholders or shareholders, are not liable for the debts of the corporation, they have limited liability. In fact, the most that stockholders can lose is their initial investment.
- *Ease of ownership transfer.* For publicly held corporations, stockholders can readily sell their stock in the open market.
- *Ability to raise funds.* The previous three advantages enhance the corporation's ability to raise large sums of money. That is, corporations can raise funds by selling additional shares of stock.
- *Proportional distribution of income.* Corporations distribute income, often by paying dividends, in proportion to ownership interest. This differs from a sole proprietor who receives all income from the business or partners who receive income based on the terms of the partnership agreement.

Disadvantages of Corporations

Despite its advantages, the corporate form also has drawbacks.

- *Cost and complexity to start.* A corporation is more difficult and costly to set up than are other forms of business organization. In the United States, a corporation is incorporated in a specific state. Forming a corporation requires preparing a charter and a set of bylaws.

Public corporations must incur the expense of preparing and disclosing information to their shareholders and various regulatory bodies.

- *Double taxation.* Unlike income from a sole proprietorship and general partnership, which is taxed once, income paid to owners is subject to double taxation. That is, the corporation pays taxes on taxable income and individual shareholders pay taxes on the income received.

- *Separation of ownership and management.* In many corporations, especially larger ones, managers and owners represent separate groups. In theory, managers should run the corporation's affairs in the best interests of its stockholders. In practice, the interests of managers and owners may not always be the same. For example, managers may place their own interests ahead of those of the shareholders. We discuss these agency conflicts later in this chapter.

Concept Check 1.2

1   What are the major advantages and disadvantages of corporations?
2   Why can the separation of ownership and management potentially lead to conflicts?

1.3 The Goal of Financial Management

So far we have seen that financial managers are primarily concerned with long-term investment and financing decisions as well as with working capital management decisions within a firm. To make effective decisions, the financial manager needs a clear objective or goal to serve as a standard for evaluating performance and deciding between alternative courses of actions. Without such a criterion, the financial manager would be unable to keep score – that is, to measure better from worse.

What should be the fundamental purpose of a business firm, specifically a corporation? More directly, what should be the goal of financial management? The number of potential goals is extensive. A few possibilities include maximizing revenues, profits, earnings per share, returns, market share, or social good; minimizing costs; maintaining steady earnings growth; avoiding financial distress and bankruptcy; and surviving. Each of these possibilities has serious defects as a corporate goal. For example, profit maximization focuses on accounting profits, lacks a time dimension, and ignores risk. Although much division of opinion exists on the goal of financial management, two leading contenders are stakeholder theory and value (wealth) maximization.

Stakeholder Theory

Stakeholder theory is the main contender to value maximization as the corporate goal. Stakeholder theory asserts that managers should make decisions that take into account the interests of all of a firm's stakeholders. Such stakeholders include not only financial claimholders but also employees, managers, customers, suppliers, local communities, and the government. The major problem with stakeholder theory is that it involves multiple objectives. Telling the financial manager to maximize multiple objectives, some of which may be conflicting, would leave that manager with no way to make a reasoned decision. That is, corporate managers cannot effectively serve many masters. Purposeful behavior requires the existence of a single-valued objective function.

Value or Wealth Maximization

Most corporate financial theorists agree that the primary corporate goal is to maximize long-term firm value or wealth. Some dissent exists on whether the criterion should be maximization of the market value of the stockholders or the firm. Maximization of shareholder wealth focuses only on stockholders whereas maximization of firm value encompasses all financial claim holders including common stockholders, debt holders, and preferred stockholders.

Because common stockholders are the firm's most important stakeholders, the financial manager has a fiduciary responsibility to act in their best interests. From the stockholders' perspective, a good management decision would lead to an increase in the value of the stock. This is because investors generally prefer more wealth to less. Thus, the financial goal of the firm is *to maximize shareholder wealth as reflected in the market price of the stock*. The term **shareholders** refers to the firm's current owners or stockholders. For non-publicly traded firms, the objective in decision making is *to maximize firm value*.

In practice, this goal means that the financial manager can best serve business owners by identifying goods and services that add value to the firm because the marketplace desires and values the firm's offerings. This single-valued objective serves as a prerequisite for rational behavior within an organization. In fact, maximizing shareholder wealth has become the premier business mantra.

Why focus on maximizing share price? First, using stock price maximization as an objective function permits making definitive statements about the best way to allocate resources and to finance them. Second, stock prices are a highly observable measure that can be used to evaluate performance of publicly held corporations. No competing measure can provide as comprehensive a measure of a firm's standing. Stock price takes into account present and future earnings per share; the timing, duration, and risk of these earnings; the firm's dividend policy; and other factors affecting stock price. The market price of the firm's stock is a measure of the owners' economic well-being. Finally, stock prices reflect the long-run effects of decisions made by the firm.

Does a short-term increase or decrease in a firm's stock price mean that management is doing a good or poor job? Not necessarily. Many factors that influence stock prices are beyond management's control. Thus, management can only partially influence the stock price of the firm. Despite this difficulty, managers can still strive to maximize stockholder wealth in the context of the current economic and social environment.

Shareholder wealth maximization rests on several assumptions. The corporate objective function assumes that managers operate in the best interests of stockholders, not themselves, and do not attempt to expropriate wealth from lenders to benefit stockholders.

Shareholder wealth maximization also assumes that managers do not take actions to deceive financial markets in order to boost the price of the firm's stock. Another assumption is that managers act in a socially responsible manner and do not create unreasonable costs to society in pursuit of shareholder wealth maximization. This implies that the financial manager should not take illegal or unethical actions to increase the value of the equity owners. Given these assumptions, shareholder wealth maximization is consistent with the best interests of stakeholders and society in the long run.

Practical Financial Tip 1.2

The objective of decision making in financial management is *to maximize shareholder wealth as reflected in the market value of the stock*. This single-valued objective function is superior to alternatives because it provides managers with a rational basis for making financial decisions. Thus, when making a decision, rational managers should choose the alternative that most increases the wealth of the owners of the business.

Concept Check 1.3

1 How does value (wealth) maximization differ from stakeholder theory as a corporate goal?
2 What is the practical difficulty of using shareholder theory as the corporate goal?
3 What should be the financial goal of the firm? Why?
4 What are several assumptions underlying shareholder wealth maximization?

1.4 Accounting Profit versus Economic Profit

To achieve the corporate goal of maximizing shareholder wealth, should the financial manager focus on accounting profit or economic profit? As we will illustrate shortly, the answer is economic profit. Let's distinguish between accounting profit and economic profit.

Accounting profit is the difference between revenues and usually only explicit costs, recorded according to accounting principles. **Explicit costs** are measurable costs of doing business. Typical explicit costs include operating expenses such as cost of goods sold. Accounting costs generally do not include implicit costs, which are the returns the employed resource would have earned in its next best use. **Implicit costs** include opportunity costs associated with a firm's equity, costs of assets used in production, and owner-provided services. For example, the opportunity cost of equity capital is the implied rate of return that investors could earn by investing these funds elsewhere.

Economic profit is the difference between revenues and total costs (explicit and implicit costs, including the normal rate of return on capital). **Normal profit** is the minimum rate of return that investors are willing to accept for taking the risks of investment. By earning revenues in excess of its total costs, the firm has an economic profit. When revenues equal total costs, economic profit is zero. This does not mean, however, that investors are receiving no returns. Instead, investors are getting a return that provides the appropriate compensation for bearing the risk of the investment. When accounting profit is zero, investors would be better off investing elsewhere because they are not recovering their full costs. Because accounting profit ignores implicit costs, accounting profit is generally higher than economic profit. By maximizing economic profit, the financial manager can maximize shareholder wealth.

Practical Financial Tip 1.3

Managers should understand the difference between accounting profit and economic profit. From the perspective of maximizing shareholder wealth, the relevant profit is economic profit.

Example 1.1 Accounting Profit versus Economic Profit

Suppose an entrepreneur has $100,000 in cash and also owns a small building. This individual uses the cash to start a new venture and the building as a place of business. During the next year, the business generates $200,000 in sales revenues and incurs $150,000 in operating expenditures. The entrepreneur does not take any salary. Instead of opening the business, the entrepreneur's next best opportunities were to invest the cash elsewhere and earn $10,000, lease the building for $15,000, and take a job paying $50,000 for the year. Has this entrepreneur made a profit?

Solution: The answer depends on the type of profit under consideration. From an accounting standpoint, the entrepreneur earned a profit because revenues exceed costs by $50,000. After factoring in less obvious costs such as opportunity costs, the entrepreneur actually experienced an economic loss.

Revenue	$200,000
Expenditures	−150,000
Accounting profit	$50,000
Interest forgone	−10,000
Lease payment forgone	−15,000
Salary forgone	−50,000
Economic loss	−$25,000

Concept Check 1.4

1 How do explicit costs differ from implicit costs? Give several examples of each.
2 What is the difference between accounting profit and economic profit?
3 Is accounting profit or economic profit more relevant to achieving the financial goal of maximizing shareholder wealth? Why?

1.5 The Agency Relationship

So far we have seen that the financial manager should act in the best interest of shareholders by taking actions that maximize the stock price. We also have seen that a separation of ownership and management exists within modern corporations. As a consequence of this separation, might the interests of management and shareholders differ? The answer to this question is definitely yes. The possibility of conflicts of interest between the stockholders and management of a firm is called an **agency problem**. Let's examine how agency problems may occur.

Stockholders delegate decision-making authority to managers to run the business. An **agent** is a person who is authorized to act for another person or group called a **principal**. The relationship between the agent and the principal is called an **agency relationship**. An agency relationship exists between stockholders and management.

Several agency problems may exist with this agency relationship. One problem is that managers may abuse the use of benefits called **perquisites** or "perks" such as expensive offices as well as access to private jets and company cars. The abuse of perquisites imposes costs on the firm and ultimately its owners. Another problem is that managers may act in their own self-interest rather than those of the stockholders. For example, in the case of Tyco International, shareholders alleged that certain Tyco executives enriched themselves and others with company funds, falsified financial reports, and inflated pre-tax profits. These actions greatly depressed the company's stock price.

Firms incur costs, called **agency costs**, to reduce the potential for conflict between the interests of principals and agents. These costs can be direct or indirect. Direct agency costs often result from corporate expenditures that benefit management but involve a cost to the stockholders. Incentives such as bonuses, stock options, and perquisites are examples of such costs. **Monitoring costs**, which are costs borne by stockholders to monitor or limit the actions of the managers, are another type of direct agency cost. One example is paying outside auditors to determine the accuracy of accounting information. Another example is the cost of having a board of directors whose job is to make sure that decisions are made in the best interests of shareholders. An indirect agency cost could result from management's failure to make a profitable investment because of its aversion to risk.

Several mechanisms are available to help align the interests of managers and shareholders.

- *Managerial compensation.* The firm can use incentive compensation systems to align managers' and shareholders' interests. That is, a firm can structure salaries, bonuses, performance shares, and stock options to reward superior performance and penalize poor performance. **Performance shares** are shares of stock given to managers based on their performance as measured by such criteria as earnings per share. The notion behind having managers become substantial owners of company stock is to lessen their likelihood of behaving in a manner inconsistent with maximizing shareholder wealth. For example, managers are often given options to buy stock at a bargain price. As the stock rises, the value of the option also increases.

- *Direct shareholder intervention.* Investors, especially institutions holding a large number of shares, can intervene in corporate issues through their voting power and by nominating and electing members to the board of directors to represent their interests.
- *Threat of dismissal.* Stockholders elect the board of directors. One of the responsibilities of the board is to hire and fire top management. Thus, the board can fire managers who do not meet performance expectations.
- *Threat of acquisition.* Compared with well-managed firms, poorly managed firms are more likely to be acquisition targets because such firms have not provided sufficient value to stockholders and have greater turnaround potential. After the takeover, managers exhibiting poor performance are often fired.

Concept Check 1.5

1 What is an agency relationship?
2 Why do agency problems exist in large corporations?
3 What is the difference between direct and indirect agency costs? Give an example of each.
4 Describe four mechanisms available for aligning the interests of managers and stockholders.

1.6 Organization of the Book

Now that we have completed an introduction to financial management, we can take a closer look at the organization of this book. We focus on the fundamentals of financial management for profit-oriented businesses, especially corporations. Since we believe that the best way to learn finance is by applying its models, theories, and techniques, we provide numerous examples throughout the book.

Understanding Financial Management: A Practical Guide consists of 12 chapters in four parts. Part I, "The Foundation," contains five chapters providing the underpinnings of financial management. In Chapter 1 we define financial management, discuss major types of financial decisions, and advocate shareholder wealth maximization as the financial goal of the firm. Our next aim is to provide certain background materials and tools needed to make sound financial decisions that create value. Therefore, in Chapters 2 and 3 we discuss interpreting financial statements and conducting financial statement analysis primarily using ratios. In Chapters 4 and 5 we explore the topics of the time value of money and valuation. We develop basic procedures for valuing future cash flows with particular emphasis on stocks and bonds.

In Part II we focus on working capital management decisions. In Chapter 6 we examine various approaches to managing working capital including cash, accounts receivable, inventory, and payables. We also discuss short-term financing. In the past, the management of working capital consumed much of a financial manager's time. Today, long-term investment and financing decisions have assumed an increasingly important role in financial management.

In Part III we examine long-term investment decisions. Chapter 7 provides an overview of capital investment decisions and focuses on estimating project cash flows. We give a comprehensive example of estimating cash flows for an expansion and a replacement project. In Chapter 8 we consider capital budgeting, which results in the acquisition of fixed assets. In Chapter 9 we examine common ways to describe, assess, and adjust for risk associated with capital investments.

The final part, Part IV, focuses on long-term financing decisions. In Chapter 10 we discuss how business firms raise external capital and how investors trade securities. We examine how to determine the cost of three capital components: debt, preferred stock, and common equity. We also discuss how to calculate the weighted average cost of capital and the appropriate weights to use in this process. Finally, we examine how to calculate the marginal cost of capital and to determine the firm's optimal capital budget.

Chapter 11 investigates the financing mix for a firm. We illustrate how a firm may use financial leverage to increase the expected returns to shareholders while increasing risk for the shareholders. We show how taxes and certain market frictions may make a firm's capital structure decision relevant in the real world.

Finally, in Chapter 12, we focus on dividends and share repurchases because they are the principal mechanisms by which corporations disburse cash to their shareholders. We also discuss other related matters such as dividend reinvestment plans, stock dividends, stock splits, and reverse stock splits. We conclude that dividends can matter by affecting shareholder wealth because of various market imperfections and other factors.

In this book, we focus on core topics and leave the discussion of special topics such as mergers and acquisitions, risk management, leasing, financial distress, and international aspects of corporate finance to other sources. At the core of financial management are three interrelated decision areas: long-term investment, long-term financing, and working capital management (short-term) decisions. Taken together, these decisions determine the value of the firm to its shareholders. Creating value within a firm requires an understanding of financial management.

Summary

This chapter provides an introduction to some of the basic concepts underlying financial management. In this chapter, we stressed the following points:

1 Financial management is concerned with acquiring, financing, and managing assets to achieve a desired goal.
2 The financial management process involves three broad decision areas: (1) long-term investment decisions, (2) long-term financing decisions, and (3) working capital management decisions.
3 Financial decisions involve a risk–return tradeoff in which higher expected returns are accompanied by higher risk. The financial manager determines the appropriate risk–return tradeoff to maximize the value of the firm's stock.

4 Corporations offer several advantages over other forms of business organization including unlimited life, limited liability, ease of transferring ownership, and ability to raise funds. Corporations also have shortcomings including cost and complexity, double taxation, and separation of ownership and management.

5 The primary financial goal of the firm is to maximize the wealth of its shareholders. Shareholder wealth maximization is achieved in a public corporation by maximizing the market price of the firm's stock.

6 Maximizing shareholder wealth results from focusing on economic profit, not accounting profit.

7 Agency problems result when the interests of owners (principals) differ from the interests of managers (agents). Mechanisms available to align the interests of these parties include management compensation, direct shareholder intervention, threat of dismissal, and threat of takeovers.

FURTHER READING

Brickley, James A., Clifford W. Smith, Jr, and Jerold L. Zimmerman, "Corporate Governance, Ethics, and Organizational Architecture," *Journal of Applied Corporate Finance* 15, Spring 2003, 34–45.

Chambers, Donald R. and Nelson J. Lacey. "Corporate Ethics and Shareholder Wealth Maximization," *Financial Practice and Education* 6, Spring/Summer 1996, 83–96.

Cloninger, Dale O. "Managerial Goals and Ethical Behavior," *Financial Practice and Education* 5, Spring/Summer 1995, 50–59.

Damodaran, Aswath. *Applied Corporate Finance: A User's Manual*, John Wiley & Sons, Inc., 1992.

Hu, H. T. C. "Behind the Corporate Hedge: Information and the Limits of 'Shareholder Wealth Maximization,'" *Journal of Applied Corporate Finance* 9, 39–51.

Jensen, Michael C. "Value Maximization, Stakeholder Theory, and the Corporate Objective Function," *Journal of Applied Corporate Finance* 14, Fall 2001, 8–21.

Loderer, Claudio and Pius Zgraggen. "When Shareholders Choose Not to Maximize Value: The Union Bank of Switzerland's 1994 Proxy Fight," *Journal of Applied Corporate Finance* 12, Fall 1999, 91–102.

Miller, Merton H. "The History of Finance: An Eyewitness Account," *Journal of Applied Corporate Finance* 13, Summer 2000, 8–14.

Rexer, Christian and Timothy J. Sheehan. "Organizing the Firm: Choosing the Right Business Entity," *Journal of Applied Corporate Finance* 7, Spring 1994, 59–65.

Shefrin, Hersh. "Behavioral Corporate Finance," *Journal of Applied Corporate Finance* 14, Fall 2001, 113–24.

Smith, Michael P. "Shareholder Activism by Institutional Investors: Evidence from CalPERS," *Journal of Finance* 51, March 1996, 227–52.

Wallace, James S. "Value Maximization and Stakeholder Theory: Compatible or Not?" *Journal of Applied Corporate Finance* 15, Spring 2003, 120–27.

Chapter 2

Interpreting Financial Statements

At Berkshire, full reporting means giving you the information that we would wish you to give to us if our positions were reversed. What Charlie and I would want under that circumstance would be all the important facts about current operations as well as the CEO's frank view of the long-term economic characteristics of the business. We would expect both a lot of financial details and a discussion of any significant data we would need to interpret what was presented. (Warren E. Buffett, Chairman of the Board, Berkshire Hathaway, Inc., 2000 Annual Report.)

Overview

This chapter discusses the basic financial statements issued by a firm including the balance sheet, income statement, statement of cash flows, and statement of retained earnings. We focus mainly on how financial managers can interpret the information reported in these statements. We emphasize the need to understand the difference between the accounting net income reported on the firm's income statement and the actual net cash flow generated by the firm during that same period. We discuss how to construct and interpret vertical common-size balance sheets and income statements to facilitate the analysis of trends over time and to compare firms of different size.

Learning Objectives

After completing this chapter, you should be able to:

- understand why many different stakeholders need to understand and interpret a firm's financial statements;
- describe the structure and understand the contents of a company's balance sheet, income statement, statement of cash flows, and statement of retained earnings;
- explain the differences between net income and cash flow;
- recognize the limitations of historical accounting information;
- interpret the information provided in common-size financial statements.

2.1 Basics of Annual Reports and Financial Statements

Knowing how to interpret **financial statements** is critically important to the many stakeholders of the firm. Lenders carefully scrutinize a firm's statements to assess the likelihood that the firm can repay the principal and pay the interest when due over the life of a loan. Equity investors analyze financial statements to assess the long-term profitability of a firm.

Suppliers use these statements to assess whether the company can fully pay its obligations on time. Customers are concerned with its continuing viability, both to supply new products and to maintain those already purchased. Employees may use their firm's financial statements to assess its future, knowing that their jobs depend on its immediate solvency, long-term debt-paying ability, and future long-term profitability. Employees are also concerned about whether the firm can meet its future pension obligations.

But we have left out perhaps one of the most important users of financial statements – the firm's management. Managers carefully assess data from these financial statements when making important investment, financing, and working capital policy decisions. Data from financial statements may be used to determine incentives and rewards for a firm's managers. These managers may use the financial data in these statements to allocate capital investments within a firm's various segments or divisions. Divisional managers use financial statement data to implement changes to improve the performance of their respective divisions.

Financial statements are probably the most important source of information from which these various stakeholders (other than management) can assess a firm's financial health. Our objective in this chapter is to show how to interpret the contents and to understand the limitations of the following financial statements – balance sheet, income statement, statement of cash flows, and statement of retained earnings. Like a patient's medical report issued by a physician, the information in these statements can provide important information that helps us to better understand the firm's financial condition.

Corporate Annual Reports

Most public firms in the United States (US) prepare two annual reports. These include the annual report to the Securities and Exchange Commission (SEC) and the shareholder annual report. The annual report to the SEC, known as **Form 10-K**, provides both financial and non-financial information about a firm, including a comprehensive review of the company's business. This report is much more comprehensive than the annual report to shareholders.

The shareholder annual report is the most widely read annual report. It contains financial and non-financial information that is important to the various users of financial statements discussed above. The information provided includes both aggregated financial information and sales and marketing information. The shareholder annual report typically includes a statement of corporate mission and strategy, an executive message, product information, discussion of financial performance, comparative financial information, an audit report, and selected investor information. Both the SEC and shareholder annual reports contain the firm's financial statements, which are the focus of this chapter.

Firms in the US prepare their financial statements according to **generally accepted accounting principles (GAAP)**. GAAP provides the conventions, rules, and procedures that define how firms should maintain records and prepare financial reports. The *Financial Accounting Standards Board (FASB)*, the US accounting profession's rule-making organization, provides the guidelines upon which these rules and procedures are based. The FASB also sets forth the conceptual framework for understanding the information provided by financial statements. The qualitative characteristics of accounting information include relevance, timeliness, reliability, consistency, and comparability.

Overview of Financial Statements

Public corporations in the US and many other countries are required to prepare and disclose the following financial statements to the public on a periodic basis:

- balance sheet;
- income statement;
- statement of cash flows;
- statement of retained earnings.

Firms typically prepare these statements quarterly, but many analysts and users of financial statements concentrate on a firm's fiscal year-end statements. Firms provide the annual statements in both the annual report to the SEC (Form 10-K) and the shareholder annual report. Firms provide Form 10-Q statements filed on a quarterly basis with the SEC. New US legislation requires that annual statements be filed within 60 days of the company's year-end and quarterly statements within 35 days of the close of the quarter. Only three quarterly reports are required, as the firm's year-end annual report replaces the fourth quarterly report.

In the following sections, we look at these financial statements using the consolidated financial statements for the Home Depot Corporation. Home Depot is the world's largest home improvement retailer with more than 1,500 stores, most of which are located in the US. Since being founded in 1978, Home Depot has experienced remarkable growth and profitability. To reflect its prestige as a leading US company, it was included in 2000 as one of the 30 firms in the Dow Jones Industrial Average.

Concept Check 2.1

1   Which stakeholders need to interpret a firm's financial statements?
2   How can a firm's management use its financial statements to make important decisions?
3   What are the four financial statements issued by a firm?
4   How often are financial statements produced?

2.2 Balance Sheet

A **balance sheet** reports a firm's assets, liabilities, and owners' (stockholders') equity as of a given date, usually at the end of a reporting period. A firm's assets represent its investments (what it owns), and the liabilities (what it owes), while owners' equity represents how the firm financed these investments (assets). One way to think of a balance sheet is as a financial snapshot of the firm's assets, liabilities, and owners' equity at a particular point in time.

Figure 2.1 General format of a balance sheet

Constructing a balance sheet involves the basic accounting identity:

Assets = Liabilities + Owners' equity   (2.1)

Following this identity, **assets** often appear on the left-hand side of the balance sheet, while the liabilities and owners' equity appear on the right-hand side, as shown in Figure 2.1. Sometimes balance sheets are portrayed using a top-down approach with assets at the top, followed by liabilities, and lastly by owners' equity at the bottom. Balance sheets are frequently shown with major balance sheet categories using a left-hand side and right-hand side structure.

Figure 2.2 shows the balance sheets for Home Depot at the fiscal year-end dates of February 3, 2002, and February 2, 2003. In the following sections, we briefly discuss the major areas within a balance sheet using Home Depot's balance sheet.

Let's look at the asset side of Home Depot's balance sheet. The assets are listed in order of decreasing liquidity beginning with the firm's current assets. Home Depot's **current assets** include its cash and cash equivalents, short-term investments, receivables, inventories, and other current assets such as prepaid expenses. Current assets are those assets in the form of cash or that are expected to be converted into cash within 1 year. Cash and cash equivalents include cash and other negotiable instruments such as checks and money orders that the bank does not have the legal right to demand notice before withdrawal. Short-term investments include short-term money market investments that have maturities of 1 year or less. The receivables represent those credit sales that the firm has not yet collected. They are reported on a net basis, which excludes credit sales that are overdue and unlikely to be ultimately collected. Inventories represent those items that remain unsold as of the balance sheet reporting date, but are likely to be sold within the next year. Other current assets such as prepaid expenses include payments made for benefits to be received within 1 year, such as payments for rent or insurance premiums.

Home Depot's sizable level of total current assets of about $11,917 million on the February 2, 2003 balance sheet date represent more than a third of its total assets. Maintaining a sufficient level of current assets is essential for a firm to ensure that it has enough cash and

The Home Depot, Inc. and Subsidiaries

Amounts in millions	February 2, 2003	February 3, 2002
Assets		
Current assets		
Cash and cash equivalents	$2,188	$2,477
Short-term investments	65	69
Receivables, net	1,072	920
Merchandise inventories	8,338	6,725
Other current assets	254	170
Total current assets	11,917	10,361
Property, plant and equipment (PPE), net		
Land	5,560	4,972
Buildings	9,197	7,698
Furniture, fixtures, and equipment	4,074	3,403
Leasehold improvements	872	750
Construction in progress	724	1,049
Capital leases	306	257
Gross PPE	20,733	18,129
Less accumulated depreciation and amortization	3,565	2,754
Net PPE	17,168	15,375
Long-term investments	107	83
Goodwill	575	419
Other assets	244	156
Total assets	$30,011	$26,394
Liabilities and stockholders' equity		
Current liabilities		
Accounts payable	4,560	3,436
Accrued salaries and related expenses	809	717
Sales taxes payable	307	348
Deferred revenue	998	851
Income taxes payable	227	211
Other accrued expenses	1,134	938
Total current liabilities	8,035	6,501
Long-term debt, excluding current installments	1,321	1,250
Other long-term liabilities	491	372
Deferred income taxes	362	189
Total liabilities	10,209	8,312
Stockholders' equity		
Common stock, par value $0.05	118	117
Paid-in capital	5,858	5,412
Retained earnings	15,971	12,799
Accumulated other comprehensive loss	(82)	(220)
Unearned compensation	(63)	(26)
Treasury stock	(2,000)	–
Total stockholders' equity	19,802	18,082
Total liabilities and stockholders' equity	$30,011	$26,394

Figure 2.2 Consolidated balance sheets

near-cash to meet its short-term obligations and a sufficient level of inventory to meet sales in the near term. We examine the management of a firm's current assets in Chapter 6 when we discuss the working capital decisions of a firm.

The next section of Home Depot's balance sheet contains its property, plant, and equipment (PPE). Home Depot provides substantial detail in this section with separate line items provided for its land, buildings, furniture, fixtures and equipment, leasehold improvements, construction in progress, and capital leases. Home Depot reports PPE on a net basis by subtracting the accumulated depreciation and amortization that has been taken as an expense on the income statement. However, firms generally cannot depreciate land as it represents an asset that retains its economic and productive value over time.

Long-term investments, goodwill, and other assets complete the asset side of Home Depot's balance sheet. Long-term investments include securities, bonds, and investments that Home Depot expects to hold for longer than 1 year. Goodwill is the cost in excess of the fair value of the net assets acquired. Finally, other assets may include various items such as non-current receivables and intangible assets. Non-current receivables are those receivables Home Depot expects to remain outstanding for longer than 1 year. Intangible assets, which have no physical substance, include items such as patents, copyrights, and trademarks.

The **liability** section of the balance sheet consists of current liabilities and long-term liabilities. Current liabilities include a firm's short-term maturing obligations. Home Depot's current liabilities include its accounts payable, accrued salaries, sales tax payable, deferred revenue, income taxes payable, and other accrued expenses. Home Depot expects to pay these liabilities within 1 year.

The long-term liabilities for Home Depot include the firm's long-term debt, other long-term liabilities, and deferred income taxes. The long-term debt includes only the debt due for longer than 1 year (current liabilities include the current portion of long-term debt). Deferred income taxes result when the pretax income shown on a firm's tax return is less than what is reported as income before taxes on the income statement. The difference in taxes is caused by different depreciation methods for reporting purposes and for tax purposes.

Other common long-term liabilities (not shown explicitly on Home Depot's balance sheet) include capital leases and minority interest. A lease must be classified as a **capital lease** if the lease transfers substantially all of the benefits and risks associated with ownership of the property to the lessee. If the lease meets any of the following four criteria, the firm must treat it as a capital lease: (1) the lessor transfers ownership of the property to the lessee by the end of the lease term; (2) the lease contains a bargain purchase option; (3) the lease term is equal to 75 percent of the estimated economic life of the leased property; or (4) the present value at the beginning of the lease term of the minimum lease payments equals or exceeds 90 percent of the fair market value of the property. A firm reports the present value of a capital lease as both an asset (included in plant and equipment) and as a long-term liability on its balance sheet.

Minority interest represents the proportionate stake that outside minority shareholders have in a firm's consolidated subsidiaries. This claim arises because a firm owns less than 100 percent of some firms whose assets and liabilities have been completely consolidated into the parent firm's balance sheet and income statement. The minority interest is therefore listed as a credit on the parent firm's balance sheet. Because the minority interest is not an immediate claim on any of the parent firm's resources, it typically appears between the debt and equity sections of the balance sheet.

The **stockholders' equity** section lists Home Depot's common stock and paid-in capital accounts that combine to tell how much capital has been raised through the issuance of common stock. Home Depot's **retained earnings** represent the firm's cumulative net income that has been reinvested back into the firm and not distributed to shareholders as cash dividends. Treasury stock represents shares of common stock that Home Depot repurchased from shareholders. Total stockholders' equity for Home Depot as of February 2, 2003 was $19,802 million, which represents about two-thirds of the total financing.

Historical Cost versus Current Market Value

The values of most items reported on a firm's balance sheet are reported in terms of their accounting book values, which are based on historical cost or original value. The historical cost of an asset is the price paid when the firm acquires the asset. The historical cost of a liability is the amount involved when the firm incurs the liability.

Financial managers and analysts recognize that these historical values may differ substantially from their current market values. This is especially true for real estate and stockholders' equity. For example, Home Depot reports its net property, plant, and equipment as $17,168 million on the February 2, 2003 balance sheet date. This reported value may understate the true market value of these assets. In particular, the market value of the land owned by Home Depot may be much higher due to both inflation and supply and demand conditions. This understatement problem is avoided with the long-term investments reported on the balance sheet. Long-term investments are reported at their fair market value.

The total value of stockholders' equity reported on a firm's balance sheet might also differ substantially from the current market value of the firm's equity. The market value of a firm's equity is equal to the number of shares of common stock outstanding times the price per share, while the amount reported on the firm's balance sheet is basically the cumulative amount the firm raised when issuing common stock and any reinvested net income (retained earnings).

Practical Financial Tip 2.1

A firm's balance sheet provides important information about a firm's assets, liabilities, and owners' equity. Analysts should remember that the values of most items reported on a firm's balance sheet are reported in terms of their accounting book values, which are based on historical cost or original value, not market values. As a result, some asset values on a firm's balance sheet, such as land, may be substantially undervalued following periods of high inflation. Analysts should also recognize that the shareholders' equity on a firm's balance sheet does not represent current market value.

Concept Check 2.2

1 What is the basic accounting identity followed in a firm's balance sheet?
2 An analyst suggests that firms should use market value amounts on the balance sheet. What are some of the advantages and disadvantages of this approach?
3 Why may items based on historical cost differ from their market values?

2.3 Income Statement

An **income statement**, also called a statement of earnings or a profit and loss statement, summarizes the total revenues earned and the total expenses incurred to generate these revenues over a specified period of time. The difference between total revenues and total expenses during a given period is referred to as the firm's **net income** for that period, also commonly referred to as the firm's net earnings or profits.

An income statement is usually divided into two sections: operating and non-operating. Firms report the revenues and expenses that correspond to day-to-day operations in the operating section. Subtracting operating expenses from operating income or revenue yields the **operating income (loss)** for the firm. This is an important profitability measure of a firm's business operations. The non-operating section includes income and expense items and gains and losses that are routine to most types of businesses, but viewed as peripheral to day-to-day business operations. Non-operating items include dividend and interest income earned, interest expense, and gains or losses associated with the disposal of assets or the elimination of liabilities.

Firms have some discretion in the amount of detail they disclose in their income statement. For example, some firms may condense many of their operating expenses while others may provide a more detailed breakdown of these expenses. But regardless of the amount of detail shown or the format chosen by a firm, an income statement will follow the general format discussed above.

Figure 2.3 shows the consolidated statements of earnings (income statements) for Home Depot for the fiscal years ending on January 28, 2001, February 3, 2002, and February 2, 2003. Throughout this chapter, we refer to the fiscal year ending on February 2, 2003 as fiscal year 2002 (or simply FY 2002) and the fiscal year ending on February 3, 2002 as fiscal year 2001 (FY 2001).

As we progress down an income statement, we can examine the profit or loss after each type of expense item is deducted. With sales revenue of $58,247 million and cost of merchandise sold of $40,139 million, Home Depot reports gross profit of $18,108 million. Gross profit represents the profit after subtracting costs directly related to sales. For a manufacturing firm, gross profit would be calculated by subtracting cost of goods sold from sales. Gross profit would generally not be a relevant profit figure for a service-oriented firm.

The Home Depot, Inc. and Subsidiaries

Amounts in millions, except per share data	Fiscal Year Ended		
	February 2, 2003	February 3, 2002	January 28, 2001
Net sales	$58,247	$53,553	$45,738
Cost of merchandise sold	40,139	37,406	32,057
Gross profit	18,108	16,147	13,681
Operating expenses			
Selling and store operating	11,180	10,163	8,513
Pre-opening	96	117	142
General and administrative	1,002	935	835
Total operating expenses	12,278	11,215	9,490
Operating income	5,830	4,932	4,191
Interest and investment income	79	53	47
Earnings before interest and taxes	5,909	4,985	4,238
Interest expense	37	28	21
Earnings before provision for income taxes	5,872	4,957	4,217
Provision for income taxes	2,208	1,913	1,636
Net earnings	$3,664	$3,044	$2,581
Weighted average common shares	2,336	2,335	2,315
Basic earnings per share	$1.57	$1.30	$1.11
Diluted weighted average common shares	2,344	2,353	2,352
Diluted earnings per share	$1.56	$1.29	$1.10

Figure 2.3 Consolidated statements of earnings

With total operating expenses of $12,278 million, Home Depot reports an operating income of $5,830 million for the period. Home Depot breaks down its operating expenses into selling and store operating, pre-opening, and general and administrative expenses. Analysts pay close attention to a firm's operating income because it provides an important indication of the firm's profitability from its continuing operations before considering other income or expenses. Examining the trends in a firm's operating income may provide a good indication of its past continuing operations and may also provide a basis for extrapolating future operating profitability.

As we will show later when we examine the balance sheet, Home Depot uses a limited amount of debt financing and has a low interest expense of $37 million in fiscal year 2002. When firms borrow, they repay the lender by making a debt payment that consists of both interest expense and a portion of the principal repayment. The interest expense is subtracted on the income statement to arrive at a firm's income before tax. Thus, the interest expense associated with debt financing is a tax-deductible expense. In addition to paying interest on its debt, Home Depot receives interest and income on its investments that exceed the tax-deductible interest that it pays. We find that Home Depot actually earned more interest on its investments than it paid ($79 million earned versus $37 million paid in fiscal year 2002) in the income statement periods shown in Figure 2.3.

With earnings before tax of $5,872 million and an income tax provision of $2,208 million, Home Depot reports **net earnings** (commonly referred to as **net income**) of $3,664 million for fiscal year 2002. This represents an increase of 20.4 percent over the $3,044 million net income that Home Depot earned in fiscal year 2001 and a 42.0 percent increase in the $2,581 million net income reported in fiscal year 2000. The net income generated by a firm is either paid out as dividends to common or preferred stockholders or reinvested into the firm as retained earnings (stockholders' equity account on the firm's balance sheet).

Analysts and investors pay close attention to the **earnings per share** reported on a firm's income statement. The presentation of earnings per share figures depends on whether the firm has a *simple* or *complex* capital structure. A **simple capital structure** occurs when a firm is financed only with common stock and other non-convertible senior securities. That is, the firm's financing structure does not contain any potentially dilutive securities. This firm will report **basic earnings per share**, which is calculated by dividing the net income less any preferred dividends paid out by the weighted average number of outstanding shares of common stock.

$$\text{Basic EPS} = \frac{\text{Net income} - \text{Preferred dividends}}{\text{Weighted average common shares}} \qquad (2.2)$$

Firms with **complex capital structures** have potentially dilutive securities such as convertible securities, options, and warrants that could potentially dilute earnings per share. These firms must report both basic and **diluted earnings per share** figures. The diluted earnings per share figure provides a more conservative earnings estimate by assuming the total shares of common stock in the denominator includes all shares of common stock plus future potential shares from the likely future conversion of outstanding convertible securities, stock options, and warrants.[1]

With approximately 2,336 million shares of common stock outstanding, Home Depot reports its *basic earnings per share* as $1.57 per share for fiscal year 2002. Home Depot also reports diluted earnings per share of $1.56 by using 2,344 million shares assuming dilution. The calculations are summarized below:

Basic EPS = Net income / Number of shares of common equity
Basic EPS = $3,664 million / 2,336 million = $1.57 per share

Diluted EPS = Net income / Number of shares of common equity assuming dilution
Diluted EPS = $3,664 million / 2,344 million = $1.56 per share

The calculation of diluted EPS includes potential future common shares from the likely future conversion of outstanding stock options and warrants in the denominator of the EPS calculation.

---

[1]   Most financial accounting textbooks provide explanations of how to calculate diluted earnings per share.

Net Income versus Cash Flow

The net income reported on a firm's income statement typically does not equal the actual net **cash flow** generated by that firm over the particular time period. Net income and actual net cash flow may differ because accountants use an accrual accounting process for recognizing revenues and expenses, and because of the treatment of depreciation and taxes. We discuss each of these items in the following sections.

Accrual accounting
Firms normally record revenues on their income statement when the sale is made, not when the cash is actually collected from that sale. Firms recognize the expense of producing an item when the activity that generates the expense is performed, not when the firm actually pays out the cash for that expense. Accountants refer to recognizing the timing of revenues and expenses in this manner as **accrual accounting**. Under an accrual accounting process, for a given reporting period, the cash receipts from sales will not equal the revenue reported, nor will the cash disbursed equal the expenses recognized.

We cannot tell directly from a firm's income statement how these timing differences may cause net income and cash flow to differ. But we can get a good idea if we also examine the firm's balance sheet. Home Depot, for example, lists its accounts receivable (net) in the fiscal years ending on February 3, 2002, and February 2, 2003, as $920 million and $1,072 million, respectively, an increase of $152 million. Thus, about $152 million of the $58,247 million in net sales in the fiscal year ending in February 2003 (fiscal year 2002) did not represent actual cash inflows for Home Depot. Similarly, increases or decreases in accounts payable and accrued expenses between the balance sheet dates February 3, 2002, and February 2, 2003, indicate that the expenses reported on their income statement for fiscal year 2002 do not represent the actual cash outflows associated with these expenses during the fiscal year.

Moreover, the cost of goods sold on a firm's income statement for a given year reflects only the expenses for goods that the firm actually sold during the year. Thus, any cash outflows associated with the increase in merchandise inventories are not included as expenses until the items are sold. With the large increase in merchandise inventories from $6,725 million on February 3, 2002, to $8,338 million on February 2, 2003, the expenses listed on the income statement probably understate the actual cash outflows incurred by the firm for these expenses during the year (unless, of course, Home Depot has not yet paid their suppliers for these inventories). We will examine more closely how to disentangle these differences between net income and cash flow when we examine the Statement of Cash Flows in a later section.

Depreciation
An income statement usually includes several non-cash expenses of which the most common include **depreciation** and **amortization**. When a firm makes capital expenditures for long-term fixed assets, such as for plant and equipment, it normally cannot include the entire expense for these purchases during the year in which the capital expenditures are incurred.

Instead, the firm must spread or allocate that capital expenditure over a future period of time that reflects the estimated life of the tangible asset. Thus, depreciation is the allocation of the cost of property, plant, and equipment over its useful life. Similarly, firms spread the cost of intangible assets, such as patents and brand names, over future years in a process referred to as amortization.

For example, if a firm purchased some equipment for $13 million that has an estimated life of 5 years and an estimated salvage value of $3 million, the firm might use the **straight-line method** of depreciation to obtain a depreciation expense of $2 million each year over the 5-year life of the equipment.

$$\text{Annual depreciation (straight-line)} = \frac{\text{Original cost} - \text{Estimated salvage value}}{\text{Estimated life in years}} \quad (2.3)$$

$$\text{Annual depreciation (straight-line)} = \frac{\$13 \text{ million} - \$3 \text{ million}}{5 \text{ Years}} = \$2 \text{ million}$$

Of course, these future depreciation expenses do not represent actual net cash flows in the years in which they are reported on the firm's income statement – the cash flow occurred in the year in which the firm paid for the purchased equipment. Table 2.1 summarizes these timing differences between the actual cash flows and the depreciation reported on the income statement.

Table 2.1 Timing differences: Actual cash flow versus depreciation on income statement

Year	Cash flow	Depreciation on income statement
0	$10 million	–
1	–	$2 million
2	–	$2 million
3	–	$2 million
4	–	$2 million
5	–	$2 million

Home Depot does not list its depreciation expense separately on its income statements, but includes depreciation expense under General and Administrative expenses. Home Depot reports a combined depreciation and amortization of $903 million on its Statement of Cash Flows for fiscal year 2002 (refer to Figure 2.4). In Note 1 in the *Notes to Consolidated Financial Statements* in the Annual Report, Home Depot provides some additional information on its depreciation and amortization. We discuss other useful information provided in the Notes to the Financial Statements section of an Annual Report in Section 2.7.

Taxes

Home Depot reports an income tax expense of $2,208 million on its fiscal year 2002 income statement. However, the actual income tax paid by Home Depot differs from this amount. Many differences exist between treatments of items under tax and book accounting. These differences are reflected in what is shown on the financial statements and what is paid to the Internal Revenue Service (IRS). One example is the different depreciation methods allowed for tax purposes as opposed to book (financial statement) purposes:

- When preparing the income statement for the public, firms tend to use straight-line depreciation over periods of time that reflect the estimated lives of the assets being depreciated.
- When determining taxable income for the IRS, firms can use accelerated depreciation methods that allow depreciation over shorter time periods with accelerated rates in the early years of the assets' lives. Accelerated depreciation methods allow higher depreciation rates in the early years, resulting in lower taxable income and lower immediate tax payments for the firm.

The choice of depreciation methods affects both the income statement and balance sheet, especially for capital intensive companies. When compared to accelerated methods, straight-line depreciation has lower depreciation expense in the early years of asset life, which tends to lead to a higher tax expense but higher net income. On the balance sheet, both assets and equity are higher under straight-line depreciation versus accelerated methods during the early years of an asset. Toward the end of an asset's life, these relationships reverse.

Thus, we would expect Home Depot's taxable income expense of $2,208 million in fiscal year 2002 to understate its actual tax payment made. We can confirm that this is the case by noting that the liability for deferred income taxes on the balance sheet increased by about $173 million between the February 3, 2002, and February 2, 2003, balance sheet dates.

Concept Check 2.3

1 Why should analysts pay close attention to a firm's operating income?
2 Why may a firm's net income differ from its net cash flow?
3 Some users of financial statements become frustrated that firms use varying formats for the income statements and balance sheets. What would be the advantages and disadvantages of requiring all firms to use the same format?
4 If a firm reports a wide difference between its basic and diluted earnings per share, should this difference concern investors? Why or why not?
5 How can the choice of depreciation methods affect a firm's income statement and balance sheet? Give several examples.

Practical Financial Tip 2.2

The actual cash flows generated by a firm may differ from its net income during a given period due to accrual accounting practices, noncash revenues and expenses, and taxes.

- *Accrual accounting*: revenues are normally recorded on an income statement when the sale is made and not when the cash is actually collected from that sale, and the corresponding expense of producing an item is recorded when the revenue is recorded, not when the cash is actually paid out for that expense.
- *Noncash revenues and expenses*: the income statement usually includes noncash expenses such as *depreciation* and *amortization*.
- *Taxes*: firms in the US can use one depreciation method for determining taxable income for their financial statements for reporting purposes and another method for determining their taxable income reportable to the tax authority (IRS).

2.4 Statement of Cash Flows

A firm's **statement of cash flows** summarizes changes in its cash position over a specified period of time. A firm's cash position may change during a year as it collects revenues, pays operating expenses, and generates income (or loss). Cash also decreases as the firm buys fixed assets, increases inventories, finances additional accounts receivable, reduces outstanding debt obligations, pays dividends, or buys back shares of its stock. Its cash position will improve as it generates net income, finances additional accounts payable, sells assets and investments, and issues long-term debt and stock. The statement of cash flows helps us understand how these various activities change the firm's cash position during the year.

The statement of cash flows consists of three sections: (1) operating cash flows, (2) investing cash flows, and (3) financing cash flows. Activities in each area that bring in cash represent **sources of cash** while activities that involve spending cash are **uses of cash**.

Operating Cash Flows

Cash flow from operations (CFO) reports the cash generated from sales and the cash used in the production process. Such items flow through the firm's income statement and working capital items. Under US GAAP, typical operating activities include cash collections from sales, cash operating expenses, cash interest expense, and cash tax payments.

There are two ways to calculate cash flow from operations: (1) the direct method and (2) the indirect method. Both methods result in the same cash flow from operations.

- **Direct method**. The direct method, also called the top-down approach, derives operating cash flows by taking each item from the income statement and converting it to

The Home Depot, Inc. and Subsidiaries

Amount in millions	February 2, 2003	February 3, 2002
Cash provided from operations		
Net earnings	$3,664	$3,044
Reconciliation of net earnings to net cash provided by operations		
Depreciation and amortization	903	764
(Increase) decrease in receivables, net	(38)	(119)
Increase in merchandise inventories	(1,592)	(166)
Increase in accounts payable and accrued liabilities	1,394	1,878
Increase in deferred revenue	147	200
Increase in income taxes payable	83	272
Increase (decrease) in deferred income taxes	173	(6)
Other operating activities	68	96
Net cash provided by operations	4,802	5,963
Cash flows from investing activities		
Capital expenditures	(2,749)	(3,393)
Payments for businesses acquired, net	(235)	(190)
Proceeds from sales of businesses, net	22	64
Proceeds from sales of property and equipment	105	126
Purchases of investments	(583)	(85)
Proceeds from maturities of investments	506	25
Advances secured by real estate, net		(13)
Net cash used by investing activities	(2,934)	(3,466)
Cash flows from financing activities		
Issuance (repayments) of commercial paper obligations, net	–	(754)
Proceeds from long-term debt	1	532
Repayments of long-term debt	–	–
Repurchase of common stock	(2,000)	–
Proceeds from sale of common stock, net	326	445
Cash dividends paid to stockholders	(492)	(396)
Net cash provided by financing activities	(2,165)	(173)
Effect of exchange rate changes on cash and cash equivalents	8	(14)
(Decrease) increase in cash and cash equivalents	(289)	2310
Cash and cash equivalents at beginning of year	2,477	167
Cash and cash equivalents at end of year	$2,188	$2,477
Supplemental disclosure of cash payments made for:		
Interest, net of interest capitalized	$50	$18
Income taxes	$1,951	$1,685

Figure 2.4 Statement of Cash Flows

its cash equivalent by adding or subtracting the changes in the corresponding balance sheet accounts.

- **Indirect method**. The indirect method, also called the bottom-up approach, involves several steps. This approach begins with the firm's net earnings (income) for the period, and then subtracts gains or adds losses that result from financing or investment cash flows. Next, the approach adds back any non-cash charges such as depreciation and amortization it subtracted to arrive at net income. Net income is further adjusted by accounting for any cash that the firm used to fund increases in current assets or decreases in current liabilities. As we will soon see, Home Depot uses the indirect method to calculate cash flow from operations.

Investing Cash Flows

Cash flow from investing (CFI) reports the cash used to acquire and dispose of non-cash assets. Firms acquire such assets with the expectation of generating income. Such items are found in the non-current portion of the asset section of the balance sheet. Investing activities often include purchases of property, plant, and equipment, investments in joint ventures and affiliates, payments for businesses acquired, proceeds from sales of assets, and investments in or sales of marketable securities.

Financing Cash Flows

Cash flows from financing (CFF) reports capital structure transactions. These items are located in the long-term capital section of the balance sheet and the statement of retained earnings and involve activities related to contributing, withdrawing, and servicing of funds to support the firm's business activities. Financing activities include new debt issuances, debt repayments or retirements, stock sales and repurchases, and cash dividend payments.

Figure 2.4 shows the statement of cash flows for Home Depot for fiscal years 2001 and 2002. The first section provides details on the net cash provided from operations. To arrive at its net cash provided by operations, Home Depot adds back to its net income the depreciation and amortization expense for fiscal year 2002. Remember that depreciation and amortization are non-cash expenses that Home Depot subtracted on the income statement to determine the net income. Thus, to convert net income to actual cash flow requires adding back these non-cash expenses.

Home Depot makes further adjustments to account for the accrual accounting process that causes net income to deviate from cash flows that we discussed previously. Specifically, increases (decreases) in current asset accounts such as receivables and inventories are subtracted from (added to) net income, and increases (decreases) in current liability accounts such as accounts payable and taxes payable are added to (subtracted from) net income.

The resulting cash flow provided for operations by Home Depot is $4,802 million for fiscal year 2002. Thus, the net income figure of $3,664 million underestimates the actual cash flow from the firm's operations. The chief reason for the difference is the $903 million depreciation expense. Analysts pay close attention to the operating cash flow section of the cash flow statement because large, positive cash flows provided by operations are an initial sign of good health and liquidity for a firm.[2]

The second section details Home Depot's cash flow from investing activities. The dominant figure in this section is Home Depot's sizable $2,749 million it spent on capital expenditures in fiscal year 2002. In the *Management's Discussion and Analysis of Results* section of the Annual Report, Home Depot reports that it opened 203 new stores in fiscal year 2002 (the firm owns 195 and lease the remainder) and attributes these capital expenditures to the new store openings. Total net cash used for investing activities was $2,934 million.

The third section provides details about Home Depot's financing activities. Home Depot repurchased $2,000 million of shares of common stock, paid $492 million cash dividends to common shareholders, and raised $326 million by issuing new shares of common stock and received $1 million by issuing new long-term debt in the fiscal year ending in February 2003. The net cash outflow from financing activities was $2,165 million.

Finally, by comparing the results of these three sections for fiscal year 2002, we find that Home Depot was able to finance its sizable growth (capital expenditures and payments for business acquired) largely by the cash flow generated from operations. Specifically, the $4,802 million net cash flow provided by operations for fiscal 2002 exceeds the $2,934 million used for capital expenditures and acquisitions. Thus, Home Depot did not need to seek external financing sources (debt or equity) to fund its recent aggressive growth.

Practical Financial Tip 2.3

The statement of cash flows summarizes the sources and uses of cash for a firm during the year. Cash flows are organized into operating, investing, and financing activities. Activities in each area that bring in cash represent sources of cash while activities that involve spending cash are uses of cash. Positive cash flows from operations are a good indicator of financial health and liquidity for a firm.

Concept Check 2.4

1 What are the three major sections of a firm's statement of cash flows?
2 If depreciation is a non-cash item, why is it included in a firm's statement of cash flows?
3 Morgan Development Corp. (MDC) has reported negative net cash flow from operations and negative net cash flow from investing activities for each of the last 5 years. However, MDC's cash balances have remained stable during the period because of a large positive net cash flow from financing activities. Under what conditions or situations would this cause concern for investors?
4 Why is having a positive cash flow from operations important to a firm?

---

[2] By contrast, increased profits matched by decreasing cash flows from operations may be a warning signal. That is, some of the profits may represent sales that may not be paid or where purchasers were granted less than reliable credit terms.

2.5 Statement of Retained Earnings

A firm's **statement of retained earnings**, also known as its **statement of changes in share-holders' equity**, provides additional information on the composition of the owners' equity accounts. Specifically, for the particular reporting period, it shows:

- the retained earnings balance at the start of the period;
- how much the firm earned (net income);
- how much dividends the firm paid;
- how much net income was reinvested back into the firm (retained earnings);
- any repurchases of the firm's stock;
- any new issues of the firm's stock; and
- the retained earnings balance at the close of the period.

Figure 2.5 shows the Statement of Stockholders' Equity and Comprehensive Income for Home Depot. In the second-to-last column, we can see that the increase in stockholders' equity from $15,004 million to $19,802 million from January 28, 2001 to February 2, 2003 fiscal year-end dates is mostly attributed to the $3,044 million and $3,664 million net earnings during those 2 years, less the $2,000 million stock repurchase in fiscal year 2002. Stockholders' equity also increased from shares issued under employee stock purchase and option plans ($429 million and $330 million) and was reduced by dividends paid ($396 million and $492 million) in the fiscal years 2001 and 2002, respectively. These are the major insights gained from reviewing this statement.

Concept Check 2.5

1   What information does a statement of retained earnings provide?
2   Will the value for stockholders' equity on a firm's statement of retained earnings reflect the actual market value of the firm's equity? Why or why not?

2.6 Common-size Statements

Analysts often examine income statements and balance sheets in percentage terms, rather than in absolute dollar amounts, by constructing **common-size statements**. A common-size statement facilitates comparing firms of different size and detecting trends over time. We can prepare a **vertical common-size balance sheet** by dividing all components on the balance sheet by total assets. Thus, we display all items as a percentage of total assets. Figure 2.6 shows vertical common-size balance sheets for Home Depot.

The Home Depot, Inc. and Subsidiaries

Amounts in millions, except per share data	Common Stock — Shares	Amount	Paid-in Capital	Retained Earnings	Accumulated Other Comprehensive Income (Loss)	Treasury Stock — Shares	Amount	Unearned Compensation	Total Stockholder Equity	Comprehensive Income
Balance, 1/28/01	2,324	$116	$4,810	$10,151	$ (67)	–	$ –	$ (6)	$15,004	
Net earnings	–	–	–	3,044	–	–	–	–	3,044	$3,044
Shares issued under Employee Stock Purchase and Option Plans	22	1	448	–	–	–	–	(23)	426	
Tax effect of sale of option shares by employees	–	–	138	–	–	–	–	–	138	
Translation adjustments	–	–	–	–	(124)	–	–	–	(124)	(124)
Unrealized loss on derivatives	–	–	–	–	(29)	–	–	–	(29)	(18)
Stock compensation expense	–	–	16	–	–	–	–	(3)	19	
Cash dividends ($0.17 per share)	–	–	–	(396)	–	–	–	–	(396)	
Comprehensive income										$2,902
Balance, 2/3/2002	2,346	$117	$5,412	$12,799	$ (220)	–	–	$ (26)	$18,082	
Net earnings	–	–	–	3,664	–	–	–	–	3,664	$3,664
Shares issued under Employee Stock Purchase and Option Plans	16	1	366	–	–	–	–	(40)	327	
Tax effect of sale of option shares by employees	–	–	68	–	–	–	–	–	68	
Translation adjustments	–	–	–	–	109	–	–	–	109	109
Realized loss on derivatives	–	–	–	–	29	–	–	–	29	18
Stock compensation expense	–	–	12	–	–	–	–	3	15	
Repurchase of common stock	–	–	–	–	–	(69)	(2,000)	–	(2,000)	
Cash dividends ($0.21 per share)	–	–	–	(492)	–	–	–	–	(492)	
Comprehensive income										$3,791
Balance, 2/2/2003	2,362	$118	$5,858	$15,971	$ (82)	(69)	(2,000)	$ (63)	$19,802	

Figure 2.5 Consolidated Statement of Stockholders' Equity and Comprehensive Income

	February 2, 2003	February 3, 2002
Assets	%	%
Current assets		
Cash and cash equivalents	7.29	9.38
Short-term investments	0.22	0.26
Receivables, net	3.57	3.49
Merchandise inventories	27.78	25.48
Other current assets	0.85	0.64
Total current assets	39.71	39.26
Property, plant and equipment (PPE), net		
Land	18.53	18.84
Buildings	30.65	29.17
Furniture, fixtures, and equipment	13.58	12.89
Leasehold improvements	2.91	2.84
Construction in progress	2.41	3.97
Capital leases	1.02	0.97
Gross PPE	69.08	68.69
Less accumulated depreciation and amortization	11.88	10.43
Net PPE	57.21	58.25
Long-term investments	0.36	0.31
Goodwill	1.92	1.59
Other assets	0.81	0.59
Total assets	100.00	100.00
Liabilities and stockholders' equity		
Current liabilities		
Accounts payable	15.19	13.02
Accrued salaries and related expenses	2.70	2.72
Sales taxes payable	1.02	1.32
Deferred revenue	3.33	3.22
Income taxes payable	0.76	0.80
Other accrued expenses	3.78	3.55
Total current liabilities	26.77	24.63
Long-term debt, excluding current installments	4.40	4.74
Other long-term liabilities	1.64	1.41
Deferred income taxes	1.21	0.72
Total liabilities	7.25	6.87
Stockholders' equity		
Common stock, par value $0.05	0.39	0.44
Paid-in capital	19.52	20.50
Retained earnings	53.22	48.49
Accumulated other comprehensive income	(0.27)	(0.83)
Unearned compensation	(0.21)	(0.10)
Treasury stock	(6.66)	–
Total stockholders' equity	65.98	68.51
Total liabilities and stockholders' equity	100.00	100.00

Figure 2.6 Vertical common-size balance sheets for Home Depot, Inc.

	February 2, 2003 %	February 3, 2002 %	January 28, 2001 %
Net sales	100.00	100.00	100.00
Cost of merchandise sold	68.91	69.85	70.09
Gross profit	31.09	30.15	20.91
Operating expenses			
Selling and store operating	19.19	18.98	18.61
Pre-opening	0.16	0.22	0.31
General and administrative	1.72	1.75	1.83
Total operating expenses	21.08	20.94	20.75
Operating income	10.01	9.21	9.16
Interest income (expense)			
Interest and investment income	0.14	0.10	0.10
Earnings before interest and taxes	10.14	9.31	9.27
Interest expense	0.06	0.05	0.05
Earnings before provision for income taxes	10.08	9.26	9.22
Provision for income taxes	3.79	3.57	3.58
Net earnings	6.29	5.68	5.64

Figure 2.7 Vertical common-size statement of earnings for Home Depot, Inc.

We can construct a **vertical common-size income statement** by dividing all components of the income statement by net sales. Thus, each item is presented as a percentage of net sales. Figure 2.7 shows vertical common-size income statements for Home Depot. We can compare common-size statements of various firms because the reported figures will be relative to each firm's net sales and total assets.

Consider the vertical common-size balance sheet for Home Depot in Figure 2.6. Although no alarming or dramatic trends stand out, we find that Home Depot increased its holdings of merchandise inventories from 25.48 percent of total assets on February 3, 2002 to 27.78 percent on February 2, 2003. On the right-hand side of the balance sheet, we find that a relative increase in accounts payable from 13.02 percent to 15.19 percent, which causes a similar relative increase in total current liabilities (from 24.63 percent to 26.77 percent). We also find a relative increase in retained earnings from 48.49 percent to 53.22 percent. These relative changes are obscured if one simply examines the unscaled consolidated balance sheets in Figure 2.2.

Now suppose we wanted to know whether Home Depot's gross profits on its income statement in Figure 2.3 have been stable over time. Determining this from the income statement is difficult because the components of gross profit (net sales and cost of merchandise sold) both increase over time. But if we examine the common-size income statement in Figure 2.7, when expressed as a percentage of sales, gross profit has actually increased from 30.15 percent in fiscal year 2001 to 31.09 percent in fiscal year 2002. Net earnings as a percentage of sales increased from 5.68 percent in fiscal year 2001 to 6.29 percent in fiscal year 2002. The vertical common-size income statement reveals these underlying trends more clearly than the (unscaled) income statement.

Concept Check 2.6

1 What is a common-size financial statement?
2 How are vertical common-size balance sheets and income statements constructed?
3 How do common-size statements help provide a better understanding of a firm's financial condition?

2.7 Notes to Financial Statements

An important but often overlooked source of information is the **Notes to the Financial Statements**. Firms report important information in these notes about such items as their accounting policies, long-term debt structure, income taxes, employee stock plans, leases, employee benefit plans, basic and diluted earnings per share calculations, commitments and contingencies, and acquisitions. Annual reports also include management's discussion of recent operating results, which is usually included along with the financial statements. In addition, most annual reports include a letter to the stockholders. This letter, which is usually presented at the front of the annual report, may provide helpful insights about management's strategy and philosophy.

For example, Home Depot reports important information about its leases in note 5 of its Notes to Consolidated Financial Statements. Home Depot has short-term and long-term obligations for capital leases that are included in their balance sheet under other accrued expenses and long-term debt, respectively. The net PPE in the fiscal year 2002 balance sheet includes $235 million for these capital leases. Home Depot also reports two operating leases totaling $882 million that are off-balance sheet items.

Users of financial statements should pay close attention to the discussion of the firm's accounting policies as they can have a substantial impact on the performance reported in the financial statements. Firms adopting more conservative accounting policies such as accelerated depreciation and last-in last-out (LIFO) inventory valuation would likely report lower net income figures than firms adopting more liberal methods such as straight-line depreciation and first-in first-out (FIFO) inventory valuation, especially during periods of high inflation.

In an inflationary environment, LIFO inventory valuation will bring the more recent inventory produced at a higher cost to the income statement, leaving older, lower cost inventory on the firm's balance sheet. Accelerated depreciation will lead to higher depreciation expenses in the early years following capital expenditures. The resulting higher expenses will lead to lower reported net income. Home Depot reports in Note 1 that the majority of inventory is stated at the lower of cost (FIFO) or market, as determined by the retail inventory method.

Following the Notes to the Financial Statements is an independent auditors' report that attests the statements were prepared in accordance with GAAP, were audited in accordance with appropriate auditing standards, and reflect the financial position of the company. Such an affirming statement, however, should not lull stakeholders into a false sense of security as perhaps millions of the shareholders, lenders, suppliers, customers, and workers of Enron Corporation discovered in the late summer of 2001.

Concept Check 2.7

1   What important information do firms disclose in the Notes to Financial Statements?

2.8 Quality of Earnings

Compliance with GAAP does not necessarily ensure that a firm's reported earnings accurately reflect its economic earnings. The **quality of earnings** reported may vary among firms because GAAP provides management considerable flexibility in its choice of accounting principles and applications. A firm's quality of earnings refers to the *conservativeness* and *clarity* of that firm's reported earnings.

In recent years some firms have adopted accounting practices that result in lower earnings quality. We review some of the more common practices below.

- *Front-end income loading and cost deferral.* Firms may report income for a given period that should be spread over future periods (**front-end income loading**). A firm may also prop up its current reported earnings by deferring costs to future periods that pertain to the current period.
- *Restructuring charges.* Firms may distort their reported earnings by taking inappropriate **restructuring charges**. By timing these charges (delaying, reversing, or writing them off immediately), managers may distort or manipulate current reported earnings.
- *Reserve accounts.* Some firms use **reserve accounts** to manage reported earnings. By establishing a reserve account in a highly profitable period (thereby reducing earnings for that period), managers can later reverse the decision and boost earnings in a less profitable year. Such reserves are often appropriately called **cookie jars**, as managers can draw from these accounts during periods of poor performance.
- *Adopting less conservative accounting principles.* Firms may adopt less conservative accounting principles and thereby increase reported income and lower their earnings quality. For example, by switching from accelerated to straight-line depreciation, the firm can lower its current depreciation charge and increase reported earnings for the current year (at the expense of later years when the situation will reverse).
- *Stock option compensation.* Many firms compensate managers by giving them stock options. Stock options are typically issued with an exercise price below the current stock price. Even though the **intrinsic value** of these options is zero, they have value. However,

GAAP allows firms to avoid reporting any compensation cost on the income statement when they have no intrinsic value.[3]

Analysts look for indications that managers may be managing earnings, thereby lowering earnings quality. These indications may include the firm firing its auditors, an increasing gap between earnings and cash flow, adopting less conservative accounting principles, reducing managed costs such as R&D and advertising, under-reserving for future expenditures such as allowances for bad debts, writing off investments soon after they were made, increasing financial leverage, and declining inventory turnover. Analysts usually look for information to assess a firm's quality of earnings in the Notes to the Financial Statements.

Concept Check 2.8

1 What is meant by the term quality of earnings?
2 What are some of the common methods used by managers that may boost current reported earnings and thereby lower a firm's quality of earnings?

2.9 Other Issues

Public firms in the US follow generally accepted accounting principles (GAAP) that go a long way toward standardizing accounting procedures. Yet, firms still have substantial leeway in the way they account for book values and report earnings that may lead to major differences in the financial statements of otherwise similar firms. Some of the more important reasons these statements may differ include:

- Firms may differ in how they account for intangible assets such as patents, copyrights, and trademarks. Including these intangible assets on the balance sheet provides a better estimate of the accounting value of the firm as an ongoing concern. On the other hand, excluding such assets may provide a more conservative estimate of the firm's accounting value in measuring its liquidation value.

---

[3] The market value of options can be estimated using option-pricing models. The most common model is the Black–Scholes option-pricing model. The formula for this model can be obtained from most standard investments textbooks. However, experts are currently debating whether the cost of these options should be recognized as an expense on a firm's income statement. Some argue that these stock options represent a financing cost that is borne by the existing shareholders, and thus should not be reported as an expense on the income statement. The eventual exercise of these options will dilute the ownership of current stockholders and reduce the value of their ownership claim by allowing new shareholders to possibly purchase new shares at exercise prices below market value in the future.

- Firms may not include all of their liabilities on their balance sheet such as some lease obligations, warrants sold to investors or issued to employees, and other off-balance sheet financings.

Furthermore, analysts also differ in the way they interpret a firm's financial performance from these financial statements. Some analysts, for example, exclude profits and losses from extraordinary or nonrecurring events when determining a firm's net income, while others include them.

International Comparisons

Differences in international accounting standards can greatly complicate the analysis and comparison of firms from different countries. For example, while accounting standards in the US are more stringent than in many countries, firms in the US may use one set of accounts for financial reporting purposes and another set of accounts for tax purposes. This would not be allowed in most other countries. Accounting standards differ in terms of the degree of flexibility and rigidity. German firms, for example, have much greater flexibility to hide money in reserve accounts.

The desire of some firms to list their stocks on major stock exchanges such as the New York Stock Exchange (NYSE) has led to greater uniformity in accounting standards among firms from different countries. NYSE regulations require all firms to conform to US GAAP accounting standards. When Daimler-Benz AG decided to list on the NYSE, the revision of its financial statements to conform to US accounting standards turned its modest profit in 1993 using German accounting standards to a loss of nearly $600 million.

Negotiations are ongoing among countries to adopt a uniform set of accounting rules. The International Accounting Standards Board (IASB) working together with the International Organization of Securities Commissions (IOSCO) has garnered wide support for adopting congruous accounting rules. The continuing integration of the world's capital markets has produced considerable momentum for adopting a set of uniform international accounting standards.

Financial Reforms

With all of the national attention given to various financial scandals such as Enron during late 2001, many expect the accounting profession to enact some important reforms. At the top of the list are changes in the ways firms can keep debt off their balance sheets through off-balance sheet financing methods. Other needed reforms include creating a firewall between the auditing and consulting services that many of the large accounting firms provide to the same firm or even instituting term limits for auditing of a particular firm. Whether these efforts will lead to any major reforms in the financial reporting process for firms is uncertain. Financial analysts and managers who are responsible for interpreting financial statements need to keep abreast of these and other potential reforms.

E-sources of Financial Information

For years, investors trekked to libraries to view a company's financial statements or to collect other financial information. The Internet age has now dramatically altered how we can access financial information. The Securities and Exchange Commission (SEC) has developed an Internet-based database (www.sec.gov/edgar.shtml) where it posts the Form 10-K and quarterly 10-Q filings made by firms. Most companies now have their own websites that contain a wealth of financial information including complete financial statements in their 10-K and 10-Q filings, press releases, stock price charts and other financial news. Other websites, including MoneyCentral (moneycentral.msn.com) and Bloomberg[4] (www.bloomberg.com), provide detailed historical information including financial statements, earnings estimates, analysts' ratings, stock price quotes and charts, and other useful information. An increasing level of financial services is becoming available online. For example, Lowes, a major competitor to Home Depot, allows investors to purchase shares of its common stock online from the company web page (www.lowes.com).

Concept Check 2.9

1 What are some of the differences in international accounting standards and the US GAAP?
2 What are some important financial reforms that will likely be adopted in the near future?

Summary

This chapter discussed how to interpret financial statements issued by firms. The major points are as follows.

1 Interpreting the information provided in a firm's financial statements is an important task to the many stakeholders including the firm's lenders, equity investors, suppliers, customers, employees, and executive management.
2 The financial statements issued by a firm include its income statement, balance sheet, statement of cash flows, and statement of retained earnings.
3 An income statement summarizes the total revenues earned and the total expenses incurred to generate these revenues during a particular time period. The bottom line of an income statement is the firm's net income (earnings).
4 A balance sheet reports a firm's assets, liabilities and stockholders' equity as of a given date, usually at the end of a reporting period. The balance sheet is constructed according to the basic accounting identity: assets = liabilities + stockholders' equity.

---

[4] We are not recommending or promoting these two sites over the many others that exist.

5 A statement of cash flows reports changes in the cash position for a firm over a specified period of time. The statement is divided into three main sections including operating cash flows, investing cash flows, and financing cash flows.

6 A statement of retained earnings provides information on the composition of the stockholders' equity accounts for a firm and the amounts of any stock or cash dividends issued during the period.

7 The net income reported by a firm for a particular time period will differ from the actual net cash flow generated by the firm during that period due to the accrual accounting process, depreciation, and taxes. Although financial analysts pay close attention to both net income and net cash flow, more attention should be given to the net cash flow.

8 The items reported on a balance sheet are typically reported at their book values, which are based on historical cost. Analysts need to understand that these historical values may differ substantially from their current market values. This is especially true for real estate and for stockholders' equity.

9 Common-size statements provide a basis for interpreting trends and comparing firms of different size. A vertical common-size balance sheet is constructed by dividing all items for a given year by the total assets for that year. A vertical common-size income statement is constructed by dividing all items for a given year by the net sales for that year.

FURTHER READING

Bernstein, Leopold A. and John J. Wild. *Financial Statement Analysis: Theory, Application, and Interpretation*, 6th edn, Irwin McGraw-Hill, 1998.

Brigham, Eugene F. and Michael C. Ehrhardt. *Financial Management: Theory and Practice*, 11th edn, Thomson, 2005.

Fraser, Lyn M. and Aileen Ormiston. *Understanding Financial Statements*, Prentice-Hall, 2001.

Schilit, Howard. *Financial Shenanigans*, 2nd edn, McGraw-Hill, 2002.

White, Gerald I., Ashwinpaul C. Sondhi, and Dov Fried. *The Analysis and Use of Financial Statements*, 3rd edn, Wiley, 2003.

Chapter 3

Interpreting Financial Ratios

Financial ratios are used to compare the risk and return of different firms in order to help equity investors and creditors make intelligent investment and credit decisions. Such decisions require both an evaluation of performance over time for a particular investment and a comparison among all firms within a single industry at a specific point in time. (Gerald I. White, Ashwinpaul C. Sondhi, and Dov Fried, *The Analysis and Use of Financial Statements*, 3rd edn, Wiley, 2003, p. 111.)

Overview

In this chapter we show how lenders, investors, analysts, and managers can use information from a firm's balance sheet, income statement, and statement of cash flows to calculate financial ratios that provide useful insights into particular aspects of a firm's performance. These ratios allow the firm's stakeholders to better understand its liquidity and long-term debt paying ability, efficiency in employing its various assets, profitability, and how the market is valuing the firm relative to key financial variables. We show how to calculate and interpret various ratios related to each of the above areas using the financial statement information from Home Depot, Inc. We compare the performance of Home Depot to that of its closest competitor, Lowe's Companies, Inc. We discuss several uses and limitations of financial ratio analysis.

Learning Objectives

After completing this chapter, you should be able to:

- calculate and interpret commonly used ratios;
- understand how to use financial ratios to assess the liquidity, solvency, efficiency, and profitability of a firm;
- understand how financial ratios can be used to estimate the likelihood of bankruptcy for a firm that uses debt financing;
- conduct a DuPont analysis to decompose a firm's return on equity into other ratio subcomponents;
- discuss the uses and limitations of financial ratio analysis.

3.1 Financial Ratio Analysis

Many stakeholders analyze a firm's financial ratios before making important decisions involving the firm. A **financial ratio** is a mathematical relationship among several numbers often stated in the form of percentage, times, or days. Lenders assess liquidity and debt ratios to determine whether to lend money to a firm and at what rate. Rating agencies, such as Moody's and Standard & Poor's, use financial ratios when assigning a credit rating to a firm's debt issues. Lenders try to protect the bondholders' interest by incorporating some ratios into the restrictive covenants in the firm's bond indenture to constrain some of its financial and operating activities. Other investors review certain financial ratios to assess the firm's future profitability when contemplating investment opportunities. Regulators often use financial ratios as performance targets when determining the appropriate prices that firms may charge in regulated industries.

Managers frequently use financial ratios to identify their own firm's strengths and weaknesses and to assess its performance. They may use certain financial ratios as targets that guide their firm's investment, financing, and working capital policy decisions and to determine incentives and rewards for managers.

Financial Ratio Categories

Financial ratios are often categorized according to the type of information they provide. We organize our presentation by discussing financial ratios in each of the following five categories:

- Liquidity
- Debt management
- Asset management (efficiency)
- Profitability
- Market value.

Analyzing Financial Ratios

Before we turn our attention to defining, computing, and interpreting these ratios, some preliminary comments are warranted. First, financial ratios are not standardized. A perusal of the many financial textbooks and other sources that are available will often show differences in how to calculate some ratios. When comparing ratios provided by various financial services or your own computations, biases may result if computational methods differ. We will point out a few of the more common computational differences.

Second, analyzing a single financial ratio for a given year may not be very useful. Analysts usually examine financial ratios over the most recent 3 or 5-year period and then compare them with industry averages or key competitors. Keep in mind the limitations of making comparisons with other firms, because many firms are diversified across different industry groups. Also, combining or decomposing ratios can be helpful in predicting bankruptcy or for assessing underlying strengths or weaknesses in certain ratios.

Third, some of a firm's financial accounting practices or choices such as inventory valuation method and depreciation will affect its financial statements and, therefore, its financial ratios. As a result, firms with very similar operating and financial characteristics but with different accounting conventions will have income statements, balance sheets, and financial ratios that reflect these differences. Analysts often make appropriate adjustments in order to compare such ratios in a meaningful way.

Finally, financial ratios do not provide analysts with all of the answers about a firm's condition. Rather, this information provides important clues that the financial analyst, as a detective, uses to further investigate and ask pertinent questions about a firm's financial condition.

Concept Check 3.1

1   What are the different motivations that lenders, investors, and managers have when they interpret financial ratios?
2   Why should financial ratios not be analyzed in isolation?
3   What are some important caveats to remember when interpreting financial ratios?

Practical Financial Tip 3.1

Managers and analysts should exhibit caution when interpreting financial ratios:

- Financial ratio computations are not standardized. Many financial services that report ratios use slightly different formulas. Be careful when making comparisons.
- Financial ratios should not be analyzed in isolation. Trends over time should be examined with comparison made to relevant competitors.
- The accounting conventions adopted by a firm affect its financial ratios. Firms with similar operating and financial characteristics may report very different financial ratios if they use different accounting conventions for inventory valuation and depreciation.
- Financial ratio analysis may lead to more questions than answers about a firm's condition. A financial analyst should consider financial ratios important clues in trying to uncover the truth about a firm's financial condition.

3.2 Liquidity Ratios

Liquidity ratios indicate a firm's ability to pay its obligations in the short run. Potential lenders carefully scrutinize these ratios before making short-term loans to the firm. Financial managers must pay close attention to liquidity ratios to ensure they reflect a high probability of the firm being able to promptly and fully pay its bills without undue stress.

The most commonly used liquidity ratios include the current ratio, quick ratio, cash ratio, and net working capital to total assets ratio. We discuss each in turn.

Current ratio

The most widely used liquidity ratio is the current ratio. The **current ratio** is computed by dividing the firm's current assets by its current liabilities.

$$\text{Current ratio} = \frac{\text{Current assets}}{\text{Current liabilities}} \tag{3.1}$$

The firm's current liabilities in the denominator show the amount of short-term obligations the firm faced at the balance sheet date; the current assets in the numerator indicate the amount of short-term assets the firm could use to pay these obligations. For example, a current ratio of 1.5 implies that a firm has $1.50 in current assets for every $1 in current liabilities and thus has 1.5 times the current assets, or has its current liabilities covered 1.5 times over. This does not necessarily mean, however, that the firm will be able to pay its debts when they come due because of the timing of the current assets and liabilities. For example, a large portion of a firm's current liabilities may be due now but the company has much of its current assets tied up in accounts receivable and inventories, which take time to convert into cash in order to pay current obligations.

A declining current ratio may indicate a declining trend in a firm's liquidity. Excessively high current ratios, however, may indicate a firm may have too much of its long-term investor-supplied capital invested in short-term, low-earning current assets.

A firm's accounting methods, particularly inventory valuation, may affect its current ratio. In an inflationary environment, firms that use last-in, first-out (LIFO) inventory valuation will likely have lower current ratios than firms that use first-in, first out (FIFO). With LIFO inventory valuation, firms determine the value of cost of goods sold on the income statement by the cost of the inventory most recently produced; the value of the inventory reported on the balance sheet reflects remaining inventory produced in prior periods. Except in some declining cost industries, inflation will likely cause the value of this "older" inventory carried on the balance sheet to be less than the more recent cost of producing that inventory. On the other hand, firms that employ FIFO inventory valuation will value the cost of goods sold on the inventory produced in the most distant periods. The value of inventory reported on the balance sheet is from more recent periods and will be based on more recent (higher) cost data than the inventory balance of similar firms that use LIFO.

Firms can also *manage* their current ratio to some degree. To illustrate, consider a firm that has $1.6 million in current assets, $1 million in current liabilities, and a resulting current ratio of 1.6. If the firm were to pay off $100,000 in accounts payable with cash, it would then have $1.5 million in current assets, $0.9 million in current liabilities, and an apparently *improved* current ratio of 1.67. Yet, if a firm has a current ratio that is less than one, the same transaction would lead to a lower current ratio: If a firm with $0.8 million in current assets, $1 million in current liabilities, and a current ratio of 0.8 pays off $100,000 in accounts payable with cash, its current ratio would decline to 0.78. This example serves as a caution for the analysis of other ratios. Equal absolute changes in the numerator and denominator may lead to apparent improvements or deterioration in ratios that do not reflect real changes in performance. Analysts should be aware that a firm's managers may undertake year-end transactions, such as the one described above, to make certain ratios appear better following a period of disappointing performance. This process is often called "window dressing" because it makes specific ratios from the financial statements look better than without making such changes.

Finally, current ratios may hide important liquidity differences among firms. For example, suppose two firms have identical current ratios. Should we conclude the firms have nearly identical liquidity positions? Not necessarily. One of the firms may have a substantial portion of its current assets tied up in inventories, while the other firm may have largely cash and marketable securities. But the current assets in the numerator of the current ratio calculation would hide these important differences in liquidity. All else equal, the latter firm has stronger liquidity. Managers or analysts can examine a firm's common-size balance sheet over time to see relative changes in the composition of both current assets and current liabilities and assess changes or differences in liquidity.

Quick ratio

A more conservative measure of liquidity for a firm is the **quick ratio**, sometimes referred to as the acid test ratio. The quick ratio is similar to the current ratio except inventory is excluded from the current assets in the numerator.[1]

$$\text{Quick ratio} = \frac{\text{Current assets} - \text{inventory}}{\text{Current liabilities}} \qquad (3.2)$$

The rationale for excluding inventory is that it is the least liquid of a firm's current assets and may not be as readily available to meet a short-term maturing obligation as the other more liquid current assets.

For any firm carrying an inventory balance, the quick ratio will be lower than the current ratio. Analyzing the current ratio and quick ratio together may allow analysts to understand how changes in relative inventory levels may affect a firm's liquidity. For example, suppose a firm's current ratio has been fairly stable and consistent with industry averages over the past three years. But during the same period, the firm's quick ratio has declined and is now below industry averages. Analysts would then logically focus on relative increases in the firm's inventory: whether the increase is likely temporary or permanent, how the firm financed the inventory, and how the relative increases in inventory would affect the firm's liquidity and overall performance.

Cash ratio

The **cash ratio** is a more conservative liquidity measure than the current or quick ratio. The cash ratio only includes cash and marketable securities in the numerator:

$$\text{Cash ratio} = \frac{\text{Cash and marketable securities}}{\text{Current liabilities}} \qquad (3.3)$$

---

[1] Some analysts compute the numerator by adding cash, marketable securities, and accounts receivable, thereby excluding prepaid items such as prepaid insurance and other current assets.

The cash ratio is too conservative to accurately reflect a firm's liquidity position because it assumes that firms can fund their current liabilities with only cash and marketable securities. Analyzing a cash ratio, however, could be helpful for assessing a firm's liquidity when the firm will need to pay most or all of its current liabilities with cash in the near term. As with the other liquidity ratios, a higher cash ratio indicates a stronger liquidity condition.

Net working capital to total assets ratio
The **net working capital to total assets ratio** is computed by dividing net working capital (current assets minus current liabilities) by total assets.

$$\text{Net working capital to total assets} = \frac{\text{Current assets} - \text{Current liabilities}}{\text{Total assets}} \tag{3.4}$$

This ratio provides additional liquidity information because it indicates the percentage of total assets the firm carries as net working capital. A higher ratio indicates a stronger liquidity condition. It also indicates that the firm finances a higher percentage of its total assets with lower-earning excess current assets net of its current liabilities.

Assessing liquidity ratios for Home Depot
We compute the liquidity ratios discussed above for Home Depot for fiscal year 2002 below.

$$\text{Current ratio} = \frac{11,917}{8,035} = 1.48 \text{ times}$$

$$\text{Quick ratio} = \frac{11,917 - 8,338}{8,035} = 0.45 \text{ times}$$

$$\text{Cash ratio} = \frac{2,253}{8,035} = 0.28 \text{ times}$$

$$\text{Net working capital to total assets} = \frac{11,917 - 8,035}{30,011} = 0.13 \text{ times}$$

The quick ratio and cash ratio, which appear to suggest poor liquidity, are probably not effective liquidity measures for retail firms like Home Depot that must carry high levels of merchandise inventory in their stores. Merchandise inventory of $8,338 million for the fiscal year ending on February 2, 2003 represented about 70 percent of Home Depot's total current assets. Home Depot carries large amounts of accounts payable, which are presumably used to finance merchandise inventories. The quick and cash ratios exclude inventories from current assets in the numerator, but keep accounts payable in the current liabilities in the denominator. This biases these ratios downward. Also, unlike most manufacturing firms, which must sometimes wait 30 to 60 days to receive cash payment from credit sales of finished goods from inventory stock, the sale of inventory for retail firms usually results in receipt of cash either immediately (cash sales) or within a few days (credit card sales). This readily available source of cash should be considered when analyzing Home Depot's liquidity.

Home Depot's liquidity position is also bolstered by a commercial paper program that provides up to $1 billion of available borrowings and a back-up credit facility with a consortium of banks for up to $800 million. Because Home Depot has no borrowings against the commercial paper program as of the February 2, 2003 balance sheet date, the firm has quick access to a large amount of cash if any liquidity problems arise.

To further assess Home Depot's liquidity position, we need to compare these ratios to industry norms or key competitors. Finding meaningful comparisons for Home Depot is difficult. Value Line Investment Survey reports seven firms with a SIC Code of 5211 for retail building and supply companies. Home Depot is the giant among these firms with annual sales and total assets more than half of the aggregate industry totals. Moreover, the two largest firms, Home Depot and Lowe's, had combined total assets of about 95 percent of aggregate industry total assets. Thus, industry norms are not particularly helpful because Home Depot and Lowe's are so dominant. Therefore, we simply compare Home Depot and Lowe's.

Table 3.1 shows the liquidity ratios for Home Depot and Lowe's. Looking at just 1 year of liquidity ratios may be insufficient.

Table 3.1 Liquidity ratios for Home Depot and Lowe's for FY 2002 (fiscal year ending February 2, 2003)

Liquidity ratios	Home Depot	Lowe's
Current ratio	1.48x	1.56x
Quick ratio	0.45x	0.45x
Cash ratio	0.28x	0.31x
Net working capital to total assets	0.13x	0.12x

Figure 3.1 illustrates the current ratio for Home Depot and Lowe's for the period 1998–2002.

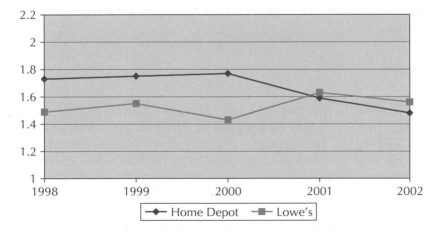

Figure 3.1 Current ratios for Home Depot and Lowe's, FY 1998–2002

The plot shows that the current ratios for Home Depot and Lowe's have essentially converged over the past 5 years, with slight decreases for Home Depot and slight increases for Lowe's. Both firms have evidence of strong liquidity with acceptable current ratios, strong cash flow from operations, and quick access to cash through commercial paper programs and back-up credit facilities.[2]

Concept Check 3.2

1   What do liquidity ratios tell us about a firm? What are the most commonly used ratios that measure a firm's liquidity?
2   What are some end-of-year transactions a firm's management could undertake to bolster its current ratio?
3   How would a firm's decision to use LIFO or FIFO inventory accounting affect its current ratio in a period of rising prices? Would it make a difference in a period of stable prices?

3.3 Debt Management Ratios

Debt management ratios characterize a firm in terms of the relative mix of debt and equity financing and provide measures of the long-term debt paying ability of the firm. The two basic types of debt management ratios are **leverage ratios** and **coverage ratios**. The leverage ratios include the debt ratio, debt-to-equity ratio, and long-term debt ratio, while the coverage ratios include the interest coverage ratio and cash flow coverage ratio.

Debt Ratio

The **debt ratio** is computed by dividing a firm's total (current and non-current) liabilities by its total assets.

$$\text{Debt ratio} = \frac{\text{Total liabilities}}{\text{Total assets}} \tag{3.5}$$

This ratio measures the percentage of a firm's total assets financed by debt. For example, if a firm has $1 million in total liabilities and $2 million in total assets, its debt ratio is 50 percent, meaning that the firm finances 50 percent of its assets with debt. The higher the debt ratio, the more of a firm's assets are provided by creditors relative to owners. It is a

---

[2]   Similar to Home Depot, Lowe's has a commercial paper program that provides up to $800 million of available borrowings and a back-up credit facility with a consortium of banks for up to $800 million.

generalized debt ratio in the sense that debt includes all current liabilities, non-current liabilities, and long-term borrowings of the firm. Creditors prefer a low or moderate debt ratio because it provides more protection if the firm experiences financial problems.

Two useful variations of the debt ratio are the **debt-to-equity ratio** and the **equity multiplier**. The debt-to-equity ratio is computed by dividing the firm's total liabilities by its total equity.

$$\text{Debt-to-equity ratio} = \frac{\text{Total liabilities}}{\text{Total equity}} \tag{3.6}$$

Returning to our example, a firm with $1 million in liabilities and $1 million in equity would have a debt-to-equity ratio of 100 percent, meaning that the firm has $1 in debt financing for each $1 in equity financing.

The equity multiplier is computed by dividing total assets by total equity.

$$\text{Equity multiplier} = \frac{\text{Total assets}}{\text{Total equity}} \tag{3.7}$$

With $2 million in assets and $1 million in equity, the firm's equity multiplier is 2.0 times, which means for every dollar in equity a firm has $2 in assets.

Long-term Debt Ratio

The **long-term debt ratio** is computed by dividing a firm's long-term debt, usually defined as all noncurrent liabilities, by its total assets. By excluding current liabilities, this ratio may provide better insight into a firm's debt management policy. Some current liabilities, such as accounts payable, result from operations and may not be relevant to the firm's debt management policy.

$$\text{Long-term debt ratio} = \frac{\text{Long-term debt}}{\text{Total assets}} \tag{3.8}$$

When computing the debt ratio and long-term debt ratio, some managers and analysts use total capital in the denominator in place of total assets. The resulting ratios are defined as the debt-to-total-capital and long-term debt to total capital ratios, respectively. Total capital includes all noncurrent liabilities plus equity, and thus excludes short-term debt. We exclude short-term debt because it usually does not represent a permanent source of financing and is thus constantly changing, and because some current liabilities, such as accounts payable, reflect the firm's trade practice more than its debt management policy.

The debt ratio, debt-to-equity ratio, equity multiplier, and long-term debt ratio for Home Depot for the fiscal year ending February 2, 2003 are as follows.

$$\text{Debt ratio} = \frac{10{,}209}{30{,}011} = 0.3402 = 34.02\%$$

$$\text{Debt-to-equity ratio} = \frac{10{,}209}{19{,}802} = 0.5156 = 51.56\%$$

$$\text{Equity multiplier} = \frac{30{,}011}{19{,}802} = 1.52 \text{ times}$$

$$\text{Long-term debt ratio} = \frac{1{,}321 + 491 + 362}{30{,}011} = 0.0724 = 7.24\%$$

Leverage ratios characterize a firm in terms of its relative amount of debt financing, but the ratios do not indicate the firm's ability to meet its debt obligations. In fact, the possibility exists that a firm with a higher debt ratio could actually be in a stronger position to service its debt due to stronger earnings and cash flows than a firm with a lower debt ratio and weaker earnings. The next group of debt management ratios provides a measure of the firm's ability to meet its long-term debt obligations by relating them to earnings and cash flow measures. These ratios include the interest coverage and cash flow coverage ratios.

Interest Coverage Ratio

The **interest coverage ratio**, also called **times interest earned**, is computed by dividing the firm's earnings before interest and taxes (EBIT) by its interest expense.

$$\text{Interest coverage ratio} = \frac{\text{EBIT}}{\text{Interest expense}} \qquad (3.9)$$

This ratio measures the margin by which the firm can pay interest expense from its operating earnings. A firm with EBIT of 100 and interest expense of 50 would have twice the EBIT it needs to meet its interest expense payment and would have an interest coverage ratio of 2.0 times.

What is an acceptable interest coverage ratio? This largely depends on the expected level of the firm's future EBIT, as well as the volatility of EBIT. Firms with stable operating earnings can typically borrow more because of the lower probability of operating earnings dipping below the level of interest expenses. Firms with more volatile and unpredictable operating earnings should rely less on debt financing to avoid potential financial distress and bankruptcy.

Cash Flow Coverage Ratio

The interest coverage ratio is an earnings-based ratio. Since firms pay debt and other financial obligations with actual cash (not earnings), cash flow ratios may provide a better indication of a firm's ability to meet these obligations. One version of a **cash flow coverage ratio** is computed by adding back depreciation to the firm's EBIT in the numerator:

$$\text{Cash flow coverage ratio} = \frac{\text{EBIT} + \text{depreciation}}{\text{Interest expense}} \qquad (3.10)$$

Depreciation is added back to EBIT to estimate cash flow because depreciation is a noncash expense subtracted from revenues to calculate EBIT on the income statement.

The interest coverage and cash flow coverage ratios for Home Depot for fiscal year 2002 are shown below.

$$\text{Interest coverage ratio} = \frac{5,909}{37} = 159.70 \text{ times}$$

$$\text{Cash flow coverage ratio} = \frac{5,909 + 903}{37} = 184.11 \text{ times}$$

Using reported interest expense may overstate coverage ratios because firms may capitalize some interest costs incurred during the construction period of long-lived assets.

Note 2 of the Home Depot's financial statements states that the $37 million interest expense for fiscal year 2002 is net of $59 million of capitalized interest. Using $96 million in interest expense considerably lowers the coverage ratios. Home Depot's Statement of Cash Flows shows a depreciation expense of $903 million that was added back to net earnings in the "Cash Provided from Operations" section.

Assessing Debt Management Ratios for Home Depot

Table 3.1 shows the debt management ratios for Home Depot and Lowe's. Lowe's is more highly leveraged than Home Depot with relatively more long-term liabilities and long-term debt financing than Home Depot. Home Depot is conservative in using leverage. Its interest coverage and cash flow coverage ratios of 159.70 times and 184.11 times, respectively, show little likelihood of default. Not surprisingly, Standard & Poor's has assigned a credit rating of AA to Home Depot's long-term debt. The long-term debt for Lowe's has a rating of A.

Table 3.2 Debt management ratios for Home Depot and Lowe's for FY 2002

Debt management ratios	Home Depot	Lowe's
Debt ratio	34.02%	48.46%
Debt-to-equity ratio	51.56%	94.04%
Equity multiplier	1.52x	1.94x
Long-term debt ratio	7.24%	26.25%
Interest coverage ratio	159.70x	13.96x
Cash flow coverage ratio	184.11x	17.40x

Concept Check 3.3

1 What do debt management ratios tell us about a firm? What are the most commonly used ratios that measure a firm's liquidity?
2 What is the major limitation of leverage ratios (such as the debt ratio and long-term debt ratio) that are based solely on the balance sheet items?
3 Ambient Technologies has liquidity and debt management ratios that either exceed or are consistent with industry norms. Yet, analysts fear that rating agencies may lower Ambient's bond rating. Why might such a downgrade occur despite apparent strength in liquidity and debt management ratios?

3.4 Asset Management Ratios

Asset management ratios, also referred to as asset utilization or asset efficiency ratios, measure a firm's ability to manage the assets at its disposal. Commonly used asset management ratios include the accounts receivable turnover ratio, inventory turnover ratio, accounts payable turnover ratio, fixed asset turnover ratio, and the total asset turnover ratio.

Accounts Receivable Turnover Ratio

The **accounts receivable turnover ratio** is computed by dividing net credit sales by the average accounts receivable outstanding. When the financial statements do not separate cash and credit sales, total net sales are often used in the numerator. Technically, the numerator should only include credit sales because the accounts receivable in the denominator arise only from credit sales.

$$\text{Accounts receivable turnover ratio} = \frac{\text{Net credit sales}}{\text{Average accounts receivable}} \qquad (3.11)$$

This ratio measures how many times a firm's accounts receivable are generated and collected during the year. In general, higher receivables turnover ratios imply that a firm is managing its accounts receivable efficiently. But a high accounts receivable turnover ratio may indicate that a firm's credit sales policy is too restrictive; management should consider whether a more lenient policy could lead to enhanced sales. Managers should analyze the tradeoff between any increased sales from a more lenient credit policy and the associated costs of longer collection periods and more uncollected receivables to determine whether changing the firm's credit sales policy could increase shareholder wealth.

A low or declining accounts receivable turnover ratio may indicate the firm is either becoming lax in its efforts to collect receivables or is not writing off receivables that are unlikely to be ultimately collected. By performing an aging of the receivables account, where receivables are sorted by the length of time outstanding, managers can assess the likelihood of collecting outstanding receivables. Those receivables that have been outstanding the longest time often have the lowest likelihood of eventual collection. We discuss the aging of accounts receivables in greater detail in Chapter 6.

Average accounts receivable is used in the denominator because the net credit sales is a cumulative sales number that reflects operations over one year, while a balance sheet item reflects the amount at the end of the fiscal year. Averaging a firm's monthly or quarterly receivables over the year typically yields a better estimate of the receivables outstanding during the year. One common approach to determining average accounts receivable is to add the beginning and ending amounts for the period and divide by two.

To compute Home Depot's accounts receivable turnover ratio requires estimating net credit sales. As mentioned previously, if a firm does not report its net credit sales, analysts sometimes use total net sales to compute the ratio. This assumption may be reasonable for a manufacturing firm whose sales are mostly credit sales, but not for a retail firm with a majority of cash sales. Most of Home Depot's sales are either immediate cash sales or credit card sales that provide cash to the company in a few days; credit sales that result in accounts receivable are probably low. Home Depot's credit sales come largely from sales to commercial customers and from sales on their private label credit card. To calculate the accounts receivable turnover ratio, we assume 25 percent of sales are on credit and get an accounts receivable turnover ratio of 14.62 times.

$$\text{Accounts receivable turnover ratio} = \frac{(58{,}247)(0.25)}{\frac{(920 + 1072)}{2}} = 14.62 \text{ times}$$

A variant of the accounts receivable turnover ratio is the **receivables collection period**, which is computed by dividing 365 by the accounts receivable turnover ratio.

$$\text{Receivables collection period} = \frac{365}{\text{Accounts receivable turnover ratio}} \qquad (3.12)$$

As its name suggests, the receivables collection period indicates how many days a firm takes to convert accounts receivable into cash. If the receivables collection period exceeds a firm's credit terms, this may indicate that a firm is ineffective in collecting its credit sales or is granting credit to marginal customers. The receivables collection period for Home Depot is 24.97 days.

$$\text{Receivables collection period} = \frac{365}{14.62} = 24.97 \text{ days}$$

Inventory Turnover Ratio

The **inventory turnover ratio** is computed by dividing the cost of goods sold by the average inventory.

$$\text{Inventory turnover ratio} = \frac{\text{Cost of goods sold}}{\text{Average inventory}} \qquad (3.13)$$

A high inventory turnover ratio, relative to some benchmark, suggests efficient management of the firm's inventory. A low, declining ratio may suggest the firm has continued to build up inventory in the face of weakening demand or may be carrying and reporting outdated or obsolete inventory that could only be sold at reduced prices, if at all. On the other hand, a manager or analyst should check to make sure that a high ratio does not reflect lost sales opportunities because of inadequate inventory levels caused by production problems, poor sales forecasting, or weak coordination between sales and production activities within the firm. The advent of computer inventory systems in recent years has allowed many firms to keep inventory levels to a minimum.

The inventory turnover ratio for Home Depot for fiscal year 2002 was 5.33 times.

$$\text{Inventory turnover ratio} = \frac{40{,}139}{\dfrac{(6{,}725 + 8{,}338)}{2}} = 5.33 \text{ times}$$

The **inventory processing period** is computed by dividing 365 by the inventory turnover ratio.

$$\text{Inventory processing period} = \frac{365}{\text{Inventory turnover ratio}} \tag{3.14}$$

The inventory processing period indicates the average number of days a firm takes to process and sell its inventory. The inventory processing period for Home Depot was 68.48 days.

$$\text{Inventory processing period} = \frac{365}{5.33} = 68.48 \text{ days}$$

Accounts Payable Turnover Ratio

The **accounts payable turnover ratio** is computed by dividing the cost of goods sold by the average accounts payable for the firm.

$$\text{Accounts payable turnover ratio} = \frac{\text{Cost of goods sold}}{\text{Average accounts payable}} \tag{3.15}$$

This ratio measures how many times a firm's accounts payable are generated and paid during the year. In general, as long as a firm pays its bills in a timely manner and satisfies its financial obligations to its suppliers, the lower the payables turnover ratio the better.

The accounts payable turnover ratio for Home Depot for fiscal year 2002 was 10.04 times.

$$\text{Accounts payable turnover ratio} = \frac{40{,}139}{\dfrac{(3{,}436 + 4{,}560)}{2}} = 10.04 \text{ times}$$

The **accounts payable payment period** can be computed by dividing 365 by the accounts payable turnover ratio.

$$\text{Accounts payable payment period} = \frac{365}{\text{Accounts payable turnover ratio}} \tag{3.16}$$

The accounts payable payment period measures how long, on average, a firm takes to pay its accounts payable. Think of the accounts payable payment period as the counterpart to the average collection period. In general, higher accounts payable payment periods are beneficial to the firm as accounts payable are a low cost source of funds for the firm. The average accounts payable payment period for Home Depot is 36.35 days.

$$\text{Accounts payable payment period} = \frac{365}{10.04} = 36.35 \text{ days}$$

When a firm produces goods or acquires inventory for sale and/or sells the items on a credit basis, it will need to have ample cash during the period between when the firm must pay for the raw materials, inventory, and labor and when it receives cash from the sale of the goods. The receivables, inventory, and payables "periods" can be combined to determine the length of time that the cash is tied up in this cycle, a time period defined as the **cash conversion cycle** for the firm:

$$\begin{array}{l}\text{Cash}\\\text{conversion} =\\\text{cycle}\end{array} \left(\begin{array}{c}\text{Receivables}\\\text{collection period}\end{array} \right) + \left(\begin{array}{c}\text{Inventory}\\\text{processing period}\end{array} \right) - \left(\begin{array}{c}\text{Accounts payable}\\\text{payment period}\end{array} \right) \tag{3.17}$$

Thus, the cash conversion cycle is the length of time a company's cash is tied up in the business. A firm's management can reduce its cash conversion cycle and free up cash for other activities by collecting its receivables more promptly, reducing the inventory processing time, or lengthening the time required to pay its suppliers. The cash conversion cycle increases when firms take longer to process inventory (buy and process raw materials, acquire inventory for sale, and make the eventual sale) and to collect the accounts receivable generated from credit sales. This cash conversion cycle correspondingly decreases by the amount of time the firm takes to pay its associated expenses associated with the sale of these goods (trades payable).

A cash conversion cycle for Home Depot is computed below:

$$\text{Cash conversion cycle} = 24.97 + 68.48 - 36.35 = 57.10 \text{ days}$$

Asset Turnover Ratios

Other asset management measures include two ratios that measure how efficiently management is using its fixed assets and total assets to generate sales. The **fixed asset turnover** and **total asset turnover ratios** are computed by dividing net sales by the appropriate asset figure:

$$\text{Fixed asset turnover ratio} = \frac{\text{Net sales}}{\text{Average net fixed assets}} \tag{3.18}$$

$$\text{Total asset turnover ratio} = \frac{\text{Net sales}}{\text{Average total assets}} \qquad (3.19)$$

The fixed asset turnover ratio indicates how effectively a firm's management uses its net fixed assets to generate sales. Similarly, the total asset turnover ratio indicates how effectively management uses total assets to generate sales. For example, a fixed asset turnover of 2.0 times would indicate that the firm generates $2.00 of net sales for each dollar invested in net fixed assets. Higher asset turnover ratios generally indicate more efficient use of the firm's assets. However, biases may occur due to the historic cost accounting principle used for a firm's fixed assets. A firm with older plant and equipment will have higher asset turnover ratios as the equipment is depreciated and reported on the balance sheet at a low book value, especially under periods of high inflation. Thus, a high asset turnover ratio may simply indicate that a firm needs to replace aging plant and equipment. Biases may also result from the depreciation method used and the extent to which a firm leases rather than owns its fixed assets.

The fixed asset and total asset turnover ratios for Home Depot are computed below:

$$\text{Fixed asset turnover ratio} = \frac{58{,}247}{\dfrac{(15{,}375 + 17{,}168)}{2}} = 3.58 \text{ times}$$

$$\text{Total asset turnover ratio} = \frac{58{,}247}{\dfrac{(26{,}394 + 30{,}011)}{2}} = 2.07 \text{ times}$$

Analyzing Asset Management Ratios for Home Depot

Table 3.3 reports the asset management ratios for Home Depot and Lowe's.[3] Both companies appear to be managing their assets efficiently with similar receivables collection periods,

Table 3.3 Asset management ratios for Home Depot and Lowe's for FY 2002

Asset management ratios	Home Depot		Lowe's	
Accounts receivable turnover	14.62	x	15.68	x
Receivables collection period	24.97	days	23.29	days
Inventory turnover	5.33	x	4.87	x
Inventory processing period	68.48	days	74.95	days
Accounts payable turnover	10.04	x	10.10	x
Payable payment period	36.35	days	36.14	days
Cash conversion cycle	57.10	days	62.10	days
Fixed asset turnover	3.58	x	2.79	x
Total asset turnover	2.07	x	1.78	x

---

[3] To calculate accounts receivable turnover, we assume that 10 percent of net sales for Lowe's are net credit sales (we assumed 25 percent for Home Depot). We assumed a lower amount because Lowe's discloses that sales made through their private label credit card are not reflected in accounts receivables.

inventory processing periods, and payables payment periods. Both firms have cash conversion cycles of around 60 days. With higher fixed asset and total asset turnover ratios, Home Depot creates more sales per dollar invested in both its fixed assets and total assets than Lowe's.

Concept Check 3.4

1 What do asset management ratios tell about a firm? What are the most commonly used asset management ratios?
2 What can a firm do to improve (shorten) its cash conversion cycle? Would you expect an improvement in a firm's cash conversion cycle to increase the value of the firm?
3 Suppose a retail firm's credit sales are only 5 percent of total net sales. If you assume all net sales are credit sales, how would this distort the calculation of the firm's accounts receivable turnover ratio and cash conversion cycle?

3.5 Profitability Ratios

Profitability ratios measure the earning power of a firm. They measure management's ability to control expenses in relation to sales and reflect a firm's operating performance, riskiness, and leverage. Some of the most commonly used profitability ratios include the gross profit margin, operating profit margin, net profit margin, return on assets, total return on assets, return on total equity, and return on common equity.

Gross Profit Margin

The **gross profit margin** is computed by dividing a firm's gross profit by net sales.

$$\text{Gross profit margin} = \frac{\text{Gross profit}}{\text{Net sales}} \qquad (3.20)$$

The gross profit margin indicates the gross profit generated per dollar of net sales. A firm with a gross profit margin of 30 percent generates $0.30 of gross profit per $1.00 of sales. Since the cost of sales is the only item subtracted from net sales to compute gross profit, the gross profit margin indicates the relationship between sales and manufacturing or production costs.

Operating Profit Margin

A firm's **operating profit margin** is computed by dividing its operating profit by net sales.

$$\text{Operating profit margin} = \frac{\text{Operating profit}}{\text{Net sales}} \qquad (3.21)$$

Operating profit is computed by subtracting cost of sales, selling, general, and administrative expenses, and depreciation expense from net sales. Thus, the operating profit margin, which indicates the operating profit generated per dollar of net sales, measures the firm's operating profitability before financing costs.

Net Profit Margin

The **net profit margin** measures the percentage of sales that result in net income, and is calculated as:

$$\text{Net profit margin} = \frac{\text{Net income}}{\text{Net sales}} \tag{3.22}$$

High net profit margins suggest a firm can control its costs or has a solid competitive position within its industry that is not threatened by cost-cutting competitors. Low net profit margins suggest a firm has not controlled its costs well or that other firms in the industry offer lower prices that threaten its competitiveness. Net profit margins vary widely by the type of industry. Firms in industries with high sales volumes (like retail grocery stores) can operate profitably with relatively low net profit margins because they experience a high turnover of their total assets, while firms in other industries require much higher margins to survive.

Using *net income from recurring operations* in the numerator avoids including changes in net profit margins caused by unusual or infrequent items, extraordinary items, discontinued operations, and changes in accounting principle. Analysts often exclude these nonrecurring items from net income to concentrate on income resulting from normal activities and operations.

The gross profit margin, operating profit margin, and net profit margin ratios are often analyzed together. For example, assume a firm's net profit margin has been declining for several years and is now lower than the industry norm. If the gross profit margin has not been declining and is on par with industry norms, but the operating profit margin has been declining and is also below industry norms, then analysis should look at indirect costs of operations and not the direct cost of goods sold. But if the gross profit margin has been declining and is below industry norms, then the decline in profitability may be associated entirely with direct production costs and perhaps also with indirect costs of production. These ratios may be analyzed by constructing a vertical common-size income statement, as discussed in Chapter 2.

The gross profit, operating profit, and net profit margins for Home Depot for fiscal year 2002 are computed below:

$$\text{Gross profit margin} = \frac{18,108}{58,247} = 0.3109 = 31.09\%$$

$$\text{Operating profit margin} = \frac{5,830}{58,247} = 0.1001 = 10.01\%$$

$$\text{Net profit margin} = \frac{3,664}{58,247} = 0.0629 = 6.29\%$$

Return on Assets

The **return on assets** (ROA) ratio measures the net income generated from each dollar invested in total assets, and is usually calculated as:

$$\text{Return on assets} = \frac{\text{Net income}}{\text{Average total assets}} \tag{3.23}$$

The net income should be from recurring operations, thereby excluding income or loss from transactions outside the ordinary course of business. Analysts often compute average total assets as the sum of the beginning and ending total assets for the period divided by two. ROA ratios are also affected by the age of a firm's plant and equipment, especially during periods of moderate to high inflation. If the firm's fixed assets are old and have been depreciated to a low book value, and the assets have not lost their productive ability, then the low figure in the denominator will inflate ROA.

Total Return on Assets

Since total assets are financed by both debt and equity and provide returns to both groups of investors, some analysts compute **total return on assets** by adding a firm's interest expense to the numerator.

$$\text{Total return on assets} = \frac{\text{Net income} + \text{Interest expense}}{\text{Average total assets}} \tag{3.24}$$

Without this adjustment, firms with high relative amounts of debt financing will have lower returns on assets.

Return on Total Equity

The **return on total equity** (ROE) ratio measures the accounting return earned on the capital provided by the firm's preferred and common stockholders. The computation of ROE is:

$$\text{Return on total equity} = \frac{\text{Net income}}{\text{Average total equity}} \tag{3.25}$$

ROE indicates how well management has used shareholder resources to generate net income. This ratio is often referred to as return on total equity (ROTE) because the equity figure includes both common and preferred equity and the net income before any dividends paid to common or preferred shareholders.

Return on Common Equity

Return on common equity (ROCE) focuses on just the return to common shareholders and is computed by removing the dividends to preferred shareholders from net income and dividing by the capital provided by common shareholders.

$$\text{Return on common equity} = \frac{\text{Net income} - \text{Preferred dividends}}{\text{Average common equity}} \qquad (3.26)$$

Both return on equity ratios are accounting-based measures that do not typically represent the actual return earned by shareholders. Net income is an accrual-based accounting measure of profit earned during the period and may differ substantially from the net cash flow generated during the period. Also, the equity amount in the denominator represents the equity capital that has been invested in the firm, including reinvestment of retained earnings, but does not represent the current market value of the firm's equity investment.

The ROA and ROE ratios for Home Depot for fiscal year 2002 are computed below. Since Home Depot has no preferred stock, the return on total equity and return on common equity are the same.

$$\text{Return on assets} = \frac{3{,}664}{\dfrac{(26{,}394 + 30{,}011)}{2}} = 0.1299 = 12.99\%$$

$$\text{Total return on assets} = \frac{3{,}664 + 37}{\dfrac{(26{,}394 + 30{,}011)}{2}} = 0.1312 = 13.12\%$$

$$\text{Return on total equity} = \text{Return on common equity} = \frac{3{,}664}{\dfrac{(18{,}083 + 19{,}803)}{2}} = 0.1934 = 19.34\%$$

Table 3.4 reports the profitability ratios for Home Depot and Lowe's. Home Depot appears to have a higher level of profitability than Lowe's does. The higher net profit margin earned by Home Depot appears to be due to both the higher gross profit and operating profit margins. Home Depot has a higher ROA than Lowe's, 12.99 percent versus 9.36 percent, respectively, but has a slightly lower ROE. This is because Lowe's makes greater use of financial leverage. The DuPont analysis of ROE discussed in the next section helps to explain how leverage affects ROE.

Table 3.4 Profitability ratios for Home Depot and Lowe's for FY 2002

Profitability ratios	Home Depot (%)	Lowe's (%)
Gross profit margin	31.09	30.30
Operating profit margin	10.01	9.67
Net profit margin	6.29	5.55
Return on assets	12.99	9.36
Total return on assets	13.12	11.08
Return on total equity	19.34	19.64
Return on common equity	19.34	19.64

DuPont Analysis of ROE

Analysts often examine return on equity more carefully by breaking it down into other ratios using a **traditional DuPont analysis** framework where:

$$\text{Return on equity} = \text{Profit margin} \times \text{Total asset turnover} \times \text{Equity multiplier} \qquad (3.27a)$$

$$\text{Return on equity} = \frac{\text{Net income}}{\text{Sales}} \times \frac{\text{Sales}}{\text{Average total assets}} \times \frac{\text{Total assets}}{\text{Equity}} \qquad (3.27b)$$

By separating ROE into these three components, an analyst can determine whether changes in a firm's ROE are attributable to changes in the level of earnings generated from sales, the sales generated from total assets, or the equity multiplier (leverage factor) employed in the financing of the firm's assets.

Table 3.5 provides a DuPont analysis of ROE for Home Depot and Lowe's for fiscal year 2002.[4]

Table 3.5 Dupont analysis of ROE for Home Depot and Lowe's for FY 2002

	Net profit margin (%)	×	Total asset turnover	×	Equity multiplier	=	Return on equity (%)
Home Depot	6.29		2.07		1.49		19.34
Lowe's	5.55		1.78		1.99		19.64

Multiplying the first two terms of Equation 3.27b (profit margin times total asset turnover) gives us the net income divided by average total assets, which is the ROA ratio. Therefore, ROE is equal to ROA times the equity multiplier. Table 3.5 shows that the higher ROA for Home Depot reported in Table 3.4 can be attributed to its higher net profit margin and higher total asset turnover ratio: $6.29\% \times 2.07 = 12.99\%$ versus $5.55\% \times 1.78 = 9.36\%$ for Lowe's. The higher ROE for Lowe's is caused by their greater use of financial leverage, with an equity multiplier of 1.99 times versus only 1.49 times for Home Depot.

A fair question to ask is whether management at Home Depot should also use more financial leverage to increase ROE for its shareholders. Has management at Lowe's increased the value of their firm by increasing ROE through the use of debt financing? Not necessarily. Increased financial leverage increases the volatility of returns to the shareholders, and will increase their required returns to compensate them for the additional risk. We cannot tell from our analysis whether the increased returns are sufficient to compensate for this additional risk. This issue will be explored in much greater detail in Chapter 11.

Return on common equity (ROCE) can also be separated in a DuPont analysis by using an adjusted profit margin and a common equity multiplier:

---

[4] Because the total asset turnover ratio uses average total assets, we use an average equity multiplier figure computed as average total assets divided by average common equity. To obtain the 19.34 percent and 19.64 percent ROE figures also requires maintaining more decimal places in the net profit margin, total asset turnover, and equity multiplier ratios than shown in Table 3.5.

$$\underset{\text{common equity}}{\text{Return on}} = \underset{\text{margin}}{\text{Adjusted profit}} \times \underset{\text{turnover}}{\text{Total asset}} \times \underset{\text{multiplier}}{\text{Common equity}} \qquad (3.28a)$$

$$\underset{\text{equity}}{\overset{\text{Return on}}{\underset{}{\text{common}}}} = \frac{\text{Net income} - \text{Pfd dividends}}{\text{Sales}} \times \frac{\text{Sales}}{\text{Average total assets}} \times \frac{\text{Average total assets}}{\text{Average common equity}}$$

$$(3.28b)$$

Because Home Depot does not have any preferred stock, the DuPont analysis for return on common equity is identical to the return on equity analysis.

Managers and analysts can obtain additional insight into a firm's ROE by performing an **extended DuPont analysis**:

$$\text{Return on equity} = \left[\left(\begin{matrix} \text{Operating} \\ \text{profit} \\ \text{margin} \end{matrix} \right) \left(\begin{matrix} \text{Total} \\ \text{asset} \\ \text{turnover} \end{matrix} \right) - \left(\begin{matrix} \text{Interest} \\ \text{expense} \\ \text{rate} \end{matrix} \right) \right] \left(\begin{matrix} \text{Financial} \\ \text{leverage} \\ \text{multiplier} \end{matrix} \right) \left(\begin{matrix} \text{Tax} \\ \text{retention} \\ \text{rate} \end{matrix} \right) \qquad (3.29a)$$

$$\text{Return on equity} = \left[\left(\frac{\text{EBIT}}{\text{Sales}} \right) \left(\frac{\text{Sales}}{\text{Assets}} \right) - \left(\frac{\text{Interest expense}}{\text{Assets}} \right) \right] \left(\frac{\text{Total assets}}{\text{Equity}} \right) (1 - t) \qquad (3.29b)$$

We can now attribute changes in return on equity to changes in the levels of operating profits generated by sales, the sales generated from total assets, the firm's interest expense relative to its total assets, the leverage factor employed in the financing of the firm's assets, and the taxation of the firm's profits.

Concept Check 3.5

1   What do profitability ratios tell us about a firm? What are the most commonly used profitability ratios?
2   Why will the net profit margin ratio, as defined in Equation 3.22, not provide a fair comparison between firms with similar operating profit margins but widely differing long-term debt ratios? Can you suggest a modification to Equation 3.22 that would adjust for different levels of debt financing?
3   Why might the ROA and ROE for a firm not be an accurate measure of the firm's profitability based on its investments in assets or equity, respectively?
4   How can traditional DuPont analysis or extended DuPont analysis provide additional insight into changes in a firm's profitability?

3.6 Market Value Ratios

Market value ratios use market data such as stock price to provide useful information about the firm's relative value. Commonly used market value ratios include the price-to-earnings ratio, market-to-book value ratio, dividend yield, and dividend payout.

Price/earnings Ratio

The **price/earnings (P/E) ratio**, one of the most widely used financial ratios, is computed by dividing the market price per share of the firm's common stock by its earnings per share.

$$\text{Price/earnings ratio} = \frac{\text{Market price per share}}{\text{Earnings per share}} \qquad (3.30)$$

The P/E ratio indicates how much investors are willing to pay per dollar of earnings for shares of the firm's common stock. It provides an important indication of how the market perceives the growth and profit opportunities of a firm. High growth firms with strong future profit opportunities will command higher P/E ratios than firms with lower expected growth and profits. The P/E ratio has several potential shortcomings. For example, a firm can have negative earnings, which produces a meaningless P/E ratio. In addition management can distort reported earnings because of the discretion allowed by accounting practices.

The P/E ratio for Home Depot is computed below.

$$\text{Price/earnings ratio} = \frac{\$35.15}{\$1.57} = 22.39 \text{ times}$$

Since our ratio analysis has focused primarily on assessing Home Depot's recent performance, we average the stock price, at the end of fiscal year 2001 and 2002. We use an estimate of the average price during the fiscal year in which the earnings occurred. Investment analysts frequently compute P/E ratios by dividing an estimate of next year's earnings by the current stock price (leading P/E ratio) or by dividing last year's earnings by the current stock price (lagging P/E ratio).

Market-to-book Value Ratio

A firm's **market-to-book value ratio** is computed by dividing the market value of the firm's equity by its book value of equity.

$$\text{Market-to-book value ratio} = \frac{\text{Market value of equity}}{\text{Book value of equity}} \qquad (3.31)$$

In this ratio, book value of equity equals total assets minus total liabilities less preferred stock. The market-to-book value ratio measures how much value the firm has created for its shareholders. To the extent the ratio exceeds 1.0 times, management has succeeded in creating value for the shareholders. If the book value of a firm's equity is understated due to inflation, the ratio will provide an imprecise measure of this relationship. Home Depot's market to book ratio is computed below:

$$\text{Market-to-book value ratio} = \frac{2{,}336 \text{ million shares} \times \$20.90 \text{ per share}}{\$19{,}802 \text{ million}} = 2.47 \text{ times}$$

Dividend Yield and Payout

Dividend yield is computed by dividing a firm's dividends per share by the market price of its common stock.

$$\text{Dividend yield} = \frac{\text{Dividends per share}}{\text{Market price per share}} \tag{3.32}$$

Dividend yield represents part of a stock's total return; another part of a stock's total return is price appreciation. The **dividend payout** is the percentage of a firm's earnings paid out as cash dividends.

$$\text{Dividend payout} = \frac{\text{Cash dividends per share}}{\text{Earnings per share}} \tag{3.33}$$

The dividend yield and dividend payout ratios for Home Depot are shown below.

$$\text{Dividend yield} = \frac{\$0.21}{\$20.90} = 0.0100 = 1.00\%$$

$$\text{Dividend payout} = \frac{\$0.21}{\$1.57} = 0.1338 = 13.38\%$$

Since we used Home Depot's stock price at the end of fiscal year 2002, this dividend yield was a current annual dividend yield on February 2, 2003.

Table 3.6 reports the market value ratios for Home Depot and Lowe's. Until FY 2002, Home Depot had much higher P/E and market-to-book ratios than Lowe's. Both ratios incorporate a firm's stock price, and Home Depot's stock price fell from $49.40 per share on February 3, 2002 to $20.90 per share on February 2, 2003. As a result, Home Depot's P/E and market-to-book ratios fell substantially. By comparison, Lowe's stock price fell from $45.70 per share on its fiscal year-end date of February 1, 2002 to $34.18 on its fiscal year-end date of January 31, 2003, a much smaller relative decline over a similar period. Both firms have relatively low dividend yields and dividend payouts.

Table 3.6 Market value ratios for Home Depot and Lowe's for FY 2002

Market value ratios	Home Depot	Lowe's
Price/earnings	22.39x	21.13x
Market-to-book value	2.47x	3.22x
Dividend yield	1.00%	0.26%
Dividend payout	13.38%	4.76%

Concept Check 3.6

1   What do market value ratios tell about a firm? What are some commonly used market value ratios?
2   What does a high P/E ratio suggest about a firm's future growth opportunities?
3   Many investment analysts define *growth stocks* as those of firms with high P/E and market-to-book value ratios. Would such firms typically have high or low dividend payouts? Would Home Depot and Lowe's be considered growth stocks?
4   Many investment analysts define *value stocks* as those of firms with low P/E and market-to-book value ratios and high dividend payouts. Would such stocks be attractive investments?

3.7 Uses of Financial Ratios

Financial ratios are widely used in the finance industry. We review some of the specific uses below including stock valuation, bond ratings, and price setting for regulated firms.

Stock Valuation

Financial ratios are commonly used to estimate the intrinsic value of a firm's common stock. **Intrinsic value** is what a stock is really worth, which could differ from the market price. Many analysts estimate the price of a firm's stock using an earnings estimate and a price-earnings multiple (P/E ratio). For example, suppose an analyst estimates a firm's earnings as $3 per share and its P/E ratio is 20 times. An estimate of the firm's stock price would be $60 per share. Return on equity ratios are commonly used to estimate sustainable growth rates in stock valuation models. Specifically, a firm's sustainable growth rate may be estimated by multiplying the firm's return on equity by its earnings retention rate. Home Depot's sustainable growth rate is computed below:

$$\text{Sustainable growth rate} = \text{ROE} \times \text{Earnings retention rate} \qquad (3.34)$$

$$\text{Sustainable growth rate} = \text{ROE} \times (1 - \text{Dividend payout})$$

$$\text{Sustainable growth rate} = 19.34\% \times (1 - 0.1338) = 16.75\%$$

Financial Ratios and Bond Ratings

As mentioned earlier in this chapter, bond rating agencies such as Standard & Poor's and Moody's assign a credit rating that reflects the likelihood of default on a firm's debt and the protection that creditors have in the event of a default. To assess the likelihood of default, these rating agencies closely examine a firm's ratios, especially the firm's leverage, coverage, liquidity, and profitability ratios.

Regulation

Regulators frequently use financial ratios to determine a target performance benchmark for a regulated firm. They then set allowed prices or price caps or these firm that are designed to allow the firm to achieve a desired level of performance. For example, the private company that is responsible for water treatment and supply in the city of Manila has its prices for water services determined based on a targeted return on assets ratio for the level of assets invested.

Concept Check 3.7

1   What are three uses for financial ratios?
2   What is the calculation of a firm's sustainable growth rate?

3.8 Limitations of Financial Ratio Analysis

While financial ratios clearly provide important information about a firm's health and profitability, such analysis has several limitations including:

- identifying appropriate industry averages for comparison purposes;
- adjusting for the effects of inflation on financial statements;
- adjusting for the effects of different accounting practices on financial statements and ratios; and
- drawing conclusions about a ratio for a particular firm.

As we discussed earlier in the chapter, analysts should examine a firm's performance within the context of its industry environment. That is, the financial ratios for a firm should be compared to either industry average ratios or to relevant competitors. Several issues arise that complicate these comparisons. Many firms are widely diversified across various industry segments. While the firm's Standard Industrial Classification (SIC) Code may place it in a particular industry segment, the firm's assets and operations within its other divisions may affect its financial statements and ratios. Other firms within the same major industry segment may also be widely diversified into other industry sectors that are different from the firm.

The question also arises as to whether to use an industry average. The industry average consists of firms in a particular industry segment, both the good and the poor performers. Comparing a leading firm within an industry to the industry average may be inappropriate. A better approach might be to compute a new industry average that leaves out the weak performers or to simply compare the ratios of the firm to those of two or three of its closest competitors.

Answers to these questions require judgment on the part of the analyst. In this chapter, comparing financial ratios of Home Depot to industry averages may be inappropriate because Home Depot is by far the largest firm in the retail building supply industry. Instead, we chose to compare Home Depot to Lowe's, its closest competitor. Was this the right choice? Arguments can be made for and against such an approach but we discussed our reasons for doing so. Other qualified analysts might have used different logic and chosen a different approach.

Finally, when using financial ratios for making comparisons, analysts should check to make sure that all ratios are computed using the same formula. Different financial services sometimes use slightly different formulas for some of the ratios. We have pointed out some of these differences in this chapter.

Financial analysts also need to consider the effects that inflation has on a firm's financial statements. Since many assets are recorded on an historic cost basis, inflation may cause some of these reported values to be understated. This is especially true for fixed assets, particularly when substantial property is included. Understating fixed assets causes biases in ratios using total assets or fixed assets. Furthermore, comparison between competitors or industry averages becomes complicated when different firms within the industry have varying degrees of distortion due to the effects of inflation on their fixed assets. Some firms may be carrying fixed assets on their balance sheets that are much older than other firms that have modernized and have newer plant and equipment. Analysts need to take into account these differences when making comparisons.

Concept Check 3.8

1 What are several important limitations of financial ratio analysis? How can these limitations be overcome?

Summary

This chapter discussed how to interpret financial ratios. The major points follow.

1 Financial ratios help users of financial statements to more carefully assess a firm's financial condition.
2 Five major categories of ratios are: liquidity, debt management, asset management, profitability, and market value.
3 Liquidity ratios indicate a firm's ability to pay its bills in the short run.
4 Debt management ratios characterize a firm in terms of the relative mix of debt-equity financing and measure the long-term debt paying ability of a firm.

5 Asset management ratios measure the ability of a firm's management to manage the assets at its disposal.
6 Profitability ratios measure the ability of a firm's management to generate profits.
7 Market value ratios provide information about a firm's relative market value.

FURTHER READING

Beaver, William H. *Financial Reporting: An Accounting Revolution*, Prentice-Hall, 1989.

Bernstein, Leopold A. and John J. Wild. *Financial Statement Analysis: Theory, Application, and Interpretation*, 6th edn, Irwin McGraw Hill, 1998.

Choi, Frederick D. S., Carol Ann Frost, and Gary Meek. *International Accounting*, Prentice-Hall, 2000.

Stickney, Clyde and Paul R. Brown. *Financial Reporting and Statement Analysis: A Strategic Perspective*, 4th edn, Dryden Press, 1999.

White, Gerald I., Ashwinpaul C. Sondhi, and Dov Fried. *The Analysis and Use of Financial Statements*, 3rd edn, Wiley, 2003.

Chapter 4

The Time Value of Money

I will gladly pay you Tuesday for a hamburger I can eat today. (Wimpie, from the *Popeye* cartoon, E. C. Segar.)

Overview

Money has time value. We know this intuitively because most of us would prefer to receive $1,000 today than 1 year or 5 years from today. By receiving it today, we can invest the money and expect to have an even greater sum in the future. The same reasoning suggests we, not unlike Wimpie, should prefer to pay money we owe later than sooner. Thus, the value of money depends on the time when it is paid or received.

Many important financial decisions of a firm involve cash flows at various points in time. Financial managers should consider how time affects the value of these cash flows. For example, when a firm issues bonds to investors, managers should compare the value of future cash payments owed to the bondholders in exchange for the cash received today. Similarly, when making capital investments, managers need to compare the value of expected cash flows in the future to the present cash outlay needed to undertake the investment. In both cases, financial managers must understand how the value of cash flows varies at different points in time.

This chapter deals with the mathematics of the time value of money. Specifically, we provide the mathematical relationships for determining the future value of a present cash amount and the present value of a specified future cash amount. These future and present value relationships are extended to incorporate multiple cash flows that are equal and periodic (annuities) and multiple cash flows that are not. We also show how to determine the implied interest rate.

Learning Objectives

After completing this chapter, you should be able to:

- explain the meaning of the time value of money and the importance of the timing of cash flows in making financial decisions;
- calculate the future value and present value of cash flows for one period and multiple periods;
- solve for the interest rate implied by a given set of present value and future value cash flows;
- apply time value of money techniques to solve basic problems facing financial managers;
- use a financial calculator to solve time value of money problems.

4.1 Central Concepts in Finance

An old saying is that "A bird in the hand is worth two in the bush." In a way, this expression refers to the time value of birds. That is, having a single bird in the hand today is worth more than the chance of catching two birds in the future. The bird-in-hand expression reflects two central concepts in finance: the risk return tradeoff and the time value of money.

- **Risk-return tradeoff**: Investors will take on additional risk only if they anticipate higher return.
- **Time value of money**: A dollar available today is worth more than a dollar available at a future date. This is because a dollar today can be invested to earn a return.

Thus, investors require compensation for both risk bearing and the time value of money (TVM). These two principles lie at the heart of the financial decision-making concepts discussed in this book. We focus on time value of money principles in this chapter and discuss risk analysis in Chapter 9, as it relates to capital investments.

The notion that money has time value associated with it is intuitively appealing. Investors prefer to receive money earlier than later because they can expect to earn a positive rate of return on invested money.[1] Knowledge of time value of money concepts is essential to an understanding of many topics in finance. In fact, most financial decisions at both the personal and business levels involve cash flows at different points in time. Common users of time value of money concepts include corporate financial managers, securities analysts, portfolio managers, bankers, and investors. Here are a few examples.

- When firms issue bonds to investors in the capital markets, they should compare the value of future cash payments to the bondholders in exchange for the cash received from them today. Analysts and investors use time value of money concepts to value many financial securities. In Chapter 5, we use time value of money concepts to value bonds, preferred stock, and common stock.
- Managers who make capital investments in long-lived fixed assets should compare the value of expected future cash flows to the present cash outlay needed to undertake the investment. In Chapter 8, we discuss applications of time value of money when evaluating capital budgeting projects.

In all cases, financial managers, analysts, and investors must understand how the value of cash flows varies at different points in time.

---

[1]   In economics, the idea that money has time value is referred to as the opportunity cost of sacrificing the earning potential of a current dollar. Stated differently, an **opportunity cost** is what funds could earn on an alternative investment of equal risk. A basic principle of investment decisions is that an investment is acceptable only if it earns at least its opportunity cost (risk-adjusted required rate of return).

4.2 Future Value of a Present Amount

Someone investing a sum of money today at a given interest rate for a given period of time would expect to have a larger sum of money at that future date. We can determine that future amount using the **future value of a present amount formula**. We define **future value** as the value of a present amount at a future date after applying compound interest over a specified period. The amount invested today is the **present value**. Equation 4.1 shows how to compute the future value of a present amount:

$$FV = PV(1 + r)^n \tag{4.1}$$

where FV is the future value of an amount n periods from now; PV is the present value of an amount – it represents the amount invested today; r is the rate of return or interest rate per period; and n is the compounding term or interval, which is the number of periods between the PV and the FV.

Thus, future value calculations answer the question: How much will an investment be worth at a specific time in the future, compounded at a specific rate of interest? Future value is a **compounded value** because of compounding of interest. Another common name for future value is **terminal value**.

Example 4.1 illustrates how to compute the future value of a present amount using Equation 4.1.

Example 4.1 Future Value of a Single Amount

An investor has the opportunity to earn an 8 percent annual interest rate for the next 15 years. Assuming an investment of $5,000, how much will the investor have 15 years from today?

Solution: This problem requires computing a future value, given a present value of $5,000, an annual interest rate of 8 percent, and a compounding term of 15 years. Substituting into Equation 4.1 we get:

$$FV = PV(1 + r)^n$$

$$FV = \$5,000(1.08)^{15} = \$15,860.85$$

Effects of Interest Rates and Compounding Terms on Future Values

The level of the interest rate (r) and the length of the compounding term (n) affect future values. Specifically, future values increase as the compound interest rate increases and/or the compounding term becomes longer. As illustrated in Example 4.2 below, substantial increases in future values can result from small changes in interest rates, especially when the compounding term is long.

Example 4.2 Effect of Interest Rates on Future Values

Sue Wang is considering two long-term investment options for an inheritance of $50,000 she has recently received. Under Option A, she expects an annual return of 10 percent for the next 30 years; under Option B, she expects an annual return of 12 percent over the same period. What are the expected future values of these two plans 30 years from today when she retires?

Option A: $FV = \$50,000(1.10)^{30} = \$872,470.11$

Option B: $FV = \$50,000(1.12)^{30} = \$1,497,996.11$

Solution: This example shows that a relatively small difference in interest rates results in a substantial difference in the future values 30 years later. The future value under Option B is about 72 percent higher than Option A.[2] This substantial difference in future value amounts explains why young investors, who have long investment horizons for their retirement savings, are often encouraged to seek the higher expected returns from long-term growth equity investments.

Time Diagrams

Using a **time diagram** is helpful to illustrate the timing of cash flows, especially for situations involving cash flows at different points in time that are not equal. For Example 4.1, our time diagram would look like this:

Year	0	15
Amount	$5,000	$15,860.85

---

[2]   Of course, the choice of Option B would need to take into account any perceived differences in risk between the two investments.

Compounding of Interest

Interest earned and paid in future years depends not only on the initial amount, but also on any interest earned that has not been withdrawn from the investment account. Thus, with compounding, interest is earned on interest, and the future value amount will increase geometrically over time, not linearly.

To illustrate, assume an investment of $100 today at 10 percent per year. One year from today, the future value grows to $110, computed as [$100 + (0.10)($100)]. Assuming no interest is withdrawn, the investor will earn interest on $110 during the second year and receive a year-end interest payment of $11.00. The future value at the end of the second year will be $121.00, computed as [$110 + (0.10)($110)]. Assuming that no interest is withdrawn, the investor will earn $12.10 during the third year and will have a future value of $133.10 at the end of three years, computed as [$121 + (0.10)($121)]. Table 4.1 summarizes these interest and future value amounts.

Table 4.1 Future value of $100 at an interest rate of 10 percent

Year	Future value of $100 investment at 10%	Interest earned
1	$110.00	$10.00
2	$121.00	$11.00
3	$133.10	$12.10

By compounding rates annually, the interest is earned throughout the year, but it is paid at the end of the year. As just discussed, the first interest payment of $10 on the $100 initial investment would be paid at the end of the first year. If the investor withdrew the principal before the year-end interest payment date, the investor would not receive any partial interest payment. The second interest payment of $11 would be paid at the end of the second year, and the third interest payment of $12.10 would be paid at the end of the third year. Thus, no partial intra-year interest payments are made under annual compounding. Later in this chapter, we examine situations where interest is compounded more frequently than once per year.

Writing the future value equation (Equation 4.1) with subscripts on the FV and PV terms is sometimes helpful. For a present value invested at time t, the equation for a future value n periods from time t may be written:

$$FV_n = PV_t(1 + r)^n$$

For example, suppose an investor expects to receive a sum of money 3 years from today and plans to immediately invest the funds in a savings account at a fixed interest rate for 5 years. We can write the future value equation to show the timing of the cash flows:

$$FV_8 = PV_3(1 + r)^5$$

where PV_3 is the amount to be invested 3 years from now and FV_8 is the future value 5 years later (8 years from today).

Future Value of Multiple Amounts

When multiple present values need to be compounded to obtain a future value, these compounded future value amounts can be summed together. For example, if an investment provides a cash flow of $100 in year 0, $250 in year 1, and $475 in year 2, the future value in year 3 could be computed by summing the future value of each. Assuming an annual interest rate of 10 percent, we get:

$$FV_3 = PV_0(1 + r)^3 + PV_1(1 + r)^2 + PV_2(1 + r)^1$$

$$FV_3 = \$100(1.10)^3 + \$250(1.10)^2 + \$475(1.10)^1 = \$958.10$$

Thus, future value of present amount calculations are additive. Of course, these calculations get tedious when we have many present value amounts. If the present value amounts are equal and periodic, they constitute what is called an *annuity* and the future value calculation is simplified. We address future value of annuity calculations in Section 4.4.

Using the BA II PLUS® Financial Calculator

Skillful use of financial calculators can greatly simplify and quicken our time value of money calculations. Throughout this chapter, we illustrate how to solve time value of money calculations on the Texas Instruments (TI) BA II PLUS® financial calculator. However, before attempting any problems, we need to check and perhaps change an important setting on your calculator. This calculator comes with a preset factory setting of 12 P/YR to accommodate the many users who compute monthly loan payments. We need to change this setting to 1 P/YR by sequentially pressing [2nd] [P/Y] "1" [ENTER] [2nd][QUIT]. These keystrokes will also automatically change the calculator setting to one compounding period per year. We recommend keeping the setting on 1 P/Y because it is easy to forget to change the setting back to 1 P/Y for future calculations.

Now we can proceed to an example. Across the third row (from the top) of this calculator, there are five TVM keys that correspond to the basic time value of money concepts: N, I/Y, PV, PMT, and FV keys.

- N = number of compounding periods.
- I/Y = interest rate per compounding period.
- PV = present value.
- FV = future value.
- PMT = annuity payments or constant periodic amount.

Refer to Example 4.1 and follow these steps:

1   2nd CLR TVM
2   15 N

3   8 I/YR

4   5,000 +/− PV

5   CPT FV (CPT refers to the *compute* key in the top row.)

Steps 2 through 5 look like the following on the BA II PLUS® calculator:

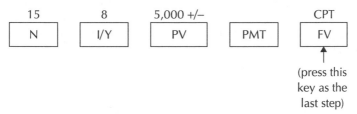

(press this
key as the
last step)

The answer is 15,860.85. Note the negative sign on PV. Specifically, the $5,000 represents the funds needed to create the account (an outflow) and the $15,860.85 represents the value of the account at the end of the period (an inflow). Although this step is unnecessary, it makes the FV come out as a positive number. If PV is entered as a positive number, the negative sign that appears on the FV should be ignored.

Practical Financial Tip 4.1

Using the BA II PLUS® calculator requires understanding the sign convention. This calculator uses the convention that cash outflows (expenditures) have negative signs (−) and cash inflows (receipts) have positive signs (+). Failing to follow this convention may yield nonsensical answers or error messages. Thus, PV and FV must have opposite signs.

Practical Financial Tip 4.2

Always start time value of money (TVM) computations on the BA II PLUS® calculator with [2ⁿᵈ] [Clear TVM]. The keys N, I/Y, PV, PMT, and PV are TVM memory registers. Many problems use only four of the five keys (three known variables and one unknown variable). This calculator has continuous memory that retains numbers in storage registers even when the calculator is turned off. Forgetting to clear the calculator's TVM memory after each use could result in the calculator's internal program solving the current problem using information stored from a previous problem. This may result in an incorrect answer. Another way to handle this situation is to enter 0 in any unused TVM memory registers such as entering 0 PMT in a single sum TVM problem.

Concept Check 4.2

1   What is meant by the term *compounding of interest*?

2   How do the length of the compounding term and the interest rate affect future values?

4.3 Present Value of a Future Amount

In Section 4.2, we learned how to compute the future value of a present amount. Financial managers are often more interested in determining the **present value of a future amount**. We will demonstrate the usefulness of this concept many times in this book, especially in the chapters where we value financial securities (Chapter 5) and capital investment projects (Chapters 8 and 9).

To solve for the present value of a future amount, we solve equation 4.1 for the present value amount:

$$PV = FV\left[\frac{1}{(1 + r)^n}\right] \tag{4.2}$$

This equation is also often written as:

$$PV = \frac{FV}{(1 + r)^n} \tag{4.2a}$$

We illustrate the calculation of the present value of a future amount in Example 4.3.

Example 4.3 Present Value of a Single Amount

The Hobbs Corporation must make a final payment of $20 million to its bondholders 5 years from today to retire the bond issue. At an interest rate of 6 percent, what is the present value of the $20 million payment?

Solution: This problem calls for computing a present value, given a future value of $20 million, an annual interest rate of 6 percent, and a term of 5 years.

The time diagram for our example is illustrated as follows:

Year	0	5
Amount	PV	$20,000,000

We can solve for the present value using Equation 4.2.

$$PV = FV\left[\frac{1}{(1 + r)^n}\right]$$

$$PV = \$20,000,000\left[\frac{1}{(1.06)^5}\right] = \$14,945,163.46$$

How should we interpret this present value amount? The $14,945,163.46 present value amount (today) is *financially equivalent* to $20 million five years from today at an annual interest rate of 6 percent. Assuming no preference for spending the money today or 5 years from now, an individual would be indifferent between receiving $14,945,163.46 today or $20 million five years from today at an annual interest rate of 6 percent. Suppose the borrower and lender decide to settle this future liability today. If they both agree that 6 percent is the appropriate annual interest rate over the next 5 years, a $14,945,163.46 payment would be the appropriate (present value) payment today.

The process of computing the present value of a future amount is called **discounting**. The interest rate used to compute the present value is called the **discount rate**, but may also be referred to as the **opportunity cost**, **required rate of return**, and the **cost of capital**. Regardless of the term used, it represents the compound rate of return that an investor can earn on an investment. In Example 4.3, we would say that $14,945,163.46 is the discounted value of a $20 million payment 5 years from now at a discount rate of 6 percent. Time value of money analysis is often referred to as **discounted cash flow analysis**.

Present values decrease as the discount rate increases. Thus, *present values are inversely related to interest rates*. The logic is simple. Suppose a person needs to have $50,000 five years from today, and wants to invest money today to meet that goal. The higher the interest rate, the lower the (present value) amount needed to be invested today. This inverse relationship is an important concept that we will return to several times in this the book, especially when we discuss valuing securities issued by firms and capital investment projects that firms adopt.

Using the BA II PLUS® Financial Calculator

The steps used for computing the future value of a present amount on the BA II PLUS® calculator are similar to those used for computing the present value of a future amount in Section 4.2. We illustrate these steps using the previous Example 4.3 where we solved for the present value of a $200,000 future value amount 5 years from now at a discount rate of 6 percent.

1   2nd CLR TVM
2   5 N
3   6 I/YR   Steps 2–4 can be done in any order.
4   20,000,000 +/− FV
5   CPT PV

Steps 2 through 5 will look like the following on a BA II PLUS® calculator:

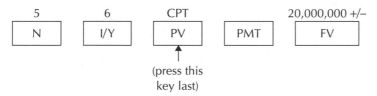

The answer should appear as $14,945,163.46. Recall from Example 4.1 that when using the BA II PLUS® calculator, entering a negative (positive) future value amount results in a positive (negative) present value amount due to the sign convention.

Present Value of Multiple Future Cash Flows

The present value of multiple future value amounts can be computed by simply summing the present value of each individual future value amount. The following example illustrates the important property that present values are additive.

Example 4.4 Present Value of Uneven Amounts

The Crusty Crumbs Company expects to receive the following payments from one of its delinquent customers: $500 one year from today, $800 two years from today, and $950 three years from today. At an interest rate of 8 percent, what is the present value of these future value payment amounts?

Year	0	1	2	3
Amount	PV	$500	$800	$950

Solution: We obtained the present value of this stream of uneven amounts as follows:

$$PV_0 = FV_1\left[\frac{1}{(1+r)^1}\right] + FV_2\left[\frac{1}{(1+r)^2}\right] + FV_3\left[\frac{1}{(1+r)^3}\right]$$

$$PV = \$500\left[\frac{1}{(1.08)^1}\right] + \$800\left[\frac{1}{(1.08)^2}\right] + \$950\left[\frac{1}{(1.08)^3}\right] = \$1{,}902.97$$

While computing the present value of multiple future value amounts is straightforward, the computations become tedious and time consuming as the number of cash flows increases. When the multiple future value amounts are equal and periodic, they constitute what is called an *annuity*. Present value of annuity calculations are discussed in Section 4.5. When the amounts are uneven (not equal or periodic), follow the steps in the example above.

Using the BA II PLUS® Financial Calculator

We illustrate two approaches for solving this example. The more tedious approach is to compute the present value of each future amount and then sum the results, as shown below:

PV_1: FV = 500 +/−; I/Y = 8; N = 1; CPT → PV = PV_1 = 462.96

PV_2: FV = 800 +/−; I/Y = 8; N = 2; CPT → PV = PV_2 = 685.87

PV_3: FV = 950 +/−; I/Y = 8; N = 3; CPT → PV = PV_3 = 754.14

PV of uneven amounts = $\sum PV_{individual}$ = 1,902.97

We can also solve for the present value on the BA II PLUS® calculator by entering the actual cash flows into the calculator and pressing the NPV key.[3] These steps are detailed in Table 4.2 below.

Table 4.2 Calculating the PV of multiple future amounts using the BA II PLUS® calculator

Key strokes	Explanation	Display	
[2nd] → [Format] → [2] → [Enter]	Display 2 decimals (Need to do this only once)	DEC =	2.00
[CF] → [2nd] → [CLR WORK]	Clear Memory Registers	CF$_0$ =	0.00
0 → [+/−] → [ENTER]	Initial Cash Outlay	CF$_0$ =	0.00
[↓] → 500 → [ENTER]	Period 1 Cash Flow	C01 =	500.00
[↓]	Frequency of Cash Flow 1	F01 =	1.00
[↓] → 800 → [ENTER]	Period 2 Cash Flow	C02 =	800.00
[↓]	Frequency of Cash Flow 2	F02 =	1.00
[↓] → 950 → [ENTER]	Period 3 Cash Flow	C03 =	950.00
[↓]	Frequency of Cash Flow 3	F03 =	1.00
[NPV] → 8 → [ENTER]	8% Discount Rate	I =	8.00
[↓] → [CPT]	Calculate NPV	NPV =	1,902.97

Concept Check 4.3

1 What steps are needed to solve for the present value of a future amount?
2 What is meant by the terms *discounting* and *discount rate*?
3 How do the length of the compounding term and the interest rate affect present values?

4.4 Future Value of an Annuity

An **annuity** is a series of equal and periodic cash flows. For example, if someone deposits $2,000 at the end of each year for 20 years into an IRA account for retirement years, these 20 payments represent a 20-year annuity of $2,000 per year. We could compute the future value of these annuity payments by applying Equation 4.1 twenty times and summing the individual results. We can simplify our work by using the future value of an annuity formula. The future value of an annuity is computed as:

$$FV = PMT\left[\frac{(1 + r)^n - 1}{r}\right] \qquad (4.3)$$

---

[3] NPV refers to net present value, a concept we address in Chapter 8. A net present value subtracts the cash flow in year 0 from the present value of the future cash flows. Since we have no cash flow in year 0 in this example, the NPV is simply equal to the present value of the future cash flows.

Future value of an annuity calculations are used to compute the future compounded value of a series of equal, periodic payments. We illustrate how to solve for the future value of an ordinary annuity in which payments occur at the end of each period in Example 4.5 below.

Example 4.5 Future Value of an Ordinary Annuity

Suppose John Early decides to save $2,000 at the end of each year for the next 10 years. If Early can earn 8 percent per year on his invested funds, what will be the future value of the investment 10 years from today?

| Year | 0 | 1 | 2 | 3 | 4 | 5 | 6 | 7 | 8 | 9 | 10 |

Amount $2,000   FV

Solution: Using Equation 4.3, the future value of the ordinary annuity is:

$$FV = \$2,000 \left[\frac{(1.08)^{10} - 1}{0.08} \right] = \$28,973.12$$

We can also solve for the future value of an ordinary annuity with the BA II PLUS® calculator for Example 4.5 using the following keystrokes:

1   2nd CLR TVM
2   10 N
3   8 I/YR
4   2,000 +/− PMT
5   CPT FV

Steps 2 through 5 look like the following on the BA II PLUS® calculator:

10	8		2,000 +/−	CPT
N	I/Y	PV	PMT	FV

(last step)

The answer is $28,973.12.

In Example 4.5, we also could have treated the 10 cash flows of $2,000 each as separate present values, computed the future value of each, and summed them to get the future value. Computing the future value of 10 separate terms and summing is more work than using the future value of an annuity formula.

Two rules or conventions must be observed when solving for the future value of an annuity.

- The value for n is the number of payments in the annuity.
- When using the future value of an annuity formula, the future value is obtained *at the time of the last annuity payment*. This convention follows from the derivation of the future

value of an annuity formula.[4] To determine the future value at some later date requires the adjustment illustrated in Example 4.6 below.

Example 4.6 Future Value of an Annuity Due

If an investor invests $2,000 at the beginning of each year (beginning today) for the next 5 years, how much will she have 5 years from now if she can earn 10 percent per year on her investment?

Solution: The time diagram looks like this:

Time	0	1	2	3	4	5
Amount	$2,000	$2,000	$2,000	$2,000	$2,000	FV

Using Equation 4.3, we obtain the future value at the time of the last payment, which is year 4:

$$FV = \$2,000\left[\frac{(1.10)^5 - 1}{0.10}\right] = \$12,210.20$$

Since we want the future value 1 year later, we need to compound this intermediate amount for 1 year:

$$FV_5 = PV_4(1 + r)^1$$

$$FV = \$12,210.20(1.10)^1 = \$13,431.22$$

Alternatively, we could have combined these two steps into a single step.

$$FV = \$2,000\left[\frac{(1.10)^5 - 1}{0.10}\right](1.10)^1 = \$13,431.22$$

Solving this problem using the BA II PLUS® calculator requires putting the calculator in the BGN mode, inputting the relevant data, and computing FV.

1 2nd CLR TVM
2 2nd BGN 2nd SET 2nd QUIT
3 5 N
4 10 I/YR
5 2,000 +/− PMT
6 CPT FV

---

[4] This derivation is beyond the scope of our discussion, but can be found in many corporate finance texts.

Steps 3 through 6 look like the following on the BA II PLUS® calculator:

(last step)

Again, the answer is $13,431.22.

Concept Check 4.4

1   What steps are involved in solving for the future value of an annuity?
2   When using the future value of an annuity formula (Equation 4.3), at what point in time is the future value computed?

4.5 Present Value of an Annuity

When computing the present value of an annuity, we need to distinguish between two types of annuities: ordinary annuities and annuities due. An **ordinary annuity** is an annuity characterized by amounts that occur at the end of each compounding period. This is the most common type of annuity. For example, a series of $1,000 payments at the end of each year for the next 5 years represent a 5-year ordinary annuity of $1,000. An **annuity due** is a type of annuity where payments or receipts occur at the beginning of each period.

The present value of an ordinary annuity can be computed as:

$$PV = PMT \left[\frac{1 - \dfrac{1}{(1+r)^n}}{r} \right] \tag{4.4}$$

where PMT is the annuity amount, and n is the number of payments or receipts in the annuity.

Example 4.7 Present Value of an Ordinary Annuity

Tastee Foods has five payments of $2,500 remaining on a loan. These payments will occur at the end of each of the next 5 years. At an annual interest rate of 6 percent, what is the present value of these loan payments?

Solution: Given an annuity amount of $2,500 each year for 5 years and an annual interest rate of 6 percent, we need to compute the present value of the loan.
   The time diagram for our loan can be depicted as follows:

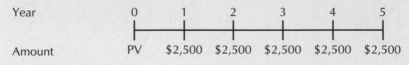

We use the present value of an ordinary annuity formula, Equation 4.4:

$$PV = PMT\left[\frac{1 - \frac{1}{(1+r)^n}}{r}\right]$$

Substituting $PMT = \$2,500$, $r = 0.06$, and $n = 5$, we get:

$$PV = \$2,500\left[\frac{1 - \frac{1}{(1.06)^5}}{0.06}\right] = \$10,530.91$$

If we had not used the present value of an annuity formula, we would have needed to solve for five individual present value amounts and added them together. Imagine the work that would be required to compute the present value of the 360 payments in a 30-year loan with monthly payments.

   We can also solve for the present value of an ordinary annuity using the BA II PLUS® calculator. For the above example, we would enter the following keystrokes:

1   2nd CLR TVM
2   5 N
3   6 I/YR
4   2,500 +/− PMT
5   CPT PV

These steps look like the following on your BA II PLUS® calculator:

5	6	CPT	2,500 +/−	
N	I/Y	PV	PMT	FV
		(last step)		

Again, the present value of this ordinary annuity is $10,530.91.

   Remember two important points when solving for the present value of an ordinary annuity.

• The value for n is the number of payments or receipts in the annuity. This definition for n differs from its definition when solving future value and present value calculations using Equations 4.1 and 4.2. When compounding or discounting with Equations 4.1 or 4.2, n refers to the compounding or discounting interval of time. This point will be clear by reviewing Examples 4.1 and 4.3. Contrast this with Example 4.7 where we used the number of payments in the annuity as our value for n.

- When using the present value of an annuity formula, the present value is obtained *one period before* the annuity begins. This convention follows from the derivation of the present value of an ordinary annuity formula.[5] End-of-year annuity payments and the present value at time 0 are often referred to as an ordinary annuity.

Thus, with an ordinary annuity, we have end-of-year payments with a time diagram as shown below, and the present value is obtained one period before where the annuity starts.

What happens if we need to compute a present value when the payments do not conform to those in the figure above? An adjustment must be made. We illustrate two such adjustments in Examples 4.8 and 4.9.

Example 4.8 Present Value of an Annuity Due

Using the data in Example 4.7, let's compute the present value of the five loan payments assuming *beginning of year* payments, with the first payment occurring today.

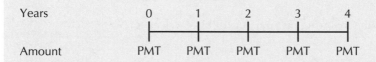

Solution: We can begin by computing the present value of the five payments in the annuity:

$$PV = \$2,500 \left[\frac{1 - \frac{1}{(1.06)^5}}{0.06} \right] = \$10,530.91$$

---

[5] This derivation is beyond the scope of our discussion, but can be found in many corporate finance texts.

Of course, we get the same result as in Example 4.7. But since the first payment in the annuity occurs today, the present value obtained at time period $t = -1$. To calculate the present value at time 0, we need to take the future value of this present amount for 1 year:

$$FV_0 = PV_{-1}(1 + r)^1$$

$$FV = \$10,530.91(1.06)^1 = \$11,162.76$$

If we combine these two steps, the present value of an annuity with beginning of year payments that begin today can be computed:

$$PV = PMT\left[\frac{1 - \dfrac{1}{(1 + r)^n}}{r}\right](1 + r)$$

This annuity scheme with beginning of year payments is called an **annuity due**. In Example 4.9, we illustrate a similar adjustment needed when computing the present value of an annuity when the payments begin in the second period or later.

We can also solve for the present value of an annuity due using the BA II PLUS® calculator. In this situation, each payment occurs at the beginning of the year. Therefore, we must set the calculator to the BGN mode ([2nd] [BGN] [2nd] [SET] [2nd] [QUIT]) before entering the relevant data and computing PV. For the above example, we would enter the following keystrokes:

1   2nd CLR TVM
2   2nd BGN 2nd SET 2nd QUIT (Note: BGN should appear in the upper right corner of the display window)
3   5 N
4   6 I/YR
5   2,500 +/− PMT
6   CPT PV

Steps 3 through 6 look like the following on your BA II PLUS® calculator:

5	6	CPT	2,500 +/−	
N	I/Y	PV	PMT	FV

(last step)

The present value of this annuity due is $11,162.76.

Example 4.9 Present Value of an Annuity Due – Extended

Compute the present value of five payments of $2,500 with the first payment occurring 5 years from today. Assume an annual interest rate of 6 percent.

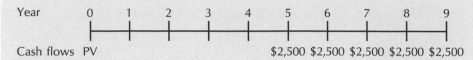

Year   0   1   2   3   4   5   6   7   8   9

Cash flows PV $2,500 $2,500 $2,500 $2,500 $2,500

Solution: When we compute the present value of the five payments, we get a "present value" in year 4 (one period before where the annuity starts). This present value amount is still a future value with respect to time 0. Thus, we must discount this amount for 4 years by taking the present value of this "future amount" for 4 years. If we combine these two steps, we get:

$$PV = PMT \left[\frac{1 - \frac{1}{(1+r)^n}}{r} \right] \left[\frac{1}{(1+r)^n} \right]$$

$$PV = \$2,500 \left[\frac{1 - \frac{1}{(1.06)^5}}{0.06} \right] \left[\frac{1}{(1.06)^4} \right] = \$8,341.47$$

Computes the "PV in year 4" of the five payments in the annuity

Discounts the "PV in year 4" back to year 0

Practical Financial Tip 4.3

After working annuity due problems using the BA II PLUS® calculator, reset the calculator to the end-of-period, END, mode. To switch between the BGN and END modes, press [2nd] [BGN] [2nd] [SET]. If the display indicates the desired mode, which in this case would be END, press [2nd] [QUIT]. If nothing appears in the upper right corner of the display window, the BA II PLUS® calculator is set in the END mode.

Concept Check 4.5

1   What are the steps involved in solving for the present value of an annuity?
2   What is the difference between an *ordinary annuity* and an *annuity due*?

4.6 Present Value of a Perpetuity

A **perpetuity** is an annuity with an infinite life. The present value of a perpetuity is computed by dividing the perpetuity payment by the discount rate:

$$PV_{perpetuity} = \frac{PMT}{r}$$ (4.5)

Example 4.10 Present Value of a Perpetuity

An investment will pay $10 per year in perpetuity. At an annual interest rate of 12 percent, what is the present value of the investment?

Solution: Using Equation 4.5, the present value this perpetuity is:

$$PV = \frac{\$10}{0.12} = \$83.33$$

As we will see in Chapter 5, we can determine the value of noncallable preferred stock, which pays a constant dividend and has no expiration date, by calculating the present value of the perpetuity payments.

We can also use Equation 4.5 to solve for the amount that can be withdrawn in perpetuity from a present value at a given interest rate, fixed indefinitely. For example, suppose someone deposits $10,000 into an account that promises to pay 8 percent per year forever. The individual could withdraw $800 per year in perpetuity (forever) from this account:

$$PMT = r(PV)$$

$$PMT = 0.08(\$10,000) = \$800.00$$

Concept Check 4.6

1 What is a perpetuity?
2 What are the steps involved in solving for the present value of a perpetuity?

4.7 Compounding Frequencies

When we introduced the time value of money formulas in Equations 4.1–4.4, we defined the interest rate as the interest rate *per period* and defined *n* as the *number of periods*. Since all of our examples so far have assumed annual compounding, the interest rate was on a per year basis (compounded annually) and n was the number of years. In many instances, interest is compounded more frequently than once per year. For example, banks often compound interest on a *daily* basis on savings accounts.

Solving a problem where interest is compounded more frequently than once a year involves adjusting the interest rate and number of periods to the appropriate compounding basis. Example 4.11 illustrates these adjustments.

Example 4.11 Future Value with Different Compounding Frequencies

Suppose an investor deposits $1,000 into an account that earns 6 percent per year. What will be the future value 5 years from today if interest is compounded semi-annually quarterly, and monthly?

Solution: With interest compounded semi-annually, we need to determine the *interest rate per semi-annual period* and the *number of semi-annual periods*.

$$r = \frac{6\%}{2} = 3\% \text{ per semi-annual period}$$

$n = 2 \times 5 = 10$ semi-annual periods

Use these values in Equation 4.1.

$$FV = PV(1 + r)^n$$

$$FV = \$1,000(1.03)^{10} = \$1,343.92$$

With annual compounding, our future value would have been $1,338.23. As expected, increasing the compounding frequency to a semi-annual basis increases the future value. With semi-annual compounding, we receive our first interest payment sooner than under annual compounding, and we begin earning interest on interest sooner and more frequently during the term of the investment.

What happens if interest is compounded quarterly? Now we need to determine the *interest rate per quarter (three-month period)* and the *number of quarterly periods*.

$$r = \frac{6\%}{4} = 1.5\% \text{ per quarter}$$

$n = 4 \times 5 = 20$ quarters

The future value is calculated as:

$$FV = \$1,000(1.015)^{20} = \$1,346.86$$

Finally, what happens if interest is compounded monthly? The interest rate would be 0.5 percent per month (6 percent/12) and n would be 60 months (12×5). The future value is calculated:

$FV = \$1,000(1.005)^{60} = \$1,348.85$

The future value increases by compounding more frequently.

The adjustments for compounding frequency can be incorporated directly into the future value of a present amount formula as follows:

$$FV = PV\left[1 + \frac{r}{m}\right]^{mn} \tag{4.6}$$

where r is the interest rate per year; n is the number of years; and m is the number of compounding periods per year.

Equation 4.6 is consistent with Equation 4.1 except that we divide the annual interest rate by the number of periods per year (m), and multiply the number of years by m. These are the same adjustments illustrated in Example 4.11.

Continuous Compounding

Another situation to consider is one where interest is continuously compounded. With continuous compounding, the value for m in Equation 4.6 is infinity (∞). Elementary calculus and the concept of limits (beyond the scope of our analysis) can be used to evaluate Equation 4.6 when m is infinite; the equation becomes:

$$FV = PV e^{rn} \tag{4.7}$$

where r is the stated annual interest rate; n is the number of years in the investment horizon; and e is the base of natural logarithm, approximately equal to 2.71828.

Example 4.12 Future Value with Continuous Compounding

Let's go back to our previous example where an investor deposited $1,000 for 5 years at 6 percent and compute the future value under continuous compounding.

Solution: Using Equation 4.7, the future value using continuous compounding is:

$FV = \$1,000 e^{(0.06)(5)} = \$1,349.86$

Continuous compounding computations on the BA II PLUS® calculator involve using the e^x key. Begin by multiplying 0.06 by 5, press [2nd] [e^x], and then multiply by 1,000.

Note that the future value with continuous compounding is larger than in the annual, semi-annual, quarterly, or monthly compounding cases. Continuous compounding provides the highest future value for a given annual rate of interest because the interest is compounded every infinitesimal part of a second.

Concept Check 4.7

1 What adjustments need to be made to the basic time value of money equations when interest is compounded semi-annually, quarterly, monthly, or daily?
2 What is continuous compounding? What steps are involved in computing the future value of a present amount when interest is continuously compounded?

4.8 Nominal and Effective Interest Rates

Financial institutions typically quote interest rates as **nominal annual interest rates** that ignore compounding effects. For example, a local bank may quote an annual interest rate of 6 percent per year on loans that require monthly payments. With monthly compounding, the bank charges 0.5 percent per month on loans quoted at 6 percent. With compounding of interest, 6 percent a year is not equal to 0.5 percent a month. Thus, the stated 6 percent annual rate does not represent the **effective annual interest rate** the bank is actually charging. The formula for the effective annual interest rate follows:

$$r_{eff} = \left[1 + \frac{r_{nom}}{m} \right]^m - 1 \qquad (4.8)$$

where r_{eff} is the effective annual interest rate; r_{nom} is the nominal interest rate, and m is the number of compounding periods per year. The variable m is the number of times per year interest is compounded (for semi-annual compounding, $m = 2$ and for monthly compounding, $m = 12$).

Example 4.13 Effective Annual Interest Rate

The situation just described calls for monthly compounding assuming a 6 percent nominal interest rate. What is the effective annual rate?

Solution: Using Equation 4.8, the effective annual interest rate would be 6.17 percent.

$$r_{eff} = \left[1 + \frac{0.06}{12}\right]^{12} - 1 = 0.0617 = 6.17\%$$

Practical Financial Tip 4.4

Financial managers and analysts should pay close attention to quoted interest rates to understand important differences that may exist. Bond yields are typically quoted as nominal yields. Since most bonds pay interest semi-annually, the effective annual yield on a bond will exceed the quoted nominal yield. The yields on other investments may be quoted on an annual, semi-annual, quarterly, or monthly basis. When comparing expected yields or returns on investment alternatives, managers need to make sure they are comparing "apples with apples."

Concept Check 4.8

1 How is the effective annual interest rate, given a nominal rate, computed?
2 Will the difference between the effective annual interest rate and the nominal rate increase or decrease as the compounding frequency (*m*) increases? Why?

4.9 Solving for an Unknown Interest Rate

A common time value of money application involves solving for an unknown interest rate that is implied by a given set of cash flows. For example, suppose a financial manager invested $1 million 1 year ago, and today it is worth $1.1 million. Making a quick mental calculation reveals that the manager earned a 10 percent rate of return on the investment: The 10 percent rate is implied from the present value ($1 million) and the future value ($1.1 million) amounts.

Most problems that involve solving for an unknown interest rate require an iterative (trial and error) approach. As a result, financial calculators or computer spreadsheets become the most efficient method for solving for unknown interest rates. We illustrate how to solve for unknown interest rates in Examples 4.14 and 4.15.

Example 4.14 Solving for the Implied Annual Interest Rate

An equipment supplier allows a firm to finance the purchase of $100,000 of equipment with a $15,000 down payment followed by five annual year-end payments of $22,000. What is the implied annual interest rate of the equipment purchase?

Solution: The firm has financed the equipment by borrowing $85,000 and promising to repay the loan with payments of $22,000 at the end of each year for 5 years.

Year	0	1	2	3	4	5
Amount	$85,000	$22,000	$22,000	$22,000	$22,000	$22,000

We need to solve for the discount rate that makes the present value of the $22,000 annuity equal to $85,000:

$$\$85{,}000 = \$22{,}000 \left[\frac{1 - \dfrac{1}{(1+r)^5}}{r} \right]$$

Unfortunately, an algebraic solution for the unknown interest rate, r, involves an iterative procedure. Using the BA II PLUS® calculator, the correct interest rate is 9.26 percent.

1   2nd CLR TVM
2   5 N
3   85,000 PV
4   22,000 +/– PMT
5   CPT I/Y

These steps look like the following using the BA II PLUS® calculator:

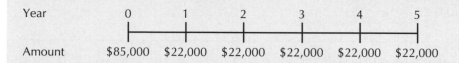

5	CPT	85,000	22,000 +/–	
N	I/Y	PV	PMT	FV
	(last step)			

Example 4.15 Solving for the Implied Interest Rate – Extended

An equipment supplier allows a firm to finance the purchase of $575,000 of equipment with a $150,000 down payment followed by ten annual (year-end) payments of $45,000, which are followed by ten annual (year-end) payments of $52,500. What is the annual interest rate implied by the supplier's financing of the equipment purchase?

Solution: The firm finances the equipment by borrowing $425,000 from the equipment supplier and repaying the loan with payments of $45,000 at the end of each year for 10 years followed by payments of $52,500 at the end of each year for years 11–20.

The time value of money equation that makes $425,000 the present value of the two annuities is written below:

$$\$425{,}000 = \$45{,}000 \left[\frac{1 - \dfrac{1}{(1+r)^{10}}}{r} \right] + \$52{,}500 \left[\frac{1 - \dfrac{1}{(1+r)^{10}}}{r} \right] \left[\frac{1}{(1+r)^{10}} \right]$$

Solving for the unknown interest rate, r, algebraically involves an iterative procedure. Using a financial calculator, we find the implied interest rate on the loan to be 9.19 percent. The steps required on the BA II PLUS® calculator are outlined in Table 4.3 below:

Table 4.3 Calculating an unknown interest rate using the BA II PLUS calculator®

Key strokes	Explanation	Display
[CF] → [2nd] → [CLR WORK]	Clear Memory Registers	$CF_0 =$ 0.00
425,000 → [+/–] → [ENTER]	Initial Cash Outlay	$CF_0 =$ −425,000.00
[↓] → 45,000 → [ENTER]	Period 1 Cash Flow	$C01 =$ 45,000.00
[↓] →10 → [ENTER]	Frequency of Cash Flow 1	$F01 =$ 10.00
[↓] → 52,500 → [ENTER]	Period 2 Cash Flow	$C02 =$ 52,500.00
[↓] →10 → [ENTER]	Frequency of Cash Flow 2	$F02 =$ 10.00
[IRR] → [CPT]	Calculate IRR[a]	$IRR =$ 9.19

[a] IRR refers to the internal rate of return. IRR computations are common in analyzing the capital expenditures (projects) that a firm is considering. An IRR is simply an interest rate that is implied by the cash flows estimated for a project.

Solving for unknown interest rates is among the most common time value of money applications. Examples include solving for the expected yield-to-maturity for a corporate bond, discussed in Chapter 5, and the internal rate of return for a capital investment project, discussed in Chapter 8. Investors often determine the interest rate that equates the present value of expected future amount with the market price of a security to identify the expected return on that investment.

4.10 Other Time Value Applications

Skillful users of time value of money principles can apply the principles and equations developed and discussed in this chapter to solve numerous practical problems. Several of these important applications are illustrated in this section including mortgage amortization, leasing, and solving for the period needed for a given present value to grow to a specified future amount.

Amortization Table

An **amortization table** shows how a loan balance is systematically reduced to zero over its life. For each loan payment, the table reports the loan balance before and after the payment and the principal and interest components of the payment. Borrowers frequently need to know the total interest paid on a loan during given years because interest payments may represent a tax-deductible expense. Principal payments are not tax deductible. Example 4.16 shows how to construct a basic amortization table.

Example 4.16 Amortization Schedule

A firm takes out a 5-year, $20,000 loan with an annual interest rate of 12 percent and monthly payments. What is the amortization schedule for this loan?

Solution: The first step is to compute the monthly loan payment by solving the present value of an annuity formula (Equation 4.4) for the annuity payment.

$$PMT = \frac{PV}{\left[\dfrac{1 - \dfrac{1}{(1+r)^n}}{r}\right]} = \frac{\$20,000}{\left[\dfrac{1 - \dfrac{1}{(1.01)^{60}}}{0.01}\right]} = \$444.89$$

The amortization table is shown in Table 4.4. The initial loan balance is $20,000. The first loan payment of $444.89 is made at the end of the first month. Since a loan balance of $20,000 has been outstanding for 1 month, and the interest rate is 1 percent per month, the interest due at the end of the month is 1 percent of the initial $20,000 loan balance, which is $200.

$$\frac{\text{Interest portion}}{\text{of loan payment}} = r \times \frac{\text{Beginning of month}}{\text{loan balance}} = 0.01 \times \$20,000 = \$200.00$$

Since the total monthly payment of $444.89 consists of both interest and principal, the principal portion of the loan payment can be computed by subtracting the interest portion of the payment from the total payment.

$$\frac{\text{Principal portion}}{\text{of loan payment}} = \text{Loan payment} - \text{Interest} = \$444.89 - \$200.00 = \$244.89$$

Now compute the end-of-month balance by subtracting the principal portion of the payment from the beginning-of-month balance:

$$\frac{\text{End of month}}{\text{loan balance}} = \frac{\text{Beginning of month}}{\text{loan balance}} - \frac{\text{Principal}}{\text{paid}} = \$20,000 - \$244.89 = \$19,755.11$$

Repeat this same process for months 2–60 to complete the amortization table. Table 4.4 contains partial results.

Table 4.4 Amortization table for a $20,000 loan at 12 percent for 60 months

Month	Beginning of month balance ($)	Loan payment ($)	Interest ($)	Principal ($)	End of month balance ($)
1	20,000.00	444.89	200.00	244.89	19,755.11
2	19,755.11	444.89	197.55	247.34	19,507.77
3	19,507.77	444.89	195.08	249.81	19,257.96
58	1,308.41	444.89	13.08	431.81	876.60
59	876.61	444.89	8.77	436.12	440.49
60	440.49	444.88	4.40	440.49	0.00

Several important patterns are illustrated in Table 4.4. First, note that in the first few months, a substantial portion of the monthly payment is interest, about 45 percent. As time elapses, the portion of the payment representing interest declines, with more of the payment going to reduce the principal balance. Toward the end of the life of the loan, nearly all of the monthly payment represents principal repayment.

Leasing

Leasing of assets has become an increasingly popular means for acquiring assets by both corporate and personal users. Basic time value of money principles can be used to determine the periodic lease payment over the term of the lease. We illustrate the calculation of the monthly payment for an auto lease in Example 4.17.

Example 4.17 Leasing

Vitel Incorporated has agreed to lease a fleet of Leopard luxury cars from Sports Motors Inc. (SMI) for its executive management. The Leopard model sells at its MSRP of $49,900. SMI estimates the residual market value of a Leopard to be $28,500 after three years. Assuming a market interest rate of 9 percent per year (compounded monthly) on auto loans and leases, what is the monthly lease payment?

Solution: In a leasing payment structure, the estimated residual payment at the end of the leasing term is essentially a final balloon payment. By returning the car, the lessee is giving an asset worth the estimated residual amount to the lessor. Thus, the time diagram for the lease can be depicted as follows:

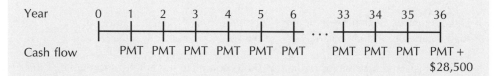

The present value of the lease ($49,900) must be equal to the present value of the lease payments and the present value of the terminal residual lease amount of $28,500 at the monthly discount rate of 0.75 percent a month:

$$49{,}900 = PMT\left[\frac{1 - \dfrac{1}{(1.0075)^{36}}}{0.0075}\right] + 28{,}500\left[\frac{1}{(1.0075)^{36}}\right]$$

The keystrokes on the BA II PLUS® calculator would be:

1 2nd CLR TVM
2 36 N
3 0.75 I/YR
4 49,900 PV
5 28,500 +/– FV
6 CPT PMT

These steps will look as follows on the BA II PLUS® calculator:

36	0.75	49,900	CPT	28,500 +/–
N	I/Y	PV	PMT	FV
			(last step)	

The lease payment should be set at $894.26.

Solving for Unknown Time Periods

Suppose a financial manager wants to know the amount of time needed for an amount of money (present value) to grow to a specified (future value) amount. We illustrate how to solve this type of problem in Example 4.18.

Example 4.18 Solving for an Unknown Time Period

A financial manager wants to know the approximate time needed to double a $1 million investment if the investment earns an annual interest rate of 5 percent.

Solution: Given a future value that is twice the size of the present value and an annual interest rate of 5 percent, what is *n*? Substituting $PV = 1$, $FV = 2$ and $r = 0.05$ into the future value of a present amount formula (Equation 4.1):

$$FV = PV(1 + r)^n$$

$$2 = 1(1.05)^n$$

Using the BA II PLUS® calculator enter:

1   2nd CLR TVM
2   5 I/YR
3   1 PV
4   2 +/– FV
5   CPT N

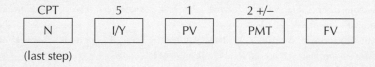

CPT   5   1   2 +/–
[N]   [I/Y]   [PV]   [PMT]   [FV]
(last step)

These keystrokes should give $N = 14.21$ years. Be careful in interpreting this number. Recall that with annual compounding, interest is paid annually. After years 14 and 15, the future value will be about $1.98 million and $2.08 million, respectively. The financial manager will not have $2 million as an intermediate amount any time during year 14 because interest is not paid during the year. Thus, the best answer is 15 years. The financial manager will have more than doubled the investment at that time.

Summary

This chapter discusses major principles and applications of time value of money. The key concepts covered are summarized below.

1 Because cash can be invested to earn a positive rate of interest, most individuals would prefer to have $1 today rather than $1 at some time in the future. Thus, money is said to have time value.
2 The most basic formulas involving time value of money include determining the future value of a present amount or the present value of a future amount.
3 Compounding is the process used to determine the future value of a current amount.
4 Discounting is the process used to determine the present value of some future amount.
5 The interest rate used to compute a present value is called a discount rate. Present values are inversely related to the discount rate.
6 An annuity is a series of payments that occur at evenly spaced intervals over time. With an ordinary annuity, payments occur at the *end* of each period. With an annuity due, payments occur at the *beginning* of each period.
7 A perpetuity is an annuity with an infinite life. Computing the present value of a perpetuity involves dividing the perpetuity payment amount by the discount rate.
8 A nominal interest rate is a quoted annual interest rate. It ignores the compounding effect when interest is compounded more frequently than once per year. An effective annual interest rate is the annual rate that takes into account the compounding frequency in the nominal rate.

FURTHER READING

Brigham, Eugene F. and Michael C. Ehrhardt. *Financial Management: Theory and Practice*, 11th edn, Thomson, 2005.
Keown, Arthur J., John D. Martin, J. William Petty, and David F. Scott, Jr. *Financial Management: Principles and Applications*, 10th edn, Pearson-Prentice Hall, 2005.

SELECTED WEBSITES

http://financenter.com is where calculators may be obtained for solving a variety of problems in finance.
http://invest-faq.com/articles/analy-fut-prs-val.html explains basic time value of money principles.

Chapter 5

Valuation

The problem in valuation is not that there are not enough models to value an asset, it is that there are too many. Choosing the right model to use in valuation is as critical to arriving at a reasonable value as understanding how to use the model. (Aswath Damodaran, *Investment Valuation*, John Wiley & Sons, 1996, p. 501.)

Overview

Major decisions of a company are all interrelated in their effect on the valuation of the firm and its securities. Corporate managers, especially financial managers, need to understand how their decisions affect the value of their firm's common stock and shareholder wealth. They also need to understand how the market values the financial instruments of a company. Finally, to achieve the goal of maximizing shareholder wealth, managers must comprehend what creates it. Thus, valuation is a fundamental issue in finance.

In the previous chapter, we discussed the basic procedures used to value future cash flows. In this chapter, we show how to use time value of money techniques to value a firm's long-term securities – bonds, preferred stock, and common stock. Although the concept of value has several meanings, we focus on determining a security's intrinsic value, which is what the security ought to be worth. We discuss two major approaches to valuation – discounted cash flow valuation and relative valuation. We focus on discounted cash flow models to estimate the value of bonds, preferred stock, and common stock. We also discuss relative valuation, which uses multiples to estimate stock values. Along the way, we discuss some terminology and features associated with bonds, preferred stock, and common stock.

Learning Objectives

After completing this chapter, you should be able to:

- explain the concept of valuation and five different types of value;
- differentiate between discounted cash flow valuation and relative valuation;
- describe the key inputs to the basic model used in the valuation process;
- estimate the intrinsic value of annual-pay, semiannual-pay, and zero coupon bonds;
- understand six fundamentals of bond pricing that relate bond prices to coupon rates, the required return, and the remaining term to maturity;
- explain the importance of interest rate risk for bonds;

- explain and calculate the current yield, yield to maturity, and yield to call of a bond;
- calculate the intrinsic value of preferred stock;
- calculate the intrinsic value of common stock using dividend discount models with different growth rate assumptions;
- discuss when using multiples is appropriate to value a stock;
- describe the major characteristics and features of bonds, preferred stock, and common stock.

5.1 Valuation Fundamentals

Valuation is the process that links risk and return to estimate the worth of an asset or a firm. The term **value** can have different meanings when applied to a financial asset or a firm. Broadly defined, a **financial asset** is a monetary claim on an issuer, typically a paper asset such as a bond, preferred stock, or common stock. These different types of value include:

- *Going-concern value*. **Going-concern value** is the value of a firm as an operating business. This type of value depends on the firm's ability to generate future cash flows rather than on its balance sheet assets. Going-concern value is particularly important when one firm wants to acquire another.
- *Liquidation value*. **Liquidation value** is the amount of money that a firm would realize by selling its assets and paying off its liabilities. A firm's assets are generally worth more as a going concern than they are worth separately. **Liquidation value per share** is the actual amount per share of common stock that stockholders would receive if the firm sells all assets, pays all its liabilities including preferred stock, and divides any remaining money among them.
- *Book value*. **Book value** is the accounting value of a firm or an asset. Book value is an historical value rather than a current value. Firms usually report book value on a per share basis. **Book value per share** of common stock is the shareholders' equity – total assets less liabilities and preferred stock as listed on the balance sheet – divided by the number of shares outstanding. Book value per share may bear little relationship to liquidation value per share or market value per share.
- *Market value*. **Market value** is the price that the owner can receive from selling an asset in the market place. The key determinant of market value is supply and demand for the asset. For stocks and bonds, market values reflect current market prices.
- *Intrinsic value*. **Intrinsic value**, also called **fundamental value**, is a measure of the theoretical value of an asset. Because determining the intrinsic value requires estimates, we may never know the "actual" or "true" intrinsic value of some financial assets. Nonetheless, intrinsic value serves as a basis for determining whether to buy or sell a financial asset when compared to its market value or price.

These various types of value – book value, market value and intrinsic value – can differ for the same financial asset. For example, in a market in which security prices rapidly reflect all information about securities, called an **efficient capital market**, the intrinsic value of a security is equal to its market value. In less than perfectly efficient markets, market value and intrinsic value may differ. Although controversy surrounds the degree of market efficiency, most experts agree that the capital markets are not perfectly efficient. Thus, mispricing may occur for financial assets.

In this chapter, we focus on estimating the intrinsic value of three types of financial assets – bonds, preferred stock, and common stock. We do not examine valuation of the overall firm.[1] Corporate managers, especially financial managers, need to know how to estimate the intrinsic value of financial assets to determine if the market properly prices these assets. Financial managers also need to estimate the price that their firms are likely to receive when issuing bonds or shares of common or preferred stock. In addition, financial managers need to understand how corporate decisions may affect the value of their firm's outstanding securities, especially common stock. For example, financial management decisions determine the risk/return characteristics of the firm. These decisions cause both cash flows and the required rate of return to change, which in turn cause changes in the firm's stock price.

Analysts and investors often compare the current market price of a security to the intrinsic value they estimate from a security valuation formula. If the estimate of intrinsic value exceeds an asset's market value (price), investors would consider buying the asset. Conversely, if the market value (price) exceeds the estimated intrinsic value, investors would not consider buying the asset (or would consider selling if they own it). Because the financial rewards from identifying an undervalued or overvalued security can be great, many analysts and investors devote substantial time and resources to developing innovative security valuation models, especially for common stock.

Valuation Approaches

There are three basic approaches to valuing financial assets – discounted cash flow (DCF) valuation, relative valuation, and contingent claim valuation. DCF valuation and relative valuation are the standard approaches to valuation.

With **discounted cash flow valuation**, the estimated value of a financial asset is the present value of the asset's expected future cash flows. The discount rate should reflect the riskiness of these cash flows. Thus, DCF valuation serves as a way to estimate the intrinsic value of a security.[2] While DCF models are considered to be theoretically correct, they often

---

[1] For a discussion of corporate valuation, see Phillip R. Daves, Michael C. Ehrhardt, and Ronald E. Shrieves, *Corporate Valuation: A Guide for Managers and Investors,* Thomson/South-Western, 2004.

[2] In addition to applying DCF valuation to stocks and bonds, this approach is also applicable to determining the value of the entire firm, which includes the value of common equity plus other claimholders of the firm such as bondholders and preferred stockholders. Using DCF valuation for valuing individual securities and the entire firm involves discounting the expected cash flows. Yet, the relevant cash flows and the appropriate discount rate differ for each. A discussion of firm valuation is outside of our scope.

provide intrinsic value estimates that differ from prevailing market prices. These differences are likely to result from the difficulty in estimating inputs for the models.

With **relative valuation**, the value of a financial asset is computed relative to how the market prices similar assets. For example, relative valuation of common stock uses firm-specific multiples such as price-to-earnings, price-to-cash flows, price-to-book value, and price-to-sales ratios. This valuation method provides information on current valuation, but it does not provide guidance on the appropriateness of the current valuations. That is, the approach measures relative value, not intrinsic value. Relative valuation techniques are appropriate to consider when a good set of comparable entities is available and when serious undervaluation or overvaluation does not prevail in the market.

In some situations, option-pricing models may give more realistic estimates of value than those obtained using DCF valuation or relative valuation models. With **contingent claim valuation**, an asset with the characteristics of an option is valued using an option-pricing model. Some cases in which managers and analysts may view equity in a firm as an option include equity in a deeply troubled firm, natural resource firms, and firms deriving much of their value from product patents. In this chapter, we focus mainly on DCF valuation, but briefly discuss relative valuation.[3]

Practical Financial Tip 5.1

Corporate managers must understand the valuation process to maximize value or shareholder wealth. Financial decisions may influence the firm's risk-return characteristics, which in turn are reflected in the price of its common stock.

Discounted Cash Flow Valuation

The valuation of any financial asset is a function of the:

1 amount of the expected cash flows (returns) generated by the asset over its life;
2 timing of the cash flows;[4] and
3 riskiness associated with these cash flows as measured by the required rate of return.

The value of a financial asset is directly related to the amount of expected cash flows, but inversely related to the amount of risk. In addition, the timing of cash flows affects the value of a financial asset. For example, a dollar in cash flow expected in 5 years is worth less than the same dollar in cash flow expected in 2 years, due to the time value of money. The basic DCF valuation model combines these variables into Equation 5.1, which shows that intrinsic

---

[3] For further discussion of option pricing approaches to equity valuation, see Aswath Damodaran, *Damodaran on Valuation*, John Wiley & Sons, Inc., 1994; and Aswath Damodaran, *Investment Valuation*, John Wiley & Sons, 1996.

[4] Cash flows can occur at any time during a year, but we will assume that they occur at the end of the year unless otherwise noted. This assumption is customary and simplifies the calculations.

value is the sum of an asset's discounted cash flows over the life of the security. With certain modifications and customization, this model serves as the basis for valuing bonds, preferred stock, and common stock.

$$V_0 = \sum_{t=1}^{n} \frac{CF_t}{(1 + k)^t}$$ (5.1)

where V_o is the intrinsic value of an asset at time zero; CF_t is the expected future cash flow at the end of year t; k is the appropriate required rate of return (discount rate); n is the remaining term to maturity; and t is the time period.

One assumption of the basic DCF valuation model is that returns in the form of cash flows consist of a point estimate or single value at a particular time, rather than a probability distribution of values. Another assumption is that the investor's required rate of return (k) reflects the risks associated with these cash flows.

Applying the basic DCF model involves a three-step valuation process:

1 Estimate the future cash flows expected over the life of the asset.
2 Determine the appropriate required rate of return on the asset.
3 Calculate the present value of the estimated cash flows using the required rate of return as the discount rate.

Practical Financial Tip 5.2

The results of DCF valuation are only as accurate as the estimates of the amount and timing of the expected future cash flows and the required rate of return. Because these variables are uncertain in many cases, the intrinsic value is only an estimate of the security's value. Users of DCF valuation should treat the results of these models with caution.

Estimating future cash flows

The nature of the cash flows differs among various financial assets. For bonds, the cash flows represent the coupon interest payments and the recovery of the principal (or par value) at maturity or retirement. For preferred stock, the cash flows are dividends. Because most bonds and preferred stock provide stable cash flows at regular intervals, the cash flows resulting from these investments are relatively easy to forecast. In the case of floating-rate securities, the coupons on bonds and the dividends on preferred stock may vary period by period, depending on conditions in the market. Estimating such cash flows requires forecasting interest rates, which is a topic that extends beyond the scope of this book.

For common stock, the cash flows can be dividends or free cash flow to equity. The more straightforward measure of cash flow is **dividends**, which are cash payments to stockholders. **Free cash flow to equity** (FCFE) is the residual cash flow remaining after meeting interest and principal payments and providing for capital expenditures to maintain existing assets and acquire new assets for future growth. Various techniques are available to forecast these different types of cash flows.

Practical Financial Tip 5.3

Using dividends instead of free cash flow to equity (FCFE) usually provides a more conservative estimate of the value of common stock because most firms pay a lower amount of dividends than they are capable of paying. Using FCFE generally provides a more realistic value of equity because FCFE is the amount that a firm can pay in dividends. In practice, FCFE may be greater or smaller than the dividend. From a practical perspective, estimating FCFE is more difficult when leverage changes over time because FCFE is net of debt issues or payments.

One popular method of deriving these estimates is the **top-down approach**. This approach to the valuation process involves three steps.[5]

1 *Economic analysis.* The analyst begins by making a forecast of the economic environment in which the company will operate. The forecast involves identifying general economic influences such as fiscal policy and monetary policy.
2 *Industry analysis.* Based on this economic forecast, the analyst projects the outlook of each industry in which the company will operate.
3 *Company analysis.* The analyst forecasts the individual company's future prospects and earnings capability. This analysis provides the basis for estimating the expected dividends to stockholders or the FCFE.

Estimating the required rate of return
The required rate of return, also known as the **discount rate**, reflects the riskiness of the estimated cash flows. Riskier cash flows carry a higher discount rate than less risky cash flows. Unlike the cash flows for bonds and preferred stock, which are contractually stated, the cash flows for common stock may exhibit substantial uncertainty. Thus, the required rate of return on a firm's common stock should be higher than on its bonds or preferred stock.

The required rate of return consists of three major components:

- **Real risk-free rate of interest** (RRFR) is a default free rate in which investors know the expected returns with certainty.
- **Expected inflation rate premium** (INF) is an adjustment to the real risk-free rate to compensate investors for expected inflation. The **nominal risk-free rate** (NRFR) is the combination of the real risk-free rate and the expected inflation rate premium.
- **Risk premium** (RP) is the "extra return" that investors demand for the uncertainty associated with the investment. The risk premium reflects the additional return demanded for internal and external risk factors. Internal risk factors are diversifiable and include factors that are unique to a particular firm such as financial risk and liquidity risk. External risk factors, known as market risk factors, are macroeconomic in nature and are nondiversifiable.

---

[5] For a detailed discussion of the top-down valuation process, see Frank K. Reilly and Keith C. Brown, *Investment Analysis and Portfolio Management*, 6th edn, Dryden Press, 2000.

In order to reflect risk, one approach is to combine all internal and external risk factors into a single risk premium. Equations 5.2 and 5.2a show that the required rate of return (k) is a function of the real risk-free rate of interest, an inflation premium, and a risk premium.

$$k = [(1 + RRFR)(1 + INF)(1 + RP)] - 1 \qquad (5.2)$$

Equation 5.2a is the approximation formula for the required rate of return.

$$k_{approximation} \cong RRFR + INF + RP \qquad (5.2a)$$

Note that the NRFR equals $(1 + RRFR)(1 + INF) - 1$ or is approximated by $RRFR + INF$.

Later in the chapter, we show how to apply these components to estimate the required rate of return for a bond, preferred stock, and common stock.

Example 5.1 Estimating the Required Rate of Return

An analyst estimates that the real risk-free rate of return for a financial asset is 4 percent, the inflation premium is 3 percent, and the risk premium is 5 percent. What is the nominal required rate of return for this asset?

Solution: Using Equation 5.2, the nominal required rate of return is:

$$k = [(1.04)(1.03)(1.05)] - 1 = 1.125 - 1 = 0.125 \text{ or } 12.5\%$$

Using Equation 5.2a, the approximation formula for the nominal required rate of return is:

$$k_{approximation} = 0.04 + 0.03 + 0.05 = 0.12 \text{ or } 12.0\%$$

In this example, the approximation formula understates the nominal required rate of return by 0.5 percentage points or 50 basis points. A **basis point** is one hundredth of 1 percent or 0.01 percent. There are 100 basis points in each 1 percentage point.

Concept Check 5.1

1   What is valuation?
2   What are five types of value? How do they differ?
3   Under what circumstances can the market value and intrinsic value of a financial asset differ?
4   Why should a financial manager understand the valuation process?
5   How does discounted cash flow (DCF) valuation differ from relative valuation?

> 6 What is the basic DCF valuation model and its three key inputs?
> 7 What are the three steps in the DCF valuation process?
> 8 How do the cash flows differ between bonds and common stock?
> 9 What are the three major components of the required rate of return?

5.2 Bond Characteristics and Features

A **bond** is a long-term debt security for which the issuer promises to make periodic interest payments and to pay back the borrowed amount (principal) on predetermined dates. Bondholders are creditors to the issuer and have prior claims to the firm's earnings and to its assets in the event of liquidation. Most bonds are **fixed-income securities** because they typically have fixed interest payments. Five major types of issuers raise funds using bonds: the federal government, federal agencies, state and local governments (known as municipalities), corporations, and foreign governments. Each sector has developed its own issue characteristics, features, and trading mechanisms. Although bonds are a major source of financing for these issuers, we focus only on corporate issuers. Bond valuation is similar for each type of bond, but the expected return and riskiness of these bonds differ.

Bonds have several intrinsic characteristics including the par value, coupon rate, and maturity. Beyond this, bonds have various features that distinguish these securities from one another. We discuss some of these characteristics and features next.

Par Value

Par value, also called the **face value** or **maturity value**, is the nominal value stated on the bond. Par value represents the amount of principal per bond that the corporation agrees to repay when the bond matures. For most corporate bonds, the par value is $1,000, but it can be any multiple of $1,000. The typical way of quoting the market value (price) of a bond is as a percent of its par value. For example, a bond with a par value of $1,000 trading at $1,020 trades at 102, which means 102 percent of par.

The par value is not necessarily equal to the bond's market value or price. The price of a bond may rise above or fall below its par value due to differences between its coupon rate and prevailing market interest rates. If interest rates move above (below) the bond's coupon rate, the bond will sell below (above) its par value. A bond that trades below its par value sells at a **discount**; a bond that sells above its par value trades at a **premium**. We explore and illustrate this feature of a bond more carefully in Section 5.4.

Coupon and Coupon Rate

Coupon is the interest rate on a debt security that the issuer promises to pay the holder until maturity. As shown in Equation 5.3, the coupon is equal to the coupon interest rate as a percent rate multiplied by the maturity or par value of the bond.

$$I = c(M) \tag{5.3}$$

where I is the coupon (annual cash interest payment); c is the coupon interest rate per year as a percentage; and M is the maturity or par value of the bond.

The **coupon interest rate**, also called the **nominal yield**, is the contractual rate of interest based on a bond's par value. Calculating the coupon interest rate involves dividing the annual coupon (I) by the maturity or par value of the bond (M).

Example 5.2 Annual Interest Rate on a Bond

Assume that a bond has an 8 percent coupon rate and a par value of $1,000. What is the annual interest payment?

Solution: Substituting $c = 0.08$ and $M = \$1,000$ into Equation 5.3, the annual cash interest payment is:

$$I = 0.08(\$1,000) = \$80$$

Many bonds issued outside of the US pay interest payments on an annual basis. These bonds are **annual-pay bonds**. In contrast, most corporate bonds in the US pay interest semi-annually and are **semiannual-pay bonds**. If the bond in Example 5.2 were a semiannual-pay bond, the interest payments would be $40 every 6 months.

Bonds often differ based on the kinds of coupons they carry. Two common bonds with different coupon rate structures are zero-coupon bonds and floating-rate bonds.

Zero coupon bonds

A **zero coupon bond** or **zero** is a bond that pays all of the cash payments, both interest and principal, at maturity. Because these bonds do not carry coupons, they sell at a substantial discount from their par values and provide capital appreciation rather than interest income. Zeros typically appreciate to their par values at maturity. Thus, the difference between the discounted initial price and the bond's par value represents the implied interest earned by the bondholder.

Floating rate bonds

A **floating rate bond** is a bond that pays a variable rate of interest. Several factors influence the coupon rate including the type, maturity, and quality of the bond. The coupon rates on floating-rate securities are reset periodically, typically every 6 or 12 months, depending on interest rate conditions in the market. The coupon setting process typically starts with a **reference rate**, such as the rate on specific US Treasury securities or the London interbank offered rate (LIBOR). An additional amount, called **quoted margin**, is then added to or subtracted from the reference rate, as shown in Equation 5.4:

$$\text{New coupon rate} = \text{Reference rate} \pm \text{quoted margin} \tag{5.4}$$

Example 5.3 New Coupon Rate

Suppose a corporation issues a floating rate bond that requires resetting the interest rate every 6 months. The reference rate is the 3-month LIBOR and the quoted margin is 125 basis points. If the current 3-month LIBOR is 5 percent, what is the relevant coupon rate for the next interest payment period?

Solution: Inserting the LIBOR = 5 percent and the quoted margin of 1.25 percent into Equation 5.4 gives a new coupon rate of 6.25 percent.

New coupon rate = 5.00% + 1.25% = 6.25%

Because the coupon rate for floating rate bonds may result in extreme fluctuations, issuers often place an upper and lower limit to reduce their potential exposure. The upper limit or **cap** is the maximum interest that the borrower pays, while the lower limit or **floor** is the minimum interest that the lender receives. When a floating rate bond has both limits simultaneously, this feature is called a **collar**.

Maturity

Term to maturity or simply **maturity** of a bond is the length of time until the agreement expires. At maturity, the bondholder receives the last coupon interest payment and the bond's par value payment from the issuer. On most bond issues, the maturity of all bonds occurs on the same date. With **serial bonds**, the maturity dates are staggered over time to avoid one very large repayment on a single date from the issuer.

Various provisions in the bond contract, called **embedded options**, may affect paying all or part of the principal before maturity. Common embedded options include call provisions, sinking fund provisions, conversion rights, and put provisions. The first two embedded options favor the issuer, while the latter two favor the bondholders.

Call provisions

A **call provision** gives the issuer the right to buy back or "call" all or a part of a bond issue before maturity (under specified terms). Most corporate bonds are callable. With a call feature, the issuer may decide to retire bonds to take advantage of lower interest rates, to get rid of restrictive indenture provisions, or to reduce indebtedness. Because a call provision is beneficial to the issuer, the issuer usually has to offer investors some enticements to sell such a bond. These enticements include a higher-than-normal coupon rate, a provision not to call the bond until after a specified period (called a **deferred call provision**), and a call premium. A **call premium** is an additional amount that the issuer agrees to pay above the bond's par value to repurchase the bond. The price at which the issuer may call a bond (par plus any call premium) is termed the **call price**.

Sinking fund provisions

A **sinking fund provision** permits the issuer to retire a bond through a series of predefined principal payments over the life of the issue. Sinking fund requirements often do not apply during the early years of a bond issue. Some bonds carry an **accelerated sinking fund provision**, which allows the issuer to retire a larger proportion of the issue at par, at its discretion. The issuer can satisfy the sinking fund requirement in one of two ways – cash or delivery. The company can either deposit sufficient cash with the trustee, who redeems the bonds generally by a lottery, or buy the required number of bonds in the open market and deliver them to the trustee. In some instances, the trustee buys the bonds in the market. The company uses the least expensive method. For example, if current interest rates are above the bond's coupon rate, the current market price of the bond will be less than its par value. That is, the bond will sell at a discount. Thus, the firm should buy the bonds on the open market to meet its sinking fund requirement.

Conversion rights
Conversion rights give the bondholder the right to convert the bond into a specified number of shares of common stock at a predetermined fixed price. Such bonds, called **convertible bonds**, typically have a lower coupon rate than non-convertible debt because they offer the bondholder a chance for capital gains in exchange for lower coupon payments. This option benefits the bondholder if the equivalent value of the common shares from conversion is greater than the value of the bond. Almost all convertible bonds are callable.

Put provisions
Some bonds have a **put provision**, which gives the bondholder the right to sell the bond back to the issuer at the put price on certain dates before maturity. The **put price** is a price at or near par. If interest rates increase, causing the bond price to fall below par, the bondholder may sell the bond back to the issuer at a higher price.

Other Features of Bonds

Other important features of bonds include the indenture, trustee, collateral, and bond rating.

Indenture
An **indenture** is a legal document between the issuer and the bondholders detailing the terms and conditions of the debt issue. The purpose of this agreement is to address all matters pertaining to the bond. In the United States, the company must register the indenture of publicly issued bonds with the Securities and Exchange Commission (SEC) under the provisions of the Trust Indenture Act of 1939.

An indenture generally contains **protective covenants**, which limit certain actions that the company might be taking during the term of the agreement. Two types of protective covenants are negative covenants and positive covenants. **Negative covenants** limit or prohibit the borrower from taking certain actions such as paying too much dividends, pledging assets to other lenders, selling major assets, merging with another firm, and adding more long-term debt. **Positive** or **affirmative covenants** are actions that the borrower promises to perform such as maintaining certain ratios, keeping collateral in good condition, and making timely payments of interest and principal. Failing to adhere to these covenants could place the bond issuer in default.

Trustee

The issuer must appoint a trustee for each bond issue of substantial size. A **trustee** is the bondholders' agent, typically a bank, in a public debt offering. The issuer appoints the trustee before selling the bonds to represent the bondholders in all matters concerning the bond issue. This is necessary because some bond issues have many bondholders. The trustee monitors the issuer to ensure that it complies with all terms of the indenture. If the borrower violates the terms, the trustee initiates action against the issuer and represents the bondholders in this action.

Collateral

Corporations can issue bonds as secured or unsecured debt. **Secured debt** is a debt backed by the pledge of assets as collateral. These assets are typically in the form of real property such as land and buildings (**mortgage bonds**) or financial assets such as stocks and bonds (**collateral trust bonds**). **Unsecured debt**, also called a **debenture**, represents bonds raised without any collateral. In the case of unsecured debt, the bondholders have a claim on the assets that the issuer has not pledged to other securities. With a **subordinated debenture**, the claims against a firm's assets are junior to those of secured debt and regular debentures.

Bond rating

A **bond rating** is an assessment of the creditworthiness of the issuer. Major rating services include Standard & Poor's Corporation (S&P), Moody's Investors Service, Inc. (Moody's), and Fitch. The purpose of bond ratings is to help investors assess **default risk**, which is the possibility that the issuer will fail to meet its obligations as specified in the indenture. Bond ratings range from AAA (S&P) or Aaa (Moody's), the highest or prime grade, to D, debt in default. **Investment-grade** securities have a rating of at least BBB by S&P or Baa by Moody's, while the remaining represent **noninvestment grade** securities, commonly referred to as **junk bonds**. An inverse relationship generally exists between the rating and quality of a bond and its interest rate or yield to maturity. That is, high-quality (high-rated) bonds have lower yields than low-quality (low-rated) bonds.

Concept Check 5.2

1　Why may the market price of a bond not equal its par value?
2　How do zero coupon bonds differ from floating rate bonds?
3　What types of embedded options favor the issuer and which ones favor bond-holders? Why?
4　What is the purpose of an indenture?
5　What are protective covenants? What are examples of negative covenants and positive covenants?
6　What is the priority of claims on the assets of the issuer for secured debt, debentures, and subordinated debentures?
7　What does a bond rating say about the potential default risk of a bond?

5.3 Bond Valuation

The value of a bond is the sum of its discounted cash flows. Bondholders receive two distinct types of cash flows: (1) the periodic coupon interest payments (1) and (2) the maturity value (M) (also called the principal, par value or face value) at the end of the bond's life. Estimating the cash flow stream of a high quality, option-free bond is simple because a high degree of certainty exists about the amount and timing of the coupon and principal payments. An **option-free** or **straight bond** is a bond without embedded options, such as a call feature and sinking fund provision. If a bond is callable, putable, or convertible, then estimating cash flows can be extremely difficult because of the uncertainty associated with the amount and/or timing of the coupon and principal payments. Figure 5.1 shows the typical cash flow structure for an option-free, finite maturity, non-zero coupon bond.

Figure 5.1 Cash flow structure of a bond

The appropriate discount rate used in this present value computation is the required rate of return (k_b) for the bond. Bond investors require a return that compensates them primarily for inflation and risk. Higher risk bonds will have higher required returns. The appropriate discount rate is a function of the nominal risk-free rate and a risk premium. A proxy for the nominal risk-free rate is the yield of Treasury securities of comparable maturities. The risk premium reflects any incremental costs to the investor in corporate bonds such as default risk and call risk. **Default risk** is the possibility that the issuer will fail to meet its obligations as specified in the indenture. **Call risk** is the possibility that the issuer will call a bond and expose the investor to an uncertain cash flow pattern. If properly priced, the bond's **yield to maturity** (YTM) should reflect these risks. The yield to maturity is the rate required in the market on a bond. We discuss this yield measure in Section 5.6.

The traditional approach to bond valuation is to discount all cash flows by the same discount rate. While the coupon interest rate is typically fixed over a bond's life, the return required by investors varies as the general level and term structure of interest rates varies and as the risk of the bond varies due to the issuing firm's financial condition. One way to overcome this flaw of the traditional approach is to use different discount rates for each cash flow. We do not examine valuation using multiple discount rates in this chapter.[6]

---

[6] For a discussion of bond valuation using Treasury spot rates, see Frank J. Fabozzi, *Fixed Income Analysis for the Chartered Financial Analyst® Program*, Frank J. Fabozzi Associates, 2000.

Valuing Annual-pay Bonds

Using the DCF approach, the intrinsic value of a bond is the sum of the present values of the annuity (future coupon or interest payments) and the future value of the principal at maturity (par value of $1,000).

$$\text{Bond value} = \left(\text{Coupon payment}\right)\left(\begin{array}{c}\text{Present value} \\ \text{of annuity formula}\end{array}\right) + \left(\begin{array}{c}\text{Maturity} \\ \text{value}\end{array}\right)\left(\begin{array}{c}\text{Present value of} \\ \text{future amount formula}\end{array}\right)$$

Using the same formulas developed in Chapter 4 for the present value of an annuity and the present value of a single amount, we can restate the above expression as:

$$V_b = I\left[\frac{1 - \frac{1}{(1 + k_b)^n}}{k_b}\right] + M\left[\frac{1}{(1 + k_b)^n}\right] \tag{5.5}$$

Equation 5.6 is another valuation formula for an annual-pay bond.

$$V_b = \sum_{t=1}^{n} \frac{I_t}{(1 + k_b)^t} + \frac{M}{(1 + k_b)^n} \tag{5.6}$$

where V_b is the intrinsic value of a bond at time zero; I is the expected annual interest payment in year t; M is the maturity or par value of the bond in period n; k_b is the investor's required rate of return on the bond; n is the length of the holding period; and t is the time period.

Example 5.4 Valuing an Annual-pay Bond

Potomac Corporation issued an annual-pay bond with a 10 percent coupon rate and a $1,000 par value 25 years ago. The bond now has 10 years remaining until maturity. Due to changing interest rates and market conditions, the required rate of return on this bond is 8 percent. That is, the discount rate on the bond is 8 percent. What is the intrinsic value of the annual-pay bond?

Solution: Using Equation 5.3, the bond will pay $100 of interest each year.

$I = 0.10(\$1,000) = \$100$

The cash flow structure of this annual pay bond is shown in Figure 5.2.
  Substituting the values $I = \$100$, $M = \$1,000$, $k_d = 8$ percent, and $n = 10$ into Equation 5.5 yields an intrinsic value of $1,134.20.

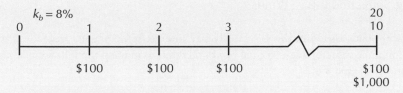

Figure 5.2 Cash flow structure of an annual-pay bond

$$V_b = \$100\left[\frac{1 - \dfrac{1}{(1.08)^{10}}}{0.08}\right] + \$1,000\left[\frac{1}{(1.08)^{10}}\right] = \$100(6.7101) + \$1,000(0.4632)$$

$$= \$1,134.20$$

Using Equation 5.6, the answer is also $1,134.20.

$$V_b = \sum_{t=1}^{10} \frac{\$100}{(1.08)^t} + \frac{\$1,000}{(1.08)^{10}} = \$1,134.20$$

Instead of using Equation 5.5 or 5.6 to get a numerical solution, another approach is to use the Texas Instruments BA II PLUS® financial calculator and to key in the following:

Inputs: 10 N; 8 I/YR; 100 +/– PMT; 1,000 +/– FV; CPT PV   *Output*: 1,134.20

Remember to clear the memory by pressing [2ⁿᵈ][CLR TVM] before doing time value of money calculations. On the BA II PLUS® financial calculator, these steps look as shown below:

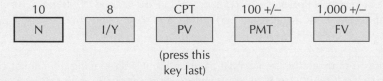

The bond's intrinsic value of $1,134.20 represents the maximum amount investors would be willing to pay for the bond. If they pay exactly that amount for the bond, investors would expect to earn the required return of 8 percent. If the intrinsic value and market value (price) were the same, the bond would be quoted at 113.42, which means that the bond is priced at 113.42 percent of its $1,000 par value, or $1,134.20. The bond would sell at a premium of $134.20 above its par value because the market's required rate of return of 8 percent is lower than its coupon rate of 10 percent.

Investors can compare this intrinsic value of the bond to its market price to determine whether to buy the bond. If the price were less than $1,134.20, investors should consider buying the bond because it is underpriced. That is, the bond's intrinsic value exceeds its market price. If the price were greater than $1,134.20, they should not buy the bond, because it is overpriced. That is, its intrinsic value is less than the purchase price.

Valuing Semiannual-pay Bonds

In practice, bonds issued in the US usually pay interest semiannually instead of annually. Determining the value of a semiannual-pay bond requires making the following adjustments to Equations 5.5 and 5.6.

1   Divide the annual interest, I, by 2 to get the semiannual interest.
2   Divide the annual discount rate, k_b, by 2 to get the semiannual discount rate.
3   Multiply the number of years until maturity, n, by 2 to get the number of 6-month periods to maturity.

Substitution of the three changes into Equations 5.5 and 5.6 yields Equations 5.7 and 5.8, respectively.

$$V_b = I/2 \left[\frac{1 - \frac{1}{(1 + k_b/2)^{2n}}}{k_b/2} \right] + M \left[\frac{1}{(1 + k_b/2)^{2n}} \right] \tag{5.7}$$

$$V_b = \sum_{t=1}^{2n} \frac{I/2}{(1 + k_b/2)^t} + \frac{M}{(1 + k_b/2)^{2n}} \tag{5.8}$$

Example 5.5 Valuing a Semiannual-pay Bond

Now assume that Potomac Corporation has a 10-year, $1,000 par, 10 percent semiannual-pay bond. If investors require an 8 percent return on this bond, what is its value?

Solution: To evaluate this semiannual-pay bond requires reducing the annual coupon payment in half ($100/2 = $50), reducing the discount rate by half (8/2 = 4 percent), and doubling the number of periods (2 × 10 = 20). The cash flow structure of the semiannual-pay bond is shown in Figure 5.3.

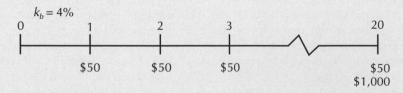

Figure 5.3 Cash flow structure of the semiannual-pay bond

Substituting $l/2 = \$50$, $M = \$1,000$, $k_b/2 = 0.04$, and $2n = 20$ into Equations 5.7 and 5.8 results in an intrinsic value of $\$1,135.90$.

$$V_b = \$100/2 \left[\frac{1 - \dfrac{1}{(1 + 0.08/2)^{2(10)}}}{0.08/2} \right] + \$1,000 \left[\frac{1}{(1 + 0.08/2)^{2(10)}} \right]$$

$$= \$50(13.5903) + \$1,000(0.4564) = \$1,135.90$$

$$V_b = \sum_{t=1}^{2(10)} \frac{\$100/2}{(1 + 0.08/2)^t} + \frac{\$1,000}{(1 + 0.08/2)^{2(10)}} = \$1,135.90$$

We can also solve for the bond price on the BA II PLUS® financial calculator as follows:

Inputs: 20 N; 4 I/YR; 50 +/− PMT; 1,000 +/− FV; CPT PV   *Output*: 1,135.90

On the BA II PLUS® financial calculator, these steps look as follows:

20	4	CPT	50 +/−	1,000 +/−
N	I/Y	PV	PMT	FV
		(press this key last)		

The market value of the semiannual-pay bond is $\$1,135.90$. Thus, the bond sells at a premium above its maturity or par value.

The market value of the semiannual-pay bond ($\$1,135.90$) is greater than that of the annual pay bond ($\$1,134.20$). This relationship, however, does not always hold. When the required rate of return is less than the coupon rate, the intrinsic value of a semi-annual pay bond would exceed that of an annual-pay bond with the same character-istics. This is the case for our example using Potomac Corporation. The opposite result would occur when the required rate of return is greater than the coupon rate. That is, the intrinsic value of a semiannual-pay bond would be smaller than that of an equivalent annual-pay bond.

Practical Financial Tip 5.4

If a bond sells at a discount (premium), its value is less (more) for a semiannual-pay bond than an annual-pay bond.

Valuing Zero Coupon Bonds

Finding the intrinsic value of a zero coupon bond is similar to that of a coupon bond, but ignores the coupon or interest component of the equation. The value of a zero coupon bond is usually computed assuming semiannual compounding, which facilitates comparisons with other semiannual coupon-paying bonds.

$$V_b = \frac{M}{(1 + k_b/2)^{2n}} \tag{5.9}$$

Example 5.6 Valuing a Zero Coupon Bond

Suppose Potomac Corporation has a 15-year zero coupon bond with a maturity value of $1,000. If investors require a 9 percent rate of return, what is the value of this zero coupon bond?

Solution: Assuming semiannual compounding, the cash flow of this zero coupon bond would be as shown in Figure 5.4.

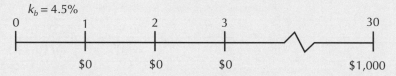

Figure 5.4 Cash flow structure of a zero coupon bond

Substituting $M = \$1,000$, $I/2 = 4.5$ percent, and $2n = 30$ into Equation 5.9 results in an intrinsic value of $267.00.

$$V_b = \frac{\$1,000}{(1 + 0.09/2)^{2(15)}} = \$267.00$$

Keying the following values into the BA II PLUS® calculator results in:

Inputs: 30 N; 4.5 I/YR; 1,000 +/– FV; CPT PV   *Output*: 267.00

These steps look like the following using the BA II PLUS® calculator:

30	4.5	CPT		1,000 +/–
N	I/Y	PV	PMT	FV

(press this
key last)

The difference of $733 between the bond's intrinsic value of $267 and its $1,000 par value represents the amount of interest that the bond would earn over its 15-year life, assuming that the bond sells for its intrinsic value.

Concept Check 5.3

1 What are the two distinct types of cash flows associated with a straight bond?
2 What is the meaning of *default risk* and *call risk*?
3 What are the three adjustments needed to convert the formula for an annual-pay bond into a semiannual-pay bond?
4 Why does a zero coupon bond typically sell at a discount to its par value?

5.4 Bond Pricing Relationships

From Equation 5.6, we know that changes in the interest rate (discount rate or yield), coupon rate, and the remaining term to maturity affect bond prices. These forces in the economy and the passage of time affect value. Thus, the value of a bond in the marketplace rarely remains constant over its life. In this section, we discuss six properties of bond prices.

The Price-yield Relationship

Perhaps the most important bond pricing property involves the **price-yield relationship**, which is the relationship between bond prices and the required rate of return (market yield).

Bond Pricing Property #1 *The price of a bond varies inversely with the bond's required rate of return (market yield).*

Thus, as the required rate of return increases (decreases), the price of the bond will decrease (increase) for debt securities that do not contain embedded options. As Figure 5.5 shows, price and yield move in opposite directions.

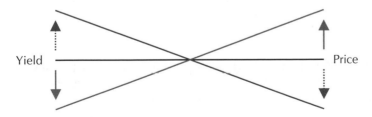

Figure 5.5 Price-yield relationship

This inverse relationship should not be surprising because a bond's value is the present value of the bond's future cash flows, and present values have an inverse relationship with interest rates. What becomes important to bond investors is the sensitivity of a bond's price to changes in interest rates, commonly referred to as interest rate risk or price volatility of a bond. We take a closer look at interest rate risk later in this section. Example 5.7 illustrates the price changes for a bond as the required rate of return (market yield) changes.

Example 5.7 Changes in Required Returns (Yields)

Returning to Example 5.5, Potomac Corporation has a 10-year, $1,000 par, 10 percent semiannual-pay bond. What is the value of the bond to an investor with a required rate of return of 8 percent, 10 percent, and 12 percent?

Solution: Use the BA II PLUS® calculator to determine the value of this bond. This semiannual-pay bond requires doubling the number of periods ($n = 2 \times 10 = 20$), reducing the coupon by half ($PMT = 100/2 = 50$), and reducing the required rate of return by half ($I/Y = 8/2 = 4$) and keying in:

Required rate of return (%)	Inputs	Output
8	20 N; 4 I/YR; 50 +/– PMT; FV +/– 1,000; CPT PV	1,135.90
10	20 N; 5 I/YR; 50 +/– PMT; FV +/– 1,000; CPT PV	1,000.00
12	20 N; 6 I/YR; 50 +/– PMT; FV +/– 1,000; CPT PV	885.30

The results show several important bond pricing properties. One property is that if the required rate of return equals the stated coupon rate, the bond price, P_o, will equal the maturity or par value, M. This relationship holds regardless of the remaining term to maturity. Using the financial calculator, we can easily verify this relationship by entering different values for N and checking the price with the PV key. In our example, when both the required rate of return and the coupon rate are 10 percent, the price of the bond is $1,000.

Bond Pricing Property #2 *If the required rate of return is equal to the coupon rate, the price of a bond will be equal to its par value.*

The logic behind this bond pricing fundamental is simple. Compare the purchase of the $1,000 bond to a $1,000 deposit at a bank. Assume the bank pays an annual interest rate of 10 percent, compounded semi-annually. You can withdraw the $50 in interest that you earn every six months and still maintain your $1,000 principal amount. You could do this for 20 years (withdrawing the $50 interest twice per year), and then withdraw your original

$1,000 at the end of the 20th year. The time diagram for this would be identical to the time diagram for our bond in Example 5.5. Thus, the amount an investor would pay for a bond with the same future payments would logically be the same as the $1,000 "deposit."

Another bond pricing property is that if the required rate of return increases, the bond price decreases. This relationship holds regardless of the remaining term to maturity. At any time during the bond's life, if the required return exceeds the bond's coupon rate, the bond will sell at a discount, which equals $M - P_0$. In our example, the required rate of return of 12 percent is greater than the coupon rate of 10 percent. As a result, the bond sells for $885.30, which is a $114.70 discount below the par value of $1,000. Investors are unwilling to pay par value because the bond pays less coupon interest than newly issued bonds with similar characteristics.

Bond Pricing Property #3	*If the required return is greater than the coupon rate, the price of a bond will be less than par value. The bond sells at a discount.*

Still another bond pricing property is if the required rate of return decreases, then the bond price will increase. Such a bond sells at a premium, which equals $P_o - M$. In this example, if the required rate of return decreases from 10 percent to 8 percent, the bond price will increase. Since the required rate of return is less than the coupon rate, the bond will sell at $1,135.90, which is a $135.90 premium above the par value of $1,000. Investors are willing to pay more than par value for this bond because of its higher coupon interest payments.

Bond Pricing Property #4	*When the required return is less than the coupon rate, the price of a bond will be greater than par value. The bond sells at a premium.*

Price-yield Curve

A **price-yield curve** is a plot of a bond's required rate of return (market yield) to its corresponding price. As Figure 5.6 illustrates, the price-yield curve is not a straight-line, but instead is convex. This price-yield curve for option-free bonds has an important property: *as bond yields rise, their prices will fall but at a decreasing rate; as bond yields fall, their prices will rise, but at an increasing rate.* This property, known as **positive convexity**, means that *bond prices go up faster than they go down.*

Bond Pricing Property #5	*As yields change for option-free bonds, bond prices go up faster than they go down.*

To illustrate this property, review the results from Example 5.7. A 2 percentage point increase in yield (from 10 percent to 12 percent) led to a $114.70 decrease in price (from

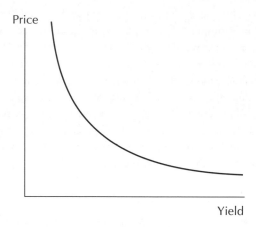

Figure 5.6 Price-yield curve

$1,000.00 to $885.30); while a 2 percentage point decrease in yield (from 10 percent to 8 percent) led to a $135.90 increase in price (from $1,000.00 to $1,135.90). These results show that bond prices increase faster than they go down with the same change in yield.

Practical Financial Tip 5.5

The extent to which bond prices move depends both on the *direction* of change in market interest rates and *the magnitude* of such change: the greater the moves in interest rates, the greater the swings in bond prices.

Maturity and Price Convergence

The final bond pricing property that we discuss relates the price of a bond to its remaining term to maturity. Regardless of its required yield, the price of a bond will converge toward par value as maturity approaches.

Bond Pricing Property #6   *As the maturity date of a bond approaches, the price of the bond will approach par value.*

Figure 5.7 shows that, holding the bond's required rate of return constant, the price of a bond selling at a premium will decline gradually over its remaining term to maturity. Similarly, the price of bond selling at a discount will gradually increase. If the required rate of return of a bond does not remain constant, the prices will still converge to par value, but not as gradually as depicted in Figure 5.7.

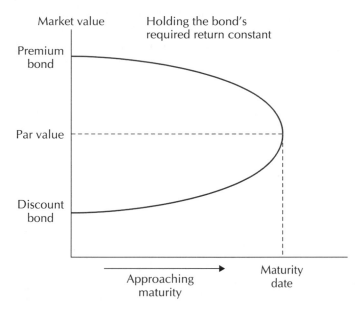

Market value

Holding the bond's
required return constant

Premium
bond

Par value

Discount
bond

Approaching
maturity

Maturity
date

Figure 5.7 Time path of a bond

Example 5.8 Maturity and Price Convergence

Returning to Example 5.7, what happens to the bond price of Potomac Corporation's
10-year, $1,000 par, 10 percent semiannual-pay bond as it approaches maturity if an
investor requires an 8 percent, 10 percent, and 12 percent yield?

Solution: Table 5.1 shows how the prices for the premium and discount bonds converge to the maturity value of $1,000 over time.

Table 5.1 Price convergence of bonds at different maturities

Time to maturity (years)	Required rate of return (yield)		
	8%	**10%**	**12%**
10	$1,135.90	$1,000.00	$ 885.30
5	1,081.11	1,000.00	926.40
4	1,067.33	1,000.00	937.90
3	1,052.42	1,000.00	950.83
2	1,036.30	1,000.00	965.35
1	1,018.86	1,000.00	981.67
0	1,000.00	1,000.00	1,000.00

Based on the expected price appreciation for discount bonds shown in Figure 5.7 and Table 5.1, can we logically conclude that investors will prefer discount bonds to premium bonds? Ignoring differences in the taxation of long-term capital gains and ordinary income, investors would not have a preference. Recall that a bond sells at a discount from par value when the coupon rate is less than the bond's required rate of return (bond pricing property #3). Thus, discount bonds pay interest income that is less than what is required for the bond to sell at par value. In order for an investor to earn the required rate of return on a discount bond, the expected price appreciation must augment the income yield (the return earned from the interest payments) so that the investor can expect to earn the required rate of return.

The opposite occurs for a premium bond. These bonds pay more interest income than investors require. As a result, such bonds sell at a premium to par value. The decrease in price over the bond's life will reduce the higher income yield offered on premium bonds such that an investor can expect to earn the required rate of return. The upshot of this argument is that both discount and premium bonds will offer investors an expected rate of return equal to the required rate of return.

Concept Check 5.4

1   Should bond prices rise or fall as the general level of interest rates in the economy rise?
2   If a bond has a coupon rate that exceeds its required rate of return, should the bond sell at a discount or a premium? Why?
3   What does the term *positive convexity* mean?
4   What happens to the price of a discount and a premium bond as it approaches maturity?

5.5 Interest Rate Risk

Investors face numerous risks associated with investing in bonds. Perhaps the most important risk is **interest rate risk**, which is the sensitivity of bond prices to changes in interest rates. The price of a fixed-coupon bond changes in the opposite direction of the change in interest rates. In particular, bond prices fall when interest rates rise. As we show below, the degree of the price change is not always the same.

For fixed-rate bonds without embedded options, two key features of a bond affect its interest rate risk: the remaining term to maturity and the coupon rate of the bond.[7] All other things being equal, *the longer the remaining time to maturity and the lower the coupon rate, the greater is the interest rate risk of the bond.* Thus, longer-term bonds with low coupon rates have greater price sensitivity (interest rate risk) to changes in the bond's required rate of return than do short-term, high coupon bonds. Examples 5.9 and 5.10 illustrate these two features of a bond.

---

[7]   Embedded options such as a call feature also affect the price volatility of a bond. When yields rise, the value of a callable bond may not fall as much as that of a similar straight bond because of the embedded call option feature. When yields fall and approach the coupon rate, callable bonds approach a ceiling value, which is the call price of the bond.

Practical Financial Tip 5.6

Bond price volatility depends on more than market yields. For bonds without embedded options, the speed or rate of change in bond prices is a function of a bond's remaining term to maturity and coupon rate. All else equal, bonds with longer maturities and lower coupons have more price volatility than bonds with shorter maturities and higher coupons.

Example 5.9 Maturity and Interest Rate Risk

To illustrate how the remaining term to maturity affects a bond's interest rate risk, consider two bonds, Bond S(hort) and Bond L(ong). Both have 8 percent coupon rates, pay interest semiannually, and have initial required returns of 8 percent. The bonds are identical except Bond S has 1 year and Bond L has 20 years remaining until maturity. With initial required returns equal to their coupon rates, both bonds will sell for par value (bond pricing property #2). Now assume that interest rates in the economy rise immediately (no time elapses) and the required returns on both bonds increase to 10 percent. What are the new prices of the bonds?

Solution: Instead of using Equations 5.7 or 5.8 to answer this question, let's use the BA II PLUS® financial calculator as follows:

Bond	Inputs	Output
S	2 N; 5 I/YR; 40 +/– PMT; FV +/– 1,000; CPT PV	981.41
L	40 N; 5 I/YR; 40 +/– PMT; FV +/– 1,000; CPT PV	828.41

The price of the long-term bond, Bond L, will decline to $828.41 while the price of Bond S will decline only to $981.41. On the other hand, if the required returns were to immediately decline to 6 percent, the prices of Bonds S and L would increase to $1,019.13 and $1,231.15, respectively. Table 5.2 summarizes these results.

Table 5.2 Price changes for 8% bonds with different terms to maturity

Bond	Term to maturity (years)	Required rate of return (yield)		
		6%	8%	10%
S	1	$1,019.13	$1,000.00	$981.41
L	20	1,231.15	1,000.00	828.41

The price of the long-term bond (Bond L) experiences greater changes in price than the short-term bond (Bond S) as the required rate of return varies from 6 percent to 10 percent.

Example 5.10 Coupon Rate and Interest Rate Risk

To illustrate how the coupon rate affects a bond's interest rate risk, consider two semiannual-pay bonds. Bond LC (low coupon) has a 6 percent coupon and Bond HC (high coupon) has a 10 percent coupon. Both bonds have 15 years to maturity and are currently selling to yield 8 percent. Table 5.3 summarizes the price changes for these two bonds.

Table 5.3 Price changes for 6% and 10% coupon bonds with 25 years to maturity currently priced to sell at 8%

| Bond | Coupon rate (%) | Required rates of return (yield) | | |
		6%	8%	10%
LC	6	$1,000.00	$785.18	$634.88
HC	10	$1,514.60	$1,214.82	$1,000.00

As Table 5.3 shows, if investors required an 8 percent yield, the price of the LC bond would be $785.18 and the price of the HC bond would be $1,214.82. Consider the following interest rate changes:

- If the yield required by investors increases by 2 percentage point to 10 percent, the price of the LC bond would fall to $634.88 and the price of the HC bond would fall to $1,000.00. These would represent percentage decreases of 19.1 percent for the LC bond and 17.7 percent for the HC bond.
- If required yields fall by 2 percentage points to 6 percent, the price of the LC bond would increase by 27.4 percent compared with a 24.7 percent increase for the HC bond.

Thus, the lower coupon bond exhibits greater price sensitivity to changes in interest rates than the higher coupon bond.

Bond investors pay close attention to the interest rate risk of their bond portfolios. When these investors expect increases in interest rates, they can reduce the interest rate risk of their portfolios by selling low-coupon, long-term bonds and buying higher-coupon bonds with shorter terms to maturity.

Concept Check 5.5

1 What does interest rate risk mean?
2 What relationship exists between changes in interest rates and bond prices?
3 How do the *term to maturity* and *coupon rate* affect the interest rate risk of a bond?
4 Two 30-year bonds are alike in all respects except Bond A's coupon rate is 6 percent and Bond B's coupon rate is 12 percent. Which of the two bonds will have the greater relative market price increase if interest rates decrease sharply? Why?

5.6 Bond Yields

As previously discussed, bond investors can make an investment decision by comparing the estimated intrinsic value of a bond to its market price. Such investors, however, generally make investment decisions based more on a bond's yield than its price. Yield affects a bond's price and serves as a measure of its expected return. Using yield as a measure of return simply involves reversing the bond valuation process and solving for yield rather than price.

In this section, we examine several traditional yield measures for fixed-rate bonds as well as their key assumptions and limitations. Specifically, we discuss the current yield, yield to maturity, and yield to call. We also show how these yield measures incorporate one or more of the basic sources of return: (1) periodic coupon interest payments, (2) recovery of the principal along with any capital gain or loss, and (3) reinvestment income.

Current Yield

Current yield (*CY*) is a return measure that relates the annual coupon interest to the bond's current price. Equation 5.10 shows the formula for current yield.

$$CY = \frac{I}{P_b} \qquad (5.10)$$

where *I* is the annual coupon interest and P_b is the current price of the bond.

Current yield does not provide an accurate measure of a bond's total expected return because it uses only one source of return: a bond's annual interest income. This yield measure does not take into account any capital gains and losses that investors may realize by holding the bond to maturity or call. For example, a zero coupon bond has a current yield of zero because it pays no cash interest income. The total return of a zero coupon bond should exceed zero due to appreciation in value over time.

Example 5.11 Current Yield on a Bond

Suppose that a 15-year, $1,000 par value, 7 percent semiannual-pay bond is currently trading at $1,100. What is the current yield on this bond?

Solution: Inserting *I* = $70 and P_0 = $1,100 into Equation 5.10 results in a current yield of 6.36 percent.

$$CY = \frac{\$70}{\$1,100} = 0.0636 \text{ or } 6.36\%$$

Yield to Maturity

Yield to maturity (YTM), also known as **promised yield**, is the rate of return that investors expect to earn if they buy a bond at its market price and hold it until maturity. YTM is probably the most widely used bond valuation measure. Unlike the current yield, YTM considers not only the coupon income but also any capital gain or loss that the investor will realize by holding the bond to maturity and reinvestment income. That is, YTM implicitly assumes that the bondholder can reinvest any interest payments received from the bond at the YTM.

In Examples 5.4 through 5.6, we computed the intrinsic value of a bond by discounting the bond's future cash flows by the required rate of return for the bond (k_b). If the market properly prices the bond, intrinsic value and market value (price) are the same and the discount rate is the bond's YTM. Thus, given the expected future cash flows for the bond, we can determine the expected return, or YTM, over the life of the bond.

To find YTM, we substitute P_0 for V_b and YTM for k_b in Equations 5.5 and 5.6 for annual-pay bonds, Equations 5.7 and 5.8 for semiannual-pay bonds, and Equation 5.9 for zerocoupon bonds and then solve for yield rather than intrinsic value. Solving for YTM using Equations 5.5 though 5.8 requires a trial-and-error approach. That is, we discount the future cash flows using a specific YTM and compare this result to the market price. If the computed amount is greater (less than) the market price, we select a higher (lower) discount rate and repeat the process until the computed amount equals the price. To avoid this time-consuming process, we show how to solve for YTM using a financial calculator.

Investors can decide whether to buy a bond by comparing its YTM to their required rate of return on the bond. When the YTM is greater or equal to the required return, the bond would be attractive for purchase. When the YTM is less than the required rate of return, investors would not buy the bond or might consider selling it if they already own it.

Example 5.12 Yield to Maturity: Annual-pay Bonds

Suppose a 15-year, $1,000 par value, 7 percent annual-pay bond is currently trading at a price of $1,100. What is the bond's yield to maturity? If an investor requires an 5.5 percent return, would this bond be attractive?

Solution: We substitute $P_0 = \$1,100$, $I = \$70$, $M = \$1,000$, and $n = 15$ into a slightly modified version of Equation 5.6. Using a trial-and-error approach to solve for YTM, the YTM is about 5.97 percent.

$$\$1{,}100 = \sum_{t=1}^{15} \frac{\$70}{(1 + YTM)^t} + \frac{\$1{,}000}{(1 + YTM)^{15}} \Rightarrow YTM = 5.97\%$$

We can easily solve for the bond's YTM by using the BA II PLUS® calculator as follows:

   Inputs: 15 N; 1,100 +/– PV; 70 PMT; 1000 FV; CPT I/Y   *Output:* 5.97

Or simply:

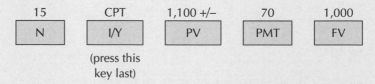

(press this
key last)

Thus, the YTM is about 5.97 percent. If the investor requires a 5.5 percent return, this bond would be attractive because the bond's YTM exceeds the investor's required rate of return.

Example 5.13 Yield to Maturity: Semiannual-pay Bonds

Now assume that the bond in the previous example is a semiannual-pay bond. If a 15-year, $1,000 par value, 7 percent semiannual-pay bond is currently trading at $1,100, what is the bond's yield to maturity?

Solution: Because this is a semiannual-pay bond, we input $P_0 = \$1,100$, $I/2 = \$35$, $M = \$1,000$, and $2n = 30$ into a slightly modified version of Equation 5.8. Using trial-and-error, we get the YTM of about 5.98 percent.

$$\$1,100 = \sum_{t=1}^{30} \frac{\$35}{(1 + YTM/2)^t} + \frac{\$1,000}{(1 + YTM/2)^{30}}$$

$$\Rightarrow YTM = 2.99\% \times 2 = 5.98\%$$

Using the BA II PLUS® calculator, key in the following and get:

Inputs: 30 N; 1,100 +/– PV; 35 PMT; 1,000 FV; CPT I/Y

Output: 2.99 × 2 = 5.98

Or simply:

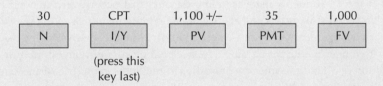

30	CPT	1,100 +/–	35	1,000
N	I/Y	PV	PMT	FV
	(press this key last)			

Because the bond involves semiannual compounding, the computed value of 2.99 percent is not the bond's YTM. Instead, it represents the semi-annual measure of yield. The market convention used to annualize the semiannual yield to maturity is to double the semiannual rate and to use that rate as the yield to maturity.[8] The term used to describe this convention is **bond-equivalent yield** (BEY). Thus, the BEY for this bond would be 2 × 2.99 = 5.98 percent. Note that the BEY is less than the YTM of the annual-pay bond (5.97 percent).

---

[8] To be technically accurate, we should find the bond's effective annual yield, as we discussed in Chapter 4: (true annual) YTM = $(1 + \text{semiannual YTM})^2 - 1 = (1.0299)^2 - 1 = 0.0607$ or 6.07%.

Practical Financial Tip 5.7

The following relationships exist among the coupon rate, current yield, and yield to maturity.

Bond selling at	Relationship
Par	Coupon rate = current yield = yield to maturity
Discount	Coupon rate < current yield < yield to maturity
Premium	Coupon rate > current yield > yield to maturity

Assumptions and limitations
Yield to maturity involves three embedded assumptions:

1   Investors will hold the bond to maturity.
2   Investors will receive all coupon payments in a prompt and timely fashion.
3   Investors will reinvest all coupons to maturity at a rate of return that equals the bond's YTM.

If these assumptions do not hold, the YTM will not equal the **realized yield**, which is the actual yield earned by investors. For example, investors may be unable to reinvest coupon payments at the YTM due to changes in interest rates that occur over the bond's life. This type of risk is **reinvestment risk**. All else equal, the reinvestment risk of a bond will increase with higher coupons because there is more interest to invest. Reinvestment risk also will increase with longer maturities because a longer period exists to reinvest interest.

A limitation of YTM and other traditional yield measures is the use of the same rate to discount all cash flows. This implies a **flat yield curve**, which means that the yield for all maturities is approximately equal. This condition rarely exists in practice. The most common relationship is a **normal** or **positively sloped yield curve** in which the longer the maturity, the higher is the yield. Occasionally, the relationship between maturities and yields is such that the longer the maturity, the lower is the yield. Such a downward sloping yield curve is an **inverted** or a **negatively sloped yield curve**.

Yield to Call

As discussed earlier, bonds are either noncallable or callable. A **noncallable bond** prohibits the issuer from calling the bond for retirement before maturity. With a **callable bond**, the issuer has the right to retire the bond before maturity. Thus, YTM may not be an appropriate measure of potential return of a bond. Another yield measure, called **yield to call** (YTC), takes into account the potential call of a bond. As with YTM, YTC considers all three sources of potential return of owning a bond. YTC assumes that:

1   Investors will hold the bond to the assumed call date.

2   The issuer will call the bond on that date.

3   Investors will reinvest all cash flows at the YTC until the assumed call date.

Calculating the YTC requires making two adjustments to the standard YTM equation. First, analysts use the length of the investment horizon as the number of years to the first call date, not the number of years to maturity. Second, they use the bond's call price instead of the bond's maturity value. The call price is typically greater than the maturity value to partially compensate bondholders for exposing them to reinvestment rate risk. Often the call price decreases over time because bondholders have less exposure to reinvestment rate risk. This is because less time remains for reinvesting cash flows before the bond matures. To calculate the YTC, solve the following equation:

$$V_b = \sum_{t=1}^{mn} \frac{I}{(1 + YTC/m)^t} + \frac{CP}{(1 + YTC/m)^{mn}}$$ (5.11)

where I is the annual or semi-annual coupon payment; CP is the appropriate call price of the bond; m is the number of coupon payments per year; and n is the number of years to first call.

In practice, bond investors generally compute both YTM and YTC for deferred-call bonds that are trading at a *premium*. A **deferred-call provision** is a stipulation in a bond indenture specifying that the issuer cannot call a bond until expiration of a specified call deferment period. Thus, the bond starts out as noncallable and becomes freely callable after the call deferment period has expired.

Example 5.14 Yield to Call: Semiannual-pay Bonds

Suppose that the 15-year, $1,000 par value, 7 percent semiannual-pay bond has a deferred call. The bond now trades at $1,100 and has 5 years before the first call at a price of $1,050. What is the yield to call?

Solution: Because this is a semiannual-pay bond, we input $P_0 = \$1,100$, $I/2 = \$35$, $M = \$1,050$, and $2n = 10$ into Equation 5.11 and solve for the YTC using a trial-and-error approach to get about 5.56 percent.

$$\$1,100 = \sum_{t=1}^{10} \frac{\$35}{(1 + YTC/2)^t} + \frac{\$1,050}{(1 + YTC/2)^{10}} \Rightarrow YTC = 2.78\% \times 2 = 5.56\%$$

Using the BA II PLUS® calculator, we input the following:

Inputs: 10 N; 1,100 +/– PV; 35 PMT; 1,050 FV; CPT I/Y

Output: 2.78 × 2 = 5.56

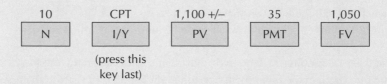

(press this
key last)

Thus, the YTM is 5.98 percent while the YTC is 5.56 percent. Market convention uses the lower of the two yield measures (YTM or YTC) as the more conservative measure of yield. In our example, the bond would be valued relative to its YTM. Why? On any premium bond, the YTC will always be less than YTM. This is because interest rates have decreased. If interest rates remain below the coupon rate, the issuer is likely to call the bond. The opposite situation exists for bonds trading at a discount.

Concept Check 5.6

1 What are three basic sources of return that may comprise the yield on a bond?
2 Which sources of return are included in calculating the current yield, yield to maturity, and yield to call?
3 What conditions cause a bond to sell at par value, a premium, or a discount?
4 Under what circumstances will the yield to maturity and the realized yield differ?
5 What is the meaning of *reinvestment rate risk*?
6 How does *yield to call* differ from *yield to maturity*?
7 For bonds selling at a premium, what is the relationship between the yield to call and the yield to maturity?

5.7 Bond Trading and Price Reporting

Firms issue bonds in a **primary market** transaction. In a primary market transaction, a firm issues securities to investors with the proceeds going to the firm. Once the issuer initially sells a bond issue, investors trade (buy and sell) them in the **secondary markets**. The *Wall Street Journal (WSJ)* provides trading data for the 40 most actively traded fixed coupon corporate bonds in its Corporate Bonds section. We present data from the August 6, 2003, *WSJ* in Figure 5.8 in a similar format to theirs.

The first column shows the name of the issuer with its ticker symbol. The second and third columns define the specific bond issue for that firm by providing the coupon rate and maturity date for the bond. Many firms have several issues outstanding. For our analysis, we focus on the Ford bond (emphasized in bold print in Figure 5.8) that has a coupon rate of 7.45 percent maturing on July 16, 2031. As of August 5, 2003, this bond had about 28 years remaining until maturity.

The "Last price" column reports the closing price for that bond on August 5. Standard practice is to report bond prices as the percentage of par value. Thus, the closing price for the Ford 7.45 percent coupon bond is 85.888 percent of par value, which would be $858.88 per $1,000 par value. The "Last yield" column reports the yield to maturity for the bond, which is 8.816 percent for the Ford bond. We can verify this to be the correct yield to maturity by solving for the unknown yield with $N = 56$, $PV = -858.88$, $PMT = 37.25$, and $FV = 1,000$. (With semiannual coupon interest payments, the yield to maturity will be a 6-month yield of 4.408 percent, which is 8.816 percent per year.)[9]

Corporate Bonds							
Tuesday, August 5, 2003							
Forty most active fixed-coupon bonds							
COMPANY (TICKER)	**COUPON**	**MATURITY**	**LAST PRICE**	**LAST YIELD**	***EST SPREAD**	**UST**	**EST $ VOL (000'S)**
General Motors (GM)	8.375	Jul 15, 2033	94.127	8.939	358	30	266,172
General Motors Acceptance (GMAC)	6.875	Aug 28, 2012	97.277	7.290	288	10	141,273
Spring Capital (FON)	8.375	Mar 15, 2012	112.415	6.469	206	10	127,549
Household Finance (HSBC)	4.750	Jul 15, 2013	92.871	5.699	130	10	101,466
Goldman Sachs Group (GS)	4.750	Jul 15, 2013	93.876	5.560	115	10	98,559
First Energy (FE)	6.450	Nov 15, 2011	101.793	6.168	177	10	97,385
General Electric Capital (GE)	5.450	Jan 15, 2013	100.626	5.364	96	10	92,664
AT&T Wireless Services (AWE)	8.750	Mar 01, 2031	115.418	7.427	207	30	82,955
Bank One (ONE)	2.625	Jun 30, 2008	94.079	3.967	72	5	82,595
General Motors (GM)	7.125	Jul 15, 2013	97.940	7.420	301	10	82,246
Meadwestvaco (MWV)	6.850	Apr 01, 2012	107.855	5.686	125	10	80,965
Bank of America (BAC)	3.875	Jan 15, 2008	100.443	3.765	48	55	79,727
General Motors Acceptance (GMAC)	8.000	Nov 01, 2031	92.826	8.683	331	30	77,375
Ford Motor (F)	**7.450**	**Jul 16, 2031**	**85.888**	**8.816**	**345**	**30**	**75,848**
Ford Motor Credit (F)	6.875	Feb 01, 2006	105.088	4.678	242	3	74,192
General Electric Capital (GE)	5.000	Jun 15, 2007	105.480	3.467	26	5	74,005
Citigroup (C)	7.250	Oct 01, 2010	114.024	4.899	49	10	71,385
Sprint Capital (FON)	8.750	Mar 15, 2032	108.726	7.970	261	30	70,221
Weyerhaeuser (WY)	6.750	Mar 15, 2012	106.209	5.821	141	10	67,977
AOL Time Warner	6.875	May 01, 2012	107.321	5.793	138	10	65,829
(partial listing only provided here)							

Volume represents total volume for each issue; price/yield data are for trades of $1 million and greater.
* Estimated spreads, in basis points (100 basis points is one percentage point), over the 2, 3, 4, 10, or 30-year on-the-run Treasury note/bond. 2-year: 1.500 07/05; 3-year: 2.000 05/06; 5-year: 2.625 05/08; 10-year: 3.625 05/13; 30-year: 5.375 02/31. UST is based on comparable U.S. Treasury issue.

Figure 5.8 Bond price quotation from the *Wall Street Journal* (partial listing)

---

[9] Small differences in the yield to maturities may result because the bond's term to maturity is not exactly 28 years. Many investment texts provide formulas that allow computing a yield to maturity for cases where the bond is trading in-between coupon payment dates.

The next two columns report the spread in basis points for the bond over US Treasury issues. A **yield spread** is the difference in yield between a bond and a reference bond such as a US Treasury bill, note, or bond. One basis point is 0.01 percent (thus, 100 basis points is equal to 1.0 percent). The footnotes at the bottom of the quotation in the *WSJ* provide the specific reference points for these spreads. Finally, the last column reports the estimated trading volume in thousands of dollars. Thus, the trading volume for the Ford bond was about $75,848,000 on August 5, 2003.

Concept Check 5.7

1   Explain the difference between primary and secondary market transactions.
2   What is a yield spread?

5.8 Preferred Stock Features and Valuation

Preferred stock is a hybrid security combining features of debt and common stock. From a legal and tax standpoint, preferred stock is a form of equity, which has preference over common stock in the payment of dividends and in the distribution of assets in the event of liquidation. Nevertheless, a good case exists to think of preferred stock as being debt in disguise. Preferred stock is similar to debt in that both securities generally have fixed payments. Preferred stock is similar to common stock in that most preferred issues have no maturity. Unlike common stockholders, preferred stockholders typically do not have voting rights or share in the residual earnings of the company. Exceptions exist to these general characteristics of preferred stock.

Preferred Stock Features

We discuss common characteristics and features of preferred stock below.

Par or no par stock
Similar to a bond, preferred stock typically has a stated par value, such as $25 or $100, which represents the size of the claim the preferred stockholders have in the event of bankruptcy. **No par preferred stock** has no par value and no specific per share liquidation claim.

No maturity date
Corporations usually intend to use preferred stock as a permanent part of their equity. Hence, most preferred stocks have no maturity date. Some issues, however, have specified maturities. Others have a sinking fund feature, which effectively creates a final maturity.

Dividends

Preferred stock typically carries a stipulated dividend that the issuer pays on a quarterly basis. Dividends are stated as a percentage of the par value or as a fixed amount for no par stock. Some preferred stock issues, called **adjustable rate**, **variable rate**, or **floating rate preferred**, do not have a fixed dividend, but peg dividends to an underlying index such as the rate on Treasury securities or other money market rates. Unlike interest payments on debt, preferred stock dividends are not a legal obligation of the firm. A corporation has no fixed obligation to pay dividends if it has insufficient earnings. Omitting the dividend will not result in a default of the obligation or force the firm into bankruptcy. From the issuer's perspective, preferred stock is less risky than bonds.

Cumulative feature

Most preferred stocks have a **cumulative** feature, requiring the company to pay all cumulative unpaid preferred dividends before resuming paying any dividends on common stock. Late or overdue dividends are **arrearages**. Many preferred stocks incur arrearages for a limited period, such as 3 years. Unpaid preferred dividends do not represent an obligation to the firm. If the corporation fails to pay a dividend on **noncumulative preferred stock**, investors generally lose this dividend.

Claims on assets and income

Preferred stockholders have a priority claim over common stockholders in the liquidation of assets resulting from bankruptcy. The basis of the amount of payment made to preferred stockholders is the par value or the liquidation value of the preferred stock. The **liquidation value** is the maximum amount that investors will receive at liquidation. Preferred stockholders also have a priority of claim to dividends before common stockholders do. Because of their prior claim on assets and income, preferred stockholders typically have no voting rights, except in special situations such as the company's inability to pay dividends for a specific period. From the perspective of investors, preferred stock is riskier than debt because creditors have a prior claim on assets and income.

Retirement of preferred stock

Similar to bond issues, preferred stock issues almost invariably have provisions for retirement. For example, almost all preferred stock issues have a call provision, which gives the issuer flexibility in retiring the issue. Many preferred stock issues also have sinking funds to facilitate the orderly retirement of the stock. Some preferred stock issues are **convertible**, which gives the holder the option to exchange preferred stock for common stock under certain conditions. Upon conversion, the corporation retires the preferred stock.

Preferred Stock Valuation

The valuation of preferred stock is relatively simple if the firm pays fixed dividends at the end of each year. If this condition holds, the stream of dividend payments represents a perpetuity discounted at the investor's required rate of return. For such preferred stock, the following perpetuity formula (discussed in Chapter 4) applies.

$$V_p = \sum_{t=1}^{\infty} \frac{D_p}{(1 + k_p)^t} \tag{5.12}$$

where V_p is the value of a share of preferred stock; D_p is the expected dividends per share on preferred stock; k_p is the investor's required rate of return on preferred stock; t is the time period; and ∞ is infinity.

Equation 5.12 says that the intrinsic value of preferred stock is the present value of all the preferred stock dividends to infinity. We can simplify this equation as follows.

$$V_p = \frac{D_p}{k_p} \tag{5.13}$$

Equation 5.13 computes the intrinsic value by capitalizing a perpetual stream of dividends. The difficult task in applying Equation 5.12 and 5.13 is estimating the required rate of return.

Example 5.15 Preferred Stock Valuation

Suppose Potomac Corporation has a $100 par value preferred stock that pays an annual dividend of $7. If investors require an 8 percent return on this preferred stock, what should be its intrinsic value?

Solution: Substituting $D_p = \$7$ and $k_p = 0.08$ into Equation 5.13 results in an intrinsic value of:

$$V_p = \frac{\$7}{0.08} = \$87.50$$

Investors interpret the results of preferred stock valuation in the same way that they do for bonds. That is, if the estimated value is greater than or equal to the current market price, say $85 a share, investors would consider buying the preferred stock. If the estimated value is less than the market price, they would decide against a purchase, or they would consider selling if they owned the stock. The formula for evaluating maturing preferred stock is identical in form to the bond value formula.

Practical Financial Tip 5.8

For a US corporation with both bonds and preferred stock, preferred stock has a lower before-tax yield than bonds due to the partial tax exclusion on dividends for corporate investors. However, the after-tax yield on the preferred is typically higher than on the firm's highest-grade bonds.

Expected Return on Preferred Stock

Determining the expected rate of return, also called a **promised yield**, on preferred stock simply involves dividing the annual dividend by the current market price.

$$\hat{k}_p = \frac{D_p}{P_p} \tag{5.14}$$

where $\hat{k}_p$ is the expected rate of return on a preferred stock; D_p is the annual cash dividend on preferred stock; and P_p is the current market price on preferred stock. Here, $\hat{k}_p$ (called "k_p hat") is the expected rate of return, as opposed to k_p, which represents the required rate of return.

Example 5.16 Expected Rate of Return of Preferred Stock

Assume the current market price of Potomac Corporation's preferred stock is $85, what would be the expected rate of return? If an investor's required rate of return is 8 percent, should the investor consider buying the preferred stock?

Solution: Using Equation 5.14, the expected rate of return on the preferred stock is:

$$\hat{k}_p = \frac{\$7}{\$85} = 8.24\%$$

Since the expected rate of return of 8.24 percent is greater than the required rate of return of 8 percent, the investor should consider buying the stock. The buy/sell decision using the expected rate of return criterion always agrees with the decision derived by comparing the intrinsic value of the preferred stock to its market price.

Concept Check 5.8

1 Why is preferred stock a hybrid security?
2 What is the importance of a cumulative dividend feature to preferred stockholders?
3 What are the components in valuing a preferred stock?
4 Is the after-tax yield on a preferred stock typically higher or lower than the after-tax yield on the firm's highest grade bonds? Why?

5.9 Common Stock Characteristics and Features

Common stock is a form of equity that represents ownership of a corporation. Common stockholders are the residual owners because their claim to earnings and assets is what remains after satisfying the prior claims of various creditors and preferred stockholders. As the true owners of the corporation, they bear the ultimate risks and realize the rewards of ownership. Stockholders have limited liability because they cannot lose more money than their investment in the common stock.

Features

Common stock has several major features. Some involve accounting terminology, which helps to explain how to record common stock on the firm's balance sheet.

Par or no par stock
Corporations can issue common stock with or without par value, based on specifications in the corporation's charter. For common stock, par value is the stated value attached to a single share at issuance. Except for accounting and legal purposes, par value has little economic significance. If a company sells stock for more than its par value, it records any issue price in excess of par as **additional paid-in capital** or **capital in excess of par**. If a company sells stock for less than its par value, any discount from par represents a legal liability of the owners to the creditors in the event of liquidation. The issuer carries no par stock on its books at the original market price or at some assigned or stated value, which is usually below the actual issuing price.

Authorized, issued, and outstanding shares
The charter of a corporation specifies the **authorized shares** of common stock, which are the maximum number of shares that the corporation may issue without amending its charter. **Issued shares** are the number of authorized shares sold by the firm. **Outstanding shares** refer to the number of shares issued and actually held by the public. The firm bases its earnings per share and dividends per share on the outstanding shares. If a firm re-purchases its shares, the number of issued shares may exceed the number of outstanding

shares. **Treasury stock** refers to common stock that the issuing company repurchases and holds. Companies often repurchase their stock when they believe that it is undervalued in the market.

No maturity

Common stock has no maturity and serves as a permanent source of long-term financing. Although common stock is not callable or convertible, the issuer can repurchase its shares through various methods discussed in Chapter 12.

Rights of Common Stockholders

As the ultimate owners of a company, common stockholders have certain rights and privileges that are unavailable to other investors.

Right to vote

Common stockholders are typically the only ones who can vote on certain key matters concerning the firm. They have a voice in management through the board of directors whom they elect annually. Other issues on which common stockholders vote include amending the corporate charter and bylaws, selecting the firm's independent auditors, changing the amount of authorized shares, and approving the issuance of securities. They also have the right to proxy their vote to others. A **proxy** is a temporary transfer of the right to vote to another party. Some corporations have more than one class of common stock and these classes often have unequal voting rights. A major reason for having dual or multiple classes of stock involves the control of the firm.

Two common systems of voting for members of the board of directors are majority voting and cumulative voting. **Straight** or **majority voting** is a voting system that entitles each shareholder to cast one vote for each share owned. If a nominee receives 50 percent plus one vote, this person has a majority of the votes and becomes a director. **Cumulative voting** is a voting system that permits the stockholder to cast multiple votes for a single director. The cumulative voting system improves the chance of minority interests to obtain representation on the board of directors.

Right to income

Common stockholders have the right to share in cash dividends only if the company's board of directors declares them. Unlike bondholders and other creditors, common stockholders have little recourse if the board decides not to distribute profits by paying dividends. If the company does distribute dividends, common stockholders have the right to dividends only after the preferred shareholders receive their dividends.

Right to residual assets

In the event of liquidation, common stockholders have the right to share in any residual assets remaining after the firm satisfies the claims of all other parties such as creditors and preferred stockholders.

Right to transfer ownership

Common stockholders can sell their ownership in the firm to another party. This generally involves selling the stock in the secondary market where the company's stock trades.

Other rights

Common stockholders have the right to inspect the corporation's books. In practice, corporations generally fulfill this limited right by providing stockholders with quarterly and annual reports. In some instances, existing stockholders have the right, but not the obligation, to share proportionately in the purchase of all new shares of common stock that the company sells. Some states require corporations chartered in the state to include this privilege, called a **preemptive right**, in their charters.

Concept Check 5.9

1   How do authorized, issued, and outstanding shares differ from one another?
2   How does majority voting differ from cumulative voting? Which method would tend to favor minority stockholders in electing members to the board of directors?
3   How can a preemptive right benefit stockholders?

5.10 Common Stock Valuation

Compared with valuing bonds and preferred stock, common stock valuation is more difficult because of the uncertainty associated with the size and timing of future cash flows and the unknown nature of the required rate of return. Future cash flows may be in the form of cash dividend payments and/or changes in the stock's price (gains or losses) over the holding period. Dividends are uncertain because corporations have no legal requirement to pay them unless declared by the board of directors. In addition, dividends may increase, remain stable, or decrease over time. Future stock prices are also uncertain. Because common stock is generally riskier than bonds or preferred stock, investors require a higher rate of return (k_s) to compensate for this risk.

Before discussing various valuation models, we want to stress that no one "best" model exists. The appropriate model to use in a specific situation depends on the characteristics of the asset being valued. These characteristics include such factors as the level of earnings, current growth rate in earnings, and the source of growth.

Discounted Cash Flow Models

Although numerous DCF valuation models are available for valuing common stock, these approaches generally differ based upon three factors:

- **measure of cash flow** – dividends and free cash flows to equity;
- **expected holding period** – finite (limited) and infinite; and
- **pattern of expected dividends** – zero (no) growth, stable (constant) growth, and supernormal growth.

We begin by narrowly defining the measure of cash flow as dividends and consider different expected holding periods and dividend patterns. Each of these models is a type of **dividend discount model** (DDM). Later, we use a broader measure of cash flow, namely, free cash flow to equity (FCFE) to estimate the value of common stock. FCFE valuation models are simply variants of the DDM, but use FCFE instead of dividends.

Dividend Discount Models

The most basic models for valuing equity are the dividend discount models. These models require two key inputs: expected dividends and the required rate of return on equity. The attractiveness of these models stems from their simplicity and intuitive logic.

Finite-period valuation model
A **finite-period valuation model** is a model that assumes an investor plans to buy a common stock and hold it for a limited period. The holding period may be for one or more periods. Equation 5.15 shows that the intrinsic value of a common stock is the present value of the expected dividends during the holding period plus the present value of the **terminal price**, which is the expected price of a stock at the end of a specific holding period. If an investor sells the stock, the buyer is still acquiring the remaining dividend stream. Therefore, the basis for determining a stock's terminal price at any point in time is the present value of the expected dividends after that point.

$$V_s = \sum_{t=1}^{n} \frac{D_t}{(1 + k_s)^t} + \frac{P_n}{(1 + k_s)^n} \tag{5.15}$$

where P_n is the terminal price of the common stock at the end of period n.

Determining the stock's intrinsic value using a limited holding period model requires the following steps.

1   *Forecast the dividends per share for each period.* Companies pay dividends from earnings or cash flows. Thus, key inputs in estimating expected dividends per share are the firm's expected earnings and dividend payout ratio. Various approaches are available for estimating earnings growth including historical growth, analyst projections, or the fundamentals of the firm. The payout ratio should reflect changes in expected earnings growth. For example, firms with high earnings growth typically have low payouts; while firms with stable earnings growth have high payouts.

    The expected growth rate should be a function of the proportion of the earnings that a firm reinvests and the returns it earns on the projects undertaken using this money. Equation 5.16 gives the retention growth rate method, which we introduced in Chapter 3. This formula shows that calculating the growth rate involves forecasting the retention rate and then multiplying the retention rate by the company's expected future rate of return on equity.

$$g = RR(ROE) \tag{5.16}$$

where g is the internal or sustainable growth rate; RR is the earnings retention rate, which is (1 – dividend payout); and ROE is the return on equity, which is net income/equity. A common approach to forecasting the dividend is to use the current dividend and to increase it by the projected growth rate (g).

2 *Forecast the expected price of the stock at the end of the holding period.* The future estimated selling price of the stock (terminal value) reflects the present value of all future dividends after the selling date to infinity.

3 *Estimate the required rate of return.* Analysts often estimate the required rate of return that stockholders demand for holding a stock based on a risk and return model called the **capital asset pricing model** (CAPM). We discuss the CAPM further in Chapters 7 and 9. Equation 5.17 presents the CAPM, which states that the required rate of return on equity is a function of the risk-free rate plus a premium based on the systematic risk of the security.

$$k_s = R_f + \beta_i(R_m - R_f) \tag{5.17}$$

where k_s is the required rate of return; R_f is the nominal risk-free rate of return (previously referred to as NRFR); R_m is the expected rate of return on the market; and β_i is the beta coefficient (a measure of systematic risk) of the stock. Note that the risk premium for a specific stock i is $\beta_i(R_m - R_f)$. Other models are available for determining the required rate of return, such as arbitrage pricing models, but these are beyond the scope of this book.

4 *Discount the expected dividends and terminal price at the required rate of return.*

Example 5.17 Two-year Holding Period

An investor plans to buy common stock of Potomac Company and to sell it at the end of 2 years. Potomac Company just paid a $1 dividend ($D_0$). The firm's return on equity (ROE) is 10 percent and the investor expects it to stay at that rate in the future. Potomac has a stable dividend payout policy of 40 percent. The investor forecasts that the stock price will be $50 at the end of the year. The current nominal risk-free rate is 5 percent, the expected market return is 11 percent, and Potomac's beta is 1.2. What is the intrinsic value of Potomac's common stock?

Solution: We can follow the four-step process to estimate the value of Potomac's common stock.

1 *Forecast the dividends per share for each period.* This step requires forecasting the dividends for the next 2 years. To determine the growth rate (g) requires first

finding the retention rate = (1 − dividend payout) = 1 − 0.4 = 0.6 and then substituting RR = 0.60 and ROE = 0.10 percent in Equation 5.16 to get g = $(RR)(ROE)$ = (0.60)(0.10) = 0.06 or 6 percent. Now calculate the dividends for the next 2 years: $D_1 = D_0(1 + g) = \$1.00(1.06) = \$1.06$ and $D_2 = D_1(1 + g) = \$1.06(1.06)$ = $1.1236 or $1.12.

2   *Forecast the expected price of the stock at the end of the holding period.* In this situation, the terminal price at the end of the first year estimated to be $50.

3   *Estimate the required rate of return.* Using Equation 5.17 for the CAPM results in a required rate of return of k_s = 0.05 + 1.2(0.11 − 0.05) = 0.122 or 12.2 percent.

4   *Discount the expected dividends and terminal price at the required rate of return.* Substituting D_1 = $1.06, D_2 = $1.12, P_2 = $50.00, and k_s = 0.122 in Equation 5.15 results in a current value of $41.55.

$$V_s = \frac{\$1.06}{(1.122)} + \frac{\$1.12 + \$50.00}{(1.122)^2} = \$0.94 + \$40.61 = \$41.55$$

Infinite-period valuation model

For investors who do not contemplate selling their stock in the near future, a finite-period valuation model would be inappropriate. Therefore, we need to accommodate long-term holders. An **infinite-period valuation model** is a model that assumes an investor plans to buy a common stock and hold it indefinitely. As Equation 5.18 shows, the **basic dividend discount model** states that the intrinsic value of a share of common stock is equal to the discounted valued of all future dividends.

$$V_s = \sum_{t=1}^{\infty} \frac{D_t}{(1 + k_s)} \tag{5.18}$$

where V_s is the intrinsic value of a share of common stock; D_t is the expected dividends per share on common stock in period t; and k_s is the investor's required rate of return on common stock (cost of equity).

The basic DDM shows that the intrinsic value of a common stock depends on the expected future dividends and the required rate of return (discount rate). Holding all other variables constant, an increase in expected dividends would cause V_s to increase, and a decrease in expected dividends would cause V_s to decrease. Likewise, an increase in k_s would cause V_s to decrease, and a decrease in k_s would cause V_s to increase (again holding all other variables constant).

This model applies both to firms that pay current dividends and to those that do not. This is because the expectations of all future dividends, not just the near ones, determine the intrinsic value of the stock. This model suggests that investors must forecast dividends to infinity and then discount them back to present value at the required rate of return to estimate the value of common stock. In practice, investors cannot accurately project dividends through infinity. This does not present an insurmountable problem if investors can efficiently model the expected dividend stream by making appropriate assumptions about future growth. Here are three growth rate cases – zero growth, constant growth rate, and variable growth rates.

Zero growth

Some companies have highly stable expected dividend streams. The zero growth valuation model is a valuation approach that assumes dividends remain a fixed amount over time. That is, the growth rate (g) of dividends is zero. Equation 5.19 for the zero growth DDM is a simplified version of the infinite-period DDM given. This formula is similar to Equation 5.13 for preferred stock because both treat dividends as a perpetuity.

$$V_s = \frac{D_s}{k_s} \qquad (5.19)$$

where D_s is the expected dividends per share on common stock.

A limitation of this model comes from the fact that companies tend to pay a different amount of dividends over the course of their life cycle. Obviously, the model is best suited for companies that pay a constant dividend over time.

Example 5.18 Zero Growth Dividend Discount Model

United Industries expects to pay a $3.60 cash dividend at the end of each year, indefinitely into the future. If investors require a 12 percent return, what is the intrinsic value of the common stock of United Industries?

Solution: Substituting D_s = $3.60 and k_s = 0.12 in Equation 5.19 results in a stock value of $30.00.

$$V_s = \frac{\$3.60}{0.12} = \$30.00$$

Constant growth

Many companies have expected dividend streams that tend to grow at a constant rate for long periods. The **constant growth valuation model** is a valuation approach that assumes dividends per share grow at a constant rate each period that is never expected to change. This model, also called the Gordon growth model, represents a **single-stage growth pattern**. Substituting $D_0(1 + g)^t$ for D_t in Equation 5.18 produces the following constant growth DDM.

$$V_s = \sum_{t=1}^{\infty} \frac{D_0(1 + g)^t}{(1 + k_s)^t} \qquad (5.20)$$

where D_0 is the dividends per share in the current period; and g is the constant dividend growth rate.

If k_s is greater than g, Equation 5.20 can be simplified as follows:

$$V_s = \frac{D_0(1 + g)}{k_s - g} = \frac{D_1}{k_s - g} \qquad (5.21)$$

Although the constant growth model is a simple and convenient way to value common stock, it has several limiting assumptions. First, in order for the dividend to increase at a constant growth rate, the firm's earnings must increase by at least that rate, because a firm pays dividends from earnings. Second, D_1 cannot be equal to zero, because the model would not apply. Third, the discount rate (k_s) must be greater than the growth rate (g). Otherwise, the model breaks down and the results are nonsense. Finally, value goes to infinity as g approaches k_s. Thus, underestimating or overestimating the growth rate can lead to large valuation errors.

Because the constant growth DDM requires using some highly restrictive assumptions, it is best suited to firms that are growing at a steady rate that is comparable to or lower than the nominal growth rate in the economy. These firms should also have well-established dividend policies. As discussed in Chapter 12, some companies have an explicit goal of steady growth in dividends. Other firms are unlikely to meet these assumptions. For example, the constant growth DDM does not work with growth stocks.

Example 5.19 Constant Growth Dividend Discount Model

Kogod Enterprises just paid a $2.00 dividend last year. Analysts expect the firm's dividends to grow at a constant rate of 6 percent a year. If investors require a 14 percent return, what is the intrinsic value of Kogod's common stock?

Solution: Substituting $D_1 = \$2.00(1.06) = \$2.12$, $k_s = 0.14$, and $g = 0.06$ in Equation 5.21 results in a stock value of $26.50.

$$V_s = \frac{\$2.12}{0.14 - 0.06} = \$26.50$$

Practical Financial Tip 5.9

An important relationship exists between the required rate of return (k_s) and the growth rate (g).

- As the difference between k_s and g widens, the stock value falls.
- As the difference between k_s and g narrows, the stock value rises.
- Small changes in the difference between k_s and g can lead to large changes in the stock's value.

Variable growth

A company may experience different levels of growth in earnings and dividends over time. A **variable growth valuation model** is a valuation approach that allows for a change in the dividend growth rate. That is, different growth rates occur during specific segments of the overall holding period. Thus, a characteristic of such a model is a **multi-stage growth pattern**. For example, a **two-stage valuation model** might involve a high growth period followed by a stable or "steady state" growth period. Because a company cannot maintain high growth forever, it is likely to return to a more sustainable rate of growth at some time in the future. The model is suitable for companies that cannot sustain high dividend payments. Limitations of such a model include the practical difficulty of defining the length of the high growth period and the abrupt drop to stable growth. To reduce these limitations, other models depend on different assumptions. For example, a **three-stage valuation model** can allow for an initial period of high growth, a transitional period where dividend growth has declined to more moderate growth, and a final stable-growth stage. Such a model could be appropriate for valuing firms with very high current growth rates.

One type of two-stage model is the **temporary supernormal growth valuation model**. As Equation 5.22 shows, the temporary supernormal growth DDM states that the value of a firm's common stock equals the present value of the expected dividends during the above-normal growth period plus the present value of the terminal price, which is the value of all remaining dividends to infinity starting at the beginning of the constant growth.

$$V_s = \sum_{t=1}^{n} \frac{D_0(1 + g_1)^t}{(1 + k_s)^t} + \frac{P_n}{(1 + k_s)^n} \tag{5.22}$$

where D_0 is the dividends per share in period 0; g_1 is the supernormal growth rate; n is the length of the supernormal growth period; P_n is the terminal price of the stock $= D_{n+1}/(k_s - g_2)$ where D_{n+1} is the first dividend at the resumption of normal growth; and g_2 is the normal growth rate.

Equation 5.22 also applies to a two-stage DDM with a delayed dividend stream. For example, a company may pay no dividends during the first stage but then pay out dividends at a constant rate thereafter.

Practical Financial Tip 5.10

Linkages exist between growth rates in earnings or cash flows and dividend payout ratios. In practice, high growth firms typically have low dividend payouts. They prefer to reinvest their earnings in profitable projects instead of paying cash to stockholders. After growth rates stabilize, firms tend to adopt more liberal dividend payout policies.

Example 5.20 Temporary Supernormal Growth Dividend Discount Model

Analysts expect dividends at LAB Corporation to grow at a rate of 20 percent for the next 4 years and 5 percent a year thereafter. The company just paid a $2 per share dividend. If investors require a 12 percent return, what is the value of the stock today?

Solution: Using Equation 5.22, finding the value of LAB Corporation's stock involves three major steps.

1 *Find the present value of the dividends during the supernormal growth period.*

$$\sum_{t=1}^{n} \frac{D_0(1 + g_1)^t}{(1 + k_s)^t} = \sum_{t=1}^{4} \frac{\$2.00(1.20)^t}{(1.10)^4}$$

Year t	Dividend $\$1.00(1.20)^t = D_t$ [1]	Discount factor $1/(1.12)^t$ [2]	Present value [1] × [2]
1	$\$2.00(1.20) = \$2.40$	0.8929	$2.14
2	$2.00(1.20)^2 = 2.88$	0.7972	2.30
3	$2.00(1.20)^3 = 3.46$	0.7118	2.46
4	$2.00(1.20)^4 = 4.15$	0.6355	2.64
			Total $9.54

2 *Find the present value of the terminal price at the end of the supernormal growth period (year 4).*
   This step involves calculating the terminal price at the end of year 4 (P_4).

$$P_4 = \frac{D_{n+1}}{k_s - g_2} = \frac{D_4(1 + g_2)}{0.12 - 0.05} = \frac{\$4.15(1.05)}{0.07} = \frac{\$4.358}{0.07} = \$62.25$$

Next, discount the terminal price to the present using the 12 percent required rate of return.

$$\text{Present value of } P_4 = \frac{P_4}{(1 + k_s)^n} = \frac{\$62.25}{(1.12)^4} = \frac{\$62.25}{1.5735} = \$39.56$$

3 Sum the present value of both the dividends during the 4-year supernormal growth period and the terminal price in year 4.

$$V_s = \$9.54 + \$39.56 = \$49.10$$

Free Cash Flow to Equity Models

An alternative measure of cash flows is free cash flow to equity (FCFE). When a firm's dividends and FCFE differ, estimates of value will also differ when using DDM versus FCFE valuation. For example, the actual amount of dividends paid to stockholders often contrasts sharply with the FCFE that firms can afford to pay. Few firms follow a policy of paying out their entire FCFE as dividends. For example, some firms desire stability or are reluctant to change dividends. If a firm pays out all FCFE as dividends, this could lead to a highly volatile payout rate. Other firms want to hold back some FCFE to provide a reserve for future needs.

Thus, FCFE valuation models are more suited to value common stock when dividends are substantially higher or lower than the FCFE. FCFE model valuation also provides a better estimate of value in valuing firms for takeovers or where changing corporate control exists.

Although several approaches are available for measuring FCFE, Equation 5.23 shows a basic measure.

$$\text{FCFE} = \text{Net income} + \text{Depreciation} - \text{Capital spending} - \text{Change in working} \\ \text{capital spending} - \text{Principal repayments spending} - \text{New debt issues} \qquad (5.23)$$

The major difference between dividend discount models and free cash flow to equity models lies in the measure of cash flows. The assumptions about growth and other inputs are similar. For example, the constant growth FCFE is the same as the constant growth DDM, except for substituting $FCFE_1$ in Equation 5.21 in lieu of D_1. Similar substitutions apply to the other DDM models. Because of the similarity between these two models, we do not repeat equations for FCFE model valuation here.

Relative Valuation Models

Another approach to valuation is **relative valuation**, which estimates value by finding similar assets that are cheap or expensive and examining how the market currently prices these assets. Relative valuation involves defining "comparable" assets and choosing a standardized measure of value to compare firms. Usually value is in the form of some multiple of earnings, cash flow, book value of equity, or sales. Thus, an asset may be cheap (expensive) based on intrinsic value but expensive (cheap) based on relative valuation.

Although relative valuation appears to require fewer assumptions than DCF valuation methods, it actually does not. A major difference between these two valuation methods is that the assumptions underlying DCF valuation are explicit whereas they are implicit with relative valuation. The same variables that affect the estimated value using DCF valuation, such as the dividend payout ratio (D_1/E_1), risk as measured by the required rate of return (k_s), and the expected growth rate of dividends (g), also affect multiples in relative valuation.

At the core of the relative valuation process is choosing comparable firms.[10] A **comparable firm** is one in the same business or sector with similar characteristics as the firm being valued. In selecting comparables, the analyst attempts to control for differences across firms, such as size. The analyst computes the multiple for each comparable firm and then averages them. Finally, the analyst compares the multiple of an individual firm to the average and attempts to explain any differences based on the firm's individual characteristics such as growth or risk. Suppose comparable firms have an average P/E of 20 but the firm's P/E is 12. If analysts cannot explain these differences by the fundamentals, they will consider the stock as cheap (undervalued) if the multiple is less than average or expensive (overvalued) if the multiple is more than the average. Below are several common relative valuation models.

---

[10] In contrast to the comparable firm approach, analysts can use multiple regression analysis using a cross-section of firms to predict various multiples such as P/E ratios.

Earnings multiplier model (P/E) *ratio*

The most commonly used multiple to estimate the value of common stock is the price-to-earnings (P/E) multiple. We show how to use the constant growth DDM to develop an earnings multiplier model for a stable firm and then explain the factors in the DDM that affect a stock's P/E ratio. Assume that intrinsic value (V_s) equals the market price (P_0). Thus, Equation 5.21 for the constant growth DDM becomes $P_0 = D_1/(k_s - g)$. Dividing both sides of the equation by next year's projected earnings (E_1) results in the P/E.

$$P/E = \frac{P_0}{E_1} = \frac{D_1/E_1}{k_s - g} \qquad (5.24)$$

where P_0 is the current stock price; and E_1 is the expected earnings per share during the next 12 months.

This equation shows that the determinants of the P/E ratio are the expected dividend payout ratio (D_1/E_1), the estimated required rate of return on the stock (k_s), and the expected growth rate of dividends for the stock (g). The P/E ratio is simply a restatement of the constant growth DDM. Thus, those factors that influence value using the DDM have the same effect on the P/E ratio.

The P/E ratio indicates how much the market is willing to pay for a dollar of expected earnings. Valuing a stock involves estimating an appropriate P/E for the industry, also called an **earnings multiple**, and then multiplying it by the firm's expected earnings per share (E_1). This popular valuation technique is the earnings multipler model. Analysts often use P/E multiples to value private or closely held corporations.

Problems with using P/E ratios include the potential manipulation of earnings, the effect of business cycles on the P/E ratio, and the possibility of negative earnings, making the P/E ratio not meaningful. Comparing P/E ratios across different markets, firms, and time is also inappropriate without controlling for differences in the underlying variables.

Example 5.21 *P/E* Multiple and Stock Price

A firm has an expected dividend payout ratio of 50 percent, an estimated required rate of return of 12 percent, and an expected dividend growth rate of 7 percent. What is the expected *P/E* ratio? If an investor expects next year's earnings to be $4.25, what is the value of the stock today?

Solution: Substituting $D_1/E_1 = 0.50$, $k_s = 0.12$, and $g = 0.07$ into Equation 5.24 results in an expected *P/E* ratio of:

$$\frac{P_0}{E_1} = \frac{0.50}{0.12 - 0.07} = 10$$

The estimated value of the stock is: $(E_1)(P_0/E_1) = (\$4.25)(10) = \$42.50$.

As before, the investor compares the estimated value of the stock to its current market price to determine whether to buy the stock.

Other price relatives

Another popular price relative is **price-to-cash flow ratio** (P/CF), which shows how much the market is willing to pay for a dollar of cash flow. Cash flows are typically more difficult to manipulate than earnings and are frequent inputs in valuation models.

$$P/CF = \frac{P_0}{CF_1} \tag{5.25}$$

where E_1 is the expected cash flow per share during the next 12 months.

The specific measure of cash flow may vary. Some analysts use earnings before interest, taxes, depreciation, and amortization (EBITDA), while others use operating cash flow or free cash flow. As with the P/E ratio, the P/CF ratio is not meaningful when cash flows are negative.

Another popular price relative is the **price-to-book value ratio** (P/BV), which shows how much the market is willing to pay for a dollar of equity. Book value equals the balance sheet value of equity, which can be estimated by subtracting the book value of liabilities from the book value of assets.

$$P/BV = \frac{P_0}{BV_1} \tag{5.26}$$

where BV_1 is the expected book value of equity per share at the end of the next period.

Book value has several advantages over other multiples. Unlike the P/E or P/CF ratio, the P/BV ratio is applicable when firms have negative earnings or cash flows. Under extreme circumstances, the book value of equity can become negative. In addition, book value provides a relatively stable, intuitive measure of value when applied to similar firms in the same industry. A limitation of this ratio is that accounting decisions on depreciation and other variables affect book values, as well as earnings. Another disadvantage is that book value is not very meaningful to service firms that do not have substantial fixed assets.

A final multiple is the **price-to-sales ratio** (P/S), which shows how much the market is willing to pay for a dollar of sales. In addition to the standard variables – the dividend payout ratio, the required rate of return, and the expected growth rate – profit margins also affect this multiple. The P/S ratio is an increasing function of the net profit margin, dividend payout ratio, and the growth rate, but a decreasing function of the riskiness of the firm. The key determinant of the P/S ratio is the profit margin.

$$P/S = \frac{P_0}{S_1} \tag{5.27}$$

where S_1 is the expected sales per share at the end of the next period.

The P/S ratio has several advantages over other multiples. First, unlike P/E and P/CF, the P/S multiple is usually positive, even for troubled firms. Second, P/S multiples are not as volatile as P/E multiples. Third, sales are more difficult to manipulate than P/E and

P/BV. A drawback of this multiple is its stability because revenues may not decline even though earnings and value may drop.

Practical Financial Tip 5.11

Directly comparing multiples can lead to erroneous conclusions without controlling for differences in fundamentals between the firm being valued and the comparable group. Usually, managers and analysts make adjustments subjectively to reflect differences.

Concept Check 5.10

1   What is the difference between an infinite-period and a finite-period dividend discount model?
2   What are two measures of cash flows used in valuation?
3   How do zero-growth, constant-growth, and variable models differ?
4   Why must the required rate of return be greater than the growth rate in the constant growth DDM?
5   How can changes in the relationship between the required rate of return and the growth rate affect the value of a stock?
6   What are the uses and limitations of the four price relatives?

Summary

This chapter focused on the valuation of financial assets, specifically bonds, preferred stock, and common stock. It also discussed the characteristics and features of these financial assets. The following summarizes key concepts covered in this chapter.

1   Valuation is the process of estimating the worth of an asset or a firm. Various ways exist to assess value, including going-concern value, liquidation value, book value, market value, and intrinsic value.
2   The two standard approaches to valuation are discounted cash flow (DCF) valuation and relative valuation.
    • *DCF valuation* estimates the intrinsic value of a financial asset as the expected future cash flow stream provided to the investor, discounted at a required rate of return appropriate for the risk involved.
    • *Relative valuation* estimates value by finding assets that are cheap or expensive by examining how the market currently prices "similar" assets.
3   The three key inputs to the valuation process are cash flows (returns), timing, and the required rate of return (risk).

4   The intrinsic value of a straight bond with a finite maturity is equal to the present value of the interest payments and principal payment at maturity, discounted at the investor's required rate of return.

5   Interest rates and bond prices move in opposite directions.

6   All other things being equal, the longer the remaining time to maturity and the lower the coupon rate, the greater the interest rate risk of the bond.

7   Three important yield measures are current yield, yield to maturity, and yield to call.

8   The intrinsic value of a preferred stock is equal to the stated annual dividend per share divided by the investor's required rate of return.

9   The intrinsic value of a share of common stock is the discounted value of all the cash flows, measured by dividends or free cash flow to equity.

10   Relative valuation multiples such as price-to-earnings, price-to-cash flow, price-to-book value, and price-to-sales are appropriate to consider when a good set of comparable entities is available and when serious under or overvaluation does not prevail in the market.

FURTHER READING

Copeland, Tom, Tim Koller, and Jack Murrin. *Valuation: Measuring and Managing the Value of Companies*, 3rd edn, John Wiley & Sons, Inc., 2001.

Damodaran, Aswath. *Damodaran on Valuation: Security Analysis for Investment and Corporate Finance*, John Wiley & Sons, Inc., 1994.

Damodaran, Aswath. *Investment Valuation: Tools and Techniques for Determining the Value of Any Asset*, John Wiley & Sons, Inc., 1996.

Daves, Phillip R., Michael C. Ehrhardt, and Ronald E. Shrieves. *Corporate Valuation: A Guide for Managers and Investors*, Thomson South-Western, 2004.

Fabozzi, Frank J. *Fixed Income Analysis for the Chartered Financial Analyst® Program*, Frank J. Fabozzi Associates, 2000.

Reilly, Frank K. and Keith C. Brown. *Investment Analysis and Portfolio Management*, 6th edn, Harcourt, Inc., 2000.

Stewart, G. Bennet, III. *The Question for Value*, HarperBusiness, 1991.

Woolridge, J. Randall, "Do Stock Prices Reflect Fundamental Values?" *Journal of Applied Corporate Finance* 8, 59–63.

PART II

Working Capital Management Decisions

Chapter 6

Working Capital Management

To maximize shareholder wealth, management should aim to set the level of the firm's cash holdings such that the marginal benefit of the incremental dollar of cash would equal the marginal cost of those holdings. There are two main benefits from holding liquid assets. First, it allows companies to avoid the transaction costs associated with raising funds or liquidating assets to make current payments. Second, the firm can use its liquid assets to finance its activities and investments when other sources of funding are not readily available or are excessively costly. (Tim Opler, Lee Pinkowitz, René Stulz, and Rohan Williamson, "Corporate Cash Holdings," *Journal of Applied Corporate Finance* 14, Spring 2001, p. 55.)

Overview

In this chapter, we focus on working capital management. We examine various approaches to managing working capital including the maturity-matching, conservative, and aggressive approaches. We also examine the importance of understanding the components of the firm's operating and cash conversion cycles. We then devote particular attention to the factors underlying a firm's cash conversion cycle including management of a firm's cash, accounts receivable, inventory, and payables. Part of short-term funds management includes short-term financing including such topics as trade credit, accruals, unsecured bank financing, commercial paper, accounts receivable financing, and inventory financing.

Learning Objectives

After completing this chapter, you should be able to:

- understand the importance of developing an effective working capital management policy that allows the firm to meet its short-term maturing obligations while avoiding excessive investments in short-term assets that lower the firm's profitability;
- describe the various philosophical approaches to managing working capital including the maturity-matching, conservative, and aggressive approaches;
- explain how to improve a firm's operating cycle and cash conversion cycle, knowing what factors comprise each;
- understand credit management and how to develop an optimal credit policy for a firm;
- apply the Baumol and Miller–Orr cash management models to estimate a firm's optimal level of cash;
- explain the importance of properly managing net float;
- understand how to monitor a firm's accounts receivable by preparing an aging schedule and computing the average age of accounts receivable;
- describe five factors that firms use to evaluate a customer's credit and how to establish an optimal credit policy;
- differentiate among the ABC, EOQ, and just-in-time inventory management systems.

6.1 Introduction to Working Capital Management

Working capital management is the administration of the firm's current assets and current liabilities. **Gross working capital** refers to a firm's current assets used in operations, including cash and marketable securities, accounts receivable, and inventory. **Net working capital** is current assets minus current liabilities. An effective working capital management policy requires that managers find appropriate investment levels of cash, marketable securities, receivables, and inventories and the appropriate level and mix of short-term financing.

Effective working capital management is important for several reasons. First, many financial managers spend a large amount of time managing current assets and current liabilities. With current assets and current liabilities comprising about 40 percent and 26 percent of the total assets of US manufacturing firms, respectively, skillful management of these short-term accounts is critical for ensuring that the firm can meet its short-term maturing obligations and provide an attractive return to its shareholders. Second, working capital assets and liabilities are the most manageable accounts and thus require frequent attention and oversight. Third, current liabilities serve as the major source of external financing for small companies.

Managers need to understand how to develop effective working capital policies to ensure growth, profitability, and long-term success for their firms. Firms experiencing rapid growth may easily fall into a growth trap with insufficient levels of current assets to support increasingly higher levels of sales. In such cases, a firm may go broke while making a profit. Small but rapidly growing firms must pay particular attention to maintaining sufficient liquidity through their working capital policies and management.

Financial managers should strive to maximize firm value by managing current assets and current liabilities in a way that balances profitability and risk. This goal involves determining both the optimal level of investment in current assets and the appropriate mix of financing sources to support the required investment in current assets. A firm needs a sufficient level of current assets (cash and marketable securities, accounts receivable, and inventory) to ensure timely payment of current liabilities (accruals, accounts payable, and notes payable). Excessive investments in current assets may diminish profitability and lower firm value. Short-term assets typically offer low returns to the firm but if managed inappropriately can have high opportunity costs. For example, while holding high inventory levels requires a firm to invest cash in assets that provide little or no return, the lost sales from inventory stockouts resulting from insufficient inventory levels can lead to sharp declines in sales and profits. Thus, determining the firm's optimal investment in working capital involves a tradeoff between liquidity and profitability. Financial managers should minimize the costs associated with working capital without jeopardizing the liquidity needed for continuing operations.

Practical Financial Tip 6.1

In managing working capital, two key tradeoffs exist. First, *profitability varies inversely with liquidity*. By increasing the level of investment in current assets, managers increase the liquidity of the firm but lower potential profitability as measured by return on investment (ROI = Net profit/total assets). On the other hand, *profitability moves together with risk*. By not maintaining sufficient current assets, the firm runs the risk of being unable to meet financial obligations when they come due, forgoing customers due to restrictive credit policies, and losing sales resulting from stockouts. The optimal level of current assets depends on management's attitudes toward these tradeoffs.

Concept Check 6.1

1   What is the meaning of the terms *working capital management, gross working capital*, and *net working capital*?
2   What is the tradeoff between profitability and liquidity and profitability and risk in working capital management?

6.2 Approaches to Working Capital Management

In the last section, we discussed the tradeoff that managers face in their working capital management decisions. Managers must maintain sufficient liquidity to ensure the firm can meet its maturing short-term obligations. On the other hand, excessive investment in current assets enhances liquidity but lowers profitability and reduces shareholder wealth. Managers have different philosophies or approaches for handling this risk-return relationship in working capital management. A **relaxed** or **conservative approach** is one that relies on greater levels of current assets; a **restricted** or **aggressive approach** relies much less heavily on investments in cash, marketable securities, and inventories. A **moderate approach** falls between these two. Figure 6.1 illustrates these three approaches.

Working capital management approaches also vary in terms of how the firm finances seasonal variations in current assets. Three common approaches include the maturity-matching approach, the conservative approach, and the aggressive approach. If sales were constant throughout the year, a firm's investment in current (operating) assets would be constant and the firm would only have a permanent funding requirement. With cyclical sales, however, current assets vary with the sales cycle, and the firm has both seasonal and permanent funding requirements. The maturity-matching, conservative, and aggressive approaches represent different philosophies about how to finance the seasonal variations in current assets. We discuss each approach below.

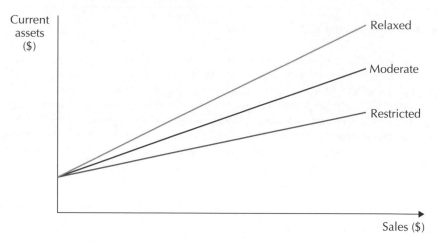

Figure 6.1 Approaches to working capital management

Maturity-matching Approach

As its name suggests, the **maturity-matching approach** involves hedging risk by matching the maturities of a firm's assets and liabilities. Under this approach, the firm finances long-term assets (fixed assets and permanent current assets) with long-term financing sources (long-term debt and equity). The firm finances seasonal variations in its current assets with current liabilities that have the same maturity. By matching the level of short-term financing to the level of temporary current assets, the firm hedges against unexpected changes in short-term interest rates. Any increases (decreases) in short-term interest rates that raise (lower) the cost of short-term financing will be offset by increases (decreases) in the return earned on an equal amount of short-term current assets. Figure 6.2 illustrates the maturity-matching approach.

Conservative Approach

Under the **conservative approach** for managing working capital, the firm uses long-term funds to finance its long-term assets, all permanent current assets, and some temporary current assets. Thus, the firm uses short-term financing for only some of the temporary current assets. Why is this a conservative approach? Short-term funds are usually less expensive than long-term funds because the yield curve is typically upward sloping. Thus, when the firm uses more long-term funds, it can lock in its cost of funds and avoid increases in short-term rates. In addition, by locking in more long-term sources of financing, the firm protects itself against the risk of a credit shutoff if either general economic conditions or the company's financial condition worsens.

Figure 6.3 depicts the conservative approach. An important point to note is that when the need for temporary current assets is low, the firm's long-term financing will exceed its total assets. During such periods, the company will invest excess funds in marketable securities.

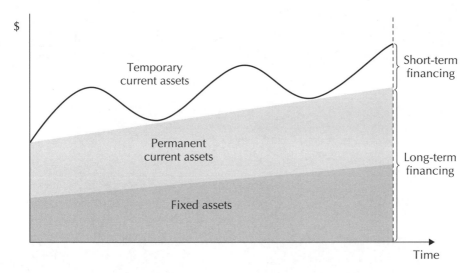

Figure 6.2 Maturity-matching approach for managing working capital

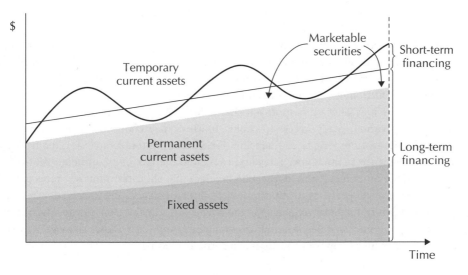

Figure 6.3 Conservative approach for managing working capital

Aggressive Approach

The **aggressive approach** for managing working capital involves using more short-term financing and less long-term financing than in the maturity-matching and conservative approaches. As shown in Figure 6.4, the firm uses short-term financing for all temporary current assets and for some of its permanent current assets. This approach is aggressive in

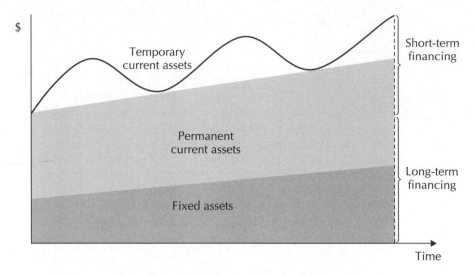

Figure 6.4 Aggressive approach for managing working capital

the sense that the firm will be less than hedged against changes in short-term interest rates. By financing some of its permanent current assets with short-term financial instruments, the firm will face an increased cost of financing if short-term interest rates rise. Of course, the firm would benefit from any declines in short-term rates.

Several factors may affect the approach that a firm chooses for managing its working capital. A firm without ready access to capital markets may choose the conservative approach and employ more long-term financing. If short-term interest rates rise, the firm will have less to refinance at the higher rates and can avoid the risk of credit being shut off by suppliers. On the other hand, a manager who believes that short-term interest rates will fall may be tempted to adopt the aggressive approach. If the manager's prediction is correct, the firm will have more funds to refinance at the lower rates in the near future. By hedging against changes in interest rates, the maturity-matching approach allows managers to concentrate on other more important value-maximizing decisions.

Concept Check 6.2

1   What are the similarities and differences among the maturity-matching, conservative, and aggressive approaches for managing working capital?
2   How would an increase in short-term interest rates affect a firm under the conservative, maturity-matching, and aggressive approaches to managing working capital?

6.3 Operating and Cash Conversion Cycles

Manufacturing firms must pay close attention to the timing of cash inflows and cash outflows. Over a typical manufacturing cycle, a firm purchases inventory and subsequently pays for it, hires and pays workers, sells finished products, and collects payment from its customers. To manage cash flows during this period, managers often focus on the firm's operating cycle and its cash conversion cycle. The **operating cycle** is the length of time it takes to acquire inventory, sell it, and collect cash from the sale. Thus, it is the period between the acquisition of the inventory and the collection of cash from accounts receivable. Computing the operating cycle involves adding a firm's receivables collection period and its inventory processing period.[1]

$$
\begin{matrix} \text{Operating} \\ \text{cycle} \end{matrix} = \left(\begin{matrix} \text{Receivables} \\ \text{collection period} \end{matrix} \right) + \left(\begin{matrix} \text{Inventory} \\ \text{processing period} \end{matrix} \right) \qquad (6.1)
$$

As defined earlier in Chapter 3, the **average receivables collection period** is the length of time needed for a firm to collect cash from a credit sale. The **average inventory processing period** is the length of time needed for a firm to acquire and then sell inventory.

The **cash conversion cycle** is the length of time the firm has cash tied up in current assets. It is the number of days between receiving cash from the sale of its products and expending cash on productive resources (materials and labor). If a firm creates accounts payable by deferring cash payment for the inventory and labor in producing finished goods, its cash conversion cycle will be less than the firm's operating cycle. Computing a firm's cash conversion cycle entails summing its average receivable collection period and average inventory processing period and subtracting its accounts payable payment period.

$$
\begin{matrix} \text{Cash} \\ \text{conversion} \\ \text{cycle} \end{matrix} = \left(\begin{matrix} \text{Receivables} \\ \text{collection period} \end{matrix} \right) + \left(\begin{matrix} \text{Inventory} \\ \text{processing period} \end{matrix} \right) - \left(\begin{matrix} \text{Accounts payable} \\ \text{payment period} \end{matrix} \right) \qquad (6.2)
$$

The **accounts payable payment period** is the average length of time between the purchase of materials and labor that go into inventory and the payment of cash for these expenses. Managers can reduce their firm's cash conversion cycle and free up cash for other activities by collecting receivables more promptly, reducing the inventory processing time, or lengthening the time taken to pay suppliers.

We show the operating cycle and cash conversion cycle for a firm whose receivables collection period is 30 days, inventory processing period is 45 days, and accounts payable payment period is 20 days. The firm's operating cycle is 75 days (30 + 45) and its cash conversion cycle is 55 days (30 + 45 − 20).

---

[1]   We discussed how to compute these ratios in Chapter 3.

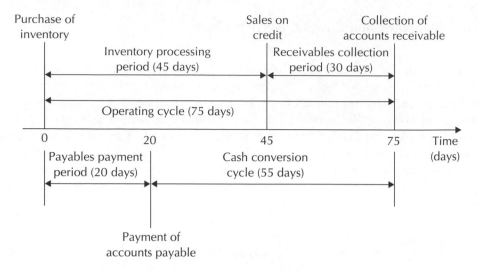

Given the above data, the manager knows when the firm starts producing finished goods that it will have to finance its outlays for a 55-day period. The firm ties up cash for 75 days when it holds inventory and later collects the receivables generated from the credit sale of finished goods, but it also conserves cash for the 20 days required to pay for materials and labor.

We take a closer look at the components of the cash conversion cycle in the following sections. In Section 6.4 we examine cash management and find how these factors affect the net float of a firm. In Sections 6.5 and 6.6, we examine issues involving both inventory and accounts receivable management.

Practical Financial Tip 6.2

A firm's cash conversion cycle is the length of time that a firm has cash tied up in its business operations. Tying up cash in operations represents a cost to the firm as it must either raise funds in the capital markets to finance this use of cash or use internally generated cash that could otherwise be invested to earn a return. Managers can reduce their firm's cash conversion cycle and free up cash for other activities by collecting receivables more promptly, reducing the inventory processing time, or lengthening the time taken to pay suppliers.

Concept Check 6.3

1   What is a firm's operating cycle? How is it calculated?
2   What is a firm's cash conversion cycle? How is it calculated?
3   How can a manager lower a firm's cash conversion cycle?

6.4 Cash Management

In this section we examine financial policies and decisions for managing a firm's cash and marketable securities. **Cash** is the currency and coin the firm keeps on hand in cash registers, petty cash drawers, or in checking accounts at commercial banks. **Marketable securities** are short-term investments in securities that the firm can quickly convert into cash. Because of their strong liquidity, marketable securities are often referred to as **near cash** or **near-cash assets**. Cash and near-cash assets comprise the **liquid assets** of a firm.

The objective in cash management is to keep the investment in cash as low as possible while maintaining the firm's efficient operations. To accomplish this objective, managers must determine the target cash balance required to maintain liquidity while minimizing the total costs related to the investment in cash. Cash management involves three major decision areas:

1   Determining appropriate cash balances.
2   Investing idle cash.
3   Managing collections and disbursements.

We investigate each of these areas below.

Cash management is a sophisticated and important aspect of working capital management. When we refer to cash management in this section, we are referring to the management of cash and marketable securities. We begin by discussing reasons firms hold cash. In his classic work, *The General Theory of Employment, Interest, and Money*, John Maynard Keynes identified three motives for holding cash: the speculative motive, the precautionary motive, and the transactions motive.

- Firms have a **speculative motive** to hold cash so that they can take advantage of bargain purchases that may arise, attractive interest rates, and favorable exchange rate fluctuations. Firms do not need to actually hold cash to meet the speculative demand for money. They can usually satisfy the speculative motive for holding cash through using reserve borrowing ability and marketable securities. This is similar to using credit cards instead of cash to make purchases.
- The **precautionary motive** for holding cash arises from the need for a safety supply of cash to act as a financial reserve. While a precautionary need for maintaining liquidity probably exists, given that the value of money market instruments is relatively certain and liquid, substantial cash holdings to satisfy the precautionary are generally unnecessary.
- Firms also have a **transactions motive** for holding cash. That is, firms need cash on hand to pay wages, trade debts, taxes, and dividends. They collect cash from product sales, asset sales, and new financing. Firms need a level of cash holdings because cash inflows and cash outflows are not perfectly synchronized. The advent of electronic funds transfers and other high-speed paperless payment methods has greatly reduced the transaction demand for cash.

Firms also hold cash as **compensating balances** at commercial banks to compensate for banking services the firm receives. Such a compensating balance requirement requires a firm to hold a minimum level of cash.

In the following sections, we discuss models for estimating the optimal cash balance level for a firm, including the Baumol and the Miller–Orr cash management models. These classic models find optimal cash balances by taking into consideration the opportunity cost of holding cash and the transactions costs incurred when selling marketable securities to increase cash balances. The **opportunity cost of holding cash** refers to the return the firm could earn if it invested the cash in marketable securities instead of holding cash. When the firm sells marketable securities, it incurs transactions costs that primarily include fees paid to brokerage firms who conduct the sales transaction.

Determining Appropriate Cash Balances

This decision involves determining the minimum levels of cash that the firm needs to provide liquidity while minimizing the total costs of holding an investment in cash. We examine two models available for determining the firm's optimal cash balances – the Baumol and the Miller–Orr cash management models.

The Baumol cash management model

The **Baumol cash management model** is a method used to determine a firm's optimal cash balance level assuming that cash disbursements are spread evenly over time, the opportunity cost of holding cash is constant, and the company pays a fixed transactions cost each time it converts securities to cash. Another assumption of the model is that a firm can predict its future cash requirements with certainty. The cash balances over time under the Baumol model will follow a saw-tooth pattern as depicted in Figure 6.5.

When cash balances in the firm's checking account reach zero, the firm sells C dollars worth of marketable securities and deposits the funds in its checking account. Cash balances

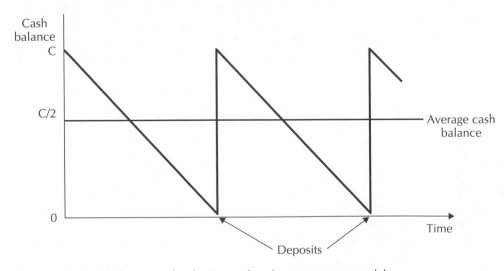

Figure 6.5 Cash balances under the Baumol cash management model

then decrease uniformly to zero as the firm spends cash and the process repeats itself. Holding cash balances has an opportunity cost that is equal to $i(C/2)$ where i is the interest rate that represents the opportunity cost of funds and $C/2$ is the average cash balance over time. The firm also incurs a transaction cost when it sells marketable securities. If the firm needs to deposit a total of T dollars in its checking account each year, and each deposit is for C dollars, the total number of deposits will be T/C. If the firm incurs a fixed transactions cost of b dollars per transaction, the annual transactions cost will be bT/C.

The total costs of cash balances consist of transactions costs plus opportunity costs.

$$\textbf{\textit{Total costs = Transactions costs + Opportunity costs}} = b\left(\frac{T}{C}\right) + i\left(\frac{C}{2}\right) \qquad (6.3)$$

where T is the total amount the firm must deposit in its checking account in a year in dollars; C is the size of each deposit, in dollars; b is the fixed cost of each transaction, in dollars; and i is the interest rate per period that the firm could earn on investments.

The firm should choose a deposit size (C) that minimizes total costs. Equation 6.4 is the formula for computing the optimal deposit size (C^*).

$$C^* = \sqrt{\frac{2bT}{i}} \qquad (6.4)$$

Equation 6.4 shows that for a given level of total cash needed in a year, the optimal deposit size increases with the size of the fixed transaction amount (b) and decreases with the opportunity cost of funds (i). Figure 6.6 shows this tradeoff and the optimal deposit amount.

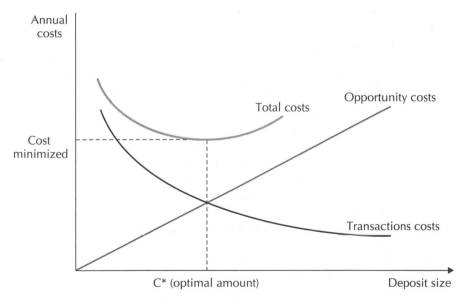

Figure 6.6 Annual costs in the Baumol model

Example 6.1 Calculating the Optimal Deposit

Sinefeld Products Incorporated needs $20 million in cash next year. The firm expects to earn 8 percent next year on the funds it invests in marketable securities. Sinefeld incurs a cost of $320 per transaction when it sells marketable securities. What are the optimal deposit size and the total annual costs?

Solution: From Equation 6.4, we find the optimal deposit size to be $400,000.

$$C^* = \sqrt{\frac{2bT}{i}} = \sqrt{\frac{2(\$320)(\$20,000,000)}{0.08}} = \$400,000$$

Using Equation 6.3, the total annual costs are $32,000.

$$\text{Total cost} = b\left(\frac{T}{C}\right) + i\left(\frac{C}{2}\right) = \$320\left(\frac{\$20,000,000}{\$400,000}\right) + 0.08\left(\frac{\$400,000}{2}\right) = \$32,000$$

The subparts in Equations 6.3 and 6.4 yield additional useful information:

- Sinefeld will have an average cash balance of $200,000.
- The total annual costs of $32,000 consist of $16,000 in transactions costs and $16,000 in opportunity costs.
- Sinefeld will make 50 deposits per year (T/C) of $400,000 each.

This relatively simplistic model assumes that the company can predict future cash inflows and outflows with certainty, cash disbursements are spread evenly over time, and interest rates are constant. Moreover, the Baumol model ignores seasonal or cyclical trends.

The Miller–Orr Cash Management Model

Instead of assuming cash balances decline uniformly over time, the **Miller–Orr cash management model** assumes that daily cash flows fluctuate randomly from day to day. Thus, this probabilistic model incorporates the uncertainty of future cash flows. Managers specify a target cash level and two control limits.

- The *lower control limit* (LCL), which management sets, may represent either a safety stock level of cash for the firm or a required compensating balance.
- The *upper control limit* (UCL) is set at 3Z above the LCL.
- The *target level* cash amount (C*) is set at a level of Z above LCL. It is the target level of cash the company returns to when cash balances reach either control limit.

As illustrated in Figure 6.7, when the cash balances fall to LCL, the firm sells Z dollars of marketable securities to replenish funds in the firm's checking account. This brings the cash balances back to the target level, C*. When the cash balances rise to UCL, the firm buys 2Z

Cash balance

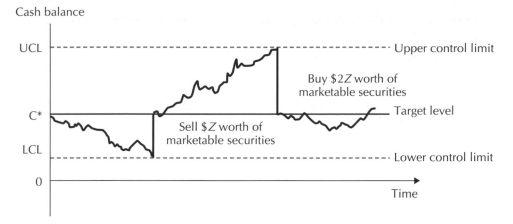

Figure 6.7 Miller–Orr cash management model

dollars worth of marketable securities with funds from its checking account. Again, the cash balances are restored to the target level, C^*. As long as the level of cash balances remains between LCL and UCL, nothing happens.

Managers also need to estimate the variance of the net cash flow per period (σ^2), the cost per transaction (b), and the interest rate per period (i). **Variance** is a statistical term used to measure the volatility of a variable. In finance, higher volatility generally reflects greater uncertainty of a future and hence greater risk.[2] The variance and the interest rate used in the model should be based on the same period of time such as a day or a week.

We can determine the target level of cash (C^*) in the Miller–Orr model by determining Z.

$$Z = \left(\frac{3b\sigma^2}{4i} \right)^{1/3} \tag{6.5}$$

where Z is the amount of cash obtained from selling marketable securities, which are then deposited in the firm's checking account; b is the cost per transaction; σ^2 is the variance of the net cash flow per period; and i is the interest rate per period the firm can earn on investments in marketable securities.

The target level of cash (C^*), upper control limit (UCL), and the average cash balance (ACB) are then computed:

$$C^* = LCL + Z \tag{6.6a}$$

$$UCL = LCL + 3Z \tag{6.6b}$$

$$ACB = LCL + (4/3)Z \tag{6.6c}$$

---

[2] Any basic statistics book contains the formula for computing variance. The more commonly used standard deviation is equal to the square root of the variance.

Example 6.2 Calculating the Optimal Cash Level with the Miller–Orr Model

Kostanza Company has established a lower control limit (LCL) of $150,000 on its cash balances. The firm incurs transactions costs for buying or selling marketable securities of $125. Management estimates the standard deviation of its daily cash flows is $50,000 per day. Assume the opportunity cost of funds is 8 percent. Use the Miller–Orr model to determine the target level of cash (C*), the upper control limit (UCL), and the average cash balance.

Solution: First, we compute Z using Equation 6.5.

$$Z = \left(\frac{3b\sigma^2}{4i}\right)^{1/3} = \left(\frac{3(\$125)(\$50,000)^2}{4(.08/365)}\right)^{1/3} = \$102,260$$

The target level of cash (C*), the upper control limit (UCL), and the average cash balance (ACB) are then computed using Equations 6.6a, 6.6b, and 6.6c, respectively.

$C^* = \$150,000 + \$102,260 = \$252,260$

$UCL = \$150,000 + 3(\$102,260) = \$456,780$

$ACB = \$150,000 + (4/3)(\$102,260) = \$286,347$

Factors other than those considered in the Baumol and Miller–Orr models may also affect a firm's optimal level of cash balances.

- If the firm has a compensating balance requirement, its average cash balance is the greater of the balance needed for transactions and the compensating balance amount.
- A firm's optimal level of marketable securities can be determined by subtracting the cash balances from the total liquidity amount desired. Some firms, however, hold large portfolios of marketable securities that exceed what they need for liquidity purposes. Others with foreign operations invest cash in marketable securities abroad to avoid paying US income taxes on the amount earned.

Focus on Practice 6.1

Do Firms with Large Cash Holdings Underperform?

A recent study by Mikkelson and Partch finds that firms with persistently high levels of cash holdings have operating performances that are comparable to or greater than the performance of similar firms matched by size and industry. They find that these firms also undertake higher levels of investment, especially in R&D, and tend to grow faster than their counterparts. Thus, they find no evidence that the operating performance of these firms suffers from such financial conservatism.

Source: Wayne H. Mikkelson and M. Megan Partch, "Do Persistent Large Cash Reserves Hinder Performance?" *Journal of Financial and Quantitative Analysis* 38, June 2003, pp. 275–93.

Investing Idle Cash

Another decision area in cash management involves developing strategies for managing marketable securities and selecting appropriate short-term investment instruments. Firms typically invest temporary surplus cash in short-term marketable securities. Why do firms have temporary idle cash? First, many firms have a predictable cash flow pattern with seasonal or cyclical variations. For example, sales revenue for many retail firms is concentrated during the year-end holiday season. Such firms may experience cash shortages in late summer and early fall as they begin to stock up for holiday sales but cash surpluses in the first few months of the year. Firms typically borrow short-term to fund the shortages and invest cash surpluses in short-term marketable securities.

Firms may also invest temporary excess cash in marketable securities to fund planned future investments for plant expansion, dividend payments, stock repurchases, bond retirement, or other large expenditures. When firms issue bonds or common stock before they actually need cash, they typically invest the proceeds in short-term marketable securities and sell the securities when they need cash for various expenditures.

When investing excess cash, firms often consider several important factors when choosing among the variety of short-term securities available. These factors include marketability, maturity, default risk, and taxes.

- **Marketability** is the ease of converting an asset or security to cash with minimum possible loss. Money market instruments vary in terms of marketability with US Treasury bills being among the most marketable (liquid).
- **Maturity** is the length of time remaining before the issuer repays the security. As we discussed in Chapter 5, securities with longer maturities have greater interest rate risk. That is, their prices are more sensitive to changes in interest rates. Many firms do not invest in securities with maturities greater than 90 days to avoid substantial price declines if interest rates increase.
- **Default risk** is the probability that the lender will not make full interest and principal payments when due. Firms typically invest temporary idle cash only in short-term securities that have negligible default risk. Various reporting agencies such as Standard & Poor's (S&P) and Moody's Investors Service publish ratings of numerous corporate and other publicly held securities to help investors assess the default risk associated with the investment.
- **Taxes** refer to the amount of taxes that the holder pays, if any, on short-term securities. Money market securities vary in their tax status. US Treasury bills are exempt from state taxes while municipal securities are exempt from federal taxes. The interest earned on other money market securities is taxed at the federal, state, and local levels.

Focus on Practice 6.2

Cash Burn

The financial press now commonly reports the *cash burn* rate for many financially distressed firms. *Cash burn* occurs when a firm is consuming more cash than it is generating; it refers to the rate at which a firm is depleting its cash balances. A frequent use of the term applies to the Internet and technology firms that gained prominence in the latter part of the 1990s. One reporter commented "It was easy to ignore the unsustainable cash burn rate of . . . dot coms when their stock prices sat in the nosebleed section . . . And loss-based business models are no longer the investor magnets they used to be. So what, exactly, are these companies planning to do?" Evidence suggests corporate liquidity of the largest 1,000 nonfinancial US companies has deteriorated. Managers and analysts should pay close attention to a firm's cash flow from operations to understand a firm's financial condition and to determine whether cash burn seriously affects the firm.

Sources: Kris Frieswick, "Cash Burn Marks," *CFO Magazine*, June 1, 2000, and Mara Der Hovanesian, "Cash: Burn, Baby, Burn," *Business Week*, April 21, 2003.

Types of money market securities

Firms generally invest any temporary surplus cash in **money market securities**, which are short-term securities that are highly marketable with a low risk of default. The most common money market securities include US Treasury bills, tax exempt instruments, certificates of deposit, commercial paper, and repurchase agreements. We briefly discuss each below.

- **US Treasury bills** are short-term debt obligations of the US government with initial maturities of 30, 90, or 180 days. Treasury bills sell at a discount to par value and do not make coupon interest payments. Thus, the interest is implied from the price increase to par value over the life of the security. Treasury bills are issued at auctions every week.
- **Short-term tax exempt instruments** are short-term debt securities issued by states, municipalities, local housing agencies, and urban renewal agencies. These securities are attractive to many investors because they are exempt from federal taxes. Examples include RANS (revenue anticipation notes), BANS (bond anticipation notes), and TANS (tax anticipation notes).
- **Commercial paper** is unsecured short-term debt obligations issued by corporations, banks, and finance companies with maturities ranging from a few days to 270 days. Usually, issuers sell commercial paper in multiples of $100,000. Default risk depends on the quality of the issue. S&P and Moody's publish quality ratings for commercial paper. The marketability of commercial paper can be low because it has no active secondary market.
- **Negotiable certificates of deposit** (CDs) are short-term loans to commercial banks with denominations of $100,000 or more. Unlike other money market securities, CDs do not sell at a discount to par value. Yields on negotiable CDs are slightly above T-bills and commercial paper because negotiable CDs contain some default risk. Active secondary markets exist for CDs with maturities of 3, 6, 9, and 12 months. Thus, holders can easily resell negotiable CDs before maturity.

- **Bankers' acceptances** are drafts (orders to pay) drawn on a bank by an exporter in order to obtain payment for goods they have shipped to a customer who has an account at that bank. Maturities typically range from a few days to 9 months. Denomination sizes depend on the amount of the export payment, but often range from $25,000 to $1 million. Like Treasury bills, they sell at a discount to par value and trade in a secondary market.
- **Repurchase agreement (repo)** is an agreement between a seller and a buyer, usually of US government securities, in which the seller agrees to repurchase the securities at an agreed upon price at a stated time. Maturities are short, usually overnight or just a few days. There are no standard denominations of repos. A common type of repo is created when an investor buys Treasury securities from a bond dealer with the simultaneous agreement to sell them back later at an agreed upon price. These agreements have little risk because of their short maturity and the promise of the borrower to repurchase the securities at a fixed price.

Managing Collections and Disbursements

A third decision area of cash management involves minimizing cash balances by accelerating receipts and slowing disbursements. Managing collections and disbursements requires a thorough understanding of float. **Float** is the amount of money represented by checks outstanding and in the process of collection. Float arises from a delay in the payment system. The three principal sources of delay are:

1 **mail float**: the time when a check is in the mail;
2 **processing float**: the time required to process a check after it is received; and
3 **clearing time float**: the time required for a check to clear through the banking system and to reduce the paying firm's account.

Paying firms have an incentive to delay in all three areas, while *receiving* firms want to speed up the process. There are two major types of float – **disbursement (positive) float** and **collection (negative) float**.

Disbursement float
Suppose a firm writes a $100,000 check to pay a supplier. After writing and mailing the check, the company immediately adjusts its ledgers to reflect a $100,000 reduction in its cash balance. The firm's checking account balance, however, will not decline until the supplier deposits the check at its own bank and that bank presents the check to the other firm's bank for payment. The extra $100,000 that remains in the firm's checking account after the firm has written and mailed a check and reduced its cash balance by that amount is called **disbursement** or **payment float**. Effective cash management tries to increase disbursement float by slowing disbursements.

Collection float
The float process described above also works in reverse. Suppose a firm receives a $60,000 check from a customer. While both the firm and its bank increase the ledger balance by the $60,000 amount, the money is unavailable to the firm immediately. The firm's bank will not receive payment from the customer's bank for one or two days. In the meantime, the firm's

bank will not include the $60,000 in the firm's available balance, but will show a **collection** or **availability float** of $60,000.

Net float is the difference between the disbursement float and the collection float.

$$\text{Net float} = \text{Disbursement float} - \text{Collection float} \tag{6.7}$$

Net float represents cash available to the firm that is not reported in the firm's ledger. The above firm would have a net float of $100,000 − $60,000 = $40,000.

Effective cash management tries to reduce collection float by accelerating collections. Equation 6.8 shows how to calculate the pretax benefit from reducing collection float.

$$\frac{\text{Pretax benefit from}}{\text{reducing collection float}} = \frac{\text{Days reduction in float time} \times}{\text{Average daily collections} \times \text{Expected return}} \tag{6.8}$$

Example 6.3 Benefit from Reducing Collection Float

Suppose a large firm has average daily collections of $10 million. If the firm could speed up its collections by one day, and could earn 0.015 percent per day on the investment of these funds, what would be the annual pre-tax benefit of reducing collection float?

Solution: Using Equation 6.8, the daily increase in earnings would be:

$$\text{Pretax benefit from reducing collection float} = 1 \times \$10,000,000 \times 0.00015$$
$$= \$1,500 \text{ per day}$$

If the firm can permanently increase its collections by one day, the present value of the perpetuity of extra interest income would be $1,500/0.00015 = $10 million.

Practical Financial Tip 6.3

If a firm manages its net float effectively, it can reduce its cash balances and keep more funds invested in interest-earning accounts or securities. Managers who do this are *playing the float*. Firms benefit when the net float increases through an increase in the disbursement float or a decrease in the collection float.

Accelerating collections

The objective of accelerating collections is to increase the speed of payment receipt without incurring excessive costs. By speeding up collections, the firm can free cash to reduce its total financing requirement. Receiving firms use various methods to speed up collections. We focus on two methods: using a lockbox system and concentration banking.

- *Use a lockbox system.* Many firms speed up collections by using lockboxes. Under a **lockbox system**, customers send incoming checks to a special post office box that a local bank maintains. For example, a firm with headquarters in Phoenix might have its east coast customers send their payments to a post office box in Philadelphia and its customers in the Midwest to a box in Chicago. A local bank collects the checks sent to a lockbox several times per day and deposits the checks directly into the firm's account. Thus, the purpose of a lockbox collection system is to eliminate processing float. In addition, a lockbox system can reduce the firm's internal processing costs because the bank handles the clerical work for a fee. A local bank typically provides a daily record of the receipts electronically in a format that easily facilitates updating the firm's accounts receivable records.
- *Use concentration banking.* Firms can also speed up collections by using **concentration banking**. The firm's customers make payments at a firm's regional offices rather than its corporate headquarters. The regional offices then deposit the checks into their local bank accounts. The firm periodically transfers surplus funds from the regional banks to a *concentration account* at one of the company's *concentration banks*. Thus, the purpose of concentration banking is to accelerate the flow of funds by instructing customers to remit payments to strategic collection centers.

Firms use several methods to transfer funds to a concentration bank. A **depository transfer check** (DTC) is a preprinted check that needs no signature and is only valid for transferring funds between specific accounts within a firm. Money becomes available to the firm within one or two days. Another method is to use electronic **automated clearinghouse** (ACH) transfers. While ACH transfers are slightly more expensive than DTCs, the funds are available to the firm the next day. A third method is to use **wire transfers**. Wire transfers are the most expensive means to transfer funds, but the funds become available the same day. The method of choice for transferring funds usually depends on the number and size of the transfers. Firms employ the less expensive DTC and ACH methods for transferring relatively small amounts from various local banks to the concentration banks. Firms typically reserve wire transfers for large amounts given their higher expense.

Slowing disbursements

Another way that firms can reduce their net float is by properly managing and controlling their cash disbursements. The objective of slowing disbursement is to delay paying suppliers and other creditors without jeopardizing the firm's credit standing or incurring any finance charges. Let's look at several ways to delay disbursements.

- *Centralize payables.* Firms can gain better control over their disbursements by centralizing their payables into a single or small number of accounts, usually maintained at the company's headquarters. Firms can maximize their use of cash by sending payments at the end of any cash discount periods or the final due date if no cash discount is available.
- *Use drafts to pay bills.* A firm can delay payments by using **payable through drafts** (PTDs). Unlike checks, the PTD is not payable on demand. Instead, the bank must present the PTD to the issuing firm for collection. Thus, the firm can delay depositing the necessary funds to cover checks until that holder presents the check to its bank. Thus, the firm can

keep smaller cash balances on hand. Firms must pay higher service charges to use PTDs than normal checks. Furthermore, many suppliers will prefer ordinary checks in order to receive funds more quickly and reduce their own net float.

- *Establish a zero balance system.* Firms can use a **zero balance account (ZBA) system** with their bank. Under a ZBA system, one master disbursement account services multiple subsidiary accounts. Subsidiary accounts are separate accounts set up for payroll, payables, and other purposes. Each day, the bank automatically transfers enough funds from the master disbursement account to the subsidiary accounts to cover all checks that holders presented to that bank on that day. Idle cash is eliminated from subsidiary accounts as a zero balance is maintained in each subsidiary account. Only the master account maintains a cash balance.

Electronic Data Interchange

An increasing number of firms use **electronic data interchange** (EDI) to process their business transactions. EDI is simply the exchange of information electronically via computer in a structured format. Using EDI can save time for a firm as well as lower its personnel costs, material costs, and costs due to errors by eliminating paper documents and mail delivery. EDI savings are so substantial that some firms charge a fee for using paper documents.

EDI is revolutionizing the way firms conduct business. Innovations will continue to affect how firms manage their working capital. Examples include electronic funds transfer and financial electronic data interchange. **Electronic funds transfer** (EFT) involves the transfer of money electronically between banks. **Financial electronic data interchange** (FEDI) involves the exchange of information between a bank and its customers regarding account balances, checks paid, and lockbox information. These types of electronic methods for transferring data serve to increase the availability and lower the cost of information.

Concept Check 6.4

1   What are three major decision areas involving cash management?
2   Why do firms hold cash balances?
3   How does the Baumol cash management model differ from the Miller–Orr cash management model?
4   What are compensating balances and how do they affect a firm's cash balances?
5   What are five different types of marketable securities?
6   What is the meaning of the terms *disbursement float, collection float,* and *net float*? Does a firm benefit from an increase or decrease in its net float?
7   How does a lockbox system speed up a firm's collections?
8   What are three advantages of using electronic funds transfers?
9   How can a firm use payable through drafts and zero balance accounts to control disbursements?
10   What is electronic data interchange (EDI)? How does EDI affect the way in which firms manage their working capital?

6.5 Accounts Receivable Management

Many firms sell goods or provide services on a credit basis. Although firms grant credit to stimulate sales, they also incur costs when granting credit. One cost is the bad debt expense that the firm incurs if the customer does not pay. Another cost of granting credit involves the interim financing needed until the customer pays the account. As we discuss later in this section, firms should grant credit as long as the net cash flows (profits) from additional sales exceed the cost of carrying the receivables.

Firms generate accounts receivable when they sell goods or provide services on credit. **Trade credit** is credit granted to other firms; **consumer credit** is credit granted to consumers. Effective management of a firm's accounts receivable is important because such receivables account for about one-sixth of the assets of US industrial firms. In this section, we consider many important aspects of accounts receivable management including the five Cs of credit, sources of credit information, credit scoring, collection policy, and optimal credit policy.

Five Cs of Credit

Credit analysts generally consider five factors when determining whether to grant credit including character, capacity, capital, collateral, and conditions.

- **Character** involves the customer's willingness to pay off debts. It is usually the most important aspect of credit analysis. An applicant's prior payment history is generally the best indicator of character.
- **Capacity** represents the customer's ability to meet its obligations. Firms granting credit typically measure capacity by looking at the customer's liquidity ratios and cash flow from operations. If meeting obligations from cash flow from operations appears weak, the credit granting firm may then look to the customer's capital.
- **Capital** refers to the relative amounts of the customer's debt and equity financing. Credit granting firms often consider the customer's debt-to-equity ratio and times interest earned ratio.
- **Collateral** refers to the customer's assets that are available for use in securing the credit. The more valuable the collateral, the lower will be the credit risk.
- **Conditions** refer to the impact of economic trends that may affect the customer's ability to repay debts. A firm that is marginally able to repay its debts in a normal or strong economy may be unable to do so during an economic downturn.

Sources of Credit Information

Firms obtain important credit information from both internal and external sources. Primary *internal sources* include a credit application with references, the applicant's previous credit history, and information from sales representatives. *External sources* include recent financial statements, credit rating agencies such as Dun & Bradstreet Business Credit Services and credit bureau reports.

Credit Scoring

Firms sometimes use **credit scoring** to assign a numerical rating for a customer based on the information they collected about the customer. The firm then bases its decision to grant or refuse credit on the numerical credit score. Credit scores for commercial firms are typically based on factors such as net worth, return on equity, operating cash flow, current ratio, and return on sales. The overall credit score for a firm is based on the individual factor scores and the weights applied to each factor. One method used to assign the factor weights is a statistical technique called **multiple discriminant analysis** (MDA).[3] Firms usually design credit-scoring systems to give quick accept/reject decisions because they know that the cost of a single bad scoring mistake is usually rather small. Firms may have to reevaluate their credit scoring formula if bad debts increase.

Collection Policy

An important aspect of a firm's collection policy involves the monitoring of its accounts receivable to detect troubled accounts and past-due accounts. Firms generally monitor their accounts receivable by tracking the receivables collection period (RCP) over time. We saw in Chapter 3 that RCP measures how many days a firm takes to convert accounts receivable into cash.[4] Taking into account expected changes in the RCP due to seasonal fluctuations, firms look carefully for unexpected increases in the RCP. Unexpected increases are usually a cause for concern.

A common method used to monitor accounts receivable is an aging schedule. An **aging schedule** classifies the firm's receivables by the number of days outstanding (the *age* of the receivable). It provides useful information about the quality of a firm's receivables. Table 6.1 provides an example of an aging schedule.

Table 6.1 Aging schedule for accounts receivable

Age of account	Receivable amount ($)	Percentage of total value
0–10 days	130,000	43.3
11–30 days	100,000	33.3
31–60 days	50,000	16.7
61–90 days	15,000	5.0
More than 90 days	5,000	1.7
Total value	300,000	100.0

---

[3]   For an example of multiple discriminant analysis used to predict bankruptcy, see Edward I. Altman, *Corporate Financial Distress and Bankruptcy*, John Wiley & Sons, New York, 1993.

[4]   Computing the receivables collection period involves dividing 365 by the receivable turnover ratio. See Equation 3.12 in Chapter 3 for more details.

Table 6.2 Calculating the average age of accounts receivable

Age of account (in days) [1]	Percentage of total value [2]	Weighted average [1] × [2]
5.0	0.433	2.17
20.5	0.333	6.83
45.5	0.167	7.60
75.5	0.050	3.78
105.5[a]	0.017	1.79
Average age of accounts receivable =		22.17 days

[a] Assumes midpoint of receivables more than 90 days outstanding.

Table 6.1 shows that 76.6 percent of the firm's accounts receivable have been outstanding for 30 days or less. If the firm allows 30 days for payment of credit sales, 23.4 percent of the receivables are past due. The firm would probably need to discover why so many of its outstanding receivables are past due. Are customers experiencing temporary financial difficulties? Are customers delaying payment because they are unhappy with the firm's products or services? Which of these customers will eventually pay and which receivables will the company have to write off as a bad debt expense?

Another tool for managing accounts receivable is the **average age of accounts receivable**. One method for computing the average age of receivables is to compute the weighted average of all individual outstanding receivables. The weight for each individual receivable is the dollar amount of that receivable divided by the total dollar amount of outstanding receivables. Managers can simplify the calculation by assuming all receivables in a given class are at the midpoint of that class. For example, in the aging schedule shown above, all receivables outstanding 0–10 days would be assumed to be 5 days outstanding; all receivables outstanding 11–30 days would be assumed to be 20.5 days outstanding, and so forth. The manager then computes the weighted average of these midpoints with the weights calculated as the percentage of receivables in each range. Using this method, the average age of accounts receivable from the above aging chart would be 22.17 days.

Another way to monitor accounts receivable is to compute the **bad debt loss ratio**, which is the proportion of the total receivables that are not paid. An increase in the bad debt loss ratio increases the cost of extending credit. Equation 6.9 shows the bad debt loss ratio.

$$\text{Bad debt loss ratio} = \frac{\text{Bad debt expenses}}{\text{Credit sales}} \qquad (6.9)$$

After identifying delinquent accounts, managers must determine the appropriate course of action. Some of the delinquent accounts may be with customers who have a long history of paying their bills on time. Other delinquencies may be with customers who do not intend to pay their bills. Many customers will fall somewhere between these two extremes.

When a firm identifies a customer whose account is overdue, it may take the following sequence of steps.

1 *The firm mails a delinquency letter* notifying the customer of the past-due account. The firm may send a polite "friendly reminder" to those customers who are just a few days late with their payment. Letters with a more serious tone may follow as the receivables remain outstanding for longer periods.

2 *The firm calls the delinquent customer to discuss payment.* Phone calls often follow after the firm has already sent several letters. The firm may agree to extend the payment period if the customer has a reasonable excuse.

3 *The firm sends a representative to meet with the delinquent customer.* Again, the firm may decide to grant a credit extension to customers with a reasonable excuse for the delinquency.

4 *The firm employs a collection agency.* The firm turns the receivables over to a collection agency. Agencies specializing in collections receive a fee for successfully collecting payment, often as much as one-half of the amount due.

5 *The firm takes legal action against the delinquent customer.* The firm may seek a legal judgment against the debtor. Because of the substantial expense involved, this action is appropriate only for the larger outstanding amounts. In addition, legal action could force the delinquent customer into bankruptcy, without securing the guarantee of eventual payment.

Optimal Credit Policy

A firm's credit decisions should focus on maximizing shareholder wealth. In light of this goal, *a firm's optimal credit policy involves the tradeoff between the incremental cash flows received*

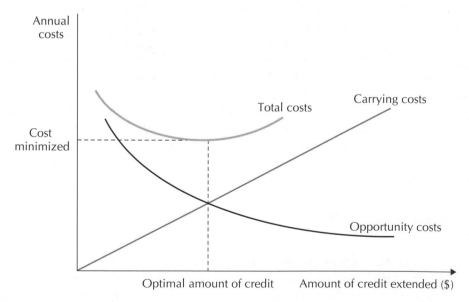

Figure 6.8 Costs of granting credit

from the additional credit sales that the firm would not otherwise realize and the incremental costs of carrying the increase in accounts receivable.

What are the costs of granting credit? One cost is the eventual nonpayment of some receivables. Another is the cost of short-term financing because the firm has to finance the receivables that it grants. A third involves the cost of managing credit and credit collections. As the firm increases the amount of credit extended to customers, these costs increase, as depicted by the increasing carrying costs curve in Figure 6.8. A final cost of granting credit is the *opportunity cost* of lost sales by not extending credit. As Figure 6.8 shows, these opportunity costs decrease as the amount of credit extended increases. The resulting tradeoff provides the optimal amount of credit the firm should provide to customers.

In practice, managers have difficulty accurately determining the optimal amount of credit to extend because of the difficulty of estimating the exact nature of the cost curves.

Concept Check 6.5

1   How can managers and analysts use a credit scoring model to assess a customer's credit?
2   List and discuss the five Cs of credit. Which Cs would be more important for commercial customers? Consumers? Why?
3   Explain two ways a firm can monitor its accounts receivable.
4   What is the tradeoff involved between carrying costs and opportunity costs in determining a firm's optimal amount of credit?

6.6 Inventory Management

Effective inventory management involves turning over inventory as quickly as possible without losing sales from inventory stockouts. Inventory management is important for two major reasons. First, inventory represents a sizable investment for some firms and affects their profitability. Second, managers often cannot correct errors in inventory management quickly because inventory is the firm's least liquid current asset.

Managers commonly use four inventory management techniques: the ABC system, the economic order quantity (EOQ) model, the just-in-time (JIT) system, and the materials requirement planning (MRP) system. We discuss each in turn.

The ABC System

Under the ABC inventory management system, a firm divides its inventory into A, B, and C groups. The firm places those items with the largest dollar investment in the A group. While the A group often includes as little as 20 percent of a firm's total inventory, it may account for as much as 80 percent of its total investment in inventory. The B group includes inventory items that account for the next largest inventory investment, and the C group includes

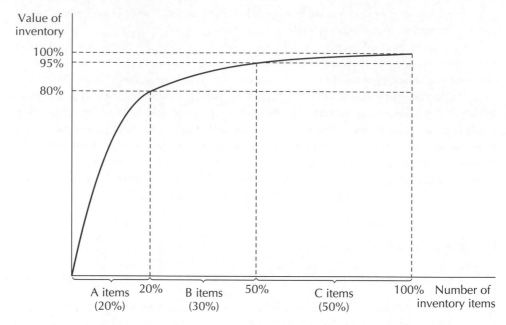

Figure 6.9 The ABC system of inventory control

a large number of inventory items that represent a relatively small inventory investment. Monitoring inventory levels differs among the three groups. Because of its high value in terms of investment, the A group logically receives the most extensive monitoring. Managers track items in the A group using a perpetual inventory system that allows for immediate, hourly, or daily inventory tracking or counts. Managers track items in the B group less frequently, often on a weekly basis. Items in the C group receive even less attention. Figure 6.9 depicts an ABC inventory control system.

For the firm shown in Figure 6.9:

- The A group of inventory items accounts for 20 percent of the number of inventory items and 80 percent of the total value of inventory.
- The B group consists of 30 percent of the number of items but only 15 percent of total inventory value.
- The C group consists of 50 percent of the number of items, but only 5 percent of total inventory value.

Because the items in the A and B inventory groups represent such large inventory investments, managers often use more sophisticated inventory management techniques. We discuss one such technique, the economic order quantity system, in the next section.

Economic Order Quantity (EOQ) Model

The **economic order quantity** (EOQ) is the order size for inventory that minimizes total inventory cost. The basic EOQ model assumes that items are removed from inventory at

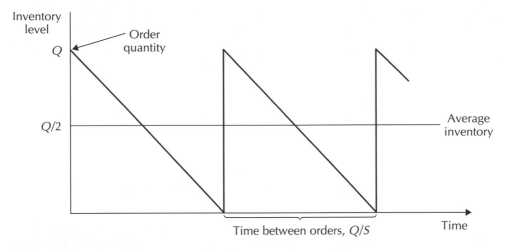

Figure 6.10 Inventory levels in an EOQ model

a constant rate (S), and that it costs the firm (C) to carry a unit of inventory for one period. The firm incurs a fixed reordering cost (F) per order that is independent of the number of items reordered. With constant inventory usage and instantaneous inventory replacement, the inventory levels under an EOQ model follow the sawtooth pattern depicted in Figure 6.10. The initial inventory level of Q falls at a constant rate to zero, is instantaneously replenished back to Q, and then repeats the same decline. The number of orders per year (S/Q) is total sales divided by the quantity ordered in units per period.

The total annual costs are equal to the ordering costs plus carrying costs. The ordering costs are the cost per order (F) times the number of orders per year (S/Q). The total annual carrying costs C(Q/2), which is the carrying cost per unit (C) times the average inventory level (Q/2). Equation 6.10 shows the formula for total costs.

$$Total\ costs = Ordering\ costs + Carrying\ costs = F\left(\frac{S}{Q}\right) + C\left(\frac{Q}{2}\right) \tag{6.10}$$

where C is the carrying cost per unit for the period; Q is the quantity ordered in units per order; S is the total sales or usage in units for the period; and F is the fixed ordering cost per order.

In Figure 6.11, we plot ordering costs and carrying costs as a function of the order size. Increasing Q increases the carrying costs but decreases the ordering costs. Thus, achieving a minimum total cost requires finding the order quantity that balances these component costs. The order quantity that minimizes total costs is the economic order quantity (EOQ).

The formula for determining EOQ is:

$$EOQ = \sqrt{\frac{2FS}{C}} \tag{6.11}$$

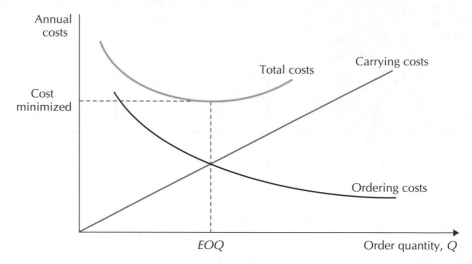

Figure 6.11 Annual costs in an EOQ model

Example 6.4 Calculating EOQ

Kramer Industrial Products sells 2,250 units of inventory per year. The cost of placing one order is $250, and the cost of carrying a unit of inventory is $50 per year. What are the EOQ, average inventory, number of orders per year, time interval between orders, annual ordering costs and annual total costs?

Solution: Using Equation 6.11, the EOQ is 150 units.

$$EOQ = \sqrt{\frac{2FS}{C}} = \sqrt{\frac{2(250)(2,250)}{50}} = 150 \; units$$

Average inventory is the $EOQ/2 = 150/2 = 75$ units.

Number of orders per year $= S/EOQ = 2,250/150 = 15$

Time interval between orders $= EOQ/S = 150/2,250 = 0.0667$ years (24.3 days)

Annual ordering costs $= F(S/EOQ) = 250(2,250/150) = \$3,750$

Annual carrying costs $= C(EOQ/2) = 50(150/2) = \$3,750$

Annual total costs of $7500 are computed using Equation 6.10.

$$Total \; costs = Ordering \; costs + Carrying \; costs = F\left(\frac{S}{Q}\right) + C\left(\frac{Q}{2}\right)$$

$$Total \; costs = 250\left(\frac{2,250}{150}\right) + 50\left(\frac{150}{2}\right) = \$7,500$$

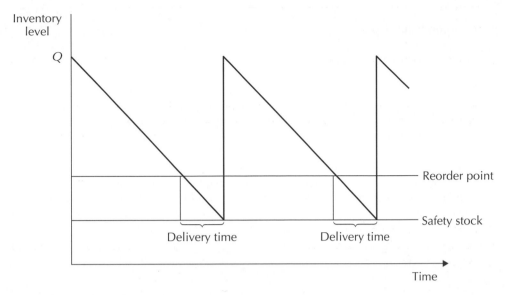

Figure 6.12 EOQ model with safety stock and reorder points

Extensions to the EOQ Model

An assumption of the EOQ model is that firms let inventory levels fall to zero before they reorder. Most firms cannot allow inventory to decline to zero without losing sales due to stockouts. Firms typically establish a minimum level of inventory, known as a **safety stock**, to prevent losing sales due to stockouts. Assuming immediate delivery of inventory upon reordering, firms would reorder inventory whenever the inventory level falls to the safety stock level. To allow for delivery time, most firms will need to reorder inventory before the inventory level reaches the critical safety stock level. The reorder points represent the times when the firm will actually place its inventory order. Two factors determine the reorder points: (1) the pace of inventory depletion and (2) the length of time for inventory delivery after placing the order. Figure 6.12 illustrates an EOQ model with safety stock and reorder point provisions.

Just-in-Time (JIT) System

Materials arrive exactly when needed in the production process in a **just-in-time** (**JIT**) system. Japanese firms popularized JIT inventory systems in the 1980s when high interest rates increased the opportunity costs of carrying high levels of inventory. JIT systems require managers to carefully plan and schedule inventory for the production process. Firms rely heavily on extensive cooperation from relatively few suppliers as they usually require frequent deliveries of the exact amounts needed in a specific order. Thus, delivery schedules, quantities, quality, and instantaneous communication with suppliers are essential factors in a JIT system. Because of the extensive planning involved, firms usually limit the number of suppliers. An effective JIT system can greatly reduce a firm's inventory carrying costs.

Focus on Practice 6.3

Just-In-Time Inventory Management

The Toyota Motor Company has been the world's leader in just-in-time (JIT) inventory systems. Most factories of Toyota and its suppliers are located in the countryside surrounding Toyota City. Suppliers deliver component parts just hours before Toyota needs them, thereby reducing the need for Toyota to carry large inventories. Effective JIT systems rely on effective total quality management systems because defective inventory has the potential to shut down the entire production line. To avoid such problems, Toyota stresses quality control that requires close coordination with its suppliers throughout the production process. JIT inventory management is now catching on in the US. Ford Motor Company has been restructuring its operating and production system with the goal of doubling its inventory turnover.

Materials Requirement Planning (MRP) Systems

Materials requirement planning (MRP) systems are computer-based systems for ordering and scheduling production of inventories that essentially work backwards through the production process. Once managers determine finished goods inventory levels, they can determine the appropriate levels of work-in-progress inventories needed for the finished goods. Then they can decide on the quantity of raw materials they need to have on hand. MRP systems are most effective for complicated products that require numerous components to create the finished product.

Concept Check 6.6

1   What is an ABC system of inventory management?
2   What is an economic order quantity (EOQ)? How is it calculated? What are the assumptions underlying the EOQ model?
3   How do safety stock levels and reorder points to allow time for delivery affect the basic EOQ model?
4   What is a just-in-time (JIT) inventory system? What type of relationship and level of cooperation must exist between manufacturers and suppliers for a JIT system to work effectively?
5   What is a materials requirement planning (MRP) system? What types of products are most suited for an MRP system?

Summary

This chapter discussed working capital management including the management of cash, marketable securities, accounts receivable, and inventory. The major points follow.

1   Three approaches for managing a firm's working capital include maturity-matching, conservative, and aggressive approaches. These approaches vary based on how the firm chooses to finance seasonal current assets.

2   A firm's operating cycle is the length of time needed to acquire inventory, sell it, and collect cash from the sale. A firm's cash conversion cycle is the length of time a company's cash is tied up in the business. It is the length of time between receiving cash from the sale of its products and expending cash on productive resources.

3   The primary reasons for holding cash involve speculative, precautionary, and transactions motives.

4   The purpose of the Baumol and Miller–Orr models is to determine the optimal cash balance for a firm.

5   Firms usually invest temporary idle cash in short-term money market securities including US Treasury bills, short-term tax-exempt securities, commercial paper, certificates of deposit, banker's acceptances, and repurchase agreements. When investing excess cash, firms consider several important factors including market-ability, maturity, default risk, and taxes.

6   A firm's net float represents cash available to the firm that is not reported in its ledger. If a firm manages its net float effectively, it can reduce its cash balances and keep more funds invested in interest-earning accounts or securities. Firms often use lockboxes and concentration banking to help reduce net float. Electronic data interchange also helps reduce both a firm's cost and its net float.

7   The decision to grant credit to a customer involves analyzing five factors – character, capacity, capital, collateral, and conditions. Firms often devise credit scoring models to assess a customer's likelihood of paying.

8   Firms frequently monitor their accounts receivable by constructing an aging schedule that classifies the firm's receivables by the number of days outstanding (the age of the receivable). An aging schedule provides useful information about the quality of a firm's receivables.

9   A firm's optimal credit policy is determined by the tradeoff between the incremental cash flows received from the additional credit sales that the firm would not otherwise realize and the incremental costs of carrying the increase in accounts receivable.

10   An ABC inventory management system classifies inventory into three classes based on the value of the inventory. The A group typically includes about 20 percent of total inventory but comprises as much as 80 percent of total inventory value. Management devotes much attention to managing these high-value inventory items.

11   The economic order quantity (EOQ) is the order size for inventory that minimizes total inventory costs. Determining the EOQ involves a tradeoff between the increasing carrying costs and decreasing ordering costs as the inventory order size increases.

12   In a just-in-time (JIT) inventory management system, management schedules inventory items to arrive exactly when needed in the production process. Reduced inventory levels in a JIT system can create substantial cost savings for a firm. JIT systems require careful planning and scheduling of inventory used in the production process to avoid stockouts.

FURTHER READING

Batlin, Cark A. and Susan Hinko. "Lockbox Management and Value Maximization," *Financial Management* 10, Winter 1981, 39–44.

Gallinger, George W. and P. Basil Healy. *Liquidity Analysis and Management*, Addison-Wesley, 1991.

Gentry, James A., "State of the Art of Short-Run Financial Management," *Financial Management* 17, Summer 1988, 41–57.

Hill, Ned C. and William L. Satoris, *Short-Term Financial Management*, 3rd edn, Prentice-Hall, 1995.

Maness, Terry S. and John T. Zietlow, *Short-term Financial Management*, 3rd edn, Thomson/South-Western, 2005.

Mian, Shehzad L. and Clifford W. Smith. "Extending Trade Credit and Financing Receivables," *Journal of Applied Corporate Finance* 7, Spring 1994, 75–84.

Opler, Tim, Lee Pinkowitz, René Stulz, and Rohan Williamson, "Corporate Cash Holdings," *Journal of Applied Corporate Finance* 14, Spring 2001, 55–66.

Phillips, Aaron L. "Migration of Corporate Payments from Check to Electronic Format: A Report on the Current Status of Payments," *Financial Management* 27, Winter 1998, 92–105.

Ricci, Cecilia Wagner and Gail Morrison. "International Working Capital Practices of the Fortune 200," *Financial Practice and Education* 6, Fall/Winter 1996, 7–20.

PART III
Long-term Investment Decisions

Chapter 7

Capital Investments and Cash Flow Analysis

In the real world, virtually all numbers are estimates. The problem with estimates, of course, is that they are frequently wrong. (Edward M. Miller, "Capital Budgeting Errors Seldom Cancel," *Financial Practice and Education* 10, Fall/Winter 2000, p. 128.)

Overview

Today's capital expenditure decisions are more critical than ever. Rapid technological advances, shorter product life cycles, and sophisticated competition make investment decisions vital to the success of a firm. Financial managers have the complex task of analyzing capital investment projects. Faced with a range of proposals, they must analyze and recommend which projects the firm should undertake to meet its goals. Making an error could be costly because many capital investment projects involve large expenditures that may have a direct impact on a firm's performance and future direction.

In this chapter, we provide an overview of capital investment decisions. After explaining the importance of capital budgeting, we discuss several ways to group capital investments. We examine six stages of the capital budgeting process but concentrate on the most complex part, estimating project cash flows. We give a comprehensive example of estimating cash flows for an expansion and a replacement project. We also discuss additional complexities of capital budgeting for multinational corporations. Completing this chapter provides the background needed to take the next step – applying different capital budgeting decision models to alternative projects to help evaluate and select which projects to undertake. We discuss these topics in Chapters 8 and 9.

Learning Objectives

After completing this chapter, you should be able to:

- explain the meaning and importance of capital budgeting;
- identify different types of capital projects;
- describe the stages of the capital budgeting process;
- understand the key guidelines in estimating cash flows;
- identify the three major cash flow components of a capital budgeting project;
- calculate the incremental after-tax cash flows of an expansion and a replacement project;
- identify the added complexities of capital budgeting for multinational corporations.

7.1 Capital Investment Decisions

Nature of Capital Budgeting

Business firms regularly make decisions involving capital goods purchases such as equipment and structures. **Capital goods** are business assets with an expected use of more than one year. The fixed asset account on a firm's balance sheet represents its net investment or capital expenditures in capital goods. Capital goods represent a major portion of the total assets of today's firms. According to the Census Bureau, US businesses invested a record $1.1 trillion in new and used capital goods in 2001. Manufacturing businesses led all industry sectors by spending $192 billion on capital goods, followed by the information sector with $146 billion. Planned future investments in capital goods make up a firm's **capital budget**.

An investment in capital goods requires an outlay of funds by the firm in exchange for expected future benefits over a period greater than one year. The proper goal in making capital investment decisions should be maximization of the long-term market value of the firm. Managers attempt to maximize value by selecting capital investments in which the value created by the project's future cash flows exceeds the required cash outlay. Capital budgeting is the process used to make this decision. Specifically, **capital budgeting** is the process of planning, analyzing, selecting, and managing capital investments.

Capital budgeting may involve other investments besides the long-term investments in capital goods. Many other long-term investments lend themselves to capital budgeting analysis. Such commitments include outlays for advertising campaigns, research and development (R&D), employee education and training programs, leasing contracts, and mergers and acquisitions. The focus of our treatment of capital budgeting centers on the decision to acquire capital goods, namely fixed assets, used for a firm's operations. However, firms can use similar procedures and processes to analyze various capital expenditures. Capital budgeting analysis also helps analysts to evaluate existing projects and operations and to decide if a firm should continue to fund certain projects.

Importance of Capital Budgeting

Capital budgeting decisions are important to a firm for three major reasons.

1 *Size of outlay.* Although a tactical investment decision generally involves a relatively small amount of funds, strategic investment decisions may require large sums of money that directly affect the firm's future course of development. Corporate managers continually face the vexing problem of deciding where to commit the firm's resources.
2 *Effect on future direction.* The future success of a business largely depends on the investment decisions that corporate managers make today. Investment decisions may result in a major departure from what the company has been doing in the past. Through making capital investments, firms acquire the long-lived fixed assets that generate the firm's future cash flows and determine its level of profitability. Thus, these decisions greatly influence a firm's ability to achieve its financial objectives.

3   *Difficulty to reverse.* Capital investment decisions often commit funds for lengthy periods, rendering such decisions difficult or costly to reverse. Therefore, capital investments are not only vital to a firm's development, but also have the capacity to lock in funds for long periods thereby reducing the firm's flexibility. The Disney example below illustrates the importance of capital budgeting.

Focus on Practice 7.1

Disney's New Theme Park

Walt Disney, Inc. has decided to make a capital investment of US$314 million in a new Disney theme park in Hong Kong. By investing US$416 million, the Hong Kong government will have a majority 57 percent stake in the project. With its investment, Disney will own the remaining 43 percent stake in the new project. The new park, Disney's fifth, is expected to open in 2006 and will be designed to resemble Disney's park (Disneyland) in Anaheim, California. Disney initially expects about 5.6 million visitors per year, with one-third expected to travel from mainland China. Disney expects annual attendance to eventually reach 10 million visitors. Disney may also later open a theme park in mainland China, near Shanghai, but has agreed not to do so until at least 2010. Disney's decision to invest in a new theme park in Hong Kong was the result of the firm's capital budgeting decision.

Capital budgeting decisions are especially critical in small businesses because they often make few capital expenditures and often have little margin for error. Making a poor decision may tie up large amounts of funds for extended periods in fixed assets while generating little, if any, value to the company. For example, suppose an entrepreneur starts a business to design and produce resumes and buys expensive computer and copying equipment to support this effort. Shortly afterward, less expensive but more efficient equipment appears on the market. Using the expensive existing equipment could put the business at a competitive disadvantage, but selling the equipment could result in a large financial loss. This is a classic example of the conflicts inherent in capital budgeting.

Proper capital budgeting analysis is critical to a firm's successful performance because sound capital investment decisions can improve cash flows and lead to higher stock prices. Yet, poor decisions can lead to financial distress and even to bankruptcy. In summary, making the right capital budgeting decisions is essential to achieving the goal of maximizing shareholder wealth.

Concept Check 7.1

1   What is capital budgeting?
2   What is the difference between a current expenditure and a capital investment?
3   How can good capital budgeting decisions increase the value of a firm?
4   How can poor capital budgeting decisions produce negative effects to the firm?
5   Why are capital budgeting decisions important to the success of a firm?

7.2 Project Classifications

A **capital budgeting project** is a proposed long-term investment that ultimately results in a capital expenditure. Firms may classify capital budgeting projects in several ways. In this chapter, we focus on classifying projects according to the nature of the project. For example, one way to classify projects is as expansion projects or replacement projects; another is to classify them as discretionary or mandated projects. In Chapters 8 and 9, we focus on classifying projects according to the degree of their dependence on other projects into independent and mutually exclusive projects.

Expansion and Replacement Projects

An **expansion project** is a capital investment designed primarily to enhance revenues by increasing operating capacity in existing products or markets or by focusing operations to expand into completely new products or markets. For example, during the 1990s, PepsiCo, Inc. expanded operations by introducing non-cola beverages into its product line when the company adopted a "total beverage strategy." This decision allowed PepsiCo to obtain market share in this fast-growing niche. Expansion projects are especially important to young or growing firms that must buy new fixed assets to meet increased demand.

A **replacement project** is a capital investment designed to improve efficiency or to maintain or increase revenues by replacing deteriorated or obsolete fixed assets. Replacing outdated equipment or facilities often benefits the firm by lowering its operating costs and preserving its efficiency. For example, when Southwest Airlines replaces old planes with new, more fuel-efficient ones, the airline often reduces the operating costs associated with servicing its fleet of planes.

Discretionary and Mandated Projects

Discretionary projects give a firm a choice of whether to undertake investment opportunities. Expansion and replacement projects typically represent discretionary projects for firms. **Mandated projects** are those in which a firm undertakes to meet social, legal, or environmental requirements. Various government regulators, labor unions, and insurance companies may require firms to meet certain standards that require capital outlays. For example, the Occupational Health and Safety Agency (OSHA) may require firms to install access ramps for the handicapped, or the Environmental Protection Agency (EPA) may require a company to install pollution abatement equipment at one of its operating facilities. These safety and environmental projects do not typically produce any revenues for the firm.

Concept Check 7.2

1 What is the primary purpose of expansion projects and replacement projects? How do they differ from one another?
2 What is the difference between mandatory and discretionary capital investments? Give an example of each.

7.3 Capital Budgeting Process

The **capital budgeting process** is a system of interrelated steps for generating long-term investment proposals; reviewing, analyzing, and selecting from them; and implementing and following up on those selected. This process is dynamic because a firm's changing environment may influence the attractiveness of current or proposed projects. Thus, managers should integrate the capital budgeting process into the firm's broader budgeting and planning cycle.

The planning process begins with top management defining the firm's goals. The main goal for capital budgeting is to make investments in long-lived assets that will maximize owners' wealth. Specifically, the firm selects those projects that it believes will maximize the firm's value for its shareholders. Because this goal is difficult to measure, managers often rely on concrete goals such as attaining a specified market share, sales growth, or level of profitability to measure their success. In turn, managers expect that achieving these goals will affect the value of their firm's stock, thereby creating wealth for their shareholders. Promising capital investments make up a **capital budget**, which is comprised of planned investment projects and a schedule of estimated outlays associated with each project.

Management then develops a **business strategy**, the plan by which the firm expects to achieve its goals in an uncertain environment. A firm's business strategy provides the framework within which it seeks capital investment opportunities and from which major capital budgeting decisions logically flow. Strategic decisions are fundamental but complex decisions because they affect the multiple variables involved in a firm's future operations, products, and services. Strategic decisions include selecting the business lines in which the company plans to concentrate and identifying competitive guidelines to use in these sectors. Project proposals should be compatible with a firm's business strategy. If not, the firm should reject them. All strategically acceptable project proposals must then survive a financial appraisal and qualitative considerations by weighing the relative value in achieving management's goals. Thus, business strategy employs capital budgeting on a grand scale resulting in strategic asset allocation decisions.

Practical Financial Tip 7.1

Strategy plays a key role in making investment decisions. Strategic planning guides the search for projects by identifying potential product lines or services and geographic areas of interest. A strategy also reflects how a firm plans to achieve its comparative advantage in a dynamically changing world. As Bierman and Smidt observed, "Strategic planning leads to a choice of the forest; project analysis studies individual trees."

Source: Harold Bierman, Jr and Seymour Smidt, *The Capital Budgeting Decision*, 7th edn, Macmillan Publishing Company, 1988, p. 5.

Although no universal consensus exists, one simple way to view capital budgeting is as a six-stage process.

1   *Identify project proposals.* Develop and provide preliminary screening of project proposals.
2   *Estimate project cash flows.* Identify and estimate the incremental, after-tax cash flows for a proposed project.
3   *Evaluate projects.* Determine the financial viability of projects by evaluating the project's incremental after-tax cash flows.
4   *Select projects.* Choose the projects that best meet the selection criteria.
5   *Implement projects.* Determine the order of implementation, initiate, and track the selected projects.
6   *Perform a post-completion audit.* Periodically compare the actual cash flows for the project to the prior estimates in the capital budgeting proposal.

Failing to complete any stage of the capital budgeting process properly may lead to detrimental capital budgeting decisions. The most challenging phase is estimating project cash flows followed by evaluating and then selecting projects. We discuss estimating cash flows in this chapter but examine the evaluation and selection stages in Chapter 8 and 9. Figure 7.1 illustrates the relationship between a company's goals and its business strategy and the capital budgeting process.

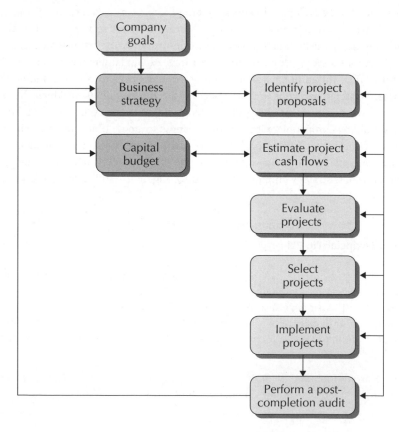

Figure 7.1 An integrated view of the capital budgeting process

Capital Budgeting Stages

Let's take a more detailed look at each of these stages.

Identify project proposals

The first stage of the capital budgeting process is identifying investment opportunities and providing a preliminary screening of project proposals. Ideas for capital investments come from sources both inside and outside the firm – planning committees, research and development groups, employees, outside consultants, and vendors. Under a **top-down approach**, major project proposals start with senior-level managers and information filters down to lower levels. Under a **bottom-up approach**, proposals "flow up" from the bottom of the organization as various departments or divisions make requests for new capital projects.

Most large and medium-sized firms have formal procedures to generate and analyze new project proposals. Initial ideas undergo preliminary screening to identify those worthy of further development. Developing all ideas into full-fledged capital budgeting proposals would be a time-consuming waste of firm resources. Consequently, decision makers use their judgment to identify potentially viable projects. Strategic considerations play a vital role in screening projects, especially for those involving large capital outlays.

Estimate project cash flows

Proposals surviving a preliminary screening usually require further development. Such development involves identifying and estimating a project's expected cash flows. Depending on the type of investment proposal, various units within a firm such as marketing, accounting, and production will ultimately provide this information. Smaller companies, which do not have expertise in all of these areas, often rely on outside consultants to provide such advice, at least for large or important projects. In practice, managers often base cash flows on informed judgment, yet there still exists a large degree of estimation.

Estimating future cash flows inevitably involves forecasting errors because managers are dealing with an uncertain future. Expansion projects are often more prone to forecasting errors than are replacement projects, because expanding into new lines of business usually involves greater uncertainty of future revenues and costs. Replacement projects, on the other hand, can rely on historical data to provide reasonable performance parameters. Thus, expansion projects may typically require more effort to obtain reliable cash flow estimates than replacement projects.

Evaluate projects

The third stage of the capital budgeting process is evaluating investment opportunities. Improper evaluation can lead to an incorrect decision, despite accurately estimating a project's cash flows. Analysts use many techniques for evaluating capital budgeting projects. As we discuss in Chapters 8 and 9, the best methods recognize the amount, the time value, and the riskiness of a project's cash flows.

Objective economic criteria should dominate the analysis of capital investments, but subjective judgment may also play a part. Sometimes, qualitative considerations such as the degree of necessity or urgency, the personal preferences of decision makers, governmental regulations or social pressures may be used to complement quantitative measures, or even overrule them. In addition, management may rearrange project priorities strictly based on internal political reasons. Thus, intangible factors are likely to play a role in capital investment decision-making.

Select projects

The fourth stage is selecting capital investments. In theory, a firm should accept all **projects** that have an expected return greater than the required rate of return. Accepting all such projects would add the most value to the firm and thus maximize shareholder wealth. In practice, however, most companies operate under capital rationing at least part of the time. **Capital rationing** occurs when a firm places an upper limit on its total capital budget. Managers may use capital rationing as a restraint mechanism on the amount and direction of a firm's growth. Capital market conditions, such as the cost and availability of funds, may inherently impose capital rationing. Under capital rationing, a firm may not maximize shareholder wealth because it is unable to accept some profitable projects.

Implement projects

Once corporate managers approve a capital investment, they must implement and closely monitor the project. Implementation involves raising capital to finance the projects, authorizing expenditures, and monitoring projects in progress. To ensure that sufficient funds are available when needed, the firm determines the amount and timing of capital investments. Management also monitors projects to avoid delays or cost overruns. If cost overruns occur, managers face three courses of action: complete the project despite its cost, delay implementation and examine the project further, or abandon it.

Perform a post-completion audit

The final stage in the capital budgeting process involves reviewing projects after a specified period. Management conducts a **post-completion audit** to compare the project's actual costs and benefits to those initially estimated earlier in the process and to decide whether the project's performance warrants its continuance. Because post audits may be costly or impractical, management does not conduct a post-completion audit of all projects. Instead, it often focuses on large capital budgeting projects.

Management post audits projects to detect errors in estimating or evaluating a project's cash flows. For example, some project planners may consistently underestimate investment outlays or overstate expected benefits. These optimistic biases may be intentional to make the project appear more attractive or simply result from a lack of experience or difficulty in estimating cash flows. Identifying systematic biases may lead to improved cash flow estimates and, therefore, to better decision making in the future. Post-completion audits succeed in holding managers accountable for their estimates and help to reduce systematic biases in future projects.

Practical Financial Tip 7.2

Successfully implementing the capital budgeting process depends on the judgment and foresight of those looking into the future. Sophisticated analysis rarely compensates for bad judgment and poor estimates. In practice, capital budgeting requires a judicious blend of theory, managerial judgment, understanding of the economic environment, knowledge of the firm's competition, among other things.

Concept Check 7.3

1   What is the link between a firm's business strategy and its capital budgeting process?
2   What are the six stages of the capital budgeting process?
3   Evaluate the following statement: "Although a firm may estimate cash flows improperly, it can resolve this deficiency by properly performing the other stages of the capital budgeting process."
4   What actions should corporate managers take before implementing a project?
5   What is the purpose of post auditing projects? Should the firm audit all capital budgeting projects after completion? Why or why not?

7.4 Guidelines for Estimating Project Cash Flows

The term **cash flow** refers to the actual flow of cash into (cash receipts or savings) and out of (cash payments) a firm during a given period. Reducing a cash outflow results in a savings. This is the same as a cash inflow. For instance, an investment in new equipment or the modernization of existing equipment may reduce operating costs. Although the equipment upgrade is a cash outflow, the reduction in costs results in a cash inflow. If the cash receipts or savings for a given year are greater (less) than the cash payments, cash flow is positive (negative) for that year. Achieving positive cash flow is a key objective for all firms, but is essential to survival for start-ups.

Cash flow and accounting profit (net income) are not necessarily the same due to the presence of certain non-cash expenditures on the firm's income statement. Accrual accounting recognizes revenues when earned and expenses when incurred, not when cash associated with those revenues or expenses actually changes hands. Thus, accounting profit includes some cash flows but excludes others. Accounting treats certain items that do not involve a flow of cash as expenses. For example, depreciation is not a cash flow, but it can reduce a firm's tax liability. This explains why profitable start-up companies find themselves in trouble if they do not have substantial positive cash flows to maintain operations. Corporate managers should use cash flows, not accounting profit, because these flows directly affect the firm's ability to pay bills and buy assets. As we discuss in Chapters 8 and 9, the value of a project depends on the amount, timing, and riskiness of the *cash flows* of that project.

Estimating project cash flows is critical because inaccurate or unreliable data can corrupt the entire capital budgeting process. Accurately forecasting cash flows can be an arduous task. Experience helps identify factors influencing the cash flows of some projects, but historical data may be unavailable on others. Estimating a new project's cash flows involves great uncertainty and may be little more than educated guesswork. Therefore, those individuals who prepare cash flow estimates should explicitly state the assumptions underlying their estimates. Corporate managers should thoroughly evaluate and test these assumptions, because faulty assumptions can easily translate into bad investment decisions. The financial staff plays a key role in the cash flow estimation process by coordinating with other departments, maintaining consistency of assumptions, and eliminating biases in the forecasts.

Firms use several methods to estimate cash flows. Some firms rely on sophisticated mathematical models and computer simulation. Others use more qualitative methods to forecast cash flows including management's subjective estimates and a survey of expert opinions. Large corporations often combine quantitative and judgmental forecasts to improve their estimates.

When estimating project cash flows, there are three key guidelines to consider:

- Identify incremental cash flows,
- Focus on after-tax cash flows, and
- Postpone considering financing costs.

Identify Incremental Cash Flows

The most important guideline is to consider only those changes in a firm's cash flows that will result if a firm undertakes a project. Specifically, what *changes* in present and future cash flows are *directly attributable* to the decision to invest in the project? This requires comparing a firm's cash flow with and without a proposed project. Managers are interested in the additional dollars the firm will receive in the future for the dollars they invest today. Therefore, the incremental cash flows generated by a project, not its total cash flows, are what matters for a project's success.

Incremental cash flows are the changes in cash flows that are attributable to the decision to invest in a given project. Cash flows not attributable to a new project are irrelevant to the investment decision-making process. When a firm decides whether to replace an old machine with a new, more efficient one, the relevant cash flows consist of those generated by the new machine less those that would have been retained by keeping the old machine. The decision should hinge on the differences in cash flows between the two machines. Thus, not all of the cash flows received are attributable to the new machine. Favorable incremental net cash flows resulting from making the decision will provide the relevant data needed to make the decision. Although the principle of incremental analysis is a simple idea, applying it in practice is often difficult.

Incremental cash flows occur during all phases of a project's life. Managers often classify such cash flows based on the stage in which they occur. These classifications include the initial cash outlay, the operating cash flows realized during a project's life, and any cash flows resulting from ending a project.[1] We discuss these different phases of a project's life later in this chapter.

---

[1] Sometimes analysts add another phase, which includes non-operating cash flows over the life of a project. Non-operating cash flows include the planned replacement of some short-lived equipment during the life of a long-term project.

Focus on After-Tax Cash Flows

The only cash flows relevant to capital budgeting are those generated by a project and still remaining after paying taxes. This is true for all phases of a project's life. Considering a project's untaxed revenues overstates its benefit because the firm cannot invest all these funds in other projects or pay them out to shareholders. Some more common tax provisions influencing cash flows involve depreciation expense as well as gains and losses from the sale of existing fixed assets. We discuss the tax effects of selling depreciable assets in Section 7.6.

Postpone Considering Financing Costs

A common mistake in estimating cash flows involves the treatment of interest expense and other financial cash flows attributable to financing the project. **Financing costs** are payments that the company makes to the parties supplying capital to finance the project. These costs may include interest paid to lenders or dividends paid to shareholders. As a general principle, capital budgeting analyses require separating investment (capital budgeting) and financing decisions. That is, analysts should evaluate a capital budgeting project independently of the source of funds used to finance the project. Analysts should include operating cash flows (cash flows from the project's operating activities) and investment cash flows (cash flows associated with acquiring or disposing of the project's assets) in their estimations, but not financing cash flows (cash flows associated with financing the project). That is, analysts should exclude financing costs from the cash flows used to evaluate projects.

As we discuss in Chapter 10, a project's required rate of return reflects financing costs. The process of deducting financing charges as cash flows and then discounting these flows by the required rate of return effectively double-counts these costs. The general rule in capital budgeting is not to deduct financing costs from a project's cash flows. The reason for postponing consideration of financing costs will become evident when we describe the discounting techniques used to evaluate capital budgeting projects in Chapters 8 and 9.

Other Cash Flow Considerations

The following are other considerations that further complicate estimating cash flows.

Net operating working capital

Adopting a project may require a change in a firm's **net operating working capital** (NOWC), which is the change in all current assets that do not pay interest less the change in all current liabilities that do not charge interest. For example, a project that entails producing and selling a new product will probably require the firm to increase its inventories and to hold more cash to conduct additional transactions. The firm's accounts receivable are also likely to increase due to rising sales. These increases in current operating assets necessitate cash outlays by the firm. However, the firm would also expect to realize an increase in accrued wages and taxes and an increase in accounts payable due to the firm's acquisition of more raw materials on trade credit. These increases in current liabilities may help the firm finance some of the increase in current assets. The excess of the increase in current operating assets over the increase in current operating liabilities represents a net cash outflow in NOWC for the firm.

If a new project increases NOWC, this increase causes a net cash outflow. Assuming this increase in NOWC must occur before the project can begin or early in its first year, it can be included as part of the project's initial cash outlay. In actuality, changes in NOWC can occur any time during a project's life. Expansion projects normally require increases in NOWC, but replacement projects often require little or no change in NOWC.

At the end of a project, the firm may recover the accumulated NOWC invested during the life of the project. Recovering NOWC results from selling remaining inventory, collecting outstanding accounts receivables, and drawing down any increases in cash balances caused by the project. This recovery of NOWC represents a one-time cash inflow in the final year of the project's life. In this situation, current operating assets and current operating liabilities may return to their pre-project levels. In other situations, a firm may be unable to recapture its full investment in accumulated NOWC because the firm cannot sell all inventories or collect all accounts receivable. The recapture of NOWC has no tax effects because the firm makes NOWC investments using after-tax dollars. Section 7.7 gives an example of an expansion project involving changes in NOWC.

Sunk costs

A **sunk cost** is an outlay incurred before making an investment decision and represents an historical cost. Past expenditures on a project should not influence the decision whether to undertake, continue, or end a project because they are not incremental cash flows. Instead, decision makers should base their decision on future costs and benefits. Sunk costs are irrelevant because the decision to adopt or reject the proposed project will not result in any change in the project's cash flows related to these costs. The firm has already incurred the sunk cost with or without the project. Because these sunk costs are irrevocable and have no bearing on a new project, they are not incremental cash flows. Thus, sunk costs are not part of the evaluation process.

Example 7.1 Sunk Costs

A pharmaceutical company is considering whether to introduce a new drug. During the past 5 years, the company invested $20 million in research and development (R&D) to create a new anti-inflammatory drug. Researchers report that the drug in its current form is unlikely to gain approval of the Food and Drug Administration (FDA) because it has some negative side effects. Corporate managers must now decide whether to incur the additional costs needed to gain FDA approval and to bring the new product to market. Analysts estimate that the potential market for the new drug is immense with potential sales of $50–75 million a year. Should the pharmaceutical company include the $20 million R&D expense in evaluating the project's incremental cash flows?

Solution: The firm should exclude the R&D costs because it has already spent the $20 million. Because these costs are irreversible, corporate managers should make the investment decision independently of the sunk costs. The only relevant data are the future costs and benefits of undertaking the project.

> **Practical Financial Tip 7.3**
>
> All relevant cash flows are future cash flows so forget sunk costs. Sunk costs are similar to spilled milk: they are past and irreversible outflows. Because sunk costs are historical costs, they should not affect the decision to accept or reject a project. Yet, decision makers often, but incorrectly, treat sunk costs as relevant. They are prone to sink more money into a failing project especially when others view them as responsible for a highly visible failure. Investing more funds is not justified by the sunk cost represented by the asset unless the incremental funds promise a return greater than their cost.

Opportunity costs

Estimating project cash flows requires considering both direct outlays and opportunity costs. An **opportunity cost** is the most valuable alternative use of a resource or an asset that the firm gives up by accepting a project. By using the asset or resource in the proposed project, the firm forgoes the opportunity to employ the asset in its alternative use. The cash flows that the firm forgoes represent an opportunity cost to the proposed project. Opportunity costs can be difficult to estimate, but they are important to recognize when estimating the relevant cash flows for analyzing a project.

> **Example 7.2 Opportunity Costs**
>
> Suppose Wal-Mart Stores, Inc., a major retailer, is considering a project proposal that requires storing additional merchandise. The firm now has excess storage capacity suitable for the new proposal. If Wal-Mart does not use the storage capacity for the new project, it could rent the space for $250,000 a year. Should Wal-Mart attach a cost to this storage space if corporate managers decided to go ahead with the new project?
>
> *Solution*: Analysts should charge the after-tax loss of revenue against the new project because it entails an opportunity cost or a loss of alternative income for using the storage space instead of renting it. Thus, if Wal-Mart's combined federal and state tax rate were 40 percent, the $150,000 [$250,000 × (1 − 0.40)] per year opportunity cost reduces the firm's annual cash inflow by this amount. If the firm cannot rent the unused storage space to outsiders or put it to another productive use, the opportunity cost of using the excess storage capacity is zero. Therefore, analysts should not assign a storage cost to the new project.

Allocated overhead

For internal reporting purposes, accountants often allocate existing overhead, such as general and administrative expenses, to each unit or division that undertakes a project. However, if the firm's current overhead will remain unchanged by accepting a project, the firm should exclude this allocated overhead from the project's cash flows in the capital budgeting analysis. Here, overhead is an existing (fixed) cost, not an incremental cost. Managers should recognize only an increase in overhead that will result from accepting the project, such as hiring a new accountant, as part of a project's cash flows.

Side effects

Adopting and implementing new projects may have important **side effects** because they affect the cash flows of other products or divisions. Project planners should consider these potential side effects, or externalities, in the capital budgeting analysis for the project. Side effects are **complements** if they enhance the cash flows of existing assets and **substitutes** if the effect is negative.

Example 7.3 Side Effects

Suppose Total Nutrition Company plans to introduce a new product that would compete directly with some of the other health fitness products it sells. The firm's analysts expect that accepting the new product will reduce sales of existing products and, therefore, the cash flows, by $1 million each year over the next 5 years. Should the company consider this reduction in cash flow when making the decision about the new product?

Solution: Yes, the lost cash flow from the lost sales is an incremental cash flow attributable to the proposed project. Therefore, analysts should incorporate this erosion in cash flows called **cannibalization** in estimating the new product's cash flows.

Concept Check 7.4

1 Why should the capital budgeting process use cash flows instead of accounting profit? How can accounting profit be misleading when considering a new project?
2 Why should corporate managers consider only incremental, after-tax cash flows?
3 Should financing costs be considered when measuring a project's cash flows? Why or why not?
4 Should sunk costs be included when estimating cash flows? Why or why not?
5 Under what circumstances would an analyst include each of the following items as an incremental cash flow for a capital budgeting project?
   a Net operating working capital.
   b Allocated overhead.
   c Opportunity costs.
   d Side effects.
6 An independent petroleum refiner decides to build a new refinery on some land it bought 5 years ago for $5 million. The firm can sell the land today for $10 million. Should the firm include the cost of the land in estimating the cash flows of the project? If so, what is the appropriate cost – $5 or $10 million? Should improvements made to the land be included?
7 An international oil company spent $1 million drilling a dry hole when searching for oil. An official argues that the company should continue drilling because the $1 million spent on the drilling is too large to simply write off. Is the $1 million a relevant cost in deciding whether to continue drilling? Explain.

7.5 Cash Flow Components

The cash flows of any project can include three basic components. Each component represents incremental, after-tax cash flows after netting any inflows and outflows of cash.

- Initial investment.
- Operating cash flows.
- Terminal cash flows.

Project planners typically can forecast the initial investment more accurately than they can forecast the other components because the initial investment estimates involve forthcoming cash flows that are more predictable than other future cash flows. Operating cash inflows during the project's life are more difficult to forecast accurately because economic, marketing, production, and other factors may cause such inflows to change. These cash flows typically vary from year to year as revenues, operating expenses, and depreciation expense change. Estimating the terminal cash flow can be especially difficult because it may require projecting cash flows many years in the future.

These cash-flow components form two types of cash-flow patterns. A **conventional (normal) cash flow pattern** is a time series of incoming and outgoing cash flows that has only one change in direction or sign. For example, a project may require one or more net cash outflows (−), such as −$100,000 in Year 0, followed by a stream of cash inflows (+), such as $50,000 each for the next 3 years.

Conversely, an **unconventional cash flow pattern** in a project is a series of cash flows having more than one sign change. For example, the pattern −, + + +, −, + + + has three sign changes. In this chapter, we limit our discussion to capital budgeting projects with conventional cash flow patterns. In Chapter 8, we discuss the evaluation of projects with unconventional cash flow patterns.

Focus on Practice 7.2

Cash Flow Forecast Biases

In a study of large US industrial firms, Pruitt and Gitman report the presence of cash flow forecast biases. Project managers and analysts often overstate revenue forecasts but tend to understate forecasts of costs. These biases may result from a lack of experience or intentional manipulation of the forecasting procedure to improve a project's chance of acceptance. By giving biased forecasts, managers may increase their span of control by controlling a larger share of the firm's investment resources. This effect often presents itself when a firm ties compensation to a manager's responsibilities. Therefore, managers have a financial incentive to provide biased forecasts.

Source: Stephen W. Pruitt and Lawrence J. Gitman, "Capital Budgeting Forecast Biases: Evidence from the Fortune 500." *Financial Management*, Spring 1987, 46–51.

Table 7.1 Format for calculating the initial investment

	Purchase price of a new asset (e.g. land, buildings, and equipment)
+	Expenses associated with placing the asset in service
+	Opportunity cost of any existing assets employed in the project
+	Initial net operating working capital (NOWC) required
−	Proceeds from selling an existing asset
+/−	<u>Tax effects from selling an existing asset</u>
	Initial investment

Initial Investment

The **initial investment** is the after-tax net cash outlay required at the beginning of an investment project. For simplicity, we often assume that the initial investment occurs immediately ($t = 0$) when the inflows and outflows of cash making up the initial investment occur over a period less than a year. If the initial investment period is less than a year, this assumption is unlikely to have an adverse impact on a project's evaluation.[2] If the period is more than a year, the analyst should estimate the capital outlay amount each year and account for the time value of money of these cash outlays in the initial investment.

The initial cash outflows generally include the cost of any land, buildings, and equipment required to undertake the project. The firm should also include any other costs associated with placing any assets into service such as delivery fees, setup expenses, and testing expenses, and any related initial increase in net operating working capital. In addition, including the opportunity cost of any assets already owned that would be employed in the project may be necessary. Although there are no tax effects associated with a change in NOWC, taxes may affect other costs. For example, training costs are tax-deductible expenses. Thus, the analyst should multiply such costs by one minus the firm's marginal tax rate $(1 − T)$ to get the after-tax cash flow.

For replacement projects, where the proposal involves replacing an existing asset with a new asset, the estimated net proceeds from selling the old asset represent a cash inflow that partially offsets the initial cash outlays. The tax impact of selling a depreciable asset may increase (decrease) a firm's tax liability, which adds to (reduces) the initial outlay. As we show later in Section 7.6, the tax implications from selling a depreciable asset depend on the relationship between the selling price and the book value of the old asset.

Operating Cash Flows

Operating cash flows are the expected after-tax net cash flows that result from any changes in operating revenue and associated expenses over a project's life. These cash flows normally

---

[2] If the project's initial investment occurs in less than a year and the project's life is short, the firm may decide to estimate all cash flows, including the initial investment, in quarterly intervals. Many short-lived, high technology projects require such attention.

vary from year to year due to changing revenues, expenses, and depreciation. Although operating cash flows occur throughout the year, analysts often estimate them over annual intervals. In many instances, however, analysts must adjust the cash flows to reflect the actual timing of the cash inflows and outflows. In our examples, we assume that operating cash flows occur at the end of each year. This also serves as a conservative assumption because cash flows received at the end of a year are not worth as much as those received during a year because of the time value of money.

Forecasting a project's operating cash flows begins with a pro forma (projected) income statement. For an expansion project, the estimates of revenues and expenses are incremental to the results the firm would achieve if the project were not to be accepted. Forecasting the operating results for a replacement project requires analysts to estimate incremental revenues and expenses as follows:

- **Incremental revenue** is equal to the expected revenue from the new project assets minus the revenue generated by keeping the existing assets in operation.
- **Incremental operating expense** is equal to the expected operating expense incurred with the new project assets minus the revenue generated by keeping the existing assets in operation.
- **Incremental depreciation** is equal to the depreciation expense associated with the new project assets minus the depreciation expense that remains for the existing (old) assets. If the firm replaces the existing assets, it would forgo the remaining depreciation expense on these assets.

The issue of depreciation requires special attention. As a non-cash expense, depreciation represents cash that never left the firm. As a rule, depreciation generates a cash flow due to its positive effect (reduction) on taxes paid. Because depreciation expense reduces taxable income, this also reduces the tax outflow, effectively resulting in a cash inflow. The decrease in the tax liability due to the depreciation charge is called the **depreciation tax shield**. This tax shield equals the depreciation amount times the tax rate. Theoretically, the depreciation expense plus the tax shield is the total amount to be added back to net income. As stated, the depreciation expense must be reversed because it is a non-cash book entry not affecting the firm's cash flows. The cash flows must also reflect depreciation's related tax benefits. Although there may be other non-cash charges against income, such as amortization and depletion expenses, depreciation expense is the most common non-cash charge.

Practical Financial Tip 7.4

A firm should generally charge as much depreciation as possible in the early years of a project's life unless it has tax losses larger than it can use to offset taxable income. Using accelerated depreciation methods results in retaining more cash in the early years and deferring taxes to later years. Because money has a time value, doing otherwise would not be in the best interests of the firm's stockholders.

Example 7.4 Depreciation Tax Shield

Bemis Company, Inc., a container and packaging company, expects a new project to increase its depreciation expense by $100,000 in the first year. If the firm's marginal tax rate is 34 percent, what is the depreciation tax shield or tax savings of the new project during its first year of operation?

Solution: The depreciation tax shield would be $34,000 = ($100,000)(0.34).

MACRS system

US firms depreciate assets for tax purposes under the **modified accelerated cost recovery system** (MACRS), enacted by Congress in the Tax Reform Act of 1986. Each item of depreciable property is assigned to a property class. An asset's recovery period (depreciable tax life) depends on the property class. Examples of MACRS property classes are:

- *3-year property:* small tools and assets used in research and development activities.
- *5-year property:* automobiles, trucks, computers and peripheral equipment, and office machines.
- *7-year property:* office furniture and fixtures, agriculture equipment, oil exploration and development equipment, railroad track, manufacturing equipment, and any property not designated by law as being in any other class.

Under MACRS, firms may use either straight-line or accelerated depreciation. Firms typically prefer to use an accelerated method because it results in larger deductions earlier in the asset's life than does straight-line depreciation. Because of the time value of money, the

Table 7.2 Depreciation rates using the modified accelerated cost recovery system

| Year | MACRS property class | | |
	3-year (%)	5-year (%)	7-year (%)
1	33.33	20.00	14.29
2	44.45	32.00	24.49
3	14.81[a]	19.20	17.49
4	7.41	11.52[a]	12.49
5		11.52	8.93[a]
6		5.76	8.93
7			8.93
8			4.45

[a] Switches to the straight-line method in the first year in which the straight-line depreciation exceeds the accelerated depreciation (double-declining balance method).

deduction from the depreciation tax shield is more valuable to the firm under accelerated depreciation versus straight-line depreciation.

For each asset class excluding real estate, the second year's depreciation exceeds the first year's depreciation rate because MACRS assumes that the firm placed assets into service at mid-year. For the same reason, the last year's depreciation rate is about half the previous year's rate. This **mid- or half-year convention** causes the term under which the asset is depreciated, its **recovery period**, to exceed its tax life, by 1 year. For example, a firm depreciates an asset with a 5-year MACRS recovery period over 6 years.

Computing the depreciation expense for a given year using MACRS involves multiplying the depreciation rate for that year (from Table 7.2) by the depreciable basis of the asset being depreciated. The **depreciable basis** of an asset is its original cost plus the costs related to its purchase, including delivery and installation costs. Under MACRS, firms depreciate assets to a zero book value. Consequently, firms do not consider **salvage value**, the expected worth of an asset at the end of its life, when calculating depreciation.

Example 7.5 Computation of MACRS Depreciation

Assume the following facts for a computer and peripheral equipment purchased by Anderson Company on January 1, 2005, and disposed of on January 2, 2012.

Cost including delivery and installation	$100,000
Estimated salvage value	$10,000
Estimated useful life	7 years
MACRS property class	5 years

What is the MACRS depreciation for this 5-year class of property?

Solution: Table 7.3 shows the computation of depreciation for tax purposes.

Table 7.3 MACRS depreciation

Year	Depreciable basis ($) [1]	Depreciation rate [2]	Depreciation amount ($) [1] × [2]
2004	100,000	0.2000	20,000
2005	100,000	0.3200	32,000
2006	100,000	0.1920	19,200
2007	100,000	0.1152	11,520
2008	100,000	0.1152	11,520
2009	100,000	0.0576	5,760
	Total depreciation		100,000

Table 7.4 Format for calculating operating cash flows

Operating revenues
− Operating expenses
− <u>Depreciation</u>
Taxable income
− <u>Income taxes</u>
Net income
+ Depreciation
− <u>Increase in net operating working capital (NOWC)</u>
Operating cash flows

Computing operating cash flows

Table 7.4 presents a format for computing operating cash flows. Calculating net income requires subtracting the incremental operating expenses, income taxes, and depreciation from incremental revenues. As noted earlier, financing costs are excluded in the process of calculating operating cash flows, but are considered in the evaluation stage of the capital budgeting process. Because depreciation does not represent an actual expenditure of cash in computing a firm's profit, depreciation is added back to net income to get operating cash flows. The firm incurs a cash outlay when it buys a fixed asset and this cash outlay is part of the initial investment. To consider an annual depreciation expense as a cash outlay would double count investment costs.

Except for ignoring financing costs, this format for estimating a project's cash flows follows a basic income statement approach. The analyst then derives the project cash flow from the project net income by adding back depreciation and subtracting (adding) any increases (decreases) in net operating working capital.

Equation 7.1 shows the formula for calculating the changes in operating cash flows using the above format. All incremental cash flows are "with the project" minus "without the project." With a replacement decision, for example, the change in cash flows is the cash flow if the firm acquires a new asset less the cash flow if the firm does not. Rearranging the terms in Equation 7.1 and applying some basic algebra allows us to develop another useful format for calculating operating cash flows.

$$\Delta \text{Operating cash flows} = (\Delta R - \Delta OC - \Delta D)(1 - T) + \Delta D$$

$$= [(R_{new} - R_{old}) - (OC_{new} - OC_{old}) - (D_{new} - D_{old})](1 - T) \qquad (7.1)$$

where Δ is the Greek symbol delta meaning "change in" or "incremental"; ΔR is the change in revenues ($R_{new} - R_{old}$); ΔOC is the change in operating costs ($OC_{new} - OC_{old}$); ΔD is the change in depreciation ($D_{new} - D_{old}$); and T is the marginal tax rate (%).

Another approach explicitly recognizes that depreciation is a non-cash charge and not part of the cash outflows. However, this method recognizes that depreciation has an indirect influence on the tax expense of the company. Equation 7.2 defines operating cash flows as the after-tax incremental net income plus the incremental depreciation tax shield, $T\Delta D$. For

Equations 7.1 and 7.2, we assume that the firm neither defers its tax liabilities, paying them when they are due, nor has any changes in NOWC.

$$\Delta \text{Operating cash flows} = (\Delta R - \Delta OC)(1 - T) + T\Delta D$$

$$= [(R_{new} - R_{old}) - (OC_{new} - OC_{old})](1 - T) + T(D_{new} - D_{old}) \quad (7.2)$$

Determining the changes in operating cash flows using Equation 7.2 offers several advantages. First, this approach requires fewer computations than the previous income statement format. Second, Equation 7.2 highlights the effect that depreciation has on operating cash flows. Specifically, we see directly how a higher depreciation amount for a given year yields a higher operating cash flow for that year. This result is not as obvious in the income statement approach.

Example 7.6 Computing Incremental Operating Cash Flows

A firm plans to replace an old machine with a new, more efficient one, which has greater production capacity. An analyst estimates that adopting the new machine will result in the following revenues, operating costs, and depreciation. For simplicity, assume that the changes in revenues, expenses, and depreciation are the same each year and that the marginal tax rate is 34 percent.

	With new machine	With old machine	Incremental change
Sales revenue (R)	$110,000	$100,000	$10,000
Operating costs (OC)	55,000	60,000	−5,000
Depreciation (D)	15,000	14,000	1,000

The operating costs of the new machine are lower than the old machine. The lower incremental operating costs result in an operating savings, which in turn increases cash inflows. Using Equation 7.2, the change in the operating cash flows is:

$$\Delta \text{Operating cash flows} = (\Delta R - \Delta OC)(1 - T) + t\Delta D$$

$$= [\$10,000 - (-\$5,000)](1 - 0.34) + (0.34)(1,000)$$

$$= \$9,900 + \$340 = \$10,240$$

Focus on Practice 7.3

Cash Flow Estimation Practices of Large Firms

Based on a survey of chief financial officers from *Fortune* 500 corporations, the results show that most firms follow a systematic approach in generating cash flow information for capital investments. That is, firms have representatives who coordinate or supervise the process using predetermined company-wide procedures in preparing cash flow data. Most firms use several forecasting methods in generating project cash flows. The following survey results show that large corporations seem to combine judgmental and quantitative forecasts to improve their estimates.

Forecasting methods used to generate cash-flow estimates

Method	Responses (%)
Management's subjective estimates	90.5
Sensitivity analysis	69.0
Consensus of experts' opinion	67.2
Computer simulation	52.2
Sophisticated mathematical models	48.3
Probability theory	43.1
Other	9.5

Source: Adapted from Randolph A. Pohlman, Emmanuel S. Santiago, and F. Lynn Markel, "Cash Flow Estimation Practices of Large Firms," *Financial Management*, Summer 1988, 71–79.

Terminal Cash Flows

Because capital budgeting projects have a finite life, the **terminal cash flow** is the cash flow associated with ending a project. A set of terminal cash flows occurs in the project's final year, along with a set of operating cash flows for that year.

In the final year of an expansion project, a firm may receive cash inflows from two major sources. The first source is the release of any accumulated NOWC necessary to operate the project through the sale of inventory, collection of accounts receivable, or freeing up of cash invested in the project. The second source is the sale of any capital assets (an asset's actual value as opposed to estimated salvage value) needed to support the project. Any taxes on the sale of the asset are calculated after subtracting removal costs because removal costs are an operating expense. As we discuss in Section 7.6, the tax effects of the sale of an asset depend on the price received, its original cost, and the current book value (cost less accumulated depreciation).

Table 7.5 Format for calculating terminal cash flows

	Salvage value
−	Cost of removing assets and shutting down
	Salvage value before taxes
±	Tax effects on disposal of an asset
	Net salvage value
+	Recovery of NOWC
	Terminal cash flows

The firm usually recovers all additions to NOWC that have occurred during the project's life, not simply the initial increase in NOWC. Recaptured NOWC is added to the final period's after-tax cash flow to compute the terminal cash flows. As a practical matter, financial managers generally assume the firm will liquidate current assets at book value. In such cases, the disposal of NOWC has no taxation implications. Table 7.5 gives the format for calculating the terminal cash flows.

So far, we have examined many guidelines involved in estimating cash flows. The following checklist covers some of the more important guidelines.

Checklist for estimating cash flows

☑ Use incremental cash flows of a project, not accounting profit
☑ Adjust for changes in NOWC, opportunity costs, and side effects
☑ Use future cash flow and ignore sunk costs
☑ Exclude interest and other financial flows to avoid double-counting
☑ Exclude any allocation of existing overhead
☑ Include depreciation tax-shield benefits in cash flow calculations
☑ Add back salvage value adjusted for removal costs and taxes in expansion decisions

---

Practical Financial Tip 7.5

Estimating cash flows is a complex task because it involves forecasting. Each project involves distinctive flows. Comparing each situation "with" and "without" the project can help to identify the relevant cash flows. Accurate estimates of cash flows are essential as inputs to evaluating proposed capital expenditures.

Concept Check 7.5

1 What are the three major categories of cash flows in a capital budgeting project? What is the format for calculating each type of cash flow?

2 What is the difference between conventional and unconventional cash flow patterns? Give an example of each.

3 Comment on the statement: "Depreciation is a non-cash expense and simply can be ignored when estimating a project's relevant cash flows."

4 What are the tax benefits of depreciation and how do they play into cash flow calculations?

5 Tuggle Toy Company plans to expand its production capacity by adding a new machine costing $25,000, including installation and transportation costs. The new machine requires an estimated $2,000 increase in NOWC. What is the initial outlay for this project?

6 What is the appropriate treatment of recaptured NOWC in terms of computing terminal cash flows?

7 Management at Harrington Corporation wants to build a fitness center for use by its employees. The analyst in charge of analyzing this proposed project recommends rejecting it because "the fitness center would require a large initial outlay but would not generate any cash inflows to the firm." Comment on this situation.

7.6 Tax Effects of Selling Depreciable Assets

Depreciable assets such as plant and equipment, owned for more than 6 months, get special tax treatment under Section 1231 of the Internal Revenue Code.[3] Each year, gains and losses from sales of depreciable assets are offset against each other. A net loss from the sale of a depreciable asset is fully deductible from the corporation's ordinary income. A net gain is generally treated as a long-term capital gain (currently taxed as ordinary income).

When a firm sells a depreciable asset, the difference between the sales price and the **book value** (installed cost less accumulated depreciation) of the asset represents an accounting gain or loss to the firm. For a fully depreciated asset, the book value is zero. If a firm sells an asset before fully depreciating it, the assumption is that the firm sells the asset at midyear and can expense only half the year's depreciation.

Four different tax situations can occur when selling depreciable assets.

- *Selling a depreciable asset at its book value.* There is no impact on corporate taxes. The firm realizes neither a gain nor a loss on the sale.

---

[3] Section 1231 applies to all depreciable assets (personal and real) and land used in a trade or business but not as an investment.

- *Selling a depreciable asset below its book value.* This results in a Section 1231 loss to be netted with all other Section 1231 gains and losses for the year. If there are no other Section 1231 transactions, the loss is fully deductible from ordinary income subject to certain exceptions. A net loss effectively reduces the firm's tax liability by an amount equal to the difference between the sales price and the book value of the asset times its marginal tax rate.

- *Selling a depreciable asset above its book value but below or equal to its depreciable basis.* The **depreciable basis** is the total amount that the Internal Revenue Service recognizes as depreciable. In this situation, the Internal Revenue Service treats the gain on the depreciable asset as recaptured depreciation, which is taxed as ordinary income. **Recaptured depreciation** represents the amount by which the firm has effectively over-depreciated the asset during its life. The firm's income tax liability on the recaptured depreciation equals the difference between the sales price and the book value of the asset times its marginal tax rate.

- *Selling a depreciable asset above its initial depreciable basis.* Here, the gain consists of (1) recaptured depreciation and (2) a Section 1231 gain to be netted with other Section 1231 gains and losses. If there are no other Section 1231 transactions, the net Section 1231 gain is a long-term capital gain (currently taxed as ordinary income if there are no capital losses with which to be netted), assuming the asset is held for 6 months. The portion of the gain representing recaptured depreciation is treated as ordinary income for tax purposes. The amount of recaptured depreciation equals the difference between the depreciable basis of the asset and its current book value. The capital gains portion is the amount by which the selling price exceeds the depreciable basis.

Table 7.6 summarizes the tax treatment of these four situations involving the sale of depreciable assets.

Table 7.6 Tax effects of the sale of depreciable assets used in a business

Selling a depreciable asset at:	Tax effect
Book value	None
Below book value	(Sales price − Book value)(Marginal tax rate) = Ordinary loss resulting in reduction of tax liability
Above book value but below or equal to the initial depreciable basis	(Sales price − Book value)(Marginal tax rate) = Recaptured depreciation resulting in increase of tax liability
Above the initial depreciable basis	(Initial depreciable basis − Book Value)(Marginal tax rate) + (Sales price − Initial depreciable basis)(Capital gains rate) = Recaptured depreciation taxed at ordinary income rate plus Section 1231 gain taxed at capital gains rate

Example 7.7 Gain and Loss from Selling a Depreciable Asset

Eagle Company bought a delivery truck with a 5-year recovery period on April 1, 2003, for $20,000 and sold it on September 15, 2005. Under the modified accelerated cost recovery system (MACRS) the total depreciation for 2003, 2004, and 2005 is $12,320 [0.20($20,000) + 0.32($20,000) and 0.096($20,000)].[4] The current book value is $7,680 [$20,000 − $12,320]. The firm's marginal tax rate on both ordinary income and capital gains is 34 percent. The firm has no other Section 1231 gains or losses during the current year or Section 1231 losses during the preceding 5 years. What is the tax treatment and tax effect if Eagle Company sells the truck for $7,680, $6,080, $10,080, and $21,000?

Solution: Table 7.7 summarizes the tax treatment for each situation.

Table 7.7 Tax treatment of selling a delivery truck: Eagle Company

Situation	Tax treatment	Tax effect
Sales price $7,680 Book value 7,680 Gain (loss) $0	No gain or loss	None
Sales price $6,080 Book value 7,680 Loss ($1,600)	Loss deductible from ordinary income	Tax saving = 0.34($1,600) = $544
Sales price $10,080 Book value 7,680 Gain $2,400	Gain is considered recaptured depreciation and is treated as ordinary income	Tax liability = 0.34($2,400) = $816
Sales price $21,000 Book value 7,680 Gain $13,320	Gain of $12,320 (limited to MACRS depreciable basis) is recaptured depreciation and is treated as ordinary income	Tax liability = 0.34($12,320) = $4,189
	Gain of $1,000 (in excess of MACRS depreciable basis) is treated as a long-term capital gain	Tax liability = 0.34($1,000) = $340 Total $4,529

---

[4] In the year of disposition, the firm gets a half-year's deduction under MACRS, which is called the half-year convention. In this example, the asset was sold in year 3, which gives a depreciation percentage of $0.5 \times 19.2\% = 9.6\%$ or 0.096.

Concept Check 7.6

1 What constitutes a Section 1231 asset? How does the Internal Revenue Service (IRS) treat multiple Section 1231 gains and losses?
2 What does the IRS use for its depreciable basis guidelines?
3 What is the tax treatment of selling a depreciable asset:
    a   Below its book value?
    b   Above book value but below or equal to its depreciable basis?
    c   Above its depreciable basis?
4 How does the IRS treat recaptured depreciation for tax purposes?

7.7 Applying Cash Flow Analysis

In this section, we use the ideas presented earlier in this chapter to calculate the three parts of a cash flow analysis – initial investment, operating cash flows, and terminal cash flows – for both an expansion project and a replacement project. In presenting these two examples, we make several simplifying assumptions. We assume that:

- any assets are bought and put to work immediately (year 0);
- cash flows occur at the end of the year when calculating operating cash flows and terminal cash flows.

Once analysts have identified and calculated the cash flows, decision makers can evaluate and select the appropriate projects needed to meet the firm's goals. In Chapters 8 and 9, we discuss various approaches for evaluating and selecting capital budgeting projects.

The Expansion Decision

Firms often engage in asset expansion decisions such as expanding one of its product lines. The following example illustrates the calculation of incremental cash flows for an asset expansion project.

Example 7.8 Expansion Project

Carolina Freight Company is considering expanding its current operations by adding new trucks to its fleet. Based on the firm's forecasts, its current fleet is inadequate to meet demand. Carolina Freight expects to increase revenues with this asset expansion project. The firm plans to depreciate the trucks over a 5-year economic life using MACRS and to sell the trucks after 6 years. The firm's marginal tax rate is 34 percent. The following are estimates of the project's incremental cash flows.

- Purchase price of $495,000
- Delivery costs of $5,000
- Initial net operating working capital required of $25,000
- Revenues of $300,000 in year 1, $350,000 in years 2 and 3, and $375,000 in years 4 through 6
- Operating expenses, excluding depreciation, 40 percent of cash revenues
- Salvage value of $100,000 in year 6

Given these estimates, what are the initial investment, operating cash flows, and terminal cash flows for Carolina Freight Company?

Solution: Table 7.8 summarizes the cash flow calculations for Carolina Freight Company.

- *Initial investment.* Estimating the initial investment in this expansion project involves only initial cash outflows. The direct cash flows are the purchase price of the trucks ($495,000) plus the delivery costs ($5,000). Therefore, the depreciable basis of the new trucks is $500,000. Concurrently, the project requires additional NOWC ($25,000). In practice, additional changes in NOWC could take place over the life of the project as revenues and expenses increase. Using the format shown in Table 7.1, Panel A of Table 7.8 shows an initial investment of $525,000.
- *Operating cash flows.* Estimating the operating cash flows associated with the project requires calculating the annual revenues, operating expenses, MACRS depreciation, and taxes. The depreciable basis of the new trucks is $500,000, consisting of the $495,000 purchase price plus $5,000 in delivery costs, depreciated using MACRS depreciation rates for 5-year assets (year 1 = 20.00 percent, year 2 = 32.00 percent, year 3 = 19.20 percent, year 4 = 11.52 percent, year 5 = 11.52 percent, and year 6 = 5.76 percent). Using the format shown in Table 7.4, the operating cash flows after taxes for this expansion project are shown in Panel B of Table 7.8.
- *Terminal cash flows.* The trucks are fully depreciated at the end of year 6 and have a book value of zero. Selling an asset at more than its book value ($0), but less than its depreciable basis ($500,000), results only in the recapture of depreciation. The $100,000 salvage value of the additional trucks is considered recaptured depreciation and is taxable as ordinary income at the firm's 34 percent tax rate. Therefore, the firm realizes a net cash inflow of $66,000 from the sale. Carolina Freight also recovers $25,000 in net operating working capital in year 6. Using the format shown in Table 7.5, Panel C of Table 7.8 shows a terminal value of $91,000. Panel D of Table 7.8 shows the composite cash flows for the project.

Table 7.8 Calculating cash flows for Carolina Freight Company's expansion project

Panel A. Initial investment

Incremental cash flows	Year 0
Purchase price of new trucks	$495,000
+ Delivery costs	5,000
Depreciable basis	$500,000
+ Change in NOWC	25,000
Initial investment	$525,000

Panel B. Operating cash flows

Incremental cash flows	Year 1	Year 2	Year 3	Year 4	Year 5	Year 6
Operating revenues	$300,000	$350,000	$350,000	$375,000	$375,000	$375,000
– Operating costs (40%)	120,000	140,000	140,000	150,000	150,000	150,000
– Depreciation	100,000	160,000	96,000	57,600	57,600	28,800
Taxable income	$80,000	$50,000	$114,000	$167,400	$167,400	$196,200
– Taxes (34%)	27,200	17,000	38,760	56,916	56,916	66,708
Net income	$52,800	$33,000	$75,240	$110,484	$110,484	$129,492
+ Depreciation	100,000	160,000	96,000	57,600	57,600	28,800
Operating cash flows	$152,800	$193,000	$171,240	$168,084	$168,084	$158,292

MACRS depreciation

Year	Depreciable basis [1]	Depreciation rate [2]	Depreciation amount [1] × [2]
1	$500,000	0.2000	$100,000
2	500,000	0.3200	160,000
3	500,000	0.1920	96,000
4	500,000	0.1152	57,600
5	500,000	0.1152	57,600
6	500,000	0.0576	28,800
	Total depreciation		$500,000

Panel C. Terminal cash flows

Incremental cash flows	Year 6
Salvage value	$100,000
– Income taxes (34%)	34,000
Net salvage value	$66,000
+ Recovery of NOWC	25,000
Terminal cash flows	$91,000

Panel D. Composite cash flows

Incremental cash flows	Year 0	Year 1	Year 2	Year 3	Year 4	Year 5	Year 6
Initial	−$525,000						
Operating		$152,800	$193,000	$171,240	$168,084	$168,084	$158,292
Terminal							$91,000

The Replacement Decision

A special type of capital budgeting decision involves replacing a currently owned asset. In many cases, decision makers decide to replace assets such as equipment based on economics, not on physical deterioration or collapse. The following example applies the principles and procedures discussed earlier in this chapter to determine the initial investment, operating cash flows, and terminal cash flows for a replacement project.

Example 7.9 Replacement Project

Carolina Freight Company is considering upgrading its current loading equipment at one of its depots with more efficient equipment. Analysts do not expect the new equipment to affect the firm's revenues or its net operating working capital. However, they do project a decrease in operating expenses due to the greater operating efficiency of the new equipment. Thus, this replacement project is purely a cost-saving proposal. The firm's ordinary tax rate remains at 34 percent.

Six years ago, Carolina Freight bought the old equipment for $75,000, but it has now fully depreciated the asset, leaving a book value of zero. The old equipment would continue to operate for 6 more years if not replaced. The current market value of the old equipment is now $10,000, but analysts expect this value to decline to zero in 6 years. The annual operating costs of the old equipment are now $66,000 (year 0), but analysts forecast that these costs will increase by $4,000 per year if Carolina Freight does not replace the equipment. These increases are due primarily to increased salaries for operators.

The proposed equipment costs $95,000 plus $5,000 in delivery and installation costs. Carolina Freight also expects to incur a $2,000 cost for training an operator. The firm plans to depreciate the new equipment using MACRS over a 5-year life and ultimately sell it for $20,000 at the end of year 6. Analysts forecast operating costs of $30,000 during the first year but expect such costs to increase by $2,000 per year over the remaining life of the asset.

- *Initial investment.* As Panel A of Table 7.9 shows, the initial investment has several parts. The equipment's depreciable basis of $100,000 consists of its purchase price ($95,000) plus delivery and installation costs ($5,000). This project does not require any initial increases in net operating working capital, but it does require an operating expenditure of $2,000, which is $1,320 = ($2,000)(1 − 0.34) after considering the tax benefit for training an equipment operator. The firm can get $10,000 from selling the old equipment. This amount decreases to $6,600 [$10,000 − ($10,000)(0.34)] because Carolina Freight must pay taxes on the proceeds (treated as recaptured depreciation). The initial investment is $94,720, which is a cash outflow.
- *Operating cash flows.* Because this is purely a cost-reduction project, the incremental sales are zero, or $\Delta S = 0$. However, the new equipment will reduce incremental operating costs, resulting in a cost savings or a cash inflow. The old equipment is fully depreciated, but the new equipment will be depreciated using MACRS for 5-year property. Panel B of Table 7.9 shows the depreciation schedule for the new equipment. Using Equation 7.2, we derive the yearly operating cash flows by

taking the change in revenues, operating costs, and depreciation between the new and old equipment for each year over a 6-year period. The operating costs for the new equipment are $30,000 in year 1, but increase by $2,000 each year thereafter. The operating costs are $66,000 in year 0 of the old equipment but these costs increase by $4,000 each year after year 0. For simplicity, we round the following operating cash flows to the nearest dollar.

Year   Changes in operating cash flows

1   [$0 − ($30,000 − $70,000)](1 − 0.34) + (0.34)($20,000 − $0) = $33,200
2   [$0 − ($32,000 − $74,000)](1 − 0.34) + (0.34)($32,000 − $0) = $38,600
3   [$0 − ($34,000 − $78,000)](1 − 0.34) + (0.34)($19,200 − $0) = $35,568
4   [$0 − ($36,000 − $82,000)](1 − 0.34) + (0.34)($11,520 − $0) = $34,277
5   [$0 − ($38,000 − $86,000)](1 − 0.34) + (0.34)($11,520 − $0) = $35,597
6   [$0 − ($40,000 − $90,000)](1 − 0.34) + (0.34)($ 5,760 − $0) = $34,958

- *Terminal cash flows.* Carolina Freight expects to sell the new equipment for its estimated salvage value of $20,000 in year 6. The firm treats the salvage value as ordinary income because it represents a recapture of depreciation for tax purposes (selling a depreciable asset above its book value of zero but below or equal to its depreciable basis of $100,000). Panel C of Table 7.9 shows the calculation of the terminal cash flows of $13,200. Panel D of Table 7.9 shows the composite cash flows for this replacement project.

Concept Check 7.7

1   In the expansion decision, how does Carolina Freight Company account for changes in net operating working capital (NOWC)?
2   Why is depreciation added back to net income in Panel B of Table 7.8?
3   Why are income taxes substracted from the salvage value in Panel C of Table 7.8?
4   What are the major differences between cash flow analyses for an expansion project and those for a replacement project?

7.8 Capital Budgeting for the Multinational Corporation

Multinational corporations (MNCs) seek investment opportunities in other countries for many reasons – strategic, economic, behavioral, competitive, and financial.[5] For example, some MNCs desire to preempt competitors by gaining a strategic advantage over them by

---

[5]   For further discussion of topics involving international aspects of financial management, see, for example, Jeff Madura, *International Financial Management*, 6th edn, South-Western College Publishing, 2000; and Michael H. Moffett, Arthur I. Stonehill, and David K. Eiteman, *Fundamentals of Multinational Finance*, Pearson Education, Inc., 2003.

Table 7.9 Calculating cash flows for Carolina Freight Company's replacement project

Panel A: Initial investment

Incremental cash flows	Year 0
Purchase price of new equipment	$95,000
+ Delivery and installation costs	5,000
Depreciable basis	$100,000
+ Training costs of an operator after taxes ($2,000)(1 − 0.34)	1,320
− Proceeds from sale of old equipment	−10,000
+ Tax on recapture of depreciation on old equipment ($10,000 × 0.34)	3,400
Initial investment	$94,720

Panel B: Operating cash flows

Incremental cash flows	Year 1	Year 2	Year 3	Year 4	Year 5	Year 6
Operating revenues	$0	$0	$0	$0	$0	$0
Operating cost savings	40,000	42,000	44,000	46,000	48,000	50,000
− Depreciation	20,000	32,000	19,200	11,520	11,520	5,760
Taxable income	$20,000	$10,000	$24,800	$34,480	$36,480	$44,240
− Taxes (34%)	6,800	3,400	8,432	11,723	12,403	15,042
Net income	$13,200	$6,600	$16,368	$22,757	$24,077	$29,198
+ Depreciation	20,000	32,000	19,200	11,520	11,520	5,760
Operating cash flows	$33,200	$38,600	$35,568	$34,277	$35,597	$34,958

MACRS depreciation

Year	Depreciable basis [1]	Depreciation rate [2]	Depreciation amount [1] × [2]
1	$100,000	0.2000	$20,000
2	100,000	0.3200	32,000
3	100,000	0.1920	19,200
4	100,000	0.1152	11,520
5	100,000	0.1152	11,520
6	100,000	0.0576	5,760
	Total depreciation		$100,000

Panel C: Terminal cash flows

Incremental Cash Flows	Year 6
Salvage value	$20,000
− Income taxes (34%)	6,800
Terminal cash flows	$13,200

Panel D: Composite cash flows

Incremental cash flows	Year 0	Year 1	Year 2	Year 3	Year 4	Year 5	Year 6
Initial	−$94,720						
Operating		$33,200	$38,600	$35,568	$34,277	$35,597	$34,958
Terminal							$13,200

taking advantage of lower labor or input costs in other countries. MNCs typically expand into foreign operations gradually, normally beginning with export activities, followed by using a sales and distribution affiliate or by acquiring a licensing agreement for local production. Some MNCs engage in **direct foreign investment**, which is the acquisition by a firm of physical assets in the form of plant and equipment in other countries, by using a foreign subsidiary.

For both MNCs and domestic firms, the goal of capital budgeting is the same – to maximize shareholder wealth as reflected by the market price of common stock. The value of foreign capital investments to stockholders depends on the amount and timing of the cash flows made available to the parent MNC. That is, a US corporation should value only those cash flows that are, or can be, repatriated net of any transfer costs such as taxes. The parent MNC depends on the accessibility to funds for such purposes as paying dividends, satisfying debt obligations, and investing in new projects. Therefore, the relevant cash flows of a foreign project are measured only on cash flows received by the parent company, not based on a foreign project's individual cash flows. A foreign project that is profitable when valued from the subsidiary's perspective may not be profitable from the parent firm's standpoint.

Although capital budgeting theory does not change, the capital budgeting process is more complicated in a global environment. Added complexities faced by MNCs evaluating foreign investments, but not encountered by domestic firms, include:

- different local economic conditions and customs;
- regulatory and tax rate differences;
- restrictions on capital flows;
- exchange rate changes;
- special financing opportunities;
- cost of capital differences;
- added sources of risk.

MNCs must consider each of these variables in foreign investment analysis. The differences between foreign and domestic investments require modifying the capital budgeting process presented in Section 7.3 to include both cash flow adjustments and risk adjustments. We discuss cash flow adjustments below but postpone our discussion of risk adjustments until Chapter 9.

Cash Flow Adjustments

Estimating the cash flows from the parent's perspective involves three steps.

- Identify cash flows generated by a foreign project.
- Determine the cash flows available for repatriation to the MNC.
- Convert the cash flows using exchange rates.

Identify cash flows generated by a foreign project
The first step in the adjustment process is to compute the project's cash flows denominated in the host country's currency. Cash flows of a foreign project consist of cash inflows and cash outflows over a designated evaluation period. These initial cash flows include the cost of property, plant, and equipment associated with the project as well as other start-up costs

such as initial working capital and organizational costs. The MNC often makes additional investments beyond its initial investment such as additions to net operating working capital for expansion projects.

Operating cash flows are the incremental revenues and expenses associated with a project. The major component is the cash flows generated by sales from the endeavor. Although not an operating cash flow, other remittable cash flows include royalties and fees agreed upon by the parent and subsidiary. Keep in mind that tax adjustments must be made to the various cash flows because only after-tax cash flows are relevant to the investment analysis.

Tax adjustments affect the project's cash flows at the host country and again when the profits are repatriated to the US. Most countries tax the income of foreign companies operating within their borders. Both the methods of measuring and taxing income differ markedly among non-US countries. This income, however, is not subject to double taxation because the foreign tax paid by a US corporation in the foreign country directly reduces the amount of US tax it owes. Because the US tax laws applicable to foreign investments are complex and change over time, they are beyond the scope of this book.[6]

Example 7.10 Coordinating Taxes between Countries

Suppose that a corporation earns $1,000,000 in Mexico and pays Mexican income tax equivalent to $250,000. Assuming a 34 percent tax rate, how much would the corporation owe in US taxes?

Solution: The tax burden would be $340,000 less the $250,000 paid to the Mexican government. Thus, the corporation would owe only $90,000 ($340,000 − $250,000) to the US government.

A firm may expect to have terminal cash flows at the end of a project's life. These cash flows may result by liquidating the assets at the end of the planning horizon or by selling a going concern to another company. Estimating these cash flows, however, can be quite complex.

Determine the cash flows available for repatriation to the MNC
In the next step, the perspective shifts from project to parent cash flows. The cash flows remitted to the parent often consist of both a project's operating cash flows and its financial cash flows (fees and royalties as well as interest on loans provided by the parent). Capital budgeting theory stipulates that the basis for evaluating a project is the net after-tax

---

[6] The actual tax paid depends on many factors, including the treaties between home and host countries, the time and form of remittance, the foreign income tax rate, and the existence of withholding taxes and foreign tax credits.

operating cash flows generated by that investment. In practice, however, this could lead to faulty decision making because it ignores other potential cash flows and benefits, such as diversification, to the parent. Considering fees, royalties, and other payments as well as non-quantifiable benefits could make the project attractive. Therefore, the relevant cash flows are all those flows available to the parent MNC.

Although some countries permit the free flow of their currency to and from that country, others impose exchange controls that specifically block the transfer of funds to external destinations. To ensure the repatriation of funds produced by foreign projects, MNCs have developed strategies to counteract any international cash flow restrictions. For example, MNCs may charge royalties and fees that require periodic remission of funds by a subsidiary to the parent company. Another technique for the successful international transfer of funds is for the subsidiary to declare a cash dividend. Here, the MNC is simply a stockholder of a foreign corporation. In addition, the MNC can supply debt capital to its subsidiary resulting in payments of interest and principal that accomplish the seamless transfer of funds.

Convert the cash flows using exchange rates
After forecasting cash flows in a foreign investment's local currency, the MNC must estimate their value in US dollars based on expected exchange rates. An **exchange rate** is the domestic price of one unit of foreign currency. Several factors complicate this step including the inherent volatility of exchange rates and the difficulty of predicting factors specially affecting the currency in question.

Capital budgeting for the MNC involves many complexities not found in domestic capital budgeting. We have identified some important issues to consider when making foreign investments. Various books on international finance contain the quantitative framework for making capital budgeting decisions in an international environment.

Concept Check 7.8

1 What is the primary goal of capital budgeting for MNCs?
2 What are the primary distinctions between foreign capital investments and domestic investments?
3 Should analysts measure cash flows of capital budgeting projects from the viewpoint of the subsidiary or the parent? Why?
4 What obstacles do MNCs face when procuring cash flows from foreign projects and how can they avoid these problems?
5 Why is converting cash flows from international capital investments to the currency of the parent firm necessary?

Summary

This chapter focused on the capital investments and cash flow analysis. The key points of the chapter are as follows:

1 Capital budgeting is the process of planning, analyzing, selecting, and managing capital investments. Capital investment decisions are crucial to a firm's welfare because they often involve large expenditures, have a long-term impact on performance, are not easily reversed once started, and are vital to a firm's ability to achieve its financial objectives.

2 The capital budgeting process is a key part of a firm's strategic planning. The financial manager evaluates individual proposals, normally the larger ones, against the strategic concerns of the firm. Thus, capital budgeting serves as a direct link between financial analysis and corporate strategy.

3 The capital budgeting process requires identifying project proposals; estimating project cash flows; evaluating, selecting, and implementing projects; monitoring performance results; and performing a post-completion audit.

4 Capital budgeting analysis uses only a project's incremental, after-tax cash flows. Cash flows resulting from accepting a project can be both direct (the purchase price of equipment and installation costs) and indirect (changes in net operating working capital, opportunity costs, and side effects). Managers generally exclude interest payments and other financial flows when computing a project's net cash flows.

5 A project's relevant cash flows consist of three components: initial investment, operating cash flows, and terminal cash flows.

6 After estimating the amount and timing of the relevant cash flows, corporate managers evaluate and select appropriate projects. Each step contains a degree of subjectivity because capital budgeting is not a mechanical process.

7 The capital budgeting process is more complicated in a global environment because multinational corporations face added complexities (foreign taxes, repatriation barriers, and exchange rate volatility).

In the next two chapters, we discuss techniques and tools for valuing a proposed project. We also stress the importance of both quantitative and qualitative considerations when making capital budgeting decisions.

FURTHER READING

Dammon, Robert M., and Lemma W. Senbet. "The Effect of Taxes and Depreciation on Corporate Investment and Financial Leverage," *Journal of Finance* 43, June 1988, 357–73.

Kroll, Yoram. "On the Differences between Accrual Accounting Figures and Cash Flows: The Case of Working Capital," *Financial Management* 14, Spring 1985, 75–82.

Metha, Dileep R., Michael D. Curley, and Hung-Gay Fung. "Inflation, Cost of Capital, and Capital Budgeting Procedures," *Financial Management* 13, Winter 1984, 48–54.

Seitz, Neil, and Mitch Ellison. *Capital Budgeting and Long-Term Financing Decisions*, 4th edn, Thomson South-Western, 2005.

Statman, Meir, and Tyzoon T. Tyebjee. "Optimistic Capital Budgeting Forecasts," *Financial Management* 14, Autumn 1985, 27–33.

Chapter 8

Capital Budgeting

According to theory, firms should use discounted cash flow methods to analyze capital budgeting alternatives. Within this theoretical framework, however, firms might evaluate somewhat similar projects differently. (Janet D. Payne, Will Carrington Heath, and Lewis R. Gale, "Comparative Financial Practice in the US and Canada: Capital Budgeting and Risk Assessment Techniques," *Financial Practice and Education 9*, Spring/Summer 1999, p. 16.)

Overview

In previous chapters, we discussed how to estimate the cash flows of a project and we illustrated time value of money concepts needed for project evaluation. This chapter discusses how to use these elements to conduct investment analysis. When evaluating potential capital investments, corporate managers should consider four key questions.

1 Are the projects independent or mutually exclusive?
2 Are the projects of the same size, cash flow pattern, and life?
3 Are the projects subject to capital rationing?
4 Are the projects of the same risk?

In this chapter, we discuss the first three questions but deal with risk analysis in Chapter 9. In answering this chapter's questions, we will show how to apply various capital budgeting techniques to *evaluate* and *select* independent and mutually exclusive projects, deal with conflicts among methods, and make decisions under capital rationing.

When conducting project analysis, decision makers should understand the assumptions made, the techniques used, and the real meaning of the results. The best decision models should help management achieve the goal of shareholder wealth maximization. That is, a firm should primarily undertake a capital investment if it creates value for the owners. Conceptually, the best technique for accomplishing this goal is the net present value (NPV) criterion. In practice, decision makers often use other methods. Therefore, we compare and contrast NPV with other methods used to assist in choosing among alternative investment proposals. At a minimum, a good decision model should consider all relevant cash flows, the time value of money, and risk as reflected in the project's required rate of return.

To simplify our presentation, we make the following assumptions:

- Financial decision makers are economically rational in that they are risk-averse wealth maximizers.
- All projects have the same level of risk to the firm as a whole.
- The firm's cost of capital is constant over time and unaffected by the amount of funds invested in capital projects.
- No resource constraints exist – that is, the firm can accept all profitable projects. Later in the chapter, we relax this assumption and consider investment decisions under capital rationing.

Learning Objectives

After completing this chapter, you should be able to:

- apply reliable capital budgeting techniques for independent and mutually exclusive projects;
- understand the advantages and disadvantages of various capital budgeting techniques;
- resolve conflicts among techniques used to rank mutually exclusive projects;
- describe the selection process under capital rationing;
- explain the trends in using capital budgeting techniques in practice.

8.1 Project Classifications and Analysis

Before managers can apply decision rules, they need to be able to distinguish between independent and mutually exclusive projects. **Independent projects** are those in which the acceptance or rejection of one project does not prevent the acceptance or rejection of other projects under consideration. That is, implementing independent projects is unrelated to each other. Analysts can evaluate the effects of an independent project on a firm's value without having to consider its effect on other investment opportunities. **Mutually exclusive projects** are those in which the acceptance of one project precludes the acceptance of the others.

Managers use a variety of techniques to evaluate and select capital investments including:

- Net present value (NPV)   } Superior approach
- Profitability index (PI)
- Internal rate of return (IRR)
- Modified internal rate of return (MIRR)   } Supplementary approaches
- Payback period (PP)
- Discounted payback period (DPP)

The basic premise of investment analysis is that an investment is worth undertaking if it creates value for its owners. Net present value (NPV) is the most appropriate approach for measuring project desirability because only this model consistently leads to shareholder wealth maximization. In practice, analysts often use other measures to evaluate capital investments because each measure provides some relevant information not contained in any of the other methods. When compared to the NPV, each of the other profitability measures has serious flaws, especially when evaluating mutually exclusive projects. We begin by discussing NPV and then explore other supplementary project appraisal techniques.

All these methods evaluate projects based on cash flows.[1] Managers seek projects in which the present value of expected future cash flows exceeds the amount of the invested funds. This chapter focuses on **discounted cash flow (DCF) techniques**, which consider the time value of money. Only the NPV, PI, IRR and MIRR methods recognize both the time value of money and also consider cash flows over the entire useful life of an investment. Although these four techniques for evaluating cash flows always give the same accept-reject decision for independent projects, they can give conflicting rankings for mutually exclusive decisions. We discuss this point in more detail later in the chapter. Other measures of capital investment desirability are the payback period, which ignores the time value of money, and the discounted payback period, which considers the time value of the cash flows only until the project recovers its initial investment.

Practical Financial Tip 8.1

Applying capital budgeting techniques is a mechanical process once the analyst estimates the cash flows and appropriate discount rate. These inputs are often difficult to determine accurately. In addition, people tend to game the system in order to obtain funding for their projects. Thus, the results from the various methods are indeed estimates, which may be too low or too high. An important point to consider when evaluating capital budgeting projects is the GIGO principle – "garbage in, garbage out." That is, the reliability of the results of capital budgeting techniques hinges on the accuracy of the estimates and assumptions.

We use Projects A and B below to illustrate and evaluate the six capital budgeting techniques in Examples 8.1 to 8.6.

---

[1] Decision makers sometimes use accounting-based profitability measures in capital budgeting analysis. This approach divides some measure of accounting profit by some measure of investment. For example, return on investment is often calculated as a project's net income divided by the investment. We do not discuss accounting-based profitability measures because they represent unsophisticated and unreliable measures that may lead to incorrect investment decisions. A major shortcoming of these measures is that they use accounting data, not cash flows. Recall from Chapter 7 that the relevant basis for evaluating capital budgeting projects is incremental after-tax cash flows, not net income.

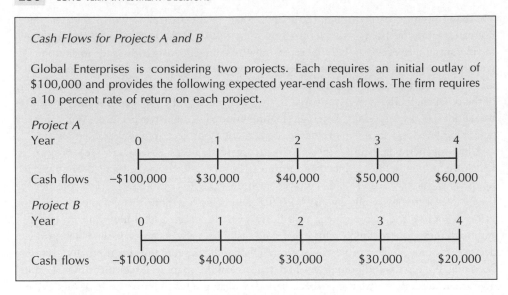

Cash Flows for Projects A and B

Global Enterprises is considering two projects. Each requires an initial outlay of $100,000 and provides the following expected year-end cash flows. The firm requires a 10 percent rate of return on each project.

Project A

Year	0	1	2	3	4
Cash flows	−$100,000	$30,000	$40,000	$50,000	$60,000

Project B

Year	0	1	2	3	4
Cash flows	−$100,000	$40,000	$30,000	$30,000	$20,000

Projects A and B have *conventional* cash flows. That is, the initial investment is a single lump sum occurring in time 0 (the beginning of year 1) followed by a series of cash inflows, conservatively assumed to occur at year-end.[2] In reality, cash flows are likely to occur throughout the year, not simply at year-end. The two projects are of equal size and have the same life span.

Concept Check 8.1

1   What is the difference between independent and mutually exclusive projects?
2   How do the results of the NPV technique relate to the goal of maximizing share-holder wealth?

8.2 Net Present Value

Net present value (NPV) is the sum of the present values of the project's expected cash inflows (benefits) and cash outflows (costs). That is, the NPV is the amount of cash flow in present value terms that the project generates after repaying the invested capital and paying

---

[2]   Assuming future cash flows occur at the end of each year is a conservative assumption because it reduces the present value of the cash flows.

the required rate of return on that capital. The **required rate of return** is the minimum percentage return acceptable to cover a project's cost of capital and risk. If we are measuring cash flows in dollars, NPV is an absolute dollar amount that represents the expected dollar change in value and, therefore, the expected dollar change in shareholder wealth created by undertaking an investment. In theory, the NPV method is considered the best approach because, as an *absolute measure* of a project's profitability, it leads to conceptually correct capital budgeting decisions.

Calculating the Net Present Value

Computing NPV requires discounting the relevant cash flows by the appropriate required rate of return and then summing these discounted cash flows. Equation 8.1 shows the general formula for the NPV:

$$NPV = CF_0 + \frac{CF_1}{(1 + k)^1} + \frac{CF_2}{(1 + k)^2} + \ldots + \frac{CF_n}{(1 + k)^n} = \sum_{t=0}^{n} \frac{CF_t}{(1 + k)^t} \tag{8.1}$$

where CF_t is the expected cash flow for period t; k is the required rate of return (also called the discount rate, hurdle rate, opportunity cost or cost of capital); and n is the expected life of the project. In Equation 8.1, cash outflows will have negative signs and cash inflows will have positive signs.

Another way of viewing the NPV calculation is to simply subtract the present value of the cash outflows directly from the present value of the cash inflows (initial investment). The difference between these two flows is the net cash flow or NPV. In our example for Global Enterprises, all of the cash outflows for Projects A and B occur in year 0 and are already in present value terms. Given the initial investment (I_0), another way to write Equation 8.1 is:

$$NPV = \sum_{t=1}^{n} \frac{CF_t}{(1 + k)^t} - I_0 \tag{8.1a}$$

Managers often use their firm's overall cost of capital as the minimum required rate of return for projects having risk equal to the risk of the firm itself. In Chapter 9, we show that some projects may be more or less risky than the firm as a whole. When this situation occurs, analysts often use a discount rate that differs from the firm's overall cost of capital in order to reflect the risk of the project under consideration. For now, however, we assume that all capital budgeting projects have the same level of risk as the firm. Therefore, the firm's cost of capital is the appropriate discount rate. In Chapter 10, we discuss how to calculate a firm's cost of capital.

Example 8.1 Calculating the NPVs of Projects A and B: Global Enterprises

What are the NPVs of Projects A and B assuming a 10 percent cost of capital?

Solution: At a 10 percent cost of capital, Project A's NPV is $38,877.13 and Project B's NPV is –$2,643.26.

Project A

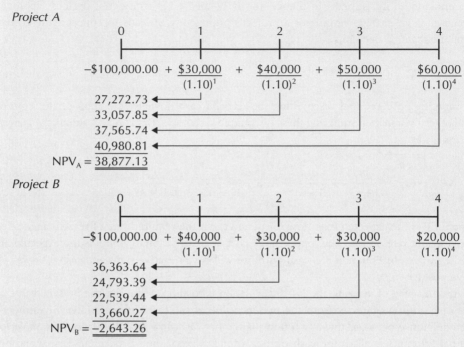

Project B

Another way to calculate the NPV is to use a financial calculator or spreadsheet application such as Excel. Tables 8.1 and 8.2 show how to calculate the NPV for Project A using a Texas Instruments (TI) BA II PLUS® and an Excel spreadsheet, respectively. Calculating the PV for Project B follows a similar procedure.

Table 8.1 Calculating the NPV of Project A using the BA II PLUS® calculator

Key strokes	Explanation	Display	
[2nd] → [Format] → [2] → [Enter]	Display 2 decimals (Need to do this only once)	DEC =	2.00
[CF] → [2nd] → [CLR WORK]	Clear Memory Registers	CF_0 =	0.00
100,000 → [+/–] → [ENTER]	Initial Cash Outlay	CF_0 =	–100,000.00
[↓] → 30,000 → [ENTER]	Period 1 Cash Flow	C01 =	30,000.00
[↓]	Frequency of Cash Flow 1	F01 =	1.00
[↓] → 40,000 → [ENTER]	Period 2 Cash Flow	C02 =	40,000.00
[↓]	Frequency of Cash Flow 2	F02 =	1.00
[↓] → 50,000 → [ENTER]	Period 3 Cash Flow	C03 =	50,000.00
[↓]	Frequency of Cash Flow 3	F03 =	1.00
[↓] → 60,000 → [ENTER]	Period 4 Cash Flow	C04 =	60,000.00
[↓]	Frequency of Cash Flow 4	F04 =	1.00
[NPV] → 10 → [ENTER]	10% Discount Rate	I =	10.00
[↓] → [CPT]	Calculate NPV	NPV =	38,877.13

Table 8.2 Calculating the NPV of Project A using Excel

	A	B	C	D	E	F
1	Project A					
2	k =	10%				
3	Time	0	1	2	3	4
4	Cash flow	−100,000	30,000	40,000	50,000	60,000
5	NPV =	$38,877.13				
6	IRR =					
7	MIRR =					

In Excel, the formula in Cell B5 is as follows: **=B4+NPV(B2,C4:F4)**, which produces a value of $38,877.13. Because the Excel NPV function assumes the cash flows occur at the end of the period, the −$100,000 cash flow in year 0 cannot be included as part of the NPV range.

Decision Rules for NPV

For accepting or rejecting projects based on NPV, the reference point is zero. Theoretically, a firm should accept a project in the case where NPV = 0 because a project has earned its required rate of return. A positive NPV project increases wealth and a negative NPV project decreases wealth.[3]

Decision Rules for the Net Present Value

- For *independent projects,* accept the project if the NPV is zero or positive and reject the project if the NPV is negative.
- For *mutually exclusive projects,* accept the project with the highest positive NPV.

---

[3] Some contend that the rule of accepting projects with positive NPVs may be too lenient because it fails to consider the bias introduced from there being typically more poor projects than good projects. Thus, the traditional NPV criterion may reject too few projects. For this argument, see Edward M. Miller, "Capital Budgeting Errors Seldom Cancel," *Financial Practice and Education*, Fall/Winter 2000, 128–35.

Theoretically, by selecting a project with a positive NPV, the value of the firm should increase by the amount of the NPV. Projects with a positive NPV do not just happen. They typically result from some competitive advantage that the firm has developed. For example, this competitive advantage may result from product differentiation and/or cost advantages. Conversely, if a firm selects a project with a negative NPV, both its stock price and shareholder wealth should decrease. Rational managers should accept all projects with a positive NPV and reject all those with a negative NPV. Even a project with an NPV of $1 would be acceptable if managers were confident about the accuracy of the inputs to the NPV model. In practice, a small NPV may not provide an adequate cushion against forecast errors. In the unlikely event that the NPV is exactly zero, the firm should technically be indifferent to the project. That is, the project would add nothing to shareholder wealth beyond the required return although it does fully compensate the firm for the time value of money and the risk involved.

In practice, forecasting biases sometimes exist. For example, those proposing projects may overstate cash inflows and understate cash outflows. These biases inflate the NPV of projects. Unless decision makers are aware of this problem and make adjustments for it, they are likely to accept too many projects that appear to have positive NPVs.

If the two projects are independent, Global Enterprises should accept Project A but reject Project B. Undertaking Project A is a good investment because it should add $38,877 to shareholder wealth. Because Project A has a positive NPV, it provides an expected return that exceeds the required rate of return of 10 percent. Based on the estimates, accepting Project B should reduce the total value of the firm's stock by $2,643. If the two projects were mutually exclusive, Global Enterprises would prefer Project A because it has both a positive and higher NPV compared with Project B.

Strengths and Weaknesses

The NPV approach has four major strengths.

- *The NPV method provides an objective criterion for making decisions that maximize shareholder wealth.* NPV is a direct measure of a project's dollar benefit to a firm's shareholders.
- *The NPV approach fully accounts for time value of money and considers all cash flows over the life of the project.*
- *The NPV method implicitly assumes that the firm can reinvest all of a project's cash inflows at the project's required rate of return throughout the life of the project.* This reinvestment rate assumption is generally more realistic than the reinvestment rate assumption used in the internal rate of return (IRR). The IRR method assumes that the firm can reinvest cash inflows at the project's IRR over its useful life.
- *The NPV approach provides theoretically correct accept-reject decisions* for both independent and mutually exclusive projects based on their effect on shareholder wealth.

The NPV has a few weaknesses.

- *The NPV does not provide a gauge for relative profitability.* For example, an NPV of $1,000 is highly desirable for a project costing $2,000 but not for a project costing $1 million.

- *Some people have difficulty understanding the meaning of the NPV measure.* In practice, managers often prefer a percentage return to a present value dollar return.

Concept Check 8.2

1 What is the typical discount rate used with the NPV technique when project risk is the same as firm risk? Why?
2 In theory, why is NPV the most appropriate technique for making capital budgeting decisions?
3 If a firm selects a project with an NPV of $75,000, what impact should this decision have on shareholder wealth?
4 If a project's NPV is positive, what does this suggest about the required versus estimated return on the project? What does this suggest about accepting the project?
5 If a project's NPV is negative, what does this suggest about the desirability of the project? Why?
6 How does the reinvestment rate assumption of the NPV method differ from IRR? Which reinvestment assumption is generally considered to be more realistic? Why?

8.3 Profitability Index

The **profitability index** (PI), also called the **benefit/cost ratio**, is the ratio of the present value of an investment's expected cash inflows (benefits) to the present value of its expected cash outflows (costs). The PI shows the *relative profitability* of any investment, or the value increase per present value dollar of costs. In a sense, the profitability index shows how much "bang for the buck" an investment provides. For some, the profitability index as a relative measure has greater intuitive appeal than the NPV criterion. PI is simply a variant of NPV because both methods use the same inputs.

Calculating the Profitability Index

The general formula for calculating the profitability index is:

$$PI = \frac{PV \text{ cash inflows}}{PV \text{ cash outflows}} = \frac{\sum_{t=0}^{n} \frac{CIF_t}{(1 + k)^t}}{\sum_{t=0}^{n} \frac{COF_t}{(1 + k)^t}} \tag{8.2}$$

Here CIF_t and COF_t represent the expected cash inflows and cash outflows, respectively. If the investment outlay occurs only in year 0, another way of writing Equation 8.2 is:

$$PI = \frac{\sum\limits_{t=1}^{n} \dfrac{CF_t}{(1 + k)^t}}{I_0} \tag{8.2a}$$

Example 8.2 Calculating the PIs of Projects A and B: Global Enterprises

Assuming a 10 percent cost of capital, what is the PI of Projects A and B?

Solution: At a 10 percent cost of capital, the PI for Projects A and B is calculated as:

Project A

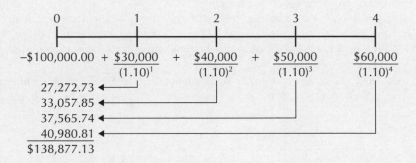

Project B

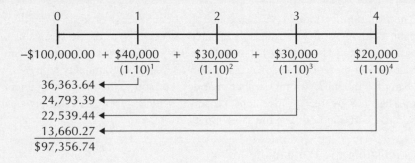

$$PI_A = \frac{\$138,877.13}{\$100,000.00} = 1.39 \qquad PI_B = \frac{\$97,356.74}{\$100,000.00} = 0.97$$

What do these PIs mean? A PI of 1.39 suggests that Project A will generate $1.39 of present value for every dollar initially invested in the project. Project B's PI is 0.97, which means that it should produce $0.97 of present value for each dollar invested. Analysts sometimes view the PI as a project's margin of error and risk indicator. For example, Project A's PI suggests that cash inflows are 39 percent greater than what is required to generate a NPV of zero and merely break even on the project. Thus, the PI gives an indication of how much cash inflows can fall below expectations before the project begins to destroy wealth. Project B's PI suggests that cash inflows are only 97 percent of what is required for this project just to break even. Hence, the firm should not implement Project B.

Decision Rules for PI

For accepting or rejecting an independent project based on the PI, the reference point is 1. An independent project is acceptable if its PI is greater than 1 because the present value of a project's benefits exceeds the present value of its costs. A project with a PI greater than 1 will have a positive NPV and enhance the wealth of the owners. If a project's PI is less than 1, the present value of the costs exceeds the present value of the benefits, so the NPV is negative. If a project's PI equals 1, the decision maker technically should be indifferent between accepting and rejecting the project.

Managers should avoid using the PI technique for mutually exclusive projects. When evaluating such projects, the project with the highest PI may not be the project with the highest NPV. Differences in ranking between the two techniques may occur for projects of different size or for projects with substantial timing differences in the future cash inflows.

Decision Rules for the Profitability Index

- For *independent projects,* accept the project if the PI is equal to or greater than 1 and reject the project if the PI is less than 1.
- For *mutually exclusive projects,* accept the project with the highest PI greater than or equal to 1. (This decision rule assumes that no conflict in ranking exists with the NPV. If a conflict in ranking occurs between the PI and NPV, accept the project with the highest positive NPV.)

If the projects are independent, management should accept Project A with a PI of 1.39 because the benefits exceed the costs but should reject Project B because its PI of 0.97 is less than 1. If the projects are mutually exclusive, Project A is acceptable and ranks ahead of Project B. In this example, no conflict exists in project rankings between using the NPV and PI.

As previously mentioned, a close relationship exists between PI and NPV. Table 8.3 shows the relationships among NPV, PI, and the required rate of return.

Strengths and Weaknesses

The PI approach has several desirable qualities.

- *The PI method reveals the ratio by which an investment should increase shareholder wealth per dollar invested.* This approach, however, does not indicate the total amount of wealth creation.

Table 8.3 Relationships among NPV, PI, and the required rate of return

Net present value	Profitability index	Required rate of return (k)
Negative	Less than 1	Less than k
Zero	Equal to 1	Equal to k
Positive	Greater than 1	Greater than k

- *The PI approach fully accounts for time value of money and considers all cash flows over a project's life.*
- *The PI serves as a measure of the margin for error.* Compared to projects with low PIs, projects with high PIs have a greater ability to absorb estimation errors and still break even (in a present value sense).

The PI method has several drawbacks.

- *Decision makers trained in interpreting NPV amounts or IRR percentages may have difficulty understanding why an investment is good because its PI is greater than 1.*
- *The PI technique may not lead to correct decisions when used to compare mutually exclusive projects.* PI ignores the *amount* of NPV generated. Thus, one project may have a higher PI than another but have a lower NPV (generate less wealth for shareholders).

Concept Check 8.3

1   What is the meaning of the profitability index?
2   Why does the profitability index fail to consider total wealth creation?
3   Why would a decision maker use the profitability index?
4   What is the relationship between PI and NPV?
5   Is the higher PI of two projects always superior? Under what circumstances can this be misleading?

8.4 Internal Rate of Return

The **internal rate of return** (IRR) is the rate of return that equates the present value of all cash flows to zero. This is equivalent to saying that the IRR is the rate of return for which the NPV is zero. Alternatively, the IRR is the rate of return that equates the present value of a project's future cash inflows to the present value of the project's costs: PV (inflows) = PV (investment outlays). Thus, a project's IRR is its **expected rate of return**. Because IRR is a percentage, managers cannot relate the IRR directly to an absolute dollar change in value or shareholder wealth. Having a clear understanding of this concept is important because managers and analysts often use the IRR.

Calculating the Internal Rate of Return

In calculating the IRR, the IRR model implicitly assumes that the firm can reinvest the cash flows at the project's IRR. The formula used to solve for the IRR is:

$$CF_0 + \frac{CF_1}{(1 + IRR)^1} + \frac{CF_2}{(1 + IRR)^2} + \ldots + \frac{CF_n}{(1 + IRR)^n} = \sum_{t=0}^{n} \frac{CF_t}{(1 + IRR)^t} = 0 \qquad (8.3)$$

If all investment outflows occur in year 0 followed by a series of cash inflows, Equation 8.3 becomes:

$$\sum_{t=1}^{n} \frac{CF_t}{(1 + IRR)^t} = I_0 \qquad (8.3a)$$

Three methods available for calculating the IRR are by using: (1) trial-and-error, (2) a financial calculator, and (3) a spreadsheet application. To calculate the IRR using the trial-and-error method requires several steps.

1 Pick a discount rate that might reflect the project's IRR. For example, the firm's cost of capital can serve as the starting discount rate.
2 Compute the project's NPV using this discount rate and see if the NPV is zero. If the NPV is not zero, pick a higher discount rate if the NPV is positive or a lower discount rate if the NPV is negative.
3 Repeat this process until NPV is zero.

Example 8.3 Calculating the IRR of Projects A and B: Global Enterprises

Returning to Global Enterprises, calculate the IRR for Projects A and B.

Solution: Using an iterative, trial-and-error process, the IRR for Projects A and B eventually results in the following:

$$0 = -\$100,000 + \frac{\$30,000}{(1 + IRR_A)^1} + \frac{\$40,000}{(1 + IRR_A)^2} + \frac{\$50,000}{(1 + IRR_A)^3} + \frac{\$60,000}{(1 + IRR_A)^4}$$

$$0 = -\$100,000 + \frac{\$40,000}{(1 + IRR_B)^1} + \frac{\$30,000}{(1 + IRR_B)^2} + \frac{\$30,000}{(1 + IRR_B)^3} + \frac{\$20,000}{(1 + IRR_B)^4}$$

Trial and error gives an $IRR_A = 24.89$ percent and an $IRR_B = 8.64$ percent.

Table 8.4 Calculating the IRR_A using the TI BA II PLUS® calculator

Key strokes	Explanation	Display	
[CF] → [2ⁿᵈ] → [CLR WORK]	Clear Memory Registers	$CF_0 =$	0.00
100,000 → [+/−] → [ENTER]	Initial Cash Outlay	$CF_0 =$	−100,000.00
[↓] → 30,000 → [ENTER]	Period 1 Cash Flow	$C01 =$	30,000.00
[↓]	Frequency of Cash Flow 1	$F01 =$	1.00
[↓] → 40,000 → [ENTER]	Period 2 Cash Flow	$C02 =$	40,000.00
[↓]	Frequency of Cash Flow 2	$F02 =$	1.00
[↓] → 50,000 → [ENTER]	Period 3 Cash Flow	$C03 =$	50,000.00
[↓]	Frequency of Cash Flow 3	$F03 =$	1.00
[↓] → 60,000 → [ENTER]	Period 4 Cash Flow	$C04 =$	60,000.00
[↓]	Frequency of Cash Flow 4	$F04 =$	1.00
[IRR} → [CPT]	Calculate IRR	$IRR =$	24.89

In practice, computing the IRR is easier using a financial calculator or spreadsheet model with a built-in IRR function. Table 8.4 illustrates how to calculate the IRR for Project A using a BA II PLUS® calculator.

Returning to Table 8.2, which is the Excel spreadsheet we used to solve for the NPV, enter the following formula in Cell B6: **=IRR(B4:F4)**. The IRR function in Excel assumes that the first cash flow occurs at $t = 0$. Thus, Excel allows specifying the full range. The result is an $IRR_A = 24.89$ percent.

What does an IRR of 24.89 percent mean? It means that Project A should provide a rate of return of about 24.89 percent of the initial investment of $100,000, assuming that projects with comparable returns materialize in the future. Recall that the IRR method assumes that the firm can reinvest cash in flows generated by the investment at the project's own IRR.

Decision Rules for IRR

Unlike the NPV, calculating the IRR does not require estimating the appropriate discount rate. In most cases, however, using the IRR decision rule necessitates establishing a required rate of return or hurdle rate as a benchmark for evaluating the acceptability of the project. This rate is the minimum acceptable IRR that would result in the project increasing shareholder wealth. This hurdle rate is usually the firm's overall cost of capital when the projects under consideration are equally as risky as the firm's average project. As we show in Chapter 9, the analyst can adjust the hurdle rate upward or downward to compensate for risk differences between the project and the firm. The decision maker then compares the project's IRR with the required rate of return.

Decision Rules for the Internal Rate of Return

- For *independent projects,* accept the project if the IRR is equal to or greater than the required rate of return and reject the project if the IRR is less than the required rate of return.
- For *mutually exclusive projects,* accept the project with the highest IRR that is greater than the required rate of return. (This decision rule assumes that no conflict in ranking exists between the IRR and the NPV. If a conflict in ranking occurs, accept the project with the highest positive NPV.)

The rationale for the IRR method is that if the IRR exceeds the cost of capital used to finance the project, the excess return remains to boost shareholders' returns and wealth. If Projects A and B were independent, Project A would be acceptable because its IRR of 24.89 percent exceeds the 10 percent cost of capital. The firm should reject Project B because its expected IRR of 8.64 percent is less than the cost of capital. If the two projects were mutually exclusive, the firm should select Project A because it ranks higher than Project B. In this particular situation, no conflict in ranking occurs between IRR and NPV.

Strengths and Weaknesses

As an evaluation technique, the IRR method has several strong points.

- *The IRR measures profitability as a percentage showing the return on each dollar invested.* Like the PI, the IRR shows whether a project contributes to the value of the firm. This measure is intuitively appealing to many managers because they can readily compare the rate of return on an investment with the cost of funds to get a "margin of profit."
- *The IRR approach fully accounts for time value of money and considers all cash flows for the life of the project.* The NPV and PI methods share these attributes.
- *The IRR provides safety margin information to management.* The IRR indicates how much the return on a project could fall in percentage terms before it begins to destroy firm value. Thus, the higher the IRR is relative to the cost of capital, the higher is the safety margin.
- *Some managers prefer the IRR because they like dealing with percentage rates of return more than with the dollar values in NPV.* Because the IRR refers to a percentage rate of return, managers can easily compare the IRR to the firm's minimum acceptable rate of return or hurdle rate when making investment decisions.

The IRR has several pitfalls.

- *The IRR method can produce no IRR, one IRR, or multiple IRRs if a project has a non-conventional cash flow pattern.* Recall from Chapter 7 that a non-conventional cash flow pattern has more than one sign change (from positive to negative and/or negative to positive) in its series of cash flows. If a project has multiple IRRs, more than one discount rate can equate the NPV to zero. Thus, determining the appropriate rate of return is not obvious. When multiple IRRs occur, their economic significance is meaningless. We do not discuss how to calculate or handle multiple IRRs because decision makers can bypass this problem by using the NPV method when faced with non-conventional cash flows.

- *The IRR method implicitly assumes that the firm can reinvest all of a project's cash inflows at the project's IRR throughout the life of the project.* This assumption may be unrealistic, especially for projects with high IRRs, because the IRR does not necessarily represent the rate of return that a firm can earn on reinvested cash flows. The firm's cost of capital is probably a more tenable reinvestment rate assumption for investment opportunities.
- *The IRR can lead to potentially conflicting accept or reject decisions when compared to NPV for mutually exclusive projects.* When the cash flows of mutually exclusive projects differ in size, timing of cash flow, or lives, the rankings can be inconsistent. The IRR method delivers only a percentage rate of a project's earnings power, not the magnitude or duration of its cash flows.

Practical Financial Tip 8.2

Managers should carefully investigate projects with an exceptionally large NPV or IRR, especially if these projects have long lives. Because the source of positive NPV projects is typically some competitive advantage, maintaining the levels of early cash flows could be a challenge. In highly competitive markets, competitors may be able to replicate these projects, which, in turn, can limit the sustainability of any competitive advantage.

Concept Check 8.4

1 What does the IRR measure?
2 Why may using the IRR method as a decision criterion not lead to maximizing shareholder wealth? What factors can cause misleading results when comparing the IRR with the NPV?
3 Under what conditions can a project have more than one IRR?
4 What reinvestment rate assumption does IRR implicitly make?

8.5 Modified Internal Rate of Return

One way to overcome some of the conceptual and computation problems with using IRR is to develop and apply an improved rate of return measure. This enhanced measure of relative profitability uses a more realistic reinvestment rate assumption than the IRR. The preferred method also avoids the multiple-IRR problem resulting from non-conventional cash flows by developing a single IRR measure. The **modified internal rate of return** (MIRR) is the rate of return that equates the present value of cash outflows for a given capital project (present value of costs) with the present value of the terminal value.[4] **Terminal value** (TV) is the value that would accumulate at the end of a project's life by compounding the project's cash inflows at a specified rate, typically the cost of capital, between the time the cash flows occurred (t) and the end of the project's life (n).

Compared to the IRR, the MIRR is a superior indicator of a project's "true" rate of return. This is because the MIRR generally assumes that the firm reinvests the cash inflows at the cost of capital instead of at the IRR. The NPV method is still better for choosing among competing projects because it provides a superior indicator of how much each project will increase the value of the firm.

Calculating the Modified Internal Rate of Return

Calculating the MIRR requires three steps: (1) computing the present value of the cash outflows; (2) compounding a project's future cash inflows at the forecast reinvestment rate (typically the firm's cost of capital) to a terminal value; and (3) determining the discount rate (MIRR) that equates the terminal value to the present value of the cash outflows. The general formula for MIRR states that the present value of the cash outflows is equal to the present value of the terminal value.

$$
\left.\begin{array}{c}
\sum_{t=0}^{n} \dfrac{COF_t}{(1+k)^t} = \dfrac{\sum_{t=0}^{n} CIF_t(1+k)^{n-t}}{(1+MIRR)^n} \\[2em]
PV \text{ cash outflows} = \dfrac{TV}{(1+MIRR)^n}
\end{array}\right\}
\qquad (8.4)
$$

As defined when discussing Equation 8.2, COF refers to the cash outflows (negative numbers) and CIF represents the cash inflows (positive numbers). For investments involving an initial cash outflow in $t = 0$, followed by a stream of cash inflows from year 1 to year n, the following formula applies:

$$
I_0 = \dfrac{TV}{(1+MIRR)^n}
\qquad (8.4a)
$$

---

[4] There are several other variations of the MIRR. For a detailed discussion of alternative yield-based capital budgeting techniques, see William R. McDaniel, Daniel E. McCarty, and Kenneth A. Jessell, "Discounted Cash Flow with Explicit Reinvestment Rates: Tutorial and Extension," *The Financial Review*, August 1988, 369–85; and David M. Shull, "Interpreting Rates of Return: A Modified Rate of Return Approach," *Financial Practice and Education*, Fall 1993, 67–71.

Example 8.4 Calculating the MIRR of Projects A and B: Global Enterprises

Using the cost of capital of 10 percent as the reinvestment rate, what is the MIRR of Projects A and B for Global Enterprises?

Solution: We illustrate the MIRR calculation for Projects A and B as follows:

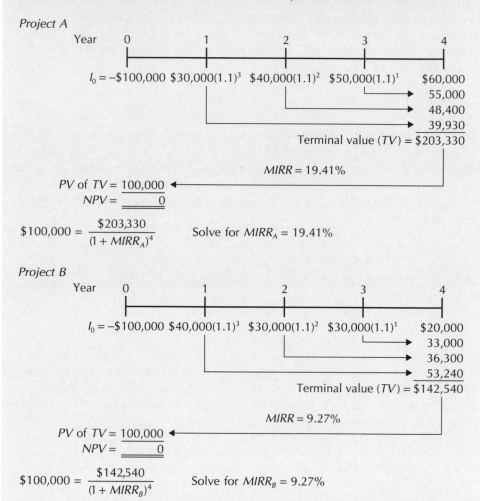

Project A

Year	0	1	2	3	4

$I_0 = -\$100,000$ $\$30,000(1.1)^3$ $\$40,000(1.1)^2$ $\$50,000(1.1)^1$ $\$60,000$

55,000

48,400

39,930

Terminal value $(TV) = \$203,330$

$MIRR = 19.41\%$

PV of $TV = 100,000$
$NPV = \underline{\qquad 0}$

$$\$100,000 = \frac{\$203,330}{(1 + MIRR_A)^4}$$ Solve for $MIRR_A = 19.41\%$

Project B

Year	0	1	2	3	4

$I_0 = -\$100,000$ $\$40,000(1.1)^3$ $\$30,000(1.1)^2$ $\$30,000(1.1)^1$ $\$20,000$

33,000

36,300

53,240

Terminal value $(TV) = \$142,540$

$MIRR = 9.27\%$

PV of $TV = 100,000$
$NPV = \underline{\qquad 0}$

$$\$100,000 = \frac{\$142,540}{(1 + MIRR_B)^4}$$ Solve for $MIRR_B = 9.27\%$

To solve for the *MIRR* for Project *A* using the BA II PLUS® calculator, input the relevant data and compute I/Y.

$N = 4$; $PV = -100,000$; $FV = 203,330$; $CPT \rightarrow$ I/Y = 19.41%.

In Excel, return to Table 8.2 and enter the following formula in Cell B7: **=MIRR(B4:F4,10%,10%)**. The result is a value of 19.41 percent. In the formula, the first 10 percent is the cost of capital used for discounting, and the second 10 percent is the reinvestment rate used for discounting. In this example, we assume both the cost of capital and the reinvestment rate are the same, but this does not necessarily have to be the case. For example, a firm may believe that it will be able to reinvest future cash flows at 12 percent, instead of at its current 10 percent cost of capital.

What is the relationship between the MIRR and the IRR for Projects A and B? Project A's MIRR (19.41 percent) is lower than its IRR (24.89 percent). This result occurs because the reinvestment rate of 10 percent using MIRR is *lower* than the assumed reinvestment rate of 24.89 percent using the IRR. On the other hand, Project B's MIRR (9.27 percent) is higher than its IRR (8.64 percent). In this case, the reinvestment rate using the MIRR (10 percent) is *higher* than assumed using the IRR (8.64 percent). Thus, a project's MIRR can be higher or lower than its IRR depending on the assumed reinvestment rate.

Decision Rules for MIRR

To determine whether to accept or reject a project, the analyst compares the MIRR to the firm's required rate of return (the hurdle rate). The following decision rules apply to the MIRR.

Decision Rules for the Modified Internal Rate of Return

- For *independent projects*, accept the project if the MIRR is equal to or greater than the required rate of return and reject the project if the MIRR is less than the required rate of return.
- For *mutually exclusive projects*, accept the project where the highest MIRR is equal to or greater than the required rate of return. (This decision rule assumes that no conflict in ranking exists between the MIRR and the NPV. If a conflict in ranking occurs, accept the project with the highest positive NPV.)

Returning to Projects A and B, Global Enterprises expects to reinvest the cash inflows from each project at its cost of capital of 10 percent. Which projects, if any, should the firm accept using the MIRR as the decision criterion? If Projects A and B are independent, managers at Global Enterprises should accept Project A because its MIRR of 19.41 percent exceeds the firm's cost of capital of 10 percent. By contrast, managers should reject Project B because its MIRR of 9.27 percent is less than the required rate of return. For mutually exclusive projects, Project A is preferred over Project B due to its higher and acceptable MIRR. Both the MIRR and NPV methods rank Project A ahead of Project B so no conflict in ranking exists.

Strengths and Weaknesses

The MIRR shares similar strengths with the IRR but overcomes several of its weaknesses. Additional strengths of the MIRR over the IRR are as follows:

- *MIRR incorporates a better reinvestment rate assumption than the IRR technique.* The MIRR assumes that the firm can reinvest a project's cash inflows at some explicit rate, typically the firm's cost of capital, while the IRR implicitly assumes that the firm can invest these cash inflows at the project's computed IRR. Using the firm's cost of capital as the reinvestment rate provides a conservative estimate of the firm's rate of return.
- *MIRR provides an unambiguous accept-reject signal when multiple IRRs are possible.* Thus, MIRR overcomes the potential problem of multiple IRRs.

The major weakness of the MIRR follows:

- Similar to the conventional IRR approach, MIRR may not give a value-maximizing decision when used to compare mutually exclusive projects with different investment scales or different risk.

Practical Financial Tip 8.3

Discounted cash flow models including NPV, PI, and IRR implicitly assume that the firm can reinvest a project's cash inflows to earn a return that is equal to the rate used to discount the cash flows. This reinvestment rate assumption applies to each cash inflow between the time it occurs and the end of the project's life. Managers should understand and examine the appropriateness of the reinvestment rate assumption for specific capital expenditures.

Concept Check 8.5

1   Why is the MIRR an improved measure of relative profitability compared with the IRR?
2   What is the typical reinvestment rate used in calculating the MIRR? Why?
3   What advantages does the MIRR have over the IRR when making capital budgeting decisions?

8.6 Payback Period

Financial managers are often concerned about how long a capital expenditure project takes to break even. The **payback period** (PP) is the amount of time required for an investment to generate sufficient cash flows to recover its initial cost. Underlying this method is the notion that a firm is more inclined to adopt a project if it can recover its initial outlay quickly. For example, suppose a company plans to make a large capital investment in a country with an unstable government. In this situation, management may want a short payback to ensure that it recovers its investment in the event circumstances change and the firm must abandon the project. Nevertheless, a rapid payback does not guarantee a good investment.

Calculating the Payback Period

One way to express the length of time needed for the cash flows to equal the amount of the investment is:

$$0 = \sum_{t=1}^{PP} CF_t - I_0 \tag{8.5}$$

Here *PP* is the payback period. If the operating cash flows occur evenly throughout each year, Equation 8.6 provides an operational formula for calculating the payback period by adding up the future cash flows.

$$\text{Payback period} = \text{Year before full recovery} + \frac{\text{Unrecovered cost at start of the year}}{\text{Cash flow during the year}} \tag{8.6}$$

Example 8.5 Calculating the Payback Period of Projects A and B: Global Enterprises

The manager now wants to calculate the payback period for Projects A and B.

Solution: As shown in Table 8.5, finding the payback period for Projects A and B involves determining when the cumulative net cash flows (NCF) of each project equal zero.

$$PP_A = 2 + \frac{30,000}{50,000} = 2.6 \text{ years} \qquad PP_B = 3.0 \text{ years}$$

Although the payback for these two projects is easy to calculate, some peculiarities may exist when computing the payback for other projects. For example, a project may never pay for itself because its cash flows do not add up to the initial investment. In addition, a project may have more than one payback when it has non-conventional cash flows (flows that contain more than one sign change). Thus, the method of calculating the payback does not guarantee a single answer.

Table 8.5 Cumulative net cash flows for Projects A and B

Project	Year (*t*)	0	1	2	3	4
A	Net cash flow	−100,000	30,000	40,000	50,000	60,000
	Cumulative NCF	−100,000	−70,000	−30,000	20,000	80,000
B	Net cash flow	−100,000	40,000	30,000	30,000	20,000
	Cumulative NCF	−100,000	−60,000	−30,000	0	20,000

Decision Rules for PP

When using the payback period approach, management should first set a maximum acceptable payback period or "cutoff period" for a project. Managers rely on their experience and judgment when establishing the maximum payback period. This ad hoc benchmark varies among firms and different types of investments. Comparing a project's expected payback period to the cutoff period provides the following decision rules.

Decision Rules for the Payback Period

- For *independent projects*, accept the project if the payback period is less than or equal to the maximum payback period, otherwise reject the project.
- For *mutually exclusive projects*, accept the project with the shortest payback period, when the payback period is less than or equal to the maximum payback period.

Suppose that management at Global Enterprises sets a maximum payback period of 2.5 years. What is the appropriate decision involving these projects? If the projects were independent, the firm should reject both Projects A and B. This decision occurs because the expected paybacks of 2.6 and 3.0 years, respectively, exceed the maximum payback period of 2.5 years. If the projects were mutually exclusive, managers would prefer Project A over Project B due to its shorter payback period. The firm should still reject Project A because its payback exceeds the maximum payback set by the firm's management of 2.5 years. If, on the other hand, management set a maximum payback of 3 years, both projects would be acceptable. This illustrates the arbitrary nature of the benchmark.

Strengths and Weaknesses

The payback period has two major redeeming qualities.

- *The concept of a payback period is intuitive and easy to understand.* Firms often use the payback method to screen minor investment decisions that do not warrant a detailed analysis.
- *The payback period is an indicator of liquidity and risk for a project.* That is, the shorter the payback period, the greater is the liquidity because the project generates cash inflows more quickly to recover the initial investment. Rapid payback periods can be critical for severely capital-constrained firms and those in industries with rapid technological developments. Payback provides a crude measure of project risk since distant cash flows are inherently riskier than near cash flows. Thus, the payback period rule provides an unsophisticated adjustment for uncertainty of later cash flows. Yet, the decision rule ignores risk differences because the payback method calculates risky and safe investments in precisely the same way.

The payback period has numerous shortcomings.

- *No firm cutoff guidelines exist for establishing a maximum payback period.* Management bases the designated payback period primarily on its experience and judgment.
- *Payback ignores the timing of the cash flows within the payback period.* The failure to consider the time value of money understates the true payback period. That is, the payback period would be longer if the firm discounted the cash flows to get a payback measure. The downward bias of the regular payback may lead to accepting investments that are actually worth less than they cost. In addition, projects with different cash flow patterns may have the same payback but not be equally desirable in an economic sense.
- *Payback neglects the expected cash flows that occur beyond the payback period.* This means that the payback method fails to consider some operating and terminal cash flows. The payback method may bias capital budgeting decisions towards accepting short-term projects while rejecting profitable long-term investments such as research and development and new projects.
- *Payback provides no objective criterion consistent with shareholder wealth maximization.* The payback method may lead to selecting projects that do not contribute the most to maximizing the firm's value. This results from failing to discount all cash flows and establishing an arbitrary cutoff criterion.
- *Payback does not measure profitability, only the speed of recovering the initial investment.* The decision rule for the payback method does not ask the right question. The relevant issue is how a project contributes to a firm's value, not how long a project takes to cover its initial cost. Because the payback period has a bias towards liquidity, it also has a bias against long-term projects. Payback would lead to selecting projects with heavy early cash flows at the expense of long-term projects that maximize a firm's wealth.

The inability of the payback method to resolve these problems makes it an unsophisticated and misleading measure. Little economic rationale exists for looking at the payback period. At best, the payback method serves as a supplementary method to the NPV criterion. Yet, firms, especially small ones, continue to use payback as an evaluation criterion for capital budgeting projects.

Concept Check 8.6

1 What supplementary information does the payback period provide beyond discounted cash flow techniques such as NPV or IRR?
2 If a project has a payback period of 3.5 years, what does this mean?
3 What decision rule applies when using the payback period to evaluate independent and mutually exclusive projects?
4 Why do some decision makers use the payback period to evaluate projects?
5 What are the disadvantages of the payback method as a capital budgeting technique?

8.7 Discounted Payback Period

To incorporate time value of money concepts, analysts sometimes use the **discounted payback period** (DPP), which is the length of time required for an investment's cumulative discounted cash flows to equal zero. Thus, the discounted payback is the length of time required to recover the initial investment from the present value of the expected future cash flows. Due to this important distinction, the discounted payback is a more realistic measure of recouping the initial investment than the standard payback method.

Calculating the Discounted Payback Period

Calculating the DPP requires discounting a project's cash flows at an appropriate discount rate, usually the firm's cost of capital, and then comparing the discounted cumulative cash flows to the initial investment. The DPP involves solving the following formula:

$$0 = \sum_{t=1}^{DPP} \frac{CF_t}{(1 + r)^t} - I_0 \qquad (8.7)$$

Equation 8.8 provides another way of stating the discounted payback period.

$$DPP = \text{Year before full recovery} + \frac{\text{Unrecovered cost at start of the year}}{\text{Discounted cash flow during the year}} \qquad (8.8)$$

Example 8.6 Calculating the Discounted Payback Period of Projects A and B: Global Enterprises

Let's return to Projects A and B and calculate the discounted payback period.

Solution: Using a discount rate of 10 percent, Table 8.6 shows the cumulative discounted net cash flows (NCF) of each project.

$$DPP_A = 3 + \frac{2,103.68}{40,980.81} = 3.05 \text{ years} \qquad DPP_B \text{ does not exist.}$$

For Project A, the present value of the net cash flows matches the $100,000 initial investment in about 3.05 years.[5] The discounted payback period is longer for Project A (3.05 years)

---

[5]   Calculating a fractional year for the discounted payback period is more complex than shown due to issues involving the time value of money. The method illustrated above generally serves as a reasonable approximation.

Table 8.6 Cumulative discounted net cash flows for Projects A and B

Project	Year (t)	0	1	2	3	4
A	Net cash flow	−100,000	30,000.00	40,000.00	50,000.00	60,000.00
	Discounted NCF		27,272.73	33,057.85	37,565.74	40,980.81
	Cumulative discounted NCF	−100,000	−72,727.27	−39,669.42	−2,103.68	38,877.13
B	Net cash flow	−100,000	40,000.00	30,000.00	30,000.00	20,000.00
	Discounted NCF		36,363.64	24,793.39	22,539.44	13,660.27
	Cumulative discounted NCF	−100,000	−63,636.36	−38,842.97	−16,303.53	−2,643.26

than for the regular payback (2.6 years). That is because discounting results in smaller cash flows, which require more time to recoup the initial costs. The discounted payback for Project B does not exist because the cumulative discounted NCF is still negative at the end of the project's life in year 4.

Decision Rules for DPP

The discounted payback period shares the same decision rule with the payback period. However, management may set an extended or higher cutoff for the discounted payback period.

Decision Rules for the Discounted Payback Period

- For *independent projects*, accept the project if the discounted payback period is less than or equal to the maximum discounted payback period, otherwise reject the project.
- For *mutually exclusive projects*, accept the project with the shortest discounted payback period, when the discounted payback is less than or equal to the maximum discounted payback period.

If management at Global Enterprises establishes a maximum discounted payback of 3.0 years, neither Project A nor Project B would be acceptable in the case of independent projects. If the projects were mutually exclusive, management would prefer Project A over Project B due to Project A's shorter discounted payback period. Nonetheless, because Project A's payback slightly exceeds the maximum payback period, management would likely reject the project.

If a discounted payback exists, this indicates that the project will have a positive NPV. To understand why, consider the cumulative discounted NCF rows for Projects A and B in

Table 8.6. The cumulative discounted NCF in the final year (4) is equal to the NPVs that we calculated for these projects. This is not surprising because a project's NPV is simply the sum of a project's discounted cash flows. Thus, as long as the cumulative discounted NCF is greater than zero by the end of a project's life, a discounted payback period exists and the firm should accept the project because it has a positive NPV. Table 8.6 shows how the NPV of the project "progressively develops" over the life of the project based on the cumulative discounted NCFs in years 2 through 4. Thus, the DPP represents a time-specific NPV break-even point.

Strengths and Weaknesses

If managers use an arbitrary cutoff rate, the discounted payback has similar strengths and weaknesses as the ordinary payback, but considers the time value of the cash flows within the payback period. If managers use an arbitrary cutoff and ignore cash flows beyond that point, they may reject a project because its DPP exceeds the cutoff despite having a positive NPV. Specifically, if managers set an arbitrary cutoff, they will be safe from accepting any projects they should reject, though they may reject some projects they should accept. Conversely, if managers use a decision rule that leads to accepting *any independent project with a defined discounted payback*, they are merely employing the discounted payback method in a manner that is consistent with the NPV technique. The decision rule will always lead to shareholder wealth maximization.

For mutually exclusive projects, the project with the shorter discounted payback does not necessarily have the larger NPV. Thus, for mutually exclusive projects, the discounted payback provides a compromise between the payback period and NPV, but lacks the theoretical merits of the NPV method.

Concept Check 8.7

1 If a project has a discounted payback of 4.0 years, what does this mean?
2 What major advantage does the discounted payback have over the regular payback period?
3 Can a project be acceptable based on the discounted payback period but be unacceptable using the NPV method? Why or why not?
4 Under what conditions will the discounted payback method result in the same accept/reject decisions as the NPV?

8.8 Summary of Capital Budgeting Techniques

We have discussed six methods used for evaluating capital budgeting projects (NPV, PI, IRR, MIRR, PP, and DPP). Although the NPV technique should be the primary decision criterion, other methods also have merit. Estimating the inputs needed to compute NPV, as well as

Table 8.7 Comparing decisions for independent Projects A and B

Technique	Project A	Project B	Decision rule: Accept if	Decision Project A	Project B
NPV	$38,877.13	–$2,643.26	NPV greater than 0	Accept	Reject
PI	1.39	0.97	PI greater than 1	Accept	Reject
IRR	24.89%	8.64%	IRR greater than 10%	Accept	Reject
MIRR	19.41%	9.27%	MIRR greater than 10%	Accept	Reject
PP	2.60 years	3.00 years	PP 2.5 years or less	Reject	Reject
DPP	3.05 years	Does not exist	DPP 3.0 years or less	Reject	Reject

Table 8.8 Comparing decisions for mutually exclusive Projects A and B

Technique	Project A	Project B	Decision rule: Accept the	Decision
NPV	$38,877.13	–$2,643.26	Higher positive NPV	Accept Project A
PI	1.39	0.97	Higher PI greater than 1	Accept Project A
IRR	24.89%	8.64%	Higher IRR above 10%	Accept Project A
MIRR	19.41%	9.27%	Higher MIRR above 10%	Accept Project A
PP	2.60 years	3.00 years	Shorter PP if 2.5 years or less	Accept neither
DPP	3.05 years	Does not exist	Shorter DPP if 3.0 years or less, if a DPP exists	Accept neither

other decision criteria, entails potential estimation errors. Consequently, managers often use multiple criteria for evaluating projects because each technique provides some additional information.

Table 8.7 summarizes the results of the six capital budgeting techniques assuming Projects A and B are independent. The results illustrate an important point. When a firm evaluates a single, independent project with conventional cash flows, the NPV, PI, IRR, and MIRR lead to the same accept-reject decision. As we have shown, the payback period and discounted payback period are inferior techniques and may lead to incorrect decisions. That is, a project with an acceptable regular payback or discounted payback period does not necessarily maximize shareholder wealth. In our example, the payback criterion rejects both Projects A and B. Rejecting Project A, however, is inconsistent with the results obtained from the four DCF techniques and is not in the best interest of the shareholders.

Table 8.8 shows the results if Projects A and B are mutually exclusive. In this case, the NPV, PI, IRR, and MIRR decision rules recommend accepting Project A but the payback and discounted payback recommend against accepting either project. Under certain conditions, discounted cash flow measures may give conflicting rankings for mutually exclusive projects. In the next section, we discuss the reasons for conflicting rankings for mutually exclusive projects and ways to resolve these conflicts.

Practical Financial Tip 8.4

Quantitative methods provide valuable information in making informed decisions about capital budgeting projects, but they are not a substitute for sound managerial judgment. Qualitative factors may also play a role in the decision-making process. After reviewing the calculations, the decision maker should include judgmental insights in the analysis to determine whether to accept or reject a project.

Concept Check 8.8

1 What is the difference between an absolute and a relative measure of project attractiveness? Give an example of each.
2 What is the relationship between NPV and PI? Under what circumstances do these techniques give the same accept-reject decision?
3 How does an increase in the firm's required rate of return affect a project's IRR and NPV?
4 What are the reinvestment rate assumptions of NPV, PI, IRR, and MIRR?
5 What are the similarities and differences in decision rules when using NPV versus IRR?
6 Do discounted cash flow techniques give the same accept-reject decision when evaluating independent projects with conventional cash flows? Why or why not?

8.9 Mutually Exclusive Project Decisions

If capital investments are mutually exclusive, selecting one project means rejecting the others. Such investments are often alternative ways to achieve the same result. Evaluating mutually exclusive projects requires ranking them. The decision rules for capital budgeting techniques that we have discussed so far may lead to different rankings and, therefore, different decisions. The three major reasons for these conflicting rankings of mutually exclusive projects result from differences in:

1   initial investments (size or scale);
2   cash flow patterns; and
3   life spans (unequal lives).

If a conflict occurs, the critical issue is to identify the technique that the firm should use to maximize shareholder wealth. Decision makers can use the standard NPV model to correctly rank mutually exclusive projects with differences in size and timing of cash flows. However, correctly ranking projects with different lives requires modifying the basic NPV model. Thus, the ability to correctly evaluate mutually exclusive projects allows the NPV model to be superior to the PI, IRR, or MIRR methods. That is, the basic or extended versions of the NPV model give correct rankings of mutually exclusive investment projects that will maximize the value of the firm.[6] In this section, we examine some of the complications that managers often encounter when grappling with capital budgeting projects.

Comparing Projects with Different Initial Investments

Ranking conflicts may result between NPV and other DCF techniques when one project is larger than another. This size disparity may result in a conflict because NPV and PI are different types of measures – absolute versus relative measures, respectively. NPV measures the total present value of dollar return, while PI measures the present value of the return for each dollar of initial investment. Therefore, PI does not reflect differences in investment scale because it ignores the size of the project.

For example, one project may have a higher positive NPV due to a larger initial investment but a lower PI than another mutually exclusive project with a smaller initial investment. Selecting the project with the higher positive NPV will add more dollars to shareholder wealth than the larger PI. The PI method can be a misleading measure of investment worth for projects of differing size because it may lead to an incorrect selection. When project rankings differ between the NPV and PI methods, NPV is preferred because it always selects the project that will add the most value to the firm.

Differences in the size of the initial investment may also cause a conflict in rankings between the NPV and IRR or MIRR. A rate of return expressed in percentage terms cannot discriminate between projects of different sizes. The NPV can discriminate between projects with different sizes because it measures return in absolute dollars. When such a conflict occurs, once again the NPV provides the decision consistent with the goal of maximizing shareholder wealth.

Example 8.7 Ranking Projects with Different Initial Investments

Global Industries is considering two mutually exclusive projects. Project S(mall) costs only half as much as Project L(arge). Table 8.9 shows the cash flows for each project. If the firm's required rate of return is 10 percent, which project is preferable?

Solution: Table 8.9 shows that conflicting rankings occur between Projects S and L. Project S is preferred using the PI method because it has a higher PI than Project L. The PI measure shows that Project S generates $1.24 for each $1 invested but Project L generates only $1.14 for each $1 invested. Thus, Project S contributes $0.24 to shareholder wealth per dollar invested compared with $0.14 for Project L. The IRR and MIRR also favor Project S above Project L. The NPV method produces a conflicting result. Due to the size of the initial investment, Project L has a higher NPV than Project S, $28,790 versus $24,343, respectively. Selecting Project L is the better choice because it will increase the wealth of Global's shareholders by $4,447 more than Project S.

---

[6] We consider only mutually exclusive projects with conventional cash flows. As we mentioned earlier, projects with non-normal cash flows can pose unique problems due to multiple IRRs.

Table 8.9 Conflicting rankings for mutually exclusive projects with different initial investments (size)

Year	Project S	Rank	Project L	Rank
0	−$100,000		−$200,000	
1	50,000		92,000	
2	50,000		92,000	
3	50,000		92,000	
NPV @ 10%	$24,343	2	$28,790	1
PI @ 10%	1.24	1	1.14	2
IRR	23.38%	1	18.01%	2
MIRR @ 10%	18.29%	1	15.04%	2
Decision: Select Project L over Project S.				

Comparing Projects with Different Cash Flow Patterns

Another ranking problem may occur when projects have the same size but differ in the timing of cash flows. That is, one project may have most of its cash flows in the early years while another may have most of its cash flows in later years. When timing differences occur, the firm will have different amounts of cash flows to invest in various periods depending on which project the firm selects.

Different rankings sometimes result from the reinvestment rate assumption. The **reinvestment rate** is the assumed rate of return a firm can earn by reinvesting the cash inflows from the project. DCF techniques typically assume that the firm can reinvest a project's cash inflows to earn a return equal to the rate used to discount the cash flows. The NPV method implicitly assumes reinvestment of a project's cash flows at the firm's required rate of return (cost of capital), while the IRR approach assumes reinvestment of cash inflows at the project's IRR. Therefore, the assumed reinvestment rate differs for projects with different IRRs.

The reinvestment assumption underlying the NPV approach tends to be more realistic than the IRR's assumption. A firm can use funds generated by a project to earn a return equal to its cost of capital by repaying the sources of capital. On the other hand, there is no assurance that a firm can reinvest cash flows at the IRR expected on a project generating those cash flows. The higher the IRR on a project, the less likely will the firm be able to reinvest the cash flows at a project's IRR. The cost of capital is generally a better reinvestment rate assumption than the IRR because it more closely approximates the firm's actual reinvestment rate. When the rankings based on IRR and NPV conflict with one another, the NPV method is the preferred approach.

As we discussed earlier, the MIRR has an advantage over the IRR because the MIRR explicitly assumes that the firm can reinvest a project's cash inflows at the firm's cost of capital. If two mutually exclusive projects have the same initial investment and expected life, NPV and MIRR will always result in selecting the same project. However, if the initial investment of two mutually exclusive projects differs, a conflict may still occur. In this situation, NPV is the better method because it is a superior indicator of how a project will affect the value of the firm.

Example 8.8 Ranking Projects with Different Cash Flow Patterns

Global Enterprises is considering two mutually exclusive projects with identical initial investments of $100,000 but different expected cash flows. As Table 8.10 shows, the expected cash flows of Project D(ecrease) drop over time but rise for Project I(ncrease). If the firm requires a 10 percent return on these investments, which project is preferred?

Table 8.10 Conflicting rankings for mutually exclusive projects with different cash flow patterns

Year	Project D	Rank	Project I	Rank
0	−$100,000		−$100,000	
1	70,000		20,000	
2	60,000		50,000	
3	20,000		100,000	
NPV @ 10%	$28,249	2	$34,636	1
PI @ 10%	1.28	2	1.35	1
IRR	28.70%	1	24.57%	2
MIRR @ 10%	19.51%	2	21.46%	1

Decision: Accept Project I over Project D.

Solution: Projects D's IRR is 28.70 percent compared with 24.57 percent for Project I. Therefore, Project D is preferred using the IRR method. Using a 10 percent required rate of return, the NPV, PI, and MIRR methods rank Project I higher than Project D. By selecting Project I, Global will increase the firm's value by $34,636 versus only $28,249 for Project D. Again, the NPV method is the better choice because it identifies the project that has the most favorable effect on shareholder wealth.

Different discount rates can cause potential conflicts in rankings between the NPV and IRR. As Table 8.11 indicates, the NPV of each project declines as the discount rate rises. The **crossover rate**, also called Fisher's intersection, is the discount rate at which the NPV profiles intersect and the NPVs of the two projects are equal. At discount rates *below* the crossover rate, a conflict in ranking occurs between NPV and IRR because Project D has the higher IRR but a lower NPV than Project I. At discount rates *above* the crossover rate, NPV and IRR yield the same ranking and no conflict in ranking exists. Thus, the NPV rankings depend on the discount rate.

Table 8.11 Discount rates and project rankings for Projects D and I

Discount rate (%)	NPV		Decision
	Project D	**Project I**	
10	$28,249	$34,636	Accept I
12	24,567	28,895	Accept I
14	21,071	23,514	Accept I
16	17,748	18,465	Accept I
16.89 Crossover	16,328	16,328	Accept either
18	14,586	13,721	Accept D
20	11,574	9,259	Accept D
22	8,703	5,057	Accept D
24	5,963	1,096	Accept D
26	3,347	−2,642	Accept D
28	845	−6,174	Accept D
30	−1,548	−9,513	Neither
IRR	28.70%	24.57%	Accept D

In this example, Project I is preferred at rates below the crossover rate but Project D is preferred at rates above the crossover rate. Notice that Project I's NPV is more sensitive to changes in the discount rate than is Project D's NPV. This is because high discount rates impose a greater (discounting) penalty on distant cash flows than on near-term cash flows. This logically follows in that the time value of money causes discounting to have a greater influence on later cash flows.

To find the crossover rate, calculate the differences (deltas or Δs) between the cash flows of the two projects and then find the IRR of these incremental cash flows. For Projects D and I, these cash flow differences are: $\Delta CF_0 = \$0$, $\Delta CF_1 = \$50,000$, $\Delta CF_2 = \$10,000$, and $\Delta CF_3 = -\$80,000$. The $IRR_{(D-I)}$ is the crossover rate, which is 16.89 percent when rounded to two decimal places.

A useful way to show this conflict is to plot the NPV profile of each project. The **NPV profile** is a graphical representation of the change in NPV relative to the change in the discount rate. Discount rates appear on the horizontal axis and the corresponding NPVs appear on the vertical axis. The NPV profile intersects the horizontal axis at the project's IRR. Why? This is because the IRR is the discount rate that causes the NPV to be zero. For an investment with conventional cash flows, the NPV profile slopes downward to the right. Notice that the slope of Project I's NPV profile is steeper than that of Project D. This indicates that a given change in the discount rate (k) has a greater effect on NPV_I than on NPV_D. Figure 8.1 graphically shows the NPV profiles for Projects D and I.

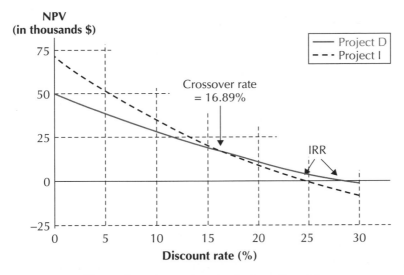

Figure 8.1 NPV Profiles and Crossover Rate for Projects D and I

Comparing Projects with Different Lives

A third potential conflict occurs when ranking mutually exclusive projects with unequal lives. DCF techniques do not provide reliable decisions unless the manager can evaluate the projects for equal periods. In particular, projects lack comparability on an NPV basis because the firm would be in a different financial position depending on which project it selects. Example 8.9 illustrates the problem of unequal useful lives.

Example 8.9 Different Lives: Preliminary Analysis

Suppose that Global Enterprises is planning to modernize its production facilities by buying one of two alternative machines. Table 8.12 shows the initial investment and the estimated future net cash flows for the mutually exclusive alternatives. Machine F(ar) is more expensive and it has an expected life that is twice that of Machine N(ear). The firm requires a 10 percent rate of return on these projects. Which machine should the firm select?

Preliminary Solution: The results show that the NPV of Machine N is $32,066 compared with $40,658 for Machine F. Although a conflict in ranking occurs, the NPV analysis suggests that Global Enterprises would prefer Machine F above Machine N. This decision is premature, however, without first determining what will happen at the end of the shorter-lived project, Machine N. If Global does not plan to replace Machine N after its useful life, management should select the project with the higher NPV. In this situation, comparing Machine N's NPV to that of Machine F is appropriate although it takes Machine F twice as long to generate its NPV.

Table 8.12 Conflicting rankings for mutually exclusive projects with different lives

Year	Machine N	Rank	Machine F	Rank
0	−$50,000		−$90,000	
1	33,000		30,000	
2	33,000		30,000	
3	33,000		30,000	
4			30,000	
5			30,000	
6			30,000	
NPV @ 10%	$32,066	2	$40,658	1
PI @ 10%	1.64	1	1.45	2
IRR	43.81%	1	24.29%	2
MIRR @ 10%	29.76%	1	17.05%	2

Preliminary Decision: Accept Machine F over Machine N based on its higher NPV.

If Global expects to continue the investment and replace Machine N after 3 years, management should consider the additional investment and subsequent cash flows in its calculations. In this situation, comparing the NPV generated by Machine F over 6 years against the NPV generated by Machine N over just 3 years would be unfair to Machine N and result in a flawed evaluation.

Two procedures available for handling the ranking problem for mutually exclusive projects with unequal lives are: (1) the replacement chain and (2) the equivalent annual annuity methods. Both approaches are extensions of the basic NPV model. Underlying these methods is the assumption that the firm's future reinvestment and cash flows will be similar to its current ones. Both the replacement chain and equivalent annual annuity methods give the same ranking when comparing mutually exclusive projects with unequal lives. These methods lead to wealth maximization when the firm can repeat the investment to a comparable time horizon.

Replacement chain
A **replacement chain** is the series of replacements of each asset by other assets having identical or at least similar characteristics until the lives of the two investments are equal. This method requires finding a **common ending period**, which is a time when both projects end simultaneously. This date can be no earlier than the end of the project with the longer life. Moreover, the replacement chains must be of equal length to make a valid comparison. After identifying the cash flows of the replacement chain, the task is to calculate the NPV of

the extended cash flows. As in previous NPV calculations, this involves finding the present value of all cash flows and then subtracting the initial outlay. After comparing both projects adjusted for equal lives, the decision rule is to accept the project with the higher NPV.

Using the replacement chain method is appropriate when the activity served by the investment continues over time. For example, a firm may plan to continue producing a product beyond the original useful life of the machine designed to produce the product. A typical assumption in using the replacement chain method is that a firm can repeat projects without changing the initial investment, net cash flows, and required rate of return. This assumption may be unrealistic. For example, the cost of a machine may change over time.

Using the replacement chain method can sometimes be tedious and unrealistic. For example, if two projects have lives of 5 and 7 years, the analyst must take each project out to 35 years to make their lives match because 35 is the lowest common denominator of 5 and 7. From a practical perspective, repeating these projects a large number of times would be unrealistic. In such cases, a quicker and easier method, called the **equivalent annual annuity**, is available and results in the same decision.

Practical Financial Tip 8.5

Using a replacement chain approach is appropriate when a high probability exists that the company will actually repeat the projects to a common life. The applicability of this method also depends on producing the same product with the same production technology that will produce identical cash flows as the current equipment. In practice, this latter assumption is likely to be unrealistic if projects are repeated more than just a few times.

Example 8.10 Different Lives: Replacement Chains

Let's return to Global Enterprises and reexamine Machines N and F using the replacement chain approach. If the firm plans to continue producing the product after Machine N's useful life, it must replace Machine N at the end of year 3. This will permit Global to generate cash inflows with the replacement machine during years 4 through 6. The common ending period becomes 6 years because the life of two Machine Ns and one Machine F is 6 years. In this case, Global must develop a replacement chain only for Machine N. Assuming the replacement has the same cash flows as the original machine, the firm will incur a $50,000 cash outflow at the end of year 3. In year 3, the $33,000 cash inflow partially offsets the $50,000 cash outflow. The replacement machine will generate another 3 years of identical cash flows during years 4 through 6. Note that the project will now have cash outflows of $50,000 in year 0 and *at the end* of year 3. It also will have cash inflows of $33,000 at the end of years 1 through 6. Table 8.13 summarizes the net cash flows and the NPVs of Machines N and F.

Table 8.13 Using replacement chains for mutually exclusive projects with different economic lives

Year	Machine N	Rank	Machine F	Rank
0	-$50,000		-$90,000	
1	33,000		30,000	
2	33,000		30,000	
3	-17,000[a]		30,000	
4	33,000		30,000	
5	33,000		30,000	
6	33,000		30,000	
NPV @ 10%	$56,158	1	$40,658	2

Decision: Accept Machine N over Machine F.

[a] $33,000 cash inflow -$50,000 cash outflow = -$17,000

Solution: Using the replacement chain method for Machine N makes the lives of the two machines equal and permits comparing their NPVs. Because the new analysis shows that Machine N now has a higher NPV than Machine F, the appropriate decision is to select Machine N. This decision conflicts with the preliminary decision shown in Table 8.12.

Equivalent annual annuity

Another approach is available for dealing with projects with unequal lives. The **equivalent annual annuity** (EAA), also called the **annualized NPV**, indicates how much NPV per year the firm expects the project to generate for as long as the firm maintains the project. The EAA is not an alternative to the NPV, but simply a direct way to develop the NPV ranking for mutually exclusive projects with unequal lives. Equation 8.9 provides the formula for computing the EAA.

$$EAA = \frac{NPV}{PVIFA_{n,k}} \tag{8.9}$$

Here, $PVIFA_{n,k}$ is the present value interest factor of an annuity for n periods at an interest rate of k per period, which is computed as $[1 - 1/(1 + k)^n]/k$. An easier way to calculate the EAA is by using a financial calculator.

When examining mutually exclusive projects, using the EAA approach leads to a decision that maximizes NPV and shareholder wealth. This approach assumes that the firm can repeat the investment to a comparable time horizon, or that the firm can repeat at least one of the two investments indefinitely. The project with the higher EAA will inevitably have the higher NPV when extended out to any common life. Two projects with identical NPVs but different lives will have different EAAs. In this situation, the project with the shorter life will have a higher EAA because the total NPV generated occurs over a shorter period. The decision rule is to accept the project with higher EAA.

Example 8.11 Different Economic Lives: Equivalent Annual Annuity

Using a 10 percent cost of capital, Table 8.14 shows that the NPVs for Machines N and F are $32,066 and $40,658, respectively. Machine N has a 3-year life and Machine F has a 6-year life. Which machine is preferred using the EAA?

Table 8.14 Using the EAA for mutually exclusive projects with different economic lives

Year	Machine N	Rank	Machine F	Rank
0	−$50,000		−$90,000	
1	33,000		30,000	
2	33,000		30,000	
3	33,000		30,000	
4			30,000	
5			30,000	
6			30,000	
NPV @ 10%	$32,066	2	$40,658	1
EAA @ 10%	$12,894	1	$9,335	2

Decision: Accept Machine N over Machine F.

Solution: Let's first illustrate how to calculate the EAA using Equation 8.9.

$$EAA_N = \frac{\$32,066}{1 - \dfrac{1}{(1+0.10)^3}} = \frac{\$32,066}{2.4869} = \$12,894$$

$$EAA_F = \frac{\$40,658}{1 - \dfrac{1}{(1+0.10)^6}} = \frac{\$40,658}{4.3553} = \$9,335$$

This approach can become tedious. A faster and easier procedure for calculating the EAA using a financial calculator is similar to that discussed in Chapter 5 in solving for an ordinary annuity. The steps using the BA II PLUS® calculator are:

	Machine N		Machine F
1	2nd CLR TVM	1	2nd CLR TVM
2	3 N	2	6 N
3	10 I/Y	3	10 I/Y
4	32,066 PV	4	40,658 PV
5	CPT PMT	5	CPT PMT

For Machine N, these steps look like the following on a BA II PLUS® calculator:

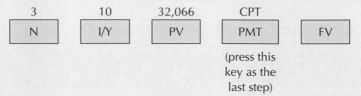

3	10	32,066	CPT	
N	I/Y	PV	PMT	FV
			(press this key as the last step)	

Solving for PMT results in an EAA_N = \$12,894 and EAA_F = \$9,335, ignoring the sign. Thus, Machine N is preferred over Machine F because Machine N has a higher EAA. Note that both the replacement chain and EAA methods give the same ranking when comparing mutually exclusive projects with unequal lives. What happens if we calculate the EAAs for 6 years for each project? The resulting NPVs are the same as those obtained in Table 8.13 using replacement chains. Some analysts find the replacement chain method easier to understand, but the ease of calculating the EAA can offset this advantage.

Equivalent annual charge

Some mutually exclusive projects do not generate cash flows directly and involve only costs. For such *cost-only* projects with unequal lives that require replacement to continue to provide the service, the appropriate measure for ranking is the **equivalent annual charge** (EAC). The decision rule is to accept the project with the lowest EAC.

Example 8.12 Different Economic Lives: Equivalent Annual Charge

Global Enterprises is considering two copiers for one of its offices. This office uses 1,000 photocopies each working day for 200 working days a year. Copier 1 costs \$15,000 and will produce 1 million copies before it wears out. Copier 2 costs \$20,000 and will produce 2 million copies in its life. Maintenance and materials costs are \$0.02 a copy for either machine. Analysts do not expect either machine to have any salvage value. The required rate of return is 10 percent a year. Assuming year-end cash flows for simplicity, which copier should Global select using the EAC?

Solution: Because annual operating costs for each machine are the same, the analysis focuses on the initial outlays. Copier 1 has a life of 5 years [1,000,000/(200 × 1,000)] and an initial outlay of \$15,000. Copier 2 has a life of 10 years [2,000,000/(200 × 1,000)] and an initial outlay of \$20,000. Instead of using Equation 8.8, which also applies for the EAC, let's use the BA II PLUS® financial calculator.

Copier 1		Copier 2	
1	2nd CLR TVM	1	2nd CLR TVM
2	5 N	2	10 N
3	10 I/Y	3	10 I/Y
4	15,000 PV	4	20,000 PV
5	CPT PMT	5	CPT PMT

Solving for PMT results in an EAC_1 = \$3,957 and EAC_2 = \$3,255, ignoring the sign. Therefore, the decision is to select Copier 2 because of its lower EAC.

Practical Financial Tip 8.6

Managers should exercise caution whenever mutually exclusive projects have differences in size, cash flow patterns, and life spans and when they expect substantial differences between their company's current and expected future reinvestment opportunities. Mechanically applying ranking techniques without considering the underlying assumptions can lead to inappropriate decisions.

Abandonment Decisions

Conventional NPV analysis assumes that a firm will use assets over a specified period. In practice, firms often do not hold a project until the end of its full physical life. Instead, they may decide to terminate the investment. When this occurs, managers make an **abandonment decision**, which is a type of real option. A **real option** occurs when the investment in a "real" asset confers the right but not the obligation to take further action in the future. Firms may abandon projects for various reasons such as changing costs and/or benefits over a project's life. For example, the expected operating cash flows of a project may turn out to be less than originally anticipated. In addition, the market or salvage value of an asset may rise more rapidly than the cash inflows resulting from using the asset.

Abandonment decisions are a type of mutually exclusive investment analysis because they require deciding between several streams of cash flows. A project's true value may be more than the NPV based on its physical life if managers abandon a project at the end of its *economic life*, which is earlier than its physical life. **Economic life** is the life that maximizes a project's NPV and consequently maximizes shareholder wealth.

If a firm can realize some abandonment value (AV) upon terminating a project, the firm should abandon the project at the point that maximizes the NPV of all cash benefits, including the abandonment value.[7] Equation 8.10 shows the NPV with abandonment at the end of the year d.

$$NPV = \frac{\sum_{t=1}^{d} CF_t}{(1 + k)^t} - I_0 + \frac{AV_d}{(1 + k)^d} \tag{8.10}$$

where AV_d is the abandonment value at the end of year d.

One way to view abandonment value is as the project's salvage value. Computing the NPV involves using Equation 8.10 for all values of d from 1 to t (the physical life of the investment). The economic life of the investment is the project life (d) that results in the greatest NPV. This approach assumes that the firm cannot invest in an identical asset. If, however, the firm can invest in an identical asset, the abandonment time that maximizes the EAA would be optimal.

---

[7] Under conditions of changing risk posture, techniques such as decision trees and simulation are available to handle abandonment values. These techniques are beyond the scope of this book.

An often-cited decision rule is to abandon a project when the abandonment value is greater than the present value of all cash flows beyond the abandonment year, discounted to the abandonment decision point. This rule is technically incorrect because it ignores future abandonment opportunities.

Practical Financial Tip 8.7

Managers should routinely analyze the abandonment option in the capital budgeting process because this real option can materially affect a project's estimated desirability. Failure to abandon projects at the financially prudent time could be costly. The firm could use the funds generated from abandonment to invest in better investment opportunities.

Example 8.13 Abandonment Decision #1

Global Enterprises is considering a machine with a physical life of 3 years. If the firm abandons the project before year 3, the machinery will have a positive abandonment value. Table 8.15 shows the yearly cash flows and abandonment values.

Table 8.15 Cash flows and abandonment value for a 3-year machine

Year (t)	Cash flows	Abandonment value
0	−50,000	50,000
1	22,000	35,000
2	20,000	20,000
3	16,000	0

The firm's cost of capital is 10 percent. If Global cannot invest in an identical asset, what is the project's economic life?

Solution: Table 8.16 shows the NPV for each abandonment time. The results indicate that Global maximizes the NPV by abandonment at the end of year 2. This project's economic life (2 years) does not equal its physical life (3 years). This example also shows that having the ability to abandon a project may turn an otherwise unattractive project into an acceptable project.

Being able to invest in identical assets would change this decision. Using the EAA approach, the option with the higher positive EAA ($2,000) is abandoning the project after 1 year and investing in an identical asset.

Table 8.16 NPVs of abandonment options

Abandonment period	Cash flows for each year				No investment in identical asset	Invest in identical asset
	0	**1**	**2**	**3**	**NPV**	**EAA**
No abandonment	−$50,000	$22,000	$20,000	$16,000	−$1,450	−$583
Abandon after 2 years	−50,000	22,000	40,000		3,058	1,762
Abandon after 1 year	−50,000	57,000			1,818	2,000

Decision: Abandon after 2 years if the firm cannot invest in an identical asset but after 1 year if the firm can invest in an identical asset.

Example 8.14 Abandonment Decision #2

Let's now look at a slightly different abandonment problem. Global Enterprises faces only the following alternatives: (1) sell an asset today for $1 million or (2) keep the asset for another 5 years generating annual cash flows of $200,000 and then sell the asset at the end of the fifth year for an estimated $250,000 (abandonment value). Because the firm expects the price of the asset to decline rapidly, it does not plan to sell the asset until the fifth year if it does not sell the asset immediately. Thus, the firm has no other abandonment opportunities. If Global requires a 10 percent rate of return, should the firm sell the asset now or keep it for another 5 years?

Solution: One way to solve this problem is to compare the present value of the future cash flows to the current abandonment value. As Table 8.17 shows, Global would receive $1 million if it sells the asset now versus a present value of $913,388 if it keeps the asset for an additional 5 years. Therefore, Global should abandon now.

Table 8.17 Present value of abandonment options

Year	0	1	2	3	4	5	Present value
Abandonment now	$1,000,000	$0	$0	$0	$0	$0	$1,000,000
Abandon after 5 years	0	200,000	200,000	200,000	200,000	450,000	$913,388

Decision: Abandon now.

Another approach is to treat this situation as a single NPV problem. In this case, the firm would forgo $1,000,000 today, which is treated as an outflow in the form of an opportunity cost, if it keeps the asset for another 5 years and then scraps it. Table 8.18 shows how to calculate the NPV for the two abandonment options using the BA II PLUS®. Global should abandon now because keeping the asset for an additional 5 years results in a negative NPV of −$86,612.

Table 8.18 Calculating the NPV of the abandonment option using the BA II PLUS®
calculator

Key strokes	Explanation	Display	
[CF] → [2nd] → [CLR WORK]	Clear Memory Registers	CF$_0$ =	0.00
1,000,000 → [+/–] → [ENTER]	Initial Cash Outlay	CF$_0$ =	−1,000,000.00
[↓] → 200,000 → [ENTER]	Period 1 Cash Flow	C01 =	200,000.00
[↓] 4 ENTER	Frequency of Cash Flow 1	F01 =	4.00
[↓] → 450,000 → [ENTER]	Period 2 Cash Flow	C02 =	450,000.00
[↓]	Frequency of Cash Flow 2	F02 =	1.00
[NPV] → 10 → [ENTER]	10% Discount Rate	I =	10.00
[↓] → [CPT]	Calculate NPV	NPV =	−86,612.32

Concept Check 8.9

1   What are three major reasons for conflicts in rankings among DCF techniques for
mutually exclusive projects?
2   Given the following information, which mutually exclusive project is preferred
when using the PI approach? Which project is preferred using the NPV approach?
Which project should management accept? Why?

	Project A	Project B
PV of net cash flows	$70,000	$130,000
Initial investment	50,000	100,000

3   What are the reinvestment rate assumptions of the NPV, PI, IRR, and MIRR
methods?
4   What does the term "crossover rate" mean? Why is this rate important in evaluating mutually exclusive projects?
5   Which DCF technique, NPV, PI, IRR or MIRR, is theoretically superior when
evaluating mutually exclusive projects of differing size or differing cash flow
patterns? Why?
6   What are two methods for evaluating mutually exclusive projects with unequal
lives?
7   If two mutually exclusive projects with unequal lives have equal NPVs, which
project will have the higher equivalent annual annuity? Why?
8   How does the equivalent annual annuity (EAA) differ from the equivalent annual
charge (EAC)?
9   What are the decision rules for determining the optimal abandonment value of
an asset?
10   How does a project's economic life differ from its physical life?

8.10 Capital Rationing Decisions

Until now, we have assumed that a firm can undertake all acceptable projects based on the appropriate DCF decision rules. That is, firms should accept all independent projects with positive NPVs and choose between mutually exclusive projects based on the project with the higher NPV. Such decisions would maximize the value of the firm and the wealth of its shareholders. Accepting all positive NPV projects assumes no limit exists on the size of the capital budget. In practice, firms often operate under capital constraints. A common name for dealing with this constraint is **capital rationing**, which is the process of allocating a limited amount of capital to acceptable capital budgeting projects. Thus, capital rationing forces managers to choose among capital investments with positive NPVs.

Why would a firm forgo capital investments that should increase shareholder wealth? Theoretically, capital rationing should not exist, but due to capital constraints, it often does in reality. Capital rationing can take two major forms:

1 externally imposed by suppliers of funds; and
2 internally imposed by managerial decisions.

Constraints imposed by capital markets include the inability to raise additional debt or equity beyond some designated amount. For example, loan provisions may limit additional borrowing. Self-imposed capital rationing may result from: (1) the firm's reluctance to issue external financing, (2) the risk-averse behavior of the firm's senior managers, (3) non-monetary constraints, and (4) the presence of biased cash flow forecasts. Management typically makes the decision to limit capital spending. Survey evidence is supportive of the reluctance to issue external financing as being the primary reason for the prevalence of capital rationing.[8]

Let's examine more closely these reasons for internal capital rationing. Management may prefer to limit the use of outside funding for capital projects because of the desire to avoid taking on additional debt or because of the unwillingness to raise new equity. For example, managers may want to reserve borrowing capacity to finance high-NPV projects in the future. They may also want to avoid adding external equity if doing so results in an undesirable dilution of existing equity. Managers are frequently under great pressure to improve the highly scrutinized earnings-per-share figure and often issue additional shares only as a last resort. Risk-averse managers may impose capital rationing to avoid accepting low-NPV projects with high downside risk. A non-monetary constraint is that a firm may lack qualified personnel necessary to successfully implement the projects. By limiting the size of the capital budget, the firm can avoid potential problems associated with overextending human

---

[8] Survey evidence on capital rationing decisions can be found in the following: Tarun K. Mukherjee and Vineeta L. Hingorani, "Capital-Rationing Decisions of *Fortune 500* Firms: A Survey," *Financial Practice and Education*, Spring/Summer 1999, 7–15; Tarun K. Mukherjee, H. Kent Baker, and Rajan D'Mello, "Capital Rationing Decisions of *Fortune 500* Firms – Part II," *Financial Practice and Education*, Fall/Winter 2000, 69–77.

resources and can control the amount and direction of growth. Finally, senior managers may use capital rationing as a tool to discourage overzealous cash flow projections by junior managers.

When determining the initial ceiling for investment capital, firms often tie this cap to the level of internally generated funds available, but some also consider external sources of financing. Under some circumstances, firms allow flexibility when setting the ceiling level. For example, firms may lower their initial capital ceiling when adherence to the original ceiling would require accepting low NPV projects when management expects higher NPV projects in the future. By contrast, firms may raise the initial allocation to accommodate high NPV projects and to implement projects when sufficient debt capacity is available.

When a budget constraint exists, the firm should select those projects that maximize future wealth over the time that capital is available for use. Several methods are available for ranking projects under capital rationing. When capital rationing is for a single period and available projects are indivisible, the preferred method is to accept a combination of projects that maximizes NPV within the budget constraint.[9] If a project is indivisible, a firm must undertake the whole project and remain within the budget constraint.[10] This approach is theoretically sound because NPV shows the net benefit realized by the firm from adopting selected capital budgeting projects.

Other approaches, such as ranking projects by their NPVs, PIs or IRRs and then selecting the most highly ranked projects down to the budget constraint, can be unreliable indicators in the case of capital rationing. These procedures may seem to give a reliable ranking of investments, but that appearance may be only an illusion. For example, selecting projects with the largest PIs may not maximize the combined NPVs when projects are indivisible.[11] These indivisibility problems suggest that a firm probably can get a higher combined NPV by selecting several smaller projects with lower NPVs than a larger project with a higher NPV.

If properly applied, the PI and IRR methods can help to maximize value under capital rationing. This requires initially ranking by either the PI or IRR and then selecting the bundle of projects that maximizes NPV. Example 8.15 illustrates the superiority of the combined NPV approach over various ranking methods.

---

[9] Under multi-period capital rationing, methods such as mathematical programming may be required to select investment proposals. These methods are beyond the scope of this book but discussions of them are available in advanced capital budgeting books. See, for example, Harold Bierman, Jr. and Seymour Smidt, *The Capital Budgeting Decision – Economic Analysis of Investment Projects*, 8th edn, Pearson Education, 1992; Don Dayananda, Richard Irons, Steve Harrison, John Herbohn, and Patrick Rowland, *Capital Budgeting: Financial Appraisal of Investment Projects*, Cambridge University Press, 2002.

[10] A firm could relax the budget constraint to allow accepting the last project for which funds are not fully available.

[11] When projects are divisible under capital rationing, the profitability index can lead to the correct decision. Using the PI technique involves ranking projects from the highest to the lowest PI, and choosing all the highest-ranked projects within the capital budget. This approach maximizes the increment in wealth per dollar invested. Those projects with high PIs have more NPV per dollar invested and are more likely to be included in the total capital budget. This approach fails when projects are mutually exclusive and during multi-period capital rationing.

Example 8.15 Project Selection under Capital Rationing Using the Highest Combined NPV Approach

Advanced Technology has allocated $1 million for next year's capital expenditures. The firm has identified five projects meeting the minimum acceptance criteria for DCF techniques. It cannot adopt all five projects because this would exceed the capital budget. Table 8.19 shows the five capital budgeting projects and their rankings by NPV, PI, and IRR. Which set of projects should the firm choose to get the highest NPV and remain within its budget?

Table 8.19 Ranking projects by NPV, PI, and IRR

Project	Initial investment	NPV	Rank	PI	Rank	IRR (%)	Rank
A	$750,000	$375,000	1	1.50	3	20	3
B	400,000	280,000	2	1.70	1	21	2
C	300,000	120,000	4	1.40	4	16	4
D	250,000	162,500	3	1.65	2	24	1
E	250,000	25,000	5	1.10	5	11	5
Total	$1,950,000	$962,500					

Solution: Table 8.20 shows several project combinations within the $1 million budget constraint.

Table 8.20 Combined NPVs of various project combinations

Project combinations	Total investment	Combined NPV
A and D	$1,000,000	$537,500
A and E	1,000,000	400,000
B, C, and D	950,000	562,500
B, C, and E	950,000	425,000
B, D, and E	900,000	467,500
C, D, and E	800,000	307,500

Advanced Technology should select Projects B, C, and D because this combination has the largest NPV of $562,500. Choosing these projects uses only $950,000 of the $1,000,000 capital budget. The firm could use the remaining $50,000 for other purposes such as paying dividends, repurchasing stock, or reducing outstanding debt.

Ranking projects by their highest NPVs, PIs or IRRs and then selecting the most highly ranked projects can provide inferior results. For example, using the highest ranked NPV method, Advanced Technology would first select Project A with an initial investment of $750,000. With $250,000 remaining within its capital budget, the firm cannot adopt Project B, which has the second highest NPV ranking, because its initial investment is $400,000. The only other investments within its budget are Projects D or E. Combining Project A and either Projects D or E gives a lower NPV than combining Projects B, C, and D. Selecting projects based only on the most highly ranked PIs or IRRs presents similar problems.

As Table 8.19 shows, the combined NPV of the five projects is $962,500. By limiting the capital budget to $1,000,000, the firm is passing up Projects A and E, which, if undertaken, would increase shareholder wealth by $400,000. This amount represents an opportunity cost of capital rationing, assuming Advanced Technology has sufficient resources to oversee the projects. The firm could implement flexibility and relax the budget constraint by accepting one or both projects. If, on the other hand, Advanced Technology lacks sufficient resources to undertake all five projects, the firm may be unable to realize the expected NPV.

Concept Check 8.10

1 What is the meaning of the term "capital rationing"?
2 What are some common reasons for capital rationing within a firm?
3 How does capital rationing affect project selection?
4 What is the preferred method for choosing among indivisible projects under capital constraints? Explain why.

8.11 Capital Budgeting Techniques in Theory and Practice

As we have already discussed, many techniques are available for evaluating capital expenditure projects. According to theory, firms should use discounted cash flow methods to analyze capital budgeting alternatives. Although the fundamental principles of capital budgeting evaluation should be the same for all firms, the question remains "Does practice conform to theory?"

Superiority of the NPV Technique

A major tenet of modern financial theory is that the value of an asset (or of a firm) equals the discounted present value of its expected future cash flows. Thus, firms considering investing in capital projects should use the NPV method to maximize the value of the firm. As a general guideline, NPV is the best approach on theoretical grounds for two reasons. First,

NPV results in an absolute measure of the project's worth, while both PI and IRR are relative measures. NPV focuses on absolute dollar returns, not the return for each dollar of investment or the percentage rate of return. NPV is merely the estimated amount by which the investment increases wealth. Therefore, using the NPV criterion to measure project attractiveness will guide firms to maximize shareholder wealth. On the other hand, relative measures of project attractiveness sometimes do not lead to shareholder wealth maximization. For example, the main problem with using the IRR is that, in some cases, managers wanting to maximize IRR may actually reduce value by rejecting positive-NPV projects or choosing projects with an inferior NPV.

Second, NPV has more a realistic reinvestment rate assumption than IRR. Discounted capital budgeting techniques implicitly assume that the firm can reinvest any operating cash flows to earn a return that equals the discount rate. The NPV approach implicitly assumes reinvestment of cash inflows at the required rate of return, while the IRR approach assumes reinvestment of cash flows at the project's own IRR.[12] The reinvestment rate assumption of the NPV approach is generally more realistic. That is, the firm can use funds generated by the project to earn a return equal to the firm's cost of capital by merely repaying the sources of capital. No assurance exists that a firm can reinvest the cash flows generated by a project at the IRR expected on the project. The higher the IRR on a project, the less likely a firm can reinvest the cash flows at the IRR. Therefore, when conflicts in rankings occur between NPV and IRR, NPV is the preferred approach.

Figure 8.2 provides guidelines for determining the appropriate DCF techniques to use for independent and mutually exclusive projects with and without capital rationing. We discussed the rationale for each approach in previous sections of this chapter.

Capital Budgeting Techniques in Practice

For more than four decades, researchers have surveyed corporate executives to document their capital budgeting practices. Early survey evidence shows that managers generally favored the payback period and accounting rate of return, but usage of these techniques has declined over time. Although relying solely on non-DCF techniques can result in poor investment decisions, some firms continue to use them especially as secondary measures. These methods have survived due to their simplicity and intuitive appeal. In some cases, top management's unfamiliarity with more sophisticated techniques has hindered the adoption of these methods.

Surveys suggest that the use of DCF techniques has increased over time, particularly among larger firms. For example, NPV is much more widely used as a project evaluation method than it was 10 or 20 years ago. This increase is largely due to the widespread use of personal

---

[12] This claim about reinvestment rate assumptions is inexact but is not likely to be harmful. The DCF methods can be computed without any assumptions about the use of the funds generated by the investment. For example, an investment generating cash flows that are consumed will have the same IRR as an investment whose cash flows are reinvested. Yet, knowing the reinvestment rates is important when comparing mutually exclusive projects.

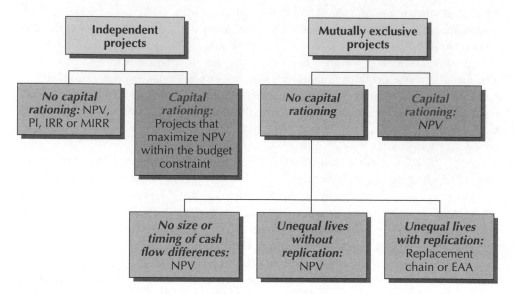

Figure 8.2 Determining the appropriate DCF technique

computers with spreadsheet programs that reduce the knowledge and effort required to calculate DCF measures.

Most large firms use several techniques to provide management with the information necessary to make capital budgeting decisions. Although the frequency of usage varies with the type of project under consideration, a common practice is to use IRR and NPV along with non-DCF methods. Due to the difficulty in making estimates for inputs such as cash flows and the cost of capital, financial managers often use multiple methods when examining projects. Because these estimates can be inaccurate, managers use several methods to provide additional information about the acceptability of a project. For example, in an uncertain world, payback can serve as a useful supplemental screening device.

Among the DCF techniques, surveys find that managers sometimes prefer to use IRR over NPV, despite the theoretical superiority of the NPV method. When making pragmatic decisions, practitioners tend to find the yield-based IRR method intuitively more appealing. Managers also like to examine the differential between the proposed project's IRR and the required rate of return.

Smaller firms are less likely to use the more theoretically recommended methods of capital budgeting analysis. Such firms tend to place a high priority on recovering their investment in a short period and therefore rely on the payback method. Others do no formal analysis of proposed capital expenditures whatsoever. There are many reasons firms fail to use DCF techniques or fail to conduct formal analysis of any kind. For example, small business owners may find that the cost of developing and maintaining a sophisticated capital budgeting system outweighs its benefits.

Focus on Practice 8.1

Common Capital Budgeting Techniques

Graham and Harvey report responses about numerous capital budgeting techniques from 392 chief financial officers (CFOs) representing a wide variety of firms and industries. Figure 8.3 shows only the responses regarding techniques discussed in this chapter. As shown in Figure 8.3, IRR and NPV are the most often used capital budgeting techniques. Payback is another highly ranked technique but fewer companies use the discounted payback. They also find that size affects the usage of various techniques. For example, large firms are more likely to use NPV than are small firms, while small firms use the payback period almost as often as they use IRR and NPV.

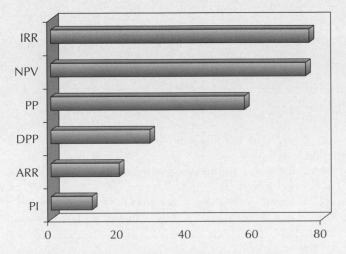

Figure 8.3 Popularity of capital budgeting techniques

Source: Adapted from John Graham and Campbell Harvey, "How Do CFOs Make Capital Budgeting and Capital Structure Decisions," *Journal of Applied Corporate Finance,* Spring 2002, p. 11.

Focus on Practice 8.2

Capital Budgeting Techniques in the United States and Canada

In 1994 Payne, Heath, and Gale surveyed managers of US firms and Canadian firms about their capital budgeting techniques. Table 8.21 shows the rankings of six capital budgeting techniques when conducting formal capital budgeting evaluation procedures. The results are highly similar. US firms appear to prefer IRR to NPV while Canadian firms appear to prefer NPV to IRR.

Table 8.21 Ranking of capital budgeting techniques by US and Canadian firms

	Rank	
Technique	United States	Canada
Internal rate of return	1	2
Net present value	2	1
Payback period	3	3
Discounted payback period	4	4
Accounting rate of return	5	5
Modified internal rate of return	6	6

Source: Adapted from Janet D. Payne, Will Carrington Heath, and Lewis R. Gale, "Comparative Financial Practices in the US and Canada: Capital Budgeting and Risk Assessment Techniques," *Financial Practice and Education*, Spring/Summer 1999, p. 19.

Concept Check 8.11

1 What are two reasons for the superiority of the NPV method in evaluating capital investment projects?
2 Which capital budgeting techniques are increasing in popularity? Which are decreasing in popularity? Why?
3 Which capital budgeting methods do managers of large firms use the most? Why?
4 Why do small firms use DCF techniques less often than large firms do?

Summary

In this chapter, we discussed issues involving the evaluation and selection of capital budgeting projects. We covered the following concepts in this chapter.

1 Financial managers use many different techniques to evaluate the economic attractiveness of making capital investments because each method provides additional information about the project.
2 DCF methods (NPV, PI, IRR, and MIRR) are superior to the payback methods (PP and DPP) because the former techniques use the time-value-of-money principle to discount all project cash flows and offer project estimates past the recovery of the initial estimate.
3 Quantitative measures serve as a mere guide to management, not as the sole basis for making capital budgeting decisions. The more challenging task is to estimate accurately the inputs for the various decision models.
4 For single, independent projects with conventional cash flows, the four DCF methods give the same accept-reject signal when firms do not face a capital constraint.

5 Conflicting rankings may occur among the DCF methods when comparing mutually exclusive projects with differing initial investments (size or scale), cash flow patterns, and economic lives.
   - When conflicts occur due to size or timing differences, the NPV is the preferred ranking method because it enables management to choose from among mutually exclusive investments with the objective of maximizing the firm's value, and therefore, shareholder wealth.
   - When conflicts occur due to unequal economic lives, the replacement chain or equivalent annual annuity (EAA) methods can be used to maximize wealth (provided that at least one alternative can be repeated). Both methods give the same rankings, but the EAA method is usually easier to compute.

6 Capital rationing, due to market or management imposed constraints, may not allow a firm to undertake all acceptable projects. When projects are indivisible, the preferred method to maximize shareholder wealth is to choose that combination of projects offering the highest NPV within the limits imposed by the constraints.

7 In theory, NPV is the preferred method of evaluating capital investments because other techniques have been shown to contain flaws. In practice, managers sometimes prefer using IRR. Ultimately, firms often use multiple approaches, including non-DCF methods, when evaluating capital budgeting projects.

FURTHER READING

Childs, Paul D., Steven H. Ott, and Alexander J. Triantis, "Capital Budgeting for Interrelated Projects: A Real Options Approach," *Journal of Financial and Quantitative Analysis 33*, September 1998, 305–34.

Damodaran, Aswath. "The Promise of Real Options," *Journal of Applied Corporate Finance 13*, Summer 2000, 29–44.

Dayananda, Richard Irons, Steve Harrison, John Herbohn, and Patrick Rowland, *Capital Budgeting: Financial Appraisal of Investment Projects*, Cambridge University Press, 2002.

Graham, John R. and Campbell R. Harvey, "The Theory and Practice of Corporate Finance: Evidence from the Field," *Journal of Financial Economics 60*, May/June 2001, 187–233.

Grinyer, John R., C. Donald Sinclair, and Daing Nasir Ibrahim. "Management Objectives in Capital Budgeting," *Financial Practice and Education 9*, Fall/Winter 1999, 12–22.

Harris, Milton and Artur Raviv, "The Capital Budgeting Process: Incentives and Information," *Journal of Finance 51*, September 1996, 1139–74.

Mun, Johnathan, *Real Options Analysis*, John Wiley & Sons, Inc., 2002.

Peterson, Pamela P. and Frank J. Fabozzi, *Capital Budgeting: Theory and Practice*, John Wiley & Sons, Inc. 2002.

Schrieves, Ronald E. and John M. Wachowicz, Jr. "Proper Risk Resolution in Replacement Chain Analysis," *Engineering Economist 34*, Winter 1989, 91–114.

Seitz, Neil and Mitch Ellison, *Capital Budgeting and Long-term Financing Decisions*, 4th edn, South-Western, 2005.

Shapiro, Alan C., *Capital Budgeting and Investment Analysis*, Pearson Education Inc., 2005.

Stein, Jeremy C., "Rational Capital Budgeting in an Irrational World," *Journal of Business 69*, October 1996, 429–55.

Stultz, René M. "What's Wrong with Modern Capital Budgeting?" *Financial Practice and Education 9*, Fall/Winter 1999, 7–11.

Chapter 9

Risk Analysis

The reason why corporations do not enter gambles with volatile payoffs and small positive expected returns is that managers know that generally volatility matters. (René M. Stulz, "What's Wrong with Modern Capital Budgeting?" *Financial Practice and Education 9*, Fall/Winter 1999, p. 8.)

Overview

In Chapter 8, we examined how to analyze capital investments under the implicit assumption that the projects under consideration are equally risky as the firm. For such normal-risk or average-risk projects, the appropriate discount rate is the firm's cost of capital, *k*, which reflects the risk of the firm. If the risk associated with a project differs from that of the firm, managers should adjust for risk. We also used a single value to represent the estimated cash flow for each period. In practice, managers cannot estimate future cash flows with absolute accuracy. A range of possible outcomes is likely for each cash flow. As a result, the payoffs associated with capital expenditures are risky. An important part of project evaluation is measuring the risk associated with cash flows and incorporating this risk into the evaluation process. Ignoring or improperly accounting for risk can result in improper investment decisions, which in turn can reduce the value of the firm's common stock and thus prevent maximizing shareholder wealth.

In this chapter, we focus on project analysis under risk. The formal treatment of risk is often quite complicated. As a result, low cost projects generally do not merit elaborate risk analysis because of the extensive time and cost involved. In such cases, managers may use less formal methods to account for risk. The methods described in this chapter are applicable mainly to moderate and large-scale projects.

None of these approaches eliminates risk, but they can provide a rational way of dealing with it. Each method has limitations and involves some subjective judgment. Although many firms use risk analysis in capital budgeting, the topic remains a complex and evolving area. In this chapter, we examine common ways to describe, assess, and adjust for risk associated with capital investments.

Learning Objectives

After completing this chapter, you should be able to:

- explain the role of risk in the capital budgeting decisions;
- identify three perspectives for viewing risk;
- describe sensitivity analysis and scenario analysis for assessing single-project risk;
- discuss the use of CAPM in capital budgeting;
- apply the risk-adjusted discount rate method and the certainty equivalent method to adjust the level of risk;
- understand additional risks associated with international capital investments projects;
- explain how practitioners assess and adjust for risk in capital budgeting.

9.1 Types of Risk in Capital Budgeting

Although the term "risk" is multi-faceted, we use risk in a general sense to refer to situations in which the outcomes are not known with certainty. In capital budgeting, **risk** refers to the uncertainty of a project's future profitability. Financial theory typically views decision makers as being **risk averse**. A risk averse decision maker considers a risky investment only if it provides compensation for risk through a risk premium. That is, a positive relationship should exist between expected risk and expected return. An investment's payoffs should have expected values sufficiently in excess of its costs to induce a decision maker to take risks.

Risk is inherent in most capital investment decisions. Project analysts must forecast both costs and benefits often for long periods and can seldom make these predictions with certainty. Analysts can sometimes base their risk analysis on historical data, but most of the time they cannot. Thus, risk analysis in capital budgeting usually involves subjective judgments. The simplest forms of risk analysis are qualitative, but all the quantitative methods involve some degree of judgment at some stage.

There are three different perspectives for considering the risk of a capital budgeting project.

1 **The single-project perspective** views each project as a stand-alone unit.
2 **The company perspective** views each project according to its contribution to the firm's total risk.
3 **The shareholders' perspective** views each project according to its contribution to the riskiness of a shareholder's portfolio.

The first perspective considers the risk of a single project in isolation, while the others consider risk from a portfolio viewpoint either the company or the shareholders' perspective. Different theories exist about which type of risk is most important. One theory contends that managers should focus on single-project risk and leave diversification up to the shareholders. Another theory holds that managers should be concerned with risk from a portfolio context. No clear answer exists about what risk perspective is "right" for the firm to use. The proper risk measure depends on the firm's goals and the circumstances surrounding the decision. Managers often examine risk from more than one perspective.

Single-project Risk

Single-project risk, also called **stand-alone risk**, is the risk of a project as a stand-alone unit. It disregards the fact that a project is only one asset within a firm's portfolio of assets and that a firm's stock is only one stock in most investors' portfolios. Single-project risk results from anything affecting a project's cash flows. For example, analysts must predict both costs and benefits, sometimes for long periods, and they seldom can make estimates with certainty. Some factors affecting a project's cash flows include competition, customer demand, and economic changes.

In evaluating a capital budgeting project, managers often focus on single-project risk for several reasons. First, estimating a project's stand-alone risk is easier than estimating other types of risk. Evaluating projects from a portfolio perspective is complex, time consuming, and costly. In many cases, managers making capital budgeting decisions lack sufficient information about the firm's other assets to analyze the project from other viewpoints. The time delay and cost for extra analysis often do not justify the extra benefits received. Therefore, the smaller the project, the more likely managers will confine their evaluation to single-project risk. Second, a high correlation often exists among all three types of risk. That is, if the general economy does well, so should the firm; and if the firm does well, so should most of its projects. Thus, stand-alone risk is generally a good proxy for other types of risk. Finally, stand-alone risk is important when an investor is a firm's owner-manager who lacks a diversified portfolio.

Analysts use various methods of assessing single-project risk, including sensitivity analysis and scenario analysis. We discuss these techniques later in this chapter. Based on information obtained from these various risk assessment methods, analysts may be able to construct probability distributions about possible outcomes. If analysts can estimate probability distributions, they can calculate several probability-based risk measures for measuring single-project risk. These measures include the standard deviation of a project's estimated cash flows or returns and the coefficient of variation.

The **standard deviation**, σ, is a statistical measure of the variability of a distribution about its mean or expected value. Analysts use the standard deviation as a measure of absolute or total risk. This measure applies to symmetrical distributions, also called normal or "bell-shaped" probability distributions. The normal distribution is a frequently encountered frequency distribution. The most obvious property of a normal distribution is that it is symmetrical about its mean or expected value.

For a capital budgeting project, the basis for computing the standard deviation is usually a project's expected future cash flows or returns. An input in calculating the standard deviation is the **expected value**, $E(X)$, which is the probability-weighted average amount of all outcomes. Equation 9.1 shows the formula for the expected value.

$$E(X) = \sum_{i=1}^{n} p_i X_i \qquad (9.1)$$

where X_i is the return associated with the ith outcome; p_i is the probability of amount X_i occurring; and n is the number of possible outcomes.

Having computed a project's expected value, the analyst can now use Equation 9.2 to calculate its standard deviation.

$$\sigma = \sqrt{\sum_{i=1}^{n} p_i[X_i - E(X)]^2} \qquad (9.2)$$

Some distributions are "tight," suggesting little variability around the expected outcome and a small standard deviation. Other distributions are "flat," suggesting much uncertainty of the expected outcome and a large standard deviation. For example, the cash flows of an equipment replacement project are likely to be more certain or less variable than those for a new product or service. Projects with greater variability of expected outcomes have more single-project risk and, therefore, require higher expected rates of return.

As a risk measure, standard deviation has several major strengths.

- *Combines many possible outcomes and probabilities in a single risk measure.*
- *Has the same units as the original project.* The standard deviation is easy to interpret because if an analyst states the project's cash flows in dollars, the standard deviation of these cash flows will also be in dollars. Because the standard deviation and expected value are both expressed in the same units, these values are easy to relate.
- *Serves as the basis for estimating the probabilities of outcomes in various ranges if the distribution is normal.* For normal frequency distributions, about 68 percent and 95 percent of the observations should be within plus and minus one and two standard deviations of the mean (expected value), respectively.

The chief deficiencies of the standard deviation are:

- *Fails to adjust for size or scale.* As an absolute measure of risk, the standard deviation does not consider the relative size of the cash flows or returns. For example, an analyst could view Project X with an expected NPV of $100,000 and a standard deviation of $12,000 as more risky than Project Y with an expected NPV of $1,000 and a standard deviation of $10,000.
- *Treats outcomes above and below the expected value as equally desirable.* Many view risk as the chance of receiving less than expected (downside variability), not the chance of receiving more than expected (upside variability). The standard deviation measures both the upside and downside variability around the expected outcome.[1]

Another risk measure overcomes this first limitation of the standard deviation by adjusting for differences in size or scale. The **coefficient of variation**, CV, is a measure of relative risk

---

[1] Measures of downside risk are the semi-variance and semi-standard deviation. Calculating the semi-variance is the same as the variance except consideration is given only to outcomes below the expected value. The **semi-standard deviation** is the square root of the semi-variance.

or risk per unit of return (expected value). Equation 9.3 shows the formula for calculating the coefficient of variation, which is the standard deviation divided by the expected value.

$$CV = \frac{\sigma}{E(X)}$$ (9.3)

We illustrate the calculation of the expected value, standard deviation, and coefficient of variation in Section 9.2.

Company Risk

So far, we have focused on the risk of capital investments on an individual basis. Some managers are interested in the impact that a project will have on the riskiness of the company as a whole, without considering the effects of the stockholders' personal diversification. This type of risk is **company risk** or **within-firm risk**. Evaluating company risk is particularly important if undertaking a project can adversely affect a firm's stability or increase the threat of bankruptcy. In addition, company risk is important because it influences the firm's ability to use debt and to maintain smooth operations over time. Such investment projects frequently involve strategic capital budgeting decisions with large outlays.

Managers can reduce risk through diversification because not all investments respond identically to factors affecting them. Thus, the firm gains diversification benefits when managers add a project to the firm's existing portfolio of capital investments whose future cash flows or returns do not have a high, positive correlation with the firm's existing cash flows or returns. Some projects that appear risky in isolation may contribute little risk to the company and could actually decrease the firm's total risk. Therefore, the financial manager may want to consider how adopting a given project affects the firm's risk from a portfolio perspective. For example, manufacturers of highly cyclical products often diversify into consumer goods to help stabilize their cash flows.

The risk measure for a portfolio is generally the standard deviation of the probability distribution of expected returns.[2] The contribution to portfolio risk depends on the relationship between investments and the way investments react to different factors affecting returns. One widely used measure of the relationship among investments is the **correlation coefficient**, which shows the strength of the relationship between the returns of two investments. Correlation coefficients range from +1 (a perfect positive relationship) to −1 (a perfect negative relationship). If the returns of the proposed project are not perfectly positively correlated with the firm's other capital investments, adding the project will reduce the firm's risk as measured by the standard deviation of the firm's existing portfolio of investments. An important principle to remember is: the lower (less positive) the correlation coefficient, the greater is the risk reduction potential.

Figure 9.1 illustrates the possible benefits of adding a project to a firm's existing portfolio of capital investments. In this case, a negative correlation exists between Project X's cash

---

[2] Further discussion of risk from a company perspective is available in more advanced textbooks on capital budgeting such as Neil Seitz and Mitch Ellison, *Capital Budgeting and Long-term Financing Decisions*, 4th edn, Thompson, 2004.

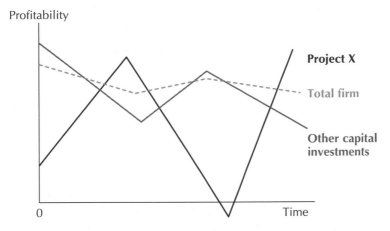

Figure 9.1 Effects of diversification on the variability of total firm profitability

flows (returns) and the cash flows (returns) on the firm's other assets. That is, Project X's returns move in the opposite direction of the returns on the firm's other assets. Hence, the overall risk or volatility of the total firm's profitability diminishes.

Much controversy surrounds the twin issues of whether firms should diversify to reduce risk and whether corporate diversification creates or destroys shareholder value. Some contend that with well-developed capital markets, investors are unwilling to pay more for the common stock of diversified firms because they can easily diversify their own portfolios. The conventional wisdom is that corporate diversification, especially conglomerate diversification, destroys shareholder wealth because the shares of diversified companies sell at a discount. Others argue that shareholder diversification is not a perfect, costless substitute for corporate diversification, even in highly developed markets. Internal corporate diversification may be beneficial because it can reduce large swings in earnings and thus lower the firm's cost of raising capital by reducing bankruptcy risk. Many companies view stabilizing their cash flows as an important goal of corporate financial strategy and engage in risk-reducing combinations of investments. Recent research challenges the evidence that diversification destroys shareholder value.[3]

Practical Financial Tip 9.1

Adding a new project may increase shareholder wealth and reduce total company risk due to diversification and portfolio effects. Managers should consider company risk because others hold them accountable for the success or failure of major projects introduced while they are in charge.

---

[3] For additional discussion involving corporate diversification and shareholder value, see John D. Martin and Akin Sayrak, "Corporate Diversification and Shareholder Value: A Survey of Recent Literature," *Journal of Corporate Finance*, January 2003, 37–57.

Market Risk

Until now, we have viewed risk from the perspective of someone within the firm. If the financial goal is shareholder wealth maximization, managers should ultimately view risk in terms of how it affects shareholders. Equation 9.4 provides a useful way of understanding risk from the stockholders' perspective.

$$\text{Total risk} = \text{Systematic} + \text{Unsystematic risk} \tag{9.4}$$

Total risk has two components. **Systematic risk** or **market risk** is the variability of investment returns caused by market fluctuations. Because systematic risk tends to affect all investments, it is undiversifiable. Thus, investors cannot diversify away systematic risk by combining investments in portfolios. **Unsystematic risk** or **non-market risk** is unique to a particular firm or investment and can be reduced or eliminated by combining various investments in a portfolio. Because investors can diversify away the unsystematic portion of total risk, only systematic risk should concern a firm's shareholders who hold fully diversified portfolios.

Systematic and Unsystematic Factors: An Analogy

An analogy may help to illustrate the difference between systematic (undiversifiable) risk and unsystematic (diversifiable) risk. As individuals, we all have differing characteristics such as physical appearance, gender, nationality, and background. These characteristics represent our unique or unsystematic factors that help make us who we are. Yet, despite our many differences, we have one thing in common – we are all human. We cannot get rid of our "humanity." In a similar fashion, companies cannot diversify away their market risk. Just as some people may be more "human" than others, some companies may have more market risk than others.

The capital asset pricing model (CAPM), discussed later in this chapter, provides a way to adjust the required return on investments for market risk. When stockholders have highly diversified portfolios, market risk, as measured by **beta**, may be the appropriate risk measure for capital projects. Some view the CAPM as a highly simplified model that only approximates the risk-return tradeoff occurring in the marketplace. In practice, many investors do not hold well-diversified portfolios. Thus, they may consider factors other than market risk when determining required rates of returns. Such investors may be more concerned with total risk than with market risk. Therefore, beta may not be the proper risk measure in all circumstances. In addition, serious problems exist in measuring the beta of a single project.

Concept Check 9.1

1 What are the three general perspectives from which to evaluate risk in capital budgeting?
2 What is the justification for viewing risk from each of the three risk perspectives?
3 How can analysts measure single-project risk, company risk, and market risk?
4 What are the two components of total project risk? How do they differ?
5 What are examples of diversifiable and undiversifiable risk?
6 Under what circumstances is beta an appropriate risk measure of a new project?

9.2 Assessing Single-Project Risk

A good starting point for assessing risk in capital budgeting begins with single-project or stand-alone risk. For small capital investment projects, financial managers may prefer to rely on subjective judgment to get a "feel" for project risk. For major capital investments, managers may want to spend the time and effort necessary to conduct a more complete analysis of project risk. The goal of conducting any risk analysis is to assess the degree of variability in future cash flows from a project and to identify the most critical variables to the success or failure of the investment.

Although many "direct" methods are available for assessing single-project risk, we focus on two of the most common approaches:[4]

1 sensitivity analysis; and
2 scenario analysis.

Direct methods attempt to directly measure the risk of each investment proposal. No one method fits every situation. Although sensitivity analysis and scenario analysis can help managers gain insights about risk, these techniques do not provide decision rules for making accept-reject decisions.[5]

---

[4] Other more complex techniques for assessing single-project risk are simulation and decision tree analysis. **Monte Carlo simulation** is a risk analysis technique that uses a computer to simulate probable future events and to estimate a project's profitability and riskiness. In capital budgeting, simulation is a procedure used to evaluate the impact on a project's cash flows of simultaneous changes in several variables. A **decision tree** is a method of graphing the set of decision points and possible alternatives. This approach is useful to help investment decision-making involving risk when the project involves a sequence of decisions at various points of time over the project's life. The decision-tree approach provides the decision maker with a probability distribution of possible NPVs for a project. We do not examine these approaches because of their complexity and relatively infrequent use in practice.

[5] For a detailed discussion of project risk analysis, see Dan Dayananda, Richard Irons, Steve Harrison, John Herbohn, and Patrick Rowland, *Capital Budgeting: Financial Appraisal of Investment Projects*, Cambridge University Press, 2002.

Sensitivity Analysis

The variables affecting a project's cash flows are subject to uncertainty. A change in any input variable that affects cash flows or a firm's cost of capital will affect the net present value (NPV).[6] Important questions that managers often ask when examining risky investments are:

- What are the critical variables?
- How might these variables change?
- How will potential changes affect the success of the project?

Managers can use sensitivity analysis to help answer these questions.

Sensitivity analysis is a technique that measures the change in one variable as a result of a change in another variable. By using sensitivity analysis, analysts can determine which variables have the greatest impact on the project's outcome. This method lets analysts conduct a "what-if analysis." For example, *what* happens to a project's NPV *if* the unit selling price is 20 percent higher than expected? *What* happens to the NPV *if* unit production costs are 10 percent less than forecasted? Sensitivity analysis permits examining a lengthy list of questions about how changes in one variable, while holding others constant, affect a project's NPV.

Having information about the critical variables can be particularly useful in at least two stages of the capital budgeting process. In the cash flow estimation stage, management can decide whether to devote additional resources to developing improved forecasts for the variables critical to the project's success. In the implementation stage, management can pay particular attention to the behavior of these critical variables.

Using the results of the sensitivity analysis, the financial manager can construct sensitivity graphs, which show the impact of changes in different variables, one at a time, on a project's NPV. A sensitivity graph typically places the input variable on the horizontal axis and the project's NPV on the vertical axis. The steeper the slope of the sensitivity line, the more sensitive a project's NPV is to a change in a specific input variable. Based on the results of the sensitivity graphs, managers can focus on improving the accuracy of estimates of critical variables or attempt to control and influence critical values if they accept the project.

Steps in using sensitivity analysis
Sensitivity analysis for a capital investment involves the following steps:

1   *Calculate a project's NPV using the most likely value estimated for each variable.* The **most likely value** is management's best guess value, which often corresponds to the expected value of the variable.
2   *Identify key variables that are likely to affect the NPV of the project.* Some variables are under management's control while others are not. In conducting sensitivity analysis, managers

---

[6]   Analysts can also use sensitivity analysis to determine how changes in input variables may affect the internal rate of return. We limit our discussion to NPV because of its superiority as a capital budgeting technique as discussed in Chapter 8.

sometimes focus on the uncontrollable variables because they feel more confident in handling the controllable variables, whatever happens in the future.

3 *Change one of the selected input variables by a fixed percentage, say plus and minus 10 or 20 percent, of the most likely value while holding the other variables constant, and recalculate the NPV based on the revision.* Management's experience and judgments serve as a guide in selecting the actual percentage change. This ad hoc approach is simple and straight-forward to apply.

4 *Repeat the process described in Step 3 by revising the estimate of each of the other selected variables one at a time.*

5 *Identify the sensitive variables by plotting the NPVs for each variable against the fixed percentage change.*

Using these steps to conduct a complex sensitivity analysis can involve many tedious calculations. Because spreadsheet computer applications such as Excel can lessen this burden, these applications are ideal for conducting this mechanical type of sensitivity analysis. In addition, managers can use spreadsheets to recalculate the NPV and to plot sensitivity graphs.

Practical Financial Tip 9.2

When selecting a set of variables for sensitivity analysis, management should consider several factors. These considerations include management's ability to control the variables, its confidence in forecasts of the variables, and its historical experience, if any, in dealing with similar projects. In addition, managers should consider the time and cost needed to conduct the analysis.

Example 9.1 Using Sensitivity Analysis: Carolina Freight Company

Let's return to Example 7.8 discussed in Chapter 7 in which Carolina Freight Company is considering whether to expand its truck fleet. Table 9.1 shows the project's expected cash flows.

Using the firm's 10 percent cost of capital to discount the project's cash flows gives the most likely NPV of $261,958 (PI = 1.50, IRR = 24.82 percent, and MIRR = 17.67 percent). Although a positive NPV suggests adopting this project, the firm is still concerned about the risk of the project.

To gain a better understanding of project risk, the financial manager identifies four input variables – operating revenues, operating costs, discount rate, and salvage value – and then conducts a sensitivity analysis to see how changes in each variable affect the project's NPV. Specifically, the manager examines a 10 percent deviation above and below the most likely value for each variable. Table 9.2 shows how changes in each variable affect the project's NPV.

Table 9.1 Carolina Freight Company's incremental cash flows

Year	0	1	2	3	4	5	6
Investment in:							
Fixed assets	(500,000)						
Net working capital (NWC)	(25,000)						
Operating revenues		300,000	350,000	350,000	375,000	375,000	375,000
− Operating costs (40%)		120,000	140,000	140,000	150,000	150,000	150,000
− Depreciation		100,000	160,000	96,000	57,600	57,600	28,800
Taxable income		80,000	50,000	114,000	167,400	167,400	196,200
− Taxes (34%)		27,200	17,000	38,760	56,916	56,916	66,708
Net income		52,800	33,000	75,240	110,484	110,484	129,492
+ Depreciation		100,000	160,000	96,000	57,600	57,600	28,800
Operating cash flows		152,800	193,000	171,240	168,084	168,084	158,292
Salvage value							100,000
Tax on salvage value (34%)							(34,000)
Recovery of NWC							25,000
Net cash flows	(525,000)	152,800	193,000	171,240	168,084	168,084	249,292

Table 9.2 Sensitivity analysis: Carolina Freight Company

	Net present value			
Change from most likely value	Operating revenues	Operating costs	Discount rate (most likely value = 10%)	Salvage value
−10%	$201,544	$302,296	$286,819	$258,232
Most likely	261,958	261,958	261,958	261,958
+10%	322,271	221,682	238,263	265,683

Plotting these NPVs for each input variable results in four sensitivity lines on a sensitivity graph. A **sensitivity graph** is a plot of a project's NPVs for changes in an input variable, holding all other input variables constant. The slope of the sensitivity line shows the sensitivity of the project's NPV to each variable, with a steeper slope suggesting greater sensitivity. Using the most likely value as the reference point, Figure 9.2 shows that the project's NPV is most sensitive to changes in operating revenues, followed by operating costs, discount rate, and salvage value. Thus, a small error in forecasting the project's operating revenues can result in a larger error in its NPV than with a similar error in forecasting any of the other three variables. The manager could construct similar graphs for other input variables.

How can managers use this information in making the capital budgeting decision? If the manager expects operating revenues or salvage value to decrease or operating

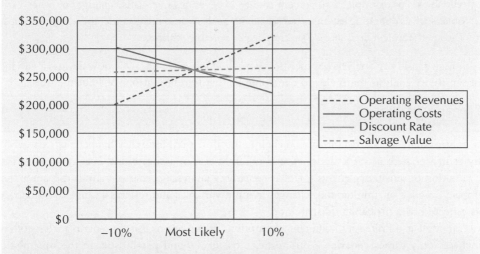

Figure 9.2 Sensitivity analysis: Carolina Freight Company

costs or the discount rate to increase by no more than 10 percent, Carolina Freight should accept the project because the project's NPV is still highly positive. If the likelihood of any of these variables changing is greater than 10 percent, the manager can reevaluate how such a change will affect the project's NPV.

Strengths and weaknesses
Sensitivity analysis has both redeeming features and drawbacks.
   Sensitivity analysis has several major strengths.

• *Helps to identify the key input variables affecting a project's NPV.* This method helps pinpoint where forecasting errors will do the most damage. Managers can then concentrate on measuring the accuracy of these variables before making a decision.
• *Is easy to conduct and the results are easy to interpret.* This method gives managers a simple picture of possible outcomes without requiring complex probability estimates. The use of spreadsheet programs facilitates this type of "what-if analysis."
• *Can provide useful insights about project risk when comparing two projects.* A project with steeper sensitivity lines is more risky than one with flatter sensitivity lines on the same variables. Information about the sensitivity of key input variables can help managers make informed decisions about risky projects.

Sensitivity analysis has several limitations.

• *Provides only a limited amount of information.* Sensitivity analysis does not include probabilities of any of the outcomes.
• *Does not show the impact on NPV of simultaneous changes in variables, but only the sensitivity of a project's NPV to changes in one variable at a time.* This approach ignores relationships among

variables. For example, a 10 percent change in revenues may cause changes in other variables such as operating expenses but sensitivity analysis does not consider these relationships.

- *Does not provide a decision rule for accepting or rejecting projects.*

Although sensitivity analysis has merits, the method is incomplete. We now discuss a variant of sensitivity analysis that helps to overcome its first two limitations but not the third.

Scenario Analysis

Scenario analysis is a risk analysis technique used to examine what happens to profitability estimates such as NPV under several different sets of assumptions. Scenario analysis is a variation of sensitivity analysis. Unlike sensitivity analysis, scenario analysis measures the impact on NPV of simultaneous changes in input variables and reflects a range of outcomes as reflected by a probability distribution.

Although an infinite set of different assumptions or conditions exists, scenario analysis often includes only three scenarios – optimistic, most likely, and pessimistic. In the **optimistic scenario**, the financial manager assumes that the outcomes of some variables are better than the most likely values. Operating revenues and salvage value, for instance, could be greater than anticipated. In the **pessimistic scenario**, the financial manager assumes that the outcomes of some variables are worse than the most likely values. For example, the initial outlay and the tax rate could be greater than expected and the project life could be less than expected. These two scenarios provide a range of possible forecast values around the **most likely scenario**.

Sometimes financial managers identify best-case, base-case, and worst-case scenarios. These are special cases of scenario analysis. In the **best-case scenario**, the manager would use all the optimistic values for each variable. The best-case scenario answers the question, "What is the best possible NPV from the project?" In the **worst-case scenario**, the manager would use all the pessimistic values for each variable. The worst-case scenario answers the question, "What is the worst possible NPV from the project?" While the worst-case and best-case scenarios emphasize extreme values, the **base case** reflects the NPV given the most likely set of conditions for all input variables. Under these special conditions, scenario analysis gives a range of potential NPVs with the worst-case scenario setting the lower bound and the best-case scenario setting the upper bound for the project.

Steps in using scenario analysis
Scenario analysis consists of the following steps.

Required

1   Identify the number of scenarios and the cash flows for each.
2   Calculate the NPV for each scenario.

Optional

3   Assign a probability of occurrence to each scenario.
4   Calculate the expected NPV, the standard deviation of the NPV, and the coefficient of variation using the probability distribution of NPVs, and then interpret the results.

Developing optimistic and pessimistic scenarios

Two basic approaches are available for developing the optimistic (or best-case) and pessimistic (or worst-case) scenarios. The **ad hoc approach**, discussed under sensitivity analysis, takes a fixed percentage above or below the most likely (or base) case. Although the financial manager can apply this approach to all variables, extensive analysis of all variables could waste resources. The **forecasting approach** emphasizes the process of forecasting and attempts to develop values that represent probable events. Because this method is more time consuming and costly to apply than is the more mechanical ad hoc approach, it forces managers to select from a full range of possibilities from those variables deemed worthy of consideration.

Several approaches are available for developing optimistic and pessimistic values using the forecasting approach. One approach is to gather expert opinions on the upper and lower values. Another approach is for managers to set upper and lower bounds based on their experience with similar projects or with risk analysis in general. A third approach is to employ statistical techniques based on descriptive statistics or inferential statistics such as regression analysis.

Example 9.2 Developing Optimistic and Pessimistic Values: Carolina Freight Company

Let's illustrate developing optimistic and pessimistic values from average values using descriptive statistics. If the distribution of values of a variable is normally distributed, the manager could establish upper and lower bounds based on a fixed number of standard deviations around the mean (expected value). Under a normal curve, about 68 percent and 95 percent of the outcomes should be within plus and minus one and two standard deviations of the mean, respectively. Thus, the manager could use the upper and lower boundaries of this range of values as the optimistic and pessimistic value for a specific variable.

As Table 9.1 shows, Carolina Freight Company's expected operating revenues for the project in year 1 are $300,000. Suppose that the standard deviation of these operating revenues is $25,000. Assuming the range of plus or minus two standard deviations from the mean, the optimistic forecast for operating revenues in year 1 is estimated to be $350,000 [$300,000 + 2($25,000)] and the pessimistic forecast in year 1 would be $250,000 [$300,000 − 2($25,000)]. The financial manager could take a similar approach to estimate optimistic and pessimistic forecasts for other input variables.

Using the information obtained from scenario analysis, managers can then assess the likelihood of occurrence of each scenario. If, for example, the probability of the pessimistic (or worst-case) scenario is high and results in a highly negative NPV, this may suggest a high level of stand-alone risk. Of critical importance is whether the firm can live with or survive the pessimistic (or worst-case) outcome. If the pessimistic outcome would seriously weaken the firm or increase its danger of bankruptcy, this would be useful information to management in assessing the project's riskiness. If the chance of the pessimistic (or worst-case) scenario is small and its NPV is positive, then management may have little concern about the project's stand-alone risk.

Example 9.3 Using Scenario Analysis: Carolina Freight Company

Let's now use scenario analysis to assess the risk of the truck fleet expansion project for Carolina Freight Company. Besides using the most likely scenario, the financial manager develops optimistic and pessimistic scenarios. Table 9.1 contains the cash flows for the most likely scenario. For simplicity, the manager assumes the initial investment remains $525,000 and focuses on three variables – operating revenues, operating costs, and salvage value. In the pessimistic case scenario, management expects the revenues to be 20 percent less than the most likely case, operating costs are 50 percent of revenues, and before-tax salvage value is $25,000 in year 6. In the optimistic scenario, revenues are estimated to be 20 percent more than the most likely case, operating costs are 35 percent of revenues, and before-tax salvage value $150,000 in year 6. If the firm's cost of capital is 10 percent, what is the project's NPV under each scenario?

Table 9.3 Scenario analysis: Carolina Freight Company

A. Cash flows under three scenarios

Scenario	0	1	Expected year-end cash flows 2	3	4	5	6[a]
Pessimistic	−$525,000	$113,200	$146,800[b]	$125,040	$118,584	$118,584	$150,292
Most likely	−525,000	152,800	193,000	171,240	168,084	168,084	249,292
Optimistic	−525,000	188,440	234,580	212,820	212,634	212,634	326,842

B. Net present value

Scenario	NPV @ 10% [1]	Scenario probabilities, P_i [2]	Probability distribution of returns [1] × [2]
Pessimistic	$32,638	0.2	$6,528
Most likely	261,958	0.6	157,175
Optimistic	461,826	0.2	92,365
		Total 1.0	Expected NPV = $256,068

[a] Year 6 includes both operating and terminal cash flows.
[b] Operating losses are assumed to result in tax savings by offsetting operating gains from other projects.

Referring to Table 9.3, Panel A shows the cash flows and Panel B presents the NPV under each scenario. How can the financial manager use these results to assess single-project risk? In this situation, the results suggest that the proposed project's NPV is positive even under the pessimistic scenario. If the chance of the pessimistic scenario occurring is small, say 10 or 20 percent, the financial manager is unlikely to be highly concerned about the single-project risk.

Now assume that the financial manager can assign a probability to each NPV. In this case, the manager estimates scenario probabilities of 60 percent for the most likely scenario and 20 percent each for the pessimistic and optimistic scenarios. The total probabilities must equal 100 percent or 1.0. The possible NPVs and their associated probabilities constitute a **discrete probability distribution**. Such a probability distribution is discrete because it has a limited number of outcomes (in this case NPVs), each with its own probability. Using Equation 9.1 permits calculating the expected NPV, which is a profitability measure. Panel B of Table 9.3 presents the calculation of the expected NPV of $256,068, which involves multiplying each NPV by its assigned probability and summing the products. Equations 9.2 and 9.3 can be used to calculate two risk measures – the standard deviation of the NPV and the coefficient of variation.

The standard deviation of the NPV is $135,913.

$$\sigma_{NPV} = \sqrt{\sum_{t=1}^{n} P_i(NPV_i - E(NPV))^2}$$

$$= \sqrt{0.2(\$32{,}638 - \$256{,}068)^2 + 0.6(\$261{,}958 - \$256{,}068)^2 + 0.2(\$461{,}826 - \$256{,}068)^2}$$

$$= \$135{,}913$$

The coefficient of variation is 0.53.

$$CV_{NPV} = \frac{\sigma_{NPV}}{E(NPV)} = \frac{\$135{,}913}{\$256{,}068} = 0.53$$

To find the relative riskiness of this expansion project, the financial manager can compare the project's coefficient of variation, $CV_{NPV} = 0.53$, to that of average-risk projects for the firm. If the expansion project has a larger CV_{NPV} than that for the firm's average risk projects, this suggests a higher risk project than average. For example, if Carolina Freight Company's average projects have a CV_{NPV} ranging from 0.25 to 0.40, the expansion project would be high risk.

Strengths and weaknesses
As with any risk analysis measure, scenario analysis has both pros and cons.
  Scenario analysis has two key benefits as a measure of single-project risk.

- *Scenario analysis provides a range of outcomes.* As a form of what-if analysis, scenario analysis focuses attention on other possible outcomes besides the most likely case. For example, developing a pessimistic scenario can help management avoid surprises and the tendency for forecasting optimism. Sometimes, performing worst-case analysis may lead to rejecting a project because its consequences are so severe.
- *Managers can use the outputs of scenario analysis to determine the expected NPV, standard deviation of NPV, and CV_{NPV}.* In turn, managers can use these statistical measures to help assess a project's stand-alone risk and develop risk adjustments.

Despite these advantages, scenario analysis has several major weaknesses.

- *Scenario analysis is generally limited to a few discrete outcomes, when many other possible outcomes exist.* As with any technique requiring subjective judgment, different managers may disagree on what forms pessimistic and optimistic scenarios may take.
- *Estimating scenario probabilities precisely is difficult.* If the financial manager decides to assign probabilities to the various scenarios, this process involves judgment.
- *The best-case and worst-case variant of scenario analysis assumes a perfect correlation between the inputs.* With this approach, the assumption is that all "good" values occur together and all "bad" values occur together. In practice, this situation is unlikely to occur.
- *Scenario analysis does not provide a decision rule for making accept-reject decisions.* Scenario analysis does not indicate whether the project should be accepted or rejected, but it can provide valuable information for making effective capital budgeting decisions. Ultimately, the decision of whether to accept the project depends on the confidence that the decision maker has in the assumptions underlying the scenario analysis including the probabilities assigned to each scenario.

Concept Check 9.2

1 What are the steps required in conducting sensitivity analysis?
2 How does sensitivity analysis differ from scenario analysis?
3 What is the difference between the optimistic scenario and the best-case scenario and between the pessimistic scenario and the worst-case scenario?
4 What are two methods for developing optimistic and pessimistic scenarios? Explain each.
5 What are the advantages and disadvantages of sensitivity analysis and scenario analysis?

9.3 Assessing Market Risk

Until now, we have focused on single-project risk. The risk analysis methods discussed so far do not consider portfolio risk from either the perspective of the company or its shareholders. Although sensitivity analysis and scenario analysis can help managers gain insights about risk, these techniques do not provide a decision rule for making accept-reject decisions. We now turn to the capital asset pricing model to help overcome these shortcomings, but we encounter other problems in doing so.

The **capital asset pricing model** (CAPM) measures the relationship between risk and required rate of return for assets held in well-diversified portfolios.[7] In theory, CAPM is an

---

[7] For further discussion of the CAPM, see Diana R. Harrington, *Modern Portfolio Theory, The Capital Asset Pricing Model and Arbitrage Pricing Theory: A Users' Guide,* 2nd edn, Prentice-Hall, Inc., 1987.

expectational model because its inputs are expected future values. This model deals only with a single factor – systematic or market risk, as measured by beta, because it assumes diversification can greatly reduce or eliminate unsystematic risk. Although analysts and others typically apply the CAPM at the firm level, the model may be applicable at the project level. Equation 9.5 shows the CAPM equation applied to capital investments, not to the firm.

$$k_i = R_f + \beta_i(R_m - R_f) \tag{9.5}$$

where k_i is the return on project i; R_f is the risk-free rate of return; R_m is the expected rate of return on the market; and β_i is the beta coefficient of project i.

Equation 9.5 says that a project's expected or required rate of return is the sum of the risk-free rate, R_f, plus the product of the risk premium $(R_m - R_f)$ and the project's beta coefficient, β_i. Based on this single-factor model, market risk (beta) is the only factor that explains the positive relationship between risk and return. In practice, other factors, in addition to the market, appear to affect the required return. For example, one well-known study found that firm size and book-to-market equity are explanatory variables that possibly serve as surrogates for risk.[8] Unfortunately, no consensus exists on either the number of factors or the identification of economic surrogates for those factors.[9] Although the CAPM oversimplifies reality, it is easy to understand and widely used in practice.

The CAPM is a simplified approximation of complex behavior in a multifaceted world. As such, constructing the CAPM requires numerous assumptions. In the real world, violations of all assumptions occur to various degrees. For example, the CAPM assumes perfect capital markets (that is, no taxes, transaction costs or other market imperfections) and the ability of investors to borrow and lend unlimited amounts at the risk-free rate. The presence of unrealistic assumptions is insufficient to condemn the model if the model is useful in practice. Unfortunately, the risk-return relationship predicted by CAPM is not fully consistent with empirical observation. Nonetheless, many practitioners continue to use the CAPM to find the required return for a company, a division, and a single asset (project). In this section, we use the CAPM to determine hurdle rates for corporate investments.

Although the CAPM looks precise, using it requires estimating R_f, R_m, and β_i. Because no single best way exists to estimate these values, the financial manager must deal with approximations or proxies. Let's now turn our attention to estimating the three inputs of the CAPM.

Estimating the Risk-free Rate

The financial manager typically uses yields on government securities as suitable proxies for the risk-free rate. The main question is: What is the appropriate maturity to use? Because

---

[8] Eugene F. Fama and Kenneth R. French, "The Cross-Section of Expected Stock Returns," *Journal of Finance* 57, June 1992, 427–65.

[9] Other models consider more factors, including arbitrage pricing theory, APT. As an alternative to CAPM, APT is used to find the required return of a risk investment, based on systematic risk. The discussion of APT is beyond the scope of this book. For a classic discussion of the standard APT, see Stephen A. Ross, "The Arbitrage Theory of Capital Asset Pricing," *Journal of Economic Theory*, December 1976, 341–60.

capital budgeting involves evaluating long-term investments, the recommended risk-free rate, R_f, is the yield on those government bonds with a term to maturity similar to the project life of the capital investment. For example, if the project has an expected life of 10 years, the financial manager should use the yield on 10-year US Treasury bonds.

Estimating the Market Return

Estimating the expected return on the market is difficult because we are trying to estimate what investors expect the return to be, not what it has been. Recall that the CAPM is an expectational model. Despite this fact, managers often attempt to estimate the expected market return based on its historical average stock returns over a long period. This approach assumes the past is the best proxy for investors' expectations of future market returns. Selecting the proper benchmark as a market proxy is subject to debate. For a large market capitalization (cap) company, analysts often use the S&P 500 but the Russell 2000 for a small cap company. **Market capitalization** is computed as the price per share times the number of outstanding shares.

Another approach is to use surveys of expectations for the market published by investment advisory services. Having estimated the market rate return and the risk-free rate, the financial manager can calculate the market risk premium, $R_m - R_f$. Studies suggest an historical average market risk premium of about 5 or 6 percent, but this risk premium is not particularly stable in the short run.

Estimating a Project's Beta

Unlike the beta of most common stocks, a project's beta is not directly observable, except when the project involves the purchase of a publicly traded company. A project's beta, β_i, measures the sensitivity of changes in the project's returns to changes in the market's returns. There are several ways to estimate a project's beta. One way is by regressing its historical holding-period returns against the returns on a market portfolio. Because historical return data on projects are seldom available, we ignore this procedure.

A second method of estimating a project's beta, especially for a new project, is to use comparable companies or **pure-play method**. This method begins by identifying several publicly traded companies in the same or similar line of business as the proposed project and determining their betas. Although finding pure-play firms that exactly match a particular project is often difficult, beta estimates are readily available from published or online sources on thousands of common stocks.[10] These services include Bloomberg, S&P, and Value Line. After finding the beta for the common stock of several comparable firms, the financial manager can average their betas as a proxy for a project's beta and use this information to compute the cost of capital.

---

[10] Research evidence shows that individual company betas are unstable over time.

Example 9.4 Using the CAPM to Estimate a Project's Required Rate of Return: Global Enterprises

For simplicity, assume that Global Enterprises, which we introduced in Chapter 8, wants to invest in capital projects and uses only equity capital. Project A involves introducing a new product for Global that differs from the existing product mix. Project B involves replacing old equipment with new labor saving equipment. Now suppose the financial manager can identify only one pure-play firm and its beta is 2.0. For the time being, we assume that the pure-play firm is financed entirely by equity. The financial manager estimates that the beta for the new labor-saving equipment is the same as the company as a whole and the market, namely 1.0. The financial manager uses the following estimates to calculate the required rate of return (cost of capital) for Projects A and B.

- Risk-free return, $R_f = 5\%$.
- Expected return on the market, $R_m = 10\%$.
- Estimated pure-play beta, $\beta_A = 2.0$ and $\beta_B = 1.0$.

Assume these values remain constant over the life of each capital investment. If the firm's beta is 1.0, Project A is riskier than the firm is, but Project B has the same market risk. Using the CAPM, the required rate of return for each project is:

- Project A: $k_A = 5\% + 2.0(10\% - 5\%) = 15.0\%$
- Project B: $k_B = 5\% + 1.0(10\% - 5\%) = 10.0\%$

The firm should evaluate Project A and B using 15 percent and 10 percent discount rates, respectively.

The CAPM method presents several difficulties in estimating a project's required rate of return. First, estimating the parameters of the model can be difficult. For example, forecasting a project's beta is difficult because historical returns on a project are often unavailable and future returns are hard to predict. Second, the CAPM includes only systematic (market) risk and ignores a project's unsystematic risk. For undiversified stockholders, total risk may be a more appropriate risk measure.

Practical Financial Tip 9.3

Detractors claim that the CAPM has serious flaws due to its unrealistic assumptions. They also assert that the model is probably wrong because empirical tests have produced results that often conflict with the theory. Finally, they contend that CAPM is practically useless because of the difficulties involved in estimating the inputs for the model. Yet, many practitioners believe that they are making better decisions by using this model. Problems exist with simple-minded use of a simple concept. In use, the CAPM can lead to diverse results. Therefore, using the CAPM requires thoroughly understanding the model and its limitations as well as using logic when applying the model. Dangers exist when using drugs without reading the warning labels. The same caveat applies for using the CAPM.

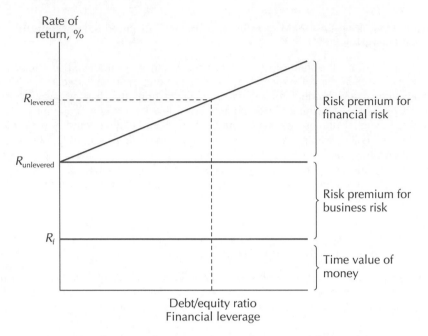

Figure 9.3 Relationship between the required rate of return and financial leverage

Required Rate of Return and Leverage

A problem with using the betas from pure-play companies is that these companies may have similar characteristics as the proposed project but different levels of financial leverage. If the pure-play firms have different levels of leverage, they are likely to have different betas because financial leverage affects beta. **Financial leverage** is the use of debt in a firm's financial structure.

Figure 9.3 shows the theoretical relationship between required rates of return and financial leverage. As we discuss further in the next section, the required rate of return consists of three components. First, the risk-free rate, R_f, measures the pure time value of money or the reward for waiting for money without taking any risk. Second, investors require a risk premium for **business risk**, which comes from the nature of the firm's normal operations. Business risk remains the same regardless of how the firm is financed. Third, investors require a risk premium for **financial risk**, which reflects how the firm finances its assets. In Figure 9.3, financial risk is measured by the debt/equity ratio.

Although business and financial risk both affect the firm's beta, a project's beta should only reflect business risk. That is, the financial manager should evaluate a project's risk based only on its operating characteristics, not on its financial considerations. Therefore, pure project risk identifies the risk without considering the financial risk associated with how the firm anticipates financing the project.[11]

---

[11]   A procedure exists for calculating a levered beta, β_L, reflecting both the pure project risk and the financial risk associated with the project. The financial manager can relever the beta to reflect the

If the pure-play firm uses debt in its capital structure, the observed beta of the levered pure-play company, β_{pp}, must be adjusted downward into an unlevered beta, β_u, using the pure-play firm's debt equity ratio. Otherwise, the financial manager will use a rate of return that is higher than required by the project. Equation 9.6 shows one way to adjust the levered beta of the pure-play firm to an unlevered beta. This equation only approximates the effect of leverage on beta because of capital market imperfections.

$$\beta_u = \frac{\beta_{pp}}{1 + (1 - T_{pp})\dfrac{D_{pp}}{E_{pp}}} \tag{9.6}$$

where β_u is the unlevered beta for a company or project; β_{pp} is the levered beta of the pure-play company; T_{pp} is the marginal tax rate of the pure-play company; and D_{pp} and E_{pp} are market values of the debt and common equity of the pure-play company.

This estimate of β_u serves as an approximation of the project beta because it ignores other firm factors that may affect beta. The financial manager should make this adjustment for each pure-play firm before averaging the betas. The financial manager may also want to take a weighted average of the pure-play betas, reflecting degrees of similarity between the project and different firms. Pure play firms that are more similar to the project should receive higher weights. Using this project beta with the CAPM provides an estimate of the required rate of return.

Example 9.5 Using the CAPM to Calculate a Project's Required Rate of Return: Global Enterprises – Extended

Global Enterprises wants to use the pure-play method to identify the beta for Project A. Suppose the financial manager identifies a single pure-play firm with a beta of 2.00 and a debt-equity ratio of 0.20 based on market values. This firm's marginal tax rate is 34 percent. Substituting these values into Equation 9.6 gives an unlevered beta of 1.77 for Project A.

---

proposed capital structure for the project or the target capital structure for the firm. The following equation reflects the levered beta, β_L.

$$\beta_L = \beta_u \left[1 + (1 - T)\left(\frac{D}{E}\right) \right]$$

where β_L is the levered beta for the project; T is the marginal tax rate of the company evaluating the project; and D and E are market values of the debt and common equity invested in the project.

Substituting the levered beta into the CAPM permits calculating the cost of equity appropriate for the project. Combining a weighted cost of equity with a weighted cost of debt yields the project's required rate of return.

$$\beta_u = \frac{2.00}{1 + (1 - 0.34)(0.20)} = \frac{2.00}{1.13} = 1.77$$

Note that β_u is always less than β_{pp}, except in the case of an all equity pure-play firm where they are equal. This unlevered beta of 1.77 corresponds to the business risk of Project A, because it excludes the effect of financial leverage on systematic risk.

If the risk-free rate is 5 percent and the expected return on the market is 10 percent, Project A's required rate of return is:

$$k_A = 5\% + 1.77(10\% - 5\%) = 13.85\%$$

Using the Security Market Line in Capital Budgeting

The **security market line** (SML) is the graphic representation of the CAPM. The positively sloped SML indicates that projects with higher market (beta) risk require higher rates of return to compensate investors for greater risk.[12] When a project's expected rate of return (IRR) is above its required rate of return, the project plots above the SML. Such a project will produce positive NPVs and, therefore, fall within the acceptance region. Similarly, a project whose expected rate of return (IRR) is below its required rate of return plots below the SML. Investing in this project will produce a negative NPV and fall within the rejection region. Projects plotting on the SML yield a NPV of zero.

Example 9.6 Using the SML to Evaluate Capital Budgeting Projects: Global Enterprises

Assume that the pure-play beta of 2.0 found in Example 9.3 is appropriate. Thus, we no longer assume that Project A is a normal or average risk project ($\beta = 1$) as we did in Chapter 8. Using this information and estimates of the expected rates of return on Projects A and B, the financial manager develops Table 9.4. Which project, if any, should Global Enterprises accept using the SML? As Figure 9.4 shows, Project A falls above the SML within the acceptance region and Project B falls below the SML within

Table 9.4 Required and expected rates of return: Global Enterprises

Project	Beta, β_i	Required rate of return, k_i (%)	Expected rate of return, IRR (%)	Decision
A	2.0	15.0	24.9	Accept
B	1.0	10.0	8.6	Reject
C	0.6	8.0	9.5	Accept

---

[12]   Research suggests that the slope of the SML is flatter than that predicted by the SML.

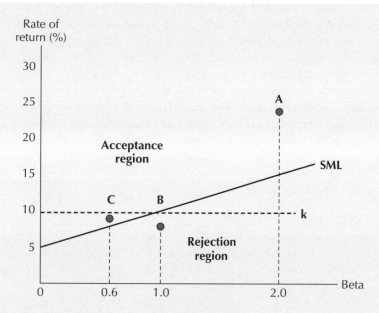

Figure 9.4 The security market line and the cost of capital

the rejection region. Project A has an expected return of 24.9 percent, but based on its systematic risk, it should earn only 15.0 percent. By contrast, Project B is expected to earn 8.6 percent, but it should earn 10.0 percent based on its systematic risk.

Now consider Project C with a beta of 0.6. Using the CAPM, this project has a required rate of return of 8 percent [$k_C = 5\% + 0.6(10\% - 5\%) = 8.0\%$] and an expected rate of return of 9.5 percent. As Figure 9.4 shows, Project C is acceptable because its expected return is above the SML, which represents the required rated of return. Notice, however, that Project C's expected return is below the firm's 10 percent cost of capital, k, represented by the dashed line in Figure 9.4. Using the firm's cost of capital of 10 percent as the hurdle rate would lead to rejecting Project C.

How can Global Enterprises afford to pay 10 percent to raise capital if it only expects to earn a 9.5 percent return on the project? The answer is simple. The cost of capital represents the return required by suppliers of capital to the firm. Some projects are less risky than the firm is, while others are more risky. Projects require a different rate of return based on their riskiness. If the firm invests in less risky projects, suppliers of capital should respond by requiring a lower return on their capital. Therefore, holding other factors constant, the firm's cost of capital should decrease. This example illustrates that using the firm's cost of capital as the required rate of return can lead to incorrect decisions for projects whose risk differs from the firm's normal or average-risk projects. The SML provides a clear decision rule for accept-reject decisions and considers market risk.

Unfortunately, the CAPM has several shortcomings when applied to capital budgeting. A major practical limitation is the difficulty of getting accurate inputs, especially beta. Using the pure-play method can provide a partial solution to estimating beta, but this approach is impractical to carry out in many situations. Another problem is applying the single-period CAPM to a capital budgeting project that involves multiple periods. That is, using the same discount rate for all periods can cause problems if the future risk-free rate, expected return on the market, or project beta change over time. The correct approach would be to estimate multi-period discount rates, which can be very complex. Despite these limitations, this simplified model has a place in the financial manager's arsenal of ways to measure risk in capital budgeting.

Concept Check 9.3

1 How can financial managers estimate the risk-free rate, the expected return on the market, and a project's beta using CAPM?
2 What are the problems of using the pure-play method to estimate a project's beta?
3 How do business risk and financial risk differ?
4 Explain how to draw the SML.
5 What is the difference between an expected rate of return and a required rate of return on a capital budgeting project? Under what condition are these two rates of return the same?
6 How can financial managers use the SML to make accept-reject decisions for capital investments?
7 Why do projects plotting above (below) the SML have positive (negative) NPVs?
8 What are several limitations of using the CAPM to calculate a project's required rate of return?

9.4 Adjusting for Risk

After recognizing and measuring stand-alone risk, the financial manager must still adjust for risk before making a decision. Various methods are available to incorporate risk into the evaluation process. For example, managers could rely on their judgment after considering subjective risk factors not captured in their numerical analysis. They could also shorten (lengthen) the payback period requirement if they consider an investment more (less) risky than the firm's average-risk projects. Although these approaches are easy, they are incomplete methods of controlling risk exposure because they do not fully account for the time value of money and risk. Therefore, we examine two indirect methods of incorporating time and risk into project analysis. **Indirect methods** attempt to indirectly measure the risk of each investment proposal. These "indirect" methods for adjusting the NPV calculations are the:

1 risk-adjusted discount rate (RADR) method; and the
2 certainty equivalent (CE) method.

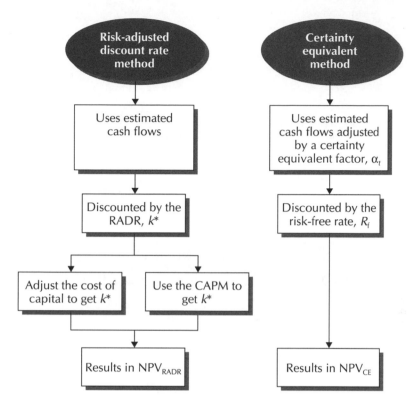

Figure 9.5 Comparison of the RADR and CE methods

The RADR method adjusts for project risk by changing the discount rate in the denominator of the NPV equation. This method is easier to use than the CE approach but has both theoretical and practical limitations. The CE method changes the cash flows in the numerator of the NPV equation and uses a risk-free discount rate. This approach is theoretically superior to the RADR method, but it is difficult to implement in practice. Although not intuitively obvious, the two methods provide the same NPV if the respective adjustments are carried out appropriately. Figure 9.5 illustrates the key elements of the RADR and CE methods of computing the NPV.

Practical Financial Tip 9.4

The suitability of the RADR and CE methods depends on a project's risk profile over time. The RADR method is suitable when the project's risk increases exponentially over time while the CE method is appropriate when a project's risk varies over time.

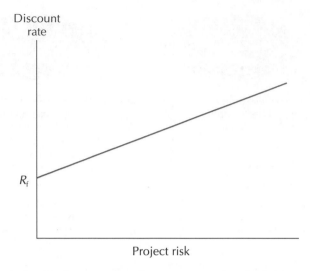

Figure 9.6 The relationship between the discount rate and project risk

Risk-adjusted Discount Rate Method

With the **risk-adjusted discount rate (RADR) method**, the financial manager discounts a project's expected future cash flows to the present using a discount rate appropriate for the degree of risk. The presumption underlying the RADR method is simple: the higher the risk of the project, the higher is the required rate of return (that is, a higher risk-adjusted discount rate), and the lower the project's risk-adjusted NPV. Figure 9.6 illustrates the relationship between the discount rate and project risk.

Using a risk-adjusted discount rate, k^*, is justified to compensate for the uncertainty of the timing and the amount of a project's cash flows. This rate also reflects the impact that risky projects can have on a firm's marginal cost of capital. The **cost of capital**, k, is the cost to firms of raising the long-term or "permanent" funds used to finance capital projects. Adopting high-risk projects will increase a firm's overall risk. In turn, suppliers of long-term funds to the firm will require higher returns, increasing the firm's cost of capital.

Calculating the risk-adjusted net present value
As Equation 9.7 shows, the RADR method adjusts the denominator of the NPV equation.

$$NPV_{RADR} = \sum_{t=1}^{n} \frac{CF_t}{(1 + k^*)^t} - I_0 \tag{9.7}$$

where CF_t is the expected net cash flow for period t; k^* is the risk-adjusted discount rate; n is the expected life of the project; and I_0 is the initial investment in period 0.

Steps in using the risk-adjusted discount method
Solving Equation 9.7 requires using steps similar to those used in computing the NPV.

1   Determine the appropriate risk-adjusted discount rate, k^*, applicable to the project being evaluated.
2   Discount the cash flows using k^* as the discount rate, and subtract the initial investment, I_0, to get the NPV_{RADR}.

Decision rules for NPV_{RADR}
The following decision rules apply to independent and mutually exclusive projects.

Decision Rules for the RADR Method

- For *independent projects,* accept the project if the NPV_{RADR} is zero or positive and reject the project if the NPV_{RADR} is negative.
- For *mutually exclusive projects,* accept the project with the highest positive NPV_{RADR}.

Accepting a project with a positive NPV_{RADR} compensates for project risk and increases the value of a firm; accepting a project with a negative NPV_{RADR} has the opposite effect. An investment with an NPV_{RADR} of zero compensates for project risk but leaves the firm's value unchanged.[13]

Determining the appropriate risk-adjusted discount rate
Using the RADR method is easy but determining the appropriate discount rate can be difficult. We discuss two ways to estimate risk-adjusted discount rates:

1   Adjust the firm's cost of capital, k, for risk.
2   Use the capital asset pricing model (CAPM).

Adjust k for risk. The cost of capital, k, is the appropriate discount rate for a firm's projects of average risk. If a project's risk characteristics differ substantially from average, the financial manager can adjust k to get a risk-adjusted discount rate, k^*. In theory, the discount rate consists of three parts:

- a risk-free rate, R_f, to account for the time value of money;
- an average risk premium, R_1, to compensate investors for a firm's business risk; and
- an additional risk factor, R_2, which can be negative, zero, or positive, to account for the difference in risk between the firm's existing business and the proposed project.

---

[13]   Risk-adjusted discount rates are also applicable in an IRR framework. The decision rule is to accept the project if the IRR is equal to or greater than the risk-adjusted discount rate, k^*; otherwise, reject it. Here, k^* acts as a **hurdle rate**, the minimum rate of return required for project acceptance. Therefore, the IRR must cross the hurdle to accept a project.

Thus, one way of stating the risk-adjusted discount rate is:

$$k^* = \overbrace{R_f + R_1}^{k} + \overbrace{R_2}^{\substack{\text{Project risk} \\ \text{adjustment}}} \tag{9.8}$$

If a proposed project has the same risk as that of the firm's existing projects, the required rate of return, k, would be $R_f + R_1$, and R_2 would be zero. If a project is more or less risky than average, the financial manager would add or subtract an additional risk factor, R_2, to k to get the risk-adjusted discount rate.

How does the financial manager make this risk adjustment? Unfortunately, no simple method exists for doing this. Using sensitivity analysis and scenario analysis can help managers form judgments about the appropriate risk adjustment. Since these methods do not lead directly to risk adjustments, managers must still use their experience and subjective judgment to determine an appropriate risk-adjusted discount rate.

Some companies group investment projects with similar risk characteristics into risk classes and then assign a discount rate to each risk class. One way to determine risk classes is by using historical data to calculate the coefficients of variation of NPVs of past projects. The financial manager then determines the range of CVs for most of a firm's projects. Suppose this range of CVs is between 0.50 and 1.00. Because projects in this range represent average-risk or normal-risk projects, the financial manager would assign the firm's cost of capital, k, as the discount rate. The financial manager would add or subtract a specific number of percentage points to the cost of capital for projects whose CVs lie outside that range to adjust for differential project risk. For example, if the cost of capital for an average-risk project is 10 percent, the financial manager could add or subtract say 3 percentage points to the cost of capital for high-risk and low-risk projects, respectively. Determining the appropriate number of percentage points to add or subtract depends largely on judgment.

Another approach is to classify projects by type (for example, replacement or expansion) and to assign a risk-adjusted discount rate for each project type. Table 9.5 lists three

Table 9.5 Hypothetical risk adjustments for project risk classes

Risk class	Project descriptions	Risk-adjusted discount rate, k^*
1	*Replacement projects*: maintenance and cost reduction. Risk is similar to the firm's current level of risk for existing projects.	k
2	*Expansion projects*: existing or related products and markets. Risk is somewhat above the firm's current level of risk for existing projects.	$k + 3\%$ to 5% risk premium
3	*Expansion projects*: new lines of business, products, and markets. Risk clearly exceeds the firm's current level of risk for existing projects.	$k + 6\%$ to 10% risk premium

hypothetical project risk classes. For typical replacement projects, the financial manager uses the firm's cost of capital, k, because such projects have average risk. Expansion projects in existing product lines call for a small risk premium because their cash flows are usually easier to predict with accuracy. Management assigns the highest risk premium to new product lines because it lacks any prior experience in predicting their cash flows.

Use the capital asset pricing model. The CAPM is another method of estimating the risk-adjusted discount rate. As we discussed in Section 9.3, using the CAPM requires estimating R_f, R_m, and β_i, and substituting these inputs into the CAPM equation to estimate the risk-adjusted discount rate. As shown in Example 9.4, Project B is an average-risk project and requires the same return as Global's cost of capital, k. Therefore, Project B requires no further risk adjustment. Project A is more risky than average. Using project betas, the $(R_f - R_m)\beta_i$ part of the CAPM Equation 9.5 represents the R_1 and R_2 of Equation 9.8. Example 9.7 shows how to use risk-adjusted discount rates to calculate a project's NPV.

Example 9.7 Using the RADR Method: Global Enterprises

In Chapter 8, we applied the NPV approach to Projects A and B for Global Enterprises assuming these projects are equally as risky as the firm's existing projects. Using k (10 percent) as the discount rate, Project A is acceptable because its NPV is $38,877. Project B is unacceptable because it has an NPV of –$2,643. No further risk adjustment is necessary because Project B is an average-risk project and properly uses 10 percent as the discount rate.

Now suppose that the financial manager uses the CAPM to determine the risk-adjusted discount rate for Project A. As Section 9.3 shows, the appropriate discount rate is 15 percent for Project A. Using a 15 percent discount rate for Project A results in the following risk-adjusted NPV:

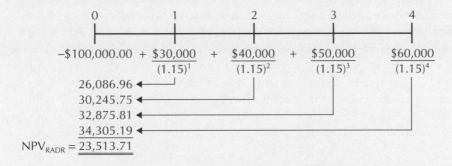

In this case, the same accept-reject decision applies when using either k (10 percent) or k^* (15 percent) as the discount rate. Using the higher risk-adjusted discount rate decreases Project A's NPV from $38,877 to $23,514. Project A is still acceptable but less attractive because it adds less value to the firm.

Using the risk adjustments shown in Table 9.5, the results would be similar to using the CAPM. Because Project B is a replacement project, the financial manager would still use the cost of capital, k, as the discount rate and get an NPV of –$2,643. Because Project A is an expansion project for a new product, the financial manager would add a 6 to 10 percentage point risk-adjustment factor to the firm's 10 percent cost of capital. This would result in a NPV$_{RADR}$ of $20,759 and $10,648 using 16 percent and 20 percent risk-adjusted discount rates, respectively.

Strengths and weaknesses
The RADR method has both strengths and weaknesses.

There are two key strengths to using the RADR method.

- *Using the RADR method is intuitively appealing because it reflects project risk by adjusting the discount rate.* Managers understand the logic of requiring a higher discount rate for more risky projects and a lower rate for less risky projects.
- *The RADR results in information that leads directly to an accept-reject decision.*

Applying the RADR approach raises several long-debated theoretical and practical issues.

- *No consensus exists on how to find an appropriate risk-adjusted discount rate.* These risk adjustments may appear arbitrary because they reflect judgments and personal values of the analyst or manager making the estimate. Different firms may establish different risk adjustments for the same type of project.
- *The RADR method uses the same discount risk premium over the entire life of the project.* This approach leads to compounding of the same risk premium over time.
- *The RADR method combines the risk-free rate and a risk premium into a single discount rate.* This approach implicitly assumes that risk increases exponentially over time because it does not make separate adjustments for time and risk. This assumption is often unjustified because risk is not necessarily an increasing function of time. For example, the uncertainty of the cash flows may remain constant or decrease over time. Using a single discount rate for all periods may result in underestimating the NPV. Some contend that a more appropriate approach is to treat the time value of money and risk separately when evaluating capital investments. Discounting future cash flows should include only time value considerations, not risk considerations. Thus, the ability to distinguish among the components constituting the risk-adjusted discount rate may be important.

Certainty Equivalent Method

An alternative approach to incorporating risk into project analysis is the **certainty equivalent (CE) method**. Rather than adjusting the discount rate to reflect risk, the CE approach adjusts the expected cash flows to account for risk and then uses the risk-free rate, R_f, as the discount rate to find the NPV. Thus, the CE method makes separate adjustments for time (by using R_f as the discount rate) and risk (by converting risky cash flows into certain cash flows). By avoiding the assumption that risk increases over time, the financial manager or analyst can apply the CE method to various business settings.

The difficult part of this approach is to convert risky future cash flows to certainty equivalent cash flows. A **certainty equivalent cash flow** is a smaller cash flow that the decision maker would accept with certainty in exchange for a risky cash flow. Although the financial manager can use the CAPM to develop the CE valuation formula, a problem with using the CAPM-derived CE is that all the limitations of the CAPM and its basic inputs transfer to the CE. Because of the many problems associated with identifying certainty equivalent cash flows, financial managers do not use the CE method very often in making capital budgeting decisions.[14] To illustrate the concept of certainty equivalent cash flows, consider the following example.

Example 9.8 Concept of Certainty Equivalent Cash Flows

Assume your rich, eccentric uncle tells you that he will flip a coin and pay you $100,000 if the coin comes up heads, but nothing if it comes up tails. The expected value of this gamble is $50,000 because the implied probability distribution is a 50 percent chance of receiving $100,000 and a 50 percent chance of receiving nothing. Instead of tossing the coin, you can elect to receive $100 with no risk. You would probably have no trouble deciding to take your chances with the coin flip. However, if your uncle offered you a choice between a certain $40,000 or the coin toss with its expected value of $50,000, you would probably elect to take the certain $40,000. Somewhere between $100 and $40,000 is an amount that would make deciding what amount to take very difficult. That is, there is an amount known with certainty that is equivalent to the expected value of the coin toss. If that amount were $20,000, then you would consider $20,000 as the certainty equivalent of the $50,000 expected value of the coin toss. Each person may have a different certainty equivalent amount. This value is the one the firm must decide upon as the certainty equivalent of each future expected cash flow from a capital investment.

Calculating the certainty equivalent net present value
The CE method adjusts the cash flows in the numerator of the NPV equation. Equation 9.9 gives the formula for the certainty-equivalent NPV, assuming that the initial investment occurs in period 0.

$$NPV_{CE} = \sum_{t=1}^{n} \frac{\alpha_t CF_t}{(1 + R_f)^t} - \alpha_0 \qquad (9.9)$$

---

[14] For a discussion of how to develop certainty equivalents, see Tarun K. Mukherjee, Magali Van Belle, and H. Kent Baker, "Using Certainty Equivalents to Evaluate Project Risk," *Corporate Finance Review*, January/ February 2003, 20–24.

where CF_t is the expected net cash flow in period t; α_t is the certainty equivalent factor associated with the risky net cash flows in period t; α_0 is the certainty equivalent factor associated with the initial investment, I, in period 0; and R_f is the risk-free rate of return assumed to remain constant over the project's life.

Multiplying the cash flows by a certainty equivalent factor produces a certainty equivalent cash flow for a specific year. A **certainty equivalent factor** is the ratio of a certain return to a risky return. This factor reflects the financial manager's perceptions of the degree of risk associated with the estimated cash flow. It also reflects the decision maker's degree of aversion to perceived risk. For cash inflows, certainty equivalent factors, α_t, range from 0 to 1. If the cash flows are known with certainty, the factor is 1. As the risk of the expected cash inflows increases, the factor decreases. That is, smaller certainty equivalent factors indicate that management views the cash flow as having more risk.

The opposite relationship exists for risky cash outflows involving the initial outlay, I_0, where the certainty equivalent factor, α_0, exceeds 1. Suppose α_0 is 1.1 for a risky cash outflow expected to be $100,000. The certainty equivalent cash flow is $110,000 (1.1 × $100,000). That is, the decision maker would be indifferent between a certain investment of $110,000 and a risky investment of $100,000. In summary, both increasing risky cash outflows and decreasing risky cash inflows use certainty equivalent factors that reduce a project's NPV.

As Equation 9.9 shows, the CE method accounts for the risk of the cash flows and, therefore, uses the risk-free rate, R_f, to discount the certainty equivalent cash flows. The risk-free rate simply accounts for the time value of money, not the risk of the project's expected cash flows. Using a discount rate containing a risk premium would result in a double counting of risk.

Steps in using the certainty equivalent method
The following steps are necessary to evaluate independent projects using the CE method.

1 Find the certainty equivalent factors for the expected cash flows, CF_t and I_0, and adjust the cash flows accordingly.
2 Find the present value of the certainty equivalent cash flows using the risk-free discount rate, R_f, and subtract the certainty equivalent initial investment.

Other than adjusting the cash flows for risk and using the risk-free rate as the discount rate, the steps involved in the CE method are the same as those in the NPV method. In practice, a firm could accept a project using the NPV method but reject it using the CE method, and vice versa. In theory, this result should not occur if the financial manager makes the appropriate adjustments to each model.

Decision rules for CE$_{NPV}$
The decision rules for the certainty-equivalent NPV method are the same as for the NPV method.[15]

---

[15] Calculating a project's certainty-equivalent IRR is also possible. The decision rule is to accept projects if the certainty-equivalent IRR is greater than the risk-free rate, R_f; otherwise, reject them.

> *Decision Rules for the CE Method*
>
> - For *independent projects*, accept the project if the NPV_{CE} is zero or positive and reject the project if the NPV_{CE} is negative.
> - For *mutually exclusive projects*, accept the project with the highest positive NPV_{CE}.

Determining certainty equivalent cash flows

Determining certainty equivalent cash flows requires considering how the risk of receiving a project's expected cash flows changes over time. With many capital budgeting projects, risk depends on the timing of the cash flows. Greater risk is often associated with expected cash flows that are farther out in the future because in these situations, certainty equivalent factors would decline as the expected cash flows become more risky over time.

Example 9.9 Using the Certainty Equivalent Method: Global Enterprises

Let's return to Project A, an expansion project for Global Enterprises. For Project A, the financial manager assigns certainty equivalent factors ranging from 0.90 for year 1 to 0.75 for year 4. These factors decline over time and reflect the manager's perception of increasing uncertainty in the cash flows. For example, the manager is willing to accept $45,000 as a certain return for the $60,000 risky return in year 4. Therefore, the certainty equivalent coefficient, α_4, is 0.75 ($45,000/$60,000). Because Project A is a new product, the manager is also unsure about the amount of the initial investment and assigns a certainty equivalent factor for Year 0 of 1.05. If the risk-free rate is 5 percent, should Global accept Project A?

Project A: Expansion Project

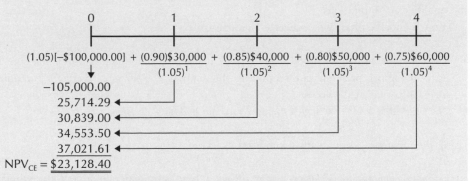

$$
\begin{array}{c}
(1.05)[-\$100,000.00] + \dfrac{(0.90)\$30,000}{(1.05)^1} + \dfrac{(0.85)\$40,000}{(1.05)^2} + \dfrac{(0.80)\$50,000}{(1.05)^3} + \dfrac{(0.75)\$60,000}{(1.05)^4}
\end{array}
$$

−105,000.00
25,714.29
30,839.00
34,553.50
37,021.61
$NPV_{CE} = \$23,128.40$

Global Enterprises should accept Project A because its NPV_{CE} of $23,128 is positive. This NPV_{CE} is similar to the NPV_{RADR} of $23,514. These methods do not necessarily produce such similar results because of the subjectivity involved in estimating the risk-adjusted discount rates and certainty equivalent cash flows.

For Project B, a replacement project, the financial manager can more accurately forecast the cash flows than for a new project. The manager assigns certainty equivalent factors ranging from 0.95 for year 1 to 0.85 for year 4. The cost of replacing the old machines is known with certainty. If the risk-free rate is 5 percent, should Global undertake Project B?

Project B: Replacement Project

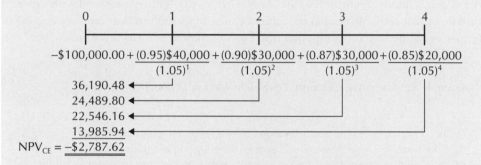

$$-\$100,000.00 + \frac{(0.95)\$40,000}{(1.05)^1} + \frac{(0.90)\$30,000}{(1.05)^2} + \frac{(0.87)\$30,000}{(1.05)^3} + \frac{(0.85)\$20,000}{(1.05)^4}$$

36,190.48
24,489.80
22,546.16
13,985.94

$\text{NPV}_{CE} = -\$2,787.62$

Because Project B's NPV_{CE} is –$2,788, management at Global Enterprises should reject the project. In comparison, the NPV_{RADR} for Project B is –$2,643.

Strengths and weaknesses
Similar to other risk analysis techniques, the certainty equivalent method has both redeeming qualities and limitations.

The CE approach has two attractive characteristics.

- *The CE approach is theoretically sound because it separates time value of money and risk.* By introducing risk preferences directly into the analysis, the financial manager can adjust for each period's cash flows.
- *The CE method leads to a single estimated value for making a decision.*

Using the CE approach involves several drawbacks.

- *Estimating appropriate CE factors can be difficult.* There is no generally accepted method of doing this estimation. Therefore, the CE factors selected, which may differ among managers, may affect the accept-reject decision.
- *The CE method is less intuitively appealing and more difficult to carry out in practice than the RADR method.*

Concept Check 9.4

1 Why is using a risk-adjusted discount rate, k^*, superior to using the firm's cost of capital, k, in calculating the NPV of a risky project?
2 How do firms develop and use project risk classes?
3 What are two ways of estimating risk-adjusted discount rates? Explain.
4 Does using a RADR method always result in a lower NPV than using the firm's cost of capital? Why or why not?
5 What is the major difference between the RADR method and CE method of incorporating risk into project evaluation? Explain.

9.5 Risk Analysis in Multinational Corporations

Many complexities confront multinational corporations (MNCs) when evaluating foreign projects. Risk analysis is far more complex for international capital investments than for domestic ones because of additional political and economic risks. The alternative methods of assessing and adjusting for risk are similar to those used by domestic firms. For example, approaches for incorporating political risk in an investment analysis often involve either adjusting the cash flows of the project or its required rate of return to reflect the impact of a particular political event. Some approaches differ from those already discussed, such as attempting to adjust for foreign project risk by borrowing locally. Instead of elaborating on these methods, we briefly discuss two additional risks faced by MNCs.

1 Political risk.
2 Exchange rate risk.

Political Risk

Political risk refers to various political events or occurrences initiated by host governments that might be unfavorable to a capital investment. Political risk takes many forms including changes in tax policy, temporary controls on repatriation of earnings of foreign firms, expropriation (the seizure of foreign assets by a host country), and political instability. Such risks often stem from conflicts between the interests of MNCs and those of the host countries.

There are three major phases of managing political risk.

• The first phase is planning before direct foreign investment. Pre-investment planning can involve avoiding investments in politically unstable countries, negotiating specific arrangements with the host government, and insuring the political risk. For example, political risk insurance is available for both US and non-US MNCs in many countries. The US government provides investment insurance through the Overseas Private Investment Corporation (OPIC).

- The second phase of managing political risk is during the life cycle of the foreign project. Political risk management strategies in this phase include maintaining a flexible relationship with the host country; developing local stakeholders; and engaging in production, market, and financial strategies that discourage expropriation by the host country. For example, the MNC can reduce political risk by controlling raw materials, patents, or transportation or by using local capital.
- The final phase of managing political risk follows expropriation or nationalization. Post-expropriation policies include negotiating with the host country, applying power, and resorting to legal remedies.

Exchange Rate Risk

Another risk of foreign investments is **exchange rate risk**, which refers to the variation in return related to changes in the relative value of the domestic and foreign currency. This risk increases the uncertainty about the number of dollars the company will eventually receive. The **exchange rate** between two currencies is the number of units of one currency required in exchange for a unit of another currency.

There are two major types of foreign exchange exposure encountered by any MNC.[16] **Translation exposure** is the risk that reported income will fluctuate because of fluctuating exchange rates. Such accounting exposure arises from the need to convert the financial statements of foreign operations from the local currencies involved to the home currency of the parent to form consolidated financial statements. Firms attempt to manage translation exposure primarily through hedging strategies. **Hedging** refers to various activities used to offset the risk of loss from a change in foreign exchange rates. For example, firms may use a forward or futures contract in foreign exchange, but completely hedging a foreign investment is extremely difficult. The discussion of hedging strategies is beyond the scope of this book.

The second type of foreign exchange exposure is **economic exposure**, the risk that changes in exchange rates will affect the firm's value. Thus, economic exposure represents any impact of exchange rate fluctuations on a firm's future cash flows. Before an MNC can manage its economic exposure, the MNC must first assess what this type of exposure is. Usually, this involves determining exposure to each currency in terms of its cash inflows and cash outflows. Once the MNC accomplishes this task, the firm may restructure its operations to reduce its economic exposure.

What does this restructuring involve? Usually, the restructuring involves shifting the sources of costs or revenues to other locations to match cash inflows and outflows in foreign currencies. How a firm restructures its operations to reduce economic exposure to exchange rate risk depends on the form of exposure. For example, assume that the firm relies on

---

[16] For further discussion of managing translation exposure and economic exposure, see Jeff Madura, *International Financial Management*, 7th edn, South-Western, 2003.

foreign suppliers. When a foreign currency has a greater impact on cash inflows, the MNC could increase foreign supply orders. If, on the other hand, a foreign currency has a greater impact on cash outflows, the MNC could reduce foreign supply orders. Another example involves an MNC having a portion of its debt structure in foreign debt. When a foreign currency has a greater impact on cash inflows, the MNC could restructure debt to increase debt payments in foreign currency. By contrast, when a foreign currency has a greater impact on cash outflows, the recommended action is for the MNC to restructure debt to reduce debt payments in foreign currency. Firms can protect operating cash flows from the negative impact of exchange rate fluctuations by effecting changes in its pricing strategies in various markets and by adapting production strategies to the new situation.

Concept Check 9.5

1 Why is risk analysis for international capital investments more complex than for domestic capital investments?
2 What is the meaning of political risk and exchange rate risk?
3 What are two types of foreign exchange exposure? Explain.

9.6 Risk Analysis in Theory and Practice

Few managers disagree with the idea that they should consider risk when evaluating capital investments. Believing in this idea and carrying it out are two different things. A major disagreement revolves around how financial managers should assess risk and incorporate it into project analysis.

Risk Analysis in Theory

A critical question facing the financial manager is: Which type of risk is most appropriate when evaluating a capital budgeting project – single-project risk, company risk, or market risk? The answer to this question is: "It depends." Strong arguments exist for using each type of risk under different situations. Current finance theory suggests that the required rate of return should be adjusted only for risks that cannot be readily diversified away by the shareholders. If the firm's shareholders have well-diversified portfolios, justification exists for using market risk. The portfolios of many shareholders, however, may not meet the criterion of full diversification. Market risk, as reflected in the project's beta, is not specific to the firm. Although managers can use a project's beta with the CAPM to find the required rate of return, estimating a project's beta can be very difficult. In practice, managers who consider risk differences most often do so on a project-by-project basis, rather than on a group basis. That is, they tend to focus on measuring single-project risk.

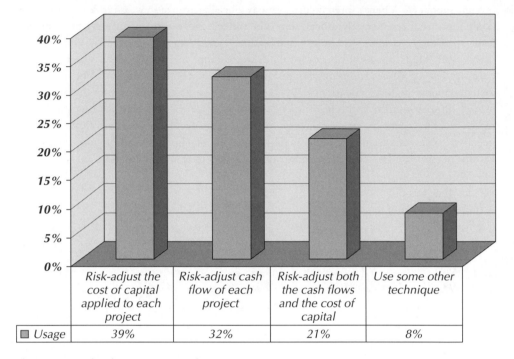

	Risk-adjust the cost of capital applied to each project	Risk-adjust cash flow of each project	Risk-adjust both the cash flows and the cost of capital	Use some other technique
■ Usage	39%	32%	21%	8%

Figure 9.7 Risk-adjustment procedures
Source: Adapted from Lawrence J. Gitman and Pieter A. Vandenberg, "Cost of Capital Techniques Used by Major US Firms: 1997 vs. 1980," *Financial Practice and Education*, Fall/Winter 2000, p. 61.

Risk Analysis in Practice

Much research exists on how managers deal with risk in evaluating capital investments.[17] These studies have examined three major aspects of risk: risk recognition, risk assessment, and risk adjustment. The results suggest that most firms recognize risk, either formally or informally, but risk assessment is often subjective. While sensitivity analysis is the most popular way that managers assess risk on individual projects, personal experience also plays an important role in risk assessment. Key risk assessment factors include the dollar size of the project, the relationship between the project's returns and the returns on the firm's other projects, and the project's payback period. In the risk-adjustment category, the most popular method is the risk-adjusted discount rate method. Figure 9.7 shows the results from

---

[17] For recent surveys about risk analysis in capital budgeting, see Lawrence J. Gitman and Pieter A. Vandenberg, "Cost of Capital Techniques Used by Major US Firms: 1997 vs. 1980," *Financial Practice and Education*, Fall/Winter 2000, 53–68; and Janet D. Payne, Will Carrington Heath, and Lewis R. Gale, "Comparative Financial Practice in the US and Canada: Capital Budgeting and Risk Assessment Techniques," *Financial Practice and Education*, Spring/Summer 1999, 16–24.

a survey sent in 1997 to the chief financial officer of each firm listed in the *Fortune* 1000. The evidence shows that more large firms use discount rate adjustments than cash flow adjustments to account for differing project risk.

Research evidence suggests that adopting sophisticated risk analysis techniques by business firms has lagged behind the theoretical literature. Yet, practitioners are clearly changing their methodology and the theory–practice gap is narrowing. Over time, more firms have moved from informal to formal methods, but intuition and subjective judgment still play a role in dealing with risk. Many firms rely on several methods when evaluating the risk of capital budgeting projects.

There are several major explanations for the increased use of risk analysis in capital budgeting. First, such techniques are becoming more widely known and understood. Evidence suggests that formal education is the primary source of learning about capital budgeting. Second, economic uncertainties have made managers more aware of the need to consider risk.

In practice, no single method of assessing or adjusting for risk in capital budgeting is clearly superior to the others in all situations. All the approaches for dealing with risk have advantages and disadvantages. This may explain why many firms use one or more techniques of risk analysis.

Practical Financial Tip 9.5

Risk is a complex and multifaceted problem. Evaluating risky projects is not a purely mechanical procedure. Much room for disagreement exists about the appropriate methods of risk assessment, measurement, and adjustment. We have not reached the point where any one measure adequately measures risk in every situation. Ultimately, these techniques are simply tools used by decision makers to make informed judgments about the risk-return tradeoffs of proposed projects.

Concept Check 9.6

1 In theory, which type of risk – single-project risk, company risk, or market risk – is most important? Why?
2 Which formal method of risk assessment do firms most commonly use in practice?
3 Which formal method of risk adjustment do firms use most widely in practice?
4 What are two reasons for the increased use of risk analysis in capital budgeting? Explain.

Summary

In this chapter, we looked at various types of risk, methods of assessing risk, and evaluation methods of incorporating risk into capital budgeting decisions. We discussed some of the problems that can occur when using these methods in practice. The main idea to carry away from reading this chapter is that different methods of assessing and adjusting for risk may lead to different estimated NPVs. Here are the key points in this chapter.

1   A major complication in analyzing capital budgeting projects is that the actual cash flows may differ from expectations. Failure to recognize risk can result in poor project selection and financial distress to the firm. Firms adopting projects with high levels of risk should be rewarded with high levels of return.
2   A financial manager can view the riskiness of an investment project from three perspectives: a single-project perspective, a company perspective, and a diversified-shareholder perspective. Each perspective involves a different type of risk.
3   Managers usually evaluate small to mid-sized capital investments on a project-by-project basis rather than from any diversified portfolio perspective. When managers are considering large capital investments, they are often interested in how projects contribute to the risk of the company and shareholders, not simply the stand-alone risk of the project.
4   Sensitivity analysis and scenario analysis are two common methods for assessing the risk present in a proposed capital project. These methods do not provide a clear accept-reject decision rule.
   • Sensitivity analysis measures the impact of changes in the values of an input variable on a project's NPV.
   • Scenario analysis examines what happens to NPV estimates under several different sets of assumptions, usually optimistic, most likely, and pessimistic scenarios.
5   Financial managers may use the information provided by sensitivity analysis and scenario analysis, along with other information, to construct probability distributions regarding possible outcomes. If managers can estimate probability distributions, they can quantify such risk measures as the standard deviation and coefficient of variation.
6   Using even more information, financial managers can examine risk from a portfolio perspective. Contribution to portfolio risk depends on the way investments respond to different factors affecting returns. Measures used to analyze risk from a portfolio perspective include the correlation coefficient and beta.
   • The correlation coefficient is not a risk measure, but it is useful in helping to assess company risk. That is, the manager can reduce risk through diversification by accepting projects whose returns are not perfectly positively correlated with other investment projects.
   • A project's beta is important from the diversified-shareholder perspective because shareholders can diversify away unsystematic risk. Therefore, they should be concerned only with market or systematic risk, which shareholders cannot

diversify away. In practice, many shareholders lack fully diversified portfolios and are more concerned about single-project or company risk.

7   After assessing and measuring risk, the financial manager must still determine if the expected return on a project is high enough to compensate for the risk. Otherwise, the investments will decrease the wealth of the shareholders.

8   Both the risk-adjusted discount rate method and the certainty equivalent method provide decision makers with tools for making accept-reject decisions. In practice, managers overwhelmingly prefer using the RADR method to the CE approach.

   • The RADR method requires using a discount rate commensurate with project risk. Managers usually determine a project's risk-adjusted discount rate by subjectively assigning a risk premium or by using the CAPM.
   • The CE approach adjusts the cash flows for risk and uses the risk-free rate as the discount rate.

9   In deciding upon which methods to use in evaluating risky investments, the financial manager should weigh the additional costs of using the technique against its perceived benefits. Some small projects do not warrant extensive risk analysis. Large-scale projects require more attention because they may result in large losses.

FURTHER READING

Ang, James S. and Wilbur G. Lewellen. "Risk Adjustment in Capital Investment Project Evaluations," *Financial Management* 1, Summer 1982, 5–14.

Arnott, Robert D. and Peter L. Bernstein. "What Risk Premium Is 'Normal'?" *Financial Analysts Journal* 58, March/April 2002, 64–85.

Butler, J. S. and Barry Schachter. "The Investment Decision: Estimation Risk and Risk Adjusted Discount Rates," *Financial Management* 18, Winter 1989, 13–22.

Eschbenback, Ted G. and Lisa S. McKeague. "Exposition on Using Graphs for Sensitivity Analysis," *Engineering Economist* 34, Summer 1989, 315–33.

Forham, David R. and S. Brooks Marshall. "Tools for Dealing with Uncertainty," *Management Accounting* 79, September 1997, 38–43.

Graham, John R., Michael L. Lemmon, and Jack G. Wolf. "Does Corporate Diversification Destroy Value?" *Journal of Finance* 57, April 2002, 695–720.

Hyland, David C. and J. David Diltz. "Why Firms Diversify: An Empirical Examination," *Financial Management* 31, Spring 2002, 51–81.

Jagannathan, Ravi and Iwan Meier. "Do We Need CAPM for Capital Budgeting?" *Financial Management* 31, Winter 2002, 55–77.

Kothari, S. P. and Jay Shanken, "In Defense of Beta," *Journal of Applied Corporate Finance* 8, Spring 1995, 53–58.

Miller, Edward. "The Cutoff Benefit-Cost Ratio Should Exceed One," *Engineering Economist* 46, Winger 2001, 312 19.

Quederni, Bechir N. and William G. Sullivan. "A Semi-Variance Model for Incorporating Risk into Capital Investment Analysis," *Engineering Economist* 35, Winter 1991, 83–106.

Roll, Richard and Stephen A. Ross. "On the Cross-sectional Relation between Expected Returns and Betas," *Journal of Finance* 47, March 1994, 101–21.

Schnabel, Jacques A. "Uncertainty and the Abandonment Option," *Engineering Economist* 37, Winter 1992, 172–77.

Sick, Gordan A. "A Certainty-Equivalent Approach to Capital Budgeting," *Financial Management* 15, Winter 1986, 23–32.

Yoon, Kwangsun Paul. "Capital Investment Analysis Involving Estimate Error," *Engineering Economist* 35, Fall 1990, 21–30.

PART IV

Long-term Financing Decisions

Chapter 10

Raising Funds and Cost of Capital

Finally our research is a reminder of the old saying that too often in business we measure with a micrometer, mark with a pencil, and cut with an ax. Despite the many advances in finance theory, the particular "ax" available for estimating company capital costs remains a blunt one. Best-practice companies can expect to estimate their weighted average cost of capital with an accuracy of no more than plus or minus 100 to 150 basis points. This has important implications for how managers use the cost of capital in decision making. (Robert F. Bruner, Kenneth M. Eades, Robert S. Harris, and Robert C. Higgins, "Best Practices in Estimating the Cost of Capital: Survey and Synthesis," *Financial Practice and Education* 8, Spring/Summer 1998, p. 27.)

Overview

Business firms must raise capital for many purposes. For example, a company may need cash to invest in capital projects and corporate acquisitions. Although firms usually generate most of their total capital internally by retaining earnings, they often rely on external sources. Senior corporate managers need to know the choices available to them when raising capital in order to use the system to their advantage. They also need to know how to determine the cost of capital if they are to make sound investment and financing decisions.

In this chapter, we discuss how business firms raise external capital, and how investors trade securities. We examine the roles of financial markets and financial intermediaries in facilitating transfer of funds between the suppliers and demanders of capital. We review different methods by which a firm can sell a new issue of securities. We also look at the markets for trading equity securities after the original sale. In raising funds, firms incur an explicit or implicit cost. We examine how to determine the cost of three capital components: debt, preferred stock, and common equity. We also discuss how to calculate the weighted average cost of capital and the appropriate weights to use in this process. Finally, we consider how to calculate the marginal cost of capital and to determine the firm's optimal capital budget.

Learning Objectives

After completing this chapter, you should be able to:

- describe the role of financial markets;
- distinguish between money and capital markets and primary and secondary markets;
- explain the services provided by investment bankers;

- discuss the advantages and disadvantages of going public;
- compare the different methods by which a firm can sell new securities;
- explain the major factors affecting the cost of issuing securities;
- explain the theoretical underpinning of analyzing the cost of capital;
- measure the component costs of debt, preferred stock, and common equity;
- determine the appropriate weights when calculating the weighted average cost of capital;
- develop an optimal capital budget.

10.1 Financial Markets

Firms wanting to raise funds or to invest surplus funds must enter the financial markets. A **financial market** is a mechanism for bringing together buyers and sellers of financial assets. A **financial asset** is a monetary claim on an issuer in the form of a paper asset such as stocks or bonds. In financial transactions, one party exchanges one paper asset (money) for another (securities or loans). For example, debt and equity securities are financial assets from the perspective of investors, but are claims on assets from the perspective of the issuing firm. Financial markets differ in several ways depending on the types of securities traded, trading practices, and buyers and sellers. These financial markets exist both inside and outside of the United States. US corporations can raise capital in both domestic and foreign financial markets.

Figure 10.1 illustrates the interaction of cash flows between a business firm and the financial markets. This interaction involves the following five major steps. The firm:

1 Raises debt and equity through the financial markets.
2 Invests these funds in various assets.
3 Generates cash flows from its investments in these assets.
4 Pays taxes to the government, dividends to shareholders, and debt payments to creditors.
5 Reinvests the remaining cash flows in its operations.

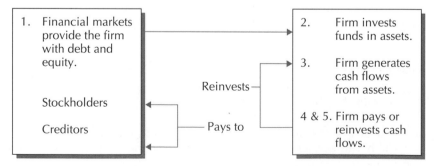

Figure 10.1 Cash flows between a firm and the financial markets

The Role of Financial Markets

Financial markets serve three important functions in a healthy economy.

1   *Help channel funds from suppliers to demanders.* Firms turn to financial markets to raise funds to support their growth. For example, corporations issue securities to raise money to buy plant and equipment. Without financial markets, firms would have to rely on internally generated funds to meet their financial needs. Yet, the financing needs of most firms exceed their ability to generate these funds internally. By turning to financial markets, these firms can raise the required funds. Besides providing mechanisms for firms to raise funds, financial markets provide suppliers of capital with an opportunity to identify and invest in suitable investments. Therefore, financial markets serve to meet the needs of both the suppliers and demanders of capital by helping the transfer of funds between them.
2   *Provide a resale market.* Well-functioning financial markets enable investors holding financial assets to sell or exchange these assets whenever they want. That is, financial markets provide **liquidity** or the ability to convert an asset easily and quickly into cash at a fair market value. Investors are more willing to buy securities that they can easily resell when needed. The absence of a resale market reduces the investors' flexibility and increases their risk of holding financial assets. The higher risk would result in a higher required rate of return for investors and, therefore, a higher cost of capital for firms.
3   *Set market prices and rates of return.* The presence of financial markets provides a mechanism for setting market prices and rates of return through the interaction of suppliers and demanders of funds. Setting market prices is useful for two major reasons. First, the market price reflects the market's assessment of the value of a financial asset. Investors use this information to decide whether they want to buy or sell a security. Second, market prices typically serve as a measure of corporate performance. That is, stock prices reflect the market's view of the expected performance of a firm. Holding other factors constant, stocks of well-managed companies should perform better in the market than less well-managed firms.

Types of Financial Markets

Because financial markets are highly diverse and complex, there are several ways to classify them. One way to categorize financial markets is by the maturity dates of assets, which classifies markets into money and capital markets. Another way to classify financial markets depends on whether the securities are new or already exist. In this chapter, we mainly focus on capital markets because our concern involves long-term financing by corporations. We begin, however, by briefly discussing money markets.

Money markets
A **money market** is a financial market for issuing and trading short-term debt securities. Money markets are decentralized markets, consisting of securities dealers who are linked by an electronic communications network. Leading money market centers include New York, London, and Tokyo.

Some corporations raise funds in money markets by issuing **commercial paper**, which is a short-term unsecured promissory note or IOU issued by financially secure firms. Corporations also temporarily invest their surplus funds in various money market instruments, including US Treasury bills (T-bills), negotiable certificates of deposit (CDs), and Eurodollar market time deposits. Besides corporations, other major participants in money markets are governments and financial institutions such as brokerage firms and insurance companies.

Capital markets

A **capital market** is a financial market for long-term securities. Corporations may raise funds in capital markets by selling bonds, preferred stock, and common stock. Other capital market instruments include US Treasury notes and bonds, mortgages, state and local bonds, term loans, and leases.

Primary markets

The **primary market**, also called the **new issue market**, is a financial market for the original sale of new securities. This market is not a physical trading exchange or location, but represents a telecommunications network for selling new securities. The issuing corporation receives the proceeds from the sale of the new securities, less any related costs of the issue. The buyers, who are mainly individual and institutional investors, receive shares of a new securities issue.

In primary markets, buyers and issuers of securities may or may not negotiate directly with one another. **Direct negotiation** occurs when a corporation arranges a term loan with a bank, leases an asset, or places debt privately. In an **indirect negotiation**, issuers usually rely upon another party in selling securities to buyers. An example of an indirect negotiation includes the public sale of bonds, preferred or common stock, in which investment bankers and brokers act as intermediaries in bringing together the sellers and the buyers.

Secondary markets

The **secondary market**, also called the **aftermarket**, is a market for trading existing securities among investors, either directly or through an intermediary. Secondary markets exist for bonds, stocks, options, futures contracts, and other financial assets. Firms do not use secondary markets to raise external funds because these markets are resale markets. Corporations may enter the secondary market to repurchase their securities or buy securities in other companies. Once a firm has issued its securities, investors may trade them in the secondary markets. The most important secondary markets in the United States are the securities exchanges such as the New York Stock Exchange (NYSE), American Stock Exchange (AMEX), and the NASDAQ Stock Market.

Concept Check 10.1

1 What are the three primary roles of financial markets? Explain.
2 What is the major difference between capital markets and money markets? Give two examples of securities in each market.
3 When would a corporation use the primary market and the secondary market?
4 How do primary markets differ from secondary markets?

10.2 Investment Banks

A corporation can issue its securities directly to the public, but such offers called **direct sales**, occur infrequently. Transferring capital between suppliers (investors) and demanders (business firms) usually takes place indirectly, through financial intermediaries such as investment banks and other financial institutions.

When issuing securities to the public, a firm usually hires an investment-banking house to do specific services. An **investment bank** is a firm that acts as an intermediary between sellers needing additional funds and buyers with surplus funds to invest. Investment bankers can perform the functions associated with issuing securities more efficiently than issuing firms can. Unlike other banks, investment banks neither take deposits nor make loans. Investment banks in the United States can also enter international financial markets by helping US firms sell new securities abroad and by helping foreign firms sell securities in the US. Investment bankers provide three major services in handling a new security issue – advising, underwriting, and marketing.

Advising

Investment bankers provide their financial and legal expertise to corporations wanting to sell new issues of stocks and bonds. They advise corporations on all specifics of a security offering. This advice may include suggestions on the type of securities to sell and its size, timing, and pricing characteristics. The investment banker also helps design new security issues with features that appeal to investors. For example, if a corporation wants to sell bonds, the investment banker helps the firm decide the bond's maturity date, coupon interest rate, collateral, payment dates, and so on. For stocks, this task involves helping a firm decide the offering size, pricing, and issuing date. Investment bankers can offer such advice because they are experts on current market conditions. They can also help firms enter the market at the right time with the right security at the right price.

Underwriting

Underwriting is the act of buying a new security from a company and reselling it to investors. An investment banker that acts to guarantee the sale of a new securities issue by buying the securities for subsequent resale to the public is called an **underwriter**. Because the underwriter bears the risk of not selling the entire securities issue, the issuer receives all the funds needed from the sale regardless of whether the underwriter sells all the securities. The underwriter also handles most of the paperwork required by the Securities and Exchange Commission (SEC).

Marketing

Investment bankers have expertise in selling and distributing securities. Because underwriting involves risk, the investment banker forms an **underwriting syndicate** to spread the risk and to help distribute the issue to the public. Depending on the size of the new issue, the size of a syndicate may range from a few firms to several hundred firms.

The underwriter may also support the issue in the aftermarket by trying to stabilize prices around the offer date of a security. During the **stabilization period**, the time elapsing between the offering of a security issue for sale and its final distribution, the underwriter stands ready to enter the secondary market to buy the security. The purpose of this activity, called **price pegging**, is to provide price support by keeping the market price from falling below the security's offering price. Therefore, if investors view the issue as overpriced, they can sell their shares into the stabilizing bid. Yet, if the issue continues to sell slowly, the underwriter may abandon the offering price for a lower price, which may result in a loss to the underwriter. Regulations prohibit issuing corporations from stabilizing their shares to prevent them from manipulating their share price.

Table 10.1 summarizes the role of investment bankers in helping corporations raise funds with new security issues.

Table 10.1 Functions of investment bankers during a public offer of a new security issue

Task	Description
Advising	Advise corporations about the type of security to issue, its features, timing, pricing, and size.
Underwriting	Assume the risk of the sale of an issue by buying a new security issue from the issuer and then reselling it to investors.
Marketing	Form an underwriting syndicate to spread the risk and to get greater financial and marketing resources. Stabilize the market price of a new security through buying and selling in the open market to insure acceptance by the market.

Concept Check 10.2

1 What are the major functions of financial intermediaries? Explain.
2 What are the three major functions of investment bankers involving a new security issue?
3 Why would an investment banking firm form an underwriting syndicate instead of keeping all the business and profits for itself?

10.3 The Decision to Go Public

Firms often begin as proprietorships or partnerships and some of them later convert into corporations. If a company grows and prospers, the owners must decide whether to keep the company privately held or become publicly held. A **privately held company** is usually a small firm with few owners, who often are also its managers. Trading shares of privately held corporations occurs infrequently. By contrast, a **publicly held company** is one in which many investors own its shares but they do not actively manage the firm. Active secondary markets exist for trading shares of publicly held stock. When a privately held company sells part of its ownership to the public through a stock offering, the process is called **going public**. New public offerings by privately held firms occur in the primary markets typically with the help of an investment banker.

When a firm makes its first equity issue available to the public, it is making an **initial public offering** (IPO). Equities offered in an IPO are typically those of young, rapidly growing companies. Thus, another name for an IPO is an **unseasoned new issue**. Not surprisingly, the costs associated with an IPO are higher than for a seasoned issue. Several other types of IPOs include spin-offs from well-established companies and old-line, privately held companies.

Going public has both advantages and disadvantages. The decision on whether to go public depends on the relative importance of these pros and cons as they relate to a firm's characteristics. Unfortunately, only rough guidelines exist for determining whether a firm should go public or when it should do so.

Advantages of Going Public

There are several advantages to going public.

1 *Broadens a firm's access to capital markets.* By limiting itself to internally generated funds and borrowing, a firm restricts its sources of capital and the extent of possible expansion. Going public provides firms with more capital for financing their growth, while simultaneously allowing the original owners to diversify their holdings. Going public also allows a firm to enhance its debt capacity because it involves issuing new shares of common stock.
2 *Increases the liquidity of a firm's stock.* The shares of a privately held company are illiquid because no ready market exists for them. By going public, a firm increases the trading of its shares and, therefore, increases its liquidity.
3 *Sets a value for a firm's shares.* Going public sets a market price for a firm's stock. The publicly traded price also provides management and shareholders with important out-side information about the firm's value. This helps in assessing a firm's cost of capital and results in a more efficient distribution of funds among firms in the economy.
4 *Increases a firm's ability to attract management.* A publicly held firm can often attract better managers by offering them **incentive stock options**, which allow managers to buy shares of the firm's stock at a predetermined price.

Disadvantages of Going Public

Despite offering many advantages, going public also has several disadvantages.

1 *Dilution of control.* Owner-managers of privately held companies often have greater auto-nomy because public ownership reduces the autonomy of management.

2   *Costs*. **Flotation costs** are the costs associated with floating a new issue. These costs include both direct costs (fees paid by the issuer to the underwriters as well as filing fees, legal fees, and taxes), indirect costs (management time spent working on the new issue), and others. Another cost for IPOs is **underpricing**, which represents "money left on the table" or losses arising from selling the stock below the correct value. One way to measure underpricing is to multiply the difference in the closing price and the offering price by the number of shares sold. The costs associated with underpricing, which we discuss below, can exceed the direct costs of going public. Flotation costs of an IPO depend on such factors as the size and risk of the issue. A publicly held company also incurs the added costs of filing annual and quarterly financial reports with the SEC and state officials.

3   *Disclosure of operating data*. Going public gives the public, including competitors, access to more information about the firm.

4   *Possible inactive trading*. Secondary trading of the stock may be inactive if the firm remains small after the public stock offering. A thin market can cause an artificially low market price of the common stock.

Pricing of IPOs

Pricing IPOs is difficult because there is no observable market price before the offering and issuing firms often have little or no operating history. If the investment banker sets the price too low, the issuer will not raise as much money as it could have and the issuer's existing shareholders will experience excessive dilution of ownership. If the investment banker sets the price too high, investors may reject the offering causing the issue to be withdrawn. Thus, the underwriter must set an offering price to satisfy both the issuer and the investors.

Research shows that the prices of unseasoned equity offerings often increase substantially after issuance. That is, underwriters typically underprice IPOs or sell the stock below the correct value, resulting in losses for the issuer. Underwriters typically underprice smaller, more speculative offerings more than larger offerings. The underpricing of a typical IPO averages at least 15 percent below the price at which the securities trade immediately after the issue. Thus, investors buying IPOs at the initial offering often earn abnormally positive returns in the early aftermarket period. Few IPO buyers get the initial high average returns. After a year or more, returns of IPOs are generally lower than those of the average stock. Younger companies show more pronounced underperformance than do more established firms.

There are several possible reasons for the underpricing or positive initial returns of IPOs. None of these explanations taken alone is entirely satisfactory in explaining the persistent and systematic underpricing of IPOs.

1   *Asymmetric information hypothesis*. One explanation attributes IPO underpricing to differences in information (or information asymmetries) between parties about the value of the new issue. For example, information asymmetry may exist between the issuer and the investment banker underwriting the IPO. If underwriters have more information about market-clearing prices than issuers do, underwriters can take advantage of issuers by setting low prices. Underpricing may damage the reputation of the underwriter and affect future business with other potential issuers.

2   *Risk-aversion underwriter's hypothesis.* Another popular theory is that investment bankers purposely underprice new common stocks to reduce their risks and costs of underwriting. Although this view has some superficial appeal, it has little empirical support.

3   *Insurance hypothesis.* A third theory proposes that investment bankers intentionally underprice unseasoned issues as a form of insurance against legal liability and the associated damage to the reputation of the investment banker. Securities underwriters have the responsibility, called **due diligence**, to investigate all aspects of an IPO-firm's operations. Carrying out this responsibility is often difficult because of the lack of information. Investment bankers, therefore, potentially face legal liabilities when floating an IPO.

4   *Fads or speculative-bubbles hypothesis.* Another explanation is that IPOs are subject to overvaluation or fads in early aftermarket trading. Investors who cannot buy shares of oversubscribed IPOs create a speculative demand, which pushes up prices in the aftermarket. This explanation has some empirical support.

5   *Regulatory and procedural hypothesis.* This explanation suggests that regulations and procedures governing the underwriting and pricing of IPOs encourage underwriters to underprice new issues. For example, regulations restrict the underwriter's commissions within a small range. The underwriter has no obligation to set the final offer price within the range shown in the preliminary prospectus. Therefore, the underwriter can increase expected income by underpricing the IPO.

Concept Check 10.3

1   How does a privately held company differ from a publicly held company?
2   What are the advantages and disadvantages of going public?
3   What are several explanations for the underpricing of IPOs?

10.4 Different Methods of Issuing New Securities

We now turn our attention from IPOs or unseasoned issues to a **seasoned new issue**, a new equity issue of securities by a company that has previously issued securities to the public. Firms may issue new securities either through a **public offer** or a **private placement** (see Figure 10.2). If management chooses a public offer, it may select either a **general cash offer** to the public at large or offer securities on a pro rata basis to existing owners through a **rights offer**. We discuss these different methods of issuing new securities later in this chapter.

If corporate management selects a general cash offer, it can structure the offering internally and then put it out for **competitive offers**. Alternatively, it can negotiate the offer terms directly with an underwriter. With a **negotiated offer**, the underwriting contract can be either a **firm commitment** to market all shares or a **best-efforts offer**, in which an investment bank does not guarantee selling all shares. Finally, the firm can register the issue with the

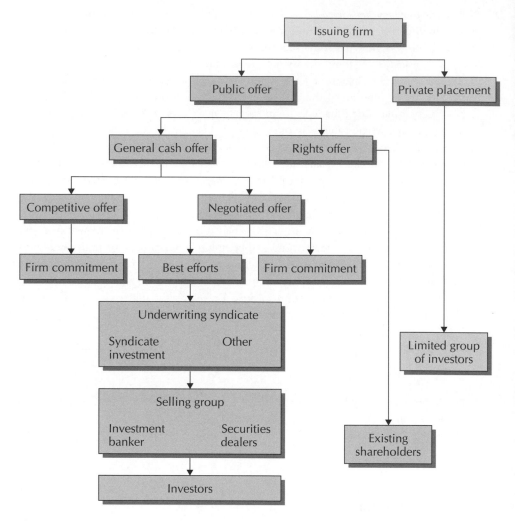

Figure 10.2 Comparison of a public offer and a private placement

Securities and Exchange Commission (SEC) under its traditional registration procedures or, if the firm qualifies, it can file a **shelf registration**.

Although a firm's shares typically command a fair price despite the method chosen, the issuer can benefit by selecting the method best fitting its own circumstances. Two important considerations in choosing the best method of raising capital are:

1   *Flotation costs* – expenses involved in selling a new security issue.
2   *Risk* – the chance of getting the desired amount of funds.

These factors help to determine the net proceeds the company receives from the sale of securities. We examine these factors when discussing the various methods of raising capital.

Competitive Cash Offer versus Negotiated Cash Offer

A firm making a public offering must decide whether to select an investment banker using a competitive offer or by engaging in negotiation. Under a **competitive cash offer**, also called **competitive bidding**, a securities issuer selects an investment banker based on the best price offered through competitive bids by the investment bankers. Only firms with large offerings use competitive offers because most investment banking firms are unwilling to bid on smaller issues. The law requires public utility companies to secure competitive bids, unless exempted by the SEC. Under a **negotiated cash offer**, a securities issuer selects an investment banking firm to help in or guarantee the sale of securities based on discussions and factors including the best price.

Which arrangement is better for firms issuing securities? The answer is unclear. Competitive offers generally have lower total flotation costs to the issuer than negotiated offers. Yet, in gaining lower costs, a firm may lose the benefits of an investment banker's expert advice and services. In turn, this may lessen the attractiveness of the issue to investors. In addition, with competitive offers, the issuer has more control over the terms and timing of the offer. Yet, outside investors value the monitoring provided by investment bankers through a negotiated contract. In practice, most firms not facing regulatory constraints choose negotiated offers, despite their greater cost. Competitive bids are more common for debt issues than for equity offerings.

Best-efforts Cash Offer versus Firm Commitment Cash Offer

A firm selecting an investment banker based on a negotiated offer may arrange a best-efforts offer or a firm commitment underwriting to market its shares. Under a **best-efforts cash offer**, the investment banker agrees to make "best efforts" to sell as much of the issue as possible at the agreed-upon price. The investment banker does not guarantee the sale but acts only as a marketing agent to the firm. The best-efforts offer reduces the risk faced by the underwriter but places much of the risk on the issuer. Firms often use a best-efforts offer because underwriters refuse to give them firm commitments. Therefore, this form of underwriting is more common with IPOs than with seasoned new issues.

Under a **firm commitment cash offer**, the issuer sells the entire issue to the underwriters, who then try to resell the issue to the public. Thus, the underwriters guarantee that the issuer will receive an agreed-upon amount of capital. Prestigious underwriters typically conduct firm commitment cash offers. The size of the average firm commitment offer is several times as large as best-efforts offers. Firm commitment underwriting is much more common for large issues than best efforts underwriting.

As we mentioned earlier, the relative attractiveness of these two types of contracts to the issuer depends on two factors – flotation costs and the risk of getting the desired funds. Best-efforts offers are usually more expensive than firm commitment offers due to higher flotation costs and greater underpricing. Issuers using best-efforts arrangements are often those whose financial performance is questionable or those with unproven records including new, speculative firms. Investment bankers do not bear the risk of underwriting or guaranteeing the offering. Therefore, the issuing firm bears the risk of getting the desired funds.

Traditional versus Shelf Registration

Some firms have two options when registering a security issue with the SEC, **traditional registration** and **shelf registration**. Under a traditional registration, a firm must register newly issued securities with the SEC at least 20 days before a public offering. A **registration statement** is a document containing detailed information about a firm (its history and nature of its business) that plans to sell securities to the public. The issuer also files the statement with the appropriate securities markets and state securities regulators.

In 1982, the SEC introduced Rule 415 allowing some corporations to streamline the process of registering future debt or equity securities by filing a shelf registration. Under a shelf registration, a qualifying company files a master registration covering a variety of potential new issues that can last up to 2 years. After the SEC approves the registration, a firm can sell the securities to the public or place them privately during the 2-year period with only a quick update of the master registration. To qualify for a shelf registration, a company must have: (1) investment grade debt, (2) no defaults on its debt within the past 3 years, (3) at least $150 million in market value of outstanding stock, and (4) not violated the Securities Act of 1934 within the past 3 years.

Advantages of shelf registration
Shelf registration has several advantages over traditional registration.

1 *Lower flotation costs.* Shelf registration is less costly than a traditional underwriting because firms avoid the costs associated with frequent filings. Shelf-registration is cost-effective for large, well-known companies that frequently issue securities, especially public debt offers.
2 *Flexibility.* Another advantage is greater flexibility in timing the issue and tailoring the amount of funds raised. For example, shelf-registration may allow a firm to sell shares of common stock more quickly to take advantage of favorable market conditions.
3 *Less risk.* Because of the shorter registration period, there is less risk that the shares will drop between the period of announcement and time of the issue. Thus, a firm "shelves" the securities it expects to issue until it needs them or until it believes the market is right for bringing out a new issue. In addition, a corporation expecting higher market interest rates can lock in its financing cost by issuing bonds right away.

Concept Check 10.4

1 What is the difference between a competitive bid and a negotiated offer?
2 How does the risk differ to an investment banker who sells new securities with a firm commitment underwriting versus a best-efforts agreement?
3 What are the benefits of using a shelf registration when issuing new securities?

10.5 Public Offer

A **public offer** is the sale of an issue of securities to the public. As we discussed earlier, an IPO is a special type of public offering. Another type involves **seasoned issues** or securities of well-established, publicly held companies sold in the primary market.

Most public offerings of debt are cash offers. When making a public offering of additional equity, a firm can issue the shares using a general cash offer and a rights offer. In the United States, firms use general cash offers much more frequently than they do rights offers.

General Cash Offer

A **general cash offer** is the public offering of securities to all interested investors. A company could directly auction its securities to the public and save underwriter fees. Although this approach may be possible for large, well-known corporations, direct public auctions are infrequent for firms of any size. Without an underwriter, the issuing company bears all the risk of selling the issue. Because the sale of securities directly to investors by firms is inefficient, corporations use the services of investment bankers for cash offers.

The most often-used method for raising equity in the United States is a general cash offer to the public using a firm commitment underwriting. The **Securities Act of 1933** sets forth the federal regulations for all new interstate securities issues. The steps involved in underwriting common stock are as follows.

1   *Make preliminary decisions.* After deciding to raise new capital, a corporation makes some preliminary decisions about the amount of capital needed, the type of securities to use, and the timing of the issue. The firm's board of directors must approve issuing new securities to the public.
2   *Select an investment banker.* Assuming a public offering, the firm usually contacts an investment banker. Well-established firms that have gone to the capital markets before already have relationships with investment bankers. Other firms may shop around.
3   *Conduct conferences.* The issuer and the investment banker hold a series of **pre-underwriting conferences** to reevaluate the firm's preliminary decisions involving the issue. They also negotiate the investment banker's fee and discuss other costs associated with the issue.
4   *Decide the method of raising capital.* The issuer decides among the various methods of raising capital. For example, if the issuer decides to use a general cash offer negotiated with an underwriter, the following steps would apply.
5   *Syndicate the underwriting.* For large offerings, the underwriter forms an **underwriting syndicate** to spread the risk of adverse price movements. Syndicate members sign an **underwriting agreement** identifying the syndicate manager, member liability, allocation of fees, and the life of the group. The **syndicate manager**, also known as the **lead** or **managing underwriter**, handles most of the transaction details such as allocating the securities among other member firms in the group and pricing the securities. Usually, the syndicate manager has the largest share of the issue and, therefore, carries the largest

share of risk. Each syndicate member assumes the risk for the portion of securities it agrees to sell. The difference in the price that an investor pays for a new security issue and the price paid the issuer by the lead underwriter is called the **gross spread**.

6 *Form a selling group.* The underwriting syndicate often seeks help from non-syndicate securities dealers to help distribute a new offering of securities. Dealers receive allotments of stock from the syndicate at wholesale prices and collect a commission or concession fee for securities placed with them. Because these dealers usually do not incur the risk of underwriting the issue, their commission is lower than that of the syndicate members. The underwriting syndicate and the securities dealers comprise the **selling group**.

7 *Register the issue.* The issuing firm, usually working with the underwriter, prepares and files a registration statement, which the SEC examines during a 20-day waiting period. Approval of the documents once filed may take longer than 20 days. Included within the required registration information is a **prospectus**, an abridged version of the firm's registration statement detailing information needed by investors to make educated decisions about whether to buy the security. A firm may issue the prospectus to prospective investors only after the SEC has approved the registration. Approval by the SEC does not guarantee safety of the new issue. It merely acknowledges that the firm is disclosing enough information to inform potential investors about itself and the new issue.

During the waiting period, the selling group cannot sell these securities before the SEC approves the registration statement. The selling group can distribute copies of a preliminary prospectus and receive non-binding bids from potential buyers on how many shares they expect to buy. A **preliminary prospectus** is a formal document given to prospective investors in a new security issue before the firm has set the selling price and before the SEC has approved the issuer's registration statement for accuracy and completeness. The preliminary prospectus carries a warning in red ink, called a **red herring**, stating that the prospectus is for information purposes only and that the securities are not yet for sale.

8 *Price the issue.* The underwriter typically does not set an **offering price**, the price at which investors can buy a security, until the end of the registration period. After SEC approval, the underwriter and the issuer hold a pricing meeting at which they agree upon an offering price. For publicly held companies, the underwriter typically sets the offering price below the market price at the time of issue. Once the SEC approves the registration statement, the issuing firm with its investment banker prepares the **final prospectus**, which includes the offering price and date of sale, for distribution to interested investors.

9 *Sell the issue.* When the registration statement becomes effective, the selling officially begins. The investment banker through its selling group distributes the prospectus to potential investors and advertises the issue to the public. The syndicate manager runs a **tombstone** advertisement in the financial press. The advertisement lists the security, some specifics about the security, and the members of the syndicate selling the issue. The underwriters' names appear in **brackets** on the tombstone, signifying the order of the underwriters' importance in a particular offering. The **major bracket**, which lists the primary underwriters in a securities offering, appears immediately under the names of the issue's co-managers. The **mezzanine bracket** is the list of underwriters playing a moderately important role in a securities offering.

10 *Dissolve the syndicate*. The syndication ends after selling the issue and turning the net proceeds over to the issuing company.

Advantages of general cash offers
General cash offers have several advantages to the issuing firm.

- *Broad distribution of stock*. With a general cash offer, the investing public, not merely a few investors, can buy a firm's securities. Having a wider distribution of ownership reduces the chance of having a few investors gain control over the firm.
- *High chance of getting the needed funds*. If the investment banker underwrites the issue, the issuer has a guarantee of getting a specific amount of financing. That is, underwriters provide insurance against a failed offering.

Disadvantages of general cash offers
General cash offers have two major disadvantages.

- *High flotation costs*. The flotation costs are typically higher for a general cash offer than for a rights offer.
- *Time required*. Unless a firm has a shelf registration, the time required to issue securities can be lengthy. Yet, the proceeds of underwritten issues are generally available sooner than when using a rights offer.

Rights Offer

Another means of issuing stock through a public offering is to use a rights offer (or rights offering). A **rights offer**, also called a **privileged subscription**, involves initially offering the securities to the firm's existing stockholders. These stockholders receive preference in buying new shares up to the proportion of shares that they already own. Thus, a stockholder with 5 percent of the issuing firm's outstanding stock could buy up to 5 percent of the new issue at a special price below the current market price. With a rights offer, the company must still go through the same SEC registration process as it does when making other public offers.

Many corporate charters include a **preemptive right** giving existing stockholders the right to buy new shares of common stock issued in proportion to their current ownership. Some states require that corporations chartered with them have the preemptive right in their charters. The purpose of the preemptive right is to protect existing shareholders from having their proportionate ownership diluted when a firm issues new common stock. If the firm's common stockholders have a preemptive right, the company must offer any newly issued common stock to existing stockholders through a rights offering.

A firm may make a rights offer directly to its shareholders (**pure rights**) or through an investment banker (**rights with a standby underwriting**). Most companies use an investment banker to issue the rights, handle the administrative aspects of the issue, and buy and resell all stock not subscribed. Generally, some shareholders will not use or sell their rights to buy the new shares, thus leaving some stock unsold even at the bargain price. The issuing firm can plan for this contingency using a **standby underwriting**, an arrangement in which an investment banker buys all unsold shares at a specific price. The underwriter typically gets a **standby fee** for agreeing to buy any unsold shares. Another alternative is to include an **over-subscription privilege**, allowing shareholders to oversubscribe in anticipation of extra available shares. Under this provision, shareholders can buy, on a pro rata basis, any unsold shares of a new stock offering at the subscription price.

Elements of rights offers
The terms of rights offer specify three major items.

1 *Number of rights needed to buy a new share*. Each stockholder receives one right for each share of stock owned. A **right** is an option allowing the owner to buy some shares, or frequently, a fractional share of new stock from the issuer at a specific price, called the **offering price**. The firm announces the number of rights needed to buy each new share. This number depends on the relationship between the number of pre-offering shares of common stock outstanding and the number of new shares the firm plans to issue. For example, a firm with 10 million shares outstanding that wants to issue 1 million new shares will require 10 rights, and cash, to buy one new share.
2 *Subscription price per share*. The **subscription price**, also called the **exercise price**, is the price at which rights holders may buy new shares. The firm normally sets the subscription price below the stock's current market price to ensure the successful sale of the issue. Otherwise, investors would prefer to buy the less costly existing shares in the secondary market than buying new shares through a rights offering. A low subscription price increases the chance that shareholders will exercise all rights, but forces the firm to issue more shares to raise the required funds.
3 *Subscription period of the offering*. The **subscription period** is the period during which investors can exercise their rights and buy shares of the new issue. A subscription period typically lasts a week or two, after which the right to subscribe expires. The **expiration date** is the last day on which the rights holder may exercise the right.

Actions of shareholders with rights
Shareholders with rights have three courses of action.

1 *Exercise the rights and buy additional shares*. Shareholders exercise the rights by completing a subscription form and sending it with their payment to the firm's subscription agent, usually a bank.
2 *Sell the rights after the date of record*. Because rights are transferable, shareholders who do not wish to buy additional stock can sell their rights to other investors.
3 *Do nothing and let the rights expire*. Shareholders may also do nothing, but this choice is inadvisable because rights have value. That is, rights typically allow investors to buy stock below market prices.

Advantages of rights offers
Compared to general cash offers, rights offers have several advantages to the issuer.

1   *Lower flotation costs*. From the firm's perspective, rights offers are cheaper than cash offers. Lower flotation costs result because investment bankers bear lower risks with a rights offer and, therefore, require less compensation. A pure rights offer involving no underwriter is less costly than a rights offer with a standby underwriting.
2   *Increases stockholder loyalty*. A rights offer may increase loyalty of existing stockholders and stimulate interest in the firm.

Disadvantages of rights offers
Rights offers have several possible disadvantages.

1   *Fail to broaden the shareholder base*. A rights offer may lead to narrower distribution of stock than a general cash offer because the firm offers the shares only to existing stock-holders. A broader stockholder base may reduce the volatility of a stock's price and help a company meet listing requirements.
2   *Lead to a possible loss to stockholders*. Stockholders will suffer a loss if they let their rights expire.

Concept Check 10.5

1   How do general cash offers differ from rights offers?
2   What are the basic steps in selling a new issue? Explain.
3   Why might a firm prefer to use a rights offer to a general cash offer?

10.6 Private Placement

Instead of having a public offer of new debt or equity securities, a firm may seek a **private placement**. With a private placement, the issuing firm or its investment banker, acting as an agent, negotiates the price and the terms of the issue with a single buyer or a few buyers. Life insurance companies and pension funds are the dominant buyers in the private placement segment of the bond market. Other buyers include commercial banks and mutual funds.

The primary legal distinction between a private placement and a public offering is that private placements are normally exempt from registration with the SEC. The rationale for this exemption is that institutional investors have the sophistication necessary to investigate thoroughly the quality of the issue. Private placements are more common for issuing bonds than stocks and investment bankers typically conduct the placement. A **direct placement** occurs when an issuer avoids using an investment banker.

Advantages of Private Placements

Private placements offer several advantages to the issuing firm over public offerings as a mechanism for getting long-term financing.

- *Flexibility*. Because a private placement involves few buyers, the issuer can tailor the terms and provisions of the new issue to meet the needs of both the issuer and the buyers. Privately placed securities typically contain nonstandard covenants to meet the special concerns of the institutional buyers. In contrast, a public offering has more standardized provisions to fit all types of potential investors. In case of financial distress, the few investors in a private placement make renegotiation of terms easier than with a public offering. Companies choosing private placements over public issues benefit from the more direct relationship between the issuer and the investors.
- *Speed*. Private placements are exempt from registration with the SEC. By avoiding the delays of registration and approval, the issuing firm can proceed quickly to sell its securities.
- *Lower flotation costs*. Private placement typically involves less expense to the issuer who can avoid underwriting fees, sales commissions, and registration expenses. The issuer also avoids the costs of continuous reporting requirements associated with SEC registration.
- *Privacy*. A private offer involves less public disclosure of information than a public offer. Although private investors may need to know more about the company than the SEC would, the issuer does not have to make this information a matter of public record.

Disadvantages of Private Placements

A private placement has several possible disadvantages to the issuer, compared with a general cash offer.

- *Higher interest and dividend rates*. The interest rates or dividend payments on private placements are usually higher than are those on a similar public issue.
- *Lower demand*. The demand for a privately placed issue may not be as strong as for a public offer because the issuer targets only a fraction of the market of potential buyers. Such investors, primarily financial intermediaries, may lack the funds to invest during certain periods.
- *Less liquidity*. Securities issued in private placements are often less liquid than public issues. The SEC restricts the sale of unregistered securities by requiring buyers of these securities to hold them for at least 2 years. Yet, liquidity is inherently less important to private investors who often intend to hold securities until maturity. As compensation for lower liquidity, investors require higher rates of return. Thus, the interest rate on debt issues is usually higher and the price on equity issues is typically lower than comparable public issues.
- *More restrictions*. In private placements, investors can reduce the risk of illiquidity by imposing more restrictions or covenants on the borrower in order to reduce the likelihood of deteriorating credit. These investors exert their bargaining power to get concessions from issuing firms that need financing or have trouble after making the placement.

Concept Check 10.6

1   Who are some typical buyers of securities through a private placement?
2   Why might a firm use a private placement instead of a public offering?
3   What are some potential disadvantages to the issue of using a private placement?

10.7 Costs of Issuing New Securities

The costs of issuing new securities, called flotation costs, can be quite large. **Flotation costs** consist of the underwriting spread and other direct issue expenses. The investment banker receives compensation as an underwriting spread for advising the issuer, underwriting the issue, and marketing the securities to investors. An **underwriting spread** or **gross spread** is the dollar difference between the price that the issuing firm receives from the underwriter and the price at which the underwriter sells the securities to the public. Other direct issue expenses include all other flotation costs incurred by the issuer, including legal and account-ing expenses, printing costs, registration fees, and taxes. The underwriting spread is the larger of the two flotation costs. Issuers also incur **indirect expenses** including the costs of management time spent working on the new issue and underpricing for IPOs.

Example 10.1 Cost of an Underwriting

Filbeck Corporation plans to issue 1 million shares of new stock. An investment banking firm guarantees a selling price of $18 per share and then expects to sell the stock to investors for $20 per share. What are the underwriting spread and the flotation cost as a percentage of the new issue?

Solution: The underwriting spread per share = $20 − $18 = $2
Gross underwriting spread = 1 million shares × $2 = $2 million
Market value of shares = 1 million shares × $20 per share = $20 million
Flotation cost as a percentage of the new issue = $2 million/$20 million = 10%

Factors Affecting Flotation Costs

Flotation costs vary widely and depend on several factors.

• *Type of security*. Flotation costs are typically higher for common stock than for bonds. The cost of issuing preferred stock falls between common stock and bonds. With com-mon stock issues, an investment banker incurs more risk and higher marketing expenses than with preferred stock or bonds.

- *Riskiness of an issue*. A close relationship exists between an underwriter's compensation and the risk of an unsuccessful offering. The quality of an issue affects its risk. Low-quality issues have higher flotation costs than high-quality issues because underwriters bear more risk and incur higher costs in selling low-quality issues.
- *Size of the issue*. Flotation costs as a percentage of the value of an issue often vary inversely with issue size. Small issues are more expensive as a percentage of total funds raised than large issues because many issuing costs are fixed.

Concept Check 10.7

1   What types of costs do corporations incur when issuing new securities?
2   What are three factors that affect flotation costs?

10.8 Cost of Capital Concept

Now that we have discussed how companies raise funds in financial markets, we turn to estimating the cost of these funds. We can view the cost of capital from two major perspectives: demanders (issuers) and suppliers (investors). The **cost of capital** is the rate that the firm has to pay, explicitly or implicitly, to investors for their capital or the minimum rate of return required by the suppliers of capital. Thus, ignoring taxes and flotation costs, the cost of capital represents two sides of the same coin – the cost to issuers is the return to investors.

Various factors affect the cost of capital. Some of these factors are within the firm's control while others are not. For example, firms have no direct control over the level of interest rates, tax rates, and the market risk premium. Conversely, managers can affect the cost of capital of their firm. For example, investment policy decisions affect the riskiness of the firm and hence the rate of return required by creditors and stockholders who provided the funds. Capital structure decisions have an effect on the financing mix of the firm, which in turn affects its cost of capital. Finally, dividend policy decisions influence the amount of earnings distributed to shareholders or retained by the firm to finance future growth. Dividend policy can affect the return investors require and the firm's cost of capital.

Uses of the Cost of Capital

The cost of capital is a central concept in financial management because it provides a way to link investment and financing decisions of a firm. An interrelationship exists between capital budgeting and cost of capital. For example, to determine the size of the capital budget, corporate managers need information about both the returns on investment opportunities and the cost of capital. Managers and analysts use estimates of the firm's cost of capital in two major ways: (1) to help identify the discount rate to be used to evaluate proposed capital investments and (2) to serve as a guideline in developing capital structure and evaluating financial alternatives. We discussed these uses of the cost of capital in Chapters 7 through 9.

Using the firm's overall cost of capital is appropriate for project evaluation only in those cases where the risk profile of the new project is the same as the risk profile for the firm. That is, the cost of capital embodies the average risk posture of the firm for its portfolio of operational projects. In cases where the risk profile of a specific project differs from that of the risk complexion of the firm, managers and analysts need to adjust the required discount rate to reflect this deviation. Ideally, the cost of capital for each project should reflect the risk of the project itself. In Chapter 8, we referred to this concept as the **risk-adjusted discount rate**.

More risky projects require a higher cost of capital (discount rate, hurdle rate, or required rate of return) than less risky projects. Failing to adjust the differences in project risk would lead a firm to accept too many value-destroying risky projects and reject too many value-adding safe ones. Over time, the riskiness of the firm would increase and lead to an increase in its cost of capital. Eventually, shareholder value would suffer.

An important point to remember is that the cost of capital (appropriate discount rate) depends mainly on the use of the funds, not on how and where the firm raises the capital. The specific source of financing for a project is not directly relevant.

Capital Components

Although some firms can finance their operations totally with common equity, most rely on other capital components that represent funds provided by various suppliers. Each capital component has a **component cost**, which is the minimum required rate of return on the component. Capital components are funds that come from investors. In capital budgeting, managers and analysts should use the weighted average of the component costs for projects of average risk. They should not use the cost of the specific source of financing employed in a particular year as the discount or cutoff rate in project evaluation. Instead, they should view companies as ongoing concerns. Firms typically raise capital from several sources in an effort to reduce the average required rate of return on the firm's overall capital. Thus, their costs of capital should be the weighted averages of the various types of funds they use.

The three major long-term components in the capital structures of most firms are straight debt, straight preferred stock, and common equity. Companies use other sources of financing to a lesser extent such as convertible debt, variable-rate debt, term loans, leases, floating-rate preferred stock, and numerous new types of securities. Estimating the cost of capital for most of these instruments is difficult. Fortunately, these financial assets usually constitute a small percentage of financing and have a relatively small impact on the cost of capital of most firms. Assigning a cost to these instruments is beyond the scope of this book. Therefore, we confine our discussion to the three major sources of financing.

Issues Involving Component Costs

Before discussing how to estimate the three major component costs of capital, four issues are important to address. Financial theory offers several important observations when estimating the component costs.

- *Should the firm focus on before-tax or after-tax capital costs?* Although the corporate tax effects associated with financing can be incorporated either in the cash flows of capital budgeting projects or in the cost of capital, most firms incorporate tax effects in the cost of capital. Therefore, managers and analysts should focus on after-tax costs. Taxes only affect the cost of debt because interest, not dividends, is an expense that reduces taxes.

- *Should the firm consider flotation costs involved in selling new bonds and stock?* If a firm raises new financing, the flotation costs are relevant. Disagreement exists on how to appropriately handle flotation costs. One approach adjusts the component costs upward to reflect these costs. This approach increases the firm's weighted average cost of capital and hence the discount rate used for capital budgeting projects. Another approach treats flotation costs as an additional outflow that increases the initial cash outlay of an investment. In the remainder of this chapter, we adopt the first approach in calculating component costs.

- *Should the firm focus on historical costs or new (marginal) costs?* A primary use of the cost of capital is to make decisions that involve raising and investing new capital. Therefore, the relevant cost is the marginal cost of any incremental funds that the firm plans to raise during the planning period, not the historical or sunk cost of capital that the firm has already raised.

- *Should the firm consider the cost of depreciation in the calculation of the cost of capital?* For many firms, depreciation is the IR largest source of funds. These so-called depreciation-generated funds are available to support the capital budget. The cost of funds generated through depreciation depends on how the firm will use the funds. If the firm plans to use these funds as part of the capital expenditure process, the cost of depreciation will be the weighted average cost of capital before issuing new equity. That is, the firm should require the same return on investments using depreciation-generated funds as for other funds. Following this logic, including depreciation in calculating the cost of capital is unnecessary.

Weighted Average Cost of Capital

The **weighted average cost of capital** (WACC) is the weighted average of the costs of debt and equity. WACC is the cost of capital for the firm as a whole. If a firm consists of various divisions, the divisional cost of capital is likely to differ from the firm's WACC depending on the riskiness of the division. Since a firm uses debt and equity capital, WACC represents a mixture of the returns needed to compensate both creditors and stockholders. If the firm earns an overall rate of return on its existing assets equal to its WACC, it can maintain the market value of its stock. If the firm fails to meet this objective, the market price of its stock should decline.

Measuring a company's WACC involves two major steps: (1) estimating the cost of each capital component, and (2) determining the weights of each component. Multiplying each capital component by its weight in the capital structure and then summing the percentages produces an estimate of the WACC. Although debate exists over which components to use in measuring the cost of capital, the traditional approach is to use only permanent short-term and long-term sources of financing. If a firm has a permanent level of short-term debt, the financial manager should include short-term debt as another component in the firm's capital structure. Otherwise, short-term debt is not part of the capital base.[1]

Others argue that all forms of debt financing, including non-interest bearing debt such as accounts payables and accruals, should be included in calculating WACC. We do not favor this approach because current liabilities affect the cash flows of a project, not its WACC. Instead, we recommend including such changes in non-permanent current liabilities as part of net operating working capital. We discussed this approach in Chapter 7. In this section, we examine only long-term sources of funds to measure the cost of capital because firms seldom use short-term debt as part of their permanent financing for capital projects.

Practical Financial Tip 10.1

There are no free sources of permanent financing. The specific cost of each capital component is the minimum rate of return required by the suppliers. Different costs occur because of the varying degrees of risk associated with each capital component. The higher the risk of a particular component, the higher will be the return required by investors and the higher the cost to the firm.

Concept Check 10.8

1 What is the meaning of cost of capital and weighted average cost of capital?
2 What factors affecting a firm's cost of capital are beyond its direct control?
3 What are two major uses of the cost of capital? Explain.
4 What is the primary determinant of the cost of capital (appropriate discount rate) for an investment?
5 Why should corporate managers measure the cost of capital on an after-tax basis?
6 Is the historical cost of capital or the marginal cost of capital more meaningful for making financial decisions? Explain why.
7 What are two ways of treating flotation costs?

10.9 Cost of Capital Components

Firms have many potential sources of capital. Unless these sources of funds come from investors, they are not capital components. For most firms, the primary sources are retained earnings from profits and the funds generated through depreciation. Firms issue new

---

[1] An appropriate approach is to treat interest on short-term debt as an expense associated with the specific project.

common stock infrequently. In addition to equity, firms use debt and preferred stock to a lesser extent to finance their investments. In this section, we focus on estimating the component costs of three capital components: debt, preferred stock, and common equity. We begin by discussing debt and preferred stock, which are easier costs to measure than the cost of equity.

Cost of Debt

The **cost of debt** (k_d) is the rate of return required by suppliers of the firm's debt. We focus only on estimating the cost of bonds because the lender typically determines the cost of other types of debt such as term loans and leases. Determining the cost of debt is straightforward because we can observe interest rates in the financial market. For a company with publicly held debt, a reasonable estimate of the cost of debt is its yield to maturity (YTM) on outstanding debt. If the firm has no publicly traded debt, the interest rate on newly issued bonds with the same bond rating is a good proxy.

Because interest expense on corporate debt in the United States is tax-deductible, a firm's **after-tax cost of debt** (k'_d) is less than its before-tax cost for any marginal tax rate greater than zero.[2] In effect, the government pays part of the total cost. Thus, the relevant component cost of debt is the after-tax cost of new debt, not the historical or before-tax cost of outstanding debt.

Unadjusted after-tax cost of debt

Assuming a company sells new debt but incurs no flotation costs, Equation 10.1 is the formula for the after-tax cost of debt.[3] The after-tax cost of debt is simply a firm's before-tax cost of debt (k_d), which is the yield to maturity, multiplied by $(1 - T)$, where T is the firm's marginal tax rate. The coupon rate on the firm's outstanding debt is irrelevant because it roughly represents the cost of debt when the firm issued the bonds, not the current cost of debt. Firms usually do not incur flotation costs because they sell most debt through private placements.

Unadjusted After-tax Cost of New Debt $k'_d = k_d(1 - T)$ (10.1)

where k_d is the before-tax cost of debt, which is the yield to maturity (YTM); and T is the firm's marginal tax rate.

---

[2]   If a firm has such large current or past losses that it does not pay taxes, the effective tax rate is zero. In this case, the after-tax cost of debt is equal to the pre-tax interest rate, assuming no flotation costs.

[3]   Another approach for estimating the before-tax cost of debt is to look at the average current yield on similar bonds. Typically, the average seasoned yield differs from the average new-issue yield due to the difference in the treatment of taxes and the inclusion of discount and premium bonds. The new issue yield typically provides a more reliable measure of the cost of debt then does the average seasoned yield. For non-publicly traded debt, using yields on publicly traded debt of similar firms may provide a reasonable estimate of the before-tax cost of debt.

Example 10.2 Estimating the Unadjusted After-tax Cost of New Debt

Chesapeake Company plans to engage in a private placement of 10-year semiannual-pay coupon bonds. Each bond has a par value of $1,000 and a coupon rate of 9 percent. The firm has a marginal federal-plus-state tax rate of 40 percent. What is the estimated unadjusted after-tax cost of the new debt?

Solution: Since the bonds sell at par and have no flotation costs, their coupon rate is the same as their yield to maturity. Substituting $k_d = 9$ percent and $T = 40$ percent into Equation 10.1 yields an unadjusted after-tax cost of debt of 5.4 percent.

$$k_d' = 9\%(1 - 0.40) = 5.4\%$$

Adjusted after-tax cost of debt

Companies issuing new debt to the public incur flotation costs. Flotation costs reduce the amount that the issuer receives from selling bonds and increase the cost of bonds to the issuer. Issuers pay flotation costs up-front, but usually amortize them over the life of the bond. The amortized expenses reduce tax liabilities. This treatment of flotation costs slightly complicates the task of determining the after-tax cost of debt. In practice, managers and analysts sometimes ignore flotation costs even for publicly placed debt because such costs are usually small in percentage terms for most debt issues. This does not mean, however, that they should not make the adjustment.

Equations 10.2 and 10.3 provide a means of measuring the adjusted after-tax cost of new debt for annual-pay and semi-annual pay bonds, respectively. These two equations are modified versions of Equation 5.6 and Equation 5.8 for the yield-to-maturity (YTM) in Chapter 5. Each involves finding the discount rate, $k_d(1 - T)$ that makes the present value of the net cash outflows equal to the net proceeds received from the sale of the bond. If a firm sells bonds at par value, the **net proceeds** of a bond issue are the maturity value of the bond (M) multiplied by 1 minus the percentage flotation costs (F).[4] The percentage flotation costs typically decrease as the size of the debt raised increases.

$$M(1 - F) = \sum_{t=1}^{n} \frac{I(1 - T) - (F^*/n)(1 - T)}{[1 + K_d(1 - T)]^t} + \frac{M}{[1 + k_d(1 - T)]^n} \tag{10.2}$$

$$M(1 - F) = \sum_{t=1}^{2n} \frac{(I/2)(1 - T) - (F^*/2n)(1 - T)}{[1 + (k_d/2)(1 - T)]^t} + \frac{M}{[1 + (k_d/2)(1 - T)]^{2n}} \tag{10.3}$$

where I is the expected interest payment; F is the percentage flotation costs; F^* is the amount of flotation costs per bond; M is the maturity or par value of the bond; k_d is the issuer's cost to maturity, which is the same as the yield to maturity in Chapter 6; n is the length of the holding period; and t is the time period.

---

[4]   If a firm sells a bond issue at discount or premium relative to their par value, some adjustment should be made in the formula. The net proceeds from the sale would be equal to the selling price (P_0) minus the amount of the flotation costs.

Example 10.3 Estimating the Adjusted After-tax Cost of New Debt

Suppose that instead of having a private placement, Chesapeake Company plans to issue $4 million in 10-year semi-annual coupon bonds. Each bond has a par value of $1,000 and a coupon rate of 9 percent. The firm expects to sell the bond at par and to incur flotation costs of 2.5 percent or $25 per bond. The firm has a marginal federal-plus-state tax rate of 40 percent. What is the estimated adjusted after-tax cost of the new bond?

Solution: The first step is to calculate the net proceeds per bond as follows.

$$M(1 - F) = \$1,000(1 - 0.025) = \$975$$

Next, substitute $M(1 - F) = \$975$, $I/2 = \$90/2 = \$45$, $F/2n = \$25/20 = \$1.25$, $M = \$1,000$, $T = 0.40$, and $2n = 20$ into Equation 10.3.[5] Using trial-and-error to solve for $k_d(1 - T)$ yields an adjusted after-tax cost of 2.7898 percent, which is the semi-annual rate. We follow the market convention of using nominal rates for all component costs. For semi-annual pay bonds, this involves doubling the semi-annual rate so that $k_b(1 - T) = 2.7898 \times 2 = 5.5796$ percent or about 5.58 percent.[6]

$$\$975 = \sum_{t=1}^{20} \frac{\$45(1 - 0.40) - \$1.25(1 - 0.40)}{[1 + (k_d/2)(1 - 0.40)]^t} + \frac{\$1,000}{[1 + (k_d/2)(1 - 0.40)]^{20}}$$

$$\Rightarrow k_d = 2.7898 \times 2 = 5.5796\%$$

Using the BA II PLUS® financial calculator, key in the following:

Inputs: 20 N; 975 PV; 26.25 +/– PMT; 1000 +/– FV; CPT I/Y

Output: 2.7898 × 2 = 5.5796

These steps look like the following on the BA II PLUS® financial calculator.

20	CPT	975	26.25 +/–	1,000 +/–
N	I/Y	PV	PMT	FV

(press this
key last)

Thus, the adjusted after-tax cost of new debt of about 5.58 percent is larger than the unadjusted after-tax cost of 5.40 percent.

---

[5] To keep the example simple, we use straight-line amortization.

[6] As an alternative, the effective annual cost would be $(1 + 0.027898)^2 - 1 = 0.056574$ or 5.6574 percent.

Practical Financial Tip 10.2

Usually the difference between the adjusted and unadjusted costs of debt is not very large. In general, the lower the percentage flotation costs or the greater the number of years to maturity, the smaller is the impact on the cost of the debt component. Because the information needed to make the adjustment is readily available and requires little effort, managers and analysts should make this adjustment.

Preferred Stock

The **cost of preferred stock** (k_p) is the rate of return required by preferred stock investors to buy a firm's preferred stock. Preferred stock is more risky to investors than debt because a company is not required to pay preferred dividends and it is less risky than common stock because preferred stockholders take priority in dividend distribution. Because of the hybrid nature of preferred stock, its riskiness to investors and its cost to issuers fall between debt and equity. Most preferred stocks have fixed dividend payments and no stated maturity dates. Unlike interest expense on debt, preferred dividends are not deductible for tax purposes, so there is no need to make a tax adjustment. Thus, the before-tax and after-tax cost of preferred stock are the same. Because flotation costs for preferred stock can be substantial, the cost of preferred stock should reflect these costs.

Equation 10.4 (derived from Equation 5.13 in Chapter 5) states that the component cost of new preferred stock is the preferred dividend divided by the net issue price. Again, we assume that the issuer can sell the preferred stock at its par value. Since all future payments are constant, Equation 10.4 is a perpetuity model. This model only approximates the cost of preferred stock because it ignores the fact that corporations usually pay quarterly dividends. Adjusting Equation 10.4 to account for the quarterly dividend payment simply requires substituting quarterly dividends into the formula and multiplying the quarterly rate by four to get the nominal annual rate.

$$\text{Cost of New Preferred Stock} \quad k_p = \frac{D_p}{P_0(1 - F)} \tag{10.4}$$

where D_p is the annual dividend per share on preferred stock; and P_0 is the price of the preferred stock.

Now consider a preferred stock that is not perpetual but instead has a sinking fund with a final redemption date. Finding the adjusted after-tax cost of preferred stock involves the same approach as in the case of debt. This requires amortizing the flotation costs and specifying the cash flows for each period. The cost of preferred stock is the rate that equates the future stream of cash flows to the net proceeds of the issue.

Example 10.4 Estimating the Cost of New Preferred Stock

Chesapeake Company expects to sell preferred stock at its par value of $100 per share. The firm intends to pay $2 in quarterly dividends and flotation costs are 5 percent of the issue. What is the cost of new preferred stock based on an annual and a quarterly dividend payment?

Solution: The expected net proceeds from the sale are $95 = $100(1 − 0.05). Substituting D_p = $8, P_0 = $100, and F = 0.05 into Equation 10.4 yields a cost of new preferred stock of about 8.42 percent.

$$\text{Annual dividend payment } k_p = \frac{\$8}{\$100(1 - 0.05)} = 0.08421 \approx 8.42\%$$

If Chesapeake Company expects to make quarterly dividend payments of $2 per share, the adjusted cost of the preferred stock is also about 8.42 percent.[7]

$$\text{Quarterly dividend payment } k_p = \frac{\$2}{\$100(1 - 0.05)} = 0.02105 \times 4 = 0.0842 \approx 8.42\%$$

In practice, companies typically do not adjust the cost of preferred stock to a quarterly basis, even though companies pay dividends quarterly.

Why is the before-tax yield on Chesapeake's preferred stock ($8/$100 = 8 percent) lower than its before-tax yield on debt (9 percent)? In the United States, corporations own most preferred stock because a large proportion of dividends are nontaxable to them. For example, if one corporation holds less than 20 percent of another, it can exclude 70 percent of the dividend income received from income. Therefore, preferred stock usually has a lower before tax-yield than the before-tax yield on debt. However, the after-tax yield to investors and after-tax cost to the issuer are higher on preferred stock than on debt. This is consistent with the higher risk of preferred stock compared with bonds.

Types of Common Equity

The **cost of common equity** is the minimum rate or return required by investors to buy a firm's common stock. Compared to estimating the cost of bonds, estimating the cost of common equity is more difficult because common equity does not represent a contractual obligation to make specific payments. The required return is an **opportunity cost** based on returns that investors can expect from alternative investments of equal risk. Unfortunately, no direct way exists to observe these returns. Therefore, measuring the cost of common equity requires using various estimation procedures. The choice of the appropriate method depends primarily on the type of information available for a given situation.

---

[7]   As an alternative, the compounded annual cost would be $(1 + 0.02105)^4 - 1 = 0.08690 \approx 8.69$ percent.

Companies can raise common equity in two ways: (1) internally by retaining earnings and (2) externally by selling new shares. Most mature firms rely on internally generated equity and raise only a small percentage of all new corporate funds from external equity markets. Due to flotation costs, the cost of raising new equity capital in the market is more expensive than that of retaining earnings. Thus, firms typically use lower-cost retained earnings before they issue more costly new common stock.

Cost of Existing Equity

Various models are available for estimating the cost of existing equity or retained earnings. The opportunity cost of retained earnings does not differ from that of other existing equity accounts such as common stock or capital in excess of par. We focus on three models to estimate the cost of existing equity: (1) capital asset pricing model (CAPM), (2) dividend discount model (DDM), and the bond-yield-plus-risk-premium approach.[8]

Capital asset pricing model
The standard capital asset pricing model (CAPM) is the dominant model used by practitioners to estimate the cost of equity. Although we already discussed CAPM in Chapters 5 and 9, we review this simple model as it applies to estimating the cost of common equity. The cost of common equity (k_e) is the required rate of return in market equilibrium. The CAPM, as applied to the cost of equity, describes this risk-return relationship as follows:

$$k_e = R_f + \beta_i(R_m - R_f) \tag{10.5}$$

where k_e is the required rate of return on common equity; R_f is the nominal risk-free rate of return; R_m is the expected rate of return on the market; and β_i is the beta coefficient (a measure of systematic risk) of the stock.

The CAPM approach has both advantages and disadvantages. The major advantages are that CAPM explicitly adjusts for risk and applies to companies other than those with constant dividend growth. Drawbacks of the CAPM include problems associated with estimating its components and relying on past data to predict the future.

According to the CAPM, the cost of equity for a company depends on three components: (1) the risk-free rate of return (R_f), (2) the market risk premium $(R_m - R_f)$, and (3) the stock's equity beta (β_i). In theory, each component requires a forward-looking estimate. In practice, managers and analysts often use historical data as a starting point for their estimates and then make adjustments as necessary. Using the CAPM to provide a reasonable measure of a company's cost of equity requires accurately estimating all three components. Substantial disagreements exist on making these estimations.

---

[8] For a discussion of alternative methods for estimating the cost of equity such as the earning/price approach, option-based approach, and multifactor models, see Michael C. Ehrhardt, *The Search for Value: Measuring the Company's Cost of Capital*, Harvard Business School Press, 1994; and James J. McNulty, Tony D. Yeh, William S. Schulze, and Michael H. Lubatkin, "What's Your Real Cost of Capital," *Harvard Business Review*, October 2002, 114–21.

Estimating the risk-free rate (R_f) requires using a proxy because no truly risk-less asset exists. Managers and analysts generally use returns on US Treasury securities as a proxy for the risk-free rate. Common choices range between the Treasury bill (T-bill) yield and a long-term Treasury bond (T-bond) yield. Probably the best proxy for the risk-free rate is the yield on long-term Treasury bonds, such as a 10-year T-bond, because it more closely reflects the default-free holding period returns available on long-lived investments than does the T-bill. Various public sources such as *The Wall Street Journal* and the *Federal Reserve Bulletin* report returns on US Treasury securities.

In addition to estimating the risk-free rate, measuring the market risk premium $(R_m - R_f)$ requires estimating the expected return for the market portfolio (R_m). Common approaches for estimating the expected return for investments in general include using historical returns and surveys of investor expectations. Each approach results in a proxy for the market risk premium.

Using the historical average approach involves examining market data such as returns on stocks and T-bonds over long periods and computing the average historical risk premium. The average can be an arithmetic average or a geometric average (compound rate of return), which is generally lower than an arithmetic average. The arithmetic average generally provides a better estimate of the current risk premium over a shorter future interval, based on the assumption that the future resembles the past. On the other hand, the geometric average is a better predictor of the risk premium over a longer future interval. Disagreement exists over which method of averaging is more appropriate. As an alternative, surveys of the investor expectations provide forward-looking risk premiums. As a general guideline, estimated market risk premiums are generally between 3 and 6 percent. Unfortunately, there is no way to prove that a particular risk premium is correct.

Practical Financial Tip 10.3

When estimating the market risk premium for the CAPM, do not mix historical returns on stocks with the current risk-free rate. This incorrect approach mixes "apples" and "oranges." To get the market risk premium, use either the difference between the historical return on common stocks (R_m) and the historical risk-free rate (R_f) or the current expected return on common stocks and the proxy for the current expected risk-free rate.

To develop a beta forecast, managers and analysts often extrapolate from history using some form of regression analysis.[9] Using historical data and regression analysis involves two major problems. The first problem is determining the best way to capture the information contained in history. This requires making judgments on different time periods, market indexes, risk-free rates, holding periods, and estimation techniques. Each of these judgments

---

[9]   For a discussion of implementation issues that arise when using the CAPM, see Justin Petit, "Corporate Capital Costs: A Practitioner's Guide," *Journal of Applied Corporate Finance*, Spring 1999, 113–20.

can result in a different estimate of beta. The second problem is determining whether a historical beta is useful in forecasting risk. In practice, managers and analysts typically rely on various investment advisory services such as Standard & Poor's, Value Line, and Bloomberg for identifying the appropriate beta or they calculate the beta of their firm's common stock. Because these advisory services use different assumptions to perform their calculations, the beta of a company may differ depending on the source. Sometimes managers and analysts adjust historical beta to get what they view as a more accurate estimate of the "true" beta. For example, over time, betas tend to regress toward the mean, which is a beta of 1.0.

Example 10.5 Using CAPM to Estimate the Cost of Existing Equity

Suppose the stock of Chesapeake Company has a beta of 1.1 according to *Value Line*. The average rate of return on long-term government bonds was 5.5 percent, and the estimated market risk premium was 6 percent. Using the CAPM, what is the estimated cost of existing equity?

Solution: Calculating the required rate of return on the market requires adding the risk premium of 6 percent to the risk-free rate of 5.5 percent. Substituting $R_f = 5.5$, $\beta_i = 1.1$, and $R_m = 11.5$ into Equation 10.5 results in a cost of existing equity of 12.1 percent.

$$k_e = 5.5\% + 1.1(11.5\% - 5.5\%) = 12.1\%$$

Dividend discount model

Another approach for estimating the cost of existing equity is the dividend discount model (DDM). We discussed various types of DDMs in Chapter 5 such as the zero growth, constant growth, and variable growth models. For the purpose of illustration, we focus on a general case in which dividends grow perpetually at a constant growth rate (*g*). Equation 10.6 presents the formula for the constant growth DDM.

$$k_e = \frac{D_1}{P_0} + g \tag{10.6}$$

where D_1 is the dividend expected to be paid at the end of year 1, $D_0(1 + g)$; P_0 is the current market price of the firm's common stock; and *g* is the expected constant dividend growth rate.

Thus, the cost of common equity is equal to the expected dividend yield (D_1/P_0) plus the growth rate of future earnings, which for a given retention policy, also constitutes the growth rate of dividends (*g*). No need exists to make any tax adjustments because dividends are not a tax-deductible expense. In situations in which a corporation pays no dividends or has an erratic growth rate, managers and analysts must turn to other methods to estimate the cost of common equity.

Applying the constant growth DDM begins by using an observed price of the stock (P_0) and last year's dividend (D_0). The difficult task is estimating the expected growth rate (g). Several approaches are available for estimating the growth rate. Not surprisingly, these methods result in different estimates because they rely on different sources of information.

The **historical time series approach** calculates year-to-year growth rates based on a firm's past earnings or dividends per share adjusted for stock splits and stock dividends and then averages them. An obvious advantage of this approach is its simplicity. Problems can arise when using historical growth rates if the growth rate has been variable and if the growth in earnings per share does not equal the growth in dividends per share. In addition, this approach does not explicitly consider risk because it does not allow for the degree of uncertainty surrounding the estimated growth rate.

The **sustainable growth method** estimates the growth rate by forecasting the retention rate (RR), which is (1 − dividend payout ratio), and then multiplies the retention rate by the company's expected future rate of return on equity (ROE). Thus, $g = (RR)(ROE)$. Using this latter method rests on several assumptions: (1) the retention rate and return on equity remain constant, (2) the firm does not plan to issue new common stock, and (3) the degree of risk of future projects remains the same as that of the firm's existing assets. We discussed this model in Chapter 5. Because both the historical time series and sustainable growth methods rely on historical data, managers and analysts may need to adjust the historical growth rate to reflect the expected growth rate.

A final technique of finding the expected dividend growth rate uses **analysts' forecasts**. Many of these forecasts involve nonconstant growth and a range of values. Although techniques are available for converting nonconstant growth estimates into an approximate average growth rate, they are beyond the scope of this book. Numerous sources for analysts' forecasts are available on the Internet. For example, these sources include www.ThomsonFM.com, www.zachs.com, and www.valueline.com.

Example 10.6 Using the Constant Growth DDM to Estimate the Cost of Existing Equity

The common stock of Chesapeake Company is currently selling at $55 per share. The company just paid an annual dividend of $4 per share and the expected growth in dividends is 4 percent a year. Using the constant growth DDM, what is the estimate of Chesapeake's cost of existing equity?

Solution: The expected dividends after one year (D_1) is ($4.00)(1.04) = $4.16. Substituting D_1 = $4.16, P_0 = $55, and g = 0.04 into Equation 10.6 yields a cost of existing equity of 11.56 percent.

$$k_e = \frac{\$4.16}{\$55.00} + 0.04 = 0.1156 \text{ or } 11.56\%$$

Bond-yield-plus-risk-premium approach

A third approach for estimating the cost of common equity is the **bond-yield-plus-risk-premium approach**. This subjective method involves adding a risk premium to some base rate such as the Treasury bonds rate or the rate on the firm's own bonds. The base rate is a before-tax cost of debt. This approach is particularly useful for non-publicly traded companies. The risk premium is a judgmental estimate but often ranges between 3 and 5 percentage points above the base rate. This risk premium is not the same as the market risk premium using CAPM. Equity risk premiums are often unstable over time. Equation 10.7 shows the bond-yield-plus-risk-premium approach.

$$k_e = k_d + RP \tag{10.7}$$

where k_d is the before-tax rate of long-term bonds (base rate or bond yield to maturity); and RP is the risk premium.

This approach produces a "ballpark" estimate of the cost of existing equity and provides a useful check with other methods.

Example 10.7 Using the Bond-yield-plus-risk-premium Approach to Estimate the Cost of Existing Equity

Chesapeake can sell long-term bonds at par with a coupon rate of 9 percent. The financial manager expects that the firm's stockholders require a risk premium of 5 percentage points above the cost of its own bonds. What is the estimated cost of existing equity?

Solution: Substituting $k_d = 9\%$ and $RP = 5\%$ into Equation 10.7 produces a cost of existing equity of 14 percent.

$$k_e = 9\% + 5\% = 14\%$$

Comparing the approaches

The various methods used to estimate the cost of existing equity may produce different results. For example, Table 10.2 shows the estimated costs of existing equity for Chesapeake Company using three approaches.

Table 10.2 Comparison of methods of estimating the cost of existing equity

Method	Estimated cost (%)
Capital asset pricing model	12.10
Constant growth dividend discount model	11.56
Bond-yield-plus-risk-premium approach	14.00
Average	12.55

Which, if any, of these estimates should the firm use as its cost of existing equity? The answer largely depends on the appropriateness of the method for a given situation and the confidence that managers have about the inputs to the models. None of the methods is very accurate. Of these three methods, large firms tend to use the CAPM, despite its many difficulties. If a company has a stable growth in dividends, the constant growth DDM can be a helpful supplement to the CAPM. The bond-yield-plus-risk-premium approach provides a general estimate of the cost of existing equity and is particularly applicable to private companies. When substantial differences exist between the cost estimates, managers may decide that further analysis is necessary. In other circumstances, they may decide that an average of the costs derived from various estimation methods suffices as a proxy. Ultimately, the financial manager must exercise judgment in deciding on the appropriate estimate for the cost of existing equity.

Focus on Practice 10.1

Cost of Capital

Graham and Harvey surveyed chief financial officers representing a wide variety of firms and industries about cost of capital practices. Some of their key results follow.

- The most popular method of estimating the cost of equity capital is the CAPM, followed by average stock returns, and a multi-factor CAPM.
- Few firms use a dividend discount model to back out the cost of equity.
- Large firms are much more likely than small firms to use the CAPM.
- Public firms are more likely than private firms to use the CAPM.

Source: John Graham and Campbell Harvey, "How Do CFOs Make Capital Budgeting and Capital Structure Decisions?" *Journal of Applied Corporate Finance*, Spring 2002, 8–23.

Cost of new common equity

The cost of new common stock (k_s) is somewhat higher than the cost of existing equity (k_e) due to flotation costs. The exact differential depends on the magnitude of the flotation costs. If a firm pays out all earnings in the form of dividends, the impact of flotation costs increases because the firm must raise external capital to fund profitable investment opportunities. If, however, a firm retains some earnings to finance operations and to provide for future growth, the impact of flotation costs decreases because the firm needs to raise less external capital.

Finding the cost of new common stock requires adjusting the cost of existing equity to account for flotation costs. Equation 10.8 includes flotation costs as part of the constant growth DDM.

$$k_e = \frac{D_1}{P_0(1 - F)} + g \qquad (10.8)$$

Example 10.8 Using the Constant Growth DDM to Estimate the Cost of New Common Equity

Suppose Chesapeake Company can issue stock for $55 per share before flotation costs of 7 percent of the issue proceeds. The first annual dividend will be $4.16 per share, and the expected annual growth in dividends is 4 percent. Using the constant growth DDM, what is the estimated cost of new equity with flotation costs?

Solution: Substituting $D_1 = \$4.16$, $P_0 = \$55$, $F = 0.07$, and $g = 0.04$ into Equation 10.8 yields an estimated cost of new equity of 12.13 percent.

$$k_e = \frac{\$4.16}{\$55.00(1 - 0.07)} + 0.04 = 0.12133 \text{ or } 12.13\%$$

Using the constant growth DDM, the cost of new equity (12.13 percent) is more costly than the cost of existing equity (11.56 percent) by about 0.57 percentage points. This difference is the **flotation adjustment factor**. Managers and analysts sometimes add this adjustment factor to the results obtained from the CAPM or bond-yield-plus-risk-premium method to estimate the after-tax cost of new equity. The most obvious weakness in this procedure is the use of an estimated growth rate in the constant growth DDM. Adding the adjustment factor (0.57 percentage points) to the average of the three methods (12.55 percent) would result in a cost of new equity of 13.12 percent.

Practical Financial Tip 10.4

Estimating the cost of capital is not an exact science, especially when involving the cost of equity. The decisions made about the inputs for various models can make a substantial difference in the estimate of the cost of a capital component. Because of the many choices available, we recommend finding a range of likely values and using this range to do sensitivity analysis when examining capital budgeting projects.

Concept Check 10.9

1   Why does the impact of a given flotation cost on the specific cost of bonds depend on the maturity of the debt?
2   Why is estimating the cost of common equity more difficult than estimating the cost of debt or preferred stock?
3   What are the advantages and disadvantages of the three methods used to estimate the cost of existing equity?
4   What are three approaches for estimating the growth rate of dividends for the dividend discount model? What are their advantages and disadvantages?
5   What effect do flotation costs have on the cost of capital components?

10.10 Weighted Average Cost of Capital

Once the manager or analyst has estimated the cost of capital components, the next step in calculating the weighted average cost of capital is to determine the appropriate weights. The **weighted average cost of capital** (WACC) is the firm's overall cost of capital. WACC represents the risks associated with the firm's "typical" or average project. Equation 10.9 provides a general formula for calculating WACC.

$$WACC = \sum_{i=1}^{n} w_i k_i \qquad (10.9)$$

where w_i is the percentage of total permanent capital represented by capital source i; k_i is the after-tax cost of each new capital component; and n is the number of types of new capital.

The sum of the weights of the capital components must equal 1.0 because WACC includes all sources of permanent financing in the firm's capital structure. Three common weighting schemes are available to compute WACC: book value weights, market value weights, and target weights.

Book Value Weights

Book value weights measure the proportion of each type of capital in a firm's capital structure based on accounting values shown on the firm's balance sheet. Calculating the book weights involves dividing the book value of a specific component by the total book value of all components. Although some advocate computing the total book value using total liabilities and shareholders' equity, we do not recommend this approach. Current liabilities, such as accounts payable and accruals, result from operating relationships with suppliers and employees. As such, these funds do not come from investors. We recommend using only permanent sources of capital in calculating book value weights. This approach excludes current liabilities such as accounts payable, accruals, and short-term debt because the firm typically does not use these as a source of permanent financing.

Book values represent historical costs. Consequently, book weights remain relatively stable over time because they do not depend on the changing market value of debt and equity. Using book values to estimate the weights for WACC may be tempting, but it can lead to substantial mistakes by misstating the WACC. This situation occurs because the book value for some sources of financing often bears little relationship with the market value. For example, the book and market values of equity can differ markedly. Thus, using book values could seriously bias the estimate of the WACC. In addition, changes in interest rates will cause the market value of long-term debt to differ from its book value. Therefore, historical accounting costs are simply irrelevant and do not provide a cost of capital that is useful for evaluating a proposed project. Nonetheless, some firms still use book values as the basis for calculating book weights to estimate the WACC, based on what they view as practical considerations.

Market Value Weights

Market value weights measure the actual proportion of each type of funds in the firm's capital structure at current market prices. Calculating the market value of the firm's equity involves multiplying the price per share by the number of shares outstanding. A similar procedure exists for long-term debt – multiplying the market price of a single bond by the number of bonds outstanding. If a firm has multiple bond issues, the analyst repeats this process for each issue and sums the results. For short-term debt, the book values and market values are likely to be similar, so book values often serve as reasonable estimates.

Compared with book value weights, market value weights are superior because they represent "true" value, if markets are efficient. An **efficient capital market** is one in which the current price of a security fully reflects all the information currently available about that security. Market value weights provide current estimates for the required rates of return of the firm's suppliers of capital. If a firm is operating at its target or optimal capital structure, the preferred approach is to use the market values of the debt and equity. A drawback of using market value weights is that market prices change frequently. In practice, firms do not recalculate their cost of capital every time the market price of the securities changes because this would be impractical. Instead, they often identify an average market price or trend.

Target Value Weights

Target value weights represent the weights based on the firm's target or optimal capital structure. Target weights and actual weights often differ due to changes in the business environment that can affect the firm's debt and equity differently. Target weights represent the best estimate of how the firm, on average, will raise money in the future. If a firm is not currently operating at its target capital structure but is moving toward it, using target weights makes sense.

Practical Financial Tip 10.5

Market value provides the only conceptually correct method for estimating the weighted average cost of capital even if the firm does not plan to issue new debt or equity. Yet, an issue exists of whether using weights based on the actual market values of debt and equity or using weights based on the target market capital structure is more appropriate. If a company is moving toward its optimal capital structure, the theoretically preferred approach is to use target weights based on market values. Using these weights should simultaneously maximize the stock price and minimize the cost of capital.

Example 10.9 The Weighted Average Cost of Capital

Managers at Chesapeake Company consider its current capital structure of 40 percent long-term debt, 10 percent preferred stock, and 50 percent common equity as optimal. The after-tax cost in these three categories is 5.58 percent, 8.42 percent, and 12.55 percent, respectively. The firm wants to maintain this target capital structure in raising future capital. Managers expect to have enough retained earnings so that the firm can use the cost of retained earnings as the common equity cost component. If Chesapeake Company raises new capital in target proportions, what is the firm's WACC?

Solution: Substituting the given weights and components costs into Equation 10.9 yields a WACC of about 9.35 percent.

$$WACC = 0.40(5.58\%) + 0.10(8.42\%) + 0.50(12.55\%) = 9.35\%$$

Focus on Practice 10.2

Best Practices in Estimating Cost of Capital

Bruner, Eads, Harris, and Higgins sought to identify the "best practice" in cost-of-capital estimation by interviewing managers at leading corporations and financial advisors. The following elements represent the best current practice in the estimation of WACC. Corporate managers should:

- base weights on market, not book value mixes of debt and equity;
- estimate the after-tax cost of debt from marginal pretax costs, combined with marginal or statutory tax rates;
- use CAPM to estimate the cost of equity;
- obtain betas from published sources using a long interval of equity returns, but apply judgment to estimate a beta;
- match the risk-free rate to the tenor of the cash flows being valued;
- use an equity market risk premium of 6 percent or lower;
- monitor for changes in WACC keyed to major changes in financial market conditions;
- risk-adjust WACC to reflect substantive differences among different businesses in a corporation.

Source: Robert F. Bruner, Kenneth M. Eades, Robert S. Harris, and Robert C. Higgins, "Best Practices in Estimating the Cost of Capital: Survey and Synthesis," *Financial Practice and Education*, Spring/Summer 1998, 13–28.

Concept Check 10.10

1 What are the steps in calculating the weighted average cost of capital?
2 What are three types of weights available to calculate the weighted average cost of capital?
3 Which type of weight is most appropriate? Why?

10.11 Marginal Cost of Capital

The **marginal cost of capital** (MCC) is the last dollar of new capital that the firm raises. If a firm uses more than one type of new financing, the MCC represents a weighted average cost of the last dollar of capital raised, reflecting higher marginal costs. Thus, the MCC represents the rate of return that a firm must earn on new investments to satisfy investors. A firm's weighted average cost of capital (WACC) equals its MCC until the cost of a capital component increases. For example, suppose a firm must issue new common stock after exhausting retained earnings as the equity portion of its capital structure to finance investment opportunities. The MCC will increase because flotation costs cause the cost of new equity to be higher than the cost of retained earnings. The graph showing how WACC changes as the volume of new financing increases during a given period is called the **marginal cost of capital schedule**.

Developing the MCC schedule involves five steps.

1 *Determine the appropriate weights of the new financing.*
2 *Calculate the component cost of capital associated with each amount of capital raised.* Externally raised capital has flotation costs, which increase the cost of capital. Investors may perceive large capital budgets as being risky, which drives up the cost of capital.
3 *Calculate the range of total new financing at which the cost of the new components change.* A **break point** (*BP*) is the total financing that a firm can raise before a specific cost of capital increases. The MCC schedule may contain several break points. Equation 10.10 is the formula for calculating the break point for each financing source.[10]

$$BP_i = \frac{TF_i}{w_i} \tag{10.10}$$

where BP_i is the break point for capital component i; TF_i is the total amount of funds available from capital component i; and w_i is the percentage of total permanent capital represented by capital component i. This formula shows that finding each break point

---

[10] If a firm has depreciation-generated funds, each break point will increase by the amount of depreciation, which in turn moves the MCC schedule to the right.

involves dividing the total amount of funds available for a particular capital component at a stated cost by its capital structure weight.

4 *Calculate the MCC for each range of total new financing.*
5 *Plot the MCC schedule.*

Example 10.10 MCC Schedule

Chesapeake Company has expected earnings of $8 a share and an expected dividend of $4 per share. If the firm has 1 million shares outstanding, it will add $4 million to its retained earnings. Table 10.3 shows the amount of funds that Chesapeake Company can raise at different costs.

Table 10.3 Marginal cost of capital for Chesapeake Company

Capital component	Target weight (%)	Range of financing (in millions)	Component cost (%)
Long-term debt (bonds)	40	Up to $4	5.58
		$4 up to $8	6.00
Preferred stock	10	Up to $1	8.42
		$1 up to $2	9.00
Common equity	50	Up to $4	12.55
		$4 up to $10	13.12

What is the MCC schedule for Chesapeake Company?

Solution: Table 10.3 provides the information needed for Steps 1 and 2. Step 3 involves calculating the break points for each capital component and the range of total new financing. Table 10.4 shows these calculations. For example, the firm can raise up to $8 million before it uses up all new retained earnings as the equity portion of its

Table 10.4 Breakpoints and range of total new financing for Chesapeake Company

Capital component	Range of new financing (in millions)	Specific cost (%)	Break point (in millions)	Range of total new financing (in millions)
Long-term debt	Up to $4	5.58	$4/0.40 = $10	Up to $10
	$4 up to $8	6.50	$8/0.40 = $20	Up to $20
Preferred stock	Up to $1	8.42	$1/0.10 = $10	Up to $10
	$1 up to $2	9.50	$2/0.10 = $20	Up to $20
Common equity	Up to $4	12.55	$4/0.50 = $8	Up to $8
	$4 up to $10	13.12	$10/0.50 = $20	Up to $20

target capital structure and has to sell new, higher-cost common stock. Once the firm goes beyond $8 million, its MCC increases because of the higher cost associated with new common stock. Up to the first break point of $8 million, the MCC is equal to the WACC. The firm must calculate new MCCs if the cost of any capital components changes.

Step 4 involves calculating the MCC over the ranges of total new financing between break points. Table 10.5 shows the MCC for each range of total new financing.

Table 10.5 MCC for Chesapeake Company

Range of total new financing (in millions)	Marginal cost of capital
Up to $8	$MCC_1 = 0.40(5.58) + 0.10(8.42\%) + 0.50(12.55\%) = 9.35\%$
$8 to $10	$MCC_2 = 0.40(5.58) + 0.10(8.42\%) + 0.50(13.12\%) = 9.63\%$
$10 to $20	$MCC_3 = 0.40(6.50) + 0.10(9.50\%) + 0.50(13.12\%) = 10.11\%$

Step 5 involves plotting the MCC schedule as shown in Figure 10.3.

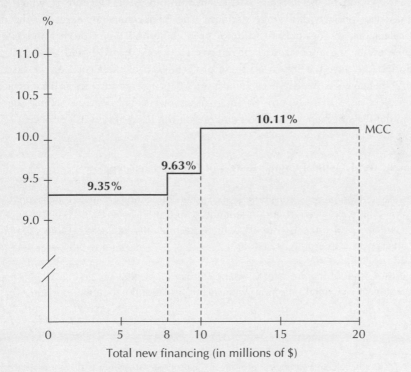

Figure 10.3 MCC schedule for Chesapeake Company

Optimal Capital Budget

The firm can use the MCC schedule in conjunction with its available investment opportunities to select acceptable capital budgeting projects. The firm places its capital budgeting projects in an **investment opportunity schedule** (IOS) in descending order according to each project's internal rate of return (IRR). If the firm has mutually exclusive projects, it has multiple investment opportunity schedules, one for each different combination of projects. By combining its IOS and MCC schedule, managers can determine the firm's optimal capital budget and cost of capital to evaluate average-risk capital budgeting projects. The firm's level of financing and investing will be optimal if the firm uses its MCC as the criterion for evaluating average-risk projects.

The **optimal capital budget** is the level of capital investment that maximizes the value of the firm. This level occurs when a firm's investment opportunity schedule (IOS) intersects its marginal cost of capital (MCC) schedule. This point is the **intersection rate**. A classic principle underlying microeconomics is that a firm should expand to the point where its marginal revenue equals its marginal cost. In the context of capital budgeting, the firm should accept all projects with rates of return above its MCC, but should reject those projects with rates of return below its MCC.[11] In practice, firms often do not choose the optimal capital budget because of capital rationing. We discussed capital rationing in Chapter 8.

The intersection of the IOS and MCC schedule represents the rate at which the firm should discount projects of average riskiness. The intersection rate serves as the discount rate in calculating the net present value or profitability index of a project and as a hurdle rate when evaluating internal rates of returns. In theory, firms should accept all positive NPV projects because the return on these projects exceeds their cost. As we discussed in Chapter 9, managers and analysts can adjust the MCC upward (downward) for projects that are more (less) risky than the firm's average-risk projects. They can also adjust the IOS, by lowering the IRRs of high-risk projects and raising the IRRs of low-risk projects.

Example 10.11 Optimal Capital Budget of Chesapeake Company

Chesapeake Company is considering six capital budgeting projects for the next year. All projects are average risk and independent, except Projects B and B*. The firm does not plan to repeat Projects B or B*, which are mutually exclusive. Table 10.6 shows the investment opportunity schedule.

What MCC should managers at Chesapeake use for capital budgeting? If Chesapeake is not subject to capital rationing, what is the firm's optimal capital budget?

---

[11] If the MCC schedule cuts through a project, the appropriate procedure is to determine the project's average cost of capital; accept the project if the IRR exceeds its average cost of capital over the interval of the project.

Table 10.6 Investment opportunity schedule of Chesapeake Company

Project	Cost ($)	Annual year-end cash flows ($)	Life	IRR (%)
A	6,000,000	1,442,162	7	15
B	3,000,000	1,270,566	3	13
B*	3,000,000	729,677	6	12
C	5,000,000	1,611,632	4	11
D	4,000,000	1,028,370	5	9
E	1,000,000	560,769	2	8

Solution: Figure 10.4 shows the IOS and MCC schedule of Chesapeake Company. The IOS plots projects in descending order of IRR and consists of two potential schedules: one with A, B, C, D, and E and another with A, B*, C, D, and E. The IOS and MCC schedule intersect at 10.11 percent, which represents the discount rate that the firm should use for average-risk capital investments.

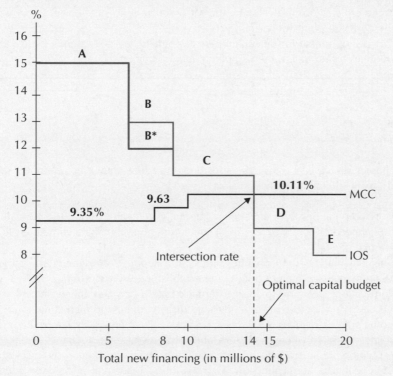

Figure 10.4 IOS and MCC schedule for Chesapeake Company

Since all projects have average risk, Chesapeake should use 10.11 percent as the discount or hurdle rate. As we discussed in Chapter 8, IRR and NPV lead to the same decisions for independent projects. Thus, the firm should accept all independent projects with IRRs above 10.11 percent. Thus, Chesapeake should accept Projects A and C, either B or B*, and reject D and E. NPV and IRR may conflict for mutually exclusive projects. Using the NPV method is better than IRR in choosing between B and B*. Here, no need exists to use the replacement chain or equivalent annual annuity methods because the firm does not plan to repeat B or B*. Therefore, managers can rely upon the NPV method in making their choice. Because NPV_{B^*} of $167,715 is greater than NPV_B of $153,601, the firm should choose Project B* over B. The optimal capital budget is $14 million, which consists of $6 million for Project A, $3 million for Project B*, and $5 million for Project C.

Concept Check 10.11

1 How does the marginal cost of capital differ from the weighted average cost of capital?
2 What are the steps in developing the MCC schedule?
3 Why do break points occur in the MCC schedule?
4 What is the formula for calculating break points?
5 How does a firm determine its optimal capital budget?

Summary

This chapter discussed how firms raise funds and how they calculate their cost of capital. We list below the key concepts covered.

1 Most corporations cannot rely on internally generated funds to meet all their capital needs. Therefore, they must sometimes go to the financial markets to raise external capital.
2 Financial markets help channel funds from suppliers to demanders, provide a resale market, set market prices, and establish rates of return.
3 Corporations deciding to raise external capital often use an investment banker whose major services include advising, underwriting, and marketing.
4 Going public broadens the firm's access to capital markets, increases the liquidity of its stock, sets a value for the firm, and increases its ability to attract management. Yet, going public leads to dilution of control, high reporting costs, disclosure of additional data about the firm, and possibly a low stock price due to inactive trading.

5 Once a firm goes public, it has many ways of raising additional long-term funds. For example, the firm may raise funds through public offerings and private placements.
   - If the firm selects a public offering, it faces the additional choice of using a general cash offer or a rights offering.
   - Other choices include deciding between a competitive bid and a negotiated offering, a best efforts arrangement and a firm commitment underwriting, and a traditional registration and a shelf registration.

6 The cost of capital is the rate that the firm has to pay, explicitly or implicitly, to investors for their capital or the minimum rate of return required by the suppliers of capital. For capital budgeting purposes, the cost of capital is a weighted average of the capital components used by the firm.

7 Compared to estimating the cost of equity, calculating the component cost of debt and preferred stock is relatively straightforward.

8 All relevant component costs are marginal, after-tax costs that include flotation costs.

9 Three methods used to estimate the cost of existing equity are: (1) the CAPM approach, (2) the dividend discount model, and (3) the bond-yield-plus-risk-premium approach.

10 Three types of weights used to calculate the weighted average cost of capital (WACC) are book value weights, market value weights, and target weights.
   - If a firm is operating at its target or optimal capital structure, the preferred approach is to use the market values of the debt and equity.
   - If a firm is not currently operating at its target capital structure but is moving toward it, the firm should use the target weights to calculate the WACC.

11 The intersection of a firm's investment opportunity schedule (IOS) and marginal cost of capital (MCC) schedule indicates the rate used to discount projects of average riskiness.

FURTHER READING

Amihud, Yakov. "The Liquidity Route to a Lower Cost of Capital," *Journal of Applied Corporate Finance* 12, Winter 2000, 8–25.

Booth, Lawrence. "Estimating the Equity Risk Premium and Equity Costs: New Ways of Looking at Old Data," *Journal of Applied Corporate Finance* 12, Spring 1999, 100–12.

Brigham, Eugene F. and Louis C. Gapenski. "Flotation Cost Adjustments," *Financial Practice and Education* 1, Fall/Winter 1991, 29–34.

Ehrhardt, Michael C. *The Search for Value: Measuring the Company's Cost of Capital*, Harvard Business School Press, 1994.

Fama, Eugene F. and Kenneth R. French. "The Corporate Cost of Capital and the Return on Corporate Investment," *Journal of Finance* 54 (December 1999), 1939–67.

Greenbaum, Staurt I. and Anjan V. Thakor. *Contemporary Financial Intermediation*, Dryden Press, 1995.

Harris, Robert S. and Felicia C. Marston. "Estimating Shareholder Risk Premia Using Analysts' Growth Forecasts," *Financial Management* 21, Summer 1992, 63–70.

Harris, Robert S., Thomas J. O'Brien, and Doug Wakeman. "Divisional Cost-of-Capital Estimation for Multi-Industry Firms," *Financial Management* 18, Summer 1989, 74–84.

Keck, Tom, Eric Levengood, and Al Longfield. "Using Discounted Cash Flow Analysis in an International Setting: A Survey of Issues in Modeling the Cost of Capital," *Journal of Applied Corporate Finance* 11, Fall 1998, 82–88.

Kidwell, David S., Richard Peterson, and David Blackwell. *Financial Institutions, Markets, and Money*. John Wiley & Sons, 2003.

Livingston, Miles. *Money and Capital Markets*. Blackwell, 1996.

O'Brien, Thomas J. "The Global CAPM and a Firm's Cost of Capital in Different Currencies," *Journal of Applied Corporate Finance* 12, Fall 1999, 73–79.

Pettit, Justin. "Corporate Capital Costs: A Practitioner's Guide," *Journal of Applied Corporate Finance* 12, Spring 1999, 113–20.

Schramm, Ronald M. and Henry N. Wang. "Measuring the Cost of Capital in an International CAPM Framework," *Journal of Applied Corporate Finance* 12, Fall 1999, 63–72.

Stultz, René M. "Globalization, Corporate Finance, and the Cost of Capital," *Journal of Applied Corporate Finance* 12, Fall 1999, 8–25.

Taggart, Robert A., Jr. "Allocating Capital among a Firm's Divisions: Hurdle Rates vs. Budgets," *Journal of Financial Research* 10, Fall 1987, 177–89.

Weaver, Samuel C., Peter J. Clemmens III, Jack A. Gunn, and Bruce D. Dannenburg. "Divisional Hurdle Rates and the Cost of Capital," *Financial Management* 18, Spring 1989, 18–25.

Chapter 11

Capital Structure

A perennial debate in corporate finance concerns the question of optimal capital structure: Given a level of total capital necessary to support a company's activities, is there a way of dividing up that capital into debt and equity that maximizes current firm value? And if so, what are the critical factors in setting the leverage ratio for a given company? (Michael J. Barclay and Clifford W. Smith, Jr, "The Capital Structure Puzzle: Another Look at the Evidence," *Journal of Applied Corporate Finance* 12, Spring 1999, p. 8.)

Overview

This chapter investigates a firm's capital structure decision. Capital structure refers to the sources of long-term financing employed by the firm. Although a firm may use various long-term securities in its financing mix, we focus on the debt-equity financing mix. We illustrate how a firm may use financial leverage to increase the expected returns to shareholders while increasing risk for the shareholders. We also discuss the Modigliani–Miller theorem of capital structure irrelevance for a firm when there are no taxes or other market frictions. We then show how taxes and certain market frictions may make a firm's capital structure decision relevant in the real world.

Learning Objectives

After completing this chapter, you should be able to:

- define what is meant by the terms financial leverage and capital structure;
- describe the concept of financial risk and the effects that financial leverage has on earnings per share and return on equity;
- explain how tax incentives and other factors may create incentives for a firm to increase the use of debt financing in its capital structure;
- understand how the costs of financial distress may cause a firm to limit its use of debt financing;
- discuss the pecking order explanation for a firm's financing choices;
- explain how different stakeholders of a firm may influence a firm's financing choices;
- recognize how the stock market typically reacts to new debt and equity issuances.

11.1 The Financing Mix

In this chapter we examine the capital structure decision, which involves determining a firm's financing mix. **Capital structure** is the mix of long-term sources of funds used by the firm. The capital structures of many firms today are complex, consisting of some combination of debt, preferred stock, common stock, leases, warrants, convertible bonds, and convertible preferred stock. We focus on the financing choice between debt and equity because they are the major sources of financing for most firms.

Financial managers need to know how their capital structure decision affects the value of their firms. They are particularly interested in whether an optimal capital structure exists for their firm. An **optimal capital structure** is the financing mix that maximizes the value of the firm. We examine whether managers can maximize the value of their firm by choosing a particular capital structure. The search for optimal capital structure is ongoing. Research has led to mixed views. Some believe that while managers can theoretically determine a firm's optimal capital structure, they cannot determine the precise percentage of debt that will maximize the market value of the firm. Others believe that a firm's value does not depend on its financing mix (and that an optimal capital structure does not exist) or that firms do not strive to attain an optimal financing mix. In either case, managers must use informed judgment to set a desired or target capital structure.

Capital Structure of US Firms

The amount of debt financing by US firms varies considerably. Table 11.1 reports the debt ratio (computed as total long-term debt to total capital) for a sample of US firms.

Table 11.1 Recent debt ratios for various US firms

Firm	Debt to total capital (%)	Firm	Debt to total capital (%)
Microsoft	0.0	Lowe's	35.9
Intel	2.8	K Mart	37.5
Home Depot	6.5	IBM	40.3
Apple Computers	7.5	AT&T	45.0
Johnson & Johnson	8.4	Verizon Communications	45.5
Exxon Mobil Corp	8.5	Commonwealth Edison	54.9
Dell Computer Corp.	9.9	Bank of America	58.4
Pfizer	12.5	American Airlines	59.1
Merck	18.7	Polaroid	60.5
Hewlett Packard	21.1	Citicorp	66.4
Wal-Mart	34.0	Sears Roebuck and Co.	75.6
SBC Communications Inc.	34.5	Nextel Communications	90.6

Source: Standard & Poor's Compustat Research Insight for the fiscal year ending in 2000.

Some of the differences in the debt ratios of the firms in Table 11.1 are surprising. Even among apparently similar firms, debt ratios vary widely. For example, look at some of the firms from the computer/software industry: Microsoft, Intel, Apple Computers, and Dell Computer have debt ratios of 10 percent or less. Industry leader Microsoft has no debt. Yet, Hewlett-Packard and IBM rely more heavily on debt financing with debt ratios of 21.1 percent and 40.3 percent, respectively. Even more divergent are the retail firms in our sample. Home Depot is only slightly leveraged with a debt ratio of 6.5 percent while its closest competitor, Lowe's, has a debt ratio of 35.9 percent. On the far extreme is Sears Roebuck with a debt ratio of 75.6 percent. While the computer firms appear to be only modestly leveraged, the communications firms rely much more on debt financing: SBC Communications, AT&T, Verizon Communications, and Nextel Communications have debt ratios ranging from 34.5 percent to 90.6 percent.

Why do these capital structures vary so markedly across different industries? Why would apparently similar firms within the same industry take such different approaches in their use of financial leverage? Does an optimal capital structure exist that these firms are seeking to employ? We address these questions and others in this chapter.

We begin our analysis by discussing financial risk in the next section. Before addressing how employing financial leverage may affect firm value, we need to understand how it affects the earnings per share (EPS) and return on equity (ROE) for the shareholders of a firm. We then proceed to the famous Modigliani–Miller theorems for capital structure.

Concept Check 11.1

1 What is meant by the term capital structure?
2 Do US firms in the same industries tend to have similar or widely divergent capital structures?

11.2 Understanding Financial Risk

Investing in a firm's common stock involves risk. A firm's earnings before interest and taxes (EBIT), also called operating income, often varies substantially as the general economy expands and contracts. The volatility of operating income, caused by the nature of the firm's business, refers to **business risk**. Many factors influence a firm's business risk, including the uncertainty of demand, uncertainty of output prices and input costs, competitive factors, and product and other types of liability. Because business risk focuses on operating income, it ignores financing effects. Some firms, such as automobile manufacturers and other durable goods producers, have high levels of business risk because they have sales that are highly correlated with the business cycle. Firms in the grocery retail industry, on the other hand, typically have sales that are much less sensitive to the business cycle and have lower levels of business risk.

When firms borrow, they incur an additional risk, referred to as **financial risk**, which further increases the risk to the investors of the firm. Financial risk has two components.

- Borrowing increases the risk of default for a firm. Interest and principal payments on debt are legal obligations for the firm. Failure to meet these payments in a timely manner may lead to default and eventual bankruptcy for the firm.
- The interest and principal payments associated with borrowing increase the volatility of a firm's earnings per share and its return on equity.

Managers sometimes overlook this latter aspect of financial risk. Because the returns to the shareholders are more volatile when firms use debt financing, the common shareholders require a higher rate of return as compensation for this increased financial risk component. Thus, while business risk refers to the volatility of a firm's operating earnings due to the nature of the firm's business, financial risk refers to the additional volatility that is translated from the operating earnings to the firm's EPS and ROE due to the fixed interest expenses associated with financial leverage. We discuss the latter aspect of financial risk in the following illustration.

Illustration of Financial Risk

Consider a firm that has $10 billion of assets that are financed entirely with equity. The firm has 200 million shares of equity that sell for $50 per share. The firm's balance sheet, in market value terms, is depicted below:

Market Value Balance Sheet
All equity financing

Assets	$10 billion	$10 billion	Equity

Analysts at the firm estimate that the firm's operating earnings (EBIT) next year will be $1.5 billion. However, sales of the firm's products are highly sensitive to the economic business cycle (the firm has a high degree of business risk), and these analysts predict that EBIT could be as low as $0.5 billion or as high as $2.5 billion depending on the strength of the economy. Assume the firm has a 40 percent marginal tax rate.

Panel A of Table 11.2 shows how the firm's net income, EPS, and ROE would vary as EBIT varies from $0.5 billion to $1.5 billion to $2.5 billion. Note that, without any interest expenses, the volatility of EPS and ROE is the same as the volatility of the firm's EBIT:

- As EBIT triples from $0.5 billion to $1.5 billion, EPS triples from $1.50 to $4.50 and ROE from 3.0 percent to 9.0 percent.
- As EBIT increases fivefold from $0.5 billion to $2.5 billion, EPS increases fivefold from $1.50 to $7.50 and ROE increases fivefold from 3.0 percent to 15.0 percent.

Now let's assume the firm finances its $10 billion in assets by using equal amounts of debt and equity. The debt carries a fixed interest rate of 8.0 percent, and the firm now incurs an interest expense of $400 million annually. The firm now has 100 million shares of equity (half as many as before) that are currently selling for $50 per share. The firm's new market value balance sheet is depicted below.

Market Value Balance Sheet
Financed with equal amounts of debt and equity

Assets	$10 billion	Debt	$5 billion
		Equity	$5 billion

Assume again that EBIT levels vary from $0.5 billion to $1.5 billion to $2.5 billion. The income statements and the resulting EPS and ROE values are shown in Panel B of Table 11.2.

Table 11.2 Variability of EPS and ROE as a function of EBIT

	Scenario		
	Low	Moderate	High
Panel A: Firm financed with 100% equity		(in million $)	
EBIT	500	1,500	2,500
Interest expense	0	0	0
EBT	500	1,500	2,500
Taxes	200	600	1,000
Net income	300	900	1,500
Earnings per share (EPS)	$1.50	$4.50	$7.50
Return on equity (ROE)	3.0%	9.0%	15.0%
Panel B: Firm financed with 50% debt and 50% equity			
EBIT	500	1,500	2,500
Interest expense	400	400	400
EBT	100	1,100	2,100
Taxes	40	440	840
Net income	60	660	1,260
Earnings per share (EPS)	$0.60	$6.60	$12.60
Return on equity (ROE)	1.2%	13.2%	25.2%

We can see the effects of debt financing in the levels and variations in EPS and ROE. Note that at the higher levels of operating earnings, when EBIT is either $1.5 billion or $2.5 billion, the resulting EPS and ROE are higher when the firm uses debt financing than when it is all equity financed. But when EBIT assumes the lower value of $0.5 billion, the EPS and ROE fall below the levels obtained when the firm uses only equity to finance its operations.

Figure 11.1 shows the relationship between ROE and EBIT for both capital structure alternatives. The volatility of ROE is greater when EBIT varies as the firm employs debt financing. While not shown in Figure 11.1, increasing levels of debt financing would increase the variability of ROE as a function of EBIT.

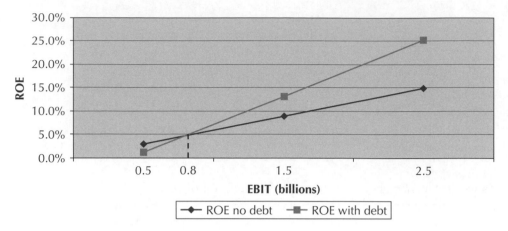

Figure 11.1 ROE versus EBIT for alternative capital structures

Based on the results in Figure 11.1, which capital structure should the firm use? As long as EBIT is greater than $800 million, the ROE (and EPS) will be higher when the firm finances with both debt and equity.[1] Would the higher level of ROE and EPS lead to a higher share price and maximize the wealth of the firm's shareholders? Not necessarily. While the firm's ROE and EPS are higher for EBIT levels above $800 million when the firm uses debt financing, the volatility of ROE and EPS to changes in EBIT is also greater! The firm has greater financial risk. We cannot tell from this analysis whether the higher ROE and EPS are commensurate with the increase in risk faced by the shareholders and would lead to a higher share price.

To summarize what we have learned to this point, financial risk has two components:

- Financial leverage increases the variability of earnings available to the common stock-holders because the interest payments often represent a fixed cost that the firm must pay. Earnings available to common stockholders represent a residual amount after the firm pays interest and taxes.
- Financial leverage increases the probability of bankruptcy because the operating earnings (EBIT) must be sufficient to meet the interest payments to the bondholders. Otherwise, the firm is in default on the debt and may have to declare bankruptcy.

Thus, investors are subject to both business risk and financial risk when they invest in the equity securities of firms that employ debt financing. The variability of returns to the stockholders (variability of EPS and ROE) is due to both the firm's business risk and financial risk. The variability of the firm's EPS and ROE caused by business risk is the variability of the firm's operating earnings, EBIT. The additional volatility in EPS and ROE is the financial risk attributed to using debt financing.

---

[1] The general rule is that as long as the return on assets exceeds the firm's after-tax cost of the debt, employing financial leverage will increase the EPS and ROE for the firm's stockholders.

Can we draw a conclusion as to which capital structure is better for the firm? As long as EBIT is greater than $800 million, the levered capital structure appears better for the firm because it results in a higher level of earnings per share and return on equity. This conclusion, however, may be incorrect. A higher level of risk accompanies the higher level of earnings and profitability, as the earnings are now more volatile. Unless we know the tradeoff between the risk and the extra return required by investors, we cannot say which capital structure is better. Only when we include both the risk and return aspects of financial leverage can we begin to understand the effect that financial leverage has on the value of a firm.

Practical Financial Tip 11.1

Firms incur financial risk when they borrow. Issuing debt with fixed interest payments will increase the volatility of the firm's earnings per share and return on equity. Managers can prepare ROE-EPS graphs to analyze the tradeoff between the higher expected return on equity (ROE) from debt financing and the increased ROE volatility.

Concept Check 11.2

1   What do the terms "business risk" and "financial risk" mean?
2   What effect does financial leverage have on the expected level and the variability of a firm's EPS and ROE?

11.3 Capital Structure and the Value of the Firm

Understanding the effects that financial leverage has on a firm's earnings per share and its return on equity is important. Yet, even more important to a financial manager is understanding the effect that financial leverage has on the value of a firm. Financial economists widely accept the premise that the managers should make decisions that maximize the value of the firm's common equity. By maximizing shareholder wealth, managers are serving the interests of the firm's owners. Under most circumstances, the premise of maximizing total firm value (debt and equity) is also consistent with maximizing shareholder wealth.

Franco Modigliani and Merton Miller (M&M) pioneered the research efforts relating capital structure and the value of a firm. Both have won the Nobel prize in economics for their life-time work in the area. In a seminal article, M&M show that in a world of perfect (or frictionless) capital markets with no corporate or personal taxes, *the value of a firm is independent of its capital structure.*[2] We discuss these important findings in the next section.

---

[2]   Franco Modigliani and Merton H. Miller, "The Cost of Capital, Corporate Finance, and the Theory of Investment," *American Economic Review*, June 1958, 251–97.

The Modigliani–Miller Theorem

The Modigliani and Miller (M&M) theorem states that in the absence of corporate and personal taxes, transaction costs, and other market imperfections, *the value of a firm is independent of its capital structure*. In other words, managers cannot alter the value of their firms by the capital structures that they choose. M&M argue that under a highly restrictive set of assumptions the value of the firm is determined solely by the size and the riskiness of the real cash flows generated by the firm's assets, and not by how these cash flows are divided between the debt and equity stakeholders of the firm. If managers want to increase the value of their firms, they should invest in real assets whose cash flows are sufficient to provide returns to shareholders in excess of their required returns.

One way to illustrate the M&M theorem is by showing the total cash flows in a pie chart with the debt and equity claims as slices of the pie. According to the theorem, the value of the firm is determined by the size of the cash flows, or as shown in Figure 11.2, by the size of the pie. According to the M&M theorem, how the firm divides the pie between the debt and equity slices does not matter because the size of the pie (the value of the firm) remains the same.

Yogi Berra and M&M

When asked by a waitress whether he wanted his pizza cut into four pieces or eight, Yogi Berra (Hall of Fame catcher of the New York Yankees) replied: "Better make it four, I don't think I can eat eight." Yogi's humor helps us understand the point that Modigliani and Miller are making as the size of the pizza does not depend on how many slices into which it is cut.

Source: Lee Green, *Sportwrit*, Fawcett Crest, 1984, p. 228. We also acknowledge the prior use of this quote in the M&M context by Michael J. Barclay, Clifford W. Smith, Jr, and Ronald D. Watts in "The Determinants of Corporate Leverage and Dividend Policies," *The New Corporate Finance: Where Theory Meets Practice*. Donald H. Chew, Jr (ed.), Irwin McGraw-Hill, 2nd edn, 1999, pp. 205–13.

This conclusion, commonly referred to as M&M's Proposition I, can be expressed as:

$$\text{Proposition I:} \quad V_L = V_U \tag{11.1}$$

where V_L represents the value of a levered firm (a firm financed with debt and equity) and V_U represents the value of an unlevered firm (firm financed entirely with equity).

Modigliani and Miller also developed another relationship, known as Proposition II, which shows how a firm's capital structure affects its cost of equity.

$$\text{Proposition II:} \quad k_S = k_A + \frac{D}{S}(k_A - k_D) \tag{11.2}$$

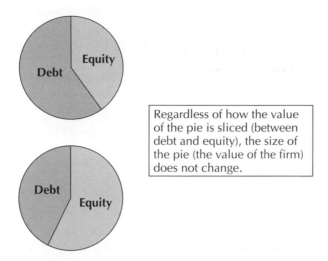

Regardless of how the value of the pie is sliced (between debt and equity), the size of the pie (the value of the firm) does not change.

Figure 11.2 Pie models of capital structure under perfect markets with no taxes

The term k_S represents the required return on equity, k_A is the required return on the firm's assets, and k_D represents the firm's cost of debt. D and S represent the market value amounts of debt and equity, respectively. This equation shows us how a firm's required return on equity increases as a firm employs increasing amounts of financial leverage.

Development of M&M's Irrelevance Argument

In the following discussion, we provide a relatively simple and intuitive development of the M&M capital structure propositions for the case where there are no taxes or other market imperfections.

In Chapter 5 we presented a formula (Equation 5.21) for determining the value of a firm's stock when the firm's dividends are expected to grow at a constant rate indefinitely:

$$V_S = \frac{D_1}{k_S - g}$$

where V_S is the value of the firm's stock, D_1 is the expected dividend one year from today, k_S is the estimated required return on the firm's stock, and g is the expected constant growth rate of the dividends. Suppose we want to value an entire firm and not just the firm's common stock. We can modify the constant growth valuation formula above by using the total real asset cash flows of the firm (not just the dividends to the stockholders) in the numerator and discount them at the firm's weighted average cost of capital (WACC), not just the firm's required return on equity. If the firm finances its assets entirely by debt and equity, the formula for the firm's WACC, given previously as Equation 10.9, can be expressed:

$$WACC = (D/V)k_D + (S/V)k_S \tag{11.3}$$

Let's assume a simple case where a firm's real asset cash flows are constant in perpetuity. Thus, we can assume the growth rate (g) is zero. We further recognize that these real asset cash flows will be the firm's operating earnings (EBIT). Our valuation formula for the firm would become:

$$\text{Firm Value} = \frac{EBIT}{WACC} \tag{11.4}$$

Under our assumptions, the firm's operating earnings are fixed by the firm's investment decision in its real assets, and are independent of the firm's financing decision.[3] *Therefore, the firm will maximize its value when it minimizes its WACC. Therefore, we can concentrate our efforts on minimizing the firm's WACC.*

Let's begin with a firm that is initially all equity financed. Assume the firm's cost of equity is 20 percent and the firm's cost of debt (if it did borrow) is 10 percent. The firm's initial weighted average cost of capital would be 20 percent.

$$WACC = (0.0)10\% + (1.0)20\% = 20\%$$

Now let's ask the question: Could the firm lower its WACC by replacing some of its "expensive" equity financing with "cheaper" debt financing? For example, if the firm replaced half of the equity with debt financing, its cost of capital may appear to be reduced to 15 percent with WACC = (0.5)(10%) + (0.5)(20%) = 15 percent.

M&M show us the fallacy of this thinking. Remember, when firms use financial leverage, their shareholders incur financial risk that magnifies the volatility of their returns (EPS and ROE). Shareholders will require a higher return as compensation for this financial risk (Proposition II). Given the new debt-equity ratio of 1.0, we find that the required return on equity will increase to 30 percent. Thus, the increase in risk exactly offsets any increase in return on equity resulting from financial leverage.

$$k_S = k_A + \frac{D}{S}(k_A - k_D)$$

$$k_S = 20\% + 1(20\% - 10\%) = 30\%$$

The firm's weighted average cost of capital would actually remain at 20 percent.

$$WACC = (0.5)10\% + (0.5)30\% = 20.0\%$$

Thus, we see how M&M Propositions I and II work together to provide the case for capital structure irrelevance in perfect markets with no taxes. If the firm's WACC is unchanged, the

---

[3] Because we are assuming no taxes, the firm's EBIT is actually equal to EBI (earnings before interest).

value of the firm will not change. M&M show that when firms borrow, the associated increase in financial risk increases the shareholders' required return on equity just enough (Proposition II) to keep the firm's WACC constant and thus leave the value of the firm (Proposition I) unchanged.

Illustration of the M&M Theorem

We can illustrate the M&M theorem with an example. Consider the Pawkett brothers, Left and Right, who invested $5 million each to become the sole (equity) owners of Pawkett Sprockets, Inc. With expected operating cash flows of $1 million each year in perpetuity and a 10 percent required return on equity for this all equity firm, the firm value is $10 million.

$$\text{Firm Value} = \frac{EBIT}{WACC} = \frac{\$1\,\text{million}}{0.10} = \$10\,\text{million}$$

Each brother shares equally in both the $1 million operating cash flow and the total value of the firm. Each has equity worth $5 million.

Assume that Left and Right decide to alter the composition of their ownership, with Left exchanging all of his equity ownership for debt. Left and Right agree that the debt should carry a 6 percent interest rate. Now, rather than splitting the expected $1 million operating cash flow each year, Left Pawkett will receive $300,000 (6 percent of his $5 million of debt) and Right Pawkett will collect the residual amount, which he expects to be $700,000. Would this decision affect the total value of their firm?

Because this financing decision does not change the amount and the riskiness of the firm's *total* operating cash flows, the value of the firm would remain unchanged at $10 million. What has changed is how these brothers now share the firm's cash flows in terms of priority and amount:

- Left Pawkett now receives only $300,000 of the expected $1 million operating cash flow. However, he has a priority claim above that of his brother. If the operating cash flow were only $300,000 in a given year, he would receive all of it and Right Pawkett would receive nothing.
- Right Pawkett receives the residual operating earnings after Left Pawkett has been paid. His residual claim is EBIT minus $300,000 and will depend on the level of EBIT each year.

The volatility of the firm's EBIT has not changed. EBIT is just as risky as it was when both brothers shared the equity value of the firm equally. But now, since Left Pawkett's claim is a fixed claim of 6 percent ($300,000), the volatility of EBIT focuses entirely on Right Pawkett.[4] This corresponds to the increased financial risk that we illustrated in Table 11.2 and Figure 11.1 earlier in the chapter. Right Pawkett will now require a higher return on equity to compensate for the increase in financial risk (M&M Proposition II).

---

[4]   This result assumes that EBIT exceeds the $300,000 debt payment owed to Left Pawkett.

This example illustrates how the value of the firm does not depend on how the firm's cash flows are split into its Left and Right (debt and equity) pockets. Instead, firm value depends only on distributing the size and riskiness of the total cash flows into the pockets of all security holders. This is the essence of the M&M theorem: under perfect capital markets with no taxes, the value of a firm depends on the level and the riskiness of the real asset total cash flows, not on how the firm "packages" these cash flows as security claims.

Graphical Illustration of the M&M Theorem

We illustrate Propositions I and II in Figure 11.3. The upper panel shows Proposition I. Notice that as the debt-equity ratio increases, the value of the firm does not change. The lower panel shows Proposition II. Let's begin with the WACC when the debt-equity ratio is zero. As the debt-equity ratio increases, WACC remains the same because of the increases in the cost of equity.

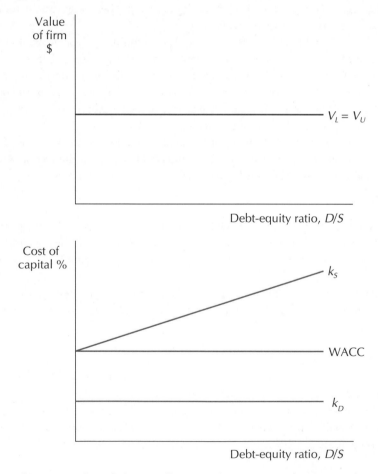

Figure 11.3 Illustration of Modigliani–Miller capital structure irrelevance under perfect capital markets with no taxes

The M&M Theorem in the Real World

Do these results hold in the real world? Probably not. Miller was quoted later as saying:

> The view that capital structure is literally irrelevant or that "nothing matters" in corporate finance, though sometimes attributed to us . . . is far from what we ever actually said about the real-world applications of our theoretical propositions.[5]

Accordingly, their results provide an important lesson. In the idealized world of M&M with no market imperfections such as taxes, capital structure does not matter. Therefore, if capital structure decisions matter in the real world, they must be responses to market imperfections. Now we know where to investigate further. What are these market imperfections? Key imperfections or factors that affect capital structure and value are taxes (corporate and personal), bankruptcy and financial distress costs, and information asymmetry. We now consider how corporate taxes may affect the capital structure decision.

Concept Check 11.3

1   What is the implication for financial managers of M&M Proposition I? What assumptions must hold for this result to be true?
2   Under perfect capital markets without taxes, why does borrowing at a rate less than the required return on equity not decrease a firm's WACC?

11.4 The Modigliani–Miller Theorem with Corporate Taxes

The interest payments associated with corporate borrowings are a tax-deductible expense for a firm. As such, they shield taxable income from federal and state taxes. At issue is whether the tax-deductibility of the interest payments associated with corporate borrowings would affect the value of the firm. Modigliani and Miller addressed this issue by considering how capital structure affected the value of a firm under perfect capital markets with corporate taxes.[6]

Assume two firms, Firm U and Firm L, which are identical in terms of their assets and operations. Firm U is an unlevered firm (all equity financed) with operating earnings (EBIT) of $1,000. With a marginal tax rate of 40 percent, the firm will pay $400 in taxes. Firm L is a

---

5   Miller Merton, "The Modigliani–Miller Propositions after Thirty Years," *Journal of Economic Perspectives*, Autumn 1988, 99–120.
6   Franco Modigliani and Merton H. Miller, "Corporate Income Taxes and the Cost of Capital: A Correction," *American Economic Review* 53, June 1963, 433–42.

levered firm that has issued $2,000 of perpetual bonds (i.e., the bonds have no maturity) with an interest rate of 10 percent. Firm L will incur an annual interest expense in perpetuity of $200, and with EBIT of $1,000, will have $800 of taxable income. The firm's tax payment will fall to $320. These two situations are illustrated below:

	Firm U	Firm L
EBIT	$1,000	$1,000
Interest expense	0	200
EBT	$1,000	$800
Taxes	400	320
Net income	$600	$480

Understanding the tax benefits associated with Firm L's debt is important. While Firm L must pay its bondholders $200 in interest payments, it also pays $80 less in taxes. The interest payments shielded some of Firm L's taxable income from taxes.

Note also that the total cash flows to both bondholders and shareholders are greater for Firm L than for Firm U, as illustrated below:

	Firm U	Firm L
Cash flow to bondholders	0	$200
Cash flow to shareholders	$600	$480
Total cash flow	$600	$680

The interest tax shield results in $80 per year in incremental cash flow to the levered firm. This amount is equal to $t_c k_D D$ which is $(0.4)(0.10)(\$2,000) = \$80$. The logic is simple: when the firm deducts its interest payment of $k_D D$ from its taxable income, it saves t_c times that amount in taxes.

The increased cash flow to the levered firm's stakeholders will increase the total value of the firm. The extra value comes from the increased cash flow from interest tax shield: $t_c k_D D$ per year in perpetuity. We can compute the present value of this cash flow perpetuity by dividing it by the firm's cost of debt[7]:

$$\text{PV of interest tax shield} = \frac{t_c k_D D}{k_D} = t_c D \tag{11.5}$$

Thus, the value of a levered firm will exceed the value of an unlevered firm by the present value of the levered firm's interest tax shield, $t_c k_D D$. M&M's Proposition I, with corporate taxes, now becomes:

$$\text{Proposition I: } V_L = V_U + t_c D \tag{11.6}$$

---

[7] Recall from Chapter 5 that the present value of a perpetuity is computed by dividing the perpetuity by the appropriate discount rate.

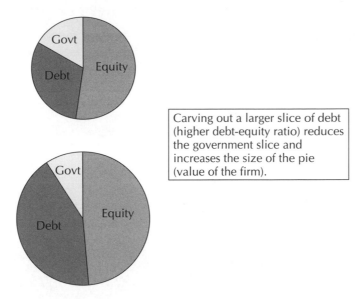

Carving out a larger slice of debt (higher debt-equity ratio) reduces the government slice and increases the size of the pie (value of the firm).

Figure 11.4 Pie models of capital structure with corporate taxes

As long as a firm can use the interest payments from debt to shield taxes, the firm can increase its value by using debt financing.

We use a pie chart to illustrate these results in Figure 11.4. Now the pie has a slice removed to represent the firm's tax payments to the government. As discussed before, the total size of the pie is unaffected by how the pie is sliced. But the firm's owners are no longer interested in the total size of the pie. They care only about the size of the debt and equity slices. These slices represent the claims that can be sold in the financial markets to security holders. To maximize firm value, the firm needs to minimize the government slice. According to the discussion above, using debt financing to shield income from taxes reduces the government slice. Thus, maximizing the size of the debt slice, as represented by the sum of the debt and equity slices, will maximize the value of the firm.

M&M also developed a version of Proposition II that accounts for the effects of corporate taxes:

Proposition II: $k_S = k_A + D/S(k_A - k_D)(1 - t_C)$ (11.7)

which is similar to the previous Proposition II we had under the no tax case.

We illustrate Propositions I and II in Figure 11.5. The upper panel shows Proposition I. As the debt-equity ratio increases, the value of the firm increases. The lower panel illustrates Proposition II. The firm's WACC declines when the debt-equity ratio increases due to the tax-deductibility of the interest payments.

The implication of the M&M case with corporate taxes is that firms should rely almost exclusively on debt financing, say almost 100 percent, to maximize the value of a firm. For

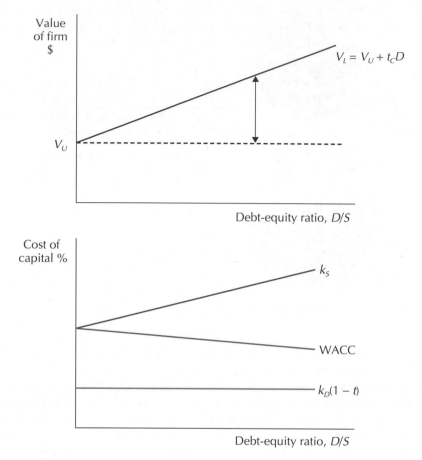

Figure 11.5 Illustration of Propositions I and II under perfect capital markets with corporate taxes

every dollar of debt that replaces equity, the value of the firm will increase by t_cD. In practice firms do not come anywhere near this reliance on debt financing.

Why Firms Are Not Leveraged to the Maximum

Why would financial managers miss out on such an opportunity to increase the value of the firm for their shareholders? The key reasons that managers do not use the excessive amount of debt financing suggested by M&M Proposition I with corporate taxes include the availability of other non-debt tax shields, the existence of personal taxes, and the costs of financial distress and bankruptcy. We discuss each in turn.

Other non-debt tax shields
The interest payments associated with corporate borrowings are not the only way a firm can shield income from taxes. Other non-debt tax shields exist of which the largest are

depreciation, amortization, and research and development (R&D) expenses. The existence of these other non-debt tax shields lower the probability that a firm can use all of its interest payments to shield taxable income.

To illustrate, consider the income statement that a firm has projected for the coming year:

Sales	$1,000
Cost of sales	400
Depreciation	200
EBIT	400
Interest expense	300
EBT	100
Tax (40%)	40
Net income	$60

The firm's depreciation expense of $200 decreases expected EBIT to $400, and the firm uses its entire annual interest expense of $300 to further reduce taxable income (EBT) to $100. In this case, since every dollar of interest expense shields taxable income from taxes, the firm saves $0.40 in taxes for every dollar of interest expense, resulting in a total tax savings of $120.

What would happen if projected EBIT fell to $100? The firm would no longer be able to use the entire interest expense to shield income from taxes. Instead, the firm could use only $100 of the interest expense to shield taxes. Therefore, the tax savings from the firm's interest expense would fall from $120 to $40.

Thus, to the extent that the firm has other tax shields or has highly uncertain operating earnings, the value of the interest tax shield decreases. This is because the probability of fully using these tax shields also decreases. Similarly, as a firm's use of debt increases, the likelihood of using the entire interest expense to shield taxes also declines. Thus, the firm reduces its tax advantage of using debt.

Personal taxes

We saw in the M&M case with corporate taxes that firms should rely extensively on financial leverage to maximize firm value. But would the personal taxes that investors pay on dividends, interest, and capital gains that we ignored in that discussion change these conclusions?

What matters to the investors who value a firm are the after-tax cash flows they receive from an investment. Most investors probably pay higher taxes on income from corporate bonds than on equity for several reasons. First, under the current tax code, long-term capital gains are taxed at a lower rate than ordinary income. While investors can realize long-term capital gains from bond and equity investments, such gains are far more common among equity investments. Furthermore, investors can defer paying taxes on long-term capital gains until they realize these gains when they sell the stock. Deferring taxes decreases the tax rate on a present value basis.

The consensus among financial economists is that the personal tax disadvantage does not eliminate the corporate tax advantage of debt, but probably reduces it. Without personal taxes, the present value of the interest tax shield is $t_C D$. With a corporate tax rate of

40 percent, firms can add $0.40 in value for every dollar of debt issued. With both personal and corporate taxes, firms can probably add only about $0.20 or so in value when issuing corporate debt.

Costs of financial distress and bankruptcy

Perhaps the strongest argument for a firm to limit its amount of debt involves the costs of financial distress and bankruptcy associated with issuing too much debt. Financial distress occurs when a firm has difficulty in meeting the contractual obligations on its debt financing. It refers to any general weakening in a company's financial condition caused by excessive financial leverage.

The extreme case of financial distress is **bankruptcy**, a formal legal proceeding where an overextended firm is placed under the protection of the bankruptcy court, allowing it to keep operating while developing a new plan to pay off creditors. When a firm declares bankruptcy, it will bear various legal, accounting, and administrative expenses and could be forced to sell certain assets at "fire sale" prices to meet creditors' claims. Lenders anticipate the risks of attendant costs of bankruptcy and require higher rates of return as compensation. Thus, the firm's shareholders bear these costs of bankruptcy. The direct costs of bankruptcy do not appear to be large enough to offset the tax advantage of debt financing. Probably more significant than the actual direct costs of bankruptcy are the indirect costs of financial distress. We discuss these costs more thoroughly in the next section.

Concept Check 11.4

1   How may corporate taxes make a firm's borrowing decision relevant? Why might debt financing increase the total cash flows that a firm distributes to its debt and equity security holders?
2   What is the value of the interest tax shield when a firm borrows?
3   What is the implication for financial managers of M&M Proposition I under perfect capital markets with corporate taxes?

11.5 The Costs of Financial Distress

Actual bankruptcy is not required for a firm to face costs of financial distress. Just the threat of bankruptcy can lead to deterioration in the firm's operating performance. The costs of financial distress involve incentives for stakeholders of the firm to act in a manner that is not most beneficial to the firm. For example, rather than planning a firm's long-term strategy, top management may spend its time devising short-term strategies to stay afloat. Key employees may leave the firm in search of a more secure future. Customers may no longer want to buy the firm's products or services fearing that the firm may not be around much longer to back up the product or service. The firm's suppliers may not be willing to supply short-term credit. Finally, financial distress can also lead to several adverse incentives for a firm's management. One such adverse incentive is for the managers to invest in higher risk projects, even if the projects have negative net present values.

In these examples, financial distress weakens the relationships between the firm and its stakeholders. Financial distress also decreases the cash flows that investors expect the firm to generate from its operations, and thus leads to a reduction in firm value. But a firm can suffer the costs of financial distress without engaging in or being affected by the activities described above. If a firm is sufficiently leveraged and future operating earnings are sufficiently uncertain, just the *expectation* by investors that the firm will incur these costs of financial distress can lead to a reduction in firm value. Investors would rationally deduct the expected future cost of financial distress from their estimate of firm value by estimating this cost and multiplying it by the probability of its occurrence. The nature of these financial distress costs makes them nearly impossible to quantify accurately.

Characteristics of Firms with High Expected Costs of Financial Distress

Financial economists widely believe that certain firm-specific characteristics make the costs of financial distress very costly or highly likely. We highlight and discuss several of these characteristics below:

- *Firms producing highly specialized products or products possibly requiring repairs.* Customers are less likely to purchase highly specialized products or products that may require repairs from firms that appear to be financially distressed. They fear the company will not remain in business to provide service, repairs, product updates, and technical advice.
- *Firms producing goods or providing services whose quality is important but difficult to assess in advance.* Consider an airline that is financially distressed. Consumers value the quality of performance as it relates to safety issues. But many customers may choose not to travel with an airline that is financially distressed, fearing the company has an incentive to lower its costs and could do so by not keeping the same maintenance and safety quality procedures as other airlines.
- *Firms having high growth opportunities.* Firms with substantial capital investment opportunities may not want to risk becoming financially distressed and thereby jeopardize their access to outside capital. A financially distressed firm may find that raising external capital from outside investors to fund these new projects is difficult, especially if investors fear the actions discussed previously that financially distressed firms might take.
- *Firms having intangible assets.* A firm whose asset values depend on its human capital, reputation for quality, and brand name may suffer greatly if it becomes financially distressed. In such cases, the values of these intangible assets may deteriorate quickly as customers and investors anticipate lower quality of service and products from the firm.

Concept Check 11.5

1   What are three reasons that firms would not maximize the use of financial leverage as predicted under M&M Proposition I with corporate taxes?
2   What does the term "financial distress" mean? What are some of the costs of financial distress for a firm?
3   Do the direct costs of bankruptcy seem to be high enough to limit the amount of financial leverage employed by a firm?

11.6 Tradeoff Theory of Optimal Capital Structure

The tax benefits of debt financing bestowed by the government and the costs of financial distress that may at some point accompany the use of financial leverage may lead to a static tradeoff that provides an optimal capital structure for a firm. According to the tradeoff theory, as depicted in the upper panel of Figure 11.5, firms with initially little or no debt should consider adding debt to their capital structure because of the tax deductibility of the interest payments. Recall that this interest tax shield, which is essentially a government subsidy, increases the value of the firm. The value does not continue to increase indefinitely as the firm continues to increase its use of debt financing. At some point, the probability of being able to fully utilize the interest deduction will decrease given the uncertainty that the firm's operating earnings will exceed the interest tax deductions. This is especially true for firms that already have a large amount of other tax shields such as depreciation, amortization, and R&D expenses.

Also, as a firm continues to employ higher levels of debt financing, the probability of incurring financial distress increases. These costs of financial distress initially offset the tax advantage of debt to some degree. Yet, such costs gradually increase as debt levels rise until they begin to completely offset the tax advantage of debt. Beyond that point, issuing more debt decreases the value of the firm. So firms will borrow only up to the point where the tax benefit from another dollar of debt financing exactly equals the cost from the increased probability of financial distress. At this point a static tradeoff exists between debt and equity financing where the firm maximizes its value.

Since the indirect costs of financial distress are difficult to measure, most financial economists agree that the optimal capital structure for a firm cannot be precisely determined. Rather, we often think of an optimal capital structure *range* for a firm. Managers determine this optimal capital structure range based on many factors including the firm's marginal tax rate, the amount of other non-interest tax shields, the variability of the firm's operating earnings, and the likelihood and the magnitude of the costs of financial distress for that firm.

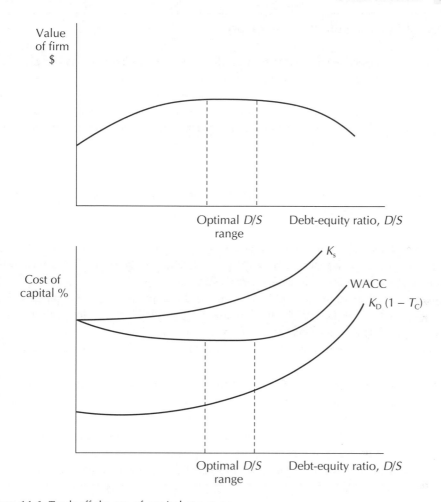

Figure 11.6 Tradeoff theory of capital structure

Optimal Capital Structure and Cost of Capital

Let's refer to our valuation formula in Equation 11.4. Since the firm's real asset cash flows are fixed, we find that the capital structure that maximizes firm value is also the capital structure that minimizes the firm's WACC. We illustrate this in the lower panel of Figure 11.6. As we have seen before, the cost of equity (K_s) increases to reflect the increased financial risk. At low debt levels, the firm's WACC decreases as the firm's debt-equity ratio increases because the deductibility of interest payments reduces the firm's after-tax cost of debt to $k(1 - T_c)$ more than offsets the higher return required by stockholders. At higher levels of debt financing, the costs of financial distress increase the after-tax cost of debt. Thus, the firm's WACC eventually begins to increase.

Empirical Evidence on Tradeoff Theory

Early studies provided evidence that firms in the same industry tend to have similar capital structures. For example, high-growth computer software firms in the US tend to have low debt ratios. For example, Table 11.1 at the beginning of this chapter shows that Microsoft, Intel, Apple Computers, and Dell Computer all have debt ratios of 10 percent or less. Recall from the same table that we found much higher debt ratios for the communications firms. Some analysts conclude that such evidence supports the tradeoff theory. This conclusion may be unwarranted because firms may adopt capital structures to conform to industry norms.

Empirical evidence for the tradeoff theory is mixed. The following evidence appears to support the tradeoff theory:

* Firms with higher tax rates tend to have higher debt ratios.
* Observed debt ratios appear to be negatively related to bankruptcy and financial distress costs, R&D expenditures, and advertising and selling expenses.
* High costs of bankruptcy and financial distress reduce optimal debt ratios for these firms. As discussed earlier, firms with other tax-deductible expenses have a lower probability of being able to fully use all tax benefits from borrowing.
* Chief financial officers often state they try to maintain an optimal capital structure.[8]

But the following empirical evidence suggests the tradeoff theory does not completely capture managers' strategy for long-term financing decisions:

* Actual debt ratios tend to vary more widely across given industries than would be suggested by the tradeoff theory.
* The explanatory power of a target capital structure in regression models is very low.

Concept Check 11.6

1   What factors may lead to an optimal capital structure for a firm?
2   Should the optimal capital structure be viewed as a point or a range? Why?
3   If a firm were operating at its optimal capital structure, what would also be true about the firm's weighted average cost of capital?
4   What empirical evidence supports the tradeoff theory of capital structure?

---

[8]   Ravinda R. Kamath, "Long-Term Financing Decisions: Views and Practices of Financial Managers of NYSE Firms," *Financial Review* 32, May 1997, 350–56.

Practical Financial Tip 11.2

Managers of firms with little or no financial leverage may be able to add value to their firm by issuing debt securities. Debt may increase total firm value because the interest payments are a tax-deductible expense for the firm. In essence, the government subsidizes debt financing through the tax code. At some point, the increase in value from issuing additional debt diminishes as the likelihood of having sufficient pre-tax income to shield from taxes decreases. In addition, the firm may begin to incur costs of financial distress. These costs of financial distress include direct costs such as bankruptcy as well as indirect costs that include damaged relationships with suppliers, shifting of management priorities, loss of key employees, and potential adverse incentives. The tradeoffs from the advantages and disadvantages of debt financing may create an optimal range of debt financing for firms. In practice, identifying this optimal range may be difficult because of the problem of quantifying the costs of financial distress caused by debt financing.

11.7 Pecking Order Theory of Capital Structure

The basis for the pecking order theory of capital structure is the notion that managers have inside information. By contrast, Modigliani and Miller assumed that managers and investors have the same information. In finance, we often refer to this inside information as asymmetric information. Despite its technical sounding name, **asymmetric information** simply means that managers as insiders know more about a firm's current situation and future prospects than do outsiders. Thus, investors may use capital structure decisions as a signal of management's expectations. Failure to choose the capital structure that sends the appropriate signal can result in an information asymmetry cost. This asymmetric information leads to a pecking order of financing choices where managers prefer internal financing to external financing and prefer debt securities to equity securities when a firm requires external financing.

At the top of the pecking order is the premise that managers prefer internal financing. When managers need funds for new investments, they prefer to reinvest the firm's earnings back into the firm. Using accounting terminology, we say the firm is financing the new projects with its retained earnings. Managers avoid seeking external financing because it may require them to divulge private information about their firm to the outside investment community and to incur expensive flotation or transaction costs. Managers would not want to release any technical or strategic information that could be useful to the firm's competitors.

Managers also may want to avoid external financing because it subjects them to the disciplining effects of these markets. The firm will likely need to release information to various accounting, legal, and financial professionals who will scrutinize the information to verify that the firm conforms to acceptable standards. Managers can lessen the likelihood of needing external financing by choosing a dividend payout policy according to the firm's future capital investment needs.

Despite management's best attempts to avoid external financing, they will likely need to do so occasionally due to the uncertainty of future cash revenues, sticky dividend policies, and future investment opportunities. When managers must raise funds externally, the pecking order theory suggests that they prefer issuing debt securities to issuing new shares of equity. Managers prefer issuing debt because of the reaction of investors in the capital markets when firms raise funds externally. Investors understand that some managers want to issue new shares of equity when they think the firm's stock is currently overpriced. Not surprisingly, the stock market typically reacts negatively to the announcement of new equity issues by firms, and managers avoid issuing new shares of equity whenever they can.[9] Thus, managers' preference for debt securities results from the information asymmetry argument where managers have inside information.

To summarize, the pecking order of financing choices for firms is as follows.

1   Managers prefer internal financing to external financing. Managers choose their target dividend payouts in light of their expected future investment opportunities, seeking to avoid the need for external financing.
2   When operating cash flows and resulting profits are higher than expected and in excess of what the firm needs to fund new capital expenditures and pay dividends, managers pay off debt or invest in marketable securities. When they are less, managers draw down cash balances and sell marketable securities in order to fund new expenditures and pay dividends.
3   After drawing down cash balances and selling marketable securities, managers need to seek external financing from time to time. This is because operating cash flows and investment opportunities are often highly unpredictable.
4   When forced to raise funds externally, firms prefer to issue debt and seek to avoid issuing new shares of equity. In between these choices are hybrid securities such as convertible bonds and convertible preferred stock.

The implication of the pecking order theory of capital structure is that a firm has no optimal capital structure. Rather, the capital structures we observe for firms simply reflect the cumulative need over time for external financing by the firm and the preference for debt financing when that need arose. Moreover, equity financing occurs at both ends of the pecking order. At the top of the pecking order is internal equity (reinvested earnings) and at the bottom of the pecking order is the issuance of new shares of equity (external equity). Thus, no natural tradeoff exists between debt and equity that provides a target capital structure for a firm under the pecking order theory of financing choice.

---

[9]   Because of the asymmetric information between managers and investors, investors cannot tell which firms are issuing equity because they think it is currently overpriced and those firms that are not. Thus, they assume the worst case and generally interpret an announcement of a new equity issue as inside information that managers perceive the firm's stock as overvalued.

Pecking Order and Financial Slack

Financial slack refers to having a sufficient level of cash, marketable securities, and real assets that are readily saleable, and ready access for obtaining debt from the financial markets (bond issues and bank financing). Financial slack is valuable to a firm. In the long run, the value of a firm is largely determined by its capital investment and operating decisions. Thus, a firm needs sufficient financial slack to ensure that it will be in position to adopt all of its positive net present value (NPV) projects.

The pecking order theory of capital structure posits that a firm prefers to be at the top of the pecking order where the firm relies on internal financing, i.e., reinvesting its earnings to fund new growth opportunities. A firm at the top of the pecking order has sufficient financial slack. A firm that is near the bottom of the pecking order may choose to pass up some positive NPV projects if the firm has to sell equity to finance these projects at a price less than what managers think is fair.[10] The lack of financial slack for such a firm may lead to decisions that do not maximize shareholder wealth. Thus, financial slack can have great value to a firm. Financial slack is probably most valuable for growth firms. Such firms are likely adopt to conservative capital structures with low to moderately low levels of debt financing.

Signaling and Pecking Order Theory

The pecking order theory described above is consistent with a signaling explanation for capital structure. Since managers, who have inside information, are reluctant to issue new shares of equity when they believe the firm's stock is undervalued, investors view a new issue of equity as a signal that managers believe the current shares are overpriced. The negative stock market reaction to announcements of new issues of common stock is consistent with this signaling explanation.

Empirical Evidence on Pecking Order Theory

Some empirical evidence supports the pecking order theory. In particular, research shows that past profitability for firms is negatively related to their observed debt ratios. The explanation behind this debt ratio-profitability relationship is that when firms are more profitable, they tend to pay down their debt. But when firms are less profitable and generate insufficient cash flows from operations to meet investment needs, they tend to issue debt to cover the shortfall.

---

[10] This is the signaling argument that we discussed above.

Concept Check 11.7

1   What is the pecking order theory of financing choices?
2   Why would managers prefer internal financing to external financing?
3   Why would managers prefer issuing debt to issuing equity?
4   Do the pecking order and optimal capital structure theories provide consistent conclusions? Discuss.
5   Why is sufficient financial slack important to growth firms?
6   What empirical evidence supports the pecking order theory of capital structure?

11.8 Stakeholder Theory of Capital Structure

As we discussed in Chapter 1, the stakeholder theory in finance considers how various decisions by a firm affect its different non-financial stakeholders in addition to the firm's lenders and shareholders. The non-financial stakeholders of a firm include its customers, employees, suppliers, the overall community in which it operates, and even the national and local government. The stakeholder theory of capital structure is based on how a firm's financing decisions interact with these non-financial stakeholders in terms of its strategic choices, including the design of its products and its employment policies.

Financial difficulties can also hurt a firm's non-financial stakeholders. For example, if many employees lose their jobs, this can adversely affect the economy of an entire community. A company in financial distress may be unable to maintain the quality of its products, service, and repairs, which negatively affects customers. As a result, many of these stakeholders will be less interested in doing business with a firm that is in financial distress.

According to the stakeholder theory of capital structure, financial distress is especially costly for firms most greatly affected by the costs of financial distress. As we discussed earlier, this would include firms that produce goods or provide services whose quality is important but difficult to assess in advance, firms producing highly specialized products or products that may require repairs, and firms whose employees and/or suppliers require specialized capital or training. For these firms, the presence of debt may reduce the firm's profits even if bankruptcy does not occur. Thus, these types of firms should, all else equal, have relatively low levels of debt financing.

A few examples serve to illustrate how financial distress affects non-financial stakeholders. One of the most notable near-bankruptcies in modern times occurred with Chrysler in the late 1970s. Chrysler offered generous rebates on its cars and trucks in 1979 to attract customers. For a brief time, the firm also offered money-back guarantees. Chrysler apparently feared that it would lose customers who believed the company would not survive to service and repair the cars and trucks.

Another example is the Eastern Airlines bankruptcy in 1990. The unions accused the company of safety violations in its efforts to cut costs. Eastern was indicted and later pleaded guilty to three counts for maintenance violations. Despite its aggressive price-cutting to attract customers, Eastern probably lost many safety-conscious customers to the other major carriers.

Government as a Stakeholder

Local and national governments are important financial and sometimes non-financial stakeholders of firms. Governments are financial stakeholders largely because of the tax revenues that they receive. Local governments sometimes rely on certain firms not only for tax revenues, but also for jobs and the continuing economic health of the region. For example, the auto plant and steel mill shutdowns in the early 1980s had adverse effects on many areas in Michigan, Ohio, and Pennsylvania.

Equally important is the role of the national government as a non-financial stakeholder. Governments sometimes deem specific firms as having strategic importance that may warrant government subsidies to prevent failure if the firm becomes financially distressed. Firms in the airline and defense industries might be prime candidates. Often, the reasons for such consideration are both financial and non-financial.

Focus on Practice 11.1

Government Loan Guarantees and Subsidies to Distressed Firms

The government provided loan guarantees to Chrysler in the early 1980s to prevent the firm from failing. After the September 11, 2001 tragedy, the US government provided $5 billion in subsidies to the airline industry to offset the huge losses incurred because people feared air travel.

An interesting question is whether a firm that knows the government considers it a strategic non-financial stakeholder would borrow more than other firms. Would the potential for receiving a government subsidy cause such firms to rely more heavily on debt financing? While smaller firms are unlikely to expect future government subsidies in the event of financial distress, larger firms, which are strategic partners with the national government, may have such expectations.

Concept Check 11.8

1   Which types of non-financial stakeholders will a firm's financing choices likely affect?
2   What are the basic predictions of the stakeholder theory of capital structure?
3   Why is the national government a potential non-financial stakeholder of a firm?
4   What empirical evidence supports the stakeholder theory of capital structure?

11.9 Capital Structure in Practice

Capital structure policy is a puzzle for financial economists. That is, we simply do not have all the answers as to how firms should determine their financing mix. When our understanding in an area is incomplete, we often turn to surveys, anecdotal evidence, and observations of what firms are doing in practice to augment our understanding.

We begin by offering several important observations on how firms set their financing mix:

- Most US firms have low or conservative debt ratios. Such firms have less total debt (short term plus long term) as a fraction of their total value (debt plus equity) in accounting terms than their counterparts in Japan, France, and Italy.[11] Moreover, US firms do not issue sufficient debt that would allow them to fully utilize the interest tax shields that are available to them.
- Changes in the debt-equity financing mix affect the value of a firm.

Recommendations for Establishing a Target Capital Structure

We have discussed in this chapter how taxes, risk, and the types of firm assets can affect a firm's capital structure choice. The following checklist, which summarizes their effects, serves as a guide for setting a firm's capital structure.

1 *Taxes.* Firms with large taxable income, which is unshielded from taxes, may want to consider employing more debt financing to increase the total cash flows distributed to both debt and equity holders and reduce the tax cash flows paid to the government. Such a financing strategy may increase the value of the firm.
2 *Risk.* Firms with volatile operating earnings (that is, greater business risk) may choose not to borrow as much as other firms with lower business risk. Volatile operating earnings lower the probability that a firm will be able to fully utilize the tax deduction from borrowing during lower income years. This is especially true for firms with other non-debt tax deductions such as depreciation and R&D expenses.
3 *Types of assets.* Firms with substantial amounts of intangible assets and growth opportunities tend to be adversely affected by the costs of financial distress and should rely more on equity financing than debt financing. As we discussed previously in this chapter, firms with substantial growth opportunities may not want to risk becoming financially distressed and thereby jeopardize their access to outside capital. Similarly, financial distress is particularly harmful to firms whose asset values depend on their human capital, reputation for quality, and brand name. In such cases, the values of these intangible assets may deteriorate quickly as customers and investors anticipate lower quality of service and products from the firm.

---

[11]   The source for this information is OECD financial statistics.

Concept Check 11.9

1 What are some of the important observations about existing capital structures for firms?
2 What do surveys of capital structure tell us about how firms choose their capital structures?
3 What three factors should financial managers consider when setting a firm's capital structure? How might each factor affect the capital structure choice?
4 What type of firm would be likely to rely more heavily on debt financing?

11.10 Bankruptcy

We complete our discussion of a firm's financing mix by returning to the topics of bankruptcy and financial distress. News of bankruptcies or threats of bankruptcies often appear in the financial press. Tens of thousands of firms in the US fail each year with a rate of 80 to 110 failures per 10,000 businesses each year since 1980. Some of the largest and more notable bankruptcies include Enron, K Mart, Montgomery Ward Holding, and Dow Corning. Perhaps the most notable near-bankruptcies in the past few decades include Chrysler in the early 1980s and United Airlines in 2002.

Dun & Bradstreet report that the major causes of bankruptcy include both economic and financial factors. Table 11.3 shows that economic and financial factors attribute to more than 80 percent of failures. Economic factors involve industry weakness and poor location and financial factors include too much debt and insufficient capital. Neglect, disaster, and fraud account for about 14 percent of failures.

Bankruptcy Definitions

Several different terms are commonly used to describe firms under financial distress. The term **business failure** is commonly used to describe a situation in which a firm has terminated its

Table 11.3 Causes of business failures

Cause of failure	Percent of total (%)
Economic factors	37.1
Financial factors	47.3
Neglect, disaster, and fraud	14.0
Other factors	1.6
Total	100.0

Source: Dun & Bradstreet, Business Failure Record (New York).

operations or business with a loss to its creditors. A firm is **bankrupt** when it files for bankruptcy in the US Federal Court.

Several other terms in the financial press relate to financial distress. Reference is commonly made to the terms technical insolvency and accounting insolvency. **Technical insolvency** occurs when a firm cannot meet its financial obligations. **Accounting insolvency** occurs when a firm has negative net worth on its balance sheet. Many savings and loans in the US were accounting insolvent in the early 1980s as rising interest rates decreased the value of their long-term assets (loans) much more than the value of their shorter-term liabilities (deposits).

Bankruptcy Laws

The first bankruptcy laws of the US were enacted in the late nineteenth century. Our current bankruptcy law incorporates modifications made in 1938, 1978, and 1986. Current bankruptcy law consists of many different *chapters* that provide general provisions and deal with specific situations relating to reorganization and liquidation for businesses, municipalities, and family-owned firms. The most common chapters are Chapter 11 and Chapter 7.

Under Chapter 11 bankruptcy, a company attempts to reorganize under the supervision of a bankruptcy court. The bankruptcy proceedings protect the firm from allowing creditors to seize control of the firm's assets if the firm experiences temporary cash flow problems. Bankruptcy proceedings also protect the creditors from allowing a firm that should be liquidated to continue operating with continuing losses that provide fewer assets available to the creditors in an eventual liquidation. The role of the bankruptcy court is to determine the fairness and feasibility of the proposed reorganization plan. If reorganization of the firm under Chapter 11 is infeasible, the bankruptcy judge will order the firm to be liquidated according to Chapter 7 bankruptcy provisions. A bankruptcy petition is **voluntary** when filed by the firm's management and is **involuntary** when filed by one or more of the firm's creditors.

Concept Check 11.10

1   What do the terms business failure, technical insolvency, accounting insolvency, and bankruptcy mean?
2   What is the difference between Chapter 11 and Chapter 7 bankruptcy?

Summary

This chapter examined how firms determine their financing mix or capital structure. We learned how various factors may affect a firm's choice as to the optimal mix. In the end, the capital structure decision will be based on a combination of analysis and informed judgment. We list below the key concepts covered.

1   A firm incurs financial risk when it borrows. Financial risk has two components. First, borrowing increases the risk of default because the interest and principal payments are legal obligations. Second, the use of debt financing carrying a fixed interest rate increases both the level and the volatility of a firm's earnings per share and return on equity.

2   The observed debt ratios of US firms vary considerably, even among similar firms within the same industry.

3   According to the M&M theorem, in the absence of corporate and personal taxes, transaction costs, and other market imperfections, *the value of a firm is independent of its capital structure*. According to M&M, the value of a firm is determined by the investment and operating decisions of the firm, not by how managers choose the relative amounts of debt and equity financing.

4   Despite the corporate tax advantage of borrowing, firms do not rely exclusively on debt financing because of the personal tax disadvantage of debt financing, the availability of other non-debt tax shields, and the costs of financial distress and bankruptcy that accompany borrowing.

5   The tax benefits of debt financing and the costs of financial distress may lead to a static tradeoff that provides an optimal capital structure for a firm. According to the tradeoff theory, a firm should borrow only up to the point where the tax benefit from another dollar of debt financing exactly equals the cost from the increased probability of financial distress. At this point, a firm obtains a static tradeoff where its value is maximized. The firm's weighted average cost of capital is minimized at the point where its value is maximized.

6   The pecking order theory provides an alternative explanation for how firms determine their financing mix. Under this theory, managers prefer internal financing to external financing. They choose their target dividend payouts in light of their expected future investment opportunities and seek to avoid the need for external financing. Because future operating cash flows and investment opportunities are often highly unpredictable, managers sometimes need to seek external financing. When forced to raise funds externally, firms prefer to issue debt and seek to avoid issuing new shares of equity. In between these choices are hybrid securities such as convertible bonds and convertible preferred stock.

7   An implication of the pecking order theory is that capital structures for firms simply reflect their cumulative need over time for external financing and their preference for debt financing when that need arises. In addition, no optimal capital structure exists under the pecking order theory because equity financing exists at both ends of the pecking order. At the top of the pecking order is internal equity (reinvested earnings) and at the bottom of the pecking order is the issuance of new shares of equity (external equity).

8   The stakeholder theory of capital structure suggests that firms consider many stakeholders including its customers, employees, suppliers, the overall community in which it operates, and government. This theory is based on how a firm's financing decisions interact with these stakeholders in terms of the strategic choices of the firm including the design of its products and its employment policies.

9   A useful checklist for setting a firm's capital structure would likely consist of a careful consideration of the tax-paying situation of the firm, its risk, and the types of the firm's assets.

10 Under Chapter 11 bankruptcy, a company attempts to reorganize under the supervision of a bankruptcy court. The bankruptcy proceedings protect the firm from allowing creditors to seize control of its assets if the firm is experiencing temporary cash flow problems. They also protect the creditors from allowing a firm that should be liquidated to continue operating with losses.

11 If reorganization under Chapter 11 is not feasible, the bankruptcy judge will order liquidation of the firm according to Chapter 7 bankruptcy provisions.

FURTHER READING

Barclay, Michael J. and Clifford W. Smith, Jr., "The Capital Structure Puzzle: Another Look at the Evidence," *Journal of Applied Corporate Finance* 12, Spring 1999, 8–20.

Barclay, Michael J., Clifford W. Smith, and Ross L. Watts, "The Determinants of Corporate Leverage and Dividend Policies," *Journal of Applied Corporate Finance* 7, Winter 1995, 4–19.

Berens, James L. and Charles J. Cuny, "The Capital Structure Puzzle Revisited," *Review of Financial Studies* 8, Winter 1995, 1185–208.

Bradley, Michael, Greg A. Jarrell, and E. Han Kim, "On the Existence of an Optimal Capital Structure: Theory and Evidence," *Journal of Finance* 39, July 1984, 857–78.

Brealey, Richard and Stewart C. Myers. *Principles of Corporate Finance*, 6th edn, Irwin McGraw-Hill, 2000.

Copeland, Thomas E. and J. Fred Weston. *Financial Theory and Corporate Policy*, Addison-Wesley, 1988.

Grinblatt, Mark and Sheridan Titman. *Financial Markets and Corporate Strategy*, McGraw-Hill Irwin, 2nd edn, 2002.

Harris, Milton and Artur Raviv, "The Theory of Capital Structure," *Journal of Finance* 46, March 1991, 297–355.

Miller, Merton H., "The Modigliani-Miller Propositions after Thirty Years," *Journal of Applied Corporate Finance* 2, Spring 1989, 6–18.

Myers, Stewart C., "Determinants of Corporate Borrowing," *Journal of Financial Economics* 5, November 1977, 147–75.

Myers, Stewart C., "The Capital Structure Puzzle," *Journal of Finance* 39, July 1984, 575–92.

Myers, Stewart C., "Still Searching for Optimal Capital Structure," *Journal of Applied Corporate Finance* 6, Spring 1993, 4–14.

Opler, Tim C., Michael Saron, and Sheridan Titman, "Designing Capital Structure to Create Shareholder Value," *Journal of Applied Corporate Finance* 10, Spring 1997, 21–32.

Patrick, Steven C., "Three Pieces to the Capital Structure Puzzle: The Cases of Alco Standard, Comdisco, and Revco," *Journal of Applied Corporate Finance* 7, Winter 1995, 53–61.

Pinegar, J. Michael and Lisa Wilbricht, "What Managers Think of Capital Structure Theory: A Survey," *Financial Management* 18, Winter 1989, 82–91.

Chapter 12

Dividend Policy

Despite exhaustive theoretical and empirical analysis to explain their pervasive presence, dividends remain one of the thorniest puzzles in corporate finance. (H. Kent Baker, Gary E. Powell, and E. Theodore Veit, "Revisiting the Dividend Puzzle: Do All the Pieces Now Fit?" *Review of Financial Economics*, 11(4) 2002, p. 242.)

Overview

Until this point, we have focused on two main categories of decisions that corporate financial managers make – investment and financing decisions. A decision interrelated to investment and financing decisions involves dividend policy. The dividend decision, as determined by a firm's dividend policy, has an effect on the amount of earnings a firm pays out versus the amount it retains and reinvests. Interactions exist among investment, financing, and dividend decisions. When a firm changes its dividend payment, it may also have to change one of these other policies. By lowering the amount of dividends paid, a firm can retain more funds for investment purposes and avoid having to raise as much external financing. Financial managers typically pay careful attention to their choice of dividend policy for their firm.

As we have repeatedly discussed, a central principle of financial management is that managers should make decisions that lead to maximizing the wealth of shareholders as reflected in the firm's stock price. At first glance, paying as much dividends as possible to shareholders seems a logical approach for a corporation to take. Upon further examination, paying cash dividends makes less sense if the firm can reinvest earnings back in the business to benefit shareholders.

The payment versus retention of earnings decision is often puzzling because it involves many conflicting forces. Much debate exists about the role, if any, of dividend decisions on share prices. Both academics and corporate managers continue to disagree about whether the value of a firm is independent of its dividend policy. The challenge facing the firm's board of directors and management is to balance these forces to maximize the contribution of its dividend policy toward increasing shareholder wealth.

Although a firm's entire after-tax earnings belong to its stockholders, a corporation usually distributes only a portion, if any, as cash dividends and reinvests the remainder in additional assets. When a firm keeps earnings, such earnings appear in the equity section on the balance sheet as retained earnings. The cash dividend paid directly to stockholders partially compensates them for investing in the firm. As an alternative to paying cash dividends, a firm can also disburse cash to shareholders by repurchasing shares of its common stock.

In this chapter, we focus on dividends and share repurchases because they are the principal mechanisms by which corporations disburse cash to their shareholders. We also discuss other related matters such as dividend reinvestment plans, stock dividends, stock splits, and reverse stock splits. We conclude that dividends can matter by affecting shareholder wealth because of various market imperfections and other factors.

Learning Objectives

After completing this chapter, you should be able to:

- explain the theory and practice of dividend policy;
- identify key factors influencing a firm's dividend decision;
- describe two major categories of dividend policies;
- explain why companies repurchase stock;
- discuss the tradeoffs between cash dividends and stock repurchase;
- explain two types of dividend reinvestment plans;
- differentiate among stock dividends, stock splits, and reverse splits;
- discuss how the market typically reacts to news of changes in cash dividends, stock repurchase, stock dividends, stock splits, and reverse stock splits.

12.1 Dividends and Dividend Policy

Dividend policy is an important topic because dividends represent major cash outlays for many corporations. Dividends are at the heart of the difficult choice that management must make in allocating their capital resources: reinvesting the money within the company or distributing it to shareholders. Although paying dividends directly benefits stockholders, it also affects the firm's ability to retain earnings to exploit growth opportunities. Dividend policy provides guidelines for balancing the conflicting forces surrounding the dividend payment versus retention decision.

During the growth frenzy of the late 1990s, corporate managers were often reluctant to introduce, increase, or even discuss dividends. In an investment world fixated on technology companies, dot-coms, and aggressive new-economy opportunities, many corporate managers believed that plowing money back into the company would be more productive than paying dividends to shareholders. During the late 1990s, managers and investors alike viewed dividends as antiquated and obsolete. Not surprisingly, investors tended to focus on only the capital gains part of total return and ignored dividend yield, the other part.

In the spring of 2000, the technology sector collapsed and pulled down most of the other markets. The ensuing bear market led to a shift in focus towards certainty, safety, and predictability. In turn, investor attitudes toward dividends started to change. Today, not only are more companies starting to pay or to increase dividends but also more investors are emphasizing stable dividends. This example illustrates the highly cyclical attitude of investors towards dividends.

Dividend policy refers to the payout policy that management follows in determining the size and pattern of distributions to shareholders over time. The dividend policy question centers on the percentage of earnings that a firm should pay out. A **dividend** is a direct payment from a corporation to its stockholders. Corporations commonly pay dividends in cash, but occasionally they pay dividends in stock, property, or some other asset. All dividends, except for stock dividends, reduce the total stockholders' equity in the corporation. The **dividend payout ratio** is the percentage of earnings paid to shareholders in cash. In this section, we focus only on cash dividends, but we discuss other forms of distributions later in this chapter.

Cash Dividends

Cash dividends return profits to the owners of a corporation. The most common type of cash dividend is a **regular cash dividend**, which is a cash payment made by a firm to its stockholders in the normal course of business. Most dividend paying companies issue a regular cash dividend four times a year. An implicit assumption is that the firm will continue regular cash dividends in future periods. Corporations may also issue **specially designated dividends**, which management labels as "extra," "special," or "year-end." Labeling dividends permits the firm to increase the dividend during a year without the implicit need to continue that dividend in future years. Firms tend to declare these specially designated dividends after experiencing good earnings over the previous year. Thus, investors should not expect the operating performance that precedes a special dividend to continue after the announcement.

Another form of dividend is a **liquidating dividend**, which is any dividend not based on earnings. Liquidating dividends imply a return of the stockholders' investment rather than of profits. For example, liquidating dividends may result from selling off all or part of the business and distributing the funds to shareholders.

Dividend Payment Procedure

A corporation's board of directors is ultimately responsible for a firm's dividend policy. This policy could vary from zero to 100 percent payout of earnings. A corporation has no legal obligation to declare a dividend. After the board declares a dividend, the declared cash dividend becomes a liability and the corporation has a legal obligation to make the payment. Once the board sets the dividend, the procedure for paying the dividend is routine. In chronological order, the four important dates associated with a dividend payment are as follows.

1   *Declaration date.* The **declaration date** is the date when the board of directors announces the dividend payment.
2   *Ex-dividend date.* The **ex-dividend date** is the cut-off date for receiving the dividend. That is, the ex-dividend date is the first date on which the right to the most recently declared dividend no longer goes along with the sale of the stock. Companies and exchanges report the ex-dividend date to remove any ambiguity about who will receive a dividend after the sale of a stock. Investors who buy the stock before the ex-dividend date are entitled to the dividend, while those who buy shares on or after the ex-dividend date are not.
3   *Record date.* The **record date** is the date on which an investor must be a shareholder of record to be entitled to the upcoming dividend. The brokerage industry has a convention that new shareholders are entitled to dividends only if they buy the stock at least two business days before the record date. This rule allows time for the transfer of the shares and gives the company sufficient notice of the transfer to ensure that new stockholders receive the dividend. Therefore, a stock sells ex-dividend two business days, not calendar days, before the record date. The board of directors sets the record date, which is typically several weeks after the declaration date.
4. *Payment date.* The **payment date** is the date when the firm mails the dividend checks to the shareholders of record. This date is usually several weeks after the record date.

Example 12.1 Key Dates Associated with Microsoft's First Dividend

On January 17, 2003, the board of directors of Microsoft Corp. declared its first dividend ever. This annual dividend amounted to $0.16 a share before a 2-for-1 stock split. Microsoft paid the dividend on March 7 to shareholders of record on February 21. The ex-dividend date was Wednesday, February 19, two business days before Friday, February 21. Figure 12.1 presents a dividend time line showing the key dates in the payment of the dividend by Microsoft.

Market Impact of Dividends

In theory, the price of a stock should drop by the amount of the dividend on the ex-dividend date. The reason for this behavior is simple. When investors buy common stock on the

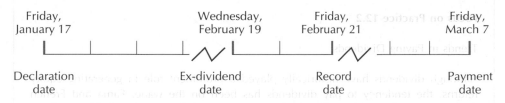

Friday,
January 17

Wednesday,
February 19

Friday,
February 21

Friday,
March 7

Declaration
date

Ex-dividend
date

Record
date

Payment
date

Figure 12.1 Key dates of Microsoft's initial dividend payment

ex-dividend date, they do not receive the cash dividend per share but the sellers do. Therefore, buyers are only willing to pay, and sellers are willing to accept, a price for the stock that excludes the dividend per share. For example, assume that a stock is selling for $50 a share before the ex-dividend date and the board of directors declares a dividend of $1 per share. The stock price should drop by $1 on the ex-dividend date, other things being unchanged, because investors who buy the stock are not entitled to the dividend.

In practice, the price drop on the ex-dividend date may not equal the dividend payment. One reason is that transaction costs and tax laws may prevent the stock price from declining by the exact amount of the dividend. For example, favorable capital gains tax treatment could cause the price drop to be less than the dividend payment. In addition, other news events may cause changes in the stock price. Empirical evidence on the amount of the price drop on the ex-dividend date is inconclusive and offers conflicting findings.

Dividend Decisions

Management must make dividend policy decisions together with financing and investment decisions due to the interaction among these decisions. Management faces numerous types of dividend decisions including:

- Should the company pay a dividend? If so, how much should the dividend be?
- What type of dividend should the company pay – cash, stock, or both?
- Should the company pay stable or irregular dividends?
- How frequently should the company pay dividends?
- Should the company announce its dividend policy?
- Should the company consider repurchasing its stock in lieu of paying or increasing its cash dividend?

The central dividend policy issue is whether freely available earnings of the company will earn more for the shareholders if left in the business to finance growth or if distributed to them as cash dividends or by share repurchases. Dividends are important because the timing and size of a firm's expected dividend payments ultimately determine the value of a firm's stock. The issue of whether the time pattern of cash dividends matters is controversial.

Focus on Practice 12.2

Trends in Paying Dividends

Although dividends have historically played a prominent role in generating equity returns, the tendency to pay dividends has been on the wane. Fama and French document a substantial decline in the percentage of firms paying dividends. From a post-1972 peak of 66.6 percent in 1978, the proportion of dividend payers among NYSE, AMEX, and NASDAQ firms fell to 20.8 percent in 1999. Three characteristics tend to affect the likelihood that a firm pays dividends: profitability, growth, and size. Large, highly profitable firms are more likely to pay dividends, and high-growth firms are less likely to do so. Fama and French conclude that the trend towards disappearing dividends is attributable not only to the changing population of firms that trade on these markets but also to a lower propensity to pay dividends.

Source: Eugene F. Fama and Kenneth R. French, "Disappearing Dividends: Changing Firm Characteristics or Lower Propensity to Pay," *Journal of Applied Corporate Finance* 14, Spring 2001, 67–79.

In Chapter 5, we presented the constant growth valuation model for common stock, $P_0 = D_1 / (k_s - g)$. This model shows that the price of common stock depends on three factors: (1) the expected dividend in the next period, D_1, (2) the required rate of return on the stock, k_s, and (3) the growth rate of the firm's dividends, g. Holding other factors constant, if a firm decides to increase its cash dividend (D_1), the firm's stock price should increase. Yet, by increasing its dividend, the firm reduces its growth rate (g), which tends to decrease the firm's stock price. The reduction in g occurs because retaining fewer earnings reduces the cash available to acquire additional assets. Because an increasing asset base is necessary to help firms grow, having a lower amount of retained earnings reduces the expected future growth rate, g, and depresses the stock price, P_0. Thus, a change in dividends results in conflicting forces that can increase or decrease the value of the firm's common stock. The **optimal dividend policy** strikes a balance between current dividends and future growth that maximizes the price of the firm's common stock.

Concept Check 12.1

1 What is the difference between regular cash dividends and specially designated dividends?
2 Who is ultimately responsible for deciding a corporation's dividend policy?
3 What are the four key dates in the dividend payment procedure? Explain the purpose of each.
4 Why does a stock go ex-dividend two business days before the record date?
5 How should the price of a stock behave when it goes ex-dividend?

12.2 The Dividend Puzzle

The questions of "Why do corporations pay dividends?" and "Why do investors pay attention to dividends?" have puzzled both academicians and corporate managers for many years.[1] Today, corporate managers face a vast and often conflicting body of research about dividends.[2] In this section, we examine the debate that has continued for almost five decades. Despite much research intended to resolve the dividend puzzle, dividend policy remains one of the most judgmental decisions that managers must make.

At the heart of the dividend puzzle is whether dividend policy affects share prices. Some financial experts contend that dividend policy does not affect the value of a firm's common stock. Others believe that dividend policy has a strong impact on stock price. Researchers have been unable to identify the "true" relationship between dividend payments and stock prices. Despite the difficulty of untangling the dividend puzzle, many firms pay cash dividends and managers typically behave as though dividend policy is relevant. We present below the major opposing views about the relevancy of dividend policy.

Dividend Irrelevance Theory

One school of thought called **dividend irrelevance theory** argues that what a firm pays in dividends is irrelevant and that stockholders are indifferent about receiving dividends. Thus, whether the dividend rate is high or low or even whether a firm pays dividends does not matter. Dividend policy is simply a way to package the return of the firm's cash flows. That is, valuation depends only upon the productivity of the firm's assets and not the form of payout. Because this packaging does not affect the common stock's market value, shareholders should be indifferent between receiving dividends today and having a claim on future earnings. If a corporation pays out dividends, the shareholders are that much richer, but the corporation is that much poorer. Therefore, a firm's dividend policy is irrelevant. According to this view, there is no optimal dividend policy. One dividend policy is as good as any other.

---

[1] Fisher Black, "The Dividend Puzzle," *Journal of Portfolio Management*, Winter 1976, 5–8 coined the phrase "the dividend puzzle."

[2] For more detailed discussion of dividends, see Ronald C. Lease, Kose John, Avner Kalay, Uri Loewenstein, and Oded H. Sarig, *Dividend Policy: Its Impact on Firm Value*, Harvard Business School Press, 2000; and George M. Frankfurter and Bob G. Wood with James Wansley, *Dividend Policy: Theory and Practice*, Academic Press, 2003.

Four Slices or Eight?

Let's return to the same whimsical example that we used to illustrate capital structure irrelevance and apply it to dividend irrelevance. Suppose that you go to a restaurant and order a pizza. The waitperson asks whether you want the pizza cut into four slices or eight. You respond, "Please cut the pizza into four slices because I can't possibly eat eight." Obviously, how the pizza is sliced does not affect its overall size. How a company slices the cash flows or earnings available to common stock investors also should not affect the firm's value. This latter statement rests on the presence of several simplifying assumptions.

The notion that dividends are irrelevant comes from the pioneering work of Nobel laureates Miller and Modigliani (M&M).[3] Under restrictive assumptions, they provide a compelling and widely accepted argument for dividend irrelevance. M&M frame their analysis in the context of a perfect capital market with rational investors. Table 12.1 lists key assumptions of this idealized version of capital markets. Such simplifying assumptions are clearly unrealistic in the real world. Yet, examining dividend policy in perfect capital markets can provide managers with useful insights about the conditions under which dividends may affect stock prices.

Table 12.1 Conditions assumed under perfect capital markets

- No flotation, transaction, and agency costs
- No taxes
- Equal and costless access to information – investors are symmetrically informed
- Investor rationality
- Price taker markets – investors cannot influence the price of a security
---

M&M argue that shareholders are indifferent to the payment of dividends because they can create any dividend policy they desire. That is, they can buy shares when the dividend payout is excessive or sell shares when the dividend payout is too low. Thus, a company's dividend decisions achieve nothing that shareholders cannot achieve for themselves. Examples 12.2 and 12.3 illustrate that investors can undo any dividend decision that the firm makes.

---
[3] Merton Miller and Franco Modigliani, "Dividend Policy, Growth, and the Valuation of Shares," *Journal of Business*, October 1961, 411–33.

Example 12.2 Reversing Dividends in a Perfect Capital Market

Suppose an investor owns 100 shares of common stock priced at $10.10 per share. The company pays a dividend of $0.10 per share, but the investor does not want the dividend. This investor can reverse the dividend by buying one new share of common stock with the cash received from the dividend. The investor receives $10 in dividends (100 shares × $0.10 per share) and uses the money to buy one additional share of the firm's common stock. Each share will now sell for $10 because the market price of the stock theoretically adjusts downward by the amount of the dividend.

As Table 12.2 shows, the investor is no worse off or better off after receiving the dividend than before receiving the dividend. Based on the M&M assumptions, this investor paid no transaction fees or taxes and the decrease in the market value of the old stock is equal in value to the newly purchased stock. After receiving the dividend, the investor owns 101 shares of common stock. Each share has a value of $10 per share for a total value of $1,010. This amount is equal in value to the 100 shares the investor owned worth $10.10 each before receiving the dividend.

Table 12.2 Illustration of dividend irrelevance by reversing dividends[a]

	Before receiving dividends	After receiving dividends
1 Shares of common stock owned	100	101
2 Price per share of common stock	$10.10	$10.00
3 Total value of common stock [1 × 2]	$1,010.00	$1,010.00

[a] Assume payment of a $0.10 per share cash dividend.

Example 12.3 Creating Dividends in a Perfect Capital Market

A shareholder who wants a dividend when the company does not pay one can create what M&M call "homemade dividends." This occurs by selling some shares of common stock equal to the amount of the desired dividend. Assume that the company in Example 12.2 now does not pay a dividend. An investor who wants a dividend can sell one share of common stock. The investor will receive $10.10 in cash and keep 99 shares of common stock valued at $10.10 each for total wealth of $1,010. In this situation, the value of the common stock does not decline, since the firm paid no cash dividend. In either instance, the investor's total wealth is $1,010. Once again, the restrictive assumptions of no transaction fees or taxes apply. Table 12.3 summarizes these transactions.

Table 12.3 Illustration of dividend irrelevance by creating dividends

	Before selling a share	After selling a share
1 Shares of common stock owned	100	99
2 Price per share of common stock	$10.10	$10.10
3 Total value of common stock [1 × 2]	$1,010.00	$999.90
4 Cash from selling 1 share		$10.10
5 Total wealth [3 + 4]	$1,010.00	$1,010.00

> **Practical Financial Tip 12.1**
>
> The conclusion that the firm's choice of dividend policy is irrelevant may not be valid under real world conditions. For dividend policy to become a relevant decision variable, market frictions and behavioral considerations must affect valuation in a systematic manner.

Dividend Relevance Theory

We know from M&M that dividend policy does not matter based on a perfect capital market. That is, perfect capital market conditions tip the balance scale toward dividend policy irrelevance. Yet, this simple world ignores several real-world factors and rests on unrealistic assumptions. In addition, M&M focus almost entirely on the impact of dividend policies on the current market value of the company, not the impact on the business itself. In analyzing dividend policy, M&M and their followers ignore the question of how a company reinvests its cash flow. No sensible manager would make such an assumption. Thus, once we leave M&M's idealized world of economic theory and enter the real world, the issue of dividend irrelevance becomes debatable.

Another school of thought on dividends argues that dividend policy is relevant. If dividend policy matters, its relevance must result from various market imperfections. That is, market frictions may tip the balance scale of dividend policy in favor of relevance. What are these market imperfections or frictions? Table 12.4 provides one classification of these imperfections.[4]

To accommodate the world in which market imperfections exist, academicians have developed various theories to explain why firms pay dividends. We focus on explanations involving the major market imperfections but also discuss other minor market frictions that potentially make the dividend decision relevant. Although the explanations of why firms pay dividends tend to focus on each market imperfection in isolation, complex interactions may exist among these factors. If the imperfections are insignificant or offsetting, the M&M

Table 12.4 Market imperfections affecting the relevance of dividend policy

Big three imperfections	Little three frictions
Taxes	Transaction costs
Asymmetric information	Flotation costs
Agency costs	Behavioral considerations (irrational investor behavior)

---

[4] For a detailed discussion of the "big three imperfections" and the "little three frictions," see Lease et al., *Dividend Policy: Its Impact on Firm Value*, Harvard Business School Press, 2000.

conclusion about dividend irrelevance may hold. Otherwise, these market imperfections may be relevant to the dividend setting process and may affect the value of the firm. Our belief is that dividend policies vary dramatically among firms because the imperfections affect firms differently.

The Tax-preference Explanation

In perfect capital markets, there are no taxes. In the real world, taxes do exist and may differ among investors. One of the earliest explanations of why dividend policy matters involves the tax effect. Tax-adjusted models assume that investors expect higher pretax returns from dividend-paying stock because of the future tax liability on dividends.

According to the tax-preference argument, investors who receive favorable tax treatment on capital gains may prefer stocks with low dividend payouts. Historically, the tax authorities in the United States have taxed dividend income more heavily than long-term capital gains. As we discuss shortly, the Tax Act of 2003 lowers and equalizes the maximum tax rate on dividends and capital gains. In addition to having a lower tax rate on long-term capital gains than on dividend income, investors can defer the capital gains tax. That is, they do not have to pay taxes on the capital gains until they sell their stock. Those investors who are subject to paying taxes on cash dividends cannot postpone the payment. The tax-preference argument suggests that firms should keep dividend payments low if they want to maximize share prices.

Because the tax effect differs among various types of investors, different dividend policies may result in tax-induced clientele effects. The **clientele effect** implies that stocks attract particular groups or clienteles based on **dividend yield**, the ratio of dividends per share to a firm's stock price. That is, investors buy stock in firms having dividend policies that meet their particular needs. Companies paying high dividend yields such as utilities may attract one group of investors while companies paying low dividend yields such as high technology firms may attract another.

Different clienteles may result from such factors as stockholder desire for additional current income, the perceived riskiness of dividends versus capital gains, and the investor tax rate. For example, many institutional investors such as pension plans favor firms with high dividend payouts because they pay no or low taxes. Some individuals favor firms with low or no dividends because such investors do not need the income or are in high tax brackets.

The tax-induced clientele effect may help explain why stock prices change after an announced change in dividend policy. If management changes a firm's dividend pattern, those stockholders who are unhappy with the new policy may sell the stock and buy stock of companies having dividend policies more to their liking. Selling pressure may lead to a decline in the firm's stock price. If more new investors like the new policy than dislike it, the net result of the clientele effect may be an increase in the price of the stock. Opponents of the clientele effect, such as M&M, argue that one clientele is simply a substitute for another. With an ample supply of firms with diverse dividend payout policies, a shift in clientele should not affect a firm's stock price. Only limited evidence supports tax-induced dividend clienteles of shareholders.

Effect of the 2003 Tax Act on Dividends

The Jobs and Growth Reconciliation Tax Act of 2003 lowers and equalizes the maximum tax rate on dividends and capital gains. Under the Act, the maximum rate on qualified dividends and long-term capital gains (those from securities held more than 1 year) is 15 percent. Dividends from real estate investment trusts (REITS), however, will continue to be taxed as ordinary income. Under the old rates, dividends were taxed as ordinary income, up to a maximum rate of 38.6 percent and long-term capital gains at a maximum rate of 20 percent. Short-term gains on securities held 1 year or less are still taxed as ordinary income. These changes are in effect only through 2008. Unless Congress acts, the rates on dividends and gains will revert in 2009 to the levels of 2002. The change in dividend taxation has already prompted some companies to initiate a dividend or raise their dividends. The tax changes could serve as a catalyst for improving how companies are financed and managed.

The Signaling Explanation

In perfect capital markets, all parties have equal and costless access to the same information. Such markets are symmetrically informed markets. In practice, information asymmetry exists. **Information asymmetry** suggests that corporate managers have an information advantage over other interested parties. If managers, as corporate insiders, have information that others do not have, they may use a change in dividends as a way to signal this private information and thus reduce information asymmetry. Another name for this type of signaling is the **information content of dividends**. In turn, investors may use dividend announcements as information to assess a firm's stock price. Thus, signaling models assume that dividend policy conveys important information to the market about the quality of a company.

Managers have an incentive to signal this private information to the investment public when they believe that the current market value of their firm's stock is below its intrinsic value. If managers accurately convey favorable information about the firm, which is unknown to the investors, the firm's stock price is likely to increase. Yet, investors are aware that management has an incentive to provide false signals if this will temporarily increase the price of the stock. In addition, dividend changes may not be perfect signals. Thus, management faces a signaling problem of transmitting information that is believable to the market.

Because of information asymmetry, stock prices are sometimes too low or too high based on information available to managers. When a firm announces an unexpectedly high or low dividend, investors may view this news as having information content about how management views the firm's expected future prospects. For example, an unexpectedly large dividend increase may signal investors that management is confident that the firm's future earnings and cash flows warrant the higher dividends. An unexpected cut or omission in dividends may signal investors that management expects the future level of earnings or cash flows to be weak. Thus, an implication of the dividend-signaling hypothesis is firms that increase (decrease) cash dividends should experience positive (negative) price reactions.

Proponents of information signaling contend that dividends help to resolve the problem of information asymmetry by serving as credible signaling devices. Much controversy still exists about what types of signal dividend changes provide. A plausible argument exists that an increase in dividends may send a negative signal to financial markets. For example, assume that a firm with an historical record of extraordinary growth and high returns decides to initiate a dividend. The market may view paying dividends as an indication that the firm's prospects are not as optimistic as in the past. Critics also suggest that dividends may not be the most cost-effective signal for managers to use. Empirical tests involving the signaling explanation yield mixed results. Although many managers agree with the basic premise outlined here, studies show that many other variables are at work.

Example 12.4 Difficulty in Sending Credible Signals: Florida Power & Light Company

FPL Group, the parent company of Florida Power & Light Company, announced a 32 percent reduction in its quarterly dividend on May 9, 1994, for strategic reasons, not problems in cash flow. Despite the company's extensive efforts to explain the reasons for the reduction in dividends, the stock market's initial reaction to FPL's announcement was negative. The stock dropped about 20 percent in value. After carefully reviewing the reasons for the reduction, analysts concluded that the action was not a signal of financial distress. Instead, the dividend decrease was a strategic decision designed by management to improve the firm's long-term flexibility and growth prospects. After the financial community adopted this view, FPL's stock began to recover.[5]

Practical Financial Tip 12.2

Dividend changes are not perfect signals and may be ambiguous. For example, a dividend increase may suggest future growth or a lack of investment opportunities, while a decrease in dividends may suggest just the opposite. Managers should clearly communicate the rationale for changing their firm's dividend policy so that the market can incorporate such information into its valuation process.

The Agency Explanation

Another view of dividend relevance is **agency theory**. This theory derives from the conflict of interests between corporate managers (agents) and outside shareholders (principals). Management may decide to retain earnings and subsequently use the money inappropriately rather than paying out dividends to shareholders. For example, managers may retain more

---

[5]   For further discussion of FPL, see Denis Soter, Eugene Brigham, and Paul Evanson, "The Dividend Cut Heard 'Round the World': The Case of FPL," *Journal of Applied Corporate Finance*, Spring 1996, 4–15.

capital than the firm needs to boost their empires, try to generate appreciation in the stock price to benefit their options, or consume excessive perquisites out of undistributed corporate earnings. They may also employ retained funds suboptimally by using the money for acquisitions that make no sense or for share repurchase at inappropriate prices. This conflict leads to **agency costs**. Agency theory posits that the dividend mechanism provides an incentive for managers to reduce these agency costs related to the principal/agent relationship. That is, agency theory models contend that dividend policy mitigates agency conflicts between managerial and stockholder priorities.

One way to reduce agency costs is to increase dividends. According to the **free cash flow hypothesis**, dividend payments can reduce the potential misuse of free cash flow generated by companies. Thus, paying dividends reduces the discretionary funds that managers could use and forces the firm to seek more external financing. Raising costly outside capital subjects the firm to the scrutiny of the capital market for new funds and reduces the possibility of suboptimal investment. This monitoring by outside suppliers of capital also helps to ensure that managers act in the best interest of outside shareholders. Thus, dividend payments may serve as a means of monitoring management performance and ensuring behavior consistent with shareholder wealth maximization. Thus, shareholders are willing to accept the higher personal taxes associated with dividends in exchange for the increase in monitoring that the professional investment community provides.

When institutional investors are relatively less taxed than individuals are, dividends result in "ownership clientele" effects. Firms paying dividends attract relatively more institutions. Because institutions are better informed than individuals, they have a relative advantage in detecting high firm quality and using this information to help the firm control agency problems. Thus, institutions are more likely to play a larger role in overseeing management than are dispersed individual investors. Mixed empirical results exist on the agency costs explanation for paying dividends.

Other Explanations for Dividend Relevance

Three other market imperfections that may make the dividend decision relevant are transaction costs, flotation costs, and behavioral considerations.

Transaction costs

In Examples 12.2 and 12.3, we show that shareholders can construct their own dividend policy without incurring costs. That is, they can undo any dividend decision made by a firm's managers. Shareholders can create their desired cash flow levels by selling shares of stock to create "homemade dividends" or using unwanted dividends to buy additional shares of the company's stock. Under the conditions of no transaction costs and taxes, one dividend policy is as good as any other. In practice, taxes and transaction costs exist so dividend policy may be relevant.

Flotation costs

Assume that a firm has a large amount of attractive investment opportunities that require more funds than are available internally after meeting dividend commitments. By assuming away flotation costs, M&M enable companies to obtain costless financing to fund new investments. Without flotation costs, the firm would be indifferent between using internally versus externally generated funds for such purposes. In real-world financial markets, companies face flotation costs if they need funds to finance desirable investment opportunities.

Getting funds from outside markets can be expensive. If financing costs are high, firms may prefer to finance investments internally by retaining earnings, not by using external sources. The cost of raising external funds suggests that firms should rely on internal equity (retained earnings) to provide the equity portion of their target capital structure. When dividends compete with investments for internally generated funds, financing costs may affect dividend policy. Therefore, as the need for investment funds increases, so will the costs associated with increasing the dividend payment.

Behavioral considerations

M&M assume that investors are economically rational in that they prefer more wealth to less wealth. Ample anecdotal evidence exists that investors are not always rational. For example, some shareholders may want to receive cash dividends for self-control reasons. That is, dividends ration out money that investors can spend without ever touching the principal. Thus, they avoid the temptation and the inconvenience of selling more stock than they need to generate cash. In addition, some firms continue to pay dividends because of habitual behavior. That is, they continue to pay dividends because old habits, which consti-tute corporate tradition, are hard to change. Solving the dividend puzzle may be impossible while ignoring the patterns of normal investor behavior.

Focus on Practice 12.3

Do Managers Think Dividend Policy Is Relevant?

The issue of whether dividend policy affects firm value remains controversial. Two surveys provide insights into this controversy. In 1997, Baker and Powell surveyed managers of dividend paying US corporations listed on the New York Stock Exchange to determine their views about dividend policy. The majority of responding managers believed that dividend policy affects firm value. Of the explanations for dividend relevance examined in this study, the respondents generally had the highest level of agreement with statements involving signaling as a way of overcoming the problem of asymmetric information. For example, the vast majority of respondents agreed that "investors regard dividend changes as signals about a firm's future prospects." In 1999, Baker, Powell, and Veit conducted a similar study of senior managers of NASDAQ firms with an established pattern of paying cash dividends. Their evidence shows that NASDAQ managers widely supported statements consistent with the concept that a firm's dividend policy matters. Managers gave the strongest support to a signaling explanation for paying dividends.

Source: H. Kent Baker and Gary E. Powell, "How Corporate Managers View Dividend Policy," *Quarterly Journal of Business and Economics*, Spring 1999, 16–35; and H. Kent Baker, Gary E. Powell, and E. Theodore Veit, "Revisiting Managerial Perspectives on Dividend Policy," *Journal of Economics and Finance*, Fall 2002, 267–83.

Wealth Effects of Cash Dividends

Cash dividend announcements would intuitively seem to affect a stock's price. The important factor is not the dividend itself but the information conveyed by the change of dividend policy. Analysts and investors develop expectations about dividend payments before a firm announces the decision by its board of directors on the size of the next dividend payment. Assuming the announced dividend approximates the expected dividend, the announcement should not affect the price of the stock. Why? The market already expects the dividend and incorporates that information in pricing the stock. The amount of the dividend or the nature of the dividend must be a surprise to move a stock's price.

Evidence shows that increases in stock prices often accompany larger than expected dividend increases. In addition, unexpected dividend cuts or omissions can send prices plummeting. Firms just beginning to pay dividends also show significant increases in stock prices. The usual interpretation of this phenomenon is that such changes in dividend policy convey information to the market about the firm's future earnings and cash flows. Research shows that stock prices quickly reflect dividend policy changes, typically on the same trading day of the announcement.

Practical Financial Tip 12.3

A problem with most existing dividend theories is that they fail to consider the potentially complex interactions among the various imperfections. Another problem is that each theory typically takes a "one-size-fits-all" approach by trying to generalize the findings. Because various imperfections affect firms differently, dividend policy may vary substantially from one firm to another. Because no single model specifies which dividend policy results in the highest value of a firm, neither managers nor investors know with certainty if a specific firm's dividend policy is optimal. Therefore, we view a firm's dividend policy as being acceptable within a range.

Concept Check 12.2

1 Why do Miller and Modigliani contend that dividend policy is irrelevant?
2 What are the key assumptions of perfect capital markets?
3 If shareholders could create their own income stream at no cost (using the argument by M&M), what type of dividend policy would a firm most likely use?
4 What are the "big three imperfections" and the "little three frictions" involving capital markets?
5 What is the clientele effect? What kind of clienteles would utility stocks paying high dividends likely attract?
6 What are the implications of the clientele effect on a firm's dividend policy?
7 How can management use a firm's dividend policy to signal information about the firm?

8 How can flotation costs in financing affect a firm's dividend policy?
9 How do stock prices typically respond to news of unexpected dividend increases and decreases?

12.3 Factors Influencing the Dividend Decision

The dividend decision involves determining whether to pay dividends and, if so, how much. Although market imperfections including behavioral and psychological influences may encourage firms to pay dividends, other factors also may affect a firm's choice. These factors change over time and differ across industries and companies. We classify these influences on the dividend decision into three broad groups.

1 Shareholder factors
2 Firm factors
3 Other constraints

To determine a proper dividend policy, management must consider many different and often conflicting and overlapping factors. The importance of these factors differs from firm to firm. The problem facing management is to balance the importance of each factor. Unfortunately, no simple or single solution exists for determining a reasonable, much less an optimal, dividend policy. Some factors favor paying high dividends while others favor low or no dividends.

Focus on Practice 12.4

Microsoft Declares its First Dividend

On January 17, 2003, Microsoft Corp., the world's largest software maker, surprised investors by announcing plans to pay its first dividend in its 28-year history. Many technology companies have long maintained that they could not pay dividends because they needed to reinvest their profits for continued growth. Microsoft's board finally bowed to mounting pressure to return some of its $43 billion cash hoard to investors. John Connors, chief financial officer of the software giant, characterized the initial dividend as a "starter dividend" but hinted that future dividends could be higher. The move was largely a symbolic gesture to shareholders but it could force other technology companies to pay at least a small portion of their earnings to shareholders as dividends. Connors said the move should allow more institutional investors, including fund managers who can only invest in stocks that pay dividends, to buy Microsoft shares. This action could boost demand and make the stock more stable in trading. The move to paying dividends highlights the evolution in Microsoft's business from a fast-moving tech start-up to a more mature business whose core software franchises are not growing as fast as they did in the past.

Shareholder Factors

Differing perceptions and preferences may affect shareholder views about dividend policy. Specifically, shareholders may differ in their needs for dividend income, their perception of the extent to which dividends reduce risk, and the tax status of dividends. The potential effect of a firm's dividend policy on dilution of ownership may also concern some shareholders.

Income needs

Some investors, such as retirees, depend on dividend income to help pay their living expenses. They want firms to provide large and stable dividends. An omission or cut in dividends could cause hardship for them. M&M say that shareholders can create homemade dividends by liquidating their share of ownership in a company. Yet, some shareholders are averse to creating homemade dividends because selling shares involves paying brokerage fees and perhaps taxes if they sell shares at prices above their original investment. In practice, homemade dividends are not perfect substitutes for cash dividends.

Risk preferences

The attitudes of shareholders about risk may affect their preferences for dividend policies. When a firm chooses to keep say $1 per share of earnings instead of paying that amount out as a dividend, investors should expect to benefit in the future by selling that stock at a price that is at least $1 higher than if the dividend is paid. Waiting to sell stock at a higher price is risky. Therefore, cautious investors may prefer to receive the cash dividend now, rather than take a chance on the future sale price of the stock. A common term for this preference is the **"bird-in-the-hand" argument**.

Opponents of this reasoning contend that the risk of future dividends and risk of capital gains are the same. M&M assert that shareholder risk lies only in the risk of a company's operating cash flows. How a company divides these cash flows between dividends and retention does not matter. An unsolved issue in finance is whether dividend payments reduce shareholders' perceived risk.

Tax status

The tax clientele argument suggests that investors in high tax brackets prefer stocks paying low or no dividends. When stockholders receive dividends, they must declare them as income and pay taxes on them in the year received. Investors in high tax brackets often prefer small dividends for two major reasons. First, they often do not need the dividends to enhance their current consumption of goods and services. Second, high tax-bracket investors generally prefer to avoid the tax liability resulting from a large dividend.

Retaining earnings may lead to an increase in a firm's stock price and to a postponement in the taxes shareholders pay on capital gains. By deferring the payment of taxes on capital gains, shareholders reduce the present value of their future tax payments.

Dilution of ownership

Another influence on investors' preferences is a concern about the dilution of ownership. When firms can support their need for common equity financing by using retained earnings, they can avoid issuing new common stock and, therefore, avert diluting each stockholder's proportionate ownership of the firm. This factor is particularly important to investors who own a large proportion of a firm's common stock.

Firm Factors

Besides trying to set dividend policy to serve shareholder interests, management should also consider several firm-related factors that may influence the dividend decision.

Stage of life cycle
A firm's dividend policy often follows the life cycle of the firm. A firm's dividend cycle consists of several stages.

- *Start-up and initial public offering (IPO) stages.* Market imperfections and frictions lead to a policy of paying no dividends. At these stages, taxes to equity holders and asymmetric information are high, agency costs are low, but transaction and flotation costs are high.
- *Rapid growth stage.* Companies tend to pay no or very low dividends. At this stage, the tax effect declines with the addition of new equity owners. The problem of asymmetric information moderates as information about the firm increases due to disclosure requirements. Agency costs grow due to increased separation between owners and managers. Transaction and flotation costs tend to moderate as the firm grows in size.
- *Maturity and decline stage.* At these stages, a growing to generous dividend payout policy tends to prevail. This change in dividend policy reflects changes in the importance of various market frictions. Taxes decline in importance as a market imperfection with growing institutional ownership because such owners often pay little or no taxes on dividends. Institutional owners have a greater ability to analyze firms than do individual investors, so asymmetric information is only moderate. Agency costs remain high due to the separation of management and ownership. Transaction and flotation costs are low, largely due to firm size.

Practical Financial Tip 12.4

Dividends often follow the life cycle of a company. Market frictions differ at various stages of the life cycle and imply different dividend payout policies. For example, young, fast-growing firms often pay no dividends or have a low dividend payout ratio, while older, slower-growing firms in mature industries frequently use a higher ratio.

Investment opportunities
The number and amount of profitable investment opportunities facing a firm can affect its capital requirements. Firms experiencing rapid growth often have large capital requirements. To support rapid growth, firms rely on both equity and debt financing. To keep the cost of capital as low as possible, rapidly growing firms often retain more earnings and have lower dividend payout ratios than companies with slow or no growth. Larger dividend payouts

often come with company maturity and the inherent slower growth. Therefore, an inverse relationship is likely to exist between the dividend payout ratio and both growth and expected capital requirements.

External financing costs

When issuing costs are high, firms often prefer to use retained earnings as a source of capital rather than to raise funds externally. Recall from Chapter 10 that using retained earnings is less costly than issuing new common stock because the cost of retained earnings does not involve flotation costs. Firm size also affects the cost of raising funds externally in that such costs are typically higher for small versus large firms. When dividends compete with investments for internally generated funds, such costs may affect dividend policy. Therefore, an inverse relationship is likely to exist between dividend payout and external financing costs.

Access to funds and reserves

Firms with greater access to external funds can have more stable and higher dividend payments because they are less dependent on internally generated funds to finance growth. Firms with less access to funds, such as many small corporations, are likely to keep more earnings and pay lower dividends than firms with greater access to funds. The amount of a firm's financial reserves can also affect the amount of dividends. If a firm has little cash, other liquid assets, or unused borrowing capacity, this may restrict the size of the dividends because a cash dividend payment reduces a firm's cash and retained earnings. Yet, if a firm has excessive financial reserves, management may decide to increase the dividend to reduce these reserves.

Profitability and earnings stability

Profitable firms with stable earning are more likely to assume the risk of having higher dividend payouts than those firms with more volatile earnings. Management is reluctant to set dividend payments at levels that may not be sustainable because lowering a dividend sometime in the future may convey negative information and cause the firm's stock price to decline at that time. Therefore, if management is sensitive to the business cycle, it may hold back earnings in good years to enable the firm to pay dividends in poor earnings years. Table 12.5 provides a summary of the shareholder and firm factors affecting dividend decisions.

Managerial Preferences and Constraints

In making dividend decisions, management may consider its preferences and constraints placed on dividend payments imposed by state law, federal tax laws, and contractual agreements. Such restrictions are especially important to smaller corporations because they have less flexibility in working around these restrictions.

Managerial preferences

Although management should keep the best interests of shareholders in mind when making dividend decisions, managerial preferences may also influence such decisions. For example, the firm may desire to smooth dividends and to avoid dividend reductions, if possible.

Table 12.5 Shareholder and firm factors affecting dividend decisions[a]

	Conditions favoring	
Type of factor	**No or smaller dividend payout**	**Larger dividend payout**
Panel A. Shareholder		
Income needs	Income not needed	Income needed
Risk preferences	Willing to assume more risk	Willing to assume less risk
Tax status	Preference to defer taxes	No preference to defer taxes
Dilution of ownership	Concerned about dilution	Not concerned about dilution
Panel B. Firm		
Stage in life cycle	Start up to rapid growth	Maturity and decline
Investment opportunities	High	Low
External financing costs	High	Low
Access to funds and reserves	Low	High
Profitability and earnings stability	Low and unstable	High and stable

[a] For further discussion of these factors, see Ronald C. Lease et al., *Dividend Policy: Its Impact on Firm Value*, Harvard Business School Press, 2000.

Evidence suggests that dividends follow a smoother path than earnings and are "sticky" in that firms do not often change their dollar dividends.

Legal constraints
Many states prohibit firms from paying dividends if doing so reduces shareholder capital. This prohibition, known as the **capital impairment rule**, protects the security interest of creditors by limiting firms from removing equity capital from the firm through dividend payments. The courts in different states have defined the term "capital" in several ways. Often this rule says that firms may pay out all their current year's net income and accumulated retained earnings, but they may not pay dividends from their common stock or paid-in capital accounts.

Improper accumulation of earnings
The Internal Revenue Service (IRS) prohibits the undue retention of earnings in excess of the present and future investment needs of the firm if done solely as a means of avoiding taxes. The IRS may impose the **accumulated earnings tax** to prevent privately owned firms from retaining earnings beyond "reasonable business needs." The tax courts must interpret "reasonable business needs" because the IRS Code does not define the term. Thus, some firms may pay dividends to avoid paying a tax penalty on the improper accumulation of earnings.

Contractual constraints
Some bond indentures and loan agreements contain provisions limiting the payment of dividends. The main reason for limiting dividend distributions is to protect creditors. Without

such provision, a firm could distribute its assets to stockholders and reduce its ability to repay creditors.

Institutional constraints

Some states prohibit financial institutions such as banks, insurance companies, and pension funds operating within the state from investing in the common stocks of companies that do not have a long history of paying dividends. These states publish legal listings showing which stocks meet certain dividend requirements and other minimum standards of acceptability. Inclusion on these legal lists may encourage firms to pay a regular dividend.

Focus on Practice 12.5

Factors Influencing Dividend Policy Decisions

In 1997, Baker and Powell surveyed chief financial officers (CFOs) of NYSE-listed firms about their views on what factors determine dividend policy. They studied three types of businesses: manufacturing, wholesale/retail trade, and utility. They asked the CFOs to indicate the level of importance of 20 factors in setting their firms' dividend policy based on a four point scale: none, low, moderate, and high. Table 12.6 shows the six mostly highly ranked factors influencing dividend policy. Based on 198 responses, they find that the most important determinants are the level of current and expected future earnings and the pattern or continuity of past dividends. Baker, Veit, and Powell conducted a 1999 survey of NASDAQ firms and found similar results. The evidence underscores the importance that managers place on maintaining the continuity of dividends.

Table 12.6 Most highly ranked factors influencing dividend policy

Factor	Moderate/High importance (%)
Level of current and expected future earnings	94.0
Pattern or continuity of past dividends	84.8
Concern about maintaining or increasing stock price	83.3
Concern that a dividend change may provide a false signal to investors	72.6
Stability of cash flows	72.2
Investment considerations such as the availability of profitable investment opportunities	64.9

Source: H. Kent Baker and Gary E. Powell, "Determinants of Corporate Dividend Policy: A Survey of NYSE Firms," *Financial Practice and Education*, Spring/Summer 2000, 29–40; H. Kent Baker, E. Theodore Veit, and Gary E. Powell, "Factors Influencing Dividend Policy Decisions of Nasdaq Firms," *The Financial Review*, August 2001, 19–38.

Concept Check 12.3

1 What characteristics affect shareholders' preferences for a high or low dividend payout ratio? How does each characteristic affect the preference?
2 What characteristics of a firm affect its preference for a high or low dividend payout ratio? How does each characteristic affect the preference?
3 What is the implied dividend policy at the start-up to rapid growth stages compared with the maturity and decline stages of the dividend life cycle?
4 How can creditors affect a firm's dividend policy? Why do creditors prefer to place constraints on a firm's dividend policy?
5 Why do some firms pay no or low dividends, even when they have funds available to pay high dividends?
6 What legal constraints may influence a firm's dividend policy?

12.4 Dividend Policies

With the input of senior management, the company's board of directors sets a corporation's dividend policy. Many companies are proud of their long-standing tradition of paying cash dividends. For example, Coca-Cola, the world's largest soft-drink company, has paid dividends since 1983; General Motors, the world's largest producer of cars and trucks, has paid dividends since 1915.

Management faces the challenge of balancing many conflicting forces to arrive at an appropriate dividend policy. Changing dividend policy can have a short-term impact on the firm's stock price. Firms often prefer to pay the same dividend as in the prior period unless strong justification exists for making a change. Most companies' boards are reluctant to cut their dividends unless conditions force them to do so or to increase their dividends unless the new dividend is sustainable. One concern is that decreasing or eliminating a dividend may convey negative information to the financial market that adversely affects a firm's stock price. The market usually interprets an increase in dividends as a lasting commitment to pay out future cash flows to shareholders.

Although dividend policies may take many forms, most fall into two broad categories.

1 Residual dividend policy
2 Managed dividend policy

Residual Dividend Policy

With a **residual dividend policy**, a firm pays dividends from earnings left over after meeting its investment needs while maintaining its target capital structure This passive approach assumes that investors prefer firms to keep and reinvest earnings. This may be true when the return firms can earn on additional equity exceeds the return investors can earn by investing the cash themselves. Management recognizes that selling new common stock is an alternative to using retained earnings as a source of common equity. Using this more expensive source of equity will increase the firm's cost of capital and may result in accepting fewer profitable projects.

Implementing a residual dividend policy requires four steps.

1   Determine the firm's planned capital spending. Assuming no capital rationing, the planned capital spending would be the firm's optimal capital budget, which we discussed in Chapter 10.

2   Determine the amount of equity needed to finance the firm's planned spending given the firm's target capital structure.

3   Use available earnings (cash flows) to the greatest extent possible to fund the equity portion of the firm's planned capital spending.

4   Pay dividends only if more earnings (cash flows) are available than the firm needs to support the equity portion of the planned capital spending.

Following a residual dividend policy has the advantage of minimizing new stock issues and flotation costs. Unfortunately, the policy can result in highly variable dividends, which can send conflicting signals to the market. For example, a policy of paying dividends as a residual could result in large dividends during periods when earnings are high and investment opportunities are poor. A residual dividend policy could also result in small or no dividends during periods when earnings are low and investment opportunities are plentiful. As a result, dividend payments may be volatile, which can lead to volatile stock prices and investor dissatisfaction. Therefore, the main drawback of a strict residual dividend approach is that it may lead to a highly unstable dividend policy.

Example 12.5 Using a "Pure" Residual Dividend Policy

Standard Manufacturing Company (SMC) forecasts $100 million in net income. SMC wants to maintain a target capital structure of 40 percent debt and 60 percent equity. Assuming the following levels of capital spending, what are the dollar amounts of cash dividends and payout ratios?

Solution: Table 12.7 illustrates the dividend amount and dividend payout for various levels of capital spending. For example, if SMC plans to spend $150 million on capital investments during the next year, the firm needs $90 million = 0.6($150 million) in equity and $60 million = 0.4($150 million) in debt to maintain its target capital structure. Because SMC expects to have $100 million in net income, the firm would retain $90 million and pay out the "left over" earnings of $10 million = $100 million − $90 million as a cash dividend. Fewer good investments (those with expected positive NPVs) would lead to a smaller capital budget and to a higher dividend payout. More good investments would lead to a lower dividend payout.

Table 12.7 Using the residual approach at different levels of capital spending

Scenario	Net income	Capital spending	Additional debt	Retained earnings	Additional stock	Dividend amount	Dividend payout (%)
			(in millions $)				
1	100	250	100	100	50	0	0
2	100	200	80	100	20	0	0
3	100	150	60	90	0	10	10
4	100	100	40	60	0	40	40
5	100	50	20	30	0	70	70
6	100	0	0	0	0	100	100

In practice, few companies follow a "pure" residual dividend policy as a guide in setting the payout for a single year. Instead, some firms use a variant of the residual policy to help set their long-run target dividend payout. Managers following a "smoothed" or "modified" residual model might attempt to smooth their firm's dividends in relation to expected cash available over time instead of using the excess cash balance as a guide to the payout in any one year. Managers can accomplish this objective of having stable, dependable dividends by taking three steps.

1 Estimate the firm's net earnings (cash flows), investment opportunities, and target capital structure over an appropriate time horizon, such as 5 years or so.
2 Use this forecasted information to find the average residual model payout ratio and dollars of dividends during the planning period.
3 Set a target payout ratio based on the average projected data. A **target payout ratio** is the desired proportion of earnings that a firm wants to pay out in dividends.

Practical Financial Tip 12.5

Despite the general notion that firms pay dividends from earnings, cash flows [operating income × (1 − tax rate) + depreciation] are a more relevant determinant of dividends. Cash flows reflect a firm's ability to pay dividends whereas accounting practices such as accrual accounting greatly influence current earnings.

Managed Dividend Policy

A **managed dividend policy** is one in which management attempts to achieve a specific pattern of dividend payments. Managed dividend policies take three major forms: (1) stable dollar dividend policy, (2) constant payout ratio policy, and (3) regular plus specially designated dividends.

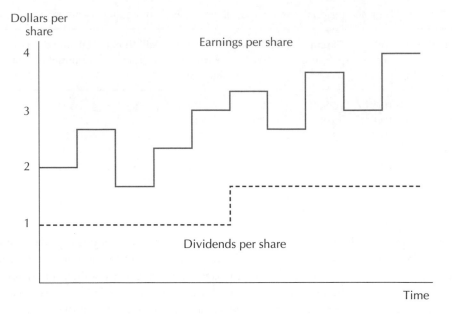

Figure 12.2 An illustration of a stable dollar dividend policy

Stable dollar dividend policy

A **stable dollar dividend policy** is one where the company maintains the same dividend per share each period unless it believes that future earnings can sustain a higher dividend. By following this policy, the firm pays a variable fraction of earnings as dividends, which results in a changing dividend payout. Earnings may change but dividends remain stable. Therefore, sudden changes in earnings do not affect the dividend payment. Dividends may grow over time if management views the new dividend as sustainable. In such cases, increases in regular cash dividends would normally lag earnings increases.

Figure 12.2 illustrates a stable dollar dividend policy. Dividends begin at $1, which is 50 percent of earnings, and remain stable until management believes that future earnings warrant a change in the dividend amount.

A firm is often reluctant to reduce dividends, even in times of financial distress. Managers realize that they may be able to affect investor expectations through the information content of dividends. A stable dividend suggests that the firm expects stable or growing dividends in the future. A stable dollar dividend policy allows the firm to send a signal by varying from that policy. Thus, the market may view dividend reductions as negative signals, which may lead to a decline in the firm's stock price. Sometimes reducing dividends is necessary when expected future earnings will not support continuing the dividend at its current level or when profitable investment opportunities are bountiful. To avoid decreasing their dividends during a year of low earnings, firms sometimes choose to pay dividends that exceed current earnings. Evidence suggests that financial markets expect a certain degree of stability in dividend payments and firms recognize this.

Most dividend-paying firms tend to follow a stable dollar dividend policy for four reasons.

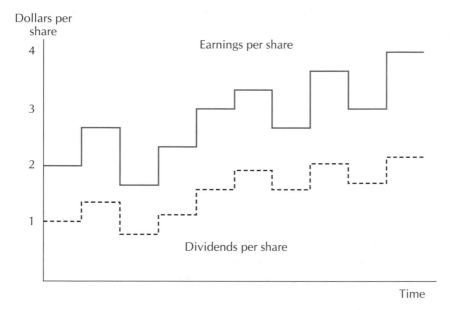

Figure 12.3 An illustration of a constant payout ratio policy

- *Many managers believe that a stable dollar dividend policy leads to higher stock prices.* The empirical evidence on the relationship between dividend policy and stock prices is inconclusive.
- *Stockholders often rely on dividends to provide a steady source of income to supplement their current consumption.* If such investors cannot depend on steady dividends, they are less likely to buy the firm's stock.
- *A stable dividend policy provides less chance of conveying erroneous information content.* Thus, management avoids reducing dividends because of the negative signal that a dividend cut might convey.
- *Legal listing in many states requires dividend stability.* Inclusion on the legal listings can raise the demand for the shares of a firm's common stock.

Constant Dividend Payout Ratio

A **constant dividend payout ratio** is a policy of paying a fixed percentage of earnings as dividends. Since a firm's earnings vary, such a policy results in unstable and unpredictable dividends. Few firms follow a constant payout ratio because highly volatile dividends may adversely affect stock prices. Figure 12.3 illustrates a constant dividend payout ratio in which a firm pays out 50 percent of its earnings as dividends.

Because using a constant payout ratio is often impractical, firms tend to develop a target payout ratio. A firm's actual dividend payout ratio may be higher or lower than the target in any given year, depending on corporate earnings and investment opportunities. Yet, the firm keeps its long-run average payout ratio near the target. Management may revise the target payout ratio in response to changes in investment opportunities and other factors that can affect the need for retaining earnings.

Low Regular Plus Specially Designated Dividends

A policy of **low regular plus specially designated dividends** is one in which a firm maintains a low regular cash dividend but pays a specially designated cash dividend ("extra," "special," or "year-end") if warranted based on the firm's earnings performance. Such a policy represents a compromise between paying a stable dividend per share and maintaining a constant payout ratio. The small, regular dividend represents a stable dividend component that investors come to expect. Having a labeled dividend permits the firm to increase the dividend without the implicit need to continue that dividend in future years. During good earnings years, the total dividend paid may be large, and during poor earnings years, the total dividend may be small. As a result, the annual dividend may be volatile, with a base-level dividend established at a low level. A policy of regular plus specially designated dividends is common among firms that experience cyclical swings in earnings. Such a policy gives the firm flexibility but leads to some uncertainty among shareholders.

Guidelines on Setting Dividend Policy

The goal of dividend policy is to maximize its contribution toward increasing shareholder wealth. The task facing the board of directors and management is deciding whether the firm or its owners can make better use of the money. What practical guidance exists for firms in trying to achieve this goal?

1   A firm should consider its investment opportunities and avoid cutting back on profitable projects to pay dividends. The crux of the analysis is determining whether the firm's opportunities are better than those available generally to investors. If expected returns from available discretionary projects exceed the opportunity cost of capital, the firm should have a lower target dividend payout. If it cannot put retained earnings to good use, a firm should distribute more to its shareholders. A higher target payout is not a confession of failure.
2   Firms should rely heavily on retained earnings as a source of equity capital. Firms should avoid issuing new equity unless needed to finance profitable investments. Selling new stock involves flotation costs and a negative market reaction to such sales.
3   If a firm pays dividends, it should contemplate paying them on a regular basis out of available cash flow. Consistency, where practicable, is important because many investors depend on dividends. Once a firm sets a dividend, it has an implicit responsibility to maintain it through the normal business cycle. Borrowing to maintain a regular dividend may be acceptable if any borrowing is within reasonable bounds and management expects earnings to increase.
4   Firms should avoid cutting or omitting dividends unless the current level of dividends is unsustainable over the long run. One of the few aspects of dividend policy on which widespread agreement exists is that management should not casually cut a dividend rate once established.

Concept Check 12.4

1 What is a residual dividend policy? What implications does this theory have for the payment of dividends?
2 Why do few firms follow a "pure" residual dividend policy in practice?
3 What are the steps in following a "smoothed" or "modified" residual dividend policy?
4 What are three types of managed dividend policy?
5 Why do firms often prefer to follow policies that result in dividend stability?
6 Why do firms with stable dividend policies avoid immediately boosting dividends when experiencing above-normal performance?

12.5 Stock Repurchases

As an alternative to paying cash dividends, corporations may choose to pay out earnings to owners by buying back shares of outstanding common stock.[6] In a **stock repurchase**, a firm exchanges assets for some portion of its outstanding shares. A stock repurchase shrinks the company's assets by the amount of cash paid out to those stockholders tendering their shares for repurchase and reduces both its borrowing base and the shareholders' aggregate equity. Common stock acquired by the issuing firm becomes **treasury stock**. Such stock has no voting rights, is not included in earnings-per-share calculations, and is ineligible for dividend payments. Although the primary source of funds used to finance the repurchase is available cash balances, firms sometimes use debt and other sources.

US corporations did not begin widely using share repurchases until the mid-1980s. Although no fully satisfactory explanation exists for changes in repurchase activity over the past several decades, numerous factors may have contributed to this development. For example, one factor is the improved regulatory environment for repurchases since the 1980s. Another factor involves the economy. Various market crashes caused stock prices to fall. Evidence suggests that the number of repurchase announcements tends to rise when stock prices fall.

Methods of Repurchasing Stock

When a firm decides to repurchase some of its outstanding shares, management may choose among several methods.

---

[6] In at least two cases, a firm should not use repurchases as a substitute for dividends: (1) when a company reissues repurchased stock to employee stock ownership plans or as executive stock options, and (2) when a company reissues repurchased stock to the acquired firm in a merger.

1   Open-market repurchase
2   Self-tender offer
3   Targeted share repurchase.[7]

Open-market repurchase

In a typical **open-market repurchase**, a firm publicly announces that it will repurchase its stock in the secondary market at the prevailing market price. As the most prevalent method, the open-market mode of repurchase usually involves a gradual buy-back of shares that can take several years. Such repurchases typically involve fewer shares than using self-tender offers.

Self-tender offer

Another repurchase method is a **self-tender offer**, in which a firm makes an open offer to its stockholders to exchange their shares for cash or other assets over a pre-established period. Firms use tender offers when they want to buy back a large percentage of their stock, say 10 to 30 percent of outstanding shares. Tender offers are important corporate events because investors perceive them as informational signals of the firm's future earnings prospects. Because tender offers are usually larger than open market repurchases, their effect on stock prices tends to be greater.

If management uses a tender offer, it has the option of considering the traditional fixed-price offer or the Dutch auction method. Introduced in the 1980s, the Dutch auction has now begun to displace the fixed-price offer.

In the conventional **fixed-price offer**, the firm announces the number of shares it wants to buy, the expiration date of the offer, and the single price it will pay. If stockholders offer to sell or tender more shares than the firm wants to buy, it will buy shares from investors on a pro rata basis. In practice, management can accept more shares (up to 2 percent of all outstanding shares) than the number stated in the offer if the offer is oversubscribed.

To induce shareholders to give up their shares, the company generally sets the tender price at a premium over the market price. Many factors influence the size of the tender offer premiums. For example, firms tend to offer larger premiums when the percentage of outstanding shares increases, in order to induce more shareholders to sell their shares. In addition, premiums are larger when the share repurchase is part of a strategy to avoid a takeover because the demand for shares among competing parties is often high. Because of premiums, a tender offer is the most expensive way to repurchase shares.

In a tender offer using a **Dutch auction**, a firm specifies a range of prices (minimum and maximum) from which tendering shareholders select a single price at which they are willing to sell their shares. Once the tender period expires, the firm counts the number of shares stockholders offered to sell back to the firm at each price within the range. Management

---

[7]   Other ways by which firms may repurchase their shares is through exchange offers and transferable put rights. In an **exchange offer**, the firm offers debt securities instead of cash in exchange for its common stock. In a share repurchase using **transferable put rights** (TPR), a firm wanting to repurchase a fraction of its outstanding shares, gives each shareholder one TPR for a specific number of shares held. A TPR gives the shareholder the right to sell back to the company one share at a pre-specified exercise price by a certain date.

finds the lowest price that allows the firm to repurchase all shares needed. All shares that the firm repurchases receive the same price, despite the bid each shareholder submitted. Dutch auctions reduce the chance of overpayments to tendering shareholders that commonly occur in fixed-price offers.

Targeted share repurchase
A **targeted share repurchase**, also called a **negotiated transaction**, is a method by which a firm purchases a large block of its shares from one or more shareholders at a negotiated price.

Motives for Stock Repurchase

Why do companies buy back their own stock? The reasons that US corporations have increasingly repurchased substantial amounts of their own common shares have been subject to numerous and often conflicting interpretations. Some of the motives are similar but not identical to those for paying cash dividends. These motives may differ based on the type of repurchase method used. Here are six explanations for stock repurchases.

Tax-motivated substitution for dividends
Managers may use share repurchases in lieu of cash dividends to minimize stockholder taxes if capital gains receive favorable tax treatment over the receipt of dividends. A problem with this rationale is that management may not know the preferences of the shareholders. The 2003 Tax Act, which equalizes the maximum tax rate on dividends and capital gains, reduces this potential tax-motivated reason for repurchasing shares in lieu of paying cash dividends. Even if the tax rates are the same, share repurchases result in less total tax paid by shareholders. The taxable portion of the capital may be much smaller than the total cash disbursed, whereas almost 100 percent of cash disbursed as dividend is taxable.

Signaling
The basis of signaling theory is that a firm's management has better information about the company's true value than do outside shareholders. Because of this informational asymmetry, prevailing stock prices may not reflect true value because investors only have access to public information as opposed to private or inside information. Managers may repurchase stock as a mechanism to signal that the company's prospects are better than the current market price suggests. That is, management's willingness to invest funds in the firm's stock may imply that its stock is depressed or undervalued (worth more than the current market price) and represents good value. Later, the firm may be able to resell treasury stock to raise funds, possibly at higher prices. A problem with this motive is that management may be able to use other less expensive ways to convey information to shareholders. Others argue that, while repurchases are not costless, they are cost effective.

Distribute excess cash
Firms may reduce the agency costs associated with managers over-investing or investing in non-productive activities by distributing excess cash to a firm's stockholders using share repurchases. **Excess cash** refers to the cash remaining after the firm has invested in all available

positive NPV projects. Firms with poor investment and growth prospects may choose to return excess cash to their shareholders through common stock repurchases instead of investing in marginal or negative NPV projects. Because management is reluctant to increase regular dividends when it believes that it cannot maintain such high dividends over the long run, it may choose to repurchase stock using excess cash.

Capital market allocations
According to the capital-market-allocation hypothesis, shareholders may benefit from share repurchases even without the agency problems of excess cash. The logic of this argument is that shareholders have a much broader view of productive opportunities in an economy and, therefore, can allocate capital in the financial markets better than a firm's management.

Capital structure adjustments
Firms may use common stock repurchases to reconfigure their capital structure by increasing the proportion of debt to equity. By moving toward a more desirable capital structure, firms receive a tax benefit by using greater leverage. Other advantages of reducing the percentage of equity in the capital structure may include lowering the average cost of capital, increasing earnings per share, and magnifying returns to common shareholders. Sometimes firms repurchase stock not with excess cash but with cash raised through issuing debt. Substituting debt for equity can increase returns by taking advantage of the tax shelter provided by tax-deductible interest expense. Using a repurchase to increase leverage has the drawback of increasing financial risk and decreasing liquid assets. Perhaps a better way to increase leverage is by borrowing rather than by repurchasing stock.

Specific reissue plans
A firm may repurchase shares in order to fulfill its obligations for such purposes as stock options, bonus and retirement plans, dividend reinvestment plans, stock distributions, and conversion of other securities. A firm may also need shares to acquire another firm in an exchange of stock. This argument assumes that the firm has insufficient authorized but not outstanding shares available for such purposes or is unwilling to seek shareholder approval to issue new shares.

Focus on Practice 12.6

Reasons for Using Open-Market Repurchases

In 2000, Baker, Powell, and Veit surveyed top executives at primarily large US corporations to learn their views about their firm's stock repurchases. They asked respondents to indicate the importance of 21 reasons for their most recent open-market repurchases on a four-point scale: none, low, moderate, and high. Table 12.8 shows the six mostly highly ranked reasons. The results show that the two mostly highly cited reasons for share repurchases are to add value to shareholders and acquire stock at a bargain price. This latter reason supports the undervaluation version of the signaling explanation for stock repurchases. Another motive is to increase earnings per share. This effect is usually a consequence of higher leverage and not of the stock repurchase.

Table 12.8 Most highly ranked reasons for open-market repurchases

Reason	Moderate/High importance (%)
Add value to shareholders	97.4
Acquire stock at a bargain price	77.7
Increase earnings per share	67.4
Increase the stock price	67.0
Best use of excess cash	63.1
Convey positive information possessed by management to the market	47.9

Source: H. Kent Baker, Gary E. Powell, and E. Theodore Veit, "Why Companies Use Open-Market Repurchases: A Managerial Perspective," *Quarterly Review of Economics and Finance* 43, 2003, 483–504.

Wealth Effects of Repurchasing Stock

Numerous studies have examined the impact of repurchase announcements on a firm's stock price. Most indicate a positive stock price reaction around the announcement date of open-market repurchases and self-tender offers. Evidence suggests that firms announcing self-tender offers realize greater increases in stock prices than those announcing open market repurchases, due primarily to the premium and the size of the repurchase. Repurchases generally result in stock price increases when a company remains adequately capitalized and is not pursuing this strategy to avoid a takeover. Apparently, the market does not appear to believe that management is engaging in false signaling because most of the stock-price effect remains for several months after the announcement.

Explaining why the market reacts favorably is difficult because many other things are occurring simultaneously. Here is one possible scenario. By repurchasing shares of its own stock, the firm has fewer shares of stock outstanding. If the company can maintain the same level of income, earnings per share will rise, increasing the value of each share of the firm's common stock. This translates into capital gains that stockholders can take at their own discretion. If the company can increase earnings and dividends in the future, shareholders will benefit because of fewer shares outstanding.

Example 12.6 Impact of a stock repurchase on stock prices

Assume that the following financial data applies to Singleton Inc.

Earnings available to common stockholders	$20 million
Number of shares outstanding	10 million
Earnings per share ($20 million/10 million shares)	$2
Market price per share ($2 EPS × 9.5 P/E)	$19
Price/earnings ratio ($19/$2)	9.5

The firm plans to distribute $10 million excess cash to stockholders by repurchasing outstanding shares at a tender offer of $1 above the current market price. What are the expected earnings per share and stock price immediately after the repurchase?

Solution: With $10 million in excess cash, the firm can buy 500,000 shares ($10 million/$20 per share), reducing the total shares outstanding to 9.5 million shares.

$$\text{EPS after purchase} = \frac{\$20 \text{ million}}{9.5 \text{ million shares}} = \$2.11$$

Stock price after repurchase = $2.11 EPS × 9.5 P/E = $20 per share

---

Concept Check 12.5

1 What is treasury stock?
2 What are three major methods for repurchasing stock?
3 How does a traditional fixed-price tender offer differ from the Dutch auction method?
4 What is the signaling motive for repurchasing shares?
5 How can a firm's repurchase of stock affect its capital structure?
6 How does the market typically respond to news of open-market repurchases and self-tender offers?

12.6 Cash Dividends versus Stock Repurchases

Why do corporations prefer to use one form of cash distribution versus another? In perfect capital markets, cash dividends and share repurchases are equivalent. Upon considering market imperfections, cash dividends and share repurchases are similar in many ways, but they are not perfect substitutes. Several reasons help to explain a firm's choice between paying cash dividends and repurchasing shares.

Comparative Advantages of Share Repurchases

A preference for share repurchase over cash dividends may arise for the following reasons.

- *Tax effects.* Repurchases may offer tax advantages to stockholders. Because shareholders only pay taxes on any capital gains realized in a repurchase, more of the total cash disbursed to shareholders in a repurchase flows through to investors untaxed. Moreover, the tax rate may be higher on dividends than on capital gains for many investors.
- *Self-selectivity.* Share repurchases provide shareholders with a choice unavailable with cash dividends. That is, share repurchases give shareholders an option to sell some or all of their shares or not sell. Cash from share repurchases goes only to those stockholders who choose to sell their shares. If stockholders do not want to convert their investments into cash, they do not have to sell their stock back to the company. By not selling, shareholders avoid realizing the capital gain and incurring transaction costs.
- *Signaling.* The signaling effects associated with the announcement of share repurchases versus cash dividends may differ. Announcements of dividend increases and share re-purchases typically generate abnormal security returns. Because firms tend to smooth dividends, they prefer not to increase dividends unless they are sustainable. Thus, firms may increase dividends if they view excess cash flows as permanent, but engage in share repurchase if the cash flows are only temporary.
- *Flexibility.* The decision to repurchase shares gives managers flexibility to reverse them-selves. Unlike regular dividends, which imply a commitment to make future payments, stock repurchases are a one-time return of cash. Thus, if management views excess cash flows as temporary, it can distribute cash to shareholders through a repurchase and avoid paying a higher dividend that the firm may be unable to maintain.
- *Ownership structure.* Common stock repurchase may affect the ownership structure of the firm because the cash distribution to shareholders is generally disproportional. Firms may prefer to use share repurchases for corporate control issues such as serving as a defensive mechanism against hostile takeovers. If managers and other insiders choose not to sell their shares in a repurchase offer, this increases their concentration of voting power and insider control.

Comparative Disadvantages of Share Repurchases

Although firms have legitimate reasons for repurchasing shares, management must balance the potential benefits against the drawbacks.

- *Wealth transfers.* If the firm repurchases undervalued shares in the open market, this transfers wealth from participating (selling) to non-participating shareholders. In a targeted repurchase, repurchasing shares at a premium over market price results in a gain to parti-cipating shareholders at the expense of non-participating shareholders. In both situations, most shareholders do not participate. Because stock repurchases increase a firm's debt ratios, this could lead to a transfer of wealth from current bondholders to shareholders.

- *Principal/agent conflicts.* Management may begin a repurchase for its own gain. If managers own the firm's stock, repurchases increase their proportional ownership in the firm and thus their control and voting power. By initiating common stock repurchases to consolidate voting rights, managers can reduce the chances of successful hostile takeovers by others and increase their entrenchment in the company.

- *IRS and SEC reaction.* Share repurchases may result in penalties, if the Internal Revenue Service (IRS) views a particular repurchase program primarily as helping stockholders avoid paying taxes on dividends. Tax laws prohibit repurchases as dividend substitutes. In addition, the Securities and Exchange Commission (SEC) may suspect a firm of trying to inflate the price of its stock through repurchases (price manipulation) before issuing new stock. Firms may avoid both potential problems by properly structuring repurchases.

- *Effect on trading activity.* Share repurchase may decrease trading activity because of fewer shares outstanding. Low trading activity may affect the liquidity of a firm's stock.

Practical Financial Tip 12.6

The net benefits of stock repurchases, as opposed to dividends, depend on various factors. Repurchases tend to be favored when: (1) excess cash flows are temporary or unstable, (2) stockholders prefer capital gains to dividends, (3) the magnitude of future investment opportunities is uncertain, and (4) managers perceive the stock as undervalued.

Concept Check 12.6

1 What are the differences in tax effects between cash dividends and share repurchases?
2 How can repurchasing stock result in wealth transfers?
3 What are the comparative advantages and disadvantages of repurchases compared with cash dividends?
4 How can managers use stock repurchases for their own gain?

12.7 Dividend Reinvestment Plans

A **dividend reinvestment plan** (DRIP) entitles shareholders enrolled in the plan to automatically buy additional shares of a firm's stock with their cash dividends.[8] Initially, DRIPs required the investor to first buy some shares through a registered broker and have the

---

[8]   For further details on DRIPs, see George C. Fisher, *All about DRIPs and DSPs*, McGraw-Hill, 2001.

shares registered in the investor's name. A growing number of companies sell initial shares directly to the public but often require a minimum purchase ranging from $10 to $3,000. These plans, called **direct stock purchase** (DSP) **plans**, enable investors who join the plans to bypass brokers.[9] Since their introduction in the late 1960s, DRIPs have undergone much growth and change. Today, about 1,000 publicly traded companies such as AT&T and General Motors offer DRIPs. Such plans offer benefits both to the firm and DRIP participants.

Focus on Practice 12.7

Microsoft's Direct Investment Program

In addition to initiating cash dividends in 2003, Microsoft decided to offer a dividend reinvestment plan. Microsoft's plan, run by Mellon Investor Services, offers a direct stock purchase option, fractional share purchases at regular intervals, and dividend reinvestment. If investors do not currently own Microsoft stock, they can enroll in the direct purchase plan by buying $1,000 worth of stock, or by agreeing to automatically purchase stock in 20 sequential purchases of at least $50. The initial purchase fee is $10 plus $0.06 per share. For subsequent purchases, the fee is $0.06 per share plus $2 per electronic purchase, or $5 per check purchase. The dividend reinvestment fee is $0.06 per share, plus 5 percent up to a maximum of $3. To sell shares, the cost is $15 plus $0.12 per share.

Companies can run their own DRIPs or use a transfer agent. Corporations administer their company-run DRIPs from corporate headquarters, typically as part of the overall shareholder relations' effort. For example, utilities have extensive investor relations departments and typically administer their own DRIPs. Instead of administering the DRIP itself, most firms appoint a third party called a **transfer agent**, usually a financial institution, to administer the plan. Because transfer agents run DRIPs for many companies, they can operate the plan at a better rate than the company itself. Some larger transfer agents include Boston EquiServe, First Chicago Trust, and Chase Mellon. The administrator performs such tasks as maintaining records, sending certificates for shares upon request, liquidating participants' shares when they leave the plan, and buying company shares for the plan.

Plan Types

Two basic types of dividend reinvestment plans are market plans and new issue plans. A key difference between these plans is the source of share purchases. The most common source is

---

[9] For further discussion about direct purchase plans, see H. Kent Baker, Walayet A. Khan, and Tarun K. Mukherjee, "Directing Investing: The Role of Stock Purchase Plans," *Financial Services Review*, Spring 2002, 47–63.

the **secondary market**, the market where shares are bought and sold after the original sale. Firms or their transfer agents can make open market purchases on any securities exchange where the stock is traded, in the over-the-counter market, or by negotiated transactions. Another source is the company itself, using either authorized but unissued shares of common stock or treasury shares.

Market plan

A **market plan** is a type of DRIP that involves purchasing shares in the open market for the accounts of shareholders reinvesting their dividends. The company or its transfer agent distributes the newly purchased shares on a pro rata basis to the accounts of the DRIP participants. Under this type of plan, the firm does not issue any new shares. Because firms or their agents purchase the shares in the secondary market, shareholders get their shares at the market price. Some companies have a service charge to participants for share purchases and pro rate broker commissions. In other instances, the company subsidizes the transaction by paying the brokerage costs.

New issue plan

A **new issue plan** is a type of DRIP that allows shareholders to buy new shares directly from the company. That is, a firm replaces the cash dividend that DRIP participants would receive with newly issued shares of common stock. New issue plans appeal to companies in capital-intensive businesses that cannot retain much of their income due to regulation, such as utilities and real estate investment trusts (REITS).

New issue plans provide an alternative way to raise new equity capital without directly using the primary market. Raising equity through new issue plans versus underwriters involves several potential tradeoffs. On the negative side, using new issue plans to raise equity avoids market scrutiny and increases investor uncertainty. In addition, firms using such plans lose underwriter certification of a new offering. Issuers using a prestigious underwriter to certify the quality of the public offering may benefit shareholders by achieving a higher offering price. Issuing new shares also dilutes the value of the firm's outstanding equity. On the positive side, using new issue plans avoids both the negative signal a new equity offering provides and the flotation costs associated with a new offering. Using new issue plans can reduce a firm's debt/equity ratio, provide funds for capital investment, and improve cash flows by reducing dividend disbursements.

Practical Financial Tip 12.7

New-issue plans compare favorably on a cost basis with other ways of raising capital. If a firm pays a dividend and needs equity capital, a new-issue DRIP is likely to raise equity capital cheaper than the alternative ways of raising new capital.

Plan Options

The basic plan offers reinvestment of dividends on all shares of stock registered in the participant's name. Some plans offer special features to increase their attractiveness.

Partial reinvestment
Some plans offer a partial reinvestment option. Participants can specify a portion of shares for dividend reinvestment and receive cash dividends on the remainder.

Optional cash payments
Many plans allow participants to buy additional shares by making minimal periodic payments such as weekly, monthly, or quarterly. Minimum payments are sometimes as low as $10. Companies typically set maximum cash purchases per period but the amount differs dramatically among companies. Depending on the plan, participants can make optional cash payments: (1) in addition to reinvesting dividends, (2) without being required to invest dividends, and (3) when a firm is not currently paying a dividend.

Automatic withdrawal
Many plans permit participants to have automatic investments made from their checking or savings accounts.

Purchase discounts
A small percentage of plans, particularly REITs, offer discounts on the price of shares purchased through the plan. These discounts can range anywhere from 1 to 10 percent. Non-participating shareholders bear this cost.

Focus on Practice 12.8

General Motors Corporation's Dividend and Cash Investment Plan

General Motors Corporation (GM) offers registered owners of at least one share of GM stock the opportunity to automatically reinvest all or part of their cash dividends in additional shares of GM stock. Participants may make optional cash investments in any amount from $25 per investment to $150,000 per year. GM pays all administrative fees for any transactions as well as the brokerage commissions for any shares purchased. GM charges a nominal brokerage commission and service fee on each sale of GM stock through the plan. GM credits accounts with fractional shares. Other plan features include an optional telephone service to enroll in the plan or sell plan shares of GM stock and optional automatic credit and debit of the participant's bank account. GM uses EquiServe as the plan administrator. The current policy of GM is to have the plan administrator purchase all GM stock on the open market.

Advantages and Disadvantages of DRIPs

The major reason firms offer DRIPs is to improve shareholder goodwill. Firms offering new issue plans gain the additional advantage of raising new equity capital whenever they pay cash dividends. Thus, new issue plans can also provide a partial solution to a firm's capital shortage problem. The major disadvantage of such plans to the firm is administrative costs. In addition, companies that issue new shares for their DRIPs dilute a shareholder's position.

DRIPs provide several benefits to participants. Plan participants can conveniently increase their holdings in a firm's stock at a low cost by making small investments or large investments if they are financially capable, on a periodic basis. Sometimes, firms increase this cost savings by issuing the stock at a discount from market value and absorbing brokerage commissions, administrative costs, and other fees.

Despite these advantages, DRIPs are not without their drawbacks to participants. A major disadvantage of DRIPs involves taxes. Although the plan participants receive additional shares of stock instead of cash, they must pay taxes on the amount of the dividends they are entitled to receive. Other disadvantages are the record keeping needed to properly calculate share purchases and the costs incurred to determine future taxable capital gains. Most companies reinvest a shareholder's dividends without cost, but some companies charge fees. Shareholders also lose control over the price paid for shares of stock.

Concept Check 12.7

1   What is a direct stock purchase plan?
2   What is the major difference between a market plan and a new issue plan?
3   What features do some DRIPs offer?
4   What are the major advantages and disadvantages of DRIPs to firms and to participants?

12.8 Stock Dividends

In addition to paying cash dividends, some companies elect to declare and issue stock distributions in the form of a stock dividend or a stock split. With stock distributions, the firm issues a percentage of outstanding stock as new shares to existing shareholders. Researchers have long puzzled over why companies make stock distributions. Conventional wisdom suggests that shareholders get no real benefits from such distributions. Although both stock dividends and stock splits increase the number of equity shares outstanding, they do not provide the firm with new funds or its stockholders with any added claims to company assets. Theoretically, a firm's economic value remains unchanged because stock distributions simply divide the corporate pie into more pieces.

Stock distributions are more than what they seem on the surface. Empirical evidence shows that the market, on average, reacts positively to news of unexpected stock dividends and stock splits. If stock distributions are merely cosmetic changes, why do some firms continue to engage in such financial practices, particularly when they incur real costs in the process? In addition, what explains the positive market reaction to these distributions? This is the stock distribution puzzle. We discuss stock dividends in this section and stock splits in the next section.

Meaning of a Stock Dividend

A **stock dividend** is a distribution of additional shares of stock to existing shareholders on a pro rata basis. Shareholders do not pay taxes on stock dividends because the IRS does not recognize them as having value. That is, stock dividends are not income to the recipients. Firms normally state the amount of a stock dividend as a percentage of the existing shares outstanding. For example, a 10 percent stock dividend means that the corporation will increase its total shares outstanding by 10 percent. Every shareholder will receive one new share of stock for each 10 shares now owned.

Motives for Issuing Stock Dividends

The reasons for issuing a stock dividend are many and varied. For example, management may simply want to use stock dividends as a publicity gesture, a way to supplement cash dividends, or a means to retain profits in the business by capitalizing a part of retained earnings. Researchers have advanced various hypotheses to explain why firms issue stock dividends. They use the signaling, trading range, liquidity, and tax hypotheses to explain both stock dividends and stock splits. Other explanations of why companies pay stock dividends involve cash substitution and retained earnings.

Signaling
One explanation for paying stock dividends involves information signaling. The **signaling hypothesis** says that the announcement of a stock dividend conveys new information to the market. That is, management may use stock dividends to signal good news or optimistic expectations to investors. The announcement of stock dividends may signal expected future increases in earnings, cash flows, cash dividends, and prices. For example, stock dividends may signal the chance of a rise in total cash dividends in the near term. The firm can increase the total cash dividend by keeping the cash dividends per share constant but increasing the shares each stockholder owns through a stock dividend. Several empirical studies generally support the signaling explanation.

Trading range
A second explanation, called the **trading range hypothesis**, suggests that stock dividends help to move a stock into a normal or preferred price range. The lower price improves the likelihood that more investors can afford to buy **round lots** (multiples of 100 shares) of a given stock. Research evidence on this hypothesis is mixed.

Trading liquidity

A third motive for stock dividends is to improve trading liquidity. According to the **liquidity hypothesis**, a stock dividend enhances liquidity by creating additional shares that generate greater trading and ownership dispersion of the firm. The announcement of stock dividends may receive extensive press coverage. Stock dividends may attract attention and, therefore, increase both the number of trades and shareholders of a firm's stock. Increases in these two factors may serve to increase a stock's trading liquidity. Academic research on the liquidity hypothesis shows mixed results.

Tax timing

A fourth explanation for paying stock dividends, called the **tax-timing hypothesis**, involves the tax code. Cash dividends are immediately taxable to recipients, but investors may delay any payments on stock dividends until they sell the shares. Therefore, recipients of a stock dividend gain at least a temporary timing advantage by deferring taxes into the future. Empirical research shows some support for the tax-timing hypothesis.

Cash substitution

A fifth explanation, called the **cash substitution hypothesis**, focuses on management's desire to conserve cash by issuing a stock dividend as a temporary substitute for an existing or contemplated cash dividend. Firms may need to conserve cash because of limited financial resources due to cash flow difficulties or asset expansion needs. Empirical studies provide some support for this hypothesis. In other cases, however, firms issuing stock dividends continue to pay the same cash dividend per share, which effectively increases the total cash dividend paid to stockholders.

Retained earnings

A final explanation for stock dividends, called the **retained earnings hypothesis**, is that stock prices do not fully adjust to a stock dividend on the ex-dividend date. Accounting for stock dividends requires reducing retained earnings and increasing the common stock and paid-in capital accounts to account for the market value of the extra shares distributed. Thus, stock dividends provide an assessment of whether a wealth transfer occurs from retained earnings to shareholders. In general, research supports this notion.

Focus on Practice 12.9

Why Companies Issue Stock Dividends

Baker and Phillips surveyed 299 managers of US corporations that issued stock dividends between 1988 and 1990. Based on 136 responses, their evidence shows that most managers believe that stock dividends have a positive psychological impact on investors receiving them. For many firms, especially those regularly issuing stock dividends, historical practice is the key motive for paying stock dividends. Of the leading hypotheses for issuing stock, the signaling hypothesis received the most support. Managers believe that stock dividends enable them to express their confidence in the firm's future prospects, suggesting that stock dividends may have some information content.

Table 12.9 Motives for stock dividends

Reason	Primary motive (%)
Maintain the firm's historical practice of paying stock dividends	42.9
Signal optimistic managerial expectations about the future	23.2
Increase the total market value of the firm's stock	7.1
Move the stock price into a better trading range	6.3
Increase trading volume	5.4
Other and don't know	15.1

Source: H. Kent Baker and Aaron L. Phillips, "Why Companies Issue Stock Dividends," *Financial Practice and Education*, Fall 1993, 29–37.

Accounting Treatment of Stock Dividends

The Securities and Exchange Commission (SEC) specifies that public companies should account for distributions of less than 25 percent as a stock dividend. A common name for such distributions is a **small stock dividend**. From an accounting point of view, a small stock dividend involves transferring an amount equal to the current market value of the additional shares of stock from retained earnings to other equity accounts.[10] The accounting treatment involves adding the par value of the new stock to the common stock account and adding the remainder to additional paid-in capital, also known as capital in excess of par (or stated value). The par value of the common stock remains unchanged. The transfer of amounts among the equity accounts involves no change in the level of total stockholders' equity, or in the asset and liability accounts.

---

[10] A **large stock dividend** usually means a transfer from retained earnings to the capital stock accounts for the par value of the stock issued as opposed to a transfer of the market value of shares issued as in the case of a small stock dividend.

Example 12.7 Accounting for a Small Stock Dividend: Haslem Industries

To illustrate a small stock dividend, assume Haslem Industries has 2 million shares of $5 par value common stock and retained earnings of $15 million. The firm declares a 5 percent stock dividend and the pre-dividend stock price is $21 per share. Table 12.10 shows the stockholders' equity accounts before the stock dividend. How does this stock dividend affect the stockholders' equity accounts?

Solution: First, determine the number of new shares by multiplying the percentage of the stock dividend by the total number of shares outstanding before the stock dividend. For Haslem Industries this means 100,000 new shares = 0.05 × 2,000,000 outstanding shares. Next, determine the amount transferred into the common stock account and additional paid-in capital account from the retained earnings account. In accounting for stock dividends, the basis for account transfers is the market price of the stock before the stock dividend. Because the firm will issue 100,000 new shares with a pre-dividend price of $21 per share, the balance sheet will reflect the movement of $2.1 million among the equity accounts:

1 Reduce retained earnings by $2.1 million = 2,000,000 × 0.05 × $21.
2 Increase the common stock account by the par value of the newly issued shares: $500,000 = 100,000 new shares × $5 per share.
3 Increase the additional paid-in capital by $1.6 million = $2.1 million − $0.5 million (the difference between the change in the retained earnings account and the change in the common stock account).

The total value of stockholders' equity remains unchanged. Table 12.10 presents these changes in the stockholders' equity accounts after the 5 percent stock dividend.

Table 12.10 Accounting for a 5 percent stock dividend: Haslem Industries[a]

Before a 5 percent stock dividend		After a 5 percent stock dividend	
Common stock ($5 par, 2,000,000 shares)	$10,000,000	Common stock ($5 par, 2,100,000 shares	$10,500,000
Additional paid-in capital	5,000,000	Additional paid-in capital	6,600,000
Retained earnings	15,000,000	Retained earnings	12,900,000
Total stockholders' equity	$30,000,000	Total stockholders' equity	$30,000,000

[a] Note that the pre-dividend stock price is $21 per share.

Wealth Effects of Stock Dividends

In theory, a stock dividend reduces the market price of each share of stock by the percentage of the stock dividend. Total market value (shareholder wealth) should not change because the increase in the number of new shares should exactly offset the decline in the share price. In practice, the change in market value may not be the same percentage as the stock dividend. Empirical studies show that a company's stock price, on average, reacts positively to the announcement of a stock dividend. This evidence suggests that the market does not view stock dividends as purely cosmetic changes. Equation 12.1 shows the theoretical price of a stock after a stock dividend.

$$P_A = \frac{P_B}{1 + SD_p} \qquad (12.1)$$

where P_A is theoretical price of a stock after a stock dividend; P_B is the price of a stock before a stock dividend; and SD_p is the percentage of the stock dividend in decimal form.

Example 12.8 Effects of Stock Dividends on Stock Price, EPS, and Total Earnings

Before Haslem Industries issues a 5 percent stock dividend, the stock is selling for $21 per share. Assume that an investor owns 1,000 shares and the firm earned $2 per share. What is the theoretical price of the stock, the earnings per share, and the total earnings after the stock dividend?

Solution: Using Equation 12.1, the theoretical market price of the stock after the stock dividend should decline to $20 per share, other things being equal.

$$P_A = \frac{\$21}{1 + 0.05} = \$20.00$$

An investor who owns 1,000 shares before the dividend has stock worth $21,000 = 1,000 shares × $21 per share and total earnings of $2,000 = 1,000 shares × $2 EPS. After the 5 percent stock dividend, this investor owns 1,050 shares valued at $20 each for a total value of $21,000 and the same proportionate earnings of $2,000. The EPS decreases from $2.00 to $1.90 = $2,000/1,050. This investor is no worse off after the stock dividend despite the stock price drop.

Concept Check 12.8

1 What are the major motives for issuing stock dividends? Explain each.
2 What is the impact of a stock dividend on (a) the total level of stockholders' equity, (b) the firm's asset accounts, and (c) the firm's liabilities?
3 In theory, what effect, if any, should a stock dividend have on the wealth of the shareholders? Why?
4 Under what conditions might the market respond positively to the announcement of a stock dividend?

12.9 Stock Splits and Reverse Splits

Stock splits are similar to stock dividends because both increase the number of shares outstanding. From a legal standpoint, a stock split differs from a stock dividend because a stock split results in a decrease in the par or stated value per share but a stock dividend does not decrease the par value. In this section, we discuss stock splits and reverse splits.

Stock Splits

A **stock split** is another method of increasing the number of shares outstanding without changing the amount of total stockholders' equity. Distributions of 25 percent or more should be considered a split-up in the form of a stock split. Companies typically express stock splits as ratios. For example, a 2-for-1 stock split results in the issuance of one new share of stock for each outstanding share. That is, a firm splits each old share into two new shares. On the surface, a 2-for-1 stock split is similar in concept to exchanging a $20 bill for two $10 bills. Therefore, stockholders have twice as many shares than before the split, and the value of each share is equal to half the pre-split value, other things being equal. Besides some accounting differences, stock splits and stock dividends differ in size. That is, the pro rata distribution of shares with a stock split is usually much higher than with a stock dividend. Many stock splits come after periods of high return, which cause the firm's stock price to rise. Therefore, the split is a reaction by the board of directors after the firm's stock price has risen.

Motives for stock splits
Several motives may explain the persistence of stock splits. Stock splits and stock dividends share four explanations – signaling, liquidity, trading range, and taxes – which we discussed in the previous section. Empirical research indicates that stock split announcements convey information to the market about the value of the company. Therefore, strong support exists for information signaling. Support also exists for the trading range hypothesis. Let us examine the rationale for this latter motive more closely.

A firm may want to decrease the market value of its common stock to make it more affordable to investors. For example, a firm may want to reduce a stock selling at $100 to about $25 by having a 4-for-1 split. With the company's price in a more accessible range, the theory suggests more shareholders should buy the stock, bidding up its price. The preferred trading range motive is likely to apply more to certain individual investors rather than to wealthier and institutional investors because they trade securities in large amounts and often have less concern for the absolute share price. Thus, the question remains "Why would a firm have a preferred trading range in the first place?"

Another argument for the preferred trading range is that it lowers transaction costs by allowing more shareholders to trade in round lots (multiples of 100 shares). Investors prefer to trade in round lots because standard commission costs are generally lower on a per share basis than they are for **odd lots** (less than 100 shares). Because institutions account for most of the trading, old lot commissions should be of little importance to the firm in determining its dividend policy. Research studies show that transaction costs actually increase as a percentage of the stock price as the price drops. These costs include both commissions and the **bid-ask spread**, the difference between the price a buyer pays and the seller receives for a stock. Commissions per share of stock typically decrease after a split, but not enough to offset a widening spread, increasing transaction costs. Evidence also shows that trading volume, which is a measure of liquidity, decreases after most splits. Thus, the rationale for a preferred trading range is dubious.

Focus on Practice 12.10

Why Companies Issue Stock Splits

Baker and Powell surveyed managers of 251 NYSE and AMEX firms that issued a stock split of at least 25 percent between 1988 and 1990. Based on 136 completed questionnaires, the evidence suggests that the major motive of a stock split is to move the stock price into a better trading range. Less important motives are to improve the stock's liquidity and to signal optimistic managerial expectations about the future.

Table 12.11 Motives for stock splits

Reason	Primary motive (%)
Move the stock price into a better trading range	50.7
Improve the stock's liquidity	22.1
Signal optimistic managerial expectations about the future	14.0
Other and don't know	13.2

Source: H. Kent Baker and Gary E. Powell, "Further Evidence on Managerial Motives for Stock Splits," *Quarterly Journal of Business and Economics*, Summer 1993, 20–31.

Accounting treatment of stock splits

From an accounting standpoint, a stock split involves increasing the number of outstanding shares and then reducing the par value of the common stock proportionately. Unlike a stock dividend, a stock split lowers the stock's par value, but it does not involve changes to the retained earnings or additional paid-in capital accounts.

Example 12.9 Accounting for a 2-for-1 Stock Split: Haslem Industries

Instead of paying a stock dividend, the board of directors of Haslem Industries declares a 2-for-1 stock split. Assume a pre-split stock price of $100 a share, not $21 as assumed in Examples 12.7 and 12.8. What effect does the 2-for-1 stock split have on the stockholders' equity accounts?

Solution: The 2-for-1 split doubles the number of outstanding shares to 4 million and decreases the par value by one-half to $2.50 per share. Table 12.12 shows these changes. In addition, the share price should decrease by about half to $50 per share.

Table 12.12 Accounting for a 2-for-1 stock split: Haslem Industries

Before a 2-for-1 stock split		After a 2-for-1 stock split	
Common stock ($5 par, 2,000,000 shares)	$10,000,000	Common stock ($2.50 par, 4,000,000 shares	$10,000,000
Additional paid-in capital	5,000,000	Additional paid-in capital	5,000,000
Retained earnings	15,000,000	Retained earnings	15,000,000
Total stockholders' equity	$30,000,000	Total stockholders' equity	$30,000,000

Wealth effects of stock splits

Stock splits pose a conundrum to finance theorists. Although these non-events appear to be purely cosmetic changes, research shows real effects associated with them. In practice, the market value per share may not change exactly in proportion to the split. Empirical evidence suggests that the market responds positively, on average, to announcements of stock splits. A firm cannot sustain the excess returns if it cannot maintain or increase its dividends per share in following periods.

Practical Financial Tip 12.8

Firms should consider using stock distributions when they do not have excess cash flows in the current period but expect to generate higher cash flows and increase dividends in future periods. Although a stock dividend is not a "true" substitute for regular cash dividends, paying a stock dividend may lessen the impact on a company's stock price during a period when a firm may be unable to maintain its regular cash dividend.

Reverse Stock Splits

A **reverse stock split** reduces the number of shares outstanding and increases the price per share. For example, with a 1-for-5 reverse split, investors receive one new share for every five they now own, boosting the share price by a factor of about five.

Motives for reverse stock splits
Some motives for reverse stock splits overlap those for regular splits. For example, a firm may use a reverse split to place its stock price in a more attractive trading range. In the instance of reverse splits, the objective is to increase the stock's price. Other motives are unique to reverse splits. These motives may be discretionary or nondiscretionary.

Management may use discretionary reverse splits to improve marketability and demand. Abnormally low share prices may harm marketability because investors may view such securities as speculative. By raising the stock price through a reverse split, management may be able to affect the image of the corporate stock and make it more attractive to institutional investors. Another potential motive for discretionary reverse splits is to increase earnings per share (EPS). That is, a firm can increase its EPS by reducing the number of shares outstanding through a reverse split.

Nondiscretionary reverse splits occur to satisfy a price-per-share listing requirement or creditors in Chapter 11 reorganization. Exchanges may require a minimum share price to satisfy initial and continued listing requirements for common stock. For example, the American Stock Exchange requires a minimum initial bid price of $3 per share. **Chapter 11** is a bankruptcy option in which the court appoints a trustee to reorganize the bankrupt firm. Under Chapter 11 reorganization, security holders often find their existing claims reduced or replaced with different claims.

Accounting treatment of reverse stock splits
From an accounting standpoint, a reverse stock split involves decreasing the number of outstanding shares and increasing the par value of the common stock proportionately. No other changes occur in the stockholders' equity section of the balance sheet.

Example 12.10 Accounting for a 1-for-5 Reverse Stock Split: Haslem Industries

Assume the common stock of Haslem Industries sells at $6 a share before the reverse split. The board of directors announces a 1-for-5 reverse stock split. How does the reverse split affect the stockholders' equity accounts?

Solution: The 1-for-5 split reduces the number of outstanding shares from 2 million to 400,000 and increases the par value from $5 to $25 per share. Table 12.13 shows these changes. Theoretically, the share price should increase fivefold from $6 a share to about $30 a share after the reverse split occurs.

Table 12.13 Accounting for a 1-for-5 reverse stock split: Haslem Industries

Before 1-for-5 reverse stock split		After 1-for-5 reverse stock split	
Common stock ($5 par, 2,000,000 shares)	$10,000,000	Common stock ($25 par, 400,000 shares)	$10,000,000
Additional paid-in capital	5,000,000	Additional paid-in capital	5,000,000
Retained earnings	15,000,000	Retained earnings	15,000,000
Total stockholders' equity	$30,000,000	Total stockholders' equity	$30,000,000

Wealth effects of reverse splits

Although reverse stock splits are theoretically non-economic events, they can result in material changes in stock price behavior. Usually, stock prices decline upon the announcement of a reverse split. In the case of Haslem Industries, the per share price should drop below $6 when the firm announces its intention of having a reverse split. Smaller companies often have stronger negative reactions than larger companies do. The stock price often continues to decline over time.

Apparently, the market interprets a reverse split as a negative signal, which may reflect management's pessimism about a stock's ability to reach an attractive trading range without a reverse split. Market participants may also view a reverse split as a desperate effort by management to prop up the firm's depressed stock price. Research evidence suggests that engaging in reverse splits may not be consistent with the maximization of shareholder wealth. Therefore, the reverse stock split strategy may be of questionable value to firms. This is especially true for firms with positive outlooks.

Concept Check 12.9

1 What is the impact of a stock split on (a) the common stock account, (b) additional paid-in capital and (c) retained earnings?
2 An investor owns 5 percent of Shaw Industries. The firm announces a 3-for-1 stock split. Will the investor's proportional ownership increase, decrease, or remain unaffected due to the stock split? Explain.
3 Why do firms choose to split their stock?
4 What are the most common reasons for firms declaring a reverse stock split?
5 What is the typical impact of a stock split on a firm's stock price? How about a reverse stock split?

Summary

In this chapter, we discussed dividend policy and various factors influencing whether companies decide to pay dividends or repurchase stock. We also examined dividend reinvestment plans and two types of stock distributions – stock dividends and stock splits – as well as reverse stock splits. The key point to derive from this chapter is that no single correct explanation exists for the prevalence of dividends or for the relationship between dividend policy and stock price. This suggests that managers should look for a combination of factors in examining investor preferences for dividends. The key points of the chapter follow.

1 Much debate exists over the relevance of dividend policy. Advocates of dividend irrelevance contend that dividend policy will not affect stock prices in the simplified world of perfect capital markets. Proponents of dividend relevance point out that, in the real world, capital markets are not perfect.
2 Management must balance many factors in setting dividends, including market imperfections, shareholder factors, firm factors, and other constraints. Dividend decisions are often complex and require tradeoffs because some factors encourage larger dividend payouts while others encourage greater retention. Unfortunately, real-world considerations provide no easy answers for determining the "right" dividend policy.
3 Dividend policies take two major forms: residual and managed. Few firms follow a "pure" residual policy because strict adherence may lead to unstable dividends. Dividend paying firms typically follow dividend policies that provide dividend stability.
4 Corporate stock repurchases are another way of distributing cash to shareholders. Firms may implement repurchases through open-market repurchases, self-tender offers, and targeted share repurchases.
5 Dividend reinvestment plans provide a way in which shareholders can automatically reinvest their dividends in shares of the company's stock. Firms can establish open market or new issue plans.

6 Firms sometimes pay stock dividends or issue stock splits. Both types of stock distributions increase the number of outstanding shares of stock and should cause a proportionate decline in the market price of the stock. Although neither type of distribution should theoretically affect shareholder wealth, the market, on average, responds favorably to news of stock dividends and stock splits.

7 Reverse stock splits reduce the number of shares outstanding. The market reaction to the announcement of reverse stock splits is usually negative.

FURTHER READING

Baker, H. Kent and Aaron L. Phillips. "Why Companies Issue Stock Dividends," *Financial Practice and Education* 3, Fall 1993, 29–38.

Baker, H. Kent, Aaron L. Phillips, and Gary E. Powell. "The Stock Distribution Puzzle: A Synthesis of the Literature on Stock Splits and Stock Dividends," *Financial Practice and Education* 5, Spring/ Summer 1995, 24–37.

Baker, H. Kent and Gary E. Powell. "Further Evidence on Managerial Motives for Stock Splits," *Quarterly Journal of Business and Economics* 32, Summer 1993, 20–31.

Bartov, Eli, Itzhak Krinsky, and Jason Lee. "Some Evidence on How Companies Choose between Dividends and Stock Repurchases," *Journal of Applied Corporate Finance* 11, Spring 1998, 89–98.

Bernstein, Peter L. "Dividends: The Puzzle," *Journal of Applied Corporate Finance* 9, 16–22.

Bierman, Harold, Jr. *Increasing Shareholder Value: Distribution Policy, A Corporate Finance Challenge*, Kluwer Academic Publishers, 2001.

Frankfurter, George M. and Bob G. Wood with James Wansley. *Dividend Policy: Theory and Practice*, Academic Press, 2003.

Grullon, Gustavo and David Ikenberry. "What Do We Know about Stock Repurchases," *Journal of Applied Corporate Finance* 13, 31–51.

Grullon, Gustavo and Roni Michaely. "The Information Content of Share Repurchase Programs," *Journal of Finance* 59, April 2004, 651–80.

Hausch, Donald E, Dennis E. Logue, and James K. Seward. "Dutch Auction Share Repurchases: Theory and Evidence," *Journal of Applied Corporate Finance* 5, Spring 1992, 44–49.

Ikenberry, David L., Graeme Rankine, and Earl K. Stice. "What Do Stock Splits Really Signal?" *Journal of Financial and Quantitative Analysis* 31, September 1996, 357–75.

Lease, Ronald C., Kose John, Avner Kalay, Uri Loewenstein, and Oded H. Sarig. *Dividend Policy: Its Impact on Firm Value*, Harvard Business School Press, 2000.

WEBSITES

www.ex-dividend.com Provides dividend data for common and preferred stocks.

www.e-analytics.com   Provides the company name, ticker symbol, amount of split and dividend, pay date, and record date of companies that announced stock splits and stock dividends.

www.dripcentral.com   Offers a comprehensive directory of online resources about dividend reinvestment plans and direct purchase stocks.

www.fool.com Provides an array of information for investors including information on dividend reinvestment plans.

Glossary

Abandonment decision   A type of real option in which a firm may decide to terminate the investment before the end of its full physical life. The firm compares the expected future benefits over the remaining life of an asset to its expected salvage value if the firm scraps the asset before the end of its life.

Accelerated sinking fund provision   A provision that allows the issuer to retire a larger proportion of the issue at par, at its discretion.

Accounting insolvency   Occurs when a firm has negative net worth on its balance sheet.

Accounting profit   The difference between revenues and usually only explicit costs, recorded according to accounting principles.

Accounts payable payment period   The average length of time between the purchase of materials and labor that go into inventory and the payment of cash for these expenses.

Accrual accounting   An accounting convention where firms record revenues when a sale is made, not when the cash is collected from the sale, and recognize the expense of producing an item when the activity that generates the expense is performed, not when the firm actually pays out the cash for that expense.

Accumulated earnings tax   A tax that the Internal Revenue Service may impose to prevent privately owned firms from retaining earnings beyond "reasonable business needs."

Additional paid-in capital   The capital received from a stock issue that exceeds the par value amount received. Also known as **capital in excess of par**.

After-tax cost of debt (k'_d) The cost of debt to a firm after adjusting for federal and state taxes.

Agency cost   A direct or indirect expense that the principal bears as a result of having delegated authority to an agent.

Agency problem   Any conflict between principals (managers) and agents (shareholders and creditors). Also called an **agency conflict**.

Agency relationship   A relationship in which one party (the principal) delegates authority to another party (the agent).

Agent   A person authorized to act on the behalf of another (the principal) to perform some duty or service.

Aging schedule   An aging schedule classifies the firm's receivables by the number of days outstanding (the age of the receivable).

Allocated overhead   The allocation of existing general overhead, such as general and administrative expenses, to each unit or division that undertakes a project for the purpose of internal reporting.

Annuity   A series of cash flows that are equal and periodic.

Annuity due   An annuity where payments or receipts occur at the beginning of each period.

Asset management ratios   A category of financial ratios that measures the ability of a firm's management to manage the assets at its disposal.

Average inventory processing period   The length of time needed for a firm to acquire and then sell inventory.

Average receivables collection period   The length of time needed for a firm to collect cash from a credit sale.

Balance sheet   A statement of a firm's financial position at a single point in time, including the firm's assets and the liability and equity claims against those assets.

Bankers' acceptance   A draft (order to pay) drawn on a bank by an exporter in order to obtain payment for goods shipped to a customer who has an account at that bank.

Bankruptcy   The state reached when a firm cannot meet its contractual debt obligations.

Basic earnings per share   The earnings calculated by dividing a firm's net income less any preferred dividends paid out by the weighted average number of outstanding shares of common stock.

Basis point   One hundredths of 1 percent or 0.01 percent. There are 100 basis points in each 1 percentage point.

Beta   A measure of a security's systematic risk relative to the market. Also called **market risk**.

Best-efforts cash offer   A type of negotiated offer in which the investment banker agrees to make "best efforts" to sell as much of the issue as possible at the agreed-upon price.

Bid-asked spread   The difference between the highest price a prospective buy is prepared to pay at a particular time for a trading unit of a given security (the bid price) and lowest price acceptable to a prospective seller of the same security (the asked price).

Bird-in-the-hand argument   The belief that investors place greater value on a dollar of dividends than a dollar of expected capital gains because dividends are less risky than capital gains.

Bond   A long-term debt security in which the issuer promises to make periodic interest payments and to pay back the borrowed amount (principal) on predetermined dates.

Bond-equivalent yield (BEY)   The market convention used to annualize a bond's semiannual yield to maturity, which involves doubling the semiannual rate and using that rate as the yield to maturity.

Bond rating   An assessment of the creditworthiness of the corporate issuer.

Bond-yield-plus-risk-premium approach   A method of estimating the cost of common equity that involves adding a risk premium to some base rate such as the Treasury bonds rate or the rate on the firm's own bonds. The base rate is a before-tax cost of debt.

Book value   The value of the assets as shown in the company's books. For a fixed asset, the book value is the installed cost less accumulated depreciation of the asset.

Bottom-up approach   A capital budgeting approach in which proposals "flow up" from the bottom of the organization as various departments or divisions make requests for new capital projects.

Break point (BP)   The total financing that a firm can raise before a specific cost of capital increases.

Business risk   The uncertainty inherent to a firm's operations, measured by the volatility of its operating income.

Business strategy   The plan by which the firm expects to achieve its goals in an uncertain environment.

Call premium   The additional amount that a firm agrees to pay above the bond's par value when the firm calls a bond.

Call price   The price at which the issuer may call a bond.

Call provision   A provision in a bond indenture that gives the issuer the right to buy back or "call" all or a part of a bond issue before maturity.

Call risk The possibility that the issuer will call a bond and expose the investor to an uncertain cash flow pattern. If properly priced, the bond's yield to maturity (YTM) should reflect these risks.

Cannabilization A type of side effect resulting in an erosion of cash flows such as the lost sales attributable to the proposed project.

Capital asset pricing model (CAPM) A model that relates the expected return of a security or portfolio to the risk-free rate and the market price of risk.

Capital budget The planned future investments in capital goods.

Capital budgeting The process of planning, analyzing, selecting, and managing capital projects.

Capital budgeting process A system of interrelated steps for generating long-term investment proposals; reviewing, analyzing, and selecting from them; and implementing and following up on those selected.

Capital budgeting project A proposed long-term investment that ultimately results in a capital expenditure.

Capital good A business asset with an expected use of more than one year such as a fixed asset.

Capital impairment rule A prohibition that protects the security interest of creditors by limiting firms from removing equity capital from the firm through dividend payments.

Capital lease A lease obligation that a firm capitalizes on its balance sheet.

Capital market A financial market for long-term securities.

Capital rationing The allocation of investment funds among a set of projects when management places an upper limit on the size of a firm's capital budget during a particular period or when a firm cannot raise enough money to acquire all profitable assets.

Capital structure The mix of debt and equity that the firm uses to finance its assets.

Cash conversion cycle The length of time that the cash is tied up in this cycle, determined by summing the receivables, inventory, and payables periods for a firm.

Cash flow The actual flow of cash into (cash receipts or savings) and out of (cash payments) a firm during a given period.

Certainty equivalent cash flow A smaller cash flow that the decision maker would accept with certainty in exchange for a risky cash flow.

Certainty equivalent factor The ratio of a certain return to a risky return.

Certainty equivalent (CE) method A risk adjustment technique that adjusts the expected cash flows to account for risk and then uses the risk-free rate as the discount rate to find the NPV.

Chapter 11 A chapter in the Bankruptcy Reform Act that provides for the reorganization, rather than the liquidation, of a business.

Clearing time float The time required for a check to clear through the banking system and to reduce the paying firm's account.

Clientele effect The notion that firms with specific dividend policies attract those investors whose particular needs are met by those dividend policies.

Coefficient of variation A measure of relative risk calculated by dividing the standard deviation by the mean.

Commercial paper A short-term unsecured promissory note or IOU issued by financially secure firms on a discount yield basis.

Common ending period A time when two projects end simultaneously.

Common-size balance sheet Balance sheet that presents all balance sheet items as a percentage of total assets.

Common-size income statement Income statement that presents all income statement items as a percentage of net sales.

Common stock A form of equity that represents ownership of a corporation.

Competitive cash offer   The process by which a securities issuer selects an investment banker based on the best price offered through competitive bids by the investment bankers.

Component cost   The minimum required rate of return on a capital component.

Concentration banking   A banking process where the firm's customers make payments at a firm's regional offices rather than its corporate headquarters; the regional offices then deposit the checks into their local bank accounts.

Constant dividend payout ratio   A policy of paying a fixed percentage of a firm's earnings as dividends in each period.

Constant growth dividend discount model (DDM)   A method of estimating the cost of existing equity, which consists of the firm's dividend yield (D_1/P_0) plus the growth rate (g). The model assumes that dividends will grow at a constant rate.

Consumer credit   Credit granted to consumers by a firm.

Contingent claim valuation   A valuation approach where an asset with the characteristics of an option is valued using an option-pricing model.

Continuous compounding   A process that involves compounding interest for an infinite number of times per interval.

Conventional (normal) cash flow pattern   A time series of incoming and outgoing cash flows that has only one change in direction or sign.

Conversion rights   A provision in a bond indenture giving a bondholder the right to convert the bond into a specified number of shares of common stock at a predetermined fixed price.

Convertible bond   A bond that gives the bondholder the right to convert the bond into a specified number of shares of common stock at a predetermined fixed price.

Corporate risk   A project's contribution to a firm's total risk.

Corporation   A legal entity created by a state separate and distinct from its owners and managers.

Correlation coefficient   A statistical measure of the relationship between changes in two variables.

Cost of capital   The rate that a firm pays, explicitly or implicitly, to investors for their capital or the minimum rate of return required by the suppliers of capital.

Cost of common equity   The minimum rate or return required by investors to buy a firm's common stock.

Cost of debt (k_d) The rate of return required by suppliers of a firm's debt.

Cost of preferred stock (k_p) The rate of return required by preferred stock investors to buy a firm's preferred stock.

Coupon interest rate   The contractual rate of interest based on a bond's par value.

Coverage ratios   Debt management ratios that measure the long-term debt paying ability of the firm.

Credit scoring   A process of assigning a numerical rating for a customer based on information collected about the customer.

Crossover rate   The discount rate at which the NPV profiles intersect and the NPVs of the two projects are equal.

Cumulative voting   A voting system that permits the stockholder to cast multiple votes for a single director.

Current asset   An asset that is either in the form of cash or is expected to be converted into cash within one year.

Current liability   A liability that either matures or is expected to be paid off within one year.

Current ratio   The most widely used liquidity ratio, computed by dividing a firm's current assets by its current liabilities.

Current yield   A return measure that relates the annual coupon interest to the bond's current market price.

Debenture A type of bond raised without any specific collateral as pledge. The bondholders have a claim on the issuer's assets that the issuer has not pledged to other securities.

Debt management ratios A category of financial ratios that characterizes a firm in terms of the relative mix of debt and equity financing and provides measures of the long-term debt paying ability of the firm.

Debt ratio A debt management ratio, computed by dividing a firm's total (current and noncurrent) liabilities by its total assets.

Declaration date The date on which a firm's board of directors announces the declaration of a dividend.

Default risk The possibility that the issuer will fail to meet its obligations as specified in the indenture.

Deferred call provision A provision in a bond indenture specifying that a firm may not call the bond until after a specified period.

Depository transfer check (DTC) A preprinted check that needs no signature and is only valid for transferring funds between specific accounts within a firm.

Depreciable basis Under MACRS, an asset's original cost plus the costs related to its purchase, including delivery and installation costs.

Depreciation A noncash charge against tangible assets, such as cost of property, plant, and equipment, over the asset's useful life.

Depreciation tax shield The change in taxes due to the depreciation charge.

Diluted earnings per share A conservative earnings estimate calculated by assuming the total shares of common stock in the denominator include all shares of common stock plus future potential shares from the likely future conversion of outstanding convertible securities, stock options, and warrants and dividing this amount by the average number of shares outstanding during the period.

Direct foreign investment The acquisition by a firm of physical assets in the form of plant and equipment in other countries, by using a foreign subsidiary.

Direct negotiation When a firm arranges a term loan with a bank, leases an asset, or places debt privately.

Direct placement A method of selling a security in which an issuer avoids using an investment banker and goes directly to the buyer.

Direct sale The sale of securities by a corporation directly to the public.

Direct stock purchase (DSP) Enables investors to bypass brokers and buy shares directly from the issuer.

Disbursement float The funds that are available in a firm's bank account until its payment check has cleared through the banking system.

Discounted cash flow (DCF) valuation A valuation approach where the estimated value of a financial asset is the present value of the asset's expected future cash flows.

Discounted payback period (DPP) The length of time required for an investment's cumulative discounted cash flows to equal zero.

Discount rate The interest rate used to compute a present value amount.

Discounting The process of computing the present value of a given future value amount.

Discrete probability distribution A probability distribution with a finite or limited number of outcomes each with its own probability.

Discretionary project One that gives a firm the choice of whether to undertake investment opportunities.

Dividend A direct payment from a corporation to its stockholders.

Dividend discount model A valuation model where the intrinsic value of a share of common stock is equal to the discounted valued of all future dividends.

Dividend irrelevance theory The theory that what a firm pays in dividends is irrelevant to either a firm's stock price or its cost of capital and that stockholders are indifferent about receiving dividends.

Dividend payout ratio The percentage of net income paid out to shareholders in cash dividends.

Dividend policy The payout policy that management follows in determining the size and pattern of distributions to shareholders over time.

Dividend principle A firm should return cash to the owners if there are not enough investments that earn the hurdle rate.

Dividend reinvestment plan (DRIP) A plan that entitles shareholders enrolled in the plan to automatically buy additional shares of a firm's stock instead of receiving cash dividends.

Dividend yield The ratio of dividends per share to a firm's stock price.

Due diligence The responsibility of the underwriter of a new offering to investigate all relevant aspects of an issuer's operations including its financial reliability and the intended use of the proceeds.

Dutch auction A type of self-tender offer in which a firm specifies a range of prices (minimum and maximum) from which tendering shareholders select a single price at which they are willing to sell their shares.

Earnings before interest and tax (EBIT) A profitability measure of a firm's day-to-day business operations calculated by subtracting operating expenses from operating income.

Economic exposure The risk that changes in exchange rates will affect a firm's value.

Economic life The life that maximizes a project's NPV and consequently maximizes shareholder wealth.

Economic order quantity (EOQ) The order size for inventory that minimizes total inventory cost.

Economic profit The difference between revenues and total costs (explicit and implicit costs, including the normal rate of return on capital).

Effective annual interest rate An annual interest rate that incorporates compounding effects when interest is compounded more frequently than once per year.

Efficient capital market A market in which the current price of a security (asset) fully reflects all the information currently available about that security (asset).

Equivalent annual annuity (EAA) A method for evaluating capital budgeting projects with unequal lives showing how much NPV per year a firm expects a project to generate for as long as the firm maintains the project.

Equivalent annual charge (EAC) A level annuity over the investment's life that has a present value equal to the investment's net present value.

Excess cash The cash remaining after a firm invests in all available positive net present value projects.

Exchange rate The number of units of one currency required in exchange for a unit of another.

Exchange rate risk The variation in return related to changes in the relative value of the domestic and foreign currency.

Ex-dividend date The first date on which the right to the most recently declared dividend no longer goes along with the sale of the stock.

Expansion project A capital investment designed primarily to enhance revenues by increasing operating capacity in existing products or markets or by focusing operations to expand into completely new products or markets.

Expected value The probability weighted average amount of all outcomes calculated by dividing the standard deviation by the mean (expected value).

Expiration date The last day on which the rights holder may exercise the right.

Explicit cost A measurable cost of doing business such as operating costs.

Final prospectus A formal document given to prospective investors in a new security issue after the SEC approves the registration statement, which includes the offering price and date of sale.

Financial asset A monetary claim on an issuer in the form of a paper asset such as stocks or bonds.

Financial electronic data interchange (FEDI) The exchange of information between a bank and its customers regarding account balances, checks paid, and lockbox information.

Financial leverage The use of debt in a firm's financial structure.

Financial management An integrated decision-making process concerned with acquiring, financing, and managing assets to accomplish some overall goal within a business entity.

Financial market A mechanism for bringing together buyers and sellers of financial assets.

Financial ratio A mathematical relationship among several numbers often stated in the form of percentage, times, or days.

Financial risk The additional risk common stockholders bear as the firm increases the use of debt as a source of financing.

Financial statements Financial reports disclosed in a firm's annual report including balance sheet, income statement, statement of cash flows, and statement of retained earnings.

Financing costs Payments that the firm makes to the parties supplying capital to finance the project.

Financing principle A firm should choose a financing mix that maximizes the value of the investments made and matches the financing to the assets being financed.

Firm commitment cash offer A type of cash offer in which the issuer sells the entire issue to the underwriters who then try to resell the issue to the public.

Fixed-price offer A form of a self-tender offer in which a firm announces the number of shares it wants to buy, the expiration date of the offer, and the single price it will pay.

Float The amount of money represented by checks outstanding and in process of collection; float arises from a delay in the payment system.

Floating rate bond A bond that pays a variable rate of interest.

Flotation adjustment factor The difference between the cost of new equity and the cost of existing equity using the constant growth dividend discount model.

Flotation costs The costs associated with selling a new issue. These costs include both **direct expenses** (fees paid by the issuer to the underwriters as well as filing fees, legal fees, and taxes), **indirect expenses** (costs of management time spent working on the new issue and underpricing), and others.

Free cash flow The cash flow available to distribute to investors after a firm makes all investments in fixed assets and working capital needed to sustain ongoing operations.

Free cash flow hypothesis The belief that dividend payments can reduce the potential misuse of free cash flow generated by companies.

Free cash flow to equity (FCFE) The residual cash flow remaining after meeting interest and principal payments and providing for capital expenditures to maintain existing assets and acquire new assets for future growth.

Future value The amount to which a given amount invested today, at a given rate of return or interest rate, will be worth at some designated future time.

General cash offer The public offering of securities to all interested investors.

Generally accepted accounting principles (GAAP) The conventions, rules, and procedures that define how firms should maintain records and prepare financial reports.

Going-concern value The value of a firm as an operating business.

Going public The process of a privately held company selling part of its ownership to the public through a stock offering in an initial public offering.

Gross underwriting spread The difference in the price that underwriters pay for a security and the price that investors pay for a new security issue.

Gross working capital A firm's current assets used in operations, which includes cash and marketable securities, accounts receivable, and inventory.

Hedging Various activities used to offset the risk of loss from a change in foreign exchange rates.

Historical time series approach   A method of estimating the year-to-year growth rate using a firm's past earnings or dividends per share adjusted for stock splits and stock dividends and then averaging the growth rates.

Hurdle rate   The minimum acceptable rate of return for investing resources in a project.

Implicit cost   The return that the employed resource would have earned in its next best use.

Incentive stock options   An option that allows managers to buy shares of the firm's stock at a predetermined price.

Incremental cash flow   The cash flow that arises solely from the decision to invest in a given project.

Income statement   The financial statement that reports the income, expenses, and profit over a period of time (usually one year).

Indenture   A legal document between the corporation and the creditors detailing the terms and conditions of the debt issue.

Independent project   A project in which the acceptance or rejection of one project does not prevent the acceptance or rejection of other projects under consideration.

Indirect negotiation   When an issuer relies upon another party in selling securities to buyers.

Infinite-period valuation model   A valuation model that assumes an investor plans to buy a common stock and hold it indefinitely.

Information asymmetry   The situation in which a firm's managers have an information advantage over other interested parties.

Information content of dividends   A theory that managers, as insiders, possess information that others do not have and use a change in dividends as a way to signal this private information and thus reduce information asymmetry. Also called the **signaling hypothesis**.

Initial investment   The after-tax net cash outlay required at the beginning of an investment project.

Initial public offering (IPO)   A special type of public offer in which a firm makes its first equity issue available to the public. Also called an **unseasoned new issue**.

Interest rate risk   The sensitivity of a bond price to changes in interest rates.

Internal rate of return (IRR)   The rate of return (discount rate) that equates the present value of all cash flows to zero.

Intersection rate   The point where a firm's investment opportunity schedule (IOS) intersects its marginal cost of capital (MCC) schedule.

Intrinsic value   A measure of the theoretical value of an asset. Also called **fundamental value**.

Investment bank   A firm that acts as an intermediary between sellers needing additional funds and buyers with surplus funds to invest.

Investment grade   Bonds suitable for purchase by prudent investors. Standard & Poor's rating service designates bonds in its top four categories (AAA down to BBB) as investment grade.

Investment opportunity schedule (IOS)   A graph showing the internal rate of return in descending order of each capital project under consideration during a specific period.

Investment principle   A firm should invest in assets and projects yielding a return greater than the minimum acceptable hurdle rate.

Just-in-time (JIT) inventory management system   An inventory system where materials arrive exactly when needed in the production process.

Leverage ratios   A category of financial ratios that characterize a firm in terms of the relative mix of debt and equity financing.

Liquid assets   Cash and the near-cash assets held by a firm.

Liquidating dividend   Any dividend that is not based on earnings.

Liquidation value   The amount of money that a firm would realize by selling its assets and paying off its liabilities.

Liquidity   The ability to convert an asset easily and quickly into cash at a fair market value.

LIquidity ratios A category of financial ratios that indicate a firm's ability to pay its obligations in the short run.

Lockbox system A collection system where customers send incoming checks to a special post office box that a local bank maintains.

Long-term financing decision A decision that involves the acquisition of funds needed to support long-term investments.

Long-term investment decision A decision that involves determining the type and amount of assets that the firm wants to hold.

Low regular plus specially designated dividends A dividend policy in which a firm maintains a low regular cash dividend but pays a specially designated cash dividend ("extra," "special," or "year-end") if warranted based on the firm's earnings performance.

Mail float The time when a check is in the mail.

Major bracket A list of the primary underwriters in a securities offering as shown in a tombstone.

Majority voting A voting system that entitles each shareholder to cast one vote for each share owned.

Managed dividend policy One in which management attempts to achieve a specific pattern of dividend payments.

Mandated project One in which a firm undertakes to meet social, legal, or environmental requirements.

Marginal cost of capital (MCC) The last dollar of new capital that a firm raises to finance new investment opportunities.

Marginal cost of capital schedule A graph showing how WACC changes as the volume of new financing increases during a given period.

Market capitalization The price per share times the number of outstanding shares.

Market plan A type of dividend reinvestment plan that involves buying shares in the open market for the accounts of shareholders reinvesting their dividends.

Market value The price that the owner can receive from selling an asset in the market place.

Market value weight A measure of the proportion of each type of capital in a firm's capital structure based on current market prices.

Marketability The ease of converting an asset or security to cash with minimum possible loss.

Marketable securities Short-term investments in securities that the firm can quickly convert into cash.

Materials requirement planning (MRP) system A computer-based system for ordering and scheduling production of inventories that essentially work backwards through the production process.

Maturity The length of time remaining before the issuer repays the security.

Maturity-matching approach The working capital management approach that involves hedging risk by matching the maturities of a firm's assets and liabilities.

Mezzanine bracket A list of underwriters in a securities offering playing a moderately important role in a securities offering as shown in a tombstone.

Mid- or half-year convention An assumption under MACRS that firms place assets into service at mid-year resulting in a reduction of depreciation during the first year of operation.

Minority interest The proportionate stake that outside minority shareholders have in a firm's consolidated subsidiaries.

Modified accelerated cost recovery system (MACRS) A depreciation method that assigns each item of depreciable property to a asset class and depreciates the asset using an accelerated method.

Modified internal rate of return (MIRR) The rate of return that equates the present value of cash outflows for a given capital project (present value of costs) with the present value of the terminal value.

Money market   A financial market for issuing and trading debt securities with original maturities of less than one year.

Money market securities   Short-term securities that are highly marketable with a low default risk.

Monitoring cost   A cost borne by stockholders to monitor or limit the actions of the managers.

Monte Carlo simulation   A risk analysis technique that uses a computer to simulate probable future events and to estimate a project's profitability and riskiness.

Mutually exclusive project   A capital budgeting project in which the acceptance of one project precludes the acceptance of the others.

Negotiated cash offer   The process by which a securities issuer selects an investment-banking firm to help in or guarantee the sale of securities based on discussions and factors including the best price.

Negotiable certificates of deposit (CDs)   Short-term loans to commercial banks with denominations of $100,000 or more.

Net float   The difference between the disbursement float and the collection float.

Net income   The bottom line on an income statement computed by subtracting total expenses from total revenues.

Net operating working capital (NOWC)   Operating current assets that do not pay interest less the operating current liabilities that do not charge interest. Operating current assets include items such as cash, accounts receivable, and inventory, but exclude short-term investments. Operating current liabilities include such items as accounts payable and accruals, but exclude notes payable and other short-term debt that charges interest.

Net present value (NPV)   The sum of the present values of the project's expected cash inflows (benefits) and cash outflows (costs). That is, the NPV is the amount of cash flow in present value terms that the project generates after repaying the invested capital and paying the required rate of return on that capital.

Net proceeds   The amount at an issuer receives from an issue of securities after deducting flotation costs.

Net profit margin   A financial ratio that measures the percentage of sales that results in net income, calculated by dividing net income by sales.

Net working capital   Current assets minus current liabilities.

New issue plan   A type of dividend reinvestment plans that allows shareholders to buy new shares directly from the company instead of receiving cash dividends.

Nominal annual interest rate   An annual interest rate quoted without regard to compounding. For example, an interest rate of 1 percent per month yields an nominal annual interest rate of 12 percent per year. Also called the **stated rate**.

Normal profit   The minimum rate of return that investors are willing to accept for taking the risks of investment.

Notes to the financial statements   A set of detailed notes that follows the financial statements and explains and expands on the information provided in the financial statements.

NPV profile   A plot of the NPVs of a project at different discount rates.

Odd lot   A securities trade made for less than the normal trading unit, which is 100 shares for actively traded stock.

Offering price   The price at which an investor can buy a security in an underwriting or the holder of a right can buy a share of common stock from the issuer.

Open-market repurchase   A method of repurchasing stock in which a firm publicly announces that it will repurchase its stock in the secondary market at the prevailing market price.

Operating cash flow   The expected after-tax net cash flow that results from any changes in operating revenue and associated expenses over a project's life.

Operating cycle The length of time needed to acquire inventory, sell it, and collect cash from the sale.

Opportunity cost The return rate of return that a firm could earn in its best alternative investment.

Optimal capital budget The level of capital investment that maximizes the value of the firm.

Optimal capital structure The financing mix that maximizes the value of the firm.

Optimal dividend policy The dividend policy that strikes a balance between current dividends and future growth that maximizes the price of a firm's common stock.

Ordinary annuity An annuity where payments or receipts occur at the end of each period.

Over-subscription privilege A provision in a rights offer allowing shareholders to over subscribe in anticipation of extra available shares. Under this provision, shareholders can buy, on a pro rata basis, any unsold shares of a new stock offering at the subscription price.

Par value The nominal value stated on a bond. Also called the **stated** or **face value**.

Partnership A business owned by two or more individuals.

Payback period (PP) The amount of time required for an investment to generate sufficient cash flows to recover its initial cost.

Payment date The date on which the firm mails the dividend checks to the shareholders of record.

Pecking order view (of capital structure) A hierarchy of long-term financing where a firm prefers internal over external financing. If a firm needs external financing, the firm will prefer the safest securities first: debt, hybrids, convertibles, and lastly new equity issues.

Performance shares Shares of stock given to managers based on their performance as measured by such criteria as earnings per share and return on assets.

Perpetuity An annuity with an infinite life.

Political risk The risk associated with various political events or occurrences initiated by host governments that might be unfavorable to a capital investment.

Post-completion audit A step in the capital budgeting process in which managers compare a project's actual costs and benefits to those initially estimated earlier in the process.

Preemptive right The right that existing stockholders have to share proportionately in buying all new shares of common stock that the company sells.

Preferred stock Hybrid security combining features of debt and common stock.

Preliminary prospectus A formal document given to prospective investors in a new security issue before the firm has set the selling price and before the SEC has approved the issuer's registration statement for accuracy and completeness.

Present value The amount that a given future amount is worth today at a specific rate of interest (discount rate).

Pre-underwriting conference A step in the underwriting process in which the issuer and investment banker meet to reevaluate a firm's preliminary decisions involving the issue, negotiate the investment banker's fee, and discuss other costs associated with the issue.

Price-to-earnings (P/E) ratio A multiple calculated by dividing price per share by earnings per share. This multiple indicates how much investors are willing to pay for a dollar of reported profits.

Primary market A financial market for the original sale of new securities.

Principal Someone who hires another (the agent) to perform a duty or service.

Private placement Selling an entire security issuance to single buyer or a few buyers, without the issue becoming available to the public.

Privately held company Usually a small firm with few owners who often are its managers.

Profitability index (PI) The ratio of the present value of an investment's expected after-tax cash inflows (benefits) to the present value of its expected after-tax cash outflows (costs).

Profitability ratios   A category of financial ratios that measures the earning power of a firm, by measuring management's ability to control expenses in relation to sales.

Prospectus   An abridged version of a firm's registration statement describing a planned security and providing the information about an issuing company needed by investors to make informed decisions about whether to buy the security.

Protective covenants   Restrictions in a bond indenture that limit certain actions that the firm might take during the term of the agreement.

Proxy   A temporary transfer of the right to vote to another party.

Public offer   A method of selling an issue of securities to the public.

Publicly held company   One that sells shares outside of a closed group of investors who do not actively manage the firm.

Pure-play method   A method of estimating a project's beta by identifying several publicly traded companies in the same or similar line of business as the proposed project and determining their betas.

Pure rights offer   A rights offer that a firm makes directly to its shareholders.

Put provision   A feature of a bond indenture that allows the holder to sell the bond back to the issuer at some predetermined price on certain dates before maturity.

Quality of earnings   A term referring to the conservativeness and clarity of a firm's reported earnings.

Quick ratio   A liquidity measure computed by subtracting inventory from a firm's current assets and then dividing by its current liabilities.

Real option   When the investment in a "real" asset confers the right but not the obligation to take further action in the future.

Realized yield   The actual yield earned on a bond investment. The realized yield will differ from the promised yield to maturity if coupon rates are reinvested at rates that differ from the bond's required return or if the issuer defaults on interest payments or principal repayment.

Real risk-free rate of interest (RRFR)   A default free rate in which investors know the expected returns with certainty. The real risk-free rate does not include an inflation premium or risk premium.

Recaptured depreciation   The amount by which a firm has effectively over-depreciated the assets during its life. The Internal Revenue Service treats the gain on the depreciable asset as recaptured depreciation, which is taxed as ordinary income.

Record date   The date on which an investor must be a shareholder of record to be entitled to the upcoming dividend. Also called the **holder-of-record date**.

Red herring   A warning in red ink in the preliminary prospectus stating that the prospectus is for information purposes only and that the securities are not yet for sale.

Registration statement   A document containing detailed information about a firm that plans to sell securities to the public.

Regular cash dividend   A cash payment made by a firm to its stockholders in the normal course of business.

Reinvestment rate   The assumed rate of return a firm can earn by reinvesting the cash inflows from the project.

Reinvestment risk   The risk that a bondholder will be unable to reinvest cash flows from a bond at interest rates that differ from the bond's required rate of return.

Relative valuation   A valuation approach where the value of a financial asset is computed relative to how the market prices similar assets.

Replacement chain   The series of replacements of each asset by other assets having identical or at least similar characteristics until the lives of the two investments are equal.

Replacement project   A capital investment designed to improve efficiency or to maintain or increase revenues by replacing deteriorated or obsolete fixed assets.

Repurchase agreement (repo)   An agreement that results from the sale of government security by a securities dealer who agrees to repurchase the security at a later date.

Required rate of return   The minimum percentage return acceptable to cover a project's cost of capital and risk.

Residual dividend policy   The view that a firm should only pay dividends from earnings left over after accepting all positive NPV projects.

Retained earnings   The portion of a firm's earnings that has been saved or reinvested rather than paid out to shareholders as dividends.

Return on assets (ROA)   A financial ratio that measures the net income generated from each dollar invested in total assets, computed by dividing net income by total assets.

Return on equity (ROE)   A financial ratio that measures the net income generated from each dollar invested in equity, computed by dividing net income by total equity.

Reverse stock split   A type of stock split that reduces the number of shares outstanding and increases the price per share.

Right   An option allowing the owner of common stock to buy some shares, or frequently, a fractional share of new stock from the issuer at a specific price.

Rights offer   An offer of securities to a firm's existing stockholders. Also called a **privileged subscription**.

Rights with a standby underwriting   A rights offer that a firm makes through an investment banker.

Risk   The probability that an investor will not receive the expected return from an investment.

Risk-adjusted discount rate (RADR) **method**   A risk adjustment technique that discounts a project's expected future cash flows to the present using a discount rate appropriate for the degree of risk.

Risk aversion   The tendency of investors to avoid risk unless they receive compensation for risk through a risk premium. Thus, investors should expect a higher return for taking on higher levels of risk.

Risk-free rate   The required rate of return on an asset free of default risk, usually measured by a US Treasury security.

Risk premium   The additional return above the risk-free rate that a risk averse investor demands to invest in risky assets.

Round lot   A generally accepted unit of trading on a securities exchange, which is 100 shares for actively traded stocks.

Safety stock   The minimum level of inventory maintained by a firm to prevent losing sales due to stockouts.

Salvage value   The expected worth of an asset at the end of its useful life.

Scenario analysis   A risk analysis technique used to examine what happens to profitability estimates such as NPV if a certain set of events, called a scenario, arises.

Seasoned issue   A new equity issue by a well-established, publicly held firm that has previously issued securities to the public.

Secondary market   The market for trading existing securities among investors, either directly or through an intermediary.

Secured debt   Debt backed by the pledge of assets as collateral.

Securities Act of 1933   An act setting forth the federal regulations for all new interstate securities issues.

Security market line (SML)   A graphical representation of the capital asset pricing model, which shows the relationship between securities' expected rates of return and their betas.

Self-tender offer   A method of repurchasing stock in which a firm makes an open offer to its stockholders to exchange their shares for cash or other assets over a pre-established period.

Selling group   A group consisting of the underwriting syndicate and securities dealers with primary responsibility for helping to sell a newly issued security.

Sensitivity analysis   A risk analysis technique that measures the change in one variable resulting from a change in another variable.

Sensitivity graph   A plot of a project's NPVs for changes in an input variable, holding all other input variables constant.

Serial bond   A bond issue in which the maturity dates are staggered over time to avoid a large repayment on a single date from the issuer.

Shareholder wealth maximization   The financial goal of the firm is to maximize shareholder wealth as reflected in the market price of the stock.

Shareholder   A corporation's current owners or stockholders.

Shelf registration   A registration of a planned security offering that allows for the issuance of a variety pf potential new issues under the same registration with the Securities and Exchange Commission.

Side effects   Externalities in the capital budgeting analysis for a project affecting the cash flows of other products or divisions. Side effects are **complements** if they enhance the cash flows of existing assets and **substitutes** if the effect is negative.

Single-project risk   The risk of a project as a stand-alone unit.

Sinking fund provision   A provision that allows the issuer to retire a bond through a series of predefined principal payments over the life of the issue.

Small stock dividend   The distribution of shares to existing shareholders, when the amount of increase in the number of shares is less than 25 percent.

Sole proprietorship   A business owned and controlled by a single person.

Specially designated dividend   A type of dividend that management labels as "extra," "special," or "year-end."

Stabilization period   The time elapsing between the offering of a security issue for sale and its final distribution in which the underwriter stands ready to enter the secondary market to buy the security.

Stable dollar dividend policy   A policy of maintaining the same dividend per share each period unless the firm believes that future earnings can sustain a higher dividend.

Stakeholder   Any party affected by a firm's decisions.

Stakeholder theory   Managers should make decisions that take into account the interests of all of a firm's stakeholders.

Statement of cash flows   A financial statement that summarizes changes in its cash position over a specified period of time.

Statement of retained earnings   A financial statement that provides information on the composition of the owners' equity accounts.

Standard deviation   A measure of the variability of a distribution about its mean equal to the square root of the variance.

Standby fee   The fee an underwriter charges for agreeing to buy any unsold shares of a rights offer.

Standby underwriting   An arrangement in which an investment banker or underwriting syndicate buys any unsold shares of stock at a specific price when a rights offering expires.

Stock dividend   A distribution of additional shares of stock at no cost to existing shareholders on some proportional basis.

Stock repurchase   A transaction in which a firm buys some portion of its own shares.

Stock split   The distribution of additional shares of stock at no cost to existing shareholders, when the amount of increase in the number of shares is greater than 25 percent. Unlike a stock dividend, a stock split increases the number of shares outstanding without changing the amount of total stockholders' equity.

Stockholders' equity   The residual ownership claims against a firm's assets.

Straight bond   A bond without embedded options, such as call features and sinking fund provisions.

Subordinated debenture   An unsecured bond where the claims against a firm's assets are junior to those of secured debt and regular debentures.

Subscription period   The period during which investors can exercise their rights and buy shares of the new issue.

Subscription price   The price at which rights holders may buy new shares. Also called the **exercise price**.

Sunk cost   Any previous incurred expenditure (a historical cost) that is irrelevant to future decision making and excluded as part of a project's cash flows.

Sustainable growth method   A method of estimating the growth rate (g) by forecasting the retention rate (RR), which is ($1 -$ dividend payout ratio), and then multiplying the retention rate by the company's expected future rate of return on equity (ROE). Thus, $g = (RR)(ROE)$.

Syndicate manager   The lead or managing underwriter of an underwriting syndicate whose responsibility is to handle most of the transaction details such as allocating the securities among other member firms in the group and pricing the securities.

Systematic risk   Risk that an investor cannot diversify away by combining investments in a portfolio. Also called **market** and **nondiversifiable risk**.

Target payout ratio   The desired proportion of earnings that a firm wants to pay out in dividends.

Target value weight   A measure of the proportion of each type of capital in a firm's capital structure based on a firm's target or optimal capital structure.

Targeted share repurchase   A method of repurchasing stock in which a firm buys a large block of its shares from one or more shareholders at a negotiated price. Also called a **negotiated transaction**.

Technical insolvency   A type of insolvency that occurs when a firm cannot meet its financial obligations.

Terminal cash flow   The cash flow associated with ending a project.

Terminal price   The expected price of a stock at the end of a specific holding period.

Terminal value (TV)   The value that would accumulate at the end of a project's life by compounding the project's cash inflows at a specified rate, typically the cost of capital, between the time the cash flows occurred and the end of the project's life.

Tombstone   An advertisement of a security issue in the financial press that lists the security, some specifics about the security, and the members of the syndicate selling the issue.

Top-down approach   A capital budgeting approach in which major project proposals start with senior-level managers and information filters down to lower levels.

Total risk   The systematic plus unsystematic risk of a security or portfolio, which is usually measured by the standard deviation of returns.

Traditional registration   A type of registration in which a firm must register newly issued securities with the SEC at least 20 days before a public offering.

Transfer agent   An agent, usually a financial institution, appointed by a corporation to serve such functions as maintain records of stock and bonds and administering its dividend reinvestment plan.

Translation exposure   The risk that reported income will fluctuate because of fluctuating exchange rates.

Treasury stock   Common stock that the issuing firm repurchases and holds.

Trustee   The agent, usually a commercial bank, for a bond issue charged with the responsibility of protecting the rights of the bondholders and monitoring a bond issuer's performance to ensure that the issuer keeps all promises.

Unconventional (non-normal) cash flow pattern   A time series of incoming and outgoing cash flows that has more than only one change in direction or sign.

Underpricing   A cost associated with and IPO in which the investment banker sells the stock below the correct value.

Underwriter   An investment bank that acts to guarantee the sale of a new securities issue by buying the securities from the issuing firm for subsequent resale to the public.

Underwriting   A process in which an investment banker buys a new security from the issuing firm and resells it to investors.

Underwriting agreement   A document signed by syndicate members of an underwriting syndicate identifying the syndicate manager, member liability, allocation of fees, and the life of the group.

Underwriting spread   The dollar difference between the price that the issuing firm receives from the underwriter and the price at which the underwriter sells the securities to the public. Also called **gross spread**.

Underwriting syndicate   A group of investment banks formed during an underwriting to spread the risk of adverse price movements and facilitate distribution of the bonds or shares.

Unsystematic risk   Risk unique to a particular firm or investment that an cannot diversify away by combining various investments in a portfolio. Also called **non-market** and **diversifiable risk**.

Valuation   The process that links risk and return to estimate the worth of an asset or a firm.

Variable growth valuation model   A dividend valuation approach that allows for a change in the dividend growth rate.

Weighted average cost of capital (WACC)   A firm's overall required rate of return determined by multiplying the weight of each capital component in a firm's capital structure by its after-tax component cost and summing these values.

Wire transfer   An electronic transfer of funds between banks.

Working capital management   Decisions involving a firm's short-term assets and liabilities.

Yield spread   The difference in yield between a bond and a reference bond such as a US Treasury bill, note, or bond.

Yield to maturity (YTM)   The rate of return that investors expect to earn if they buy a bond at its market price and hold it until maturity. Also called the **promised yield**.

Zero balance account (ZBA) system   A system where one master disbursement account services multiple subsidiary accounts. The bank automatically transfers enough funds from the master disbursement account to the subsidiary accounts to cover all checks that holders presented to that bank on that day.

Zero coupon bond   A bond that pays all of the cash payments, both interest and principal, at maturity.

Zero growth valuation model   A dividend valuation approach that assumes dividends remain fixed over time.

Index